MBA'S GUIDE TO MICROSOFT® EXCEL 2002

The Essential Excel Reference for Business Professionals

MBA'S GUIDE TO

The Essential Excel Reference for Business Professionals

MICROSOFT® EXCEL 2002

Stephen L. Nelson
David B. Maguiness

NEW AGE INTERNATIONAL (P) LIMITED, PUBLISHERS

MBA's Guide to Microsoft Excel 2002
The Essential Excel Reference for Business Professionals

Printed in India at Mehra offset, Delhi
1 2 3 4 5 6 7 8 9 10

C–05-04-007

ISBN: 81-224-1631-4
Original Edition Price: $ 39.95
Indian Edition: Rs. 345/-

PUBLISHING FOR ONE WORLD

NEW AGE INTERNATIONAL (P) LIMITED, PUBLISHERS

New Delhi • Bangalore • Chennai • Cochin • Guwahati • Hyderabad
Jalandhar • Kolkata • Lucknow • Mumbai • Ranchi

Visit us at **www.newagepublishers.com**

Contents at a Glance

Contents

INTRODUCTION

You are unique among readers. Almost nobody reads the introduction to a book like this. However, you'll richly benefit by taking a few minutes to read through this text. Its purpose is to help you maximize your return on the investment you've made in this book—your investment in money and especially your even more costly investment in time.

Why This Book

Bookstore shelves are packed with guides to Microsoft® Excel, the world's most popular spreadsheet program. So why this book? Because although many fine books have been written about Excel, there really isn't a book specifically for business users of Excel. In fact, if you don't count this title only two types of books are available: One, you have the books like *Excel for Dummies™* which are really for beginners with computer anxiety (and perhaps not something that you want out on your desk even if you fall into the targeted audience). Two, you have books like Microsoft Press's *Running Excel,* which cover at least a bit about every feature of Excel and thereby provide wonderfully encyclopedic of Excel's features but often don't give the sorts of detailed commentary and advice useful to business people.

Many of the existing books in these two standard categories are very good. We heartily recommend both *Excel for Dummies* and *Running Excel,* for example, as general references. But business users of Excel benefit by having a reference that emphasizes, talks from the point of view, and focuses on the business applications of Excel. In short, business users of Excel need a book that talks about Excel as a business tool.

MBA's Guide to Microsoft® Excel 2002 is the only book that specifically describes how you can more easily, more productively, and more powerfully use Microsoft® Excel 2002 in business.

Although this book's title references the popular business professional degree, M.B.A., this book will also be of use to people without M.B.A.s. M.B.A. students, for example, will find this book useful. People with graduate degrees in accounting, public administration, economics, and related fields will find this book useful as well.

In addition, anyone who's finished a good undergraduate program in business or a related field (like accounting) will feel comfortable and gain skills using this book as a desktop reference.

What's in This Book

The easiest way to see what's in this book is to turn to the table of contents. It lists each chapter and each chapter's contents in rich detail.

The chapters in this book fall into one of three categories:

Chapter 1, "QuickPrimer™ on Using Excel," Chapter 2, "QuickPrimer™ on Charting," and Chapter 3, "QuickPrimer™ on Databases" provide faced-paced but friendly tutorials on Excel. In a nutshell, these three QuickPrimers move you to professional proficiency in Excel—even if you're new to Excel. (If you don't need this help, of course, you can easily skip it.)

Chapters 4 through 9 provide rich, detailed coverage of topics of interest to Excel business users—topics that are short-changed in books that have to be everything to everybody. Chapter 5, "Financial Calculations," for example, describes how you easily and correctly make financial and other business calculations in Excel. Chapter 6, "Business Modeling," describes how Excel's advanced modeling tools work in business settings. Other topics covered in richer detail include statistical analysis and sharing data.

NOTE *When appropriate, discussions in Chapters 4 through 8 start with EasyRefreshers that let you update old skills or acquire new core business skills.*

Chapters 10 through 15 describe how to build real-life business workbooks using Excel and provide working examples of each (via the companion CD at the back of the book). For example, Chapter 10, "Building a Business Planning Workbook," describes how to build a business planning workbook based on the BIZPLAN.XLS starter workbook included on the companion CD. Chapter 11, "Building a Profit Volume and Break-

Even Analysis Workbook," describes how to perform profit-volume-cost analysis and break-even analysis using the PROFVOL.XLS starter workbook also included on the companion CD.

NOTE *For the paper copy of the* MBA's Guide to Microsoft Excel 2002, *a companion CD provides copies of the starter workbooks discussed in Chapters 10 through 15 and copies of each of the example workbooks discussed in the text. For the electronic copy of* MBA's Guide to Microsoft Excel 2002, *readers can download the starter and example workbooks from the Redmond Technology Press Web site at www.redtechpress.com. Just click on the Missing CDs hyperlink and then follow the instructions for downloading.*

What's Not in This Book

Two topics aren't covered to any great detail in this book. *MBA's Guide to Microsoft® Excel 2002* doesn't describe how to create and use macros, and it doesn't describe Excel's built-in programming language, Visual Basic for Applications®. However, you can download a free booklet that explains how macros work and that introduces Visual Basic for Applications. This booklet is available from the Redmond Technology Press web site at www.redtechpress.com.

That's it. That's all you need to know before you begin using this book!

Stephen L. Nelson

David B. Maguiness

Part 1

QuickPrimers™

In This Part

Chapter 1

QUICKPRIMER™ ON USING EXCEL

Featuring:

- Workbook Basics
- Using Formulas and Functions
- Editing Workbook Data
- Formatting Workbooks
- Printing Workbooks

This chapter provides a primer on Excel—which means you may not need to read this chapter if you possess a lot of experience using Excel. If your Excel skills could use a little polishing, however, or if you've never used Excel, read this chapter to learn how Excel works.

NOTE *With the information provided by this chapter and the next one, you could handily pass the Microsoft Office User Specialist (MOUS) certification at the proficient user level and perhaps even the expert user level. You might not be interested in receiving this certification yourself, but it is useful to understand just what knowledge is required to receive this certification. MOUS certification may be relevant for hiring and training decisions you make.*

Workbook Basics

If you're new to Excel, you'll benefit most from a quick tour of Excel, including how you start Excel, work with its windows, and create and save a workbook. That's what we'll do here.

NOTE *This discussion assumes you're comfortable working with Microsoft Windows. You should know, for example, how to start and stop programs, choose commands, and work with dialog boxes.*

Starting Excel

You can start Excel either by starting the program directly or by opening an existing Excel workbook. To start Excel directly, click the Start button, choose Programs, and then choose Microsoft Excel. When you do this, Excel starts and opens a blank workbook.

To open an Excel workbook—which indirectly starts Excel—double-click an Excel workbook file (which has an icon with a green x and, if you're viewing file extensions, has the extension .XLS) in the My Computer or Windows Explorer window. If you've recently used the file, you can also open it from the Documents menu by clicking the Start button, choosing Documents, and choosing the Excel file you want to open. When you do this, Excel starts and opens the workbook you selected.

Working with the Excel Windows

The Excel program looks and works very much like other Microsoft application programs and especially Microsoft Office programs.

Reviewing Excel's Geography

When you start Excel, the Excel program displays the Excel application window, or program window. Inside this application window, Excel typically displays one or more document windows, or workbook windows. Figure 1-1 shows how your screen looks after you start Excel and includes some callouts to point out features of the Excel program window that may be new to you.

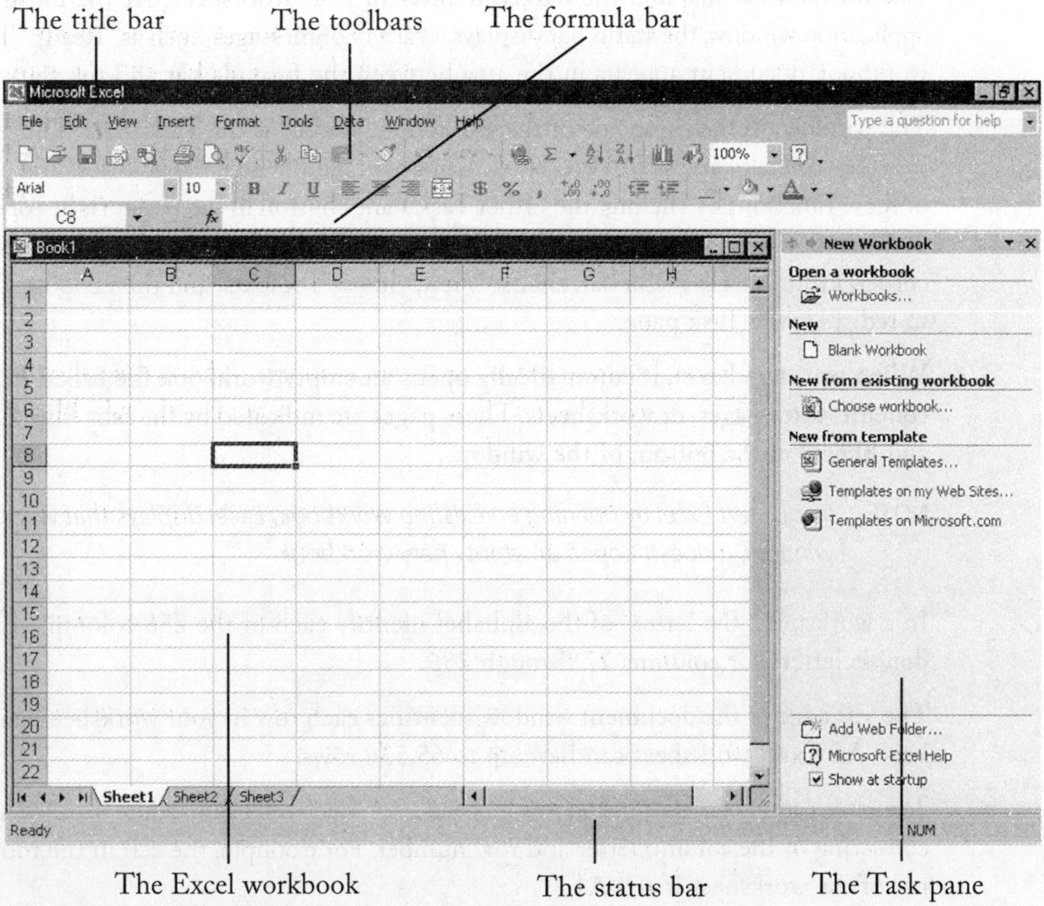

Figure 1-1 The Excel program with an Excel workbook.

The program window is the rectangle in which the Excel program displays its information. The Microsoft Excel title bar and menu bar appear at the top of the program window. The toolbar or toolbars, located just below the menu bar, provide a series of buttons that allow for faster selection of frequently used menu commands.

NOTE *Excel can personalize the menus and toolbars to show only the commands or buttons you most frequently use. If you have Excel set up to do this, and don't see a command you're looking for on a menu, click the double arrows at the bottom of the menu. Likewise, if you don't see a toolbar button on a toolbar, click the double arrows at the end of the toolbar.*

The formula bar displays the data you enter in your worksheet. At the bottom of the application window, the status bar displays a variety of messages, such as "Ready." The Excel workbook document appears in the area between the formula bar and the status bar.

The window on the right side of the workbook window is the Task pane. The Task pane provides you easy access to Workbook, Clipboard, and Search capabilities. You select one of these functions by clicking the Other Task Panes button in the upper right corner of the Task pane. If you want to close the Task pane, click the Close button in the upper right corner. From Excel's menu bar, choose View, choose Toolbars, and then choose Task Pane to redisplay the Task pane.

When you start Excel, it automatically opens an empty workbook file called Book1 that contains three pages, or worksheets. These pages are indicated by the tabs Sheet1, Sheet2, and Sheet3 at the bottom of the window.

NOTE *If you start Excel by opening an existing workbook, Excel displays that workbook in a window. It doesn't open an empty new workbook.*

In a worksheet, the letters of the alphabet identify each of the 256 columns. Excel uses double letters for columns 27 through 256.

The left edge of the document window identifies each row in your worksheet using numbers. An Excel worksheet can have up to 65,536 rows.

The intersection of a column and row is called a *cell.* Each cell has an address, called a *reference,* consisting of the column letter and row number. For example, the cell in the top left corner of the worksheet is cell A1.

A dark outline called the *cell selector* identifies the active cell. Figure 1-1 shows the cell selector in cell C8. The reference of the active cell also appears on the left side of the formula bar in the Name box. If you type a number and press the Enter key, Excel places the number in the active cell.

Moving Around a Workbook

With three (or more) sheets, 256 columns, and 65,536 rows, an Excel workbook is so large that only a small area is visible on screen at one time. Not surprisingly, Excel provides several ways for you to view different portions of the workbook displayed in the program window:

- With the mouse, you can use the vertical and horizontal scroll bars along the right and bottom edges of the document window to move through your worksheet. Just click inside the scroll bars to move one screen at a time. Click the scroll bar arrows to move one row or column.

- With the mouse, click a sheet tab to move to that worksheet in the workbook.
- The standard navigation keys, Page Up and Page Down, move through your worksheet one screen at a time. When you hold down the Ctrl key and press Page Up or Page Down, you move to the next or previous worksheet.
- The arrow keys move up and down, right and left one cell at a time. You can also move to the right one cell by pressing the Tab key; you can move to the left one cell by holding down the Shift key while pressing the Tab key.
- To move directly to a specific cell, enter that cell's name in the Name box and press the Enter key. (The Name box is located at the left end of the formula bar.) You can also choose the Edit menu's Go To command. When you choose this command, Excel displays the Go To dialog box. You can enter a cell reference in its Reference text box and then click OK to move to the cell.

Finding Help When You Need It

Excel, like other Microsoft Office programs, provides an animated character called the Office Assistant to answer any questions you may have. If you see the Office Assistant on your screen, click it to ask it a question. If you don't see the Office Assistant, choose the Help menu's Show The Office Assistant command. The Office Assistant displays a balloon you can use to enter your question, as shown in Figure 1-2. Just type your question, and click Search. The Office Assistant displays a list of topics related to your search. Click a topic to display the Microsoft Excel Help window with details on the topic you chose.

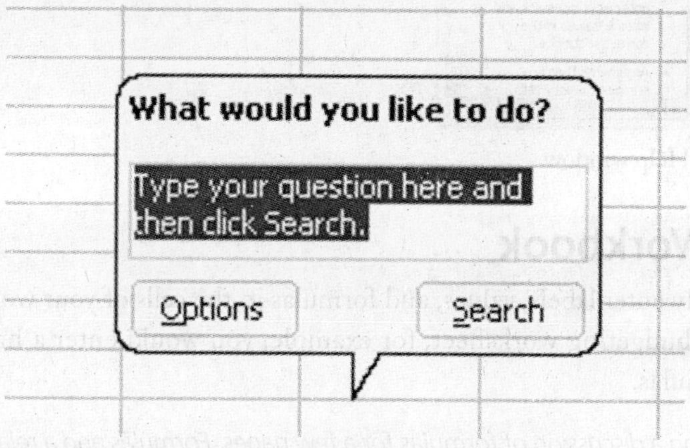

Figure 1-2 Asking the Office Assistant a question.

If the Help window doesn't answer your question, click its Show button. This displays the Contents, Answer Wizard, and Index tabs, as shown in Figure 1-3. Use the Contents tab to navigate through the help file the way you would navigate through a book by using its table of contents. Use the Answer Wizard tab to ask a question in a manner similar to the way in which you ask the Office Assistant a question. Use the Index tab to look up a keyword or phrase the way you would look up a word in a book's index.

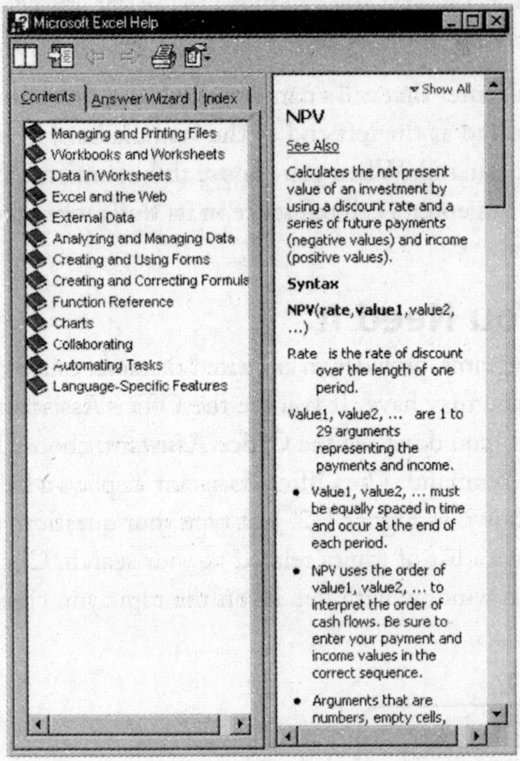

Figure 1-3 The Excel Help window.

Creating a Simple Workbook

To use Excel, you simply enter labels, values, and formulas in the cells of your worksheets. To construct a simple budgeting worksheet, for example, you would enter a handful of labels, values, and formulas.

NOTE *We're postponing a discussion of formulas for a few pages. Formulas and a related topic, functions, are described in detail in the chapter section "Using Formulas and Functions."*

Entering Labels

Labels are simply any information entered in a worksheet that you don't want to manipulatc arithmetically. They often identify the values that are subject to calculation, so you normally enter them as the first stage in setting up a worksheet. Usually, labels are pieces of text, such as the expense categories in a budgeting worksheet or the employee names in a payroll worksheet. However, they can also be numbers that won't be used arithmetically, such as telephone numbers or part or project ID numbers.

To enter a label, follow these steps:

1. **Move the cell selector to the desired location.**

   You can do this by clicking the cell, using the navigation keys to move the cell selector, or using the Name box.

2. **Type the label.**

   As you do, Excel displays what you type in the formula bar. It also adds the Enter button (the one that looks like a check mark) and the Cancel button (the one that looks like an X) to the formula bar.

3. **Set the label in the cell.**

   You can do this by pressing the Enter key, clicking the Enter button on the formula bar, or moving to another cell.

Figure 1-4 shows a simple workbook fragment with just a handful of labels. Notice that Excel aligns text to the left edge of each cell and allows long labels to spill over into adjacent cells if they are unoccupied.

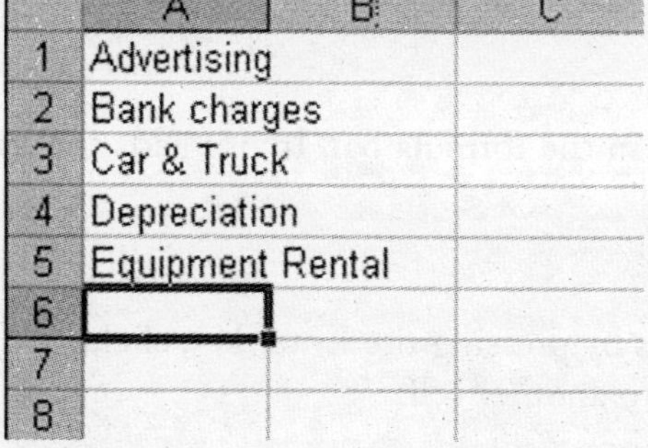

Figure 1-4 A worksheet with labels entered.

Entering Values

Values are numbers you want to add, subtract, multiply, divide, or otherwise manipulate in formulas. In a budgeting worksheet, for example, you would enter the budgeted amounts as values. Figure 1-5 shows the values, or amounts, entered beside each of the worksheet labels.

	A	B	C
1	Advertising		500
2	Bank charges		50
3	Car & Truck		500
4	Depreciation		2000
5	Equipment Rental		250
6			
7			
8			

Figure 1-5 A budgeting worksheet with labels and values.

To enter values, use the ten number keys either on the main keyboard or on the numeric keypad. To use the numeric keypad, the Num Lock key must be selected. Use the period key to show decimal places and the hyphen key to identify negative values.

To enter values, use the same three-step process you use to enter labels. For example, to enter the value 500 shown in cell C1, follow these steps:

1. **Move the cell selector to the desired cell.**

   In Figure 1-5, for example, you move the cell selector to C1 to enter the first value. You might do this by clicking.

2. **Type the value.**

   As you do, Excel displays the number in the formula bar. It also adds the Enter and Cancel buttons to the formula bar.

3. **Set the value in the cell.**

   As with setting a label, you can do this by pressing the Enter key, clicking the Enter button on the formula bar, or moving to another cell.

To enter the rest of the values shown in Figure 1-5, repeat the steps above for each value.

If a value is too large to fit into a single cell, Excel either increases the cell width or displays the cell contents using scientific notation. The number 123456789, for example, may appear as something like 1.2E+08 or 1.235E+08, depending on the width of the cell. Likewise, the number .0000001 may appear as something like 1E-07.

NOTE *Excel doesn't discard the extra digits if they don't fit in the cell. If you select the cell, you can see all the digits in the formula bar. Excel doesn't include characters such as dollar signs, percentage symbols, or commas as a part of a value (you can tell this by looking at the formula bar), but Excel does use these characters when it displays values in the worksheet. One exception to this rule concerns extremely large or extremely small values. Excel uses only the first 15 digits of a value. If you enter a value that uses more than 15 digits, Excel rewrites the value using only 15 digits. If the value uses more than 20 digits, Excel rewrites the value using scientific notation. If the value uses more than 15 digits but less than 20 digits, Excel replaces the sixteenth digit through the twentieth digit (counting from left to right) with zeros and then drops the zeros if they aren't significant. For example, the value 12345678901234567890 is rewritten to 12345678901234500000. And the value .12345678901234567890 is rewritten to .123456789012345.*

Correcting Typing Mistakes

Excel cells work like the text boxes you see elsewhere in Windows. This means that it's easy to correct any typing mistakes you make. If you make typing mistakes before setting a label or value in a cell, for example, you can use the Backspace key to erase characters to the left of the insertion point (the cursor) and then retype the correct data. You can also reposition the insertion point in the formula bar with the arrow keys and erase characters to the right with the Delete key. If you don't want to enter the data shown on the formula bar in the active cell, click the Cancel button or press the Esc key.

If you make a mistake but don't realize it until you set the label or value in the cell, move the cell selector to the cell with the erroneous content. To replace the cell's contents entirely, enter a new label or value. To edit the cell's contents, either click the formula bar or double-click the cell. Use the Backspace key to erase characters to the left of the insertion point and then retype the correct data (or reposition the insertion point with the arrow keys, erase characters to the right with the Delete key, and then retype the correct data). When the formula bar or editable text box over the cell shows the correct label or value, set it in the active cell by moving the cell selector to another cell, pressing the Enter key, or clicking Enter in the formula bar.

Saving and Opening Workbooks

To save the work you do with Excel, you save the workbooks you create. To later reuse a workbook, you open it. Neither task is difficult if you've worked with Windows a bit.

Saving Your Work for the First Time

When you first save a workbook, you must give it a name and tell Excel where to store it. If you've worked with other Windows programs, you'll find the procedure quite familiar. To save a workbook for the first time, follow these steps:

1. Choose the File menu's Save As command.

Excel displays the dialog box shown in Figure 1-6.

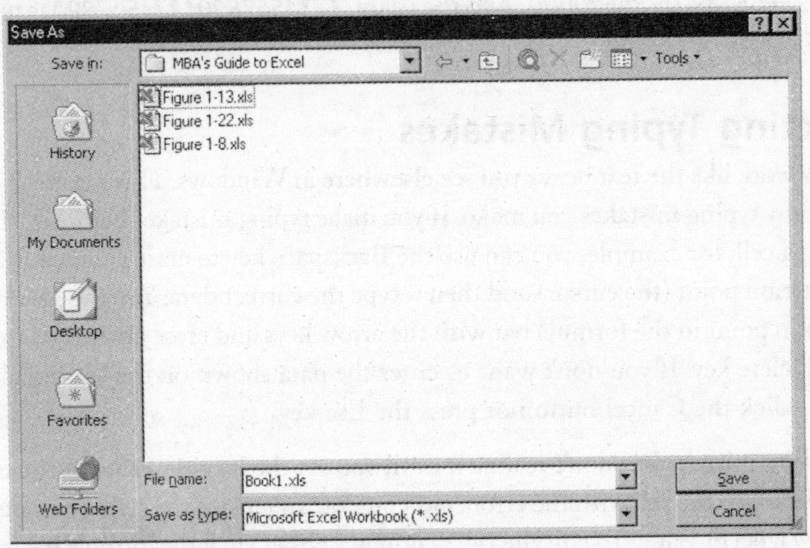

Figure 1-6 The Save As dialog box.

2. Choose a folder location for the new workbook.

To save the file in a common location for documents, click one of the icons on the left side of the Save As dialog box. For example, to save the file to the Windows desktop, click the Desktop icon. If you have Windows 95 or 98, click the My Documents icon to save the file to the default storage location for Office documents. (If you have Windows NT, click the Personal icon.) To save the file to a location other than one designated by an icon (such as a network drive), use the Save In drop-down list box and the large list box below to select the drive and folder location.

TIP *Use the Up One Level toolbar button to move up from a subfolder to its parent folder.*

3. **Name the workbook.**

   Enter a name for the file in the File Name text box. You don't need to add a file extension—Excel automatically does this for you. Excel allows you to enter very long filenames if you want, but if you do use long names, make sure that the first few characters clearly identify the workbook so it is easy to find later on.

4. **Select a file format from the Save As Type drop-down list box.**

   If you're the only one who will be using the file, accept the default format, Microsoft Excel Workbook. If you'll be sharing the file with other people, select the format they'll be using or select a format that both you and any other user can read, such as a tab-delimited or comma-delimited file.

NOTE *Selecting such a file type other than the Excel workbook format may result in the loss of formatting and functionality.*

5. **Click Save.**

   Excel saves the file in the specified location and format using whatever name you choose.

TIP *If you click the Tools button in the Save As dialog box and choose General Options, you can enter a password required to open or modify the file.*

Resaving Your Work

To save a file again and replace the previous file, click the Save toolbar button or choose the File menu's Save command. To save a file under a different name, in a different location, or in a different format, and retain the previous file, choose the File menu's Save As command. Use the Save As dialog box to specify a new name, location, or format.

Opening Workbooks

To open a workbook, follow these steps:

1. **Click the Open toolbar button.**

   Excel displays the Open dialog box shown in Figure 1-7.

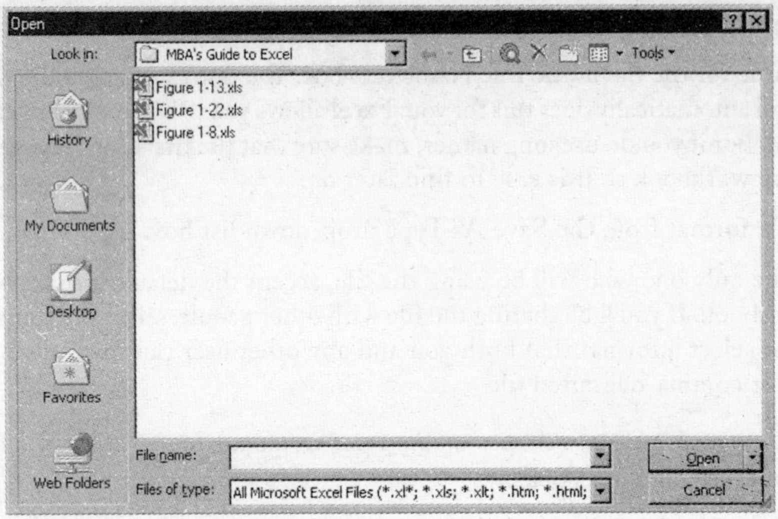

Figure 1-7 The Open dialog box.

2. Open the folder storing the file.

Use the icons along the left side, the Save In drop-down list box, and the list box of folders and files to locate the file.

3. Select the workbook.

After you find the workbook you want to open, select it by clicking it.

4. Click Open.

Excel retrieves the file from the specified location and displays it in another document window inside the Excel program window.

TIP *Excel allows you to open multiple workbooks, displaying each in its own document window, or workbook window. To move to another document window, or workbook window, choose the workbook from the Window menu.*

Using File Properties

If you choose the File menu's Properties command, Excel displays a dialog box that describes the workbook. The Properties dialog box, which isn't shown here, also lets you collect and store information about the workbook. Excel users who create or share numerous workbooks may find it useful to explore this command and its dialog box on their own.

Exiting the Program

To exit Excel, you can click the Close button (the one with an X) in the upper right corner of the Excel program window. You can also choose the File menu's Exit command.

When you exit Excel, you are asked whether you want to save any workbooks with unsaved changes. If you indicate that you want to save your changes, Excel saves the workbooks.

Using Formulas and Functions

Excel's power stems from its ability to perform calculations on the values you've stored in a workbook—something you do with *formulas* and *functions*. This section describes how to construct formulas, use Excel's predefined formulas, called functions, and use range names in formulas. It also shows how to open saved workbooks.

Entering Formulas

Excel calculates formulas automatically. You enter them in a worksheet cell in the same way that you enter labels and values. In the cell, however, Excel displays not the formula, but its result. For example, if you enter a formula that says to add 4 and 2, Excel retains the formula and displays it in the formula bar when the cell is selected, but Excel displays the result, 6, in the worksheet itself.

Formula Fundamentals

Formulas must begin with the equal sign (=); that's how Excel distinguishes them from values and labels. You can construct formulas that subtract, multiply, divide, and exponentiate. The – symbol means subtraction, the * means multiplication, the / means division, and the ^ means exponential operation. Table 1-1 shows the different mathematical operators and the results they return.

FORMULA ENTERED	RESULT DISPLAYED IN CELL
=4+2	6
=4-2	2
=4*2	8
=4/2	2
=4^2	16

Table 1-1 A list of simple formulas illustrating the standard arithmetic operators.

Figure 1-8 shows a simple budgeting worksheet built from Figure 1-5. The formula used in cell C7 appears in the formula bar and the result is displayed in the worksheet.

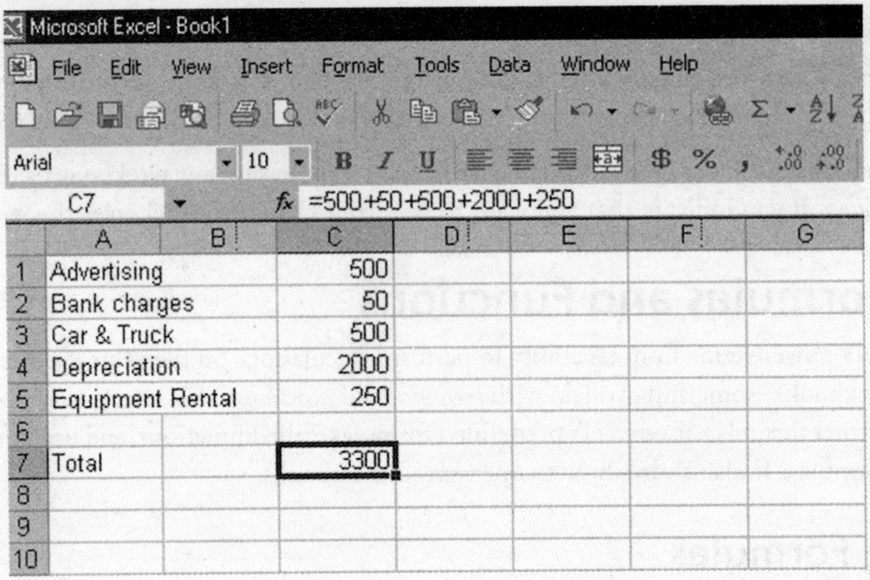

Figure 1-8 A budgeting worksheet with a formula entered and the result displayed.

To build more complicated formulas, you need to recognize the standard rules of operator precedence: Excel first performs exponential operations, then multiplication and division operations, and finally, addition and subtraction.

For example, in the equation =1+2*3^4, Excel first raises 3 to the fourth power to get 81. It then multiplies this value by 2 to get 162. Finally, it adds 1 to this value to get 163.

To override these rules, you must use parentheses. You can use multiple sets of parentheses in a formula as need be. Excel first performs the function in the innermost set of parentheses. Take the following formulas in Table 1-2 as an example:

FORMULA ENTERED	RESULT DISPLAYED IN CELL
=1+2*3^4	163
=(1+2)*3^4	243
=((1+2)*3)^4	6561

Table 1-2 A list of formulas that show how parentheses override operator procedure.

Using Cell References

In the budgeting worksheet, you could total the budgeted expenses by entering the formula =500+50+500+2000+250 in cell C7. There is, however, a practical problem with this approach: You would need to rewrite the formula each time any of the values changed. Because this approach is unwieldy, Excel also allows you to use cell references in formulas.

When a formula includes a cell reference, Excel uses the value that cell contains. For example, to add the budgeted amounts on your budgeting worksheet using a formula with cell references, follow these steps:

1. **Move the cell selector to C7.**

   You can do this by clicking cell C8. Or you can use the arrow keys.

2. **Type =C1+C2+C3+C4+C5.**

   If you make a mistake entering this formula, you can edit it in the same way that you edit any label or value.

3. **Press the Enter key, or click the Enter button.**

   Excel enters your formula in the cell, calculates the formula, and then displays the formula result.

To reference a cell on the same worksheet as the formula, you need to supply only the column-letter-and-row-number cell reference. To reference cell C1 on the same worksheet, for example, you enter C1.

You can also reference cells on other worksheets. To reference a cell on another worksheet in the same workbook, however, you need to precede the cell reference with the name of the worksheet and an exclamation point symbol. To reference cell C1 on the worksheet named Sheet2, for example, you enter Sheet2!C1.

You can reference cells in other workbooks, too. To do this most easily, open the other workbooks, begin building your formula as described earlier in this chapter, and then click the other workbook cell you want to reference at the point you want to include the reference. Excel then writes the full cell reference for you, which includes the workbook name. An external reference to cell C1 on the worksheet named Sheet2 in the workbook named Budget might be written as =[Budget.xls]Sheet2!$C$1.

Understanding Worksheet Recalculation

As you build and edit your worksheet, Excel automatically updates the formulas and recalculates their results. For example, in the budgeting worksheet, if you change the value in cell C1 from 500 to 600, Excel recalculates any formulas that use the value stored in cell C1. As a result, the formula in cell C7 returns the value 3400—an increase of one hundred.

In simple worksheets such as the one shown in Figure 1-9, recalculation takes place so quickly you won't even be aware it's occurring. In larger worksheets with hundreds or even thousands of formulas, however, recalculation is much slower. The mouse pointer changes to the hourglass symbol when Excel is busy recalculating.

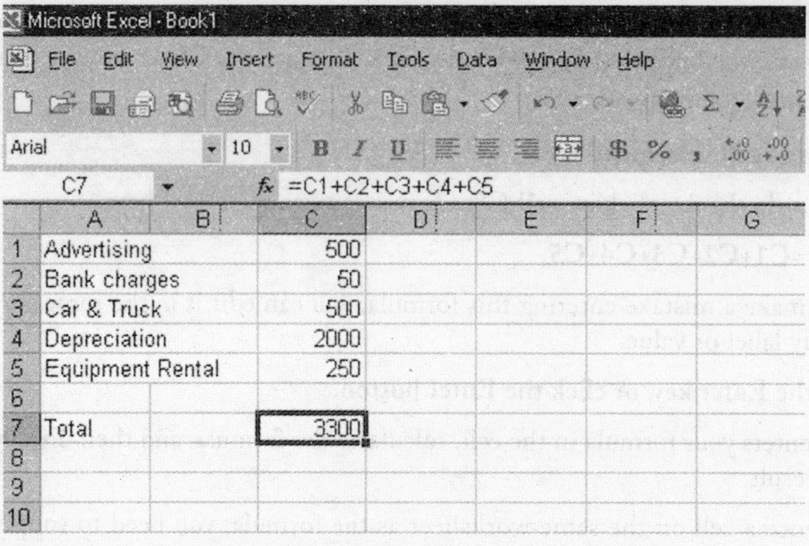

Figure 1-9 A worksheet with cell references used in a formula.

If you don't want Excel to automatically recalculate formulas as you're working, choose the Tools menu's Options command and click the Calculation tab. Then click the Manual option button under Calculation, and click OK. The word *Calculate* appears on the status bar when your worksheet needs to be recalculated. You can force recalculation by pressing the F9 key.

Formula Errors

It's possible to build an illogical or unsolvable formula. When you do, Excel displays an error message in the cell rather than calculating the result. The error message, which begins with the # symbol, describes the error. Suppose, for example, that you enter the formula =1/0 in a cell. Because division by zero is an undefined mathematical operation, Excel can't solve the formula. To alert you to this, Excel displays the error message #DIV/0!.

Another common error is a circular reference. This occurs when two or more formulas indirectly depend on one another to achieve a result. For example, if the formula in cell A1 is =A2 and the formula in cell A2 is =A1+A3+A4, A1 depends on A2 and A2 depends on A1. Excel displays a warning and the Circular Reference toolbar when you create a circular reference. Excel identifies circular references by displaying the word *Circular* on the status bar and showing the address of the cell whose formula completed the "circle." It also draws arrows between the cells causing the circle.

To fix a formula error, edit the erroneous formula using the same techniques as with label and value editing. Move the cell selector to the cell holding the formula, click the formula bar, and edit the formula. When the formula is correct, set it by moving the cell selector, pressing the Enter key, or clicking the Enter button.

NOTE *When a formula refers to a cell that contains an erroneous formula, both formulas return the error message. For example, if cell A1 attempts to divide by zero and cell A2 refers to cell A1, cell A2 returns the error message #DIV/0! as well.*

Using Functions

Excel provides several hundred pre-built formulas, called functions, that provide a shortcut to constructing complicated or lengthy formulas. In general, a function accepts input values, or arguments, then makes some calculation and returns a result.

Excel provides financial, statistical, mathematical, trigonometric, and even engineering functions. Each function has a name that describes its operation. The function that adds values is named SUM, for example, and the function that calculates an arithmetic mean, or average, is named AVERAGE.

Most functions require arguments, or input values, which you enclose in parentheses. The ROUND function, for example, rounds a specific value to a specified number of decimal places. To round the value 5.75 to the nearest tenth, you could use the function shown below:

```
=ROUND(5.75, 1)
```

Even if a function doesn't require arguments, you still need to include the parentheses. For example, the function PI returns the mathematical constant Pi. The function needs no arguments, but you still need to enter it as =PI().

Functions can use values, formulas, and even other functions as arguments. If entered in the budgeting worksheet shown in Figure 1-9, for example, each of the following functions returns the same result, 3300:

```
=SUM(C1:C5)

=SUM(C1,C2,C3,C4,C5)

=SUM(500,50,500,2000,250)

=SUM(SUM(C1),SUM(C2),SUM(C3),SUM(C4),SUM(C5))
```

NOTE *Because summing is such a common spreadsheet operation, Excel provides an AutoSum button on the toolbar; you can use it to enter an =SUM function in the active cell of a contiguous range of cells. If cell C6 in the worksheet shown in Figure 1-9 were empty, for example, and you selected the range C1:C6, you could click the AutoSum toolbar button to direct Excel to place the formula =SUM(C1:C5) in cell C6.*

TIP *To identify a toolbar button, point to the button. Excel displays the button name in a small box called a ToolTip. If you point to the button that shows the Greek sigma character, for example, Excel displays a ToolTip box identifying the button as the AutoSum button.*

To most easily insert complicated functions and reduce your chance of error, click the Insert Function button on the formula bar or choose the Insert menu's Function command. This displays the Insert Function dialog box shown in Figure 1-10. Search for a function or select a category using the upper box and select a specific function from the list in the lower box. Because some of the functions are a little difficult to recognize or distinguish by name, Excel describes what the selected function does at the bottom of the Insert Function dialog box. When you have found the function you want to use, click OK.

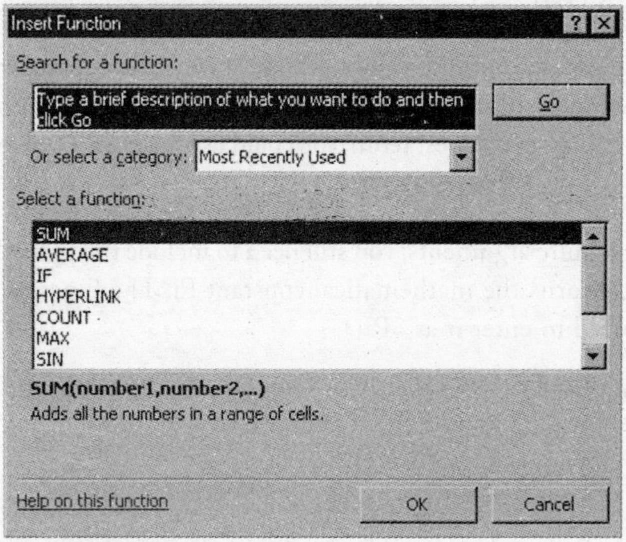

Figure 1-10 The Insert Function dialog box.

Excel displays the Function Arguments dialog box with text boxes you can use to identify or supply the arguments required for the function, as shown in Figure 1-11. If necessary, drag this dialog box to another portion of your screen to see the cells you want to include in the function. To enter cell data in an argument text box, click that box and then select the cell or range of cells in your worksheet that goes in the box. Excel highlights the cell or cells you selected with a flashing box. To enter cell data in another argument text box, click that box and select the cell or range in your worksheet that contains the data required for that box. Click OK when you're finished. Excel pastes the function in the cell.

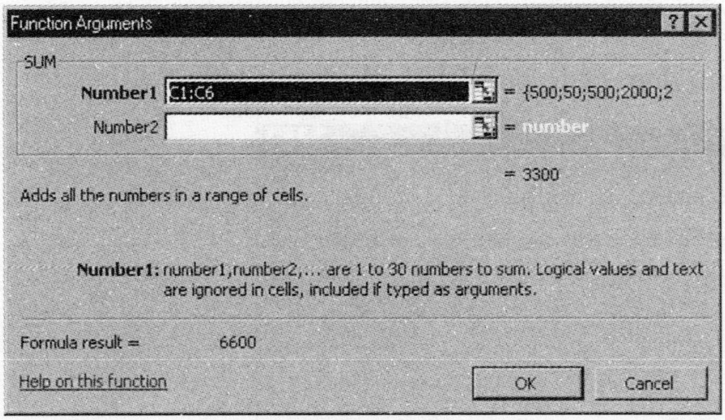

Figure 1-11 Selecting data required for a function.

NOTE *A range is simply any rectangular area of the worksheet, such as a two-cell by two-cell square, a five-cell by nine-cell rectangle, or even an entire worksheet. Excel uses opposite corner cell references and a colon to define ranges. For example, the range of cells from C1 and up to and including C5 is written as C1:C5. And the range of cells from C1 to D2 is written as C1:D2.*

Naming Cells and Ranges

In a small sample worksheet such as the one shown in Figure 1-9, it's not too difficult to remember that cell C1 contains the advertising expenses, C2 contains the bank charges, and so on. In the real world, however, Excel worksheets can be much more complex, and keeping track of what each cell represents becomes correspondingly more difficult. In this way, instead of referring to cell C1 in a formula, you could refer to Advertising if you first name the individual cell Advertising. For example, if you named cells C1, C2, C3, C4, and C5 Advertising, Bank, Car, Depreciation, and Equipment, respectively, the following two formulas would be identical:

```
=C1+C2+C3+C4+C5

=Advertising+Bank+Car+Depreciation+Equipment
```

To name a cell or range, follow these steps:

1. Select the cell or range of cells to be named.

You can select a cell by clicking it or by using the arrow keys to move the cell selector to the cell. You can select a range of cells by clicking on one corner of the range and then, while holding down the mouse button, dragging the mouse to the opposite corner of the range.

2. **Choose the Insert menu's Name command, and then choose Define.**

   Excel displays the Define Name dialog box shown in Figure 1-12.

Figure 1-12 The Define Name dialog box.

3. **Enter a name in the Names In Workbook text box.**

   Range names must begin with a letter, not a number. They cannot include spaces, and they shouldn't look like cell references or function names.

4. **Click Add.**

   To create another name, click Add and then repeat steps 1 through 3. To finish creating names, click OK.

Range names are useful in formulas and functions, but that's not their only use. Once you name a range, you can use the name in place of the range definition whenever Excel asks you for a range. For example, if you use the Go To command, you could enter a name instead of a cell address.

Editing Workbook Data

Excel supplies many helpful commands that make creating and editing your workbooks easier and more efficient. If you anticipate spending any time at all working with Excel, it makes good sense for you to learn how these tools work and when they come in handy.

Erasing Cell Contents

You can erase the contents and formatting from a single cell or a range quickly and easily. To erase, follow these steps:

1. **Select the cell or range you want to clear.**

   You can select a cell by clicking it. You can select a range of cells by dragging the mouse from one corner of the range to the opposite corner of the range.

2. **Delete the cell contents.**

   Press the Delete key to erase all contents and formatting, or choose the Edit menu's Clear command to specify what you want to erase. Choose one of the three commands from the submenu, as shown in Table 1-3.

COMMAND	DESCRIPTION
All	Erases all contents and formatting
Formats	Erases formatting but leaves contents.
Contents	Erases the contents but leaves the formatting.
Comments	Erases any comments inserted using the Insert menu's Comment command.

Table 1-3 The Clear submenu's commands.

Undoing Mistakes

If you make a mistake while entering data or editing your worksheet, you can use the Undo toolbar button to reverse the effects of your last actions. You can also undo the Undo operation by clicking the Redo toolbar button. To reverse the effects of a series of most recent actions, click the arrow beside the Undo toolbar button and select multiple actions from the list. To redo a series of last actions, click the arrow beside the Redo toolbar button and select multiple actions from the list.

Copying, Cutting, and Pasting

You can copy or cut the contents of cells and ranges and then paste them into other locations. This means you don't have to repeatedly type a label, value, or formula. You can type the entry just once and then copy or move it.

TIP *With most programs, when you copy or cut something, the program places it on the Windows Clipboard. The only catch with the Windows Clipboard is that it can hold only one copied or cut piece of information at a time. So if you copy or cut another piece of information, the program replaces what the Clipboard previously stored. Office has a nifty feature called the Clipboard toolbar that allows you to store up to 12 pieces of copied or cut information at a time. To use the Clipboard toolbar, choose the View menu's Toolbars command and then choose Clipboard.*

Copying Labels and Values

Suppose, for example, that the numbers shown in column C of the budgeting worksheet represent the budgeted expenses for January and that the same figures are projected for February and March, as shown in Figure 1-13. Rather than reenter the same values, you could copy the values already stored in column C.

	A	B	C	D	E	F
1	Advertising		600			
2	Bank charges		50			
3	Car & Truck		500			
4	Depreciation		2000			
5	Equipment Rental		250			
6						
7	Total		3400			
8						
9						

Figure 1-13 The simple budgeting worksheet.

To copy the labels and values for such an operation, follow these steps:

1. **Select the cell or range to be copied.**

   In Figure 1-13, this would mean you select the range C1:C5. The easiest method for selecting a specific cell or range is by clicking or clicking and dragging the mouse.

2. **Click the Copy toolbar button, or choose the Edit menu's Copy command.**

   When you do this, Excel places a copy of the labels and values on the Clipboard.

3. **Select the destination cell or the cell in the upper left corner of the destination range.**

   If you want to duplicate the selected cells more than once, select the multiple destination ranges in their entirety. For the worksheet shown in Figure 1-13, for example, you would select the range D1:E5.

4. **Click the Paste toolbar button, or choose the Edit menu's Paste command.**

   When you do this, Excel copies the worksheet range from the Clipboard into the specified worksheet range.

NOTE *If you paste a copy of a single cell into a multiple-cell range, the contents of the cell are duplicated in each cell in the destination range.*

TIP *You can also copy a cell or range with the mouse. Just select the cell or range, hold down the Ctrl key, point to the black border around the cell or range so that the mouse pointer changes from a cross to an arrow, and then drag the cell or range to a new location.*

Copying Formulas

When you copy labels and values, Excel duplicates the contents of the copied cell or cells and pastes the data into the selected range. When you copy a formula, however, Excel adjusts any cell references used in the formula. This important difference can be illustrated by copying the formula in cell C7 of Figure 1-14, =C1+C2+C3+C4+C5, into cells D7 and E7. To do this, follow these steps:

1. Select the cell or range with the formula(s) you want to copy.

In the example of the worksheet shown in Figure 1-14, you would select cell C7.

	A	B	C	D	E	F
1	Advertising		600	600	600	
2	Bank charges		50	50	50	
3	Car & Truck		500	500	500	
4	Depreciation		2000	2000	2000	
5	Equipment Rental		250	250	250	
6						
7	Total		3400			
8						
9						

Figure 1-14 A worksheet with two copies of C1:C5 pasted in D1:E5.

2. Click the Copy toolbar button.

Excel moves a copy of the formula in cell C7 to the Clipboard.

3. Select the destination range D7:E7.

In the example of the worksheet shown in Figure 1-14, you would select the range D7:E7.

4. Click the Paste toolbar button.

Excel adjusts the formulas for the column in question and pastes the formula =D1+D2+D3+D4+D5 into cell D7 and the formula =E1+E2+E3+E4+E5 into cell E7. Figure 1-15 shows the worksheet after copying the formula.

	A	B	C	D	E	F
1	Advertising		600	600	600	
2	Bank charges		50	50	50	
3	Car & Truck		500	500	500	
4	Depreciation		2000	2000	2000	
5	Equipment Rental		250	250	250	
6						
7	Total		3400	3400	3400	
8						
9						

Figure 1-15 The budgeting worksheet after copying the formula in cell C7 into cells D7 and E7.

The formula changes that Excel makes aren't a mistake. Excel assumes—unless you tell it otherwise—that the cell references in your formulas are *relative.* When Excel copies and pastes a formula with relative cell references, it adjusts them.

To prevent Excel from automatically adjusting the relative references of copied formulas, you can make them *absolute.* Simply place a dollar sign ($) in front of the part or parts you don't want Excel to adjust. For example, to tell Excel not to adjust the formula at all, place a dollar sign in front of both the column letter and row number like this $A$1. To allow Excel to adjust row numbers but not column letters, put a dollar sign in front of the column letter but not the row number, like this: $A1. And to allow Excel to adjust column letters but not row numbers, put a dollar sign in front of the row number but not the column letter, like this: A$1.

Special Pasting Options

If you want to specify pasting options, instead of just clicking the Paste button after copying or cutting, choose the Edit menu's Paste Special command. Excel displays the Paste Special dialog box shown in Figure 1-16. To paste a row of cells as a column of cells or vice versa, select the Transpose check box. To paste only a portion of the copied or cut cells' contents, click a Paste option button other than All. For example, to paste only the comments in a cell, click the Comments option button under Paste. To add, subtract, multiply, or divide the values in the copied range with the values in the destination range, click the Add, Subtract, Multiply, or Divide option button under Operation. To tell Excel it shouldn't paste blank cells over values, select the Skip Blanks check box.

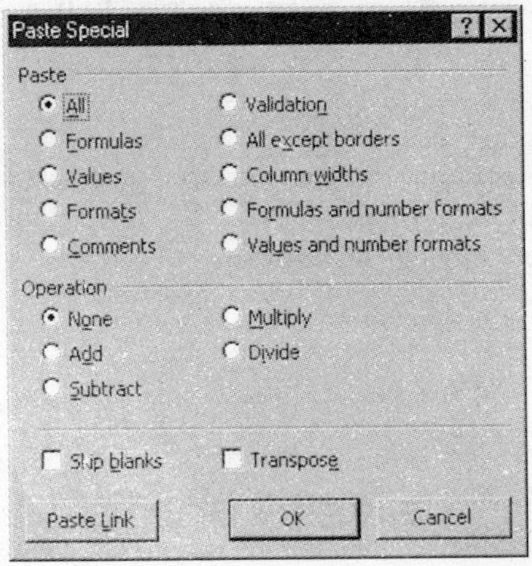

Figure 1-16 The Paste Special dialog box.

Moving Labels, Values, and Formulas

To move, rather than copy, a selected range, follow the same procedure, but click the Cut toolbar button or choose the Edit menu's Cut command instead of choosing the Copy command. Excel removes the selected contents from their original location and allows you to paste them in a new location.

NOTE *When you move a formula, Excel doesn't adjust the relative references used in the moved formula.*

You can also move a cell or range with the mouse by selecting the cell or range and pointing to the black border around the cell or range so that the mouse pointer changes from a cross to an arrow. Then drag the cell or range to a new location.

Filling Ranges

To continue a pattern you've begun, use the fill handle in the lower right corner of a cell or range. For example, if you begin the pattern 0, 5, 10 and want to continue it down a column, select the cells holding these values and click the little black square in the lower right corner of the range. The mouse pointer changes from a white outlined cross to a black cross. Now drag the mouse down the column as far as you want the pattern to go. This procedure also works for easily identifiable patterns of labels, such as months of the year and days of the week.

Inserting and Deleting Cells, Rows, Columns, and Worksheets

Excel lets you insert and delete cells, rows, columns, and worksheets in your workbook with speed and efficiency. You can easily delete what you no longer need or insert new items between existing entries when you need more space.

Using the Insert Command

To insert a row, click any cell in the row below where you want a row inserted. Then choose the Insert menu's Rows command.

To insert a column, click any cell in the column to the right of where you want a column inserted and choose the Insert menu's Columns command.

To insert a cell in a column or row, choose the Insert menu's Cells command. Excel displays the Insert dialog box shown in Figure 1-17. Click the Shift Cells Right button to insert a new cell in a row or click the Shift Cells Down button to insert a new cell in a column. After you've selected the appropriate option button, click OK.

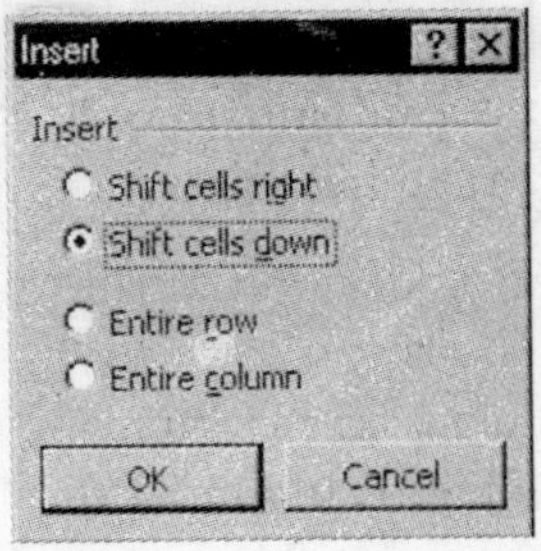

Figure 1-17 The Insert dialog box.

To insert a worksheet, display the worksheet in front of which you want to create a new worksheet and choose the Insert menu's Worksheet command.

Using the Delete Command

To delete a cell, range, row, or column, select the specific cell or range or any cell in the row or column you want to delete and choose the Edit menu's Delete command. Excel displays the Delete dialog box shown in Figure 1-18. Describe whether you want to shift the remaining cells up or to the left, or whether you want to delete the entire row or column, and click OK.

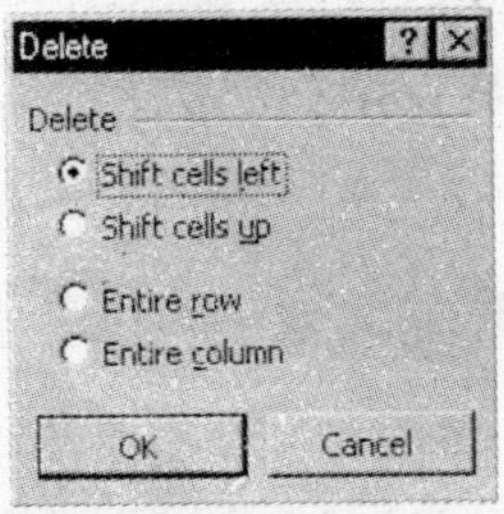

Figure 1-18 The Delete dialog box.

Excel attempts to adjust the cell references and range definitions used in formulas for row and column insertions and deletions. For example, if a formula uses values in column C and you delete column B so that column C becomes the new column B, Excel adjust the formulas to read column B. If you delete a cell referenced in a formula, however, Excel replaces the formula's reference with the error message #REF, indicating that the formula originally referenced a now-deleted cell.

Using Find and Replace

Excel provides two commands that you can use to search your workbook for specific entries. The Find command simply locates the contents you're looking for. The Replace command locates the contents and then gives you the option of replacing them with a new label, value, or formula.

Using the Find Command

To search your worksheet and locate specific entries, choose the Edit menu's Find command. Excel displays the Find And Replace dialog box with the Find tab displayed, as shown in Figure 1-19.

Figure 1-19 The Find And Replace dialog box.

Enter the label, value, or formula you want to find in the Find What text box, use the drop-down list boxes and check boxes to specify the parameters of your search, and then click Find Next to begin. If Excel finds an entry that matches your search parameters, it moves the cell selector to that cell. To resume searching, click Find Next again. Click Close when you're finished.

Using the Replace Command

When you choose the Edit menu's Replace command, Excel displays the Find And Replace dialog box with the Replace tab displayed, as shown in Figure 1-20.

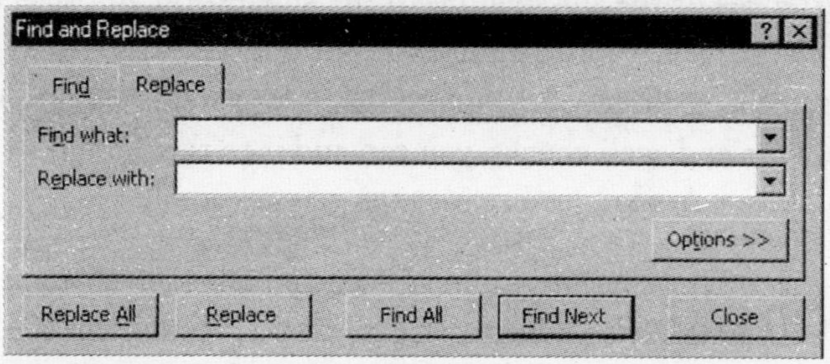

Figure 1-20 The Find And Replace dialog box.

Enter the item you want to find in the Find What text box and the label, value, or formula with which you want to replace it in the Replace With text box. Use the drop-down list box and check boxes to specify the parameters of your search.

Click Find Next and Replace to search for and replace entries one by one. Or click Replace All to have Excel automatically find and replace all occurrences of the entry without requesting verification from you. Click Close when you're finished.

TIP *With large or complex workbooks, you can streamline your find-and-replace efforts by first selecting the specific range you want to search. If you don't do this, Excel searches your entire workbook.*

Checking Your Spelling

Excel lets you check the spelling of a selected word, within a selected range or within an entire workbook. To check spelling, click the Spelling toolbar button. If Excel finds a word that's not in its dictionary, it displays the Spelling dialog box, as shown in Figure 1-21.

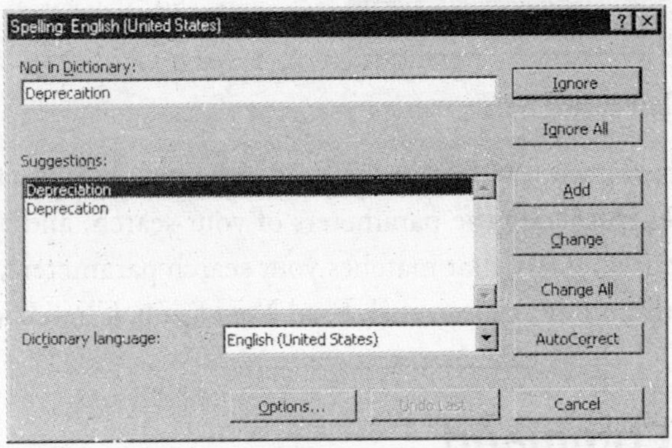

Figure 1-21 The Spelling dialog box.

If one of Excel's suggestions is correct, select it from the list box and click Change. If you want to change all occurrences of the misspelling to the suggestion you selected, click Change All. If you want to ignore the misspelling and continue, click Ignore. If you want to Ignore all occurrences of the spelling, click Ignore All. If you want Excel to recognize the word in future documents and spell checks, you can add it to the dictionary by clicking Add.

Formatting Workbooks

With proper formatting, your worksheets are easier to read and more visually attractive. Fortunately, Excel includes a rich set of easy-to-use tools for formatting your workbook data so it's more enjoyable and easier to read.

Using a Predesigned Format

Excel's AutoFormat feature performs many standard formatting tasks in a single operation: setting fonts, aligning labels, setting column width and row height, establishing numeric and date/time formats, and adding borders and rules.

To use AutoFormat, you first enter worksheet labels, values, and formulas, as shown in Figure 1-22.

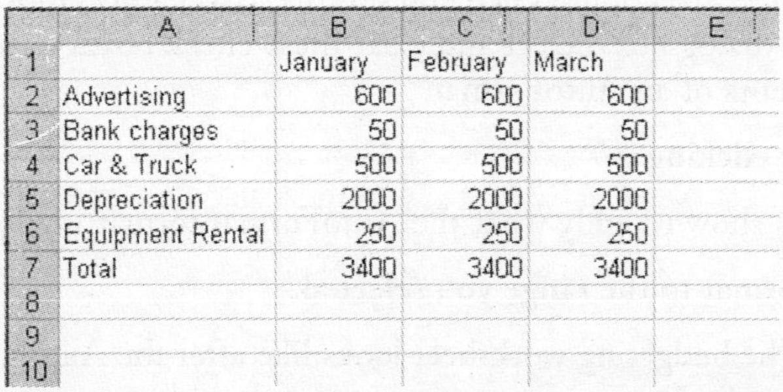

	A	B	C	D	E
1		January	February	March	
2	Advertising	600	600	600	
3	Bank charges	50	50	50	
4	Car & Truck	500	500	500	
5	Depreciation	2000	2000	2000	
6	Equipment Rental	250	250	250	
7	Total	3400	3400	3400	
8					
9					
10					

Figure 1-22 The budgeting worksheet before an AutoFormat is applied.

To use the AutoFormat command, follow these steps:

1. **Select the worksheet range you want to format.**

   In Figure 1-22, you would select the range A1:D7.

2. **Choose the Format menu's AutoFormat command.**

   Excel displays the AutoFormat dialog box shown in Figure 1-23.

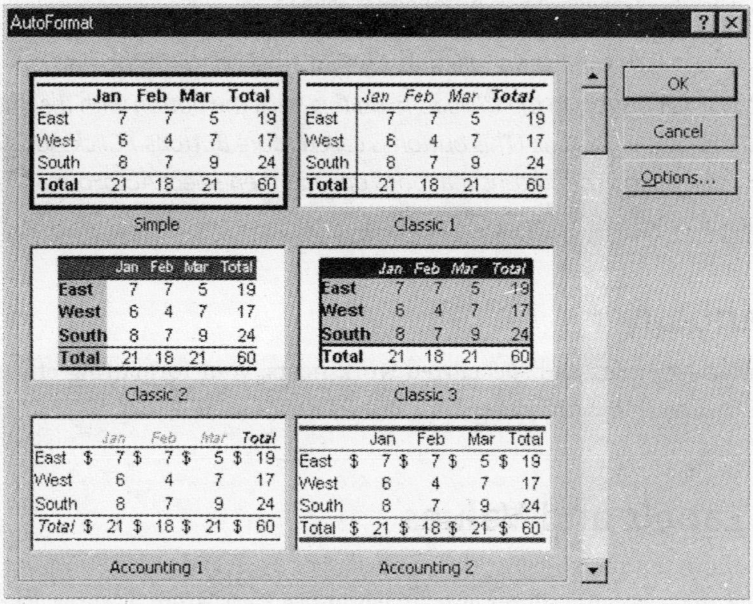

Figure 1-23 The AutoFormat dialog box.

3. **Select the AutoFormatting options you want to use.**

   Click the Options button if you want to specify which AutoFormatting options should be applied to your worksheet selection. When you do this, Excel adds Options check boxes to the AutoFormat dialog box. Select and clear these check boxes to selectively apply individual components of an AutoFormat.

4. **Select an AutoFormat by clicking it.**

   The AutoFormat pictures show roughly what the AutoFormat formatting looks like.

5. **Click OK to apply the format to the range you selected.**

   Figure 1-24 shows what the budgeting worksheet looks like after the AutoFormat selected in Figure 1-23 is applied.

	A	B	C	D	E
1		January	February	March	
2	Advertising	600	600	600	
3	Bank charges	50	50	50	
4	Car & Truck	500	500	500	
5	Depreciation	2000	2000	2000	
6	Equipment Rental	250	250	250	
7	Total	3400	3400	3400	
8					

Figure 1-24 A worksheet range with an AutoFormat applied.

TIP *If you like the AutoFormat feature and find yourself using it a lot, you can easily add the AutoFormat button to the toolbar. To do this, click the button with the arrows at the far right side of the toolbar. (This button is called More Buttons.) Click Add Or Remove Buttons from the box of buttons that pops up, and then select AutoFormat from the list of formatting buttons.*

Formatting Manually

As you create more complex and specialized worksheets, your formatting efforts require similar treatment. The following paragraphs briefly detail each of Excel's formatting features.

Aligning Labels and Values

Excel normally aligns numbers against the right edge of a cell and text against the left edge. You can override these default alignments by using the Left Align, Center, Right Align, and Merge And Center buttons on the toolbar.

The Left Align, Center, and Right Align toolbar buttons work as you might expect. For example, to left-align the contents of selected cells, click the Left Align button.

The Merge And Center toolbar button is a little more complex. It lets you center a label across a selection of cells. For example, you can enter a label in cell A1 of the budgeting worksheet, as shown in Figure 1-25, and then center it across the range A1:D1.

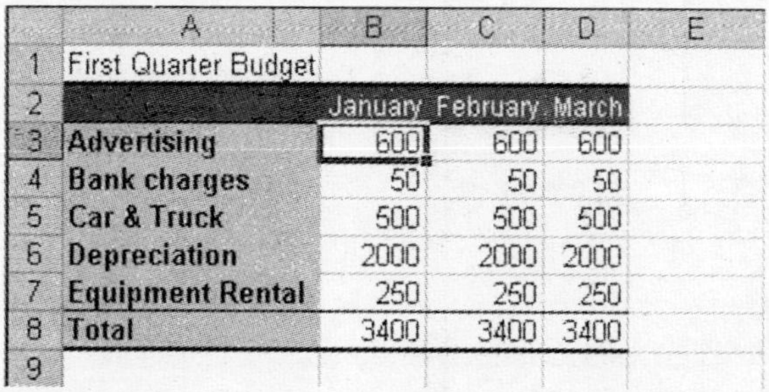

	A	B	C	D	E
1	First Quarter Budget				
2		January	February	March	
3	Advertising	600	600	600	
4	Bank charges	50	50	50	
5	Car & Truck	500	500	500	
6	Depreciation	2000	2000	2000	
7	Equipment Rental	250	250	250	
8	Total	3400	3400	3400	
9					

Figure 1-25 A label in cell A1.

To do so, first select the range and then click the Merge And Center toolbar button. Figure 1-26 shows the worksheet after making this alignment.

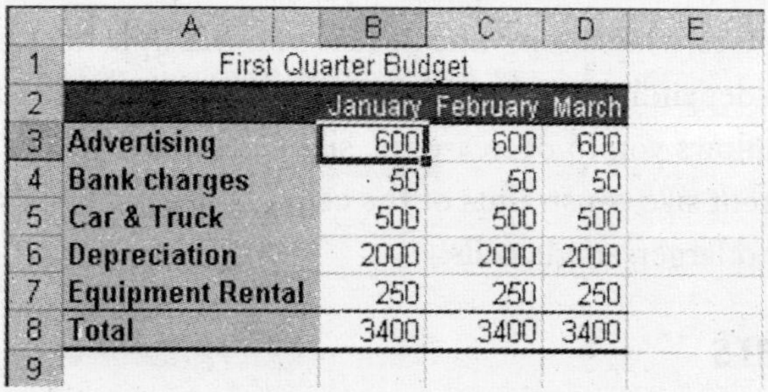

	A	B	C	D	E
1	First Quarter Budget				
2		January	February	March	
3	Advertising	600	600	600	
4	Bank charges	50	50	50	
5	Car & Truck	500	500	500	
6	Depreciation	2000	2000	2000	
7	Equipment Rental	250	250	250	
8	Total	3400	3400	3400	
9					

Figure 1-26 A label centered across the range A1:D1.

You can access a more sophisticated array of alignment features by selecting the cell or range you want to align, choosing the Format menu's Cells command, and clicking the Alignment tab, as shown in Figure 1-27. The Horizontal drop-down list box lets you align cell contents in the same ways as the Left Align, Center, Right Align, and Merge And Center tools do. The Vertical drop-down list box allows you to align cell contents at the top, center, or bottom of the cell. The Orientation box allows you to rotate the cell contents.

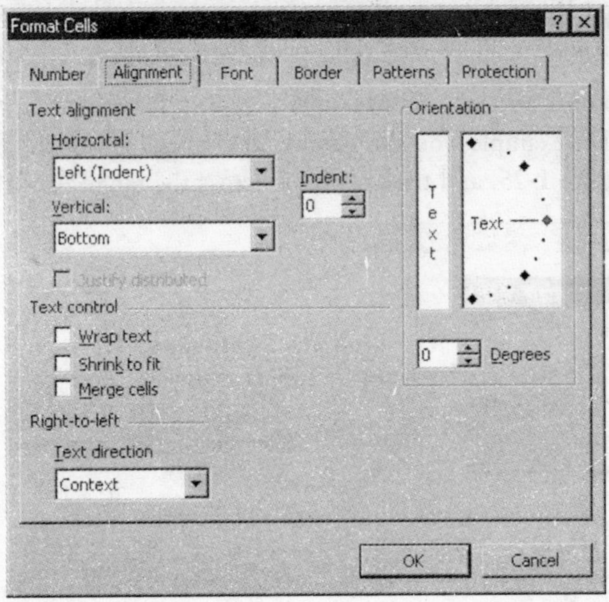

Figure 1-27 The Alignment tab of the Format Cells dialog box.

The Text Control boxes provide you with several more specialized alignment options. The Wrap Text check box allows you to wrap a long line of text into multiple lines in a single cell. The number of lines varies depending on the amount of text and the width of the cell. The Shrink To Fit check box allows you to decrease the size of the numbers or letters in a cell so that they fit in the current size constraints of the cell. The Merge Cells check box allows you to combine cells into larger, single cells.

Formatting Numbers

You can assign numeric formats such as dollar signs, percentage symbols, and commas. To quickly assign these specific common formats, select the cell or range you want to format and click the Currency Style, Percent Style, or Comma Style toolbar button. To assign other numeric formats, follow these steps:

1. Choose the Format menu's Cells command, and click the Number tab.

Excel displays the Number tab of the Format Cells dialog box, as shown in Figure 1-28.

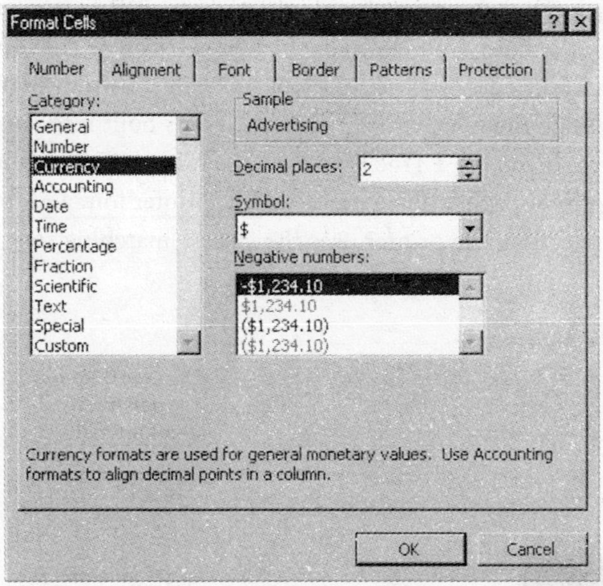

Figure 1-28 The Number tab of the Format Cells dialog box.

2. **Select a numeric formatting category from the list on the left.**

   In a budgeting worksheet, you would probably choose the Accounting category.

3. **Use the boxes and buttons for the category you chose to specify the exact formatting.**

   In a budgeting worksheet, for example, you might need to select a different currency symbol from the Symbol drop-down list box.

4. **Click OK.**

Changing Font and Font Size

Excel offers a wide variety of choices for changing a selected font's appearance, such as by adding boldfacing or underlining, for changing a font, and for specifying a different size.

To add effects such as boldfacing, italics, and underlining, you can use the Bold, Italic, and Underline font buttons on Excel's toolbar. To use any of these buttons, simply select the worksheet range you want to format and then click the button.

NOTE *If you're creating an Excel worksheet that you intend to publish on the World Wide Web, you probably don't want to use underlines in your formatting. Underlines are usually reserved for hyperlinks.*

To change the font of text, click the down arrow beside the Font toolbar button and select a font from the list. If you open the Font drop-down list box, Excel displays the font's name using the font itself, so you can preview what the font looks like, as shown in Figure 1-29. Fonts listed with a TT icon beside them are TrueType fonts. Fonts built into your printer have a printer icon next to them. If you use a TrueType font, the font you see on your screen will be the same one that the printer prints. If you use a scalable printer font and the printer you use doesn't support your selection, the printer uses the closest-matching font.

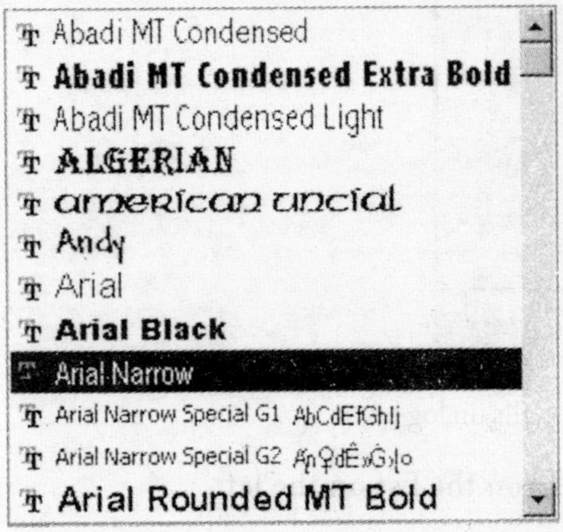

Figure 1-29 The Font drop-down list box.

To change the size of text, click the down arrow beside the Size toolbar button. Fonts are measured using points. One point is 1/72 of an inch. So a point size of 18 means that the font is ¼ inch tall. Excel's default point size is 10. You probably don't want to use fonts smaller than 10 points for legibility.

Adding Color to Cells and Text

Excel allows you to add color and shading to your data to help you organize, clarify, and emphasize the information on your worksheet—as well as to add interest.

To change the color of text, select the range you want to color, click the down arrow beside the Font Color toolbar button, and then select a color for the text.

To add a background color to a range of cells, select the range, click the down arrow beside the Fill Color toolbar button, and select a color for the cell background.

TIP *You can select a background pattern instead of, or in addition to, a background color. To do this, select the cell or range in which you want to have a background pattern, choose the Format menu's Cells command, and click the Patterns tab of the Format Cells dialog box. Select a pattern from the Pattern drop-down list box, and click OK.*

Creating Borders

To polish your worksheets and make them easy to read, you can add borders with the Borders toolbar button. To add a border to a cell or range, select the cell or range and click the down arrow beside the Borders toolbar button.

Excel displays the box shown in Figure 1-30, illustrating common border patterns and placements. To select a design for your cell or range, click it.

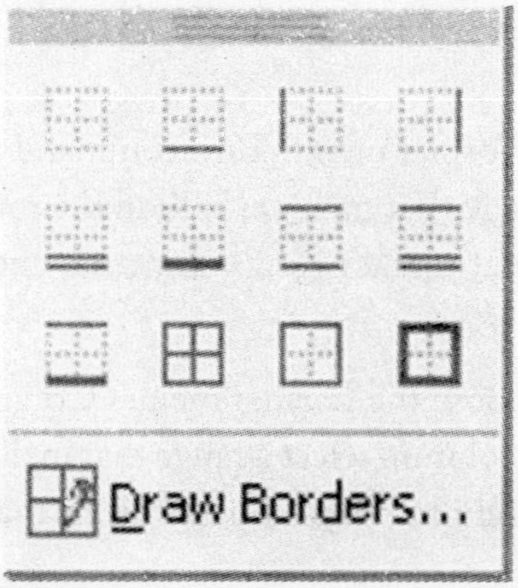

Figure 1-30 The border patterns and placements available from the Borders tool.

TIP *The border designs available from the Borders toolbar button are sufficient for most uses. If you can't find the pattern or placement you want, however, choose the Format menu's Cells command and click the Border tab. Then select a line style and place it where you want it in the range.*

Modifying Column and Row Size

As you reformat the labels and values in your worksheet, you may need to modify the standard column and row sizes to accommodate your formatting changes. To quickly increase the column width to accommodate all text in the column but include no extra white space, double-click the right border of that column heading. Normally, Excel automatically increases row height when you increase point size, but you can perform the same trick on rows by double-clicking the lower border of a row heading. This expands the row to the smallest height possible that still fits all entries within that row.

To specify exact column width, select any cell in that column, choose the Format menu's Column command, and then choose Width. Enter the width in characters in the Column Width text box, as shown in Figure 1-31, and click OK.

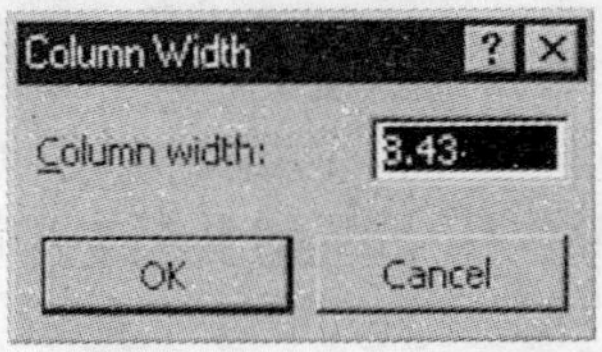

Figure 1-31 The Column Width text box.

To specify exact row height, select any cell in that row, choose the Format menu's Row command and then choose Height. Enter the height in points in the Row Height text box, and click OK.

To hide a row, select any cell in the row, choose the Format menu's Row command and then choose Hide. To redisplay a hidden row, select a range that includes cells in the rows above and below the hidden row. Then choose the Format menu's Row command, and choose Unhide.

To hide a column, select any cell in the column, choose the Format menu's Column command and then choose Hide. To redisplay a hidden column, select a range that includes cells in the columns to the left and right of the hidden column. Then choose the Format menu's Column command, and choose Unhide.

Using the Format Painter

Excel provides a feature that allows you to quickly copy the formatting from one cell to another while leaving the cell's contents intact. To copy cell formatting, select the cell with the formatting you want to copy. Next, click the Format Painter toolbar button, and then select the cell or range to which you want to apply the formatting.

Conditional Formatting

If you want to format only those cells that meet certain criteria, you can use Excel's Conditional Formatting feature. You might want to do this, for example, if you want to highlight cells in a budgeting worksheet that contain values larger than 200.

To apply conditional formatting, select the range of cells you want to include in the conditional formatting filters and then follow these steps:

1. **Choose the Format menu's Conditional Formatting command.**

   Excel displays the Conditional Formatting dialog box shown in Figure 1-32.

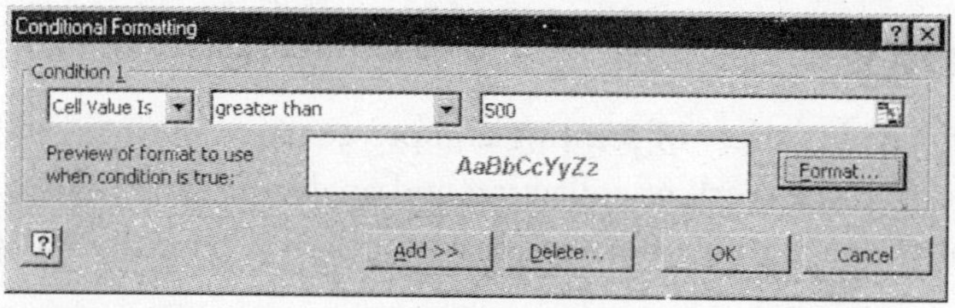

Figure 1-32 The Conditional Formatting dialog box.

2. **Enter the first criteria, using the drop-down list boxes and text boxes provided.**

   For example, if you want Excel to display values greater than $150,000 in red italic boldface, indicate that you want to conditionally format cells with values greater than 500, as shown in Figure 1-32.

3. **Click Format to describe how you want Excel to format the cells with contents that fit your criteria.**

   When you do this, Excel displays a variant of the Format Cells dialog box. Use it to specify the font, font size, font effects, and font color you want to use for cells that contain labels or values meeting your conditions. Click OK to close the Format Cells dialog box and return to the Conditional Formatting dialog box.

4. **Add the conditional formatting rule.**

   Click Add, and Excel adds the conditional formatting rule. If you want to specify multiple criteria, repeat steps 1 and 2 for the other criteria.

5. **Click OK.**

   Excel applies the conditional formatting, as shown in Figure 1-33. The budgeting worksheet displays values greater than 500 highlighted in red italic boldface.

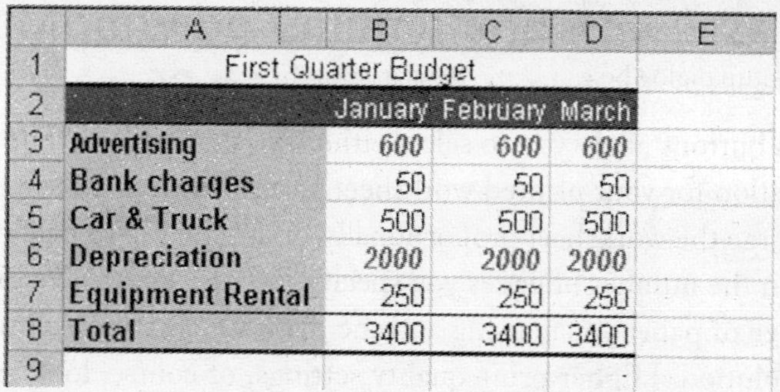

	A	B	C	D	E
1	First Quarter Budget				
2		January	February	March	
3	Advertising	*600*	*600*	*600*	
4	Bank charges	50	50	50	
5	Car & Truck	500	500	500	
6	Depreciation	*2000*	*2000*	*2000*	
7	Equipment Rental	250	250	250	
8	Total	3400	3400	3400	
9					

Figure 1-33 Conditional formatting applied to values.

Printing Workbooks

Excel provides you with a wide variety of printing and presentation options, which is fortunate. As you move beyond the work of collecting and analyzing quantitative information, you'll usually want to share your information with others—typically by printing it.

TIP *If you want to print a worksheet immediately without specifying print settings (this technique tends to work fine for small, simple worksheets), just click the Print toolbar button.*

Setting Up Pages

The Page Setup dialog box, shown in Figure 1-34, gives you precise control over how your worksheet will print. Click the Setup button in the Print Preview window or choose the File menu's Page Setup command to display the dialog box.

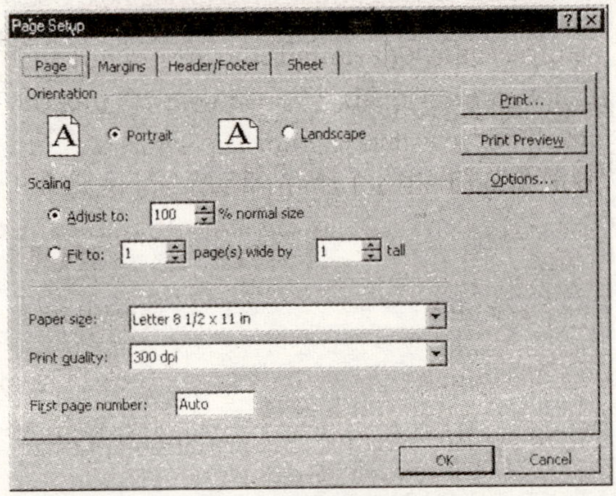

Figure 1-34 The Page Setup dialog box.

The Orientation option buttons allow you to select either the standard portrait or a horizontal landscape orientation for your printed worksheet pages. Use the Adjust To Scaling options to reduce or enlarge the worksheet proportionally, or use the Fit To Scaling options to fit the worksheet onto the number of pages you specify. Use the Paper Size drop-down list box to specify the size of paper you're using and the Print Quality drop-down list box to select the printer resolution. Higher print-quality settings, of course, look crisper and are more legible, but they take more time and toner to print. The maximum print quality setting you have available depends on your printer's capabilities.

Click the Margins tab, and use the Margins text boxes to enter the area in inches that you want to leave around the outside edges of the paper and between the spreadsheet and any header or footer. Use the Center check boxes to center your printed worksheet horizontally or vertically between the margins you specify.

Click the Header/Footer tab, and select a common header or footer from the Header And Footer drop-down list box. If you want to create your own header or footer, click Custom Header or Custom Footer and use the dialog box Excel displays to enter the header or footer text.

Click the Sheet tab, shown in Figure 1-35, to specify the print area, as well as any rows or columns you want to repeat on every page of a worksheet as titles. Select the Gridlines check box to print the gray worksheet gridlines that you see on-screen. Select the Black And White check box to print colors as black and white. Select the Draft Quality check box to print a fast, low-quality copy without most graphics. Select the Row And Column Headings check box to print the column letters and row numbers. Use the Comments drop-down list box to tell Excel if you want to print comments, and if so, where you want the text to appear on the printed page. Use the Page Order option buttons to specify the order in which multiple pages print.

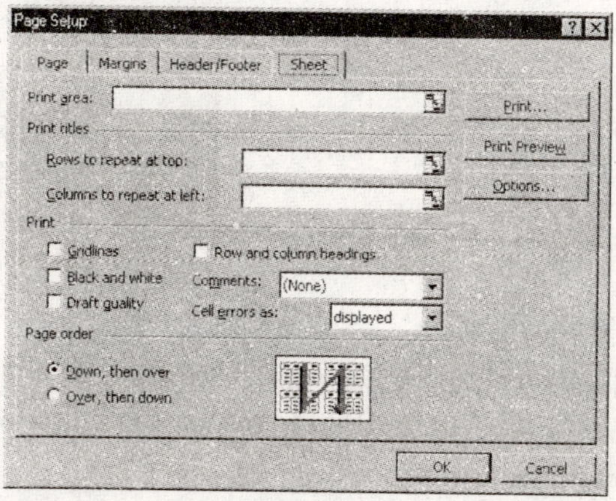

Figure 1-35 The Sheet tab of the Page Setup dialog box.

Previewing Before You Print

Previewing lets you see how a printed worksheet will look before you print it. When you preview a worksheet, for example, you can see how many pages it takes to print and whether or not all of the text fits as you think it does.

To preview a worksheet, click the Print Preview toolbar button or click Preview in the Print dialog box to display the Print Preview window, as shown in Figure 1-36.

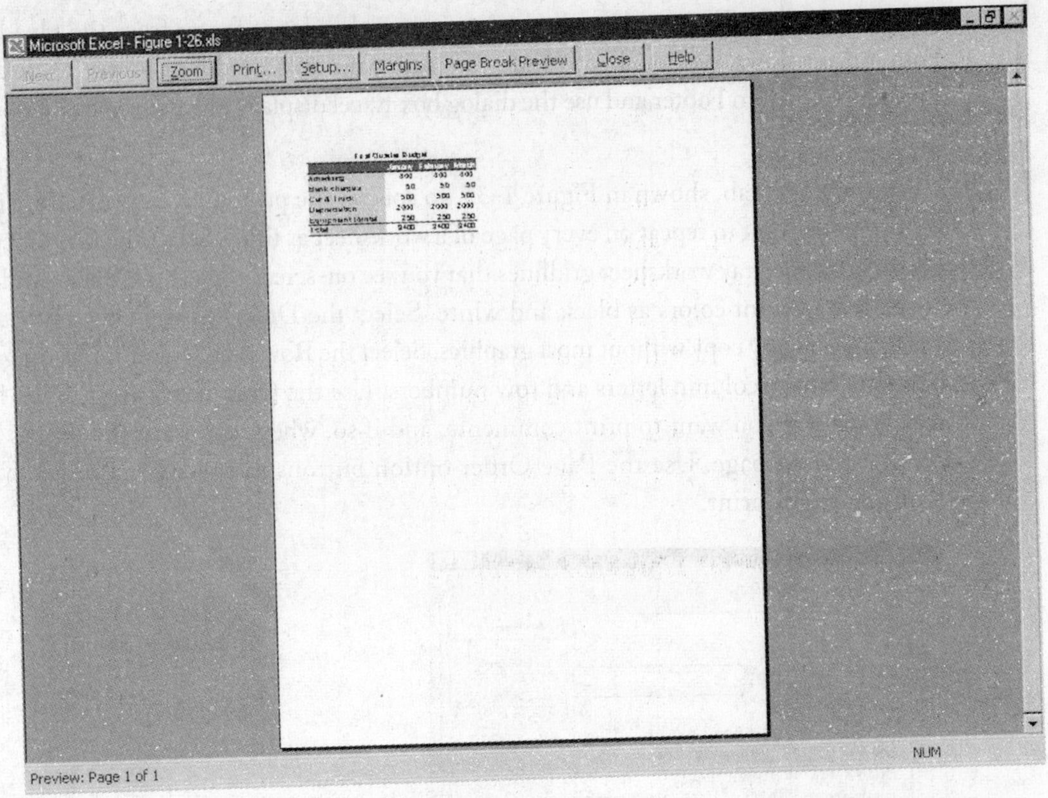

Figure 1-36 The Print Preview window.

The Next and Previous buttons allow you to page back and forth through a multipage worksheet. Click Zoom to zoom in on a page. Click Print to display the Print dialog box. Click Setup to display the Page Setup dialog box.

Click Margins to view the header, footer, and page margins. You can change these margins in the Print Preview window by dragging them. Click Page Break Preview to exit Print Preview and view the worksheet in Page Break Preview view. To change page breaks in Page Break Preview view, drag the breaks. To return to Normal view, choose the View menu's Normal command.

Click Close to go back to the regular application window. After you view a worksheet in Print Preview, Excel displays the page breaks in the worksheet as dotted lines.

Printing Workbook Pages

You have two options for printing worksheets: If you want to use Excel's default print settings, just click the Print toolbar button. If you want to specify print options, follow these steps:

1. **If you want to print only a specific area of a worksheet, select that area.**

   The easiest way to do this is by clicking and dragging the mouse.

2. **Choose the File menu's Print command.**

   Excel displays the Print dialog box, as shown in Figure 1-37.

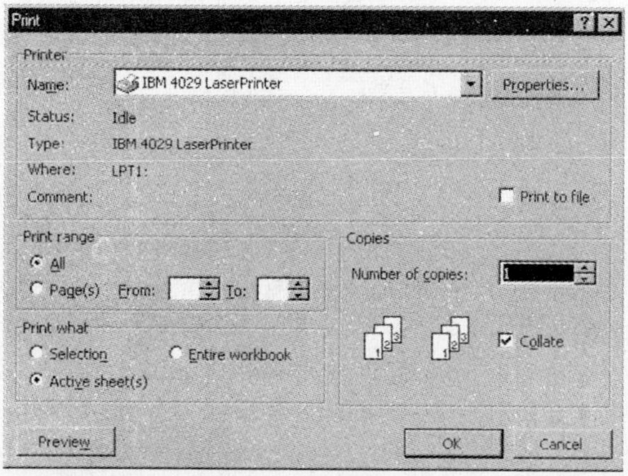

Figure 1-37 The Print dialog box.

3. **Specify which pages you want to print.**

   If a single worksheet is larger than one printed page, use the Print Range options to specify whether you want all pages or only some pages to print.

4. **Specify what portion of the workbook you want to print.**

   Use the Print What option buttons to tell Excel whether you want to print only the cells you selected, only the worksheet you currently have displayed, or all of the worksheets in the workbook.

5. **Specify how many copies Excel should print.**

   Use the Number Of Copies box to tell Excel how many copies you want to print. Select or clear the Collate check box to specify the order in which pages of multiple copies should print.

NOTE *The Print dialog box also lets you print to a file. When you print to a file, other people can print the file even if they don't have Excel. All they need to do is copy the file to their printer port.*

6. **Click OK.**

   Excel prints the workbook according to your specifications.

Chapter 2

QUICKPRIMER™ ON CHARTING

Featuring:

- Understanding Excel's Charting Terms
- Presenting Data with Charts
- Customizing Your Charts

Excel's Chart Wizard allows you to quickly and easily create professional, presentation-quality charts based on worksheet data. This chapter walks you through the steps you take to work with the Chart Wizard, paying particular attention to how you can use charts as powerful tools for better communicating complex information.

Understanding Excel's Charting Terms

In order to easily work with Excel's Chart Wizard, you'll want to learn both how Excel views to-be-plotted data and the terminology that Excel uses to refer to the parts of a chart.

How Excel Sees Chart Data

To easily use Excel for charting, you need to learn three key terms: *data points, data series,* and *data categories.*

The individual values you plot in a chart are called *data points.* Because a chart visually represents one or more numeric values, data points are always values. Note, however, that most formula results are also numeric, which means that you can also plot formulas. (Actually, in this case, you're really plotting the values that the formula calculates.)

The term *data series* refers to a collection of values that are all related—that are all part of the same set. That might sound complicated, but it's really not. If you want to chart monthly interest rates over the last 10 years, that collection of interest-rate percentages is a data series. If you want to plot advertising expenditures over the last 12 months, that collection of expense values is a data series.

Most charts you create will use more than one data series. For example, if you wanted to compare sales revenues of three competitors, each competitor's sales revenues would probably constitute its own data series. In the worksheet shown in Figure 2-1, you can see the annual sales revenues for three fictitious companies: Anderson Company, Baker Incorporated, and Carson Corporation. The data points that show Anderson's revenue represent a data series. The data points that show Baker's revenue represent another data. And the data points that represent Carson's revenue represent still a third and final data series.

	A	B	C	D	E	F	G
1		Year 1	Year 2	Year 3	Year 4	Year 5	
2	Anderson Company	1000000	1100000	1210000	1331000	1464100	
3	Baker Incorporated	3000000	2940000	2881200	2823576	2767104	
4	Carson Corporation	2000000	2050000	2100000	2150000	2200000	
5							

Figure 2-1 A simple worksheet with sales revenue data.

The term *data categories* refers to the secondary view, or perspective, on to-be-charted data. If you look at Figure 2-1 again, you can also see Year 1 data points, Year 2 data points, Year 3 data points, and so on. Each year's collection of data points represents a data category. The collection of Year 1 data points represents the Year 1 data category. Similarly, the Year 2 data points represent the Year 2 data category. The same thing is true of the Year 3, Year 4, and Year 5 data points.

People commonly get confused about the differences between data series and data categories (in part because Microsoft's product documentation typically hasn't done a very good job of defining and distinguishing these two terms). You can use the following tips to help distinguish between data series and data categories in your own charts:

- In general, if you look at a chart and ask, "What does this chart show," every concise answer identifies a data series. Figure 2-2 shows a simple line chart that plots the fictitious sales revenue from the worksheet shown in Figure 2-1. If someone asks you to describe what this chart shows, you'll probably say something like, "Well, it shows Anderson's revenue, Baker's revenue, and Carson's revenue." Which is not a coincidence; charts show data series. Anderson's revenue is a data series. And so is Baker's revenue, and so is Carson's revenue.

- Any chart that shows how some value changes over time is a time-series chart. In any time-series chart, the data categories will be some time interval, such as months or quarters or years. In Figure 2-2, for example, the chart plots sales revenue over a five-year period of time. Therefore, the chart is a time-series chart and uses time-interval data categories. In the case of Figure 2-2, the data categories are years.

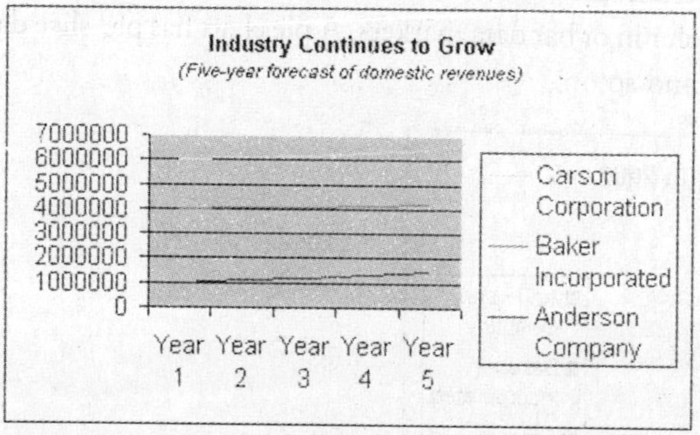

Figure 2-2 A line chart of the sales revenue data shown in Figure 2-1.

Now that you understand the three terms *data points, data series,* and *data categories,* you need to know just two final details about the to-be-charted Excel data. First, and as Figure 2-1 shows, you want not only to provide the actual data point values, but you also want to enter labels that name the data series and the data categories. In Figure 2-1, for example, you can see that cells A2, A3, and A4 hold labels that describe the names of the companies. In cells B1, C1, D1, E1, and F1, you see labels that identify the time intervals used as the data categories. Including data category and data series names in your worksheet is important. If you include this information in your worksheet, it's easily added later to your chart.

Second, note that Excel limits the number of data points and data series you can plot in a chart. A data series may hold no more than 4000 data points, for example. A chart may show no more than 255 data series. These constraints mean that you may sometimes need to arrange large data series or big sets of data series vertically by putting data series into worksheet columns rather than rows. Note that for smaller data series or small numbers of data series, a horizontal arrangement like that shown in Figure 2-1 works well.

Components of Excel Charts

Excel's Chart Wizard and documentation use several charting terms: *data markers, data-marker descriptions, legend, chart text, plot area,* and *chart area*. You'll find it useful to understand just what these words and phrases mean, so the bulleted list that follows provides definitions.

- *Data markers* are the graphical elements used to represent individual data point values in a chart. Figure 2-2, for example, uses symbols, or points, on a line to show data point values. Other types of charts in Excel use other data markers. A chart that uses columns or bars, for example, has column or bar data markers. A pie chart has pie-slice data markers, as shown in Figure 2-3, and so on.

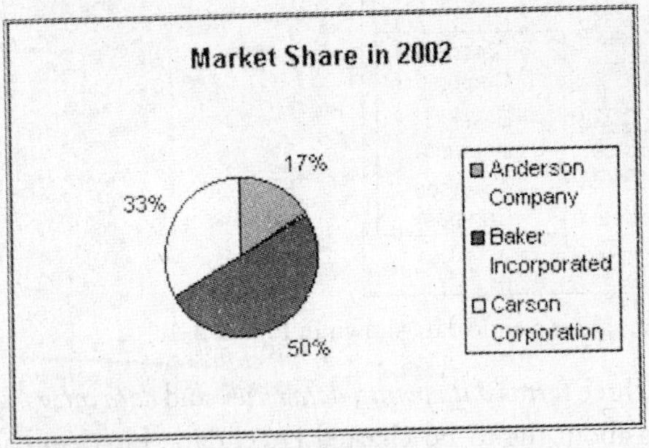

Figure 2-3 A simple pie chart.

- Excel typically describes and qualifies data markers using the *data-marker descriptions* such as axis scales and data labels. Different types of charts use different data-marker descriptions. Bar, column, and line charts use axis scales. (This is what Figure 2-2 shows, of course.) Pie and doughnut charts use data labels (see Figure 2-3).
- A *legend* names and identifies the data series you've plotted. In Figure 2-3, the legend names the data series and then shows which colors are used for which pie slices.
- *Chart text* describes a chart or some part of a chart. Figure 2-2, for example, shows a chart title (Industry Continues to Grow) and subtitle (Five-year forecast of domestic revenues).
- The *plot area* of a chart is the area that includes the data markers and data-marker descriptions. In Figure 2-2, the rectangle that shows the lines and scales represents the plot area. In the chart shown in Figure 2-3, the circle that shows the slices of pie and the data labels that identify the slices of pie comprise the plot area.
- The *chart area* includes plot area, any chart text, and a legend.

Presenting Data with Charts

Once you understand the terms that Excel uses to describe to-be-charted data and the parts of a chart, you can easily create charts. In essence, you need to simply select the worksheet data you want to chart, indicate where Excel should place the chart, and then tell the Chart Wizard to create the chart.

Using the Chart Wizard

To use the Chart Wizard, first enter your to-be-charted data in an Excel worksheet. As mentioned earlier, you want to include not only the data series data points but also the labels that identify the data series and the data categories. Figure 2-4 shows an example of how you might do this.

	A	B	C	D	E	F	G	H
1		January	February	March	April	May	June	
2	Revenues	1000000	750000	1200000	1300000	1100000	800000	
3	Expenses	550000	475000	610000	640000	580000	490000	
4								
5								

Figure 2-4 A simple worksheet with data you might plot in a chart.

Once you have the data in a worksheet, follow these steps to create a chart that visually depicts the data:

1. Select the data you want to plot in the chart.

To select the data, select the worksheet range that includes the data series and any data series names and data categories names. In Figure 2-4, you would select the worksheet range A1:G3.

NOTE *If you arrange your data series in the way shown in Figure 2-4, Excel can usually correctly guess what the data series are, what labels show data series names, and what labels show the data categories' names.*

2. Start the Chart Wizard.

You can do this by clicking the Chart Wizard button on the toolbar. Or you can choose the Insert menu's Chart command. Excel displays the first Chart Wizard dialog box, as shown in Figure 2-5.

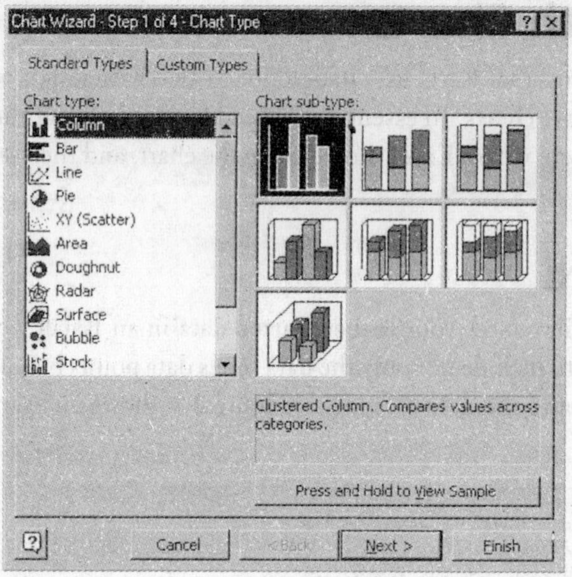

Figure 2-5 The first Chart Wizard dialog box.

3. Select the type of chart you want.

Select one of Excel's chart types from the Chart Type list box. Excel provides 14 different types of charts: Column, Bar, Line, Pie, XY (Scatter), Area, Doughnut, Radar, Surface, Bubble, Stock, Cylinder, Cone, and Pyramid.

TIP *The next section of this chapter, "Choosing the Right Chart Type," summarizes some of the rules of thumb that people often use to choose a particular chart type.*

4. Select the Chart sub-type.

After you select the Chart type, Excel displays the different versions available for the chart type as clickable buttons in the Chart Sub-type box. Excel displays a short description of the selected chart sub-type in the area below the Chart Sub-type box. To select a chart, click the button that looks like the chart you want. After making your selection, click Next.

NOTE *You can tell Excel to display a rough-draft version of the chart you're creating by clicking and holding the Press And Hold To View Sample button.*

5. **Verify that Excel has correctly interpreted the to-be-charted data.**

When Excel displays the second Chart Wizard dialog box, as shown in Figure 2-6, use it to verify that Excel is retrieving the correct data from the worksheet (this should be the case if you select the data correctly in step 1) and that it has correctly identified the data series. If Excel hasn't correctly interpreted the to-be-plotted data, click the worksheet button at the right end of the Data Range text box. When Excel minimizes the Chart Wizard dialog box, reselect the correct range. To restore the Chart Wizard dialog box, click the worksheet button a second time. If Excel has misinterpreted how you've organized your worksheet data—Excel assumes the chart has fewer data series than data categories—click the other Series In option button. Click Next when you're finished.

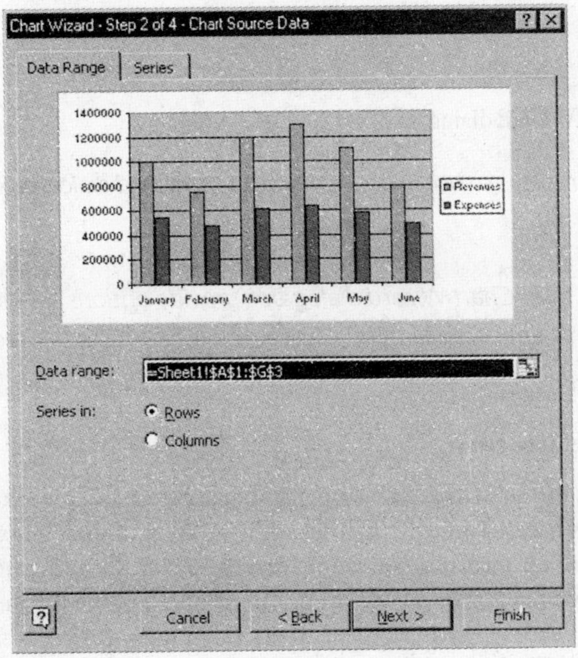

Figure 2-6 The second Chart Wizard dialog box.

NOTE *You can return to a previous Chart Wizard dialog box by clicking the Back button.*

6. **Add chart text as needed.**

When Excel displays the third Chart Wizard dialog box, as shown in Figure 2-7, you use its Titles tab to add a chart title and axis titles. To add such chart text, just click the appropriate text box and type the text you want. Click Next when you're finished.

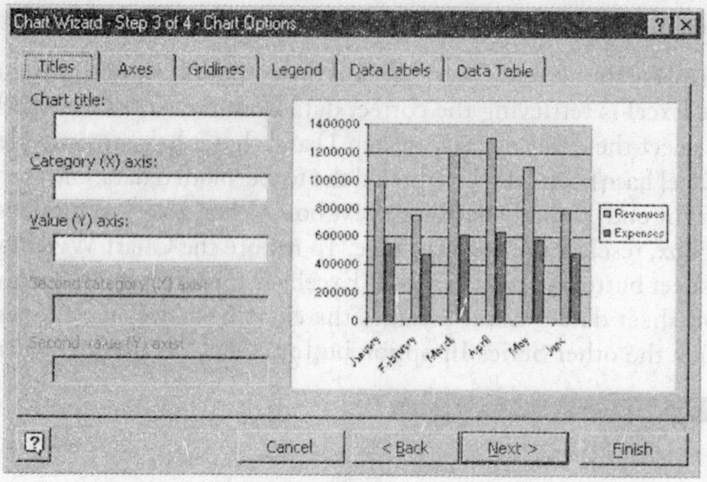

Figure 2-7 The third Chart Wizard dialog box.

NOTE *Excel updates the chart picture shown on the third Chart Wizard dialog box for any text you add.*

TIP *The other tabs of the third Chart Wizard dialog box provide options for changing and customizing the chart's appearance. The "Customizing Your Charts" section of this chapter describes how to use these tools to tailor Excel's charts to your requirements.*

7. Choose a location for the new chart.

Excel lets you place charts either as free-floating graphical objects in a worksheet or on their own individual chart sheets. You use the fourth Chart Wizard dialog box, as shown in Figure 2-8, to choose which location you want for your chart. To add a new sheet to the chart, click the As New Sheet option button and then enter a name for the new chart sheet. To add the chart as a free-floating object to an existing worksheet, click the As Object In option button and then select the worksheet from the As Object In drop-down list box. When you complete this step, you've finished creating the chart. Click Finish.

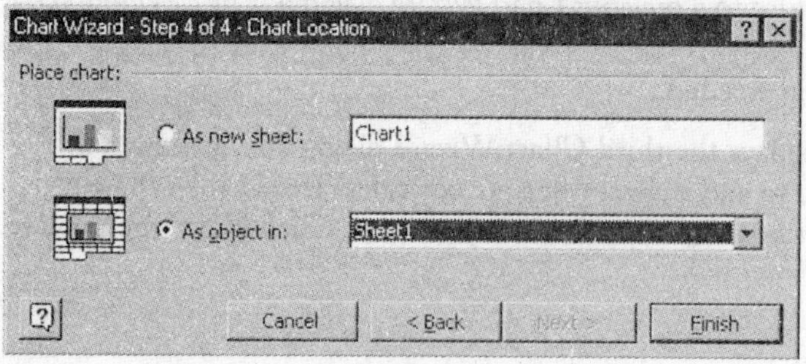

Figure 2-8 The fourth Chart Wizard dialog box.

Figure 2-9 shows how the worksheet data from Figure 2-4 looks in a column chart that resides on its own chart sheet. To view the chart, click its sheet tab. To print the chart in the selected sheet, simply click the Print toolbar button or choose the File menu's Print command.

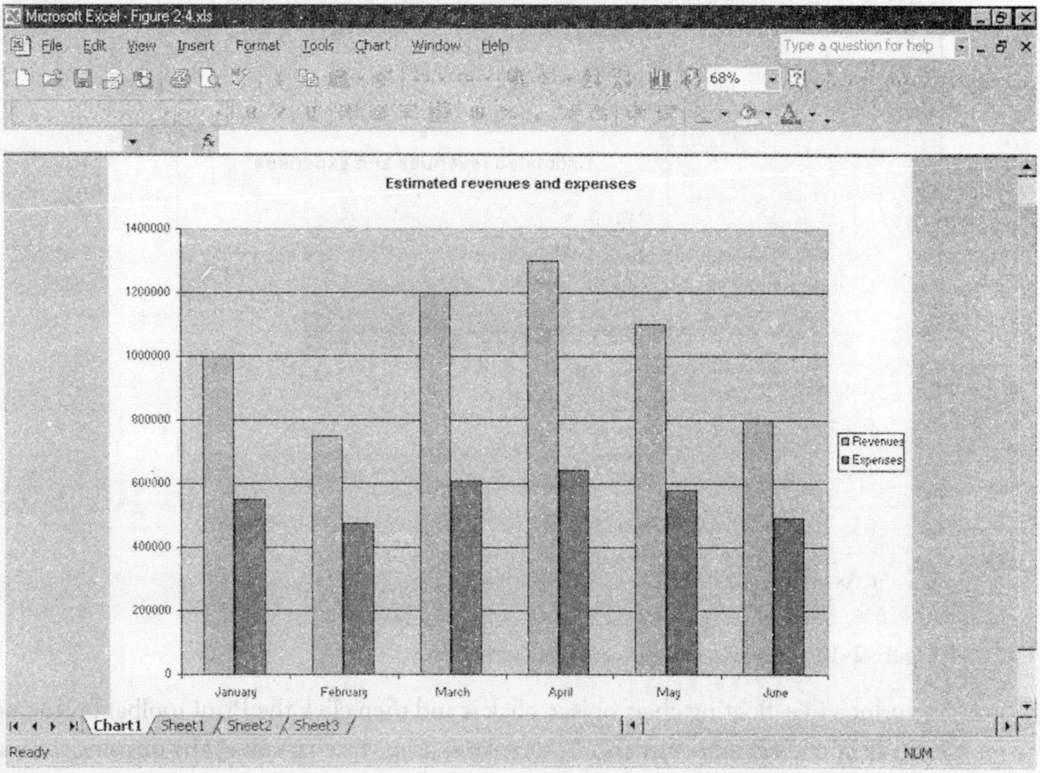

Figure 2-9 A column chart on a chart sheet.

Figure 2-10 shows the same worksheet data as that shown in Figure 2-9, except this time the worksheet data is depicted in an area chart that's free-floating as an object in a worksheet. You can resize any worksheet object, including a chart, by clicking the object and then dragging the square selection handles that appear on the sides and corners of the object.

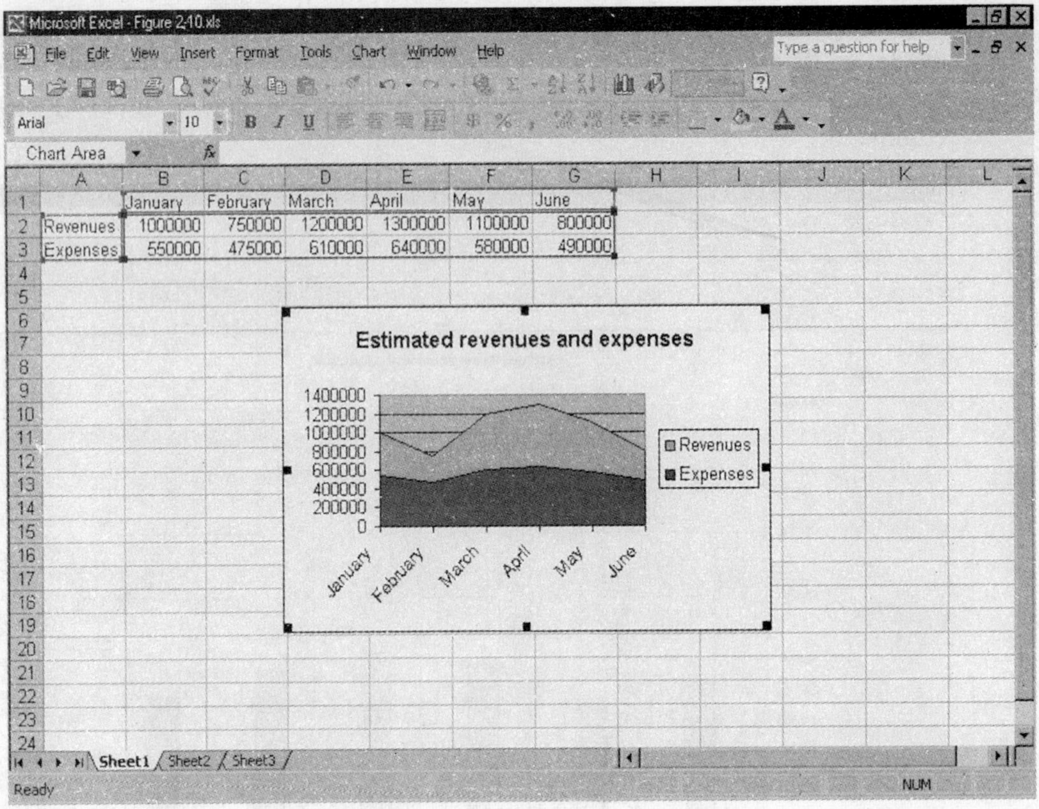

Figure 2-10 An area chart object in a worksheet.

To print a free-floating chart object, click it and then click the Print toolbar button or choose the File menu's Print command. You can also print the chart object by printing the worksheet over which it floats.

Choosing the Right Chart Type

Choosing the appropriate chart type is at least as much art as science. Nevertheless, it's still worthwhile to briefly discuss the three issues that you'll commonly want to consider as you choose a chart type: the basic data comparison that you want a chart to make, the principal message that you want a chart to communicate, and the relative strengths and weaknesses of the various chart types. All three factors greatly affect your choice of a chart type.

The Five Data Comparisons that Charts Make

Charts allow you to visually compare data in five ways, which means that your first step in determining the appropriate chart type is often simply to consider what data comparison you want to make. Suppose, for example, that you've collected detailed product sales revenue data for a golf equipment manufacturer. Using a chart, you might decide to look at this data in any of the ways summarized in Table 2-1.

COMPARISON	DESCRIPTION
Part-to-whole	Compares an individual data point value to the sum of a data series. Comparing sales of a particular golf club set to total sales, for example, is a part-to-whole comparison.
Whole-to-whole	Compares individual data point values to each other or data series to each other. Comparing sales of a starter men's golf club set to a starter women's golf club set, for example, is a whole-to-whole comparison.
Time-series	Compares data point values from different time periods to show how values change over time. Showing monthly sales over the last year, for example, is a time-series comparison.
Correlation	Compares different data series to explore correlation between the data series. Comparing industrywide sales to the average age of the population, for example, is a correlation comparison.
Geographic	Compares data values using a geographic map. Comparing sales by country, for example, is a geographic comparison.

Table 2-1 Summary of the five data comparisons made in charts.

Once you decide what data comparison you want to make, it's generally quite straightforward to identify the appropriate Excel chart types and sometimes even to identify appropriate chart sub-types.

- To make a part-to-whole comparison when working with just a single data series, you might choose a pie chart. (Pie charts plot only a single data series.) You might choose a doughnut chart or area chart if you're working with more than one data series.
- To make a whole-to-whole comparison, you might choose a chart that uses horizontal data markers, such as a bar chart or one of the cylinder, cone, or pyramid chart sub-types that uses a vertical data category axis and data markers. You might also choose a doughnut chart or radar chart.
- To make a time-series comparison, you would typically choose a chart that uses vertical data markers, such as a column chart, a line chart, or one of the cylinder, cone, or pyramid chart sub-types that uses a horizontal data category axis and data markers. You might also choose the stock chart if you're performing technical analysis of security prices. (Time-series charts typically use a horizontal data category axis because of the Western convention of using a horizontal axis to denote the passage of time.)
- To make a correlation comparison, you might choose the XY (scatter) chart if you're working with two data series or the bubble chart if you're working with three data series. You might also choose the surface chart if you want to explore trends in two dimensions.
- To make a geographic comparison, you would probably use the surface chart.

Importance of the Chart's Essential Message

A second important factor to consider is exactly what message you want to visually communicate with your chart. Typically, you can use the message as the chart title. But beyond this, you may want to experiment with different chart types and sub-types to see which best support your message.

NOTE *Of course, a chart can and should also be used to visually explore data. Oftentimes, information that's hidden in raw, tabular presentations of data suddenly becomes visible once you depict the data in a chart. This point is worth mentioning because when you are exploring data—something you might do by viewing data in different chart types—there probably shouldn't be any rules. Quite literally, thinking "outside the box" might often mean that you want to examine your data in unusual ways.*

Strengths and Weaknesses of Different Chart Types

A third factor you'll want to consider as you choose the best chart type is the relative strengths and weaknesses of each chart type. One could, of course, write an entire book on this subject. But you may find it useful to consider the strengths and weaknesses that people generally ascribe to the basic chart types as you choose a chart.

NOTE *In fact, someone has written a book—actually several books—about visually representing quantitative data. Edward Tufte has self-published several excellent books about the visual representation of data, including the bestseller* The Visual Display of Quantitative Information. *These books, available from online bookstores, will be of real interest and outstanding value to Excel users who frequently present data using charts. Note that one of Tufte's most elegantly argued points is that your charts shouldn't use more dimensions than your data—which essentially means that three-dimensional charts (with the exception of well-crafted surface charts) are usually just plain wrong.*

Area charts plot data point values using lines. Typically, they stack the lines so they show cumulative data point values and color the areas between the lines. Accordingly, area charts have two noteworthy strengths: They can show both the trend in the first data series and also the total of all the data series, and they can often create implicit total data series. Figure 2-11, for example, plots two data series: one for total expenses and one for profits. However, the total of these data series implicitly creates a third data series for total revenues.

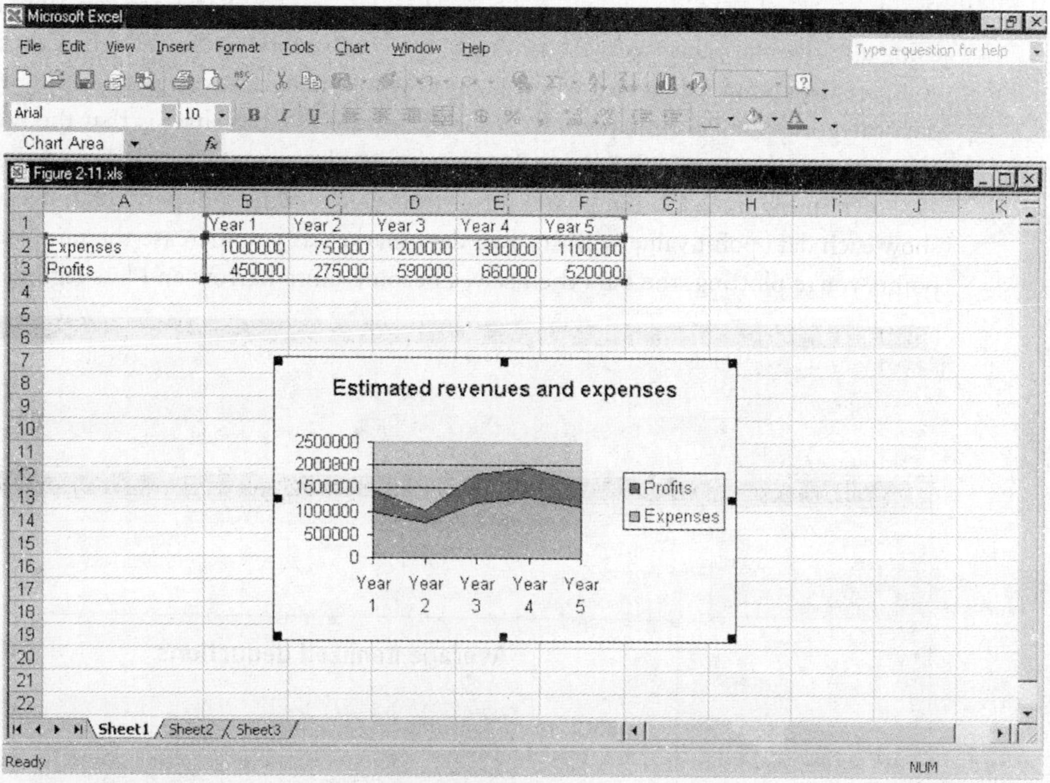

Figure 2-11 Area charts, which plot data series as stacked areas, also show the total data series.

NOTE *You have the option of not stacking the areas of an area chart, and sometimes you'll want to do this, too. In Figure 2-10, for example, an area chart plots revenues and expenses but doesn't stack the areas. Note that this arrangement also created an implied, third data series. In Figure 2-10, the visible portion of the revenue area shows profits.*

Area charts also suffer from several noteworthy weaknesses, however. They make it difficult to see the individual data point values (although this is a two-edged sword because the reduced emphasis on individual data point values also makes it possible to plot data series with large numbers of data point values). They make it next to impossible to compare data point values of the second and subsequent data series. (You can usually get a pretty good idea about the first data series data point values, though.)

NOTE *Area charts, as with any time-series graph, tend to suggest that time explains the apparent trends. This can be misleading, first, because there may not really be any trends and, second, because even if there are trends, the simple passage of time may likely not be the cause.*

Bar charts plot data point values in individual bars but arrange the bars so you calibrate them using a horizontal values axis. Accordingly, bar charts work really well when you want to compare data point values in a whole-item to whole-item data comparison and when the data categories are *not* time periods. Another feature of a bar chart is that the horizontal orientation of the chart makes it possible to comfortably use more lengthy data series names, as shown in Figure 2-12. Bar charts suffer from one weakness in particular: because they show each data point value with its own data marker, as you increase the number of data points you're plotting, the bars themselves become more narrow and less legible.

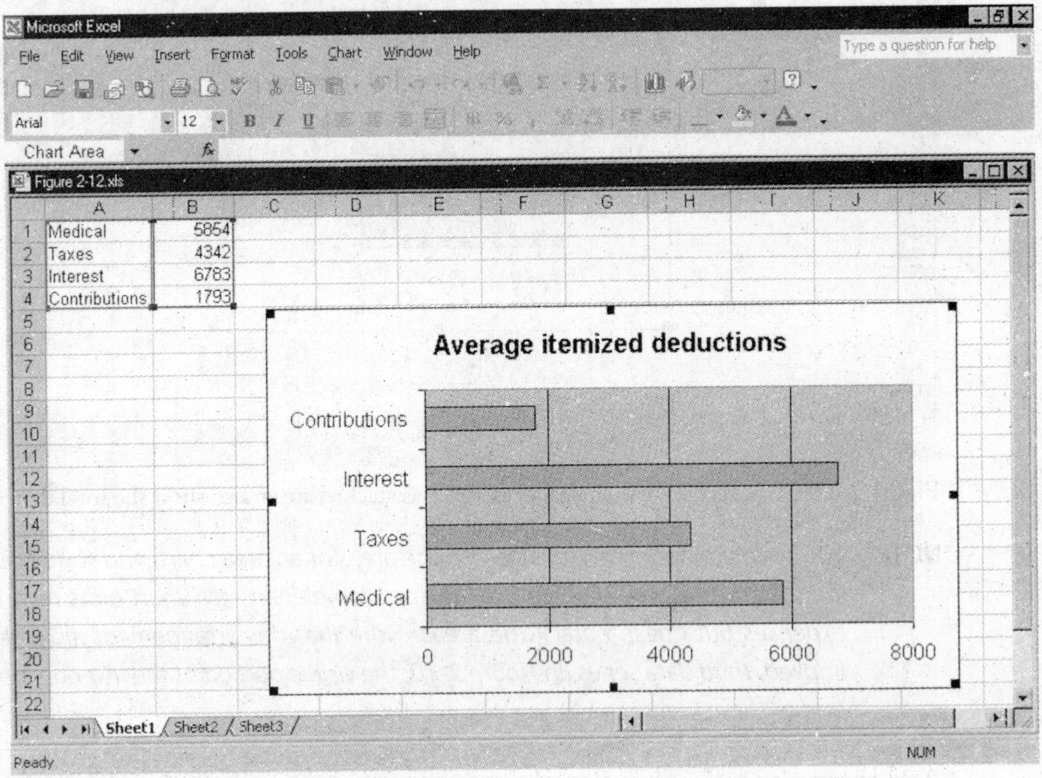

Figure 2-12 A simple bar chart that plots average tax deductions.

TIP *Cylinder, cone, and pyramid chart types possess the same general strengths and suffer from the same general weaknesses as do the bar and column charts. In addition, cylinder, cone, and pyramid chart types, because of their three-dimensionality, also suffer from an additional weakness. The added dimension, while admittedly interesting, often makes it more different to precisely compare data point values.*

Bubble charts let you visually explore the relationships between data series by treating the horizontal axis as a second values axis. To accomplish this, bubble charts plot pairs of data points. In Figure 2-13, for example, the chart shows income and contribution and suggests, perhaps surprisingly, that as people make more money, they only modestly increase their charitable giving. Bubble charts differ from XY charts, which also show this same information, in that Excel sizes the bubbles using the values of a third data point. While initially confusing, a bubble chart lets you explore the relationships between two data series. (The only other Excel chart type that lets you do this is the XY [scatter] chart.) If the bubble chart suffers from a weakness, it is that the chart may suggest correlations or relationships that don't exist.

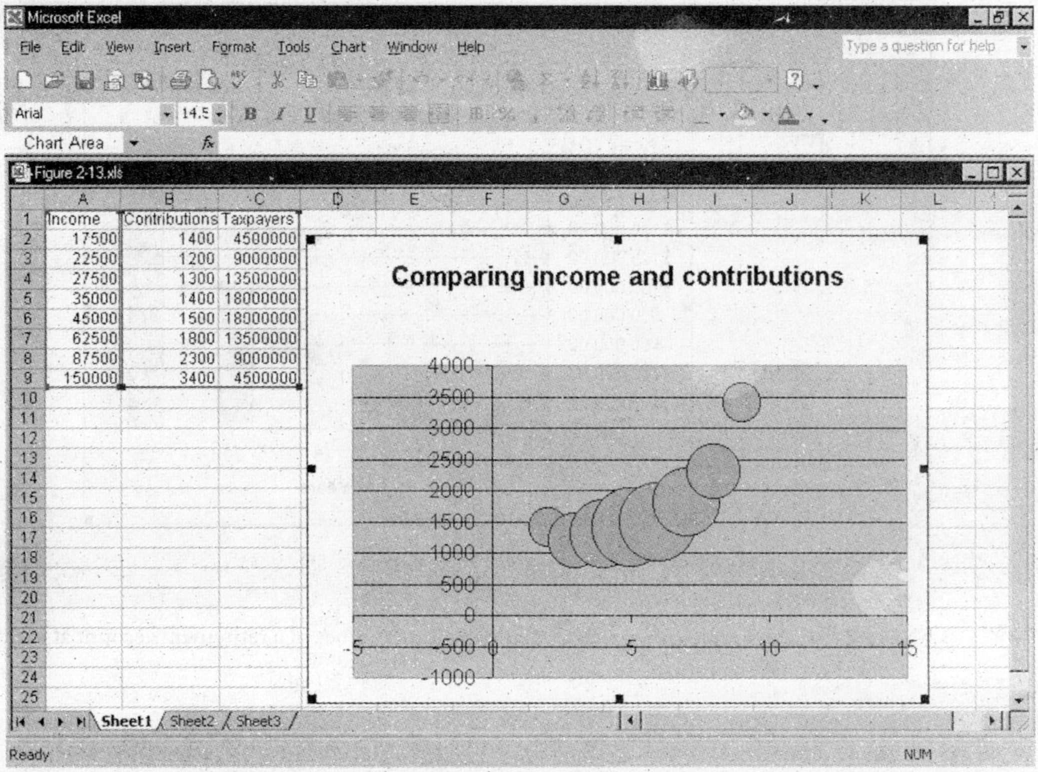

Figure 2-13 A simple bubble chart that shows U.S. Internal Revenue Service data on the relationship between income and charitable contributions.

NOTE *You can statistically examine correlations and relationships using Excel's regression analysis tools as discussed in Chapter 4.*

TIP *Compare the bubble chart shown in Figure 2-13 with the XY chart shown in Figure 2-21 on page 67 to see the other way you might choose to visually show a relationship between two data series.*

Column charts plot data point values in individual bars but arrange the bars so you calibrate them using a vertical values axis. Accordingly, column charts work really well when you want to view data point values in a whole-item to whole-item data comparison and when the data categories *are* time periods. Figure 2-14 shows a column chart that plots the future value of a retirement savings account based on $2,000-a-year contributions and a 9% annual return.

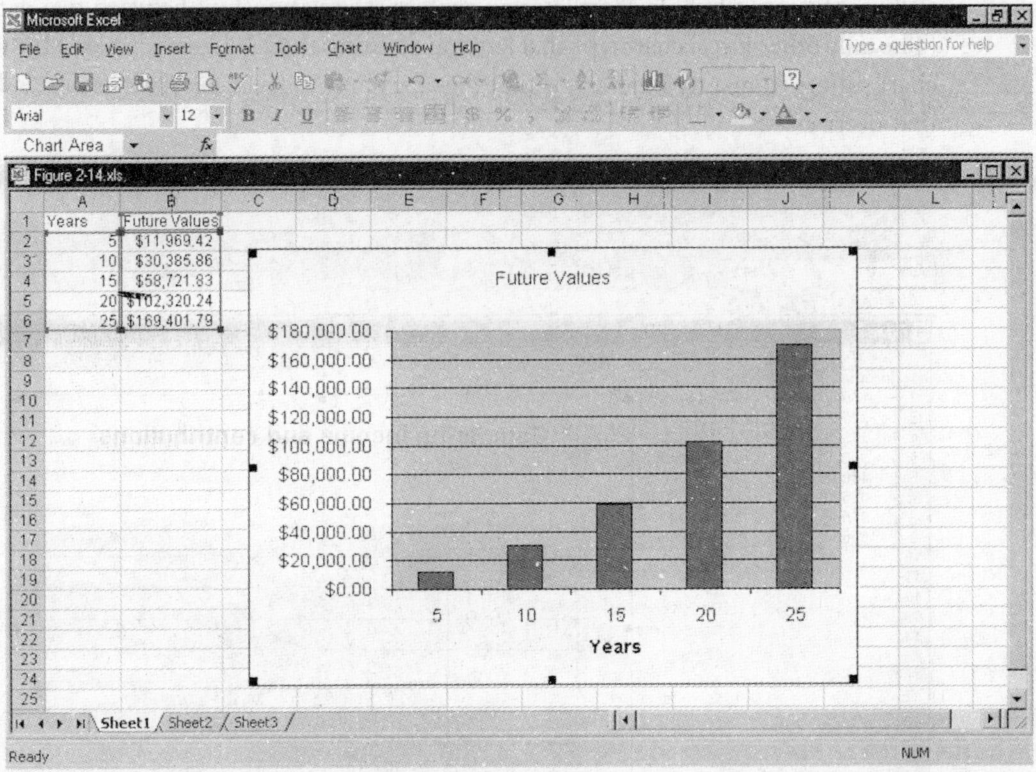

Figure 2-14 A simple column chart that plots future values of a retirement account at various points in the future.

Doughnut charts work similar to pie charts, plotting data series in concentric rings and showing each data point value as a segment, or bite, of the ring. Compared to pie charts, doughnut charts possess an advantage: they allow you to plot more than one data series. As a practical matter, they suffer from the same weaknesses as pie charts: they don't let you compare data point values between series (even though they paradoxically show multiple data series). They also limit you to small data sets. Almost always, something that appears in a doughnut chart should instead be shown with some other chart type. Figure 2-15, for example, compares the average deduction of taxpayers with $15,000 to $20,000 of adjusted gross income (shown with the inner doughnut) with those taxpayers with $100,000 to $200,000 of adjusted gross income (shown with the outer doughnut).

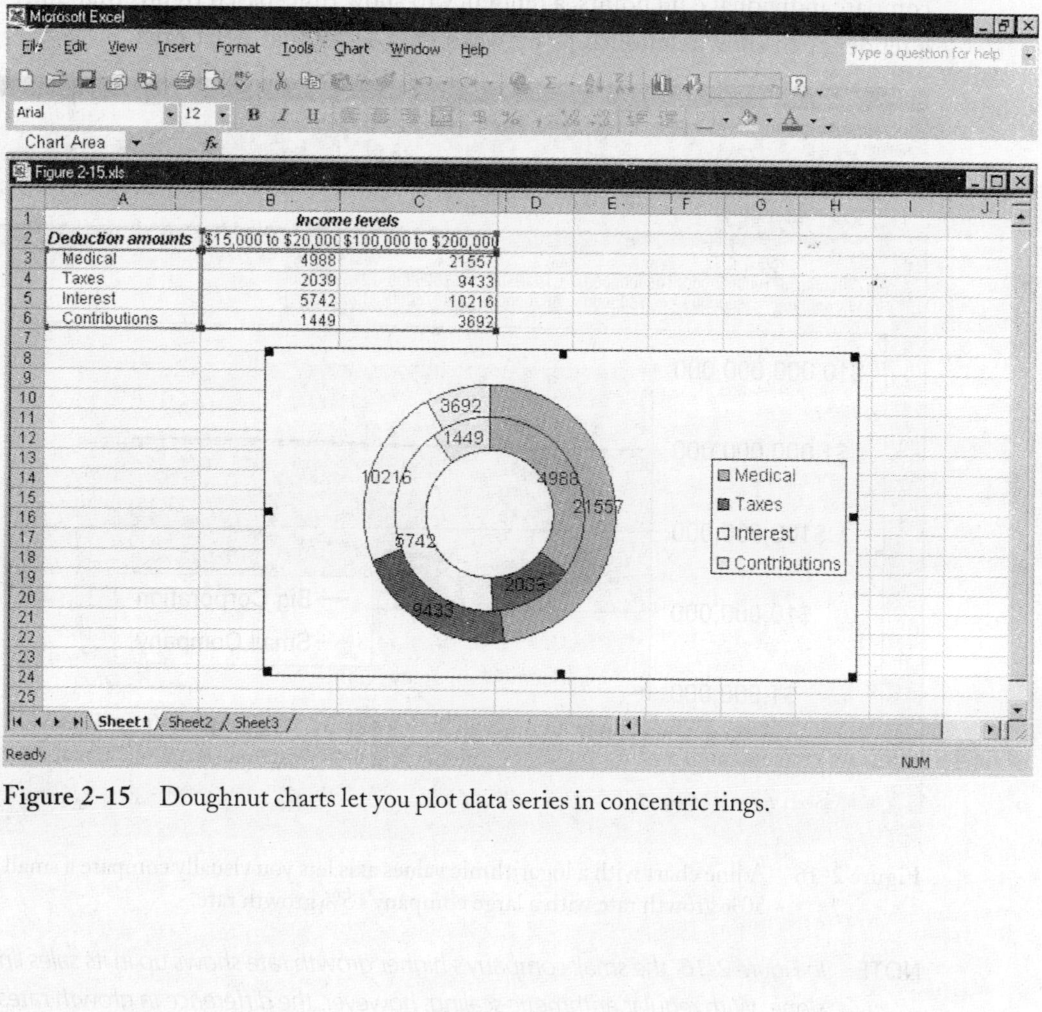

Figure 2-15 Doughnut charts let you plot data series in concentric rings.

Line charts generally plot individual data points in a line, using either different data marker symbols or different colored lines to distinguish the data series, and using a horizontal data category axis. Because line charts de-emphasize individual data point values, they work well for large data sets. With a line chart, you can literally plot thousands of data points. What's more, of all the Excel chart types, line charts tend to emphasize changes and trends in the data point values, which can be useful. Figure 2-16, for example, uses a logarithmic values axis, which means that it lets the viewer compare the rates of growth of a large company growing at 5% annually with a small company growing at 50% annually. Predictably, however, line charts suffer from some weaknesses: a de-emphasis of individual data point values which can camouflage inappropriately small data sets and make it impossible to compare individual data points, a tendency to show time-based trends that don't exist, and a tendency to show relationships between data series that don't exist.

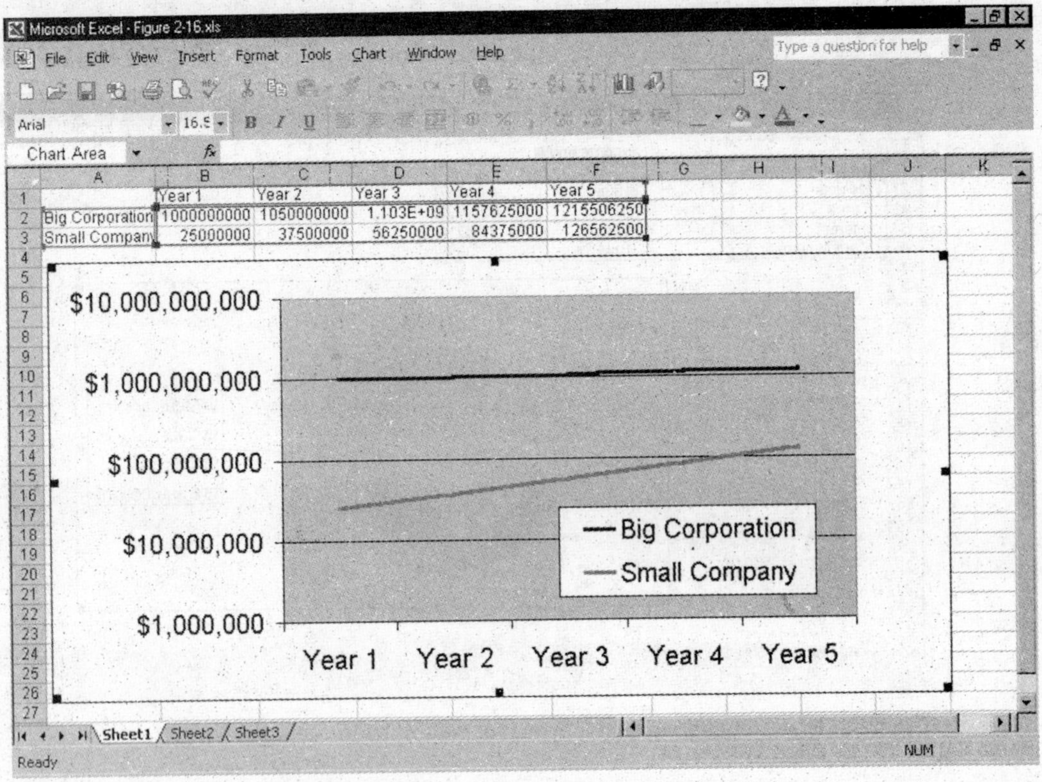

Figure 2-16 A line chart with a logarithmic values axis lets you visually compare a small company's 50% growth rate with a large company's 5% growth rate.

NOTE *In Figure 2-16, the small company's higher growth rate shows up in its sales line's greater slope. With regular arithmetic scaling, however, the difference in growth rates is hidden.*

Pie charts, as almost everybody knows, show a single data series and depict individual data points as segments of the circle, or slices of the pie. While this means that they allow people to compare individual data point values to the total of all the data point values—and one might argue this is a strength—in general, pie charts are without merit because they can show only a single small data series. Almost always, something that appears in a pie chart should instead be shown in a table. Figure 2-17, for example, uses both a table and a pie chart to show the same data set: populations of major English-speaking countries. You'll probably agree that the table shown in the worksheet range A1:B6 works much better as a communication tool than the pie chart.

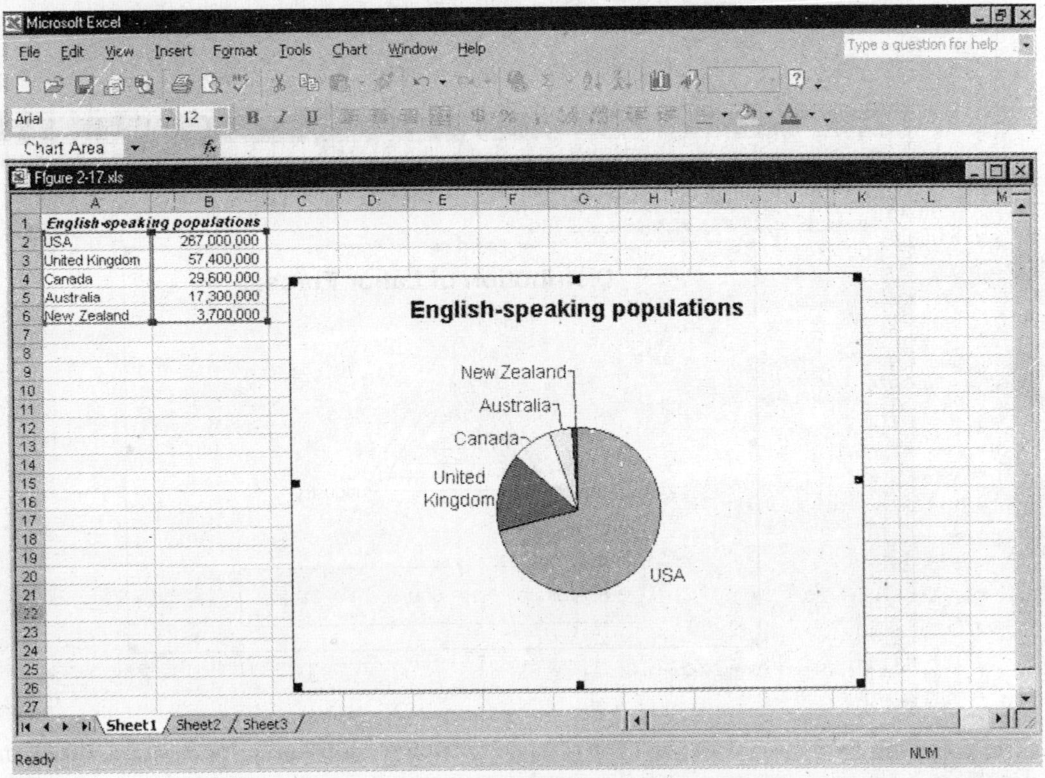

Figure 2-17 Although pie charts let you compare individual data point values to the total data point values in a data series, a table almost always presents the information more clearly.

Radar charts plot each data category's data point values on separate value axes and connect the data point values of each data series with a line, as shown in Figure 2-18. The strength of a radar chart is that it may make it possible to precisely compare individual data point values within a data category. The weakness of a radar chart is that it may make it difficult for you to compare data point values in different categories (although this isn't always a problem). You're also practically limited to a small set of data categories because the chart uses a separate value axis for each. (You obviously can't, for example, plot a set of data with two hundred categories.)

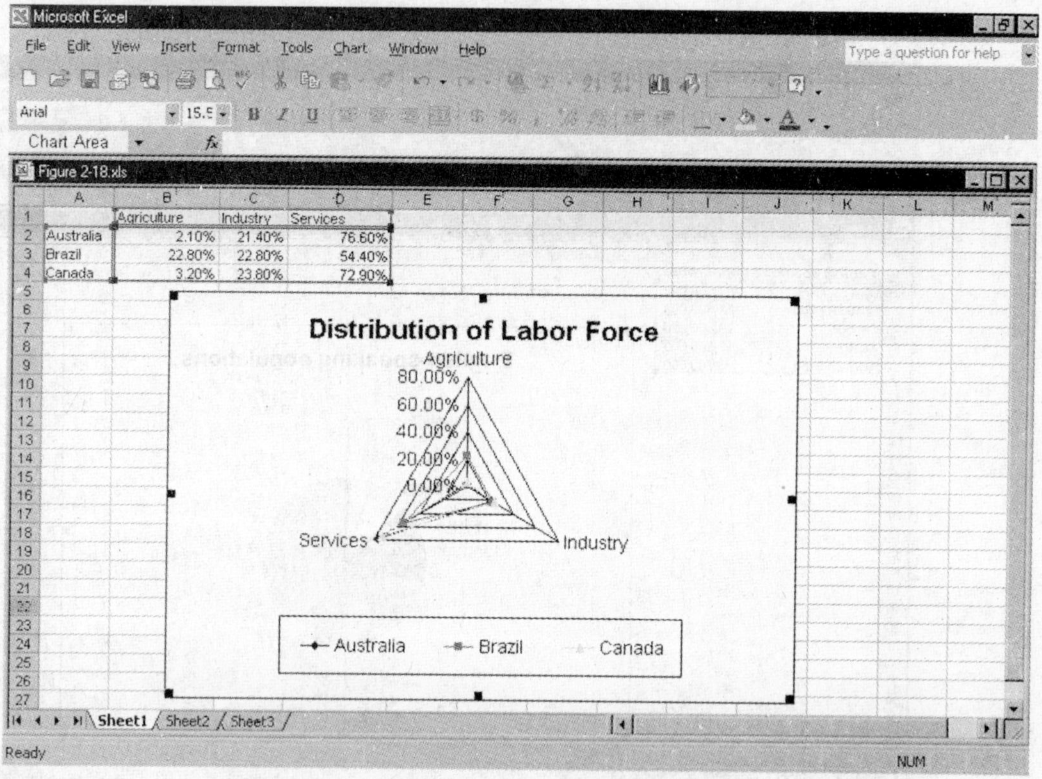

Figure 2-18 A radar chart that compares labor force distribution for Australia, Brazil, and Canada.

Stock charts plot security prices in a common open-high-low-close format, as shown in Figure 2-19. Note that if you do choose to create a stock chart, Excel expects you to organize your data series in this order: volume, opening price, high price, low price, and closing price, as shown in Figure 2-19.

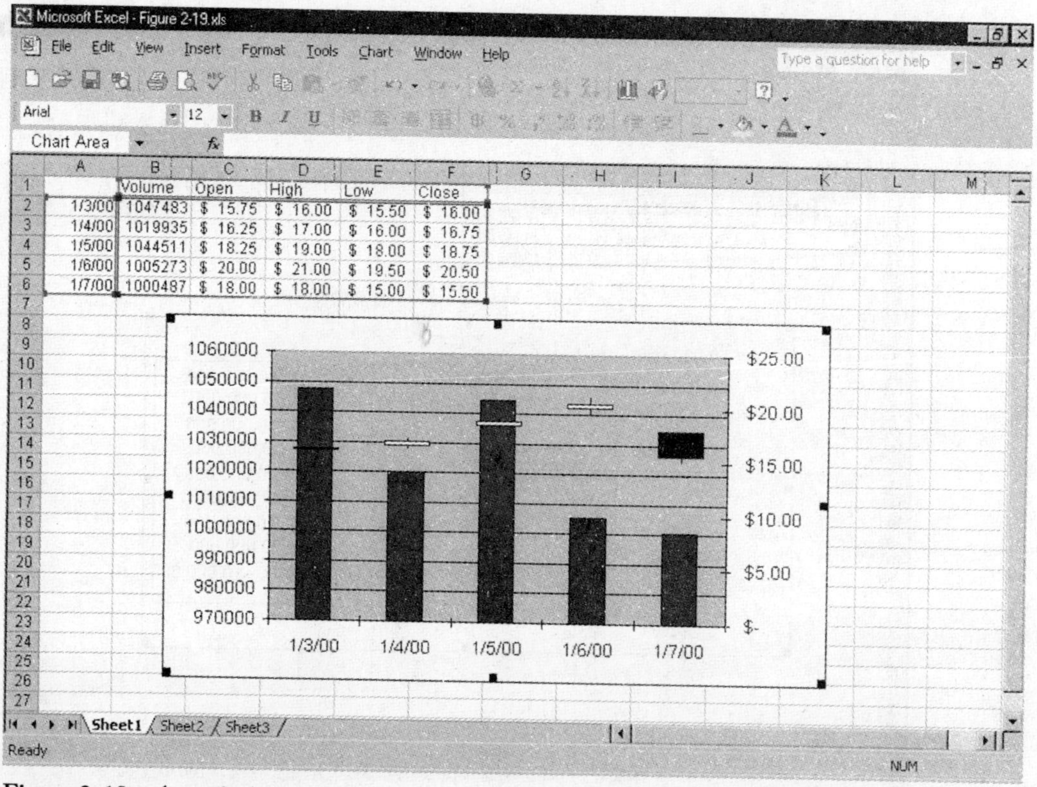

Figure 2-19 A stock chart lets you plot up to five data series in an open-high-low-close format.

NOTE *While this chart type comes from technical security analysis, the chart type can be useful even to people who don't chart security prices. One might use such a chart, for example, to plot daily temperatures.*

Surface charts plot data series in a three-dimensional grid, generally using color not to identify data series but rather to indicate value axis ranges. The principal strength of a surface chart is that it lets you show with equal emphasis both relationships within a data series and within a data category. A surface chart, however, also suffers from two weaknesses: One, because the chart does show a three-dimensional surface, it's easy for the topography of the plot area to hide data—for peaks to hide valleys. Two, although the surface uses color in its value calibrations, there isn't any agreed-upon order to colors. Is the color red "greater" than blue, for example? Is yellow "less than" green? Figure 2-20 shows a surface chart that plots labor force distribution data for Australia, Brazil, and Canada.

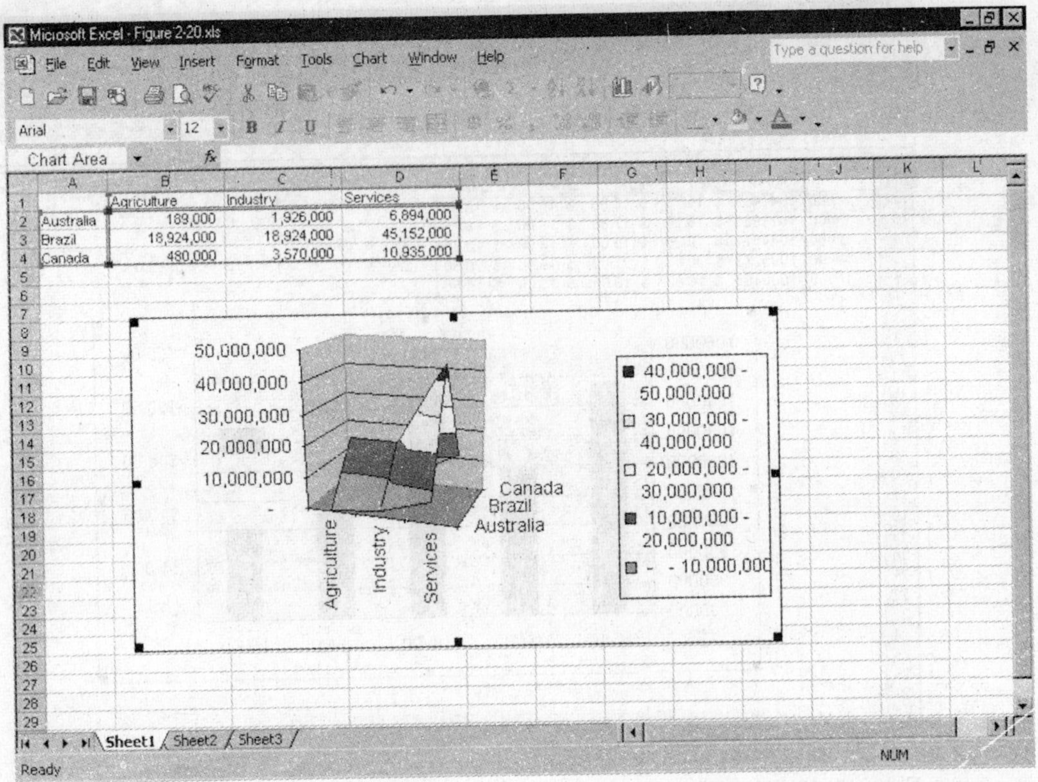

Figure 2-20 A surface chart that shows labor force distributions for Australia, Brazil, and Canada.

XY (Scatter) charts let you visually explore the relationships between data series by treating the horizontal axis as a second values axis. To accomplish this, XY charts actually plot pairs of data points. In Figure 2-21, for example, the chart shows years of education and monthly income and suggests, not surprisingly, that more educated people make more money. The huge strength of an XY chart is that it lets you explore the relationships—perhaps causation or simply correlation—between two data series. The XY chart is the only Excel chart type that lets you do this. If the XY chart suffers from a weakness, it is that the chart may suggest correlations or relationships that don't exist. (You can use Excel's regression analysis tools, discussed in Chapter 4, to examine whether two data series appear correlated.)

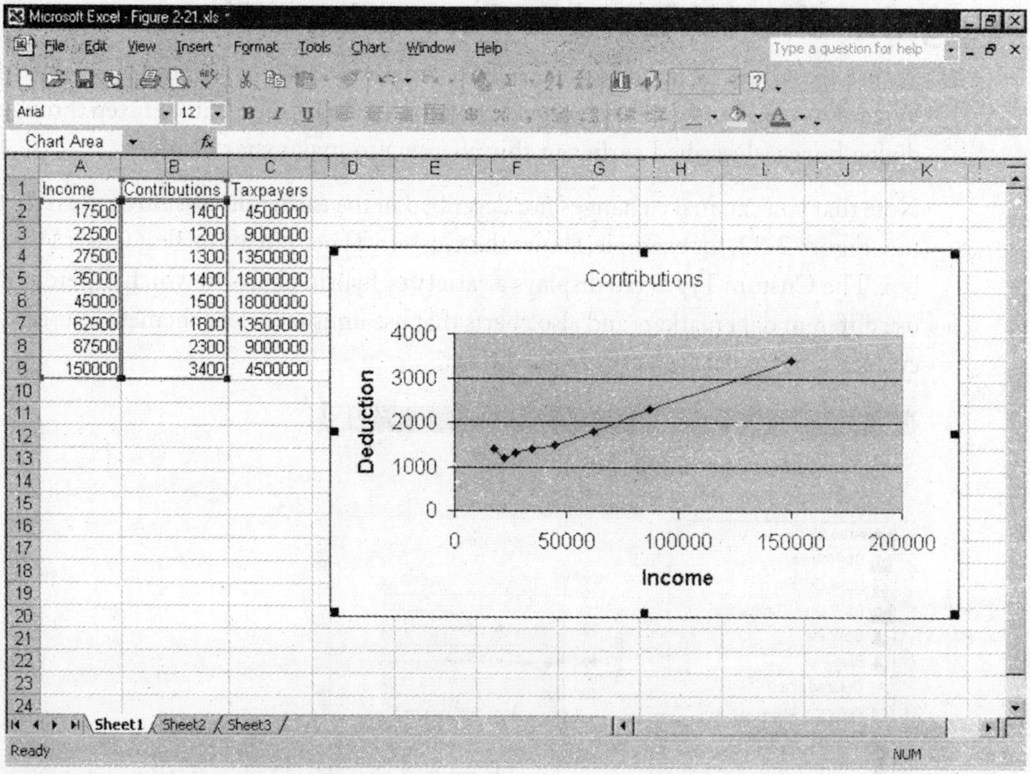

Figure 2-21 A simple XY chart that compares U.S. Internal Revenue Service data on the relation ship between education and income.

NOTE *You aren't limited to showing a single data series in an XY chart. Each data series, however, must use the same pair of data point values.*

Customizing Your Charts

You can easily customize your charts so they better fit your needs. You can, for example, rerun the Chart Wizard. This approach is usually simplest. But you can also use Chart menu commands to change specific elements of a chart. The paragraphs that follow discuss each of the two approaches, because you'll find occasion to use both.

Using the Chart Wizard to Customize a Chart

To use the Chart Wizard to customize a chart, select the chart and then click the Chart Wizard toolbar button. Excel restarts the Chart Wizard, and you can step through the four dialog boxes (described earlier in this chapter) to make your changes.

Note that you can make changes not described in the earlier discussion of the Chart Wizard, too. Figure 2-22, for example, shows the Custom Types tab of the first Chart Wizard dialog box. The Custom Types tab displays a variety of hybrid charts in which different data series use different data markers and also charts that use unusual color schemes. To use one of these custom chart types, select it from the list.

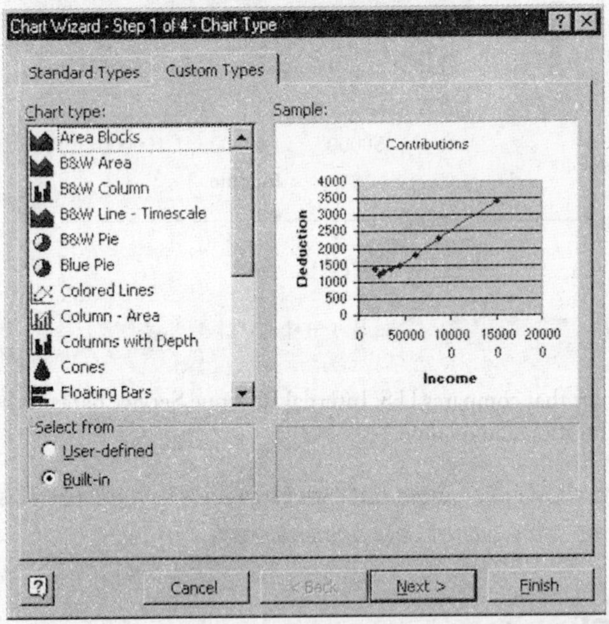

Figure 2-22 The Custom Types tab of the first Chart Wizard dialog box.

NOTE *You can also change the chart type by clicking a chart and then choosing the Chart menu's Chart Type command. When you do this, Excel displays a dialog box, which closely resembles the dialog box shown in Figure 2-22.*

You can add to or change the data series plotted in a chart using the Series tab of the second Chart Wizard dialog box, which is shown in Figure 2-23. To change a data series, click its name in the Series list box and then change the values in the Name and Values boxes. To add a data series to the chart, click Add, and then, after Excel adds the new series, use the Name and Values boxes to name the data series and identify the worksheet range holding the data series. To remove a data series, click the data series and then click Remove. Note, too, that the Series tab also provides a box you use to specify which worksheet range holds the data category names.

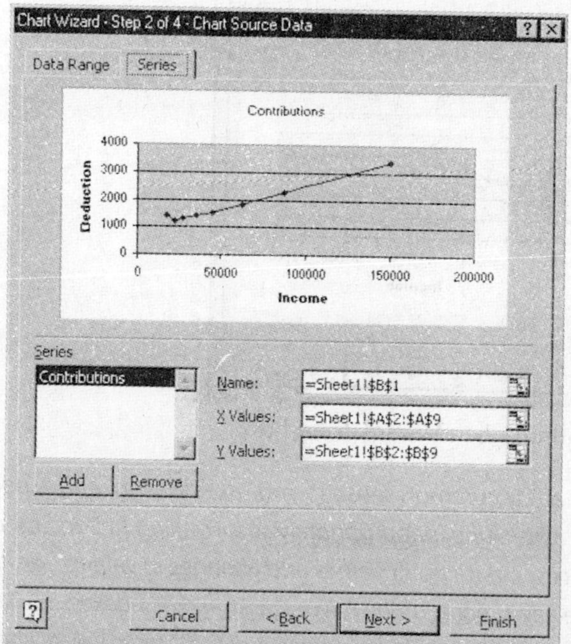

Figure 2-23 The Series tab of the second Chart Wizard dialog box.

TIP *If you click the worksheet button shown at the right end of the Name and Values boxes, Excel minimizes the dialog box. You can then select the cell or worksheet range holding the name, to-be-plotted data, or data category names.*

NOTE *You can also change the chart type by clicking a chart and then choosing the Chart menu's Source Data command. When you do this, Excel displays a dialog box, which closely resembles the dialog box shown in Figure 2-23.*

You can use the third Chart Wizard dialog box, shown in Figure 2-24, to change the text you've used to annotate the change, the appearance of the chart's axes, the gridlines used within the plot area, the location of a legend (and whether you even want one of these), whether data labels appear next to data markers, and whether a table of the plotted data also appears in the chart. Figure 2-24, for example, shows the Axes tab. You use its check boxes to indicate whether you want a Value (X) axis and a Value (Y) axis and, for the Value (X) axis, what formatting you want. Rather than reading about what each of these options does, experiment with them yourself. If your experimentation still leaves you with questions, click the Question button in the dialog box's upper right corner and then click the option you have a question about.

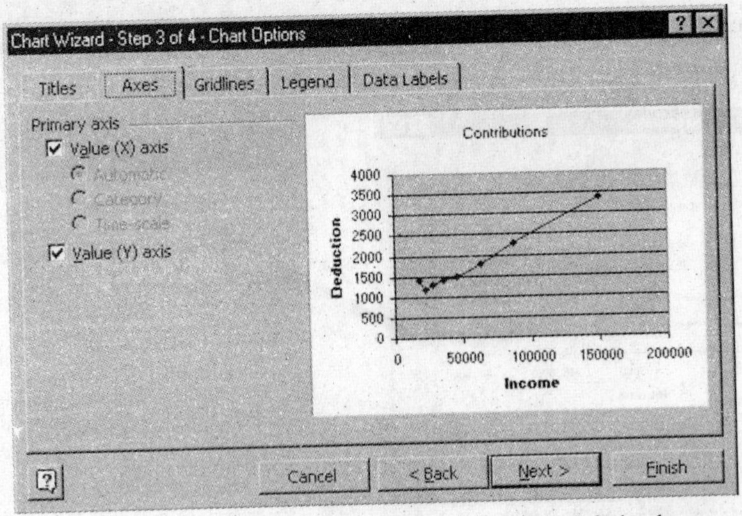

Figure 2-24 The Axes tab of the third Chart Wizard dialog box.

TIP *Typically you do want to apply common sense to your axes scaling, and especially the scaling of your Value (Y) axis. Using inappropriately small scaling factors, for example, can exaggerate differences in data point values and changes in values—as illustrated almost every night on the news report of the major stock market indexes. Similarly, using inappropriately large scaling factors can hide important differences in values and changes in values.*

NOTE *If you want to show the relative changes in values, you typically want to use logarithmic scaling of the values axis. To use the logarithmic scaling, right-click the axis you want to logarithmically scale, choose the shortcut menu's Format Axis command, click the Scale tab, and select the Logarithmic Scale check box.*

This book doesn't show pictures of the other tabs. You can easily see them yourself by clicking the appropriate tab. Note, however, what each of the other tabs allows you to do. The Gridlines tab displays check boxes you can select to add horizontal and vertical gridlines to plot the area of your chart. The Legend tab displays a Show Legend check box you can select to add a legend to the chart and then Placement option buttons—Bottom, Corner, Top, Right, or Left—which you can use to indicate where you want the legend placed. The Data Labels tab displays a set of option buttons you can use to indicate whether you want the actual data point values or equivalent percentages written next to their data markers.

Finally, the Data Table tab (if it appears) provides two check boxes you can select to add a table and, optionally, a legend of the data point values to the bottom of the chart area.

NOTE *You can also change the chart text, axes, gridlines, legend, data labels, or data table by clicking a chart and then choosing the Chart menu's Chart Options command. When you do this, Excel displays a dialog box, which closely resembles the dialog box shown in Figure 2-24.*

You can use the fourth Chart Wizard dialog box, shown in Figure 2-25, to relocate a chart. To do this, simply select the other option when you see this dialog box. For example, if the dialog box initially shows the As New Sheet option button selected, click the As Object In option button—or vice versa.

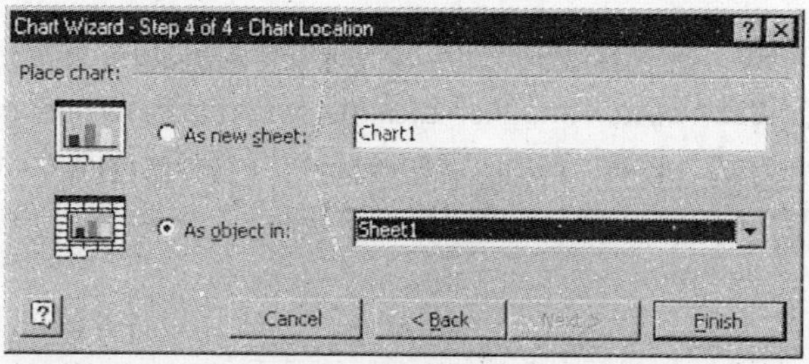

Figure 2-25 The fourth Chart Wizard dialog box.

NOTE *You can also change the chart location by clicking a chart and then choosing the Chart menu's Location command. When you do this, Excel displays a dialog box, which closely resembles the dialog box shown in Figure 2-25.*

Using the Shortcut Menu's Format Command

While you can use the Chart Wizard or some of the equivalent Chart menu commands to customize a chart, Excel doesn't allow you to make every change using just these methods. If you can't use the Chart Wizard or an equivalent command to change some element of a chart, you can right-click the part of the chart that you want to change and then choose the shortcut menu's Format command. For example, if you want to change the scaling of the values axis, you can right-click the values axis and then choose the Format Axis command. (Obviously, if you right-click other parts of a chart, Excel displays a different Format command which, in turn, displays a different dialog box.)

Some books on Excel spend pages describing the myriad changes you can make to each specific part of a chart. But you probably don't really need that level of instruction. In a nutshell, you make only a handful of changes to each part of a chart:

- *Patterns.* Many of the Format dialog boxes display a Patterns tab that you can use to select the colors and lines you want Excel to use to draw the chart object.
- *Fonts.* Any Format dialog box for an element that includes text provides a Font tab that you can use to choose font, font style, font point size, and special text effects.
- *Number.* Any Format dialog box for an element that includes numbers provides a Number tab that you can use to choose a numeric formatting style.
- *Alignment.* Any Format dialog box for an element that includes text provides an Alignment tab that you can use to align text.
- *Scale.* The Format dialog box for both the axes and the gridlines provides a Scale tab that you can use to specify how Excel should calibrate and draw the axis or grid.

TIP *Remember that if you have a question about how to work with some dialog box option, you can click the Question button and then click the option to get a brief but usually very helpful description. The Question button appears in the upper right corner of the dialog box and is marked with a question mark.*

Chapter 3

QUICKPRIMER™ ON DATABASES

Featuring:

- Understanding Databases
- Creating and Filling a Database
- Sorting and Filtering a Database
- Other Database Tools

Bcause Excel allows you to build tables quickly and easily, it is an excellent tool for creating and arranging flat databases, or basic lists of information. To create a more complex database with multiple tables linked together (called a *relational database*), you need a database management program such as Microsoft Access. Although relational databases require more time and effort to design and build, they reduce the amount of duplicate information you have to enter in the database as you work with it. For example, if you create a relational database for your customers, you can create a primary table for the customer list and related tables for customer orders. This way, when a customer places an order, you need only fill in the order information and not all of the information about the customer. However, when you use Excel's database capabilities, you are working in an environment in which you are familiar, and where you can take advantage of Excel's database tools and functions. In many cases, using Excel in this manner may be the only database you need.

Understanding Databases

A database is a table of information that you can search, sort, filter, and on which you can perform other operations. Each row of a database holds a record, and each column holds a field. For example, if you have a database of vendors, the various pieces of information about a single vendor make up a record; the rows store this information about the individual vendors. A piece of information, such as the payment term, is a field; the columns contain this same piece of information across all vendors.

Creating and Filling a Database

To work with a list of data in Excel, you first need to create the database so that Excel recognizes it as one. Then you can begin entering the data in the database. This section describes a couple of options Excel provides for doing so.

NOTE *If the data you want in your database already exists in electronic form, you can import it into Excel. See Chapter 7 for more information on how to do so.*

Creating a Database

You create a database in Excel in much the same way you create any other spreadsheet. After you have created the database, you can rename, add, or delete worksheets in the workbook, and then save the workbook.

1. **Open a new blank workbook.**

   If you don't have Excel running, start the program to create a new workbook. If you have Excel running, click the New toolbar button to create a new workbook based on the Workbook template.

2. **Determine what each record should be. The information these records' hold becomes the records' fields.**

   For example, if you want to build a database of employees, each employee is a record, and the fields are probably first name, last name, Social Security number, address, birth date, hire date, and the like.

NOTE *Even if you don't have information for every field in a record, you can still include the field. For example, you can have a mobile phone-number field for a database of contacts even though only some contacts have mobile phone entries.*

3. **Enter the field labels in the first row of the worksheet.**

   Enter the field labels in the order in which you think you want them. You can easily change the order of the fields at a later time, if you find that you need to do so. Do not leave blank columns between fields. Figure 3-1 shows a worksheet with a list of field labels in row 1.

	A	B	C	D	E	F	G	H	I	J
1	ProductID	Name	Size	Content	Color	Description	Cost	Vendor	Price	
2										

Figure 3-1 Creating a database.

TIP *For ease of use, use the shortest labels that clearly describe the contents of the field. It is not a good idea to use spaces in field labels, however, even though Excel allows it. It may cause problems if you ever need to export the database to another program.*

Filling a Database with Information

You can add information to the database the same way you add information to any other worksheet—by moving to the cell and typing the label, value, or formula. However, you can also use forms to enter the information record by record (i.e., row by row). To use forms for data entry, follow these steps:

1. **Choose the Data menu's Form command.**

   Excel displays the dialog box shown in Figure 3-2, named after the worksheet on which the form is based. The dialog box contains the form field labels you entered in the first row. If you've already entered some data in the database, Excel displays the first record you entered in the form field boxes. After you enter the first record, the upper right corner of the form tells you which record you're currently viewing and how many records you've entered (this number doesn't include the first row containing the field labels).

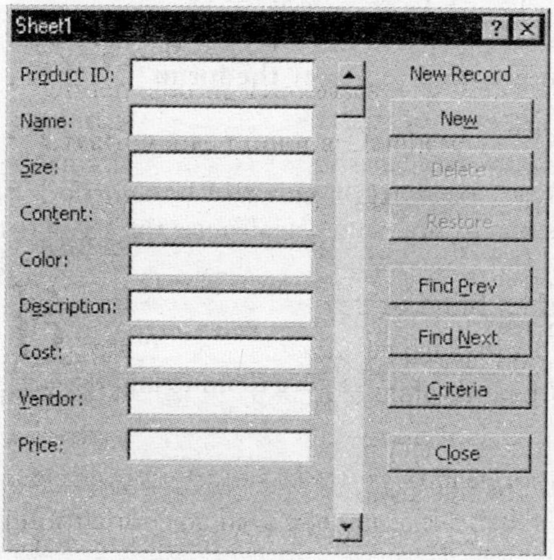

Figure 3-2 Using a form to enter data in a database.

NOTE *If you haven't yet entered any records, click OK in the warning message that Excel displays to use the first row as your field labels.*

2. **If the form field boxes are not blank, click New to create a New record.**

   Excel displays a blank form dialog box in which you can enter the new record's data.

3. **Fill in the information about the first record.**

   Enter the data in the appropriate boxes.

4. **Click New again to add the new record to the worksheet and display a new blank form.**

   When you add a new record to a database, Excel adds a new row to the worksheet.

5. **When you're finished using a form to enter records, click Close.**

   Excel closes the form and returns you to the worksheet containing the database.

TIP *To continue viewing field labels as you scroll down a database, you can use Excel's split feature. To create a horizontal pane, rest the mouse pointer over the narrow box at the top end of the vertical scroll bar so it becomes a double-sided arrow, and then drag to the line between the field label and the first record. Freeze this pane by choosing the Window menu's Freeze Panes command.*

Editing Database Records

After you've entered records, you can edit them by moving to the cell holding the information you want to change and entering new information. You can also redisplay the form and use it to edit records. To edit records using a form, follow these steps:

1. **Choose the Data menu's Form command to redisplay the form.**
2. **Move to the record you want to edit.**

   Click Find Prev to page backward through the records one by one, or click Find Next to page forward through the records one by one. You can also use the scroll bar to scroll through the database to the record you want to edit.

3. **Enter your changes in the form's fields.**

   If you make a mistake when editing a form, click Restore to undo all of your changes to the record.

NOTE *To delete a record, click Delete. Excel deletes this row from the worksheet.*

4. **Update the worksheet with your changes to the record.**

   Click Find Next or Find Prev to edit other records, click New to add a new record, or click Close to return to the worksheet.

Finding Records in a Database

To use a form to find records that match the criteria you specify, follow these steps:

1. **Choose the Data menu's Form command to display the form.**
2. **Click Criteria.**

   The upper right corner of the form now displays the word *Criteria,* as shown in Figure 3-3.

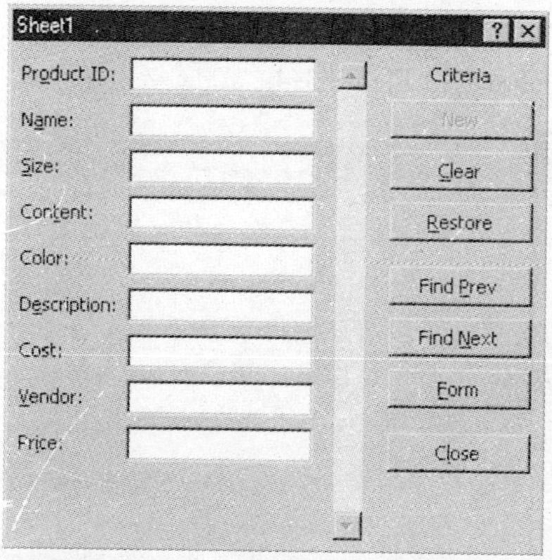

Figure 3-3 Finding a record in a database.

3. Enter the search criteria in the form's fields.

4. Click Find Prev or Find Next.

Excel finds the previous or next record matching the criteria you specified.

NOTE *You can also use Excel's Find feature to find items in a database. Just choose the Edit menu's Find command. Chapter 1 describes finding and replacing information in Excel.*

Sorting and Filtering a Database

Once you have created a database, you can begin sorting and filtering so that you can access and analyze the information you need.

Sorting a Database

To sort a database, follow these steps:

1. Click a cell in the database.

Doing so tells Excel that you want to sort all the fields in the database and keep the records intact.

WARNING *If you select a range that doesn't include all columns, Excel sorts the columns in your range but does not sort the other columns accordingly. This disassociates fields from the records to which they belong and attaches them to other records.*

TIP *To sort only a part of a database, select all rows for the records you want to sort.*

2. **Choose the Data menu's Sort command.**

Excel displays the Sort dialog box shown in Figure 3-4.

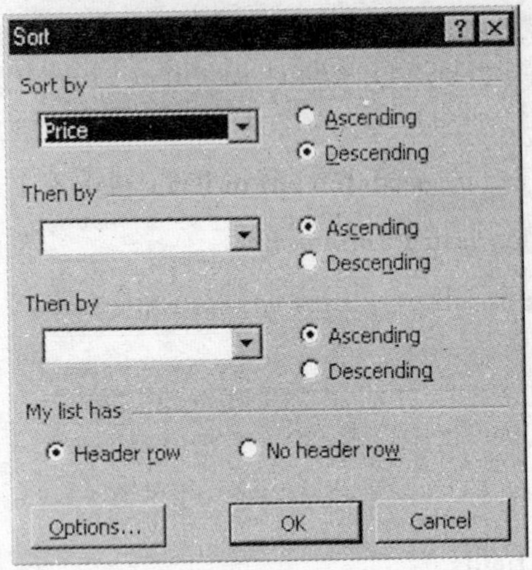

Figure 3-4 The Sort dialog box.

3. **Specify the first field by which you want to sort.**

Use the Sort By drop-down list box to select the name of the field by which you want to sort the database.

TIP *To quickly sort a database by the entries in a single field, select a cell in the field's column and click the Sort Ascending or Sort Descending toolbar button.*

4. **Specify the order by which you want to sort the field.**

Click the Ascending option button to sort with the lowest number, first letter of the alphabet, or earliest date at the top of the column. Click the Descending option button to sort in reverse numeric, alphabetic, or chronological order.

NOTE *Regardless of whether you click Ascending or Descending, blank fields appear at the bottom of the list.*

5. **Optionally, specify second- and third-level sorting.**

If multiple entries in the field you're sorting by are the same, you can specify other fields by which you want to sort using the Then By drop-down list boxes and corresponding Ascending and Descending option buttons. For example, if you sort by the price field and have multiple items selling for the same price, you can sort within this group by name, by product identification number, or by cost.

6. **Make sure that the Header Row option is selected.**

   If you don't select the Header Row option, Excel sorts your field labels along with the data in the fields.

7. **Click OK.**

Creating Custom Sort Orders

To specify a nonnumeric, nonalphabetic, or nonchronological sort order, follow these steps:

1. **Choose the Tools menu's Options command, and click the Custom Lists tab.**

   Excel displays the Custom Lists tab of the Options dialog box, as shown in Figure 3-5.

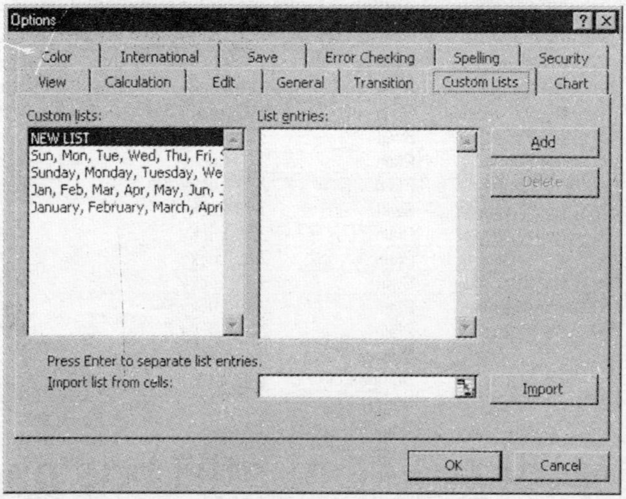

Figure 3-5 Creating a custom sort list.

2. **Select New List from the Custom Lists list.**
3. **Specify the items in the order you want to sort them.**

   To do this, enter the items in the List Entries box, pressing the Enter key after each item. Or, if you already have a range of cells in the worksheet that contains the items sorted in the order you want, click the Import List From Cells box, select the range, and click Import.

4. **Click Add.**

   Excel adds the list to the Custom Lists list.

5. **Click OK when you're finished.**

Filtering Databases

If your database contains large amounts of data, you may want Excel to display only the data you're interested in so you can focus on it better. To do this, you use Excel's Filter feature. When you filter a database, Excel doesn't delete the records that don't meet the criteria. It just hides them. To filter a database, follow these steps:

1. Select a cell in the database.

2. Choose the Data menu's Filter command, and then choose AutoFilter.

Excel adds arrow buttons to the right side of your field labels in the first row, as shown in Figure 3-6.

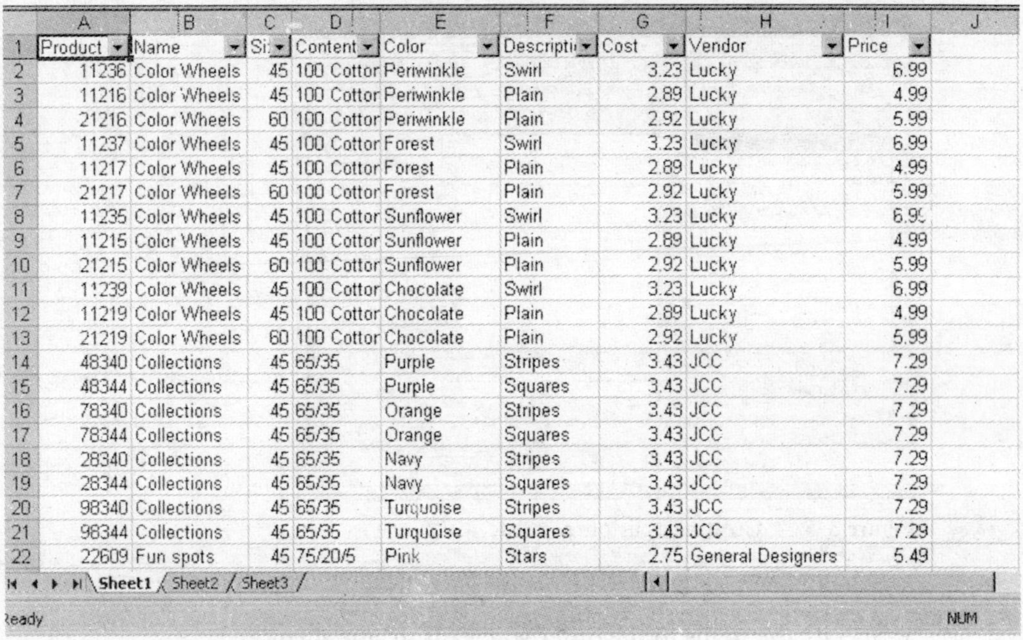

	A	B	C	D	E	F	G	H	I	J
1	Product	Name	Si:	Content	Color	Descripti	Cost	Vendor	Price	
2	11236	Color Wheels	45	100 Cottor	Periwinkle	Swirl	3.23	Lucky	6.99	
3	11216	Color Wheels	45	100 Cottor	Periwinkle	Plain	2.89	Lucky	4.99	
4	21216	Color Wheels	60	100 Cottor	Periwinkle	Plain	2.92	Lucky	5.99	
5	11237	Color Wheels	45	100 Cottor	Forest	Swirl	3.23	Lucky	6.99	
6	11217	Color Wheels	45	100 Cottor	Forest	Plain	2.89	Lucky	4.99	
7	21217	Color Wheels	60	100 Cottor	Forest	Plain	2.92	Lucky	5.99	
8	11235	Color Wheels	45	100 Cottor	Sunflower	Swirl	3.23	Lucky	6.99	
9	11215	Color Wheels	45	100 Cottor	Sunflower	Plain	2.89	Lucky	4.99	
10	21215	Color Wheels	60	100 Cottor	Sunflower	Plain	2.92	Lucky	5.99	
11	11239	Color Wheels	45	100 Cottor	Chocolate	Swirl	3.23	Lucky	6.99	
12	11219	Color Wheels	45	100 Cottor	Chocolate	Plain	2.89	Lucky	4.99	
13	21219	Color Wheels	60	100 Cottor	Chocolate	Plain	2.92	Lucky	5.99	
14	48340	Collections	45	65/35	Purple	Stripes	3.43	JCC	7.29	
15	48344	Collections	45	65/35	Purple	Squares	3.43	JCC	7.29	
16	78340	Collections	45	65/35	Orange	Stripes	3.43	JCC	7.29	
17	78344	Collections	45	65/35	Orange	Squares	3.43	JCC	7.29	
18	28340	Collections	45	65/35	Navy	Stripes	3.43	JCC	7.29	
19	28344	Collections	45	65/35	Navy	Squares	3.43	JCC	7.29	
20	98340	Collections	45	65/35	Turquoise	Stripes	3.43	JCC	7.29	
21	98344	Collections	45	65/35	Turquoise	Squares	3.43	JCC	7.29	
22	22609	Fun spots	45	75/20/5	Pink	Stars	2.75	General Designers	5.49	

Figure 3-6 Filtering field entries.

3. Click the arrow for the field by which you want to filter records.

Excel displays a drop-down list of the entries in that field.

- If you want to include only a single entry, select the entry from the list.
- To display only a given top or bottom percent or number of entries, select Top 10 from the list. Excel displays the Top 10 AutoFilter dialog box. Use it to specify whether you want to view the top or bottom entries in the field and the number or percentage of entries you want to view. Click OK when you're finished.

- To customize the filter, choose Custom from the list. Excel displays the Custom AutoFilter dialog box shown in Figure 3-7. Use the first drop-down list box to select the operator. Use the second drop-down list box to enter the text or value on which you're basing the filter. Optionally, click the And or Or option button to specify another criteria and use the second row of drop-down list boxes to describe the second criteria. Click OK when you're finished.

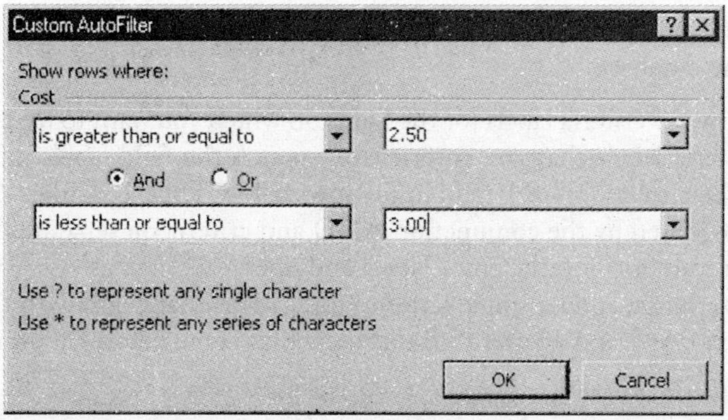

Figure 3-7 Displaying only records that show costs between \$2.50 and \$3.00.

4. If necessary, repeat the filtering procedure for another field.

For example, you could filter to display records that have cost entries fitting certain criteria and size entries fitting certain criteria.

5. Click OK.

If you want to save the filter criteria, save the database under a new name. To redisplay all records, choose the Data menu's Filter command and then choose Show All.

NOTE *You can tell that a database has been filtered because the row numbers appear in blue and skip values. The filtered field's arrow is also blue.*

Performing an Advanced Filter

For more advanced filtering options, you can use Excel's Advanced Filter feature. The Advanced Filter feature allows you to do the following:

- Filter criteria based on a computation. For example, you could display only those records with prices below the average price.
- Specify more than two criteria for a single column. For example, you may want to display all items that are from any one of three vendors.

- Specify criteria involving multiple columns and the conjunction OR. For example, you could filter to include items that either come from a particular vendor or are of a non-standard size.

To perform an advanced filter, follow these steps:

1. Enter the filter criteria in a range of cells.

Place the criteria range either above or below the database so that it doesn't get hidden when you filter the database.

Enter in a single row the criteria labels for the fields on which you want to base the filter. Make sure the criteria labels that you enter exactly match the field labels in the database. Then enter the criteria for each field in the rows below. Excel considers criteria on the same line to be joined by the conjunction AND and criteria on separate lines to be joined by OR. For numeric criteria, enter labels and operators such as <, <=, >, >=, and the value. For text criteria, enter a single letter to filter items that begin with that letter. Enter the operators < or > and a letter to filter items that come before or after that letter of the alphabet.

NOTE *Criteria based on formulas are a special case. When you use a formula to create a criterion, do not use a column label for a criteria label; either keep the criteria label blank or use a label that is not a column label in the list. For more information, choose the Help menu's Microsoft Excel Help command, click the Index tab, and select Advanced_Filter from the Keywords list.*

TIP *For filters based on computations, use absolute references to cells outside the database and relative references to cells within the database.*

Figure 3-8 shows how the criteria ranges would look for the three examples mentioned above.

M	N	O	P
Price			
=I2<AVERAGE(I2:I24)			
Vendor			
Lucky			
JCC			
General Designers			
Size	Size	Vendor	
<45	>60	Lucky	

Figure 3-8 Creating a criteria range.

2. **Select a cell in the database list, choose the Data menu's Filter command, and then choose Advanced Filter.**

   Excel selects the entire database and displays the Advanced Filter dialog box shown in Figure 3-9.

Figure 3-9 The Advanced Filter dialog box.

3. **Click an Action option button to specify where you want Excel to display the filtered database.**

   Click the first option button to display in the current database worksheet only those records that fit the filter criteria. Click the second option button to copy the records that fit the criteria to a different location.

4. **Verify that Excel selected the correct list in its entirety.**

   Make sure the List Range contains all the records and fields in the database and nothing but the database you want to filter.

5. **Enter the criteria range in the Criteria Range box.**

   You can either type the range in the box or click the box and then select the range in the worksheet.

WARNING *Make sure you don't select any blank rows in the range. When a cell in a criteria range is blank, Excel accepts any content for that field. So if a row is blank, Excel returns an unfiltered database.*

6. **If you chose to copy the filtered database to another location in step 3, specify the destination.**

   Enter the location in the Copy To box.

7. **Optionally, select the Unique Records Only check box to exclude duplicate records.**

8. Click OK.

Excel filters the database according to your criteria and displays the filtered information in the location you specified.

To redisplay all records, choose the Data menu's Filter command and then choose Show All.

Other Database Tools

You can perform several other operations on databases in Excel. This section describes how you can create subtotals, validate database entries, and use functions specific to databases.

Subtotaling Databases

After you sort and filter your database as necessary, you can create subtotals to summarize details in your database. To subtotal information in a database, follow these steps:

1. Select a cell in the database, and choose the Data menu's Subtotals command.

Excel displays the Subtotal dialog box shown in Figure 3-10.

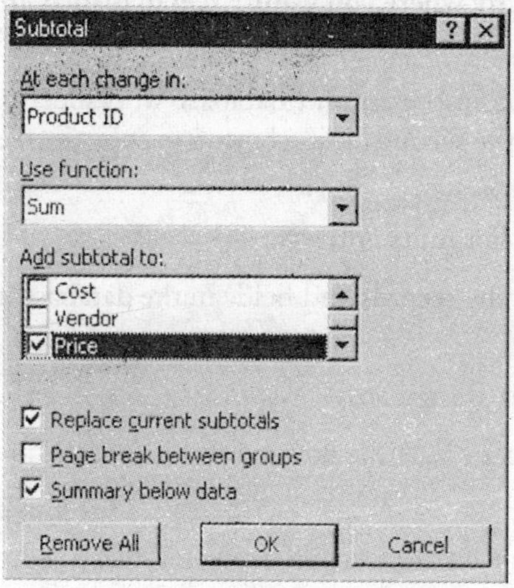

Figure 3-10 The Subtotal dialog box.

2. Use the At Each Change In drop-down list box to specify the field by which you want the subtotals grouped.

3. Select a function from the Use Function drop-down list box.

Not only can the subtotal tool add groups of entries to create subtotals, but it can also perform other functions, such as calculating the average, counting the number of entries or blank items, or calculating the standard deviation or variation.

4. Select check boxes for the fields on which you want the subtotal operation performed.
5. Select the Replace Current Subtotals check box if you've created subtotals before.
6. Leave the Page Break Between Groups check box clear.
7. Select the Summary Below Data check box unless you want the subtotals to appear above rather than below the data they summarize.
8. Click OK.

   Excel adds subtotal and grand total rows to the database, as shown in Figure 3-11. To remove subtotals, choose the Data menu's Subtotals command and click Remove All in the Subtotal dialog box.

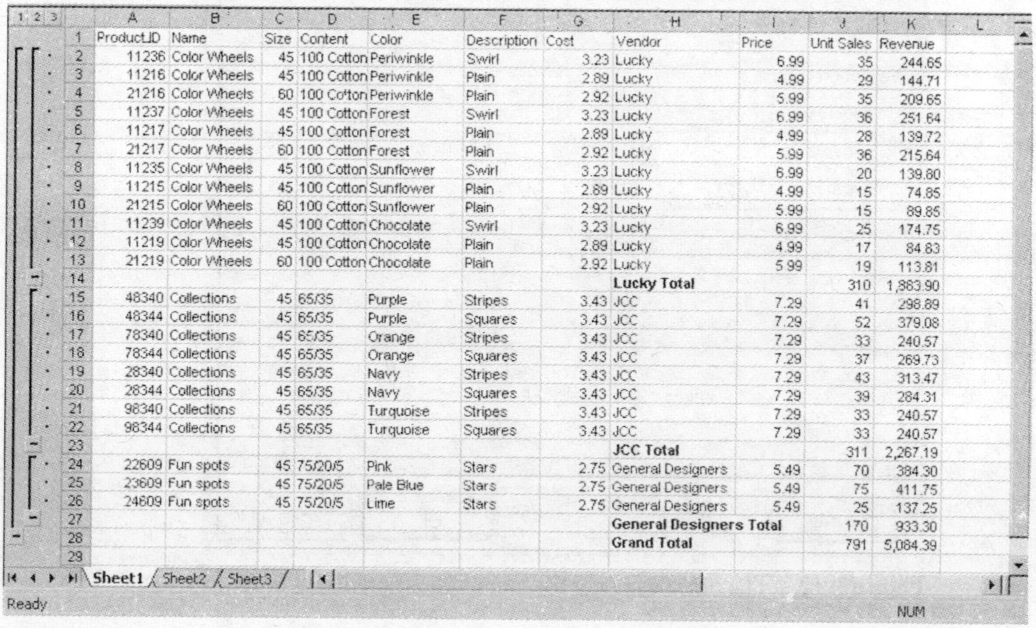

	A	B	C	D	E	F	G	H	I	J	K
1	ProductID	Name	Size	Content	Color	Description	Cost	Vendor	Price	Unit Sales	Revenue
2	11236	Color Wheels	45	100 Cotton	Periwinkle	Swirl	3.23	Lucky	6.99	35	244.65
3	11216	Color Wheels	45	100 Cotton	Periwinkle	Plain	2.89	Lucky	4.99	29	144.71
4	21216	Color Wheels	60	100 Cotton	Periwinkle	Plain	2.92	Lucky	5.99	35	209.65
5	11237	Color Wheels	45	100 Cotton	Forest	Swirl	3.23	Lucky	6.99	36	251.64
6	11217	Color Wheels	45	100 Cotton	Forest	Plain	2.89	Lucky	4.99	28	139.72
7	21217	Color Wheels	60	100 Cotton	Forest	Plain	2.92	Lucky	5.99	36	215.64
8	11235	Color Wheels	45	100 Cotton	Sunflower	Swirl	3.23	Lucky	6.99	20	139.80
9	11215	Color Wheels	45	100 Cotton	Sunflower	Plain	2.89	Lucky	4.99	15	74.85
10	21215	Color Wheels	60	100 Cotton	Sunflower	Plain	2.92	Lucky	5.99	15	89.85
11	11239	Color Wheels	45	100 Cotton	Chocolate	Swirl	3.23	Lucky	6.99	25	174.75
12	11219	Color Wheels	45	100 Cotton	Chocolate	Plain	2.89	Lucky	4.99	17	84.83
13	21219	Color Wheels	60	100 Cotton	Chocolate	Plain	2.92	Lucky	5.99	19	113.81
14								**Lucky Total**		310	1,883.90
15	48340	Collections	45	65/35	Purple	Stripes	3.43	JCC	7.29	41	298.89
16	48344	Collections	45	65/35	Purple	Squares	3.43	JCC	7.29	52	379.08
17	78340	Collections	45	65/35	Orange	Stripes	3.43	JCC	7.29	33	240.57
18	78344	Collections	45	65/35	Orange	Squares	3.43	JCC	7.29	37	269.73
19	28340	Collections	45	65/35	Navy	Stripes	3.43	JCC	7.29	43	313.47
20	28344	Collections	45	65/35	Navy	Squares	3.43	JCC	7.29	39	284.31
21	98340	Collections	45	65/35	Turquoise	Stripes	3.43	JCC	7.29	33	240.57
22	98344	Collections	45	65/35	Turquoise	Squares	3.43	JCC	7.29	33	240.57
23								**JCC Total**		311	2,267.19
24	22609	Fun spots	45	75/20/5	Pink	Stars	2.75	General Designers	5.49	70	384.30
25	23609	Fun spots	45	75/20/5	Pale Blue	Stars	2.75	General Designers	5.49	75	411.75
26	24609	Fun spots	45	75/20/5	Lime	Stars	2.75	General Designers	5.49	25	137.25
27								**General Designers Total**		170	933.30
28								**Grand Total**		791	5,084.39
29											

Figure 3-11 A database with subtotals.

TIP *You can hide and display groups by clicking the boxes with the plus and minus signs in the outline area on the left. You can also click the numbers at the top of the outline area to view specific levels of the outline.*

Validating Database Entries

Excel's Validation feature allows you to ensure that new records you add to a database fit certain criteria. This can help prevent someone from entering, for example, a product name in a numeric product ID field.

NOTE *The validation rules apply whether you enter data directly in the database worksheet or use a form.*

To set up validation criteria for your database, follow these steps:

1. **Select the range of cells to which you want the criteria to apply, and choose the Data menu's Validation command.**

   To set criteria for all entries in a field, select the entire field by clicking the column header. Excel displays the Data Validation dialog box, as shown in Figure 3-12.

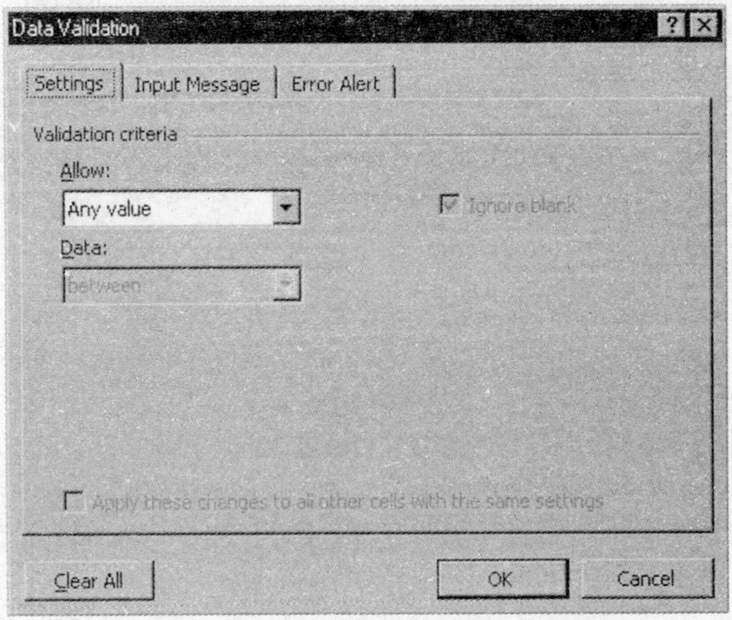

Figure 3-12 The Settings tab of the Data Validation dialog box.

2. **Click the Settings tab, and indicate which kind of data and which range of values is permissible.**

   Select a type of data from the Allow drop-down list box. After you select a data type, Excel displays other boxes, which allow you to constrain the type of data you selected. For example, if you selected Date, Excel prompts you to select the start- and end-date boundaries.

3. **Click the Input Message tab, and create a prompt to inform database users which input is allowable.**

   Optionally, enter a short title for the message in the Title box. Enter the message text in the Input Message box. If you enter records directly in the database and do not use a form, Excel displays the input message when you select a cell to which the validation criteria applies.

4. **Click the Error Alert tab to customize the pop-up error message that will appear if a person enters invalid data.**

   Select a symbol from the Style drop-down list box. Optionally, enter a title for the message in the Title box. Enter the message text in the Error Message box, as shown in Figure 3-13.

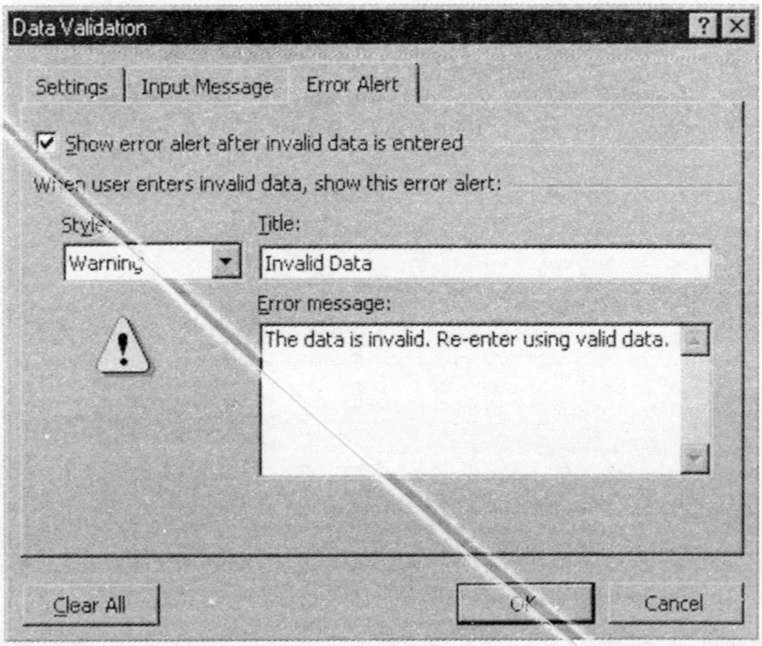

Figure 3-13 Creating an error message.

Excel's Database Functions

Excel comes with a collection of functions tailored especially for databases. To see these functions, display the Insert Function dialog box and select Database from the function category list. All of these functions begin with the letter D. The database functions work similarly to the standard worksheet functions except that they allow an extra parameter so you can specify the items to which a function applies. For example, the DSTDEV function works like the regular STDEV function to find standard deviation except that it uses the following syntax:

```
=DSTDEV(database,field,criteria)
```

where database is the range of cells that make up database, and field is the column on which you want the function performed. Enter the field parameter as text with the field label in quotation marks, such as "Product ID." Criteria is an optional range of cells containing criteria you specify.

TIP *When creating a criteria range, put it at the top or bottom of your database so that none of it is hidden if you filter the database. The "Performing an Advanced Filter" section earlier in the chapter contains more tips, information, and examples about creating criteria ranges.*

NOTE *The function DGET is unique to databases. It returns the value of any cell in a field that meets the criteria specified in the criteria range.*

Part 2

Using Excel in Business

In This Part

Chapter 4

STATISTICAL ANALYSIS

Featuring:

- EasyRefresher™: Basic Business Statistics
- Statistical Formulas
- Data Analysis Tools

Excel provides an almost countless number of tools you can use to analyze data and make meaningful statements about it. However, without understanding the purpose and design of the tools and the details of how to use them, they offer little help. This chapter supplies the background information required to determine which statistical tool to use and how to use it to find the information you need. The first part of this chapter defines some important statistical terms used in the calculations. The second part of the chapter details each function in turn and provides examples illustrating the type of data each function requires and the type of result you can expect. The last part of this chapter describes the statistical analysis tools included in the Analysis ToolPak add-in.

EasyRefresher™: Basic Business Statistics

To determine which function to use and to insert the correct variables in the correct places, you need to know some key statistical terms. This section describes these terms.

The science of statistics makes a fundamental distinction between two types of data sets: population data and sample data. A *population* is the set of all elements of interest, while a *sample* is a subset of that population, drawn to make inferences about the characteristics of the population. For example, if you want to describe the average number of televisions in American households, you can't possibly collect data for the entire population (all American households). Instead, you must draw a sample from the population and make an estimate about the whole population based on that sample. Unless otherwise stated, the

Excel functions described here make a critical assumption regarding the process used to select the sample: they assume that the sample drawn was drawn at random, so in this case, every household would have the same likelihood (probability) of being selected.

TIP *When making statements about a population, it is wise to verify the selection process used to form the sample. For example, if the sample were formed by randomly selecting entries from a phone book, this is not random selection of the sample—it excludes households with unlisted numbers or no telephones and includes households with multiple telephone book entries multiple times. The households don't have the same probability of being selected.*

When describing the data in a set, each member of the set is called an *element*. So if you're describing customers, each customer is an element. The characteristics of interest in the elements are called *variables*. So if you're looking at annual income, age, and sales, these would be your variables. The experimenter manipulates the independent variable and measures the dependent variable after the manipulation to see whether it experienced any effects. A *random variable* describes the outcome of an experiment numerically. It can take on different values or ranges with certain probabilities. The collective group of measurements obtained for an element is called an *observation*.

The term *probability* refers to the likelihood that an event will happen. Probabilities range between 0 (impossible) and 1 (inevitable). A probability distribution graphically depicts how probabilities are distributed over discrete values or ranges of the random variable. Probability distributions can take on several shapes. For example, a uniform probability distribution is rectangular—it occurs when there's an equal probability for every value of the random variable. Another common probability distribution is the normal or bell curve. This occurs when there's a relatively high probability of a random variable taking a certain value or range and a symmetrically diminishing probability as you move away from this value.

A *discrete variable* is one that can't fall to an infinite number of digits. For example, the number of children in a family is a discrete number, in this case a nonnegative integer. A *continuous variable*, on the other hand, can take on a value with any number of digits. For example, you can theoretically calculate the time it takes a person to run a mile down to the smallest fraction of a second. The probability, therefore, of a continuous random variable taking a particular value is zero. Note that statistics calculated from discrete variables are continuous variables. So you can say that the average number of children in a family is, for example, 2.3, although no family could have 2.3 children.

An *event* is a collection of outcomes that share a condition. For example, you could call all outcomes in which a project goes over budget or in which a lot of goods is rejected an event.

NOTE *In Excel, the term* logical value *refers to a value (usually textual) that Excel returns when you enter a conditional function in a cell. (A conditional function is an equation that returns a result based on whether the cell meets the condition specified.) For example, you can ask Excel to display the word TRUE if a value in a cell is greater than 100 or FALSE if it is less than or equal to 100. The most common logical values are TRUE and FALSE, but you can create your own logical values as well. For example, you can tell Excel to display the word PASS if a value in a cell is greater than or equal to 50 or FAIL if it is less than 50.*

Statistical Formulas

This section describes the basic statistical functions that come with Excel. To see which functions Excel provides or to see which arguments a function requires, click the Insert Function button and then select Statistical from the Or Select A Category list box shown in Figure 4-1.

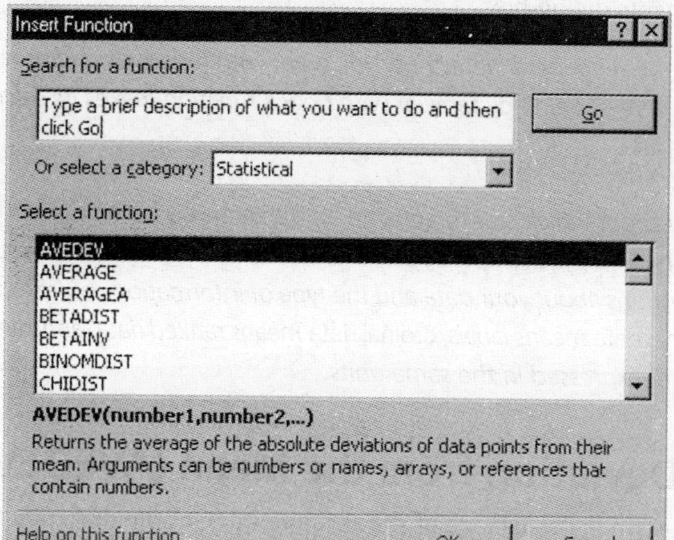

Figure 4-1 The Insert Function dialog box.

After you select a function from the Select A Function list box and click Next, the Function Arguments dialog box shows which arguments are required for the function to make its calculations, as shown in Figure 4-2.

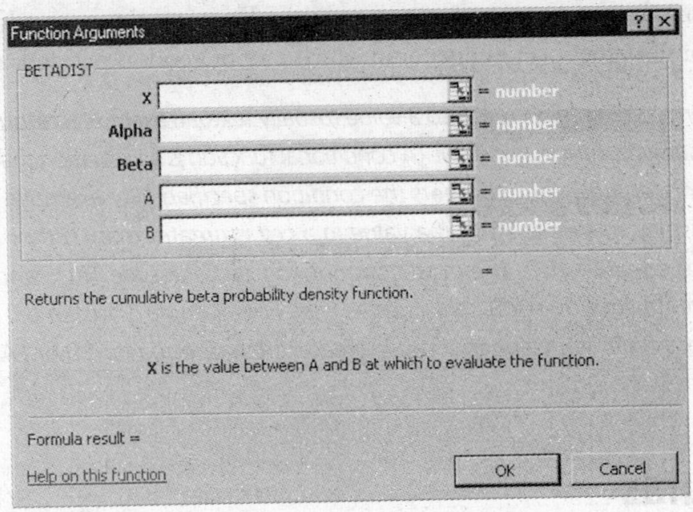

Figure 4-2 The Function Arguments dialog box.

This chapter describes the statistical functions in a way that allows you to enter them directly in a cell without using the Insert Function dialog box. However, if you want to use the Insert Function dialog box, you just enter the arguments described in this chapter in the text boxes of the Function Arguments dialog box.

NOTE *Chapter 1 describes in general detail how you work with functions and provide their arguments. If you're not already familiar with how a function makes its calculations, refer to that chapter.*

TIP *If you're unsure about which test to perform on the data you have to find the results you want, visit the web site at* http://trochim.human.cornell.edu/selstat/ssstart.htm *and answer the questions about your data and the type of information you're looking for. Note that* nominal data *means labels,* ordinal data *means ranked data, and* interval data *means a data set expressed in the same units.*

Average Absolute Deviation from the Mean (AVEDEV)

The AVEDEV function finds the average of the absolute value of the deviation from the mean for each value in a data set. The AVEDEV function uses the following syntax:

```
=AVEDEV(data set range)
```

To use the AVEDEV function, simply enter the data set range as the single argument in the function. For example, if your data set is in the range A1:C10, you would enter the function as follows:

```
=AVEDEV(A1:C10)
```

Beta Probability Density

BETADIST

The BETADIST function returns the cumulative beta probability density function. Statisticians often use the cumulative beta probability density function to study variation across samples, such as when comparing two groups of people performing the same task to see whether they have the same success rate. The BETADIST function uses the following syntax:

```
=BETADIST(x,alpha,beta,A,B)
```

where x is a value between two optional bounds A and B, and alpha and beta are the two positive parameters. For example, if x equals 2, alpha equals 85, beta equals 90, A equals 1, and B equals 3, you would enter the function as follows:

```
=BETADIST(2,85,90,1,3)
```

The formula returns the value 0.647616.

NOTE *The uniform probability distribution is a special case of the beta probability distribution where alpha=beta=1.*

BETAINV

The BETAINV function returns the inverse of the cumulative beta probability density function. That is, you use the BETADIST function if you know x and want to find the probability, and you use the BETAINV function if you know the probability and want to find x. The BETAINV function uses the following syntax:

```
=BETAINV(probability,alpha,beta,A,B)
```

Binomial Probability Distribution

The binomial distribution describes the outcome of a multistep experiment, consisting of n identical trials, where each trial ends in either a success or a failure and the probability of a success p does not change from trial to trial. The trials must also be independent so that success in one trial does not affect the probability of success in another trial. The binomial random variable x is the number of successes observed in n trials.

NOTE *If samples are not replaced, and therefore the outcome of one trial changes the probability of success in another trial, you need to use the hypergeometric probability distribution described later in the chapter.*

BINOMDIST

For example, if you flip a coin n times and "heads" is called a success, then the random variable x would be the number of heads observed in n flips. It could take the values 1,2,3,...,n with different probabilities.

The BINOMDIST function uses the following syntax:

```
=BINOMDIST(x,n,p,cumulative)
```

If you want to find the probability of exactly x successes, enter FALSE as the fourth (cumulative) argument. If you want to find the probability of x or fewer successes, enter TRUE as the fourth argument.

For example, if you were to flip a fair coin 20 times and wanted to find the probability of it turning up "heads" exactly 10 times, the function looks like this:

```
=BINOMDIST(10,20,0.5,FALSE)
```

The function returns the value 0.176197052. If you wanted to find the probability of getting 10 or fewer heads, you replace the FALSE with TRUE, and the function returns the value 0.588098526.

Figure 4-3 shows another example of this function. For this example, suppose you know that 35% of your customers are women and you select 10 customers at random. What is the probability that you won't select a woman? (In this case, it doesn't matter whether you choose TRUE or FALSE as the cumulative argument, as there are no possible outcomes less than zero.)

	A	B	C	D	E	F
1	x	0				
2	n	10				
3	p	0.35				
4		0.013463				
5						
6						

Figure 4-3 Calculating the binomial probability distribution.

CRITBINOM

The acceptance criterion function, CRITBINOM, is used for quality control of a production process. You use this function to find the maximum number of defective items that a person can find in a lot and still allow acceptance of the lot. Inspectors should accept the lot if they find this number or fewer defective items and reject the lot if they find more defective items.

To determine the acceptance criterion, you need to know the number of items in the lot, the probability of accepting each item, and the producer's allowable risk (alpha) for rejecting an acceptable lot.

The CRITBINOM function uses the following syntax:

```
=CRITBINOM(trials,probability_s,alpha)
```

where trials is the number of trials, probability_s is the probability of a success on each trial, and alpha is the criterion value. Probability_s and alpha are both between 0 and 1.

NEGBINOMDIST

If the number of successes is fixed in a binomial distribution and you want to find the number of trials, use the NEGBINOMDIST function. This function returns the probability that there will be a certain number of failures before the threshold number of successes, given the constant probability of a success.

For example, if you need to find 20 straight 2 by 4s from a stack, and you know the probability that a board in the stack is straight is 0.2 (20%), you can use the NEGBINOMDIST to find that there is about a 2% probability that you will reject 75 boards before finding all 20 straight ones.

The NEGBINOMDIST function uses the following syntax:

```
=NEGBINOMDIST(numberfailures,numbersuccesses,probability of success)
```

For this example, the function looks like this:

```
=negbinomdist(75,20,0.2)
```

Chi-Square Distribution

The chi-square distribution is commonly used to make inferences about a population variance. If a population follows the normal distribution, you can draw a sample of size N from this distribution and form the sum of the squared standardized scores (chi-square). This random variable chi-square follows the chi-square probability distribution with n degrees of freedom (df), where n is a positive integer equal to N-1. The degrees of freedom parameter determines the shape of the distribution. With more degrees of freedom, the skew is less.

NOTE *For more information about skew, see the section "Skewness" later in the chapter.*

CHIDIST

The CHIDIST function returns the area in the upper tail of the chi-square distribution. You use the CHIDIST function the same way you would use a chi-square distribution table. The CHIDIST function uses the following syntax:

```
=CHIDIST(x,df)
```

For example, if you pull a random sample of 16 from a population and want to find the probability of a sample chi-square value (x) 25 or larger, you would enter the following:

```
=CHIDIST(25,15)
```

The function returns the value 0.049943, meaning that a value of 25 or more should in the long run occur about five times in a hundred.

CHIINV

You can use the CHIINV function to create confidence interval estimates of a population variance. That is, you use the CHIDIST function if you know x and want to find the probability, and you use the CHIINV function if you have a probability and want to find x. For example, if you're creating a product and weigh a sample of 18 units to find a sample variance of 0.36, you may want to construct a 90% confidence interval estimate of the population variance for the product. With a sample size of 18, you have 17 degrees of freedom. To find the upper limit, enter the following:

```
=CHIINV(0.95,17)
```

To find the lower limit, enter the following:

```
=CHIINV(0.05,17)
```

These formulas return the values 8.67175 and 27.5871. Multiply the sample variance of 0.36 by the degrees of freedom and divide this product by each of the values returned from the CHIINV function to find the lower and upper limits of the confidence interval. You can take the square root of these values to establish interval estimates of the population standard deviation.

CHITEST

The chi-square test is used to test independence of two variables. You can use the chi-square test to determine whether there is a significant difference between observed and expected frequencies. For example, if you want to find out whether soft drink preference differs between male and female drinkers, you can construct a null hypothesis that soft drink preference is independent of the gender of the drinker, and create a table of expected results based on a sample of 93 male drinkers and 85 female drinkers as shown in Figure 4-4. You can then create a table of the results of the actual study findings.

B19 | =CHITEST(B6:C8,B14:C16)

	A	B	C	D	E
1	Soft Drink Preference				
2					
3	Expected Results				
4					
5		M	F	Total	
6	Lemon-lim	30.30337079	27.69663	58	
7	Cola	43.88764045	40.11236	84	
8	Rootbeer	18.80898876	17.19101	36	
9	Total	93	85	178	
10					
11	Actual Sample Results				
12					
13		M	F	Total	
14	Lemon-lim	25	35	60	
15	Cola	50	39	89	
16	Rootbeer	18	11	29	
17	Total	93	85	178	
18					
19	p-value	0.030981468			
20	chi-square	6.948740916			
21					

Figure 4-4 Chi-square test of independence.

NOTE *Use Fisher's test instead of the chi-square test for analyzing contingency tables with two rows and two columns. Fisher's test always returns the exact p-value, whereas the chi-square test returns only an approximate p-value. Definitely avoid the chi-square test when the numbers in the contingency table are very small (in the single digits).*

The CHITEST formula uses the following syntax:

```
=CHITEST(actual range,expected range)
```

where actual range is the data in the actual sample results table and expected range is the data from the expected results table. In the example shown in Figure 4-4, cell B19 contains the following formula:

```
=CHITEST(B6:C8,B14:C16)
```

The formula returns the value 0.03098. This is the p-value. You reject the null hypothesis if this value is less than your level of significance alpha. So if your level of significance is .05, you would reject it, but not if your level of significance is .025 or .01.

NOTE *The test for independence is a one-tailed test, so a level of significance of .05 corresponds with a 95% confidence level.*

Confidence Intervals for Population Means (CONFIDENCE)

A confidence interval is the interval around a sample mean into which you expect the population mean to fall a certain percentage of the time. If you have a sample of size n and know the sample mean m and population standard deviation sigma (s), you can find the range into which the actual population mean will fall x% of the time. Common confidence levels are 90%, 95%, and 99%. The CONFIDENCE function uses the following syntax:

```
=CONFIDENCE(alpha,s,n)
```

NOTE *Alpha is the significance level. It equals 1 minus the confidence level (expressed as a decimal).*

For example, if a sample of 500 college graduates shows that they owe an average of $12,000 in student loans at graduation and the population standard deviation is $2,000, you can find a 95% confidence interval estimate of the population mean amount owed. To do this using the CONFIDENCE function, enter alpha .05 as the first argument, the standard deviation 2000 as the second argument, and n 500 as the third argument. The function looks like this:

```
=CONFIDENCE(0.05,2000,500)
```

The function returns the value 175.30. So you can say with 95% confidence that the population mean is $12,000 plus or minus $175.30. Figure 4-5 illustrates this calculation.

B5 | fx =CONFIDENCE(B1,B2,B3)

Figure 4-5.xls

	A	B	C	D
1	Alpha	0.05		
2	Population Standard Deviation	2000		
3	Sample Size	500		
4	Sample Mean	12000		
5		175.3042		
6	Confidence Interval	11824.7	12175.3	
7				
8				

Figure 4-5 Calculating a confidence interval.

NOTE *If the value of the population standard deviation is unknown, you can use the value of the sample standard deviation as the point estimate of the population standard deviation.*

Correlation

Correlation shows the closeness of the relationship between two variables. The benefit of using a correlation coefficient to measure the relationship between two variables as opposed to using covariance is that the unit of measurement doesn't matter.

NOTE *Remember that correlation does not show causation. That is, you could easily show that as the number of ice cream cones consumed increases during a year, so does the number of drownings. But this does not mean that eating ice cream causes people to drown—more likely, these variables are both independently related to another variable—that of temperatures. Correlation is symmetrical, so you get the same coefficient if you switch the variables. Don't calculate a correlation coefficient if you manipulated one of the variables. Use linear regression instead.*

TIP *To see a graphical representation of various correlation coefficients, visit the interactive web page at* http://noppa5.pc.helsinki.fi/koe/corr/cor7.html.

CORREL

You use the CORREL function in Excel to determine whether two data sets are related, and if so, how strongly. The correlation coefficient ranges from +1, indicating a perfect positive linear relationship, to –1, indicating a perfectly negative linear relationship. To calculate a correlation coefficient for a sample, Excel uses the covariance of the samples and the standard deviations of each sample. To use the CORREL function in Excel, just select the two sets of data to use as the arguments and use the following syntax:

```
=CORREL(data set 1,data set 2)
```

For example, if you have a set of preliminary test scores for a sample of employees in column A and a set of performance feedback scores in column B, as shown in Figure 4-6, and you want to find out whether they're related and if so, how strongly, you can use Excel to find the correlation coefficient for the samples.

B8 | =CORREL(A2:A7,B2:B7)

Figure 4-6.xls

	A	B	C	D
1	Test score	Performance rating		
2	45	2.7		
3	56	3.5		
4	70	3.7		
5	62	3.3		
6	64	3.6		
7	57	3		
8		0.871303555		
9				

Figure 4-6 Testing the strength of relationship between two sets of data.

The function returns the value 0.87, indicating that the sets are positively related (as the value of one goes up, the value of the other also increases), but the relationship isn't perfect.

PEARSON

The Pearson product moment correlation coefficient function, PEARSON, uses a different equation for calculating the correlation coefficient. This formula doesn't require the computation of each deviation from the mean. Still, the correlation coefficient ranges from +1, indicating a perfect positive linear relationship, to −1, indicating a perfectly negative linear relationship. The PEARSON function uses the following syntax:

```
=PEARSON(data set 1,data set 2)
```

Using the PEARSON function on the data shown in Figure 4-6 to compute the correlation coefficient returns the same value as the CORREL function does.

RSQ

The RSQ function calculates the square of the Pearson product moment correlation coefficient through data points in the data sets. You can interpret the r-squared value as the proportion of the variance in y attributable to the variance in x. The RSQ function uses the following syntax:

```
=RSQ(data set 1,data set 2)
```

Counting Cells

If you select a range of cells, you can have Excel find how many cells are in that range using the count functions.

COUNT

To find the number of cells in a range that contain numbers (or dates, or textual representations of numbers), you use the COUNT function. This function does not count cells containing text or logical values like TRUE and FALSE, nor does it count empty cells. The COUNT function uses the following syntax:

```
=COUNT(data set range)
```

For example, if you have a database of 100 customer survey responses, and column C contains numeric responses to the question if a customer chose to respond, you can find out how many people answered the question using the COUNT function, as shown in Figure 4-7.

C102 fx =COUNT(C2:C101)

	A	B	C	D	E
82	5.5		30	1	
83	3.3	F		3	
84	7.7	M	40	4	
85	6.4	F	41	5	
86	8.9	M	33	2	
87	7.1		37	2	
88	4.0	M	34	3	
89	8.3	F	28		
90	7.3		37	2	
91	7.6	M	46	3	
92	9.9	F	38	3	
93	2.7	M	36	3	
94	1.3	M		5	
95	7.0	M	35	5	
96	2.6	F		4	
97	3.4	F	43	2	
98	10.0		38	2	
99	6.4	M		1	
100	6.1	F	36	5	
101	4.4	M	30	2	
102	# Responses	81	87	90	
103					

Figure 4-7 Counting cells.

COUNTA

The COUNTA function counts all cells in a range that aren't empty, including cells with error values, logical values, and text. The COUNTA function uses the following syntax:

```
=COUNTA(data set range)
```

COUNTBLANK

The COUNTBLANK function counts only blank cells. The COUNTBLANK function uses the following syntax:

```
=COUNTBLANK(data set range)
```

COUNTIF

The COUNTIF function counts the cells that fit the criteria you specify. The COUNTIF function uses two parameters, the data set range and the condition, in the following syntax:

```
=COUNTIF(data set range,condition)
```

For example, if you want to count cells that exactly match a number or value, just enter that number or value. To count cells that are greater than or less than a value, use the symbols >, >=, <, and <= followed by the value. If you are using any of these symbols, you need to put the condition inside quotation marks. For example, if you want to know how many numbers in cells A1:C5 are greater than one, you would use the following function:

```
=COUNTIF(A1:C5,">1")
```

Covariance (COVAR)

To determine the relationship between two data sets, you can calculate covariance using the COVAR function. The COVAR function uses the following syntax:

```
=COVAR(array 1,array 2)
```

For example, if you want to see whether there's an association between the number of advertisements you place in a local newspaper and the sales volume the following weekend, you could find the covariance between the data sets. Figure 4-8 shows these data sets.

E2 =VARP(Sheet1!$A$2:$A$11)

Figure 4-16.xls

	A	B	C	D	E	F	G
1	# of Press	Weekly Sales in Units			*Column 1*	*Column 2*	
2	2	51		Column 1	1.69		
3	5	57		Column 2	8.46	56.04	
4	1	42					
5	3	54			*Column 1*	*Column 2*	
6	4	56		Column 1	1		
7	2	38		Column 2	0.869317	1	
8	5	63					
9	3	48					
10	4	59					
11	2	46					
12							

Figure 4-8 Testing the strength of relationship between two sets of data.

A positive correlation coefficient, as shown in this example, indicates a positive relationship, that is, as the number of advertisements increases, the number of sales increases. Note, however, that a large positive value does not indicate a strong positive linear relationship, nor does a large negative value indicate a strong negative linear relationship. The value you obtain for covariance depends on the units of measurement you use. For example, if you want to test the relationship between weight and volume, you would obtain different values for covariance depending on whether you used ounces or grams, cubic inches or cubic centimeters.

Exponential Probability Distribution (EXPONDIST)

To describe the time it takes to complete a task, you use the exponential probability distribution, EXPONDIST. For example, you can describe the time between arrivals of vehicles in a drive-through or the time required to load a crate of goods. Product lifetimes also often follow an exponential probability distribution. For example, if the average lifetime of a part in a machine is 15 years, you can find the probability that the part will last less than a certain number of years, more than a certain number of years, or between numbers of years. The EXPONDIST function uses the following syntax:

```
=EXPONDIST(x,lambda,cumulative)
```

where lambda is the inverse of the mean and cumulative allows you to tell Excel whether you want the cumulative probability or the probability of exactly that value.

For example, if you want to find the probability that a part with a mean lifetime of 12 years lasts less than 6 years, enter the function as follows:

```
=EXPONDIST(6,1/12,TRUE)
```

The function returns the value 0.3935.

Exponential Regression

Exponential regression finds the equation of an exponential equation of the form $y = ab^x$ that best fits a data set.

LOGEST

The LOGEST function calculates an exponential curve that best fits your data and returns an array that describes the curve. The LOGEST function uses the following syntax:

```
=LOGEST(known ys,known xs,constant,statistics)
```

If the constant is set to False, b is set to be equal to 1. If statistics is set to True, you get an array of additional data on the error in the value of the coefficients.

GROWTH

You can use the GROWTH function in two ways: to calculate predicted exponential growth for a series of new x-values using existing x-values and y-values, or to fit an exponential curve to existing x-values and y-values. The GROWTH function uses the following syntax:

```
=GROWTH(known ys,known xs,new xs,constant)
```

If the constant is set to False, b is set to be equal to 1.

F Probability Distribution

If you want to compare the variances of two normal populations using data collected from two independent random samples of size N_1 and N_2 of these populations, it results in an F distribution with N_1-1 degrees of freedom and N_2-1 degrees of freedom.

NOTE *The more degrees of freedom, the less the skew. For more information about skew, see the section "Skewness" later in the chapter.*

FDIST

If you know a value and want to find the probability in the F distribution, you use the FDIST function. The FDIST function uses the following syntax:

```
=FDIST(x,degrees of freedom 1,degrees of freedom 2)
```

FINV

If you know the probability and want to find a value for the F distribution, you use the FINV function. The FINV function uses the following syntax:

```
=FINV(probability,degrees of freedom 1,degrees of freedom 2)
```

FTEST

The F-test finds the one-tailed probability that the variances in two data sets are not significantly different. For example, scientists use the F-test to compare pairs of data obtained from particular laboratories, analysts, or methods to determine whether one batch is significantly more precise than the other. The FTEST function uses the following syntax:

```
=FTEST(array 1,array 2)
```

Fisher Transformation

The Fisher's z' transformation converts Pearson's r to the normally distributed variable z'. You use the Fisher's z' to compute confidence intervals on Pearson's correlation and on the difference between correlations.

FISHER

The FISHER function computes from r to z'. The function has the following syntax:

```
=FISHER(r)
```

FISHERINV

The FISHERINV function computes from z' to r. The function has the following syntax:

```
=FISHERINV(z')
```

Frequency (FREQUENCY)

The FREQUENCY function calculates how often values occur within a range of values, and then returns a vertical array of numbers. For example, use FREQUENCY to count the number of test scores that fall within ranges of scores. Because FREQUENCY returns an array, you must enter it as an array formula. The frequency formula uses the following syntax:

```
=FREQUENCY(data array,bins array)
```

where data array is an array of values for which you want to count frequencies and bins array is an array of bins (listed in ascending order and as upper limits) into which you want to group the values in the data array.

For example, if you wanted to create a frequency distribution using the S&P 500 data and bins shown in Figure 4-9, you would select the range D2:D6, enter the following:

```
=FREQUENCY(B2:B21,C2:C6)
```

and press Ctrl+Shift+Enter. When Excel constructs the frequency distribution, it counts the number of items with values less than or equal to the upper limit of the each bin, and greater than the upper limit of the previous bin. The function returns the values 2, 4, 4, 4, and 6 in the corresponding cells.

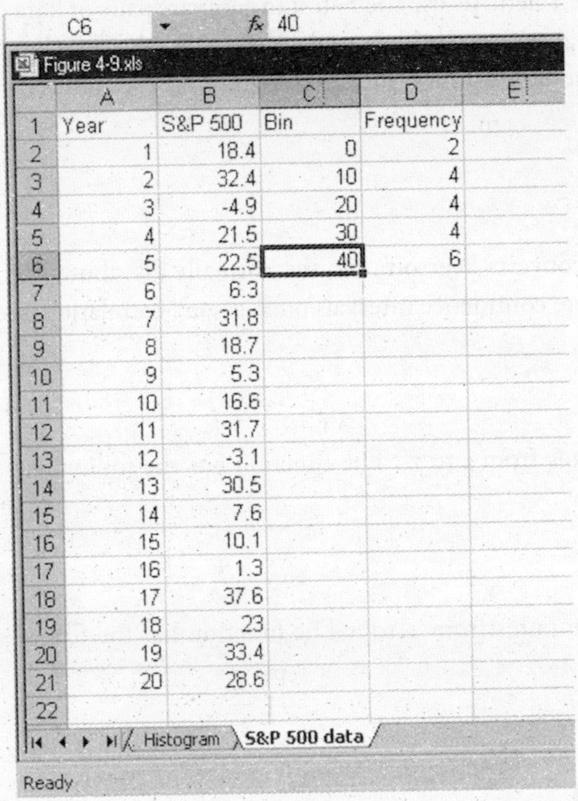

	A	B	C	D	E
1	Year	S&P 500	Bin	Frequency	
2	1	18.4	0	2	
3	2	32.4	10	4	
4	3	-4.9	20	4	
5	4	21.5	30	4	
6	5	22.5	40	6	
7	6	6.3			
8	7	31.8			
9	8	18.7			
10	9	5.3			
11	10	16.6			
12	11	31.7			
13	12	-3.1			
14	13	30.5			
15	14	7.6			
16	15	10.1			
17	16	1.3			
18	17	37.6			
19	18	23			
20	19	33.4			
21	20	28.6			
22					

Figure 4-9 Creating a frequency distribution.

NOTE *See "Histogram" under the "Data Analysis Tools" section for more information about graphically depicting frequency data.*

Gamma Probability Distribution

If a Poisson process produces successes at a constant rate of m per unit of time, then the random variable x, the elapsed time until the rth success, follows the gamma distribution. The gamma distribution is often used to determine the amount of time it takes for the rth person to arrive in a line.

GAMMADIST

If you know x and want to find the probability, you use the GAMMADIST function, which has the following syntax:

```
=GAMMADIST(x,alpha,beta,cumulative)
```

For example, if x equals 25, alpha equals 8, beta equals 9, and cumulatative is TRUE, you use the following formula:

```
=GAMMADIST(25,8,9,TRUE)
```

The function returns the value 0.007774.

GAMMAINV

If you have been given a probability and want to find x, you use the GAMMAINV function, which has the following syntax:

```
=GAMMAINV(probability,alpha,beta)
```

For example, if the probability equals .5, alpha equals 8, and beta equals 9, you use the following formula:

```
=GAMMAINV(.5,8,9)
```

The function returns the value 69.02.

GAMMALN

You use the GAMMALN function to find the natural logarithm of the gamma function, G(x). The GAMMALN function uses the following syntax:

```
=GAMMALN(x)
```

For example, if x equals 25, you use the following formula:

```
=GAMMALN(25)
```

The function returns the value 54.78.

Geometric Mean (GEOMEAN)

If you have a set of n numbers, the geometric mean of the set is the nth root of the product of the numbers. To find the geometric mean, enter the data set range as the sole parameter of the GEOMEAN function, which uses the following syntax:

```
=GEOMEAN(data set range)
```

Harmonic Mean (HARMEAN)

The harmonic mean is the reciprocal of the mean of the reciprocals of a data set. To find the harmonic mean, enter the data set range as the sole parameter of the HARMEAN function, which uses the following syntax:

```
=HARMEAN(data set range)
```

Hypergeometric Distribution (HYPGEOMDIST)

The hypergeometric probability distribution is much like the binomial probability distribution. The hypergeometric distribution describes the outcome of a multistep experiment, consisting of n trials, where each trial ends in either a success or a failure. But unlike the binomial distribution, the trials are not independent—so success in one trial affects the probability of success in another trial and the probability of success changes from trial to trial. The HYPGEOMDIST is therefore used when samples are taken from a finite population but not replaced for the next trial. The HYPGEOMDIST function uses the following syntax:

```
=HYPGEOMDIST(successes_in_sample,sample_size,number_of_successes,population)
```

For example, suppose a shipment of 10 items has 2 defective items and 8 nondefective items. If you randomly select and test the individual units and set aside the units you've tested, the probability of finding a defective unit changes depending on what's left in the shipment. Suppose that you must reject a shipment if you find a single defective unit. If you sample 3 items, what's the probability that the shipment will be accepted? To find out, you can call finding a defective item a "success," and enter the HYPGEOMDIST function to look like this:

```
=HYPGEOMDIST(0,3,2,10)
```

This means 0 "successes" in 3 trials when there are 2 "successes" in the population of 10. The function returns the value 0.4667.

The probability of rejecting the shipment is 1-0.4667, or 0.5333. To verify this, you can add the probability of getting 1 success with the probability of having 2 successes.

Kurtosis (KURT)

Kurtosis is used to help determine the size of the tails in a distribution. The kurtosis of a normal distribution is 0. A negative kurtosis value means that a distribution has smaller tails than the normal curve; a positive kurtosis indicates a distribution with larger tails than the normal curve. The KURT function uses the following syntax:

```
=KURT(data set range)
```

Linear Regression

You use linear regression functions to find a linear equation that best describes a data set. Excel uses the sum of least squares method to find the straight line of best fit. People often try to predict future amounts by assuming linear growth and extending the line forward in time. For example, if you have a series of sales data for 9 months and want to predict the sales in the 10th month, you can use Excel's linear regression functions to find the slope and y-intercept (the point on the y-axis where the line crosses) of the line that best fits the data.

To use the linear regression functions, it helps to remember the equation for a line:

$y=mx+b$

where y is the dependent variable, m the slope, x the independent variable, and b the y-intercept. If there are multiple ranges of x-values, the equation looks like this:

$y=m_1x_1+m_2x_2+...m_nx_n+b$

NOTE *To visualize and experiment with linear regression, visit the interactive web page at* http://www.math.csusb.edu/faculty/stanton/m262/regress/regress.html. *Click the graph area to add data points (x,y) to the graph. The applet draws the straight line that best fits the points you add, adjusting the line for the new data points you add.*

FORECAST

The FORECAST function predicts a future y-value for the x-value you specify using existing x- and y-values. The FORECAST function uses the following syntax:

```
=FORECAST(x,known ys,known xs)
```

where x is the x-value for which you want to predict a y-value.

INTERCEPT

If you have existing x- and y-values, Excel can find the straight line that best fits the data and then calculate the point at which the line intersects the y-axis, in other words, the value of b in the "y=mx+b" equation. The y-intercept is useful when you want to know the value of the dependent variable when the independent variable equals 0.

NOTE *The INTERCEPT function returns the same value as the FORECAST function if you enter 0 for x in the FORECAST function.*

The INTERCEPT function uses the following syntax:

```
=INTERCEPT(known ys,known xs)
```

LINEST

The LINEST function returns the value of m and b given at least one set of known ys and known xs. The LINEST function has the following syntax:

```
=LINEST(known ys,known xs,constant,statistics)
```

where known ys is the array of y-values you already know and known xs is the array of x-values you may already know. If you leave out the known xs, they are assumed to be 1, 2, 3,...n. If constant is set to FALSE, b is assumed to be 0. If statistics is set to TRUE, the LINEST function also returns the standard error for each data point.

NOTE *If the known ys are in a single column or row, then Excel considers each column of known xs to be a separate variable.*

NOTE *The array known xs can include multiple sets of variables. If you use only one set, then known ys and known xs can be ranges of any shape, as long as they have equal dimensions. If you use more than one variable, then the known ys array must be either a single column or a single row. If you don't enter known xs, Excel assumes this array is the same size as the known ys array.*

SLOPE

Use the SLOPE function to find the slope (m) of the linear regression line from the known x and known y data sets. The slope is the change in y over the change in x for any two points on the line. The SLOPE function in Excel uses the following syntax:

```
=SLOPE(known ys,known xs)
```

A positive (upward) slope means that the independent variable (such as the number of salespeople) has a positive effect on a dependent variable (such as sales). A negative (downward) slope means that the independent variable has a negative effect on the dependent variable. The steeper the slope, the more effect the independent variable has on the dependent variable.

STEYX

Use the STEYX function to find the standard error of the predicted y-value for each individual x in the regression. The STEYX function uses the following syntax:

```
=STEYX(known ys,known xs)
```

TREND

Use the TREND function to find values along a linear trend. Specify an array of new xs and the TREND function uses the method of least squares to fit a straight line to the known x and y data sets and return the y-values along the line for the new array. If constant is set to FALSE, the "b" in the y=mx+b equation is set to zero. The TREND function uses the following syntax:

```
=TREND(known ys,known xs,new xs,constant)
```

For example, in the worksheet of air pollutant values from 1986 to 1996 shown in Figure 4-10, you can predict the air pollutant values for 1997 (assuming they follow a linear equation).

F14   fx =TREND(F2:F12,A2:A12,A14)

Figure 4-10.xls

	A	B	C	D	E	F	G
1	Year	S02	NOx	VOC	CO	PM10	
2	1	11,008	78,505	107,940	544,967	218,765	
3	2	11,344	79,132	108,990	540,044	226,183	
4	3	12,267	85,187	112,939	576,232	232,331	
5	4	13,292	83,343	110,521	558,218	224,434	
6	5	11,985	81,953	104,675	533,149	130,657	
7	6	11,668	80,768	156,734	537,669	117,319	
8	7	11,386	84,610	155,072	507,138	131,654	
9	8	10,652	79,714	149,463	457,222	130,013	
10	9	9,069	81,440	150,700	461,066	141,221	
11	10	9,370	83,288	153,061	411,333	61,206	
12	11	8,550	81,833	157,346	537,688	64,868	
13							
14	12	9017.782	82747.84	169669.8	453625.6	49482.75	
15							
16	Tons of Criteria Air Pollutant Emissions for King County, Washington						
17							

Figure 4-10 Predicting values into the future.

Lognormal Distribution Function

The lognormal distribution occurs when the natural logarithm of a random variable follows the normal distribution. People commonly assume that prices for stocks and Treasury bonds are lognormally distributed, that is, that returns for these investments are normally distributed.

LOGNORMDIST

Use the LOGNORMDIST function on data that has been logarithmically transformed to find the cumulative lognormal distribution of x, where ln(x) is normally distributed around the mean with a specific standard deviation. The LOGNORMDIST function uses the following syntax:

```
=LOGNORMDIST(x,mean,standard deviation)
```

where x is the value at which you want to find the function.

LOGINV

If you know the probability and want to find the value x, you use the inverse of the lognormal cumulative distribution function, LOGINV. The LOGINV function uses the following syntax:

```
=LOGINV(probability,mean,standard deviation)
```

Maximums and Minimums

Excel provides four functions for finding the maximum and minimum values in a data set.

MAX

The MAX function returns the largest value in a set of data. It ignores blank cells and cells containing text or logical values such as TRUE and FALSE. The MAX function uses the following syntax:

```
=MAX(data set range)
```

MAXA

The MAXA function returns the largest value in a set of data, but it includes logical values and text. It counts TRUE as 1 and FALSE and all other text as 0. The MAXA function uses the following syntax:

```
=MAXA(data set range)
```

MIN

The MIN function returns the smallest value in a set of data. It ignores blank cells and cells containing text or logical values such as TRUE and FALSE. The MIN function uses the following syntax:

```
=MIN(data set range)
```

MINA

The MINA function returns the smallest value in a set of data, but it includes logical values and text. It counts TRUE as 1 and FALSE and all other text as 0. The MINA function uses the following syntax:

```
=MINA(data set range)
```

Mean

Excel provides two functions for finding the mean of a data set. Both take the sum of the values in the set and divide it by the number of values.

AVERAGE

The AVERAGE function ignores cells that contain text, that are empty, or that contain logical values. To use the AVERAGE function, simply enter the data set range as the single argument using the following syntax:

```
=AVERAGE(data set range)
```

For example, if you wanted to find the average birth rate per 1,000 people in the United States in 1996 using the data in Figure 4-11, you would use the following formula:

```
=AVERAGE(C2:C52)
```

The function returns the value 14.27.

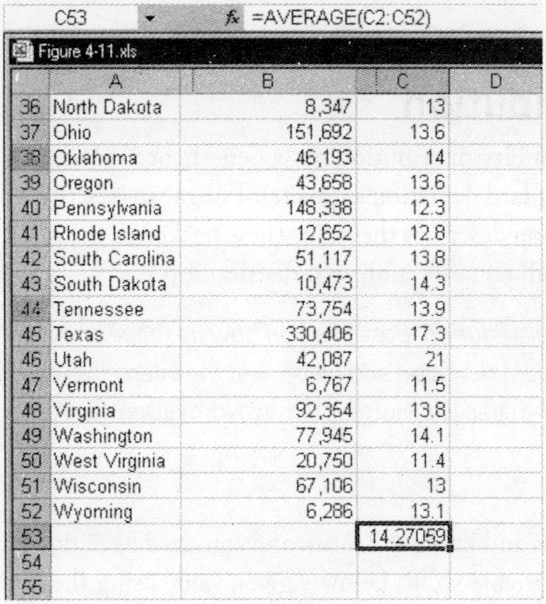
C53 =AVERAGE(C2:C52)

Figure 4-11.xls

	A	B	C	D
36	North Dakota	8,347	13	
37	Ohio	151,692	13.6	
38	Oklahoma	46,193	14	
39	Oregon	43,658	13.6	
40	Pennsylvania	148,338	12.3	
41	Rhode Island	12,652	12.8	
42	South Carolina	51,117	13.8	
43	South Dakota	10,473	14.3	
44	Tennessee	73,754	13.9	
45	Texas	330,406	17.3	
46	Utah	42,087	21	
47	Vermont	6,767	11.5	
48	Virginia	92,354	13.8	
49	Washington	77,945	14.1	
50	West Virginia	20,750	11.4	
51	Wisconsin	67,106	13	
52	Wyoming	6,286	13.1	
53			14.27059	
54				
55				

Figure 4-11 Finding the average in a data set using the Birth Rates spreadsheet.

AVERAGEA

The AVERAGEA function includes cells containing text or logical values in the calculation. Excel includes cells containing the word TRUE as the value 1 in the calculation; it includes cells containing the word FALSE or any other text as the value 0.

To use the AVERAGEA function, simply enter the data set range as the single argument in the function using the following syntax:

```
=AVERAGEA(data set range)
```

Median (MEDIAN)

The median is the middle value in a set of values. Half of the data in the set fall above this value and half fall below, so the median estimates the 50% quantile. The MEDIAN function uses the following syntax:

```
=MEDIAN(data set range)
```

If the data set contains an even number of values, Excel averages the two middle values.

Mode (MODE)

The mode is the most frequently occurring value in a set of values. When Excel calculates the mode, it ignores empty cells and cells containing text or logical values. The MODE function uses the following syntax:

```
=MODE(data set range)
```

Normal Probability Distribution

The normal, or Gaussian, probability distribution has a bell-shaped curve. It is characterized by its mean mu (μ) and standard deviation sigma (s). The mean describes the location of the curve, the standard deviation describes the shape (how peaked or flat it is). The mean, the median, and the mode are all equal in a normal distribution.

TIP *To see what the normal distribution looks like and how its shape and location change with changes in the standard deviation and mean, visit the interactive Web site at* http://www-stat.stanford.edu/~naras/jsm/NormalDensity/NormalDensity.html.

NORMDIST

If you have a normal distribution and know the mean and standard deviation, you can find the probability that a random variable x falls below a given value using the NORMDIST function. The NORMDIST function uses the following syntax:

```
=NORMDIST(x,mean,standard deviation,cumulative)
```

For example, if containers are filled with an average of 591 ml of liquid, and the volumes are normally distributed around this mean with a standard deviation of 3 ml, you can find the probability that a container has less than 586 ml of liquid. To do this, enter 586 for the first parameter x, 591 for the second parameter, 3 for the third parameter, and TRUE for the fourth parameter. The function looks like this:

```
=NORMDIST(586,591,3,TRUE)
```

The function returns the value 0.0477. So there's about a 4.8% chance that a container holds less than 586 ml. You can find the probability that a value falls between a certain range by making a few simple calculations, remembering that there's a 0.5 probability that a value falls on each side of the mean. For example, if you want to find the probability that a container holds between 585 and 593 ml of liquid, you find the probability that it contains less than 585 and subtract this from 0.5. Then you find the probability that it contains less than 593 and subtract 0.5. Then you add these two figures.

TIP *Because a normal distribution is a continuous distribution, probabilities are areas under the probability density function and the probability of any single value for the random variable is zero. However, if you set the cumulative parameter to FALSE, you can approximate the probability of a discrete value by setting a small range around that value.*

NORMINV

If instead of having a value and needing to find the probability that a random variable falls below it, you know the probability for the range into which a random variable must fall and need to find the value defining this range, you can use the NORMINV function. The NORMINV function uses the following syntax:

```
=NORMINV(probability,mean,standard deviation)
```

Using the previous example for the NORMDIST function, if the mean fill volume in a set of containers is 591 ml with a standard deviation of 3 ml, and you want to be able to say that there's a 99% probability of a container holding more than a certain volume of fluid (i.e., you want to find an amount below which the area under the curve is 0.01), enter the function as follows:

```
=NORMINV(0.01,591,3)
```

The function returns the value 584.02, meaning that there's a 1% probability of a container filled with less than this amount.

Permutations (PERMUT)

When you select a sample from a population and the order of the selection matters, this sample is called a permutation. For example, if an interviewer has four time slots for a day and 10 people to interview, then there are 10 possibilities for the first time slot, nine for the second, eight for the third, and seven for the fourth. You can easily calculate permutations with the PERMUT function, which uses the following syntax:

```
=PERMUT(number,number chosen)
```

So in the example above, you would enter the following:

```
=PERMUT(10,4)
```

The function returns the value 5,040, which is 10 x 9 x 8 x 7. So there are 5,040 possible ways the interviewer's schedule could go.

NOTE *If you select a sample from a population and the items are not replaced before the next is selected, but the order of selection does not matter, as is the case with the traditional lottery, this sample is called a combination.*

Poisson Random Variables (POISSON)

A Poisson random variable allows you to find the number of events over a given period of time or across a given distance. For example, you can use it to model how many phone calls a person receives over a certain interval of time or how many people arrive in a check-out line over a certain period of time. With a Poisson experiment, any two intervals of the same length must have the same probability of an occurrence, and occurrences in any interval must be independent of occurrences in other intervals. To calculate the Poisson distribution in Excel, you use the POISSON function. The POISSON function uses the following syntax:

```
=POISSON(x,mean,cumulative)
```

For example, if you receive 60 phone calls per hour at your service desk, you can find the probability of receiving exactly 12 calls in a 15-minute interval. You can also find the probability of receiving less than 12 calls in that interval.

To use the POISSON function, you must first determine the expected of mean value of calls in the interval. If you expect 60 calls in a 60-minute period, you expect 15 in a 15-minute period. Enter the function as follows:

```
=POISSON(12,15,FALSE)
```

The probability of receiving exactly 12 calls is 0.08285. If you enter TRUE in the cumulative, the function returns the probability of receiving 12 or fewer calls (0.2676).

Probability that Values Are Between Upper and Lower Limits (PROB)

If you have a set of values and a set of probabilities associated with these values, you can find the probability that values in the range fall between two limits using the PROB function. The PROB function uses the following syntax:

```
=PROB(x range,probability range,lower limit,upper limit)
```

NOTE *If you do not supply the upper limit, Excel returns the probability that values in the x range are equal to the lower limit.*

For example, the worksheet shown in Figure 4-12 shows the probability distribution for your company's projected profits (in $1,000s) for the coming year. You can use the PROB function to find the probability that you make between $25,000 and $100,000 by entering the function as follows:

```
=PROB(A2:A6,B2:B6,25,100)
```

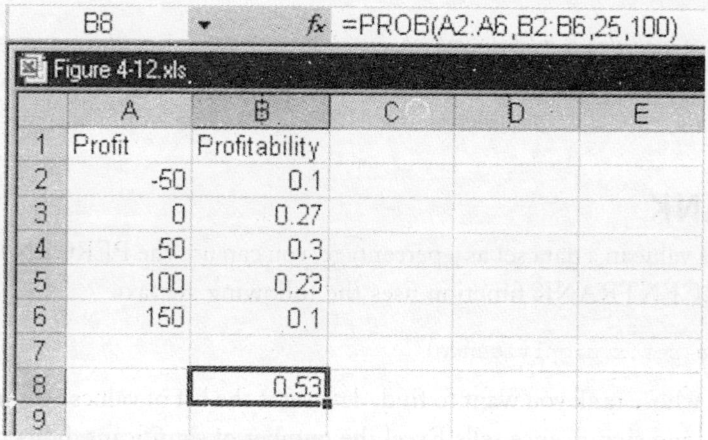

B8 =PROB(A2:A6,B2:B6,25,100)

Figure 4-12.xls

	A	B	C	D	E
1	Profit	Profitability			
2	-50	0.1			
3	0	0.27			
4	50	0.3			
5	100	0.23			
6	150	0.1			
7					
8		0.53			
9					

Figure 4-12 Profit probability distribution.

Rank and Percentile

Excel includes six functions used for finding rank and percentile on values in a data set.

LARGE

Use the LARGE function to find the kth largest value in a data set. While you can use the maximum function to find the largest value in a data set, you can use the LARGE function to find the runner up or third-place value. The LARGE function uses the following syntax:

```
=LARGE(data set range,k)
```

SMALL

Use the SMALL function to find the kth smallest value in a data set. Although you can use the MIN function to find the smallest value in a data set, you can use the SMALL function to find multiple values at the bottom. The SMALL function uses the following syntax:

```
=SMALL(data set range,k)
```

RANK

To find the rank of a value in a data set relative to other values in the data set, you can use the RANK function. The RANK function uses the following syntax:

```
=RANK(number,data set,order)
```

where number is the number whose rank you want to find, data set is the list of values against which you want to rank it, and order tells Excel to rank in ascending or descending order. Enter a nonzero value to rank the numbers in ascending order. Enter zero or leave the order parameter blank to rank in descending order.

NOTE *If the data set includes duplicate values, Excel gives these values the same rank. This affects the ranks of subsequent numbers. For example, if the value 3 appears twice and has a rank of 6, then 4 would have a rank of 8, and no value would have a rank of 7.*

PERCENTRANK

To find the rank of a value in a data set as a percentage, you can use the PERCENTRANK function. The PERCENTRANK function uses the following syntax:

```
=PERCENTRANK(data set,x,significance)
```

where x is the value whose rank you want to find, data set is the list of values against which you want to rank it, and significance tells Excel the number of significant digits it should use for the value. The value you get is between 0 and 1; you need to multiply by 100 to get the actual percent ranking.

PERCENTILE

Percentile is a measure that locates where a value stands in a data set. The kth percentile divides the data so that at least p percent are of this value or less and (100-p) percent are this value or more. If you have a set of data and need to find the value at a certain percentile, you use the PERCENTILE function in Excel. The PERCENTILE function uses the following syntax:

```
=PERCENTILE(data set range,k)
```

For example, if a score needs to be above the 80th percentile for admission, you can find which value defines that percentile by entering 0.8 for k.

QUARTILE

The QUARTILE function in Excel is closely related to the PERCENTILE function. People often use quartiles, which order the values in a data set into quarters, when dividing populations into groups based on sales and survey data. The first quartile is the 25th percentile. The second quartile is the median, or 50th percentile. The third quartile is the 75th percentile. The fourth quarter is the maximum value. The QUARTILE function uses the following syntax:

```
=QUARTILE(data set range,quartile)
```

For the quartile parameter, enter 0 for the minimum value, 1 for the first quartile, 2 for the second quartile, 3 for the third quartile, or 4 for the maximum value.

Skewness (SKEW)

Like kurtosis, skewness is used to help determine the shape of a distribution. Skewness shows whether a distribution is symmetrical or not. A symmetric distribution, such as the normal curve, has a skew of zero. A positive skewness value indicates a long tail in the positive direction. A negative skewness value indicates a long tail in the negative direction. To find the skewness of a data set, enter the data set range as the single parameter in Excel's SKEW function:

```
=SKEW(data set range)
```

Standard Deviation

Standard deviation is a common measure of describing the spread of observations in a distribution. The standard deviation is equal to the square root of the variance.

STDEV

To find the standard deviation of a sample, ignoring logical values and text, use the STDEV function. This function has the following syntax:

```
=STDEV(data set range)
```

For example, to find the standard deviation in the worksheet containing a 10-game sample of a bowler's scores, as shown in Figure 4-13, enter the following:

```
=STDEV(B2:B:11)
```

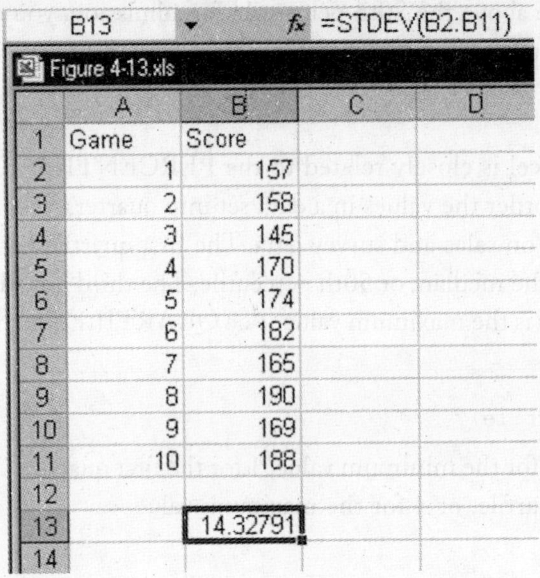

Figure 4-13 Calculating standard deviation of a sample.

STDEVA

To find the standard deviation of a sample, and include cells containing the logical value TRUE as 1 and cells containing text or the logical value FALSE as 0 (zero), use the STDEVA function. This function has the following syntax:

```
=STDEVA(data set range)
```

STDEVP

To find the standard deviation of a population, ignoring logical values and text, use the STDEVP function. This function has the following syntax:

```
=STDEVP(data set range)
```

STDEVPA

To find the standard deviation of a population, and include cells containing the logical value TRUE as 1 and cells containing text or the logical value FALSE as 0 (zero), use the STDEVPA function. This function has the following syntax:

```
=STDEVPA(data set range)
```

Standard Normal Probability Distribution

Traditionally, to find the standard normal probability distribution, you must convert the normal random variable x to the standard normal distribution using the z-value formula, and then find the area under the standard normal distribution function below z. The normal probability distribution functions described earlier in this chapter shortens this process.

The Standard Normal Probability Distribution has a mean of 0 and a standard deviation of 1.

NORMSDIST

If you already have a z-value, or if you've used the z-value formula STANDARDIZE described below to find a z-value, you can use the NORMSDIST function to find the probability that a random variable x is below z standard deviations from the mean. The NORMSDIST function uses the following syntax:

```
=NORMSDIST(z-value)
```

For example, if you create furniture that needs to fit people of various heights and know that the average American adult is 5'8" tall, and the heights are normally distributed around this mean with a standard deviation of 4", you can find the probability that one of your customers is less than 6'2".

To use this function, you must first convert the data to the standard normal distribution as described below under "STANDARDIZE." Doing so returns a z-value of 1.5, meaning that 6'2" is 1.5 standard deviations above the mean. When you enter 1.5 as the z-value parameter of the NORMSDIST function, the function returns the value 0.9331.

If you want to find the probability that a person is greater than 6'2" tall, you just subtract this value from 1. If you want to find the probability that a person is between 5'4" and 6', you must make a few calculations. The probability that a person is less than 6' tall is 0.8413. This means that the probability that a person is between the mean (5'8") and 6' is .3413 (because the probability that a person is less than 5'8" is 0.5). Likewise, the probability that a person is between 5'4" and 5'8" is .34134474. Add these together to get 0.6826.

NORMSINV

If instead of having a value and needing to find the probability that a random variable falls below it, you know the probability for the range into which a random variable must fall and need to find the value defining this range, you can use the NORMSINV function.

To use the NORMSINV function, just enter the probability (between 0 and 1, of course) and the function returns the z-value below which the probability area you entered falls. If you choose a probability less than 0.5, the function returns a negative z-value. If you enter a probability greater than 0.5, the function returns a positive z-value. The NORMSINV function uses the following syntax:

```
=NORMSINV(probability)
```

STANDARDIZE

Traditionally, to answer probability questions about a normal distribution, you first convert the distribution to the standard normal distribution. The standard normal distribution has a mean of 0 (zero) and a standard deviation of 1. To convert to the standard normal distribution, you find a z-value using the STANDARDIZE function in Excel. The STANDARDIZE function uses the following syntax:

```
=STANDARDIZE(x,mean,standard deviation)
```

For example, if you have a product that costs an average of $6,000 to produce and a standard deviation of $800, what percentage of the items should you expect to cost more than $6,600?

To find out, enter the function as follows:

```
=STANDARDIZE(6600,6000,800)
```

The function returns the value .75. You can then use the NORMSDIST function to find the probability or area under the curve between 0 and .75.

The z-value tells you how far (in terms of the number of standard deviations) an individual observation is from the mean. It therefore also allows you to determine whether an observation is an outlier (unusually large or small) and therefore suspect. Z-values of less than –3 or greater than +3 are generally treated as outliers and call for closer inspection.

Sum of Squares of Deviations from Mean (DEVSQ)

To sum the squares of the deviations of the data points in a sample from the mean, you use the DEVSQ function. The DEVSQ function uses the following syntax:

```
=DEVSQ(data set range)
```

t Distribution

If you're working with a small sample (less than about 30 or 40), you can use the Student's t-test instead of the z-value or z-score to find the probability with which a value falls below a certain number or to test how far an individual observation is from the mean. To do so, you use the TINV function.

TDIST

You can use the TDIST function to make inferences about the value of a population mean. For example, if you randomly select 20 people from a factory floor, ask them to try a new production method, and then find that they can produce 17.25 units an hour with a sample standard deviation of 3.3, you can find the probability that the population mean takes the value of 16 or less. To do so, you use Excel's TDIST function. The function uses the following syntax:

```
=TDIST(x,degrees of freedom,tails)
```

For this example, the function takes the following form:

```
=TDIST(16,19,1)
```

Depending on your level of significance, you accept or reject the hypothesis.

The hypothesis in this example is one-tailed; that is, you're interested in finding probabilities of values less than 16. If instead you need to find the probabilities of values both above and below x, your hypothesis is two-tailed.

TINV

If you know the probability and want to find the t-value, use the TINV function. This function has the following syntax:

```
=TINV(probability,degrees of freedom)
```

If this is based on a one-tailed t distribution, multiply the probability by 2.

TTEST

To find the probability associated with a Student's t-test, use the TTEST function. The t-test is most frequently used to test for a difference between two means. The TTEST function uses the following syntax:

```
=TTEST(data set 1,data set 2,tails,type)
```

where type equals 1 for paired, 2 for two samples with equal variance, or 3 for 2 samples with unequal variance.

Trimming to the Mean (TRIMMEAN)

You calculate a trimmed mean by discarding a certain percentage of the lowest and the highest values from a data set to remove outliers, and then computing the mean of the remaining values. For example, a mean trimmed 50% is computed by discarding the lowest and highest 25% of the values and taking the mean of the remaining 50% in the middle. The TRIMMEAN function uses the following syntax:

```
=TRIMMEAN(data set range,percent)
```

where percent is entered as a decimal. For example, the spreadsheet of birth rates in the United States in Figure 4-14 shows the mean and a mean trimmed 25%.

C54 | =TRIMMEAN(C2:C52,0.25)

Figure 4-14.xls

	A	B	C	D
36	North Dakota	8,347	13	
37	Ohio	151,692	13.6	
38	Oklahoma	46,193	14	
39	Oregon	43,658	13.6	
40	Pennsylvania	148,338	12.3	
41	Rhode Island	12,652	12.8	
42	South Carolina	51,117	13.8	
43	South Dakota	10,473	14.3	
44	Tennessee	73,754	13.9	
45	Texas	330,406	17.3	
46	Utah	42,087	21	
47	Vermont	6,767	11.5	
48	Virginia	92,354	13.8	
49	Washington	77,945	14.1	
50	West Virginia	20,750	11.4	
51	Wisconsin	67,106	13	
52	Wyoming	6,286	13.1	
53		mean	14.27059	
54		mean trimmed 25%	14.14615	
55				

Figure 4-14 A trimmed mean.

Variance

Excel provides four functions for calculating variance, a measure of the variability between data values in a set. Variance is based on the difference between each value and the mean.

VAR

If the data set you're working with is a sample and you do not want to include logical values or text from the set in the calculation, you use the VAR function. For example, if you're using a new production process that is supposed to increase productivity and have a series of data for the numbers of parts produced each day, you can find the sample variance. The VAR function uses the following syntax:

```
=VAR(data set range)
```

VARA

If the data set is a sample but you want to include logical values or text in the calculation, you use the VARA function. Excel counts cells containing the logical value TRUE as 1 and cells containing text or FALSE 0. The VARA function uses the following syntax:

```
=VARA(data set range)
```

VARP

If the data set you're working with is a population and you do not want to include logical values or text from the set in the calculation, you use the VARP function. The VARP function uses the following syntax:

```
=VARP(data set range)
```

VARPA

If the data set is a population but you want to include logical values or text in the calculation, you use the VARPA function. The VARPA function uses the following syntax:

```
=VARPA(data set range)
```

Weibull Distribution (WEIBULL)

The Weibull distribution is a skewed distribution commonly used to show product lifetimes, analysis of systems involving a "weakest link," and wind speed.

NOTE *To see what the Weibull distribution looks like at various wind speeds and with various standard deviations in wind speed, visit the interactive Web page at* http://www.windpower.dk/tour/wres/weibull/index.htm.

The WEIBULL function uses the following syntax:

```
=WEIBULL(x,alpha,beta,cumulative)
```

where x is the value at which to evaluate the function, alpha and beta are parameters to the distribution, and cumulative specifies whether you want Excel to return the value of the function at exactly x (in which case you enter FALSE) or up to and including x (in which case you enter TRUE).

Z-test (ZTEST)

Use the ZTEST function to find the two-tailed p-value of a z-test. The z-test standardizes x with respect to the data set, and returns the two-tailed probability for the normal distribution. You can use this function to determine the likelihood that a particular observation comes from a certain population.

The ZTEST function uses the following syntax:

```
=ZTEST(data set range,x,sigma)
```

If you don't know the population standard deviation sigma (s), leave this parameter blank and Excel uses the sample standard deviation from the data set.

Data Analysis Tools

This section describes the statistical data analysis tools that come with the Analysis ToolPak. To install the Analysis ToolPak, choose the Tools menu's Add-Ins command, select the Analysis ToolPak check box, and click OK. Excel may prompt you to insert the Microsoft Office 2002 or Excel 2002 CD if it isn't currently in your CD-ROM drive.

Analysis of Variance (ANOVA)

Analysis of variance depends on three assumptions: that the observations are independent, that the response variable is normally distributed for each population, and that the variance of the response variable is the same for all of the populations.

You can use analysis of variance to test for the equality of k population means. To use the ANOVA tools, follow these steps:

1. **Choose the Tools menu's Data Analysis command.**

   Excel displays the Data Analysis dialog box.

2. **Select an ANOVA tool from the list.**

   Select the single-factor ANOVA tool to test the hypothesis that means from two or more samples drawn from populations with the same mean are equal. Select the two-factor with replication ANOVA tool if you want to include multiple samples for each group of data. Select the two factor without replication tool if you want to perform a two-factor ANOVA and include only one sample for each group of data.

3. **Identify the data you want to analyze.**

   Enter the range of data you want to analyze in the Input Range box.

4. **Describe how the data is organized.**

   - If you're performing a single-factor test, specify whether the data is in columns or rows.
   - If you're performing an ANOVA without replication, specify whether the input range includes labels.
   - If you're performing an ANOVA with replication, enter the number of rows contained in each sample in the Rows Per Sample box. Note that the number must be the same for all samples.

5. **Enter a value for alpha.**

   Alpha gives the significance level related to the probability of rejecting a true hypothesis.

6. **Specify where you want to place the ANOVA table.**

   Figure 4-15 shows an ANOVA table beneath production sample data from three plants.

A2 fx 59

Figure 4-15.xls

	A	B	C	D	E	F	G	H
1	Houston	Miami	Detroit					
2	59	71	85					
3	64	75	76					
4	62	73	82					
5	69	75	77					
6	73	68	71					
7	67	72	86					
8	66	74	79					
9								
10	Anova: Single Factor							
11								
12	SUMMARY							
13	*Groups*	*Count*	*Sum*	*Average*	*Variance*			
14	Column 1	7	460	65.7143	21.2381			
15	Column 2	7	508	72.5714	6.28571			
16	Column 3	7	556	79.4286	28.2857			
17								
18								
19	ANOVA							
20	*Source of Variation*	*SS*	*df*	*MS*	*F*	*P-value*	*F crit*	
21	Between Groups	658.286	2	329.143	17.6928	5.63158E-05	3.55456	
22	Within Groups	334.857	18	18.6032				
23								
24	Total	993.143	20					
25								

Figure 4-15 Testing analysis of variance of populations.

Correlation

You can use the Correlation tool to create a table of Correlation coefficient data. Like covariance, a correlation coefficient also measures the linear association between two variables, but unlike covariance, correlation coefficients take values between −1 and +1. Values near −1 indicate a strong negative linear relationship. Values near zero indicate lack of relationship, and values near +1 indicate a strong positive linear relationship. Figure 4-16 shows two sets of data on PR Releases & Sales in a spreadsheet.

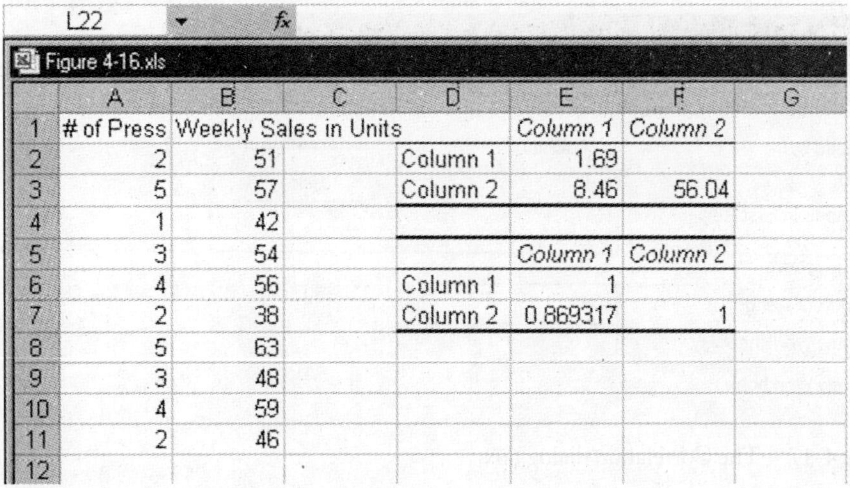

L22

Figure 4-16.xls

	A	B	C	D	E	F	G
1	# of Press	Weekly Sales in Units			*Column 1*	*Column 2*	
2	2	51		Column 1	1.69		
3	5	57		Column 2	8.46	56.04	
4	1	42					
5	3	54			*Column 1*	*Column 2*	
6	4	56		Column 1	1		
7	2	38		Column 2	0.869317	1	
8	5	63					
9	3	48					
10	4	59					
11	2	46					
12							

Figure 4-16 Determining the correlation coefficient between number of press releases and weekly sales.

To use the Correlation tool to determine the correlation coefficient between these two sets of data, follow these steps:

1. **Choose the Tools menu's Data Analysis command.**

   Excel displays the Data Analysis dialog box.

2. **Select Correlation from the list, and click OK.**

   Excel displays the Correlation dialog box.

3. **Identify the data you want to analyze.**

   In the example, you would enter *A2:B11* in the Input Range box.

4. **Describe how the data is organized.**

   In the example, you would make sure the Columns option is selected.

5. **Use the Output Options to describe the location you want for the Correlation data table.**

   Click Output Range, and enter the upper left corner of the range where you want the data table to go. Alternatively, click New Worksheet Ply to create a new worksheet in the current workbook for the data, or click New Workbook to create a new workbook for the data. The cell listed in Figure 4-17 shows where Excel places the data table when you click the Output Range option button and enter *D5* in the box.

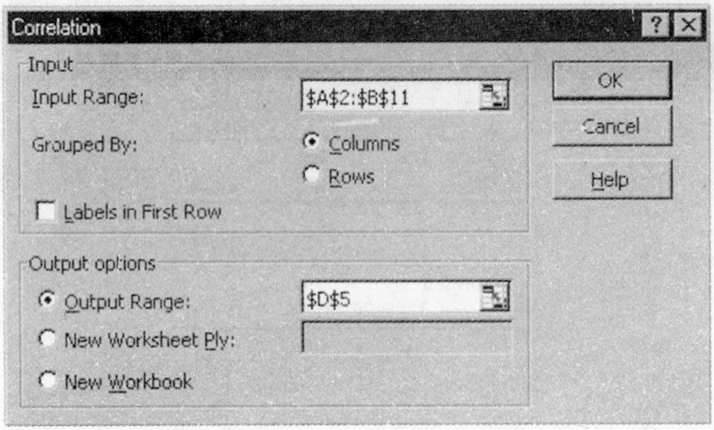

Figure 4-17 The Correlation dialog box.

6. Click OK.

The value in cell E7 is the correlation coefficient between press releases and sales. Cells E6 and F7 both hold the value 1, as a variable is always perfectly correlated with itself.

Covariance

You use covariance to measure the linear association between two sets of data. A positive covariance indicates a positive relationship, meaning that larger values of one variable tend to correspond with larger values of the other. Figure 4-18 shows two sets of data on PR Releases & Sales in a spreadsheet.

E2 =VARP(Sheet1!$A$2:$A$11)

Figure 4-16.xls

	A	B	C	D	E	F	G
1	# of Press	Weekly Sales in Units			*Column 1*	*Column 2*	
2	2	51		Column 1	1.69		
3	5	57		Column 2	8.46	56.04	
4	1	42					
5	3	54			*Column 1*	*Column 2*	
6	4	56		Column 1	1		
7	2	38		Column 2	0.869317	1	
8	5	63					
9	3	48					
10	4	59					
11	2	46					
12							

Figure 4-18 Determining the linear association between number of press releases and weekly sales.

To use the Covariance tool to measure the linear association between these two sets of data, follow these steps:

1. **Choose the Tools menu's Data Analysis command.**

   Excel displays the Data Analysis dialog box.

2. **Select Covariance from the list, and click OK.**

   Excel displays the Covariance dialog box.

3. **Identify the data you want to analyze.**

   In the example, you would enter *A2:B11* in the Input Range box.

4. **Describe how the data is organized.**

   In the example, you would make sure the Columns option is selected.

5. **Use the Output Options to describe where you want the Covariance data table to go.**

   Click Output Range, and enter the upper left corner of the range where you want the data table to go. Alternatively, click New Worksheet Ply to create a new worksheet in the current workbook for the data, or click New Workbook to create a new workbook for the data. Figure 4-19 shows where Excel places the data table when you click the Output Range option button and enter *D1* in the box.

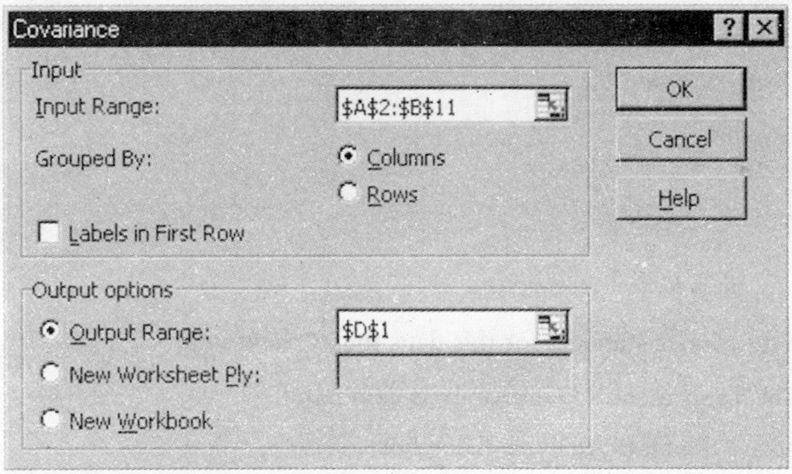

Figure 4-19 The Covariance dialog box.

6. **Click OK.**

The value in cell E2 is the variance for the number of press releases and the value in cell F3 is the variance for sales. The value in cell E3 is the covariance between press releases and sales.

Descriptive Statistics

You can use the Descriptive Statistics tool to generate several descriptive measures for a data set at once. The Descriptive Statistics tool can find the mean, standard error, median, mode, standard deviation, sample variance, kurtosis, skewness, range minimum, maximum, sum, and count. Figure 4-20 shows total yardage during a season for a sample of 25 NCAA college football receivers.

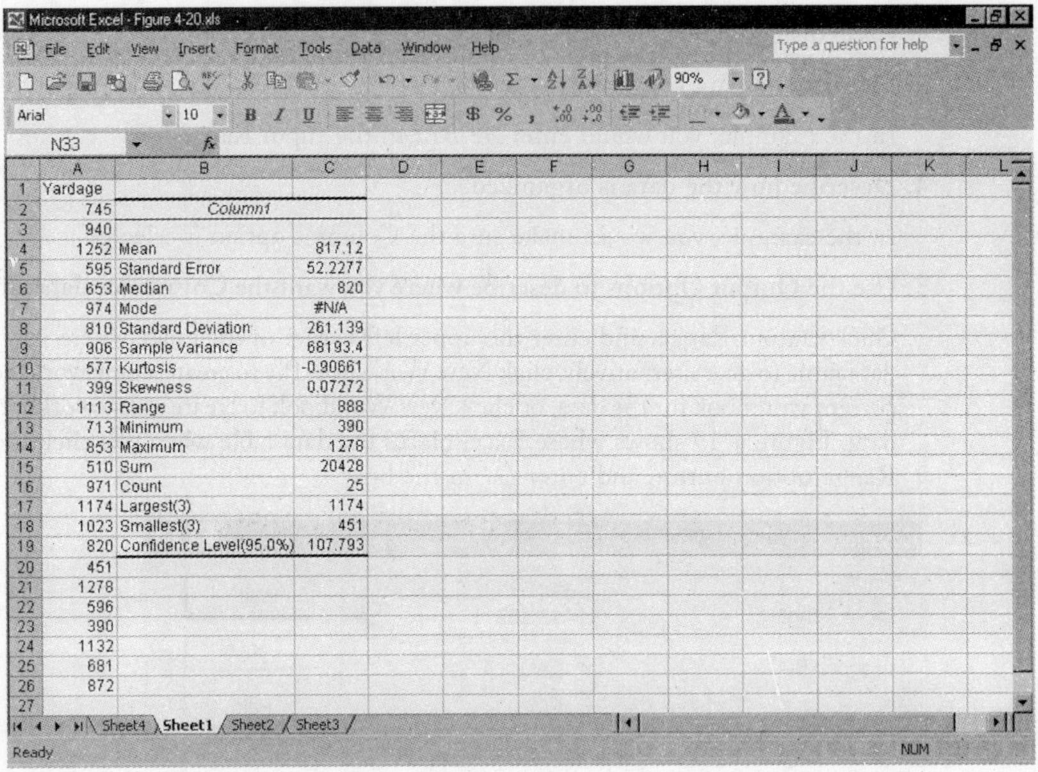

Figure 4-20 College football receiver data.

To generate descriptive statistics for this data, follow these steps:

1. **Choose the Tools menu's Data Analysis command.**

   Excel displays the Data Analysis dialog box.

2. **Select Descriptive Statistics, and click OK.**

   Excel displays the Descriptive Statistics dialog box, as shown in Figure 4-21.

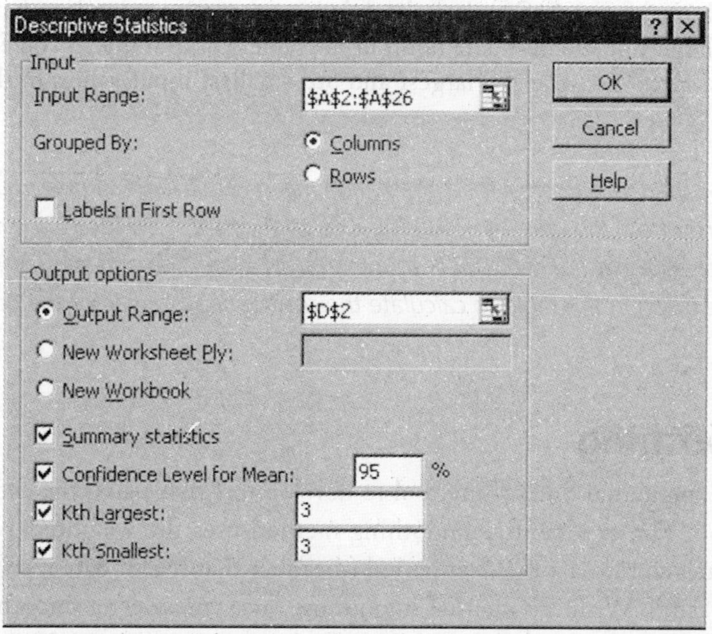

Figure 4-21 The Descriptive Statistics dialog box.

3. Enter *A2:A26* in the Input Range box.

If you want to keep the Yardage label, enter *A1:A26* in the Input Range box and select the Labels check box.

4. Describe how the data is organized.

In this example, you would click the Columns option button.

5. Use the Output Options to describe where you want the descriptive statistics table to go.

Click Output Range, and enter the upper left corner of the range where you want the data to go. Alternatively, click New Worksheet Ply to create a new worksheet in the current workbook for the descriptive statistics table, or click New Workbook to create a new workbook for the descriptive statistics table.

6. Select the Summary Statistics check box.

7. Use the other check boxes to describe other statistics you want included in the descriptive statistics table.

If you have a small sample and want to find a confidence interval for the mean, select the Confidence Level check box and enter the confidence level in the text box. When Excel returns the Confidence Level value, you can say with the percent confidence you indicated that the population mean is plus or minus this amount from the sample mean.

Select the Kth Largest or Kth Smallest check box, and enter a value k to have Excel include the kth largest or smallest data point in the table. For example, if you enter 3 in these two boxes, Excel lists the 3rd largest and 3rd smallest input values in the table.

8. Click OK.

NOTE *To find the confidence interval for a population mean with a large sample, multiply the standard error from the table by 1.645 for 90% confidence, 1.96 for 95% confidence, or 2.576 for 99% confidence. This is your margin of error. Add and subtract this from the sample mean in the table to calculate the confidence interval for the population mean.*

Exponential Smoothing

You can use the Exponential Smoothing tool to develop forecasts using the exponential smoothing method. The exponential smoothing method uses the weighted average of previous series values to forecast the next period (meaning that recent data receives more weight than older data). With exponential smoothing, once you select a smoothing constant alpha, you do not need to include past data in the forecast computation. You need only the most recent observation. Figure 4-22 shows a forecast using the exponential smoothing method based on data in a Sales spreadsheet.

D13 fx =0.7*B12+0.3*D12

	A	B	C	D	E	F
1	Week	Sales	3-week moving	Exponential Smoothing		
2	1	22	#N/A	#N/A		
3	2	18	#N/A	22		
4	3	23	21	19.2		
5	4	21	20.66666667	21.86		
6	5	17	20.33333333	21.258		
7	6	24	20.66666667	18.2774		
8	7	20	20.33333333	22.28322		
9	8	19	21	20.68497		
10	9	18	19	19.50549		
11	10	21	19.33333333	18.45165		
12	11	15	18	20.23549		
13	12	22	19.33333333	16.57065		
14						
15						

Figure 4-22 Forecasting using exponential smoothing.

To use the Exponential Smoothing tool on the Sales spreadsheet, follow these steps:

1. **Choose the Tools menu's Data Analysis command.**

   Excel displays the Data Analysis dialog box.

2. **Select Exponential Smoothing from the list, and click OK.**

   Excel displays the Exponential Smoothing dialog box.

3. **Identify the data you want to analyze.**

   In this example, you would enter *B2:B11* in the Input Range box.

4. **Enter *.3* in the Damping Factor box.**

   The damping factor is equal to 1-alpha.

5. **Describe where you want to place the smoothing forecast.**

   For example, if you enter *D2* in the Output Range box, Excel places the smoothing forecasts in Column D.

6. **Click OK.**

F-Test

You can use the F-Test tool to perform a two-sample F-test comparing two population variances. To do so, follow these steps:

1. **Choose the Tools menu's Data Analysis command.**

   Excel displays the Data Analysis dialog box.

2. **Select F-Test Two-Sample For Variances from the list, and click OK.**

   Excel displays the F-Test Two-Sample For Variances dialog box.

3. **Enter the ranges of data you want to analyze in the Variable 1 Range and Variable 2 Range boxes.**

4. **Specify whether the input ranges include labels.**

5. **Enter the confidence level for the test, *alpha*.**

   Remember to express alpha as a decimal, and that it must be between 0 and 1.

6. **Specify the location for the F-Test table, and click OK.**

   Use the Output Range option to place the table on the current worksheet, the New Worksheet Ply option to place the table on a new worksheet in the current workbook, or the New Workbook option to create a new workbook for the table.

Fourier Analysis

This tool allows you to analyze complex periodic waveforms using the Fast Fourier Transform (FFT) method to transform data. A common use for Fourier Transforms is to characterize the behavior of share prices of a company on the stock market.

To use the Fourier Analysis tool, follow these steps:

1. **Choose the Tools menu's Data Analysis command.**

   Excel displays the Data Analysis dialog box.

2. **Select Fourier Analysis from the list, and click OK.**

   Excel displays the Fourier Analysis dialog box.

3. **Enter the range of data you want to analyze in the Input Range box.**
4. **Specify whether the input ranges include labels.**
5. **Specify the output location for the Fourier table.**

   Use the Output Range option to place the table on the current worksheet, the New Worksheet Ply option to place the table on a new worksheet in the current workbook, or the New Workbook option to create a new workbook for the table.

6. **Select the Inverse check box if the data in the input range is transformed and you want to find the original inputs.**
7. **Click OK.**

Histogram

A histogram is a common graphical presentation of frequency data. Using the file containing S&P 500 returns (see Figure 4-9), you can create a histogram by following these steps:

1. **Optionally, create bins holding a set of values in ascending order.**

   Excel will count the number of occurrences in the range that are equal to or less than the value you enter in the bin, and greater than the previous bin value. The more bins you create, the smaller the bars of your histogram. Excel creates an additional bin for all values greater than the highest bin value.

TIP *It usually makes most sense to evenly space the bins.*

2. **Choose the Tools menu's Data Analysis command.**

   Excel displays the Data Analysis dialog box.

3. **Select Histogram, and click OK.**

   Excel displays the Histogram dialog box, as shown in Figure 4-23.

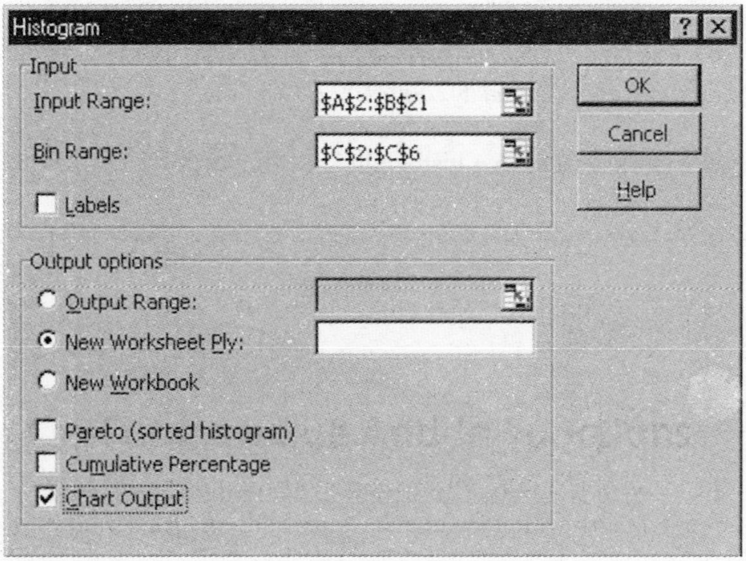

Figure 4-23 Creating a histogram.

4. Identify the data you want to analyze.

In this example, you would enter *C2:C21* in the Input Range box.

5. Enter *D2:D6* in the Bin Range box.

If you leave the bin range blank, Excel creates a set of evenly distributed bins between minimum and maximum values in your data set.

NOTE *If you want to include labels in the histogram (which can be a good idea), you must do so for both the input range and bin range. Then select the Labels check box.*

6. Use the Output Options to describe where you want the histogram and frequency distribution table to go.

Click Output Range, and enter the upper left corner of the range where you want the data to go. Alternatively, click New Worksheet Ply to create a new worksheet in the current workbook for the histogram, or click New Workbook to create a new workbook for the histogram.

7. Optionally, select the Cumulative Percentage check box.

This adds a cumulative percentage line to the histogram and a cumulative percentage line to the frequency distribution table.

8. Select the Chart Output check box.

9. Click OK.

NOTE *If you want to arrange the bars in descending order of height from left to right, select the Pareto check box. This creates a variation of a column graph called a Pareto diagram that is often used for quality control purposes.*

Figure 4-24 shows a worksheet with a histogram.

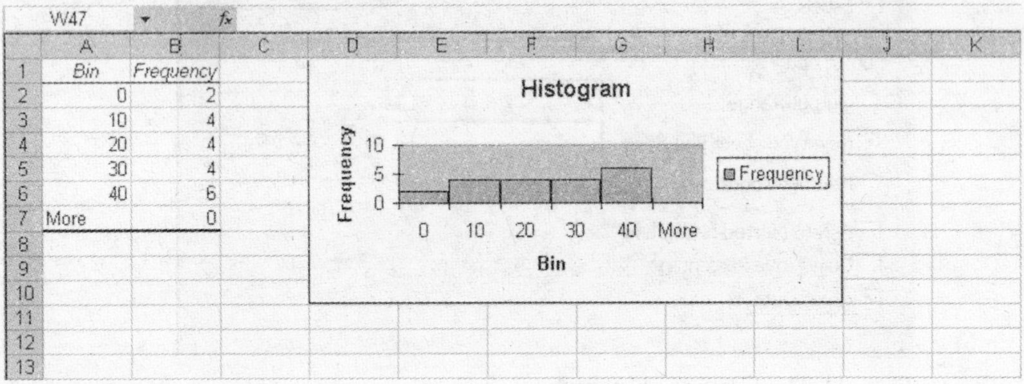

Figure 4-24 A histogram.

TIP *Technically, unlike Excel's column charts, the adjacent rectangles of a histogram shouldn't touch each other, but in Excel, they do. To correct this, right-click one of the columns and choose the shortcut menu's Format Data Series command. Then click the Options tab, and enter* 0 *in the Gap Width box.*

Moving Averages

You can use the Moving Averages tool to develop forecasts using the moving averages method. The moving averages method uses the average of a certain number of the most recent values in the time series to forecast the next period. You can specify the number of most recent values you want to use. Figure 4-25 shows a forecast using the moving averages method based on data in a Sales spreadsheet.

C13 | f_x =AVERAGE(B11:B13)

	A	B	C	D	E
1	Week	Sales	3-week moving	Exponential Smoothing	
2	1	22	#N/A	#N/A	
3	2	18	#N/A	22	
4	3	23	21	19.2	
5	4	21	20.66666667	21.86	
6	5	17	20.33333333	21.258	
7	6	24	20.66666667	18.2774	
8	7	20	20.33333333	22.28322	
9	8	19	21	20.68497	
10	9	18	19	19.50549	
11	10	21	19.33333333	18.45165	
12	11	15	18	20.23549	
13	12	22	19.33333333	16.57065	
14					

Figure 4-25 Forecasting using moving averages.

To use the Moving Averages tool on the Sales spreadsheet to produce a three-week moving average, follow these steps:

1. **Choose the Tools menu's Data Analysis command.**

   Excel displays the Data Analysis dialog box.

2. **Select Moving Averages from the list, and click OK.**

   Excel displays the Moving Averages dialog box.

3. **Identify the data you want to analyze.**

   In this example, enter *B2:B11* in the Input Range box.

4. **Specify the number of data points you are using for each moving average in the Interval box.**

   In this case, enter *3* for three weeks.

5. **Use the Output Options to describe where you want the moving averages table to go.**

   In this case, you could enter *C2* in the Output Range box to put the moving average forecasts in column C.

6. **Click OK.**

Random Number Generation

Use the Random Number Generation tool to fill a range with random numbers following the distribution you specify. To use the Random Number Generation tool, follow these steps:

1. **Choose the Tools menu's Data Analysis command.**

   Excel displays the Data Analysis dialog box.

2. **Select Random Number Generation from the list, and click OK.**

   Excel displays the Random Number Generation dialog box.

3. **In the Number Of Variables box, enter the number of columns you want Excel to fill with random numbers.**

4. **In the Number of Random Numbers box, enter the number of random numbers you want Excel to return.**

5. **Select a distribution from the Distribution drop-down list box.**

   Select Uniform if you want to specify a range within which the numbers are drawn with equal probability. Select Normal for a normal (Gaussian) distribution. You can create a standard normal distribution by selecting Normal and entering for the parameters a mean of 0 and a standard deviation of 1. Select Bernoulli for a distribution with only two event classes, "success" or "failure." Select Poisson to estimate the number of occurrences over a specified range of time or amount of space. Select Patterned to specify a range within which numbers are repeated in a sequence. Select Discrete if you have a set of values and another of their associated probabilities and want to generate numbers based on this information.

6. **Enter the parameters for the distribution you selected.**

7. **If you want to be able to produce the same set of random numbers at a later time, enter a value in the Random Seed box.**

   Note this value for future use.

8. **Specify the output location for random numbers, and click OK.**

Rank and Percentile

You can use the rank and percentile tool to create a table listing the rank, value, and percentile of data points in the data set. To do this, follow these steps:

1. **Choose the Tools menu's Data Analysis command.**

   Excel displays the Data Analysis dialog box.

2. **Select Rank And Percentile from the list, and click OK.**

   Excel displays the Rank And Percentile dialog box.

3. **Identify the data you want to analyze.**

   Enter the range of data you want to analyze in the Input Range box.

4. **Specify whether the values are organized in columns or rows.**

5. **Specify whether the input ranges include labels.**

6. **Specify the location for the Rank and Percentile table.**

   Click Output Range, and enter the upper left corner of the range where you want the table to go. Alternatively, click New Worksheet Ply to create a new worksheet for the table, or click New Workbook to create a new workbook for the table.

7. **Click OK.**

Figure 4-26 shows a rank and percentile table for a list of test scores in a class.

E1 | fx Point

Figure 4-26.xls

	A	B	C	D	E	F	G	H
1	LAST	FIRST	TEST SCORE		*Point*	*Column1*	*Rank*	*Percent*
2	ANDERSON	MARY	95		11	99	1	95.60%
3	BROWN	JOSEPH	92		23	99	1	95.60%
4	CLARK	LINDA	78		1	95	3	91.30%
5	DAVIS	RICHARD	81		5	93	4	82.60%
6	GARCIA	MARIA	93		13	93	4	82.60%
7	HARRIS	MICHAEL	86		2	92	6	73.90%
8	JACKSON	ELIZABET	84		22	92	6	73.90%
9	JOHNSON	SUSAN	59		12	91	8	69.50%
10	JONES	MARGARE	72		10	90	9	56.50%
11	LEE	DOROTHY	90		17	90	9	56.50%
12	LEWIS	LISA	99		24	90	9	56.50%
13	MARTIN	NANCY	91		20	88	12	52.10%
14	MARTINEZ	JOSE	93		16	87	13	47.80%
15	MILLER	BETTY	82		6	86	14	43.40%
16	MOORE	KAREN	85		15	85	15	34.70%
17	ROBINSON	JAMES	87		21	85	15	34.70%
18	SMITH	ROBERT	90		7	84	17	30.40%
19	TAYLOR	JENNIFER	77		19	83	18	26.00%
20	THOMAS	WILLIAM	83		14	82	19	21.70%
21	THOMPSON	DAVID	88		4	81	20	17.30%
22	WALKER	BARBARA	85		3	78	21	13.00%
23	WHITE	CHARLES	92		18	77	22	8.60%
24	WILLIAMS	PATRICIA	99		9	72	23	4.30%
25	WILSON	THOMAS	90		8	59	24	.00%

Figure 4-26 A rank and percentile table.

Regression

To perform linear regression analysis, you can use the Regression tool. The Regression tool works by using the least squares method to fit a straight line through a set of x- and y-values. To use the Regression tool, follow these steps:

1. **Choose the Tools menu's Data Analysis command.**

   Excel displays the Data Analysis dialog box.

2. **Select Regression from the list, and click OK.**

   Excel displays the Regression dialog box.

3. **Identify the data you want to analyze.**

   Enter the dependent variable range in the Input Y Range box and the independent variable range in the Input X Range box.

4. **Specify whether the input ranges include labels.**

5. **Optionally, select the Constant Is Zero check box.**

   Do this if you want to force the y-intercept constant (b) in the equation of the line (y=mx+b) to equal zero.

6. **Optionally, select the Confidence Level check box.**

   Do this if you want Excel to define a range around your line that fits the specified percentage of data.

7. **Specify the output location for the Regression table.**

   Click Output Range, and enter the upper left corner of the range where you want the table to go. Alternatively, click New Worksheet Ply to create a new worksheet in the current workbook for the table, or click New Workbook to create a new workbook for the table.

8. **Use the Residuals options.**

   Specify whether you want to include standardized residuals in the output table, chart the independent variables against the residual, or chart expected values against the observed values.

9. **Optionally, select the Normal Probability Plots.**

   Do this if you want Excel to chart normal probability.

10. **Click OK.**

Sampling

If you have population data and want to draw a sample from them, you can use the Sampling tool. To do so, follow these steps:

1. **Choose the Tools menu's Data Analysis command.**

   Excel displays the Data Analysis dialog box.

2. **Select Sampling from the list, and click OK.**

   Excel displays the Sampling dialog box.

3. **Identify the data you want to analyze.**

   Enter the range of data you want to analyze in the Input Range box.

4. **Specify whether the input ranges include labels.**
5. **Describe whether you want a periodic or random sample.**

   Click the Periodic option button to sample every kth value and enter *k* in the Period box, or click the Random option button and enter the sample size you want in the Number Of Samples box.

6. **Specify the output location for the sample values, and click OK.**

   Click Output Range, and enter the upper left corner of the range where you want the values to go. Alternatively, click New Worksheet Ply to create a new worksheet in the current workbook for the values, or click New Workbook to create a new workbook for the values.

t-Test

Use the t-Test tool to perform the Student's t-test on a small sample. The t-test is commonly used to test for a difference between means.

1. **Choose the Tools menu's Data Analysis command.**

   Excel displays the Data Analysis dialog box.

2. **Select a t-Test option from the list, and click OK.**

   Select the Paired Two Sample For Means Test if you have a pairing of observations in the data sets, for example, if the data sets show values for the same sample before and after manipulation. The Paired Two Sample For Means Test does not assume that the variances of both populations are equal. Select the Two-Sample Assuming Equal Variances test if you assume the means of both data sets are equal. Select the Two-Sample Assuming Unequal Variances test if you assume that the variances of both data sets are unequal, for instance, if the samples come from different populations.

3. **Identify the data you want to analyze.**

   Enter the ranges of data you want to analyze in the Variable 1 Range and Variable 2 Range boxes.

4. **Enter the hypothesized mean difference in the Hypothesized Mean Difference box.**
5. **Specify whether the input ranges include labels.**
6. **Specify alpha.**

   Enter .05 in the Alpha box for a 95% confidence level, .1 for a 90% confidence level, or .01 for a 99% confidence level.

7. **Specify the output location for the t-Test table, and click OK.**

   Click Output Range, and enter the upper left corner of the range where you want the table to go. Alternatively, click New Worksheet Ply to create a new worksheet in the current workbook for the table, or click New Workbook to create a new workbook for the table.

z-Test

If you have a large sample and want to conduct a hypothesis test about the difference between two population means, you can use the z-Test tool. Before you can begin, you need to find the two sample variances. You can do this by using the VAR function or by using the Descriptive Statistics tool. Figure 4-27 shows an example worksheet with the prices of an ice cream sundae in several stores in two cities.

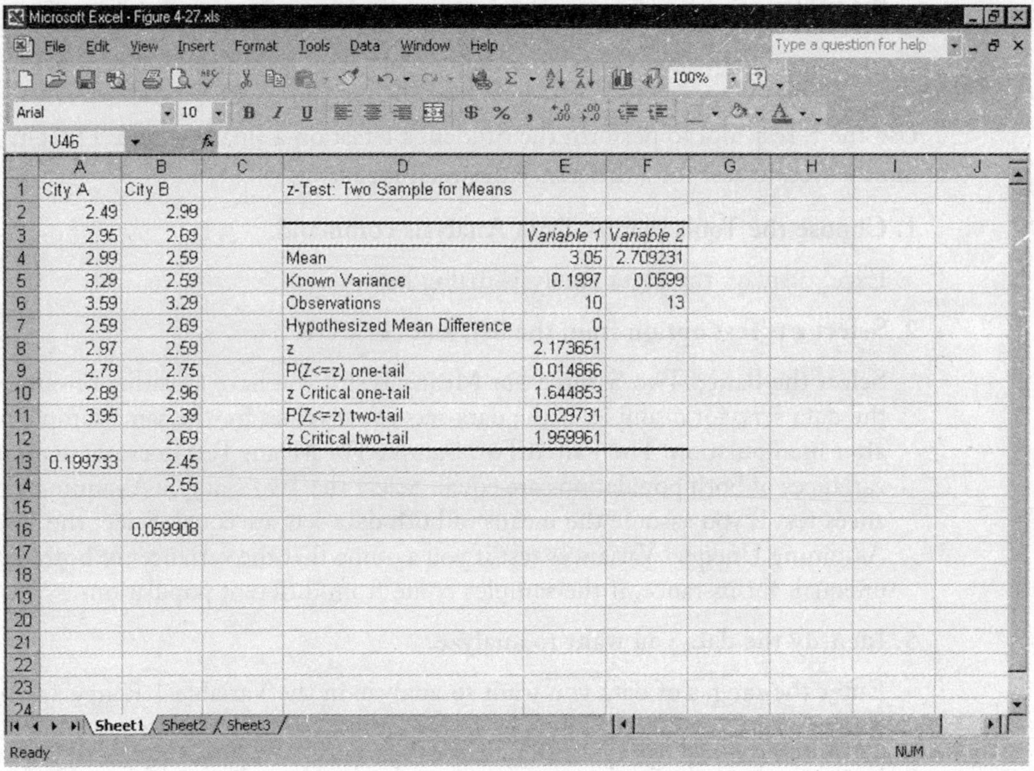

	A	B	C	D	E	F
1	City A	City B		z-Test: Two Sample for Means		
2	2.49	2.99				
3	2.95	2.69			*Variable 1*	*Variable 2*
4	2.99	2.59		Mean	3.05	2.709231
5	3.29	2.59		Known Variance	0.1997	0.0599
6	3.59	3.29		Observations	10	13
7	2.59	2.69		Hypothesized Mean Difference	0	
8	2.97	2.59		z	2.173651	
9	2.79	2.75		P(Z<=z) one-tail	0.014866	
10	2.89	2.96		z Critical one-tail	1.644853	
11	3.95	2.39		P(Z<=z) two-tail	0.029731	
12		2.69		z Critical two-tail	1.959961	
13	0.199733	2.45				
14		2.55				
15						
16		0.059908				

Figure 4-27 Testing the difference between two population means.

To use the z-Test tool to test the difference between two population means, follow these steps:

1. **Choose the Tools menu's Data Analysis command.**

   Excel displays the Data Analysis dialog box.

2. **Select z-Test: Two Sample For Means from the list, and click OK.**

   Excel displays the Sample For Means dialog box.

3. **Specify the variable ranges.**

   In the example, enter *A2:A11* in the Variable 1 Range box and *B2:B14* in the Variable 2 Range box.

4. **Enter 0 in the Hypothesized Mean Difference box.**

   This means that you are hypothesizing that the means are equal. Enter a different value if you are hypothesizing a difference between the means.

5. **Specify the variance of the samples.**

   In the example, enter .1997 in the Variable 1 Variance box and .0599 in the Variable 2 Variance box.

6. **Specify alpha.**

   Enter .05 in the Alpha box for a 95% confidence level, .1 for a 90% confidence level, or .01 for a 99% confidence level.

7. **Use the Output Options to describe where you want the Correlation data table to go.**

   Click Output Range, and enter the upper left corner of the range where you want the data table to go. Click New Worksheet Ply to create a new worksheet in the current workbook for the data, or click New Workbook to create a new workbook for the data. Figure 4-28 shows where Excel places the data table when you click the Output Range option button and enter *D3* in the box.

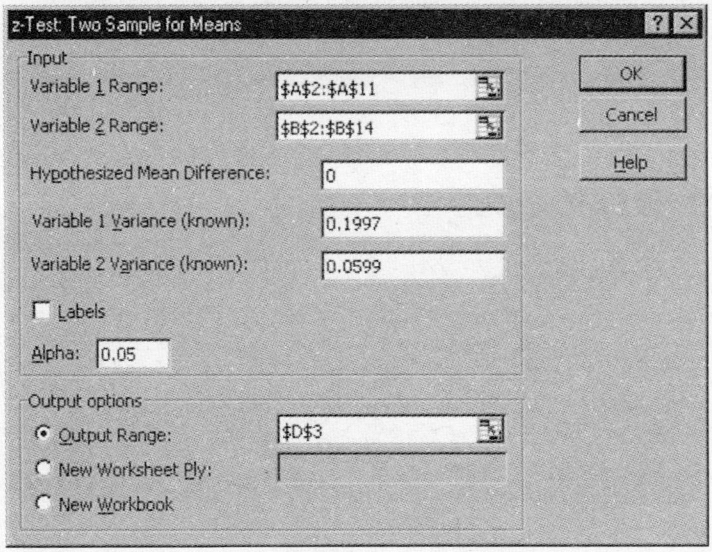

Figure 4-28 The z-Test: Two Sample For Means dialog box.

8. Click OK.

The value of z appears in the table. The two-tailed p-value also appears in the table. If this is less than alpha, reject the null hypothesis.

Chapter 5

FINANCIAL CALCULATIONS

Featuring:

- EasyRefresher™: Applying Time-Value-of-Money Concepts
- Using the Standard Financial Functions
- Using the Add-In Financial Functions

Although most Excel users—even most advanced business users—will have scant occasion to use all of the financial functions that Excel provides, almost everybody will use at least a handful of these time-saving functions. Calculating a mortgage or car loan payment requires use of the PMT function. Estimating the future value of an investment requires use of the FV function. Computing the interest rate implicit in a set of loan or investment terms requires the RATE, IRR, or MIRR functions. This chapter explains how you can use any of the financial functions that come with Excel—both those that are always available and those you can use after installing the Analysis ToolPak add-in.

NOTE *The Analysis ToolPak supplies a set of 42 additional financial functions, which you use in the same way as the standard financial functions. In general, these add-in financial functions are most useful for security analysis.*

EasyRefresher™: Applying Time-Value-of-Money Concepts

Time value of money must surely be one of the most-used phrases that people don't really understand. Almost invariably, people who don't know a discount rate from Adam use the expression to explain or question any financial complexity. The irony—and most business school students and graduates know this—is that time value of money isn't all that complicated. Or at least it isn't at the conceptual level.

Analyzing Borrowing

The time-value-of-money concept, which applies to loans, means that you need to include interest costs in any analysis of loans. In other words, to compare "loan A" to "loan B," you need to account for the interest costs of each. Note that this isn't the same thing as saying you need to compare the interest rates, however. The interest rate of a loan is important. It's the first of the three variables used to calculate the interest charges of a loan. But you need more than just the interest rate to know what, for example, "loan A" costs. You also need to know the loan balance against which the interest rate is applied. (This is the second variable.) And you need to know for how many periods—years, months, or whatever—this calculation is made. (This is the third variable.)

Interestingly, truth-in-lending laws make it easy for consumers to make time-value-of-money comparisons of different borrowing options. By comparing the annual percentage rate, or APR, of one loan with another, you can generally tell which borrowing option is cheapest. The APR wraps all of the costs of borrowing—all the time value of money—into a single, interest-rate-like number. By choosing the lowest APR, a consumer generally gets the cheapest loan. Unfortunately, it generally isn't as easy for business borrowers to get APR information. (Truth-in-lending laws, for example, apply to consumers but not to business borrowers.) Nevertheless, it's still generally most useful to make time value of money comparisons of different borrowing options by applying the APR concept.

NOTE *In the discussion of the RATE function, we'll describe how to calculate the APR of any loan.*

Analyzing Investments

The time-value-of-money concept also applies to investments, with a slight twist: When applied to investments, you need to factor in the interest or investment earnings generated by an investment. In other words, to compare "investment A" to "investment B," you need to account for the interest or investment returns of each. Note again that isn't the same thing as saying you need to compare the interest rates or investment rates of returns, however. The interest rate or rate of return on an investment is important. But as with borrowing comparisons, it's only the first of the three basic variables used to calculate the investment profits from an investment. You also need to know the investment balance against which the interest rate or rate of return is applied. (This is the second variable.) And you need to know for how many periods—years, months, or whatever—this calculation is made. (This is the third variable.)

As a general rule, when people perform time-value-of-money comparisons on investments, they compare either the present values of the two investments or the rates of return of the two investments. The rate-comparison method is easier to understand because it works very much like the APRs that lenders provide consumers. To compare "investment A" with "investment B" on the basis of interest rates or investment rates of return, you compare two percentages; whichever is larger is better, so the logic goes.

Comparing investments on the basis of their rates of return, however, creates a handful of problems, as you may already know. First, simple rate comparisons ignore the fact that the investment balance is important. For example, earning a 25% return on a billion dollars is far more profitable than earning a 100% return on a million dollars. Second, simple rate comparisons ignore the rate at which intermediate cash flows are reinvested. If you have 1 million dollars to invest for 10 years and are choosing between one investment which pays 25% for one year and another investment which pays 15% for 10 years, for example, you can't know which is better unless you know the rate at which your money can be reinvested in year two. Third, return-based investment measures sometimes suffer from a sort of mathematical phenomenon in which the return formula can't be solved with a single, unique interest rate or investment rate-of-return value.

NOTE *It turns out, as mentioned elsewhere in this book, that an investment with "N" cash flows ("N" is number of cash flows) is actually an Nth root polynomial equation with up to "N" real and imaginary solutions to the investment's internal rate-of-return equation.*

Because of the aforementioned problems with applying the time-value-of-money concept to investment calculations, business analysts commonly compare investments based on their present values. Two investments' cash flows can be evaluated on an "apples-to-apples" basis by comparing their *present values:* whichever investment provides the greater present value is better.

You can also compare the present value of an investment's cash flows to its initial cash cost, making what's known as a *net present value* calculation. A net present value is actually a simple cost benefit comparison. You compare the cost of an investment, meaning its cash price, with its benefits, calculated as the present value of its future cash flows. If the net present value is positive, it means the benefits exceed the cost. If the net present value is negative, it means the cost exceeds the benefit.

A challenging feature of present value and net present value calculations concerns the choice of a discount rate, or interest rate, used to convert future cash flows to their current-day, present value. For example, people argue in favor of using the cost of the capital used to fund an investment. If an investment is made using borrowed money that costs 8%, for example, someone taking this approach might use 8% as the discount rate. Another commonly argued approach is to use the rate of return offered by similarly risky investments. If you can make an investment that forces you to bear the same risk and pays a 12% return, some people argue that you should use a 12% discount. In practice, it's worth mentioning, that you often see discount rates set almost as a matter of management policy, or as an arbitrary decision made by a key participant in the financial analysis process. In a case like this, top management might say, perhaps explicitly, that investments must produce at least a 15% return and that would mean that present value calculations should be made with a 15% discount rate.

Dealing with Inflation

One important issue you want to consider in making time-value-of-money calculations is the effect of inflation. Over time, of course, inflation erodes the value of the currency units used to make time-value-of-money calculations. This erosion makes it difficult to compare currency values of different time periods. For example, 1 million dollars today isn't the same thing as 1 million dollars 20 years from now.

You can, fortunately, rather easily estimate the effect of inflation in your time-value-of-money calculations. To do so, you simply need to use the real rate of return rather than the nominal rate of return in your calculations. You calculate the real rate of return by subtracting the inflation rate from the nominal rate of return.

As an example of how all this works, suppose that you want to estimate the future value of a long-term investment in a stock index fund. Over long periods of time, the stock market returns about 10% and inflation runs about 3.5%, so the real return equals 6.5%. If you used 6.5% in your time-value-of-money calculations—rather than the nominal rate of return of 10%—the future value amounts you'd calculate wouldn't include inflation. In effect, by subtracting the inflation rate from the nominal return, you subtract the effects of the inflation from the compounded, future value amounts you calculate.

Using the Standard Financial Functions

Excel provides 16 standard financial functions for making depreciation, loan payment, present value, future value, and rate-of-return calculations. To see which financial functions Excel provides, or to see which arguments a function requires, choose the Insert menu's Function command and then select Financial from the Or Select A Category list box, as shown in Figure 5-1. The Insert Function dialog box shows the categories of functions that Excel provides—such as which financial functions are available.

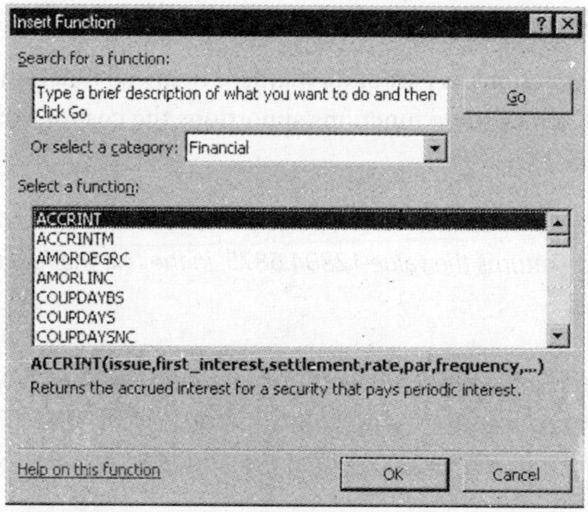

Figure 5-1 The Insert Function dialog box.

After you select a function and click OK, the Function Arguments dialog box shows which arguments are required for the function to make its calculations, as shown in Figure 5-2.

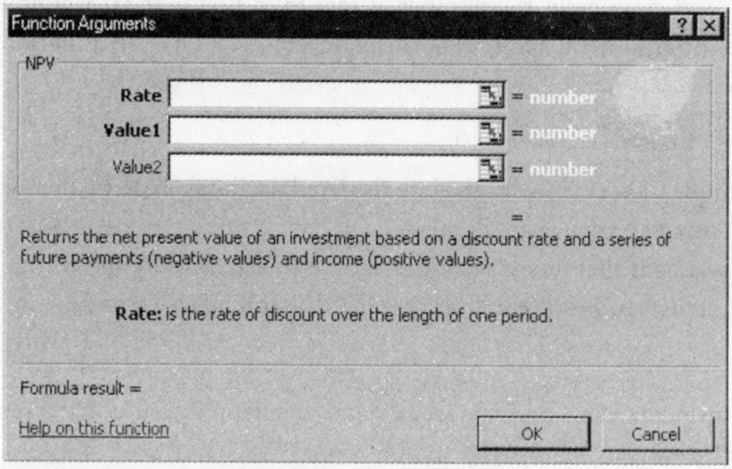

Figure 5-2 The Function Arguments dialog box.

NOTE *Chapter 1 describes how to work with functions and provide their arguments. If you're not already familiar with how a function makes its calculations, you might want to refer to that chapter.*

Using the Depreciation Functions

Excel supplies five depreciation functions as part of its standard financial function set: DB, DDB, SLN, SYD, and VDB. Each of these functions apportions the cost of a long-lived asset over its estimated economic life.

NOTE *In the examples that follow, the function results are rounded to two decimal places. For example, even if a function returns the value 12804.6875, in the text the function result is reported as 12804.69.*

TIP *Excel also supplies two add-in financial functions for calculating depreciation according to French accounting conventions, AMORDEGRC and AMORTLINC. These two functions are described in the later section "Using the Add-In Financial Functions."*

DB

The DB function calculates fixed declining-balance depreciation for an asset given the cost, its salvage value, estimated economic life, the accounting period for which depreciation is being calculated, and, optionally, the number of month in first year. (If you don't include the optional month argument, Excel sets this value to 12.) The DB function uses the following syntax:

```
DB(cost,salvage,life,period,month)
```

Suppose, for example, that you must calculate the fixed declining-balance depreciation for equipment that costs $50,000, lasts five years, will have a salvage value of $10,000 at the end of the fifth year, and that was placed into service in the third month of the first year. To calculate the depreciation for the first year, use the following formula:

```
=DB(50000,10000,5,1,3)
```

The function returns the value 3437.5. To calculate the depreciation for the second year, use the following formula:

```
=DB(50000,10000,5,2,3)
```

The function returns the value 12804.69.

The distinguishing feature of fixed declining-balance depreciation is that it calculates depreciation at a fixed rate based on the estimated cost, salvage value, and economic life of the asset. Excel calculates this rate using the following formula:

```
Fixed rate=1-((salvage/cost)^(1/life))
```

and then rounds this value to the nearest three decimal places. To calculate the depreciation for a period, Excel multiplies the rate by the sum of the original cost less the accumulated depreciation to date.

NOTE *The accumulated depreciation equals the original cost minus the previous periods' depreciation.*

Excel uses variations of the standard fixed declining-balance formula for the first and last periods. For the first period, Excel calculates the depreciation by using the following formula:

```
First-period depreciation=cost*rate*month/12
```

For the last period, Excel calculates the depreciation using the following formula (which essentially just depreciates the asset down to its salvage value):

```
Last-period depreciation=((cost-accumulated depreciation)*rate*(12-
month))/12
```

DDB

The DDB function calculates double declining-balance depreciation for an asset given the cost, its salvage value, estimated economic life, the accounting period for which depreciation is being calculated, and, optionally, the factor at which the balance declines. (If you don't include the optional factor argument, Excel sets this value to 2, indicating "double" declining balance.) The DDB function uses the following syntax:

```
DDB(cost,salvage,life,period,factor)
```

Suppose, for example, that you must calculate the double declining-balance depreciation for equipment that costs $50,000, lasts five years, and will have a salvage value of $10,000 at the end of the fifth year. To calculate the depreciation for the first year, use the following formula:

```
=DDB(50000,10000,5,1)
```

The function returns the value 20000.00. To calculate the depreciation for the second year, use the following formula:

```
=DDB(50000,10000,5,2)
```

The function returns the value 12000.00.

NOTE *A common convention when using double declining-balance depreciation is to switch to straight-line depreciation at the point in time when straight depreciation exceeds declining balance depreciation. The DDB function doesn't make this switch, but the VDB function does. Use it, therefore, if you want to use this convention.*

SLN

The SLN function calculates straight-line balance depreciation for an asset given the cost, its salvage value, and its estimated economic life. The DDB function uses the following syntax:

```
SLN(cost,salvage,life)
```

Suppose, for example, that you must calculate the straight-line depreciation for equipment that costs $50,000, lasts five years, and will have a salvage value of $10,000 at the end of the fifth year. To calculate the depreciation for the first year, use the following formula:

```
=SLN(50000,10000,5)
```

The function returns the value 8000.00. To calculate the depreciation for the second year, you use the same formula because straight-line depreciation is the same for each year period.

SYD

The SYD function calculates sum-of-the-years'-digits depreciation for an asset given the cost, its salvage value, estimated economic life, and the accounting period for which depreciation is being calculated. The SYD function uses the following syntax:

```
SYD(cost,salvage,life,period)
```

Suppose, for example, that you must calculate the sum-of-the-years'-digits depreciation for equipment that costs $50,000, lasts five years, and will have a salvage value of $10,000 at the end of the fifth year. To calculate the depreciation for the first year, use the following formula:

```
=SYD(50000,10000,5,1)
```

The function returns the value 13333.33. To calculate the depreciation for the second year, use the following formula:

```
=SYD(50000,10000,5,2)
```

The function returns the value 10666.67.

VDB

The VDB function calculates declining balance depreciation for an asset given the cost, its salvage value, estimated economic life, the starting accounting period and the ending accounting period for which depreciation is being calculated, the factor at which the balance declines, and, optionally, a switch-to-straight-line switch which is set to either TRUE or FALSE. If you set this switch to TRUE, Excel doesn't switch to straight-line at the point when straight-line depreciation exceeds declining balance depreciation. If you set this value to FALSE, Excel does switch to straight-line. If you don't set the optional switch-to-straight-line switch to TRUE, Excel sets this value to FALSE.

The VDB function uses the following syntax:

```
VDB(cost,salvage,life,start period,end period,factor,switch)
```

Suppose, for example, that you must calculate 150% declining balance depreciation for equipment that costs $50,000, lasts five years, and will have a salvage value of $10,000 at the end of the fifth year. To calculate the depreciation for the first year, you use the following formula:

```
=VDB(50000,10000,5,0,1,150%)
```

The function returns the value 15000.00. Notice that to calculate depreciation for the first year, you set the start period to 0 and the end period to 1. To calculate the depreciation for the second year, use the following formula:

```
=VDB(50000,10000,5,1,2,150%)
```

The function returns the value 10500.00. Notice that to calculate the depreciation for the second year, you set the start period to 1 and the end period to 2.

In both of the two preceding examples, Excel will automatically switch to straight-line depreciation at the point when straight-line depreciation for a period exceeds declining balance depreciation. To instruct Excel not to make this switch, use the following formula to calculate depreciation for the first year:

```
=VDB(50000,10000,5,0,1,150%,TRUE)
```

The word TRUE, which Excel interprets as 1, tells Excel not to switch to straight line. To instruct Excel not to make this switch in the second year, use the following formula to calculate depreciation:

```
=VDB(50000,10000,5,1,2,150%,TRUE)
```

Using the Payment Functions

Excel provides five standard payment functions: IPMT, ISPMT, NPER, PMT, and PPMT. Typically, you use these functions to calculate loan payment information. You can also use them for investment annuity calculations. The paragraphs that follow describe each of these payment functions and give examples of each. As you work with each, however, keep two factors in mind:

- Be sure that you stay consistent in your period assumptions between the payment and the term and rate. In other words, if you work with monthly payments, your term and interest rate must also be expressed as monthly amounts. And if you work with annual payments, your term and interest rate must also be expressed as annual amounts.
- Note that you must use the sign of a value to indicate whether it is a cash inflow or cash outflow. An initial loan balance—assuming you're the borrower—should be shown as a positive value because it represents a cash inflow. And loan payments as well as any balloon payments—again, assuming you're the borrower—should be shown as negative values because they represent cash outflows. Note, too, that Excel uses signs of values in the same ways. It shows cash inflows as positive values and cash outflows as negative values.

You must keep both of these factors in mind as you work with the financial functions and especially as you work with the payment functions.

NOTE *In keeping with the naming conventions employed by Excel, this book uses* rate *to refer to the periodic interest rate,* period *to refer to the payment period,* pmt *to refer to the regular payment or annuity amount,* nper *to refer to the term,* pv *to refer to the present value, and* fv *to refer to the future value.*

IPMT

The IPMT function calculates the interest portion of a payment given its interest rate, the period, the term (or number of payments), present value (or loan balance), future value (or balloon payment), and, optionally, the type-of-annuity switch. If you set the type-of-annuity switch to 1, Excel assumes payments occur at the beginning of the period, following the annuity due convention. If you set the annuity switch to 0, or you omit the argument, Excel assumes payments occur at the end of the period following the ordinary annuity convention.

The function uses the following syntax:

```
IPMT(rate,period,nper,pv,fv,type)
```

For example, to calculate the period interest rate for the 54th payment on a 30-year, $150,000 mortgage charging 8% annual interest, use the following formula:

```
=IPMT(.08/12,54,30*12,150000,0,0)
```

The function returns the value –957.51. Notice that to convert the 8% annual interest to a period interest, the formula divides the annual interest rate by 12. Notice, too, that to convert the 30-year term to a term in months, the formula multiplies 30 by 12. The function returns the interest payment amount as a negative value because it reflects a cash outflow you pay.

NOTE *If you set the* pv *argument to –150000, you indicate that you're loaning money. In this case, the function returns 957.51, a positive value, showing that the interest payment amount is a positive cash inflow.*

ISPMT

Provided for compatibility with Lotus 1-2-3, the ISPMT function calculates the straight-line interest portion of a payment given its interest rate, the period, the term (or number of payments), and present value (or loan balance).

```
ISPMT(rate,period,nper,pv)
```

For example, to calculate the period interest rate for the 54th payment on a 30-year, $150,000 mortgage charging 8% annual interest, use the following formula:

```
=ISPMT(.08/12,54,30*12,150000)
```

The function returns the value –850.00. Notice that to convert the 8% annual interest to a period interest, the formula divides the annual interest rate by 12. Notice, too, that to convert the 30-year term to a term in months, the formula multiplies 30 by 12. The function returns the interest payment amount as a negative value because it reflects a cash outflow you pay.

NPER

The NPER function calculates the term, or number of regular payments, on a loan or for an investment annuity given its interest rate, the payments, present value (or loan balance), future value (or balloon payment), and, optionally, the type-of-annuity switch. If you set the type-of-annuity switch to 1, Excel assumes payments occur at the beginning of the period, following the annuity due convention. If you set the annuity switch to 0, or you omit the argument, Excel assumes payments occur at the end of the period following the ordinary annuity convention.

The function uses the following syntax:

```
NPER(rate,pmt,pv,fv,type)
```

For example, to calculate the number of $1,000 monthly payments required to pay off a 9% mortgage that still has a $100,000 mortgage balance, use the following formula:

```
=NPER(.09/12,-1000,100000,0,0)
```

The function returns the value 185.53, representing roughly 185 payments and then another roughly half payment. Notice that to convert the 9% annual interest to a period interest, the formula divides the annual interest rate by 12. Notice, too, that the payment amount, as a cash outflow, shows as a negative value while the loan balance, as an implicit cash inflow, shows as a positive value.

NOTE *The NPER function rarely returns an integer, or whole-number result. As in the preceding example, it commonly returns a fractional value, indicating that after the last regular payment, an additional fractional payment will also need to be made.*

You can also use the NPER function to calculate investment terms. In this case, you calculate the number of payments that need to be made in order to reach some future value. Suppose, for example, that you want to calculate how many years a customer needs to contribute $2,000 to an Individual Retirement Account (IRA) in order to amass a $1,000,000 portfolio. If you assume the customer will earn 9% annually and will make payments at the beginning of the year, you use the following formula to make this estimate:

```
=NPER(.09,-2000,0,1000000,1)
```

The function returns the value 43.45 indicating the $2,000 payments will need to be made for slightly more than 43 years. Notice that the type switch is 1, which means that the function returns the amount that must be paid at the beginning of the year. If you instead want to calculate the amount that would need to be paid at the end of each year, you use the following formula to make this estimate:

```
=NPER(.09,-2000,0,1000000,0)
```

This formula returns the value 44.43. This value is slightly more than the annuity due value because by making payments at year-end, the customer loses interest.

If you wanted to make the same calculation but recognize the added fact that the customer already has $5,000 in his IRA, you use the following formula:

```
=NPER(.09,-2000,-5000,1000000,0)
```

This formula returns the value 42.07.

PMT

The PMT function calculates a payment given its interest rate, the term (or number of payments), present value (or loan balance), future value (or balloon payment), and, optionally, the type-of-annuity switch. If you set the type-of-annuity switch to 1, Excel assumes payments occur at the beginning of the period, following the annuity due convention. If you set the annuity switch to 0, or you omit the argument, Excel assumes payments occur at the end of the period following the ordinary annuity convention.

The function uses the following syntax:

```
PMT(rate,nper,pv,fv,type)
```

For example, to calculate the payment on a 30-year, $150,000 mortgage charging 8% annual interest, use the following formula:

```
=PMT(.08/12,30*12,150000,0,0)
```

The function returns the value −1100.65. Notice that to convert the 8% annual interest to a period interest, the formula divides the annual interest rate by 12. Notice, too, that to convert the 30-year term to a term in months, the formula multiplies 30 by 12. The function returns the interest payment amount as a negative value because it reflects a cash outflow you pay.

NOTE *If you set the* pv *argument to −150000, you indicate that you're actually loaning money. And in this case, the function returns 1100.65, a positive value, showing that the payment amount is a positive cash inflow.*

For example, to calculate the payment on a 30-year, $150,000 mortgage charging 8% annual interest that has a $25,000 balloon payment, use the following formula:

```
=PMT(.08/12,30*12,150000,-25000,0)
```

The function returns the value −1083.87. Notice that the balloon payment argument appears as a negative value because it represents a cash outflow.

NOTE *If you set the* fv *argument to 25000, you indicate that you're actually receiving a final payment from the lender. In this case, the function returns −1117.42, which is larger than required to pay off the loan. The extra payment, in effect, gets invested at the loan interest rate and future values to the $25,000.*

NOTE *You can easily calculate the total payments made on a loan. To do this, multiply the payment amount, as calculated by the PMT function, by the number of payments. Note that once you have this result, you can also easily calculate the total interest paid on a loan, too. To do this, subtract the loan balance from the total payments.*

While you'll most typically use the PMT function to calculate loan payments, you can also use it to calculate the payment required to accumulate some future value. Suppose, for example, that you want to calculate how large a contribution an employee would need to make into a 401(k) account in order to amass a $1,000,000 portfolio over 35 years. If you assume the employee will earn 9% annually, you use the following formula to make this estimate:

```
=PMT(.09,35,0,1000000,0)
```

The function returns the value −4635.84. Notice that the type switch is 0, which means that function returns the amount that must be paid at the end of the year.

If you instead want to calculate the amount that would need to be paid at the beginning of each month, you use the following formula to make this estimate:

```
=PMT(.09/12,35*12,0,1000000,1)
```

This formula returns the value −337.40. This value is slightly less than one-twelfth of the annual, ordinary annuity value because by making payments throughout the year at the start of each month, the employee earns additional interest.

If you wanted to make the same calculation but also recognize the added fact that the employee already has $10,000 in her 401(k) account, you use the following formula:

```
=PMT(.09/12,35*12,-10000,1000000,1)
```

This formula returns the value −259.58.

PPMT

The PPMT function calculates the principal portion of a payment given its interest rate, the period, the term (or number of payments), present value (or loan balance), future value (or balloon payment), and, optionally, the type-of-annuity switch. If you set the type-of-annuity switch to 1, Excel assumes payments occur at the beginning of the period, following the annuity due convention. If you set the annuity switch to 0, or you omit the argument, Excel assumes payments occur at the end of the period following the ordinary annuity convention.

The function uses the following syntax:

```
PPMT(rate,period,nper,pv,fv,type)
```

For example, to calculate the period principal payment for the 54th payment on a 30-year, $150,000 mortgage charging 8% annual interest, use the following formula:

```
=PPMT(.08/12,54,30*12,150000,0,0)
```

The function returns the value −143.13. Notice that to convert the 8% annual interest to a period interest, the formula divides the annual interest rate by 12. Notice, too, that to convert the 30-year term to a term in months, the formula multiplies 30 by 12. The function returns the principal payment amount as a negative value because it reflects a cash outflow you pay.

NOTE *If you set the* pv *argument to −150000, you indicate that you're actually loaning money. And in this case, the function returns 143.13, a positive value, showing that the principal payment amount is a positive cash inflow.*

Using the Present Value, Future Value, and Interest Rate Functions

Excel rounds out its standard financial function set with six additional functions for calculating present values, future values, and interest rates, or rates of return, including FV, IRR, MIRR, NPV, PV, and RATE.

The paragraphs that follow describe each of these functions and give examples of each. As you work with each function, remember that you need to keep two factors in mind:

- Be sure that you stay consistent in your period assumptions between the payment and the term and rate. In other words, if you work with monthly payments, your term and interest rate must also be expressed as monthly amounts. And if you work with annual payments, your term and interest rate must also be expressed as annual amounts.
- Note that you must use the sign of a value to indicate whether it is a cash inflow or cash outflow. A present value—assuming you're the investor—should be shown as a negative value because it represents a cash outflow. And annuity amounts as well as any balloon payments—again, assuming you're the investor—should be shown as positive if they represent cash inflows and as negative values if they represent cash outflows. Note, too, that Excel uses signs of values in the same ways. It shows cash inflows as positive values and cash outflows as negative values.

NOTE *In keeping with the naming conventions employed by Excel, this book uses* rate *to refer to the periodic interest rate,* period *to refer to the payment period,* pmt *to refer to the regular payment or annuity amount,* nper *to refer to the term,* pv *to refer to the present value, and* fv *to refer to the future value.*

FV

The FV function calculates the future value of a loan or investment given its interest rate, the term (or number of payments), the payment, the present value (or loan balance), and, optionally, the type-of-annuity switch. If you set the type-of-annuity switch to 1, Excel assumes payments occur at the beginning of the period, following the annuity due convention. If you set the annuity switch to 0, or you omit the argument, Excel assumes payments occur at the end of the period following the ordinary annuity convention.

The function uses the following syntax:

```
FV(rate,nper,pmt,pv,type)
```

For example, to calculate the future value of a $200-a-month savings program over 25 years assuming that the investor starts with $10,000 and earns 10% annual interest, use the following formula:

```
=FV(10%/12,25*12,-200,-10000,0)
```

The function returns the value 385936.13. Notice that to convert the 10% annual interest to a monthly interest rate, the formula divides the annual interest rate by 12. Notice, too, that to convert the 25-year term to a term in months, the formula multiplies 25 by 12. The monthly payment and initial present values show as negative amounts because they represent cash outflows. And the function returns the future value amount as a positive value because it reflects a cash inflow the investor ultimately receives.

You can also use the FV function to estimate loan balloon payment amounts. Suppose, for example, that you want to calculate the balloon payment required to pay off a $150,000 mortgage with an 8% annual interest rate after the buyer has been making $1,200-a-month payments for 10 years. Use the following formula to make this estimate:

```
=FV(8%/12,10*12,-1200,150000,0)
```

The function returns the value −113410.79. Notice that the interest rate is divided by 12 and the number of years of payments is multiplied by 12 to adjust these figures to monthly amounts. Also, notice that the monthly payment amount shows as a negative value to show it represents a cash outflow, and the initial loan balance shows as a positive value to show that it represents a cash inflow.

NOTE *Excel also supplies an FVSCHEDULE function, which lets you calculate a future value using varying annual interest rates. The FVSCHEDULE function is described in the later section "Using the Future Value Add-In Functions."*

IRR

The IRR calculates the internal rate of return implicit in a set of cash flows given a values argument (usually a worksheet range holding the cash flow values), and, optionally, a guess at the internal rate of return value. The internal rate of return of a set of cash flows is the discount rate that produces a net present value equal to zero.

NOTE *Excel also provides a net present value function, NPV.*

The function uses the following syntax:

```
IRR(values,guess)
```

For example, if you store the cash flows from an investment in a worksheet like the one shown in Figure 5-3, you can use the following formula to calculate the investment's internal rate of return:

```
=IRR(B1:B11)
```

The function returns the value 27.13%.

B13 | fx =IRR(B1:B11)

	A	B	C
1	Initial investment	-25000	
2	Year 1 cash flow	8000	
3	Year 2 cash flow	7000	
4	Year 3 cash flow	8000	
5	Year 4 cash flow	8000	
6	Year 5 cash flow	8000	
7	Year 6 cash flow	6000	
8	Year 7 cash flow	7000	
9	Year 8 cash flow	7000	
10	Year 9 cash flow	7000	
11	Year 10 cash flow	5000	
12			
13	IRR	27.13%	
14			

Figure 5-3 A simple worksheet illustrating how an IRR function works.

You'll want to consider several factors if you use the IRR function:

- The values argument needs to contain at least one positive value and at least one negative value. If your investment doesn't meet these requirements, it doesn't look enough like an investment to be measured by the IRR function.
- The order of the cash flows in the values argument should reflect their actual order: the first cash flow first, the second cash flow second, and so on.
- The cash flow periods must be consistent. In Figure 5-3, for example, the cash flow periods are all years—and that works. But you can't mix and match annual and monthly cash flow in such a values range.

NOTE *If your values range includes a cell that includes a label, a logical value, or an empty cell, that cell is ignored in the IRR calculations.*

Although you aren't required to use a guess argument because Excel assumes an initial guess of 10%, you may need to do so. Excel attempts to solve the IRR function's equation iteratively. If the equation can't be solved after 20 attempts to within .00001, the function returns the #NUM error value. Excel usually succeeds if the internal rate of return value is close to typical returns (say, between −10% and 30%), but it sometimes has trouble with returns that are outside this range. In this case, if you supply a guess argument that's close to the actual internal rate of return value, you in effect help Excel start its search close to its destination.

One consideration in using the IRR function is that theoretically it doesn't actually have a single correct solution. In practice, a set of cash flows will sometimes have as many valid internal rates of return as there are sign changes.

In the worksheet shown in Figure 5-3, only one cash flow sign change occurs (from negative cash flow at the start of the investment to positive cash flow in year one). In a case like that shown in Figure 5-4, however, the IRR function can actually return two valid internal rate-of-return values because there are two sign changes—one between the initial investment and the first-year cash flow and another between the first-year cash flow and the second-year cash flow.

C7 | =IRR(C1:C3,50%)

	A	B	C	D
1	Initial investment		-50000	
2	Year 1 cash flow		150000	
3	Year 2 cash flow		-100000	
4				
5	IRR if no guess		0%	
6				
7	IRR if guess is 50%		100%	
8				

Figure 5-4 A simple worksheet illustrating how an IRR function can sometimes malfunction.

If you don't supply a guess, Excel calculates the internal rate of return to be equal to zero. If you happen to supply a large guess value—the worksheet in Figure 5-4 uses a guess equal to 50%—Excel calculates the internal rate of return to be equal to 100%. Both calculations are right. What's happening is that Excel finds the calculation result that's closest to your guess or its guess.

NOTE *Excel also supplies an XIRR function, which lets you calculate an internal rate of return for an investment with irregular cash flows but without having to construct a worksheet schedule of the cash flows. The XIRR function is described in the later section "Using the Capital Budgeting Add-In Functions."*

MIRR

The MIRR function calculates the modified internal rate of return implicit in a set of cash flows given the cash flow values (usually a worksheet range holding the cash flow values), the finance rate, and the reinvestment rate. This rate of return calculation differs from the IRR function's calculation (described in the preceding paragraphs) in two ways: it assumes that interim cash inflows are reinvested at some specified rate of return, and it assumes that interim cash outflows are funded by borrowing at some specified interest rate.

NOTE *Unlike the IRR function, you should be able to calculate a single, unique return measure using the MIRR function—as long as the function arguments make sense.*

The function uses the following syntax:

```
MIRR(values,finance rate,reinvest rate)
```

For example, if you store the cash flows from an investment in a worksheet such as the one shown in Figure 5-5, you will borrow money at 10% to pay for the first year's cash outflow, and then you will reinvest the cash flows in years two through ten at 12%. Use the following formula to calculate the investment's modified rate of return:

```
=MIRR(C1:C11,.1,.12)
```

The function returns the value 12.43%.

C13 =MIRR(C1:C11,0.1,0.12)

	A	B	C	D	E
1	Initial investment		-100000		
2	Year 1 cash flow		-50000		
3	Year 2 cash flow		30000		
4	Year 3 cash flow		35000		
5	Year 4 cash flow		30000		
6	Year 5 cash flow		25000		
7	Year 6 cash flow		30000		
8	Year 7 cash flow		35000		
9	Year 8 cash flow		35000		
10	Year 9 cash flow		35000		
11	Year 10 cash flow		35000		
12					
13	Modified IRR		12.43%		
14					

Figure 5-5 A simple worksheet illustrating how a MIRR function works.

While it's not clear from the Excel documentation that this is the case, MIRR discounts any interim cash outflows back to an equivalent present value using the finance rate and compounds any interim cash inflows out to an equivalent future value amount using the reinvestment rate. The modified internal rate of return value, then, is the rate that equates the initial present value of the cash outflows with the future value of the cash inflows.

As with the IRR function, you'll want to consider several factors if you use the MIRR function:

- The values argument needs to contain at least one positive value and at least one negative value. If your investment doesn't meet these requirements, it doesn't look enough like an investment to be measured by the MIRR function.
- The order of the cash flows in the values argument should reflect their actual order: the first cash flow first, the second cash flow second, and so on.
- The cash flow periods must be consistent. In Figure 5-5, for example, the cash flow periods are all years.

NOTE *If your values range includes a cell that includes a label, a logical value, or an empty cell, that cell is ignored in the IRR calculations.*

NPV

The NPV function calculates the net present value of a set of cash flows given the discount rate and the cash flow values (usually a worksheet range holding the cash flow values). If you are using the NPV function to compare alternative investments, the investment opportunity with the largest NPV is the one that generates the largest profit in absolute, present value terms.

The function uses the following syntax:

```
NPV(rate,values)
```

For example, if you store the cash flows from an investment in a worksheet such as the one shown in Figure 5-6 (with the same cash flows as those shown in Figure 5-5), use the following formula to calculate the investment's modified rate of return:

```
=NPV(C13,C1:C11)
```

The function returns the value $5,798.18.

C15 | =NPV(C13,C1:C11)

	A	B	C	D	E
1	Initial investment		-100000		
2	Year 1 cash flow		-50000		
3	Year 2 cash flow		30000		
4	Year 3 cash flow		35000		
5	Year 4 cash flow		30000		
6	Year 5 cash flow		25000		
7	Year 6 cash flow		30000		
8	Year 7 cash flow		35000		
9	Year 8 cash flow		35000		
10	Year 9 cash flow		35000		
11	Year 10 cash flow		35000		
12					
13	Discount Rate		12.00%		
14					
15	Net Present Value		$5,798.18		
16					

Figure 5-6 A simple worksheet illustrating how an NPV function works.

You'll want to consider several factors if you use the NPV function:

- The NPV function assumes that the first cash flow occurs immediately, or at what's sometimes referred to as period 0.
- The rate argument needs to be the discount rate for the time period used to calibrate cash flows. In other words, if you're using monthly cash flows, your discount rate needs to be a monthly rate.
- The values argument can include more than one cell or range. You can, for example, use the NPV function NPV(.1,A1,A2,A3,A4:A8).
- The order of the cash flows in the values argument should reflect their actual order: the first cash flow first, the second cash flow second, and so on.
- The NPV function recognizes empty cells, or cells that contain text labels as zeroes in its calculations. However, if you include an array, any empty cells or cells containing text labels are ignored.

NOTE *The NPV function and the IRR functions are related and, in fact, use the same formula (although in different ways). In effect, what the IRR function does is calculate the discount rate at which the net present value equals zero. This discount rate is the internal rate of return.*

NOTE *Excel also supplies an XNPV function, which lets you calculate a net present value for an investment with irregular cash flows but without having to construct a worksheet schedule of the cash flows. The XNPV function is described in the later section "Using the Capital Budgeting Add-In Functions."*

PV

The PV function calculates the present value of an annuity, or future value, given the periodic rate, number of periods, payment, future value (or balloon payment), and, optionally, the type-of-annuity switch. If you set the type-of-annuity switch to 1, Excel assumes payments occur at the beginning of the period, following the annuity due convention. If you set the annuity switch to 0, or you omit the argument, Excel assumes payments occur at the end of the period following the ordinary annuity convention.

The function uses the following syntax:

```
PV(rate,nper,pmt,fv,type)
```

For example, if you want to estimate the outstanding balance on a mortgage loan that charges 8%, requires two hundred more $1,000-a-month payments, and also requires a $10,000 balloon payment, use the following formula:

```
=PV(.08/12,200,-1000,-10000)
```

The function returns the value $112,932.75.

NOTE *You must include either the payment (or pmt) argument or the future value argument (or fv) in order to calculate the present value. The PV function, predictably, needs something—either a payment stream or a future value—to calculate the present value of.*

RATE

The RATE function calculates the interest rate implicit in a set of loan or investment terms given the number of periods, the payment, the present value, the future value, and, optionally, the type-of-annuity switch, and also optionally, an interest rate.

If you set the type-of-annuity switch to 1, Excel assumes payments occur at the beginning of the period, following the annuity due convention. If you set the annuity switch to 0, or you omit the argument, Excel assumes payments occur at the end of the period following the ordinary annuity convention.

The function uses the following syntax:

```
RATE(nper,pmt,pv,fv,type,guess)
```

For example, suppose you want to calculate the implicit interest rate on a car lease that requires five years of $250-a-month payments (occurring as an annuity due) and also a $15,000 balloon payment. To do this, assuming you want to start with a guess of 10%, use the following formula:

```
=RATE(5*12,-250,20000,-15000,1)
```

The function returns the value .95%, which is a monthly interest rate of just less than 1%. If you annualize this monthly rate by multiplying it by 12, you get an equivalent annual interest rate of 11.41%.

NOTE *Excel solves the RATE function iteratively starting with the guess argument you provide. (If you don't provide this optional argument, Excel uses 10%.) If Excel can't solve the RATE argument within 20 attempts, it returns the #NUM! error. You can try a different guess argument, which may help because you're telling Excel to begin its search from a different starting point.*

Using the Add-In Financial Functions

In addition to Excel's 16 standard financial functions, Excel users also have access to another 42 add-in financial functions. Most business users of Excel won't need these add-in functions, but if you perform much financial analysis with Excel—especially financial analysis of investments—you'll find frequent occasion to use these tools.

NOTE *To use the add-in financial functions, you may need to install the Analysis ToolPak add-in. To install the Analysis ToolPak, choose the Tools menu's Add-Ins command, select the Analysis ToolPak check box, and click OK. Excel may prompt you to insert the Office 2002 or Excel 2002 CD if it isn't currently in your CD-ROM drive.*

Once you've installed the Analysis ToolPak, you can work with the add-in financial functions. You use these functions in the same way that you use other functions, including the financial functions described in the earlier pages of this chapter. The paragraphs that follow describe each of these add-in functions.

Using the Accrued Interest Add-In Functions

Excel provides two functions that help you with accrued interest calculations for securities that pay interest. ACCRINT calculates accrued interest for a security (such as a bond) that pays periodic interest. ACCRINTM calculates accrued interest for a security (such as a zero-coupon bond) that pays interest upon maturity.

The accrued interest functions use a similar set of arguments, including the issue date, first interest date, settlement date, maturity date, coupon rate, par value, frequency, and basis.

The date arguments are self-explanatory for the most part. The issue date is the date the security is issued. The first interest payment date is the first coupon date. The settlement date is the date you purchased, or settled, the bond. The maturity date is the date the bond matures, or expires. You may enter the date arguments either as text strings enclosed in quotation marks (for example, "7/4/99") or as serial date values (for example, 37000 for April 19, 2001).

The coupon rate and par value arguments let Excel calculate the interest. The coupon rate is the annual interest rate multiplied by the par value to calculate the annual interest. For example, if a bond pays 8% interest annually and the par value is $1,000, Excel would calculate the annual interest by multiplying the 8% by the $1,000 if the coupon is paid annually.

The frequency argument gives the number of coupon payments made each year: you specify 1 to indicate an annual coupon, 2 to indicate a semiannual coupon, and 4 to indicate a quarterly coupon.

The basis argument specifies the number of days in the month and in the year assumed for the date calculations. You specify the basis as 0 for the US (or NASD) version of 30 days in a month and 360 days in a year; as 1 for the actual number of days in the month and year; 2 for the actual number of days in the month but 360 days in a year; 3 for the actual number of days in the month and 365 days in a year; and 4 for the European version of 30 days in a month and 360 days in a year.

Both the ACCRINT and ACCRINTM functions return an error value in the following situations:

- If you enter an invalid date argument, Excel returns #VALUE.
- If the coupon rate or par value argument is less than 0, Excel returns #NUM.
- If the payment frequency is some number other than 1, 2, or 4, Excel returns #NUM.
- If the day-count-basis switch isn't 1, 2, 3, or 4, Excel returns #NUM.
- If issue date follows the settlement date, Excel returns #NUM.

ACCRINT

The ACCRINT function calculates the accrued interest for a security that pays periodic interest given the issue date, first interest payment date, settlement date, coupon rate, par value, payment frequency, and a day-count-basis switch. It uses the following syntax:

```
ACCRINT(issue,first interest,settlement,rate,par,frequency,basis)
```

For example, if you want to calculate the accrued interest on a bond that was issued on February 8, 2000, first paid interest on April 8, 2000, was purchased on May 23, 2001, pays an 8% coupon, shows a $1,000 par value, pays interest four times a year, and uses the US, or NASD, day-count-basis assumption, use the following formula:

```
=ACCRINT("2/8/00","4/8/00","5/23/01",0.08,1000,4,0)
```

The function returns the value 103.33.

ACCRINTM

The ACCRINTM function calculates the accrued interest for a security that pays interest at maturity given the issue date, the maturity date, coupon rate, par value, and a day-count-basis switch. It uses the following syntax:

```
ACCRINTM(issue,maturity,rate,par,basis)
```

For example, if you want to calculate the accrued interest on a bond that was issued on February 8, 1991, matures on May 23, 2010, accrues an 8% coupon, shows a $1,000 par value, accrues interest two times a year, and uses the US, or NASD, day-count-basis assumption, use the following formula:

```
=ACCRINTM("2/8/91","5/23/10",0.08,1000,2)
```

The function returns the value 1565.33.

Using the Bond Duration Add-In Functions

Excel provides two functions that let you make bond duration calculations: DURATION and MDURATION. Duration, a weighted average measure of the present value of a bond's cash flows, quantifies how a change in the bond yield affects the bond price.

Both duration functions use the same set of six arguments: the settlement date, the maturity date, the coupon rate, the yield, the coupon frequency, and the day-count basis. The settlement date specifies the date the bond is settled, or purchased. The maturity date specifies the date the bond matures, or expires. As with the other add-in financial functions, you may enter the date arguments either as text strings enclosed in quotation marks or as serial date values.

The coupon rate argument is the bond's interest rate and is used to calculate coupon payments. The yield argument is the bond's annual yield.

NOTE *Both duration functions assume that the bond's face, or par, value equals $100.*

The frequency argument gives the number of coupon payments made each year: you specify 1 to indicate an annual coupon, 2 to indicate a semiannual coupon, and 4 to indicate a quarterly coupon.

The basis argument specifies the number of days in the month and year assumed for the date calculations. You specify the basis as 0 for the US (or NASD) version of 30 days in a month and 360 days in a year; as 1 for the actual number of days in the month and year; 2 for the actual number of days in the month but 360 days in a year; 3 for the actual number of days in the month and 365 days in a year; and 4 for the European version of 30 days in a month and 360 days in a year.

NOTE *Excel uses only the integer portion of the arguments you supply to the add-in price and yield date functions. If you enter an argument with decimal values, Excel truncates the argument to just its integer component.*

The duration functions return an error value in several predictable cases:

- If you use an invalid date, Excel returns #VALUE. Note that this means your date arguments must make sense collectively, too. For example, your maturity date must follow the settlement date.
- If you use a frequency argument other than 1, 2, or 4, Excel returns #NUM.
- If you use a day-count-basis switch other than 0, 1, 2, 3, or 4, Excel returns #NUM.
- If the settlement day follows the maturity date, Excel returns #NUM.
- If the rate or yield is less than zero, Excel returns #NUM.

DURATION

The DURATION function calculates a Macauley duration given the settlement date, maturity date, coupon rate, yield, frequency, and basis. It uses the following syntax:

```
DURATION(settlement,maturity,coupon,yield,frequency,basis)
```

For example, suppose you want to calculate the duration of a bond you purchased on April 23, 2000, and that will mature on November 30, 2020. Further suppose that the coupon rate is 8%, which is paid in four quarterly payments, but that the bond yield is 7%. If you want to use the US (NASD) day-count basis of 30 days in a month and 360 days in a year, you use the following formula to calculate this bond's yield:

```
=DURATION("4/23/2000","11/30/2020",.08,.07,4,0)
```

The formula returns the value 10.6496.

MDURATION

The MDURATION function calculates a modified duration given the settlement date, maturity date, coupon rate, yield, frequency, and basis. It uses the following syntax:

```
MDURATION(settlement,maturity,coupon,yield,frequency,basis)
```

For example, suppose you want to calculate the duration of a bond you purchased on April 23, 2000, and that will mature on November 30, 2020. Further suppose that the coupon rate is 8%, which is paid in four quarterly payments, but that the bond yield is 7%. If you want to use the US (NASD) day-count basis of 30 days in a month and 360 days in a year, you use the following formula to calculate this bond's yield:

```
=MDURATION("4/23/2000","11/30/2020",.08,.07,4,0)
```

The formula returns the value 10.4664.

Using the Capital Budgeting Add-In Functions

Excel provides standard functions, IRR and NPV, for calculating the internal rate of return and net present value of a set of cash flows. While most often you'll want to use these two functions, they may sometimes present a practical problem: Both the IRR and NPV functions assume you've first constructed a worksheet that arranges the cash flows into equal periods. In other words, to use the IRR or NPV function, you must first construct a worksheet that shows the investment's monthly cash flows, or its annual cash flows, or the cash flows from some other consistent time period.

Unlike the IRR and the NPV functions, the XIRR and XNPV functions don't require you to first construct a worksheet schedule that arranges the investment cash flows into equal periods. With the XIRR and XNPV functions, you supply the date values that correspond to the cash flow values to the function as arguments.

NOTE *You might want to review this chapter's earlier discussion of the IRR and NPV function if you have questions about how these two capital budgeting tools work.*

The somewhat unique feature of both the XIRR and the XNPV function is that if you supply the actual date values or cash flow values inside the formula as arguments, they expect you to supply the values argument and the dates argument as arrays. (An array is just a set of numbers.)

For example, suppose that you want to calculate the internal rate of return and net present value for an investment that produces the following cash flows on the following dates:

```
1/1/2001    -1000

12/31/2001  -1000
```

```
4/15/2002    2000
12/31/2002   1000
```

If you include the actual array in the argument, you can designate the array by enclosing the values and dates arguments inside braces. To show the preceding date values in an array, for example, you would type the following:

```
{"1/1/2001","12/31/2001","4/15/2002","12/31/2002"}
```

To show the preceding cash flow values as an array, you would type the following:

```
{-1000,-1000,2000,1000}
```

If you enter the date values and cash flow values in worksheet ranges, you don't need to worry about identifying the date values and cash flow values as arrays. For example, if you enter the preceding set of date values in the worksheet range A1:A4 and the preceding set of cash flow values in the worksheet range B1:B4, you can use these worksheet ranges as the function arguments.

The XIRR and XNPV functions, predictably, require you to use date values that are valid. You must also use the same number of date values as you use cash flow values. If you supply an invalid argument or set of arguments, Excel returns the #NUM error value.

NOTE *Excel considers the first date value to be the starting date of the investment. Accordingly, the first date value in your array or worksheet range must be the earliest. Subsequent date values don't have to be in chronological order, however.*

XIRR

The XIRR function calculates the internal rate of return for an investment given its cash flows, the dates of those cash flows, and, optionally, an initial guess as to the internal rate of return. The function uses the following syntax:

```
XIRR(values,dates,guess)
```

For example, suppose that you want to calculate the internal rate of return for an investment that produces the following cash flows on the following dates:

```
1/1/2001     -1000
12/31/2001   -1000
4/15/2002    2000
12/31/2002   1000
```

To calculate the internal rate of return for this set of cash flows using the XIRR function and using a starting guess of 20%, use the following formula:

```
=XIRR({-1000,-1000,2000,1000},{"1/1/2001","12/31/2001","4/15/2002","12/31/
2002"},.2)
```

The formula returns the value .470251, which is equivalent to 47.0251% annually.

If the date values were stored in the worksheet range A1:A4 and the cash flow values were stored in the worksheet range B1:B4, you could instead use the following formula:

```
=XIRR(B1:B4,A1:A4,.2)
```

XNPV

The XNPV function calculates the net present value for an investment given its cash flows, the dates of those cash flows, and the annual discount rate. The function uses the following syntax:

```
XNPV(rate,values,dates)
```

For example, suppose that you want to calculate the net present value for an investment that produces the following cash flows on the following dates:

```
1/1/2001     -1000

12/31/2001   -1000

4/15/2002    2000

12/31/2002   1000
```

If the date values were stored in the worksheet range A1:A4, the cash flow values were stored in the worksheet range B1:B4, and you wanted to use a discount rate of 15%, you use the following formula:

```
=XNPV(.15,B1:B4,A1:A4)
```

The formula returns the value 557.17.

Curiously, the XNPV function doesn't accept date values supplied as text strings. For example, although the following formula is equivalent to the preceding one, it returns the #VALUE error value:

```
=XNPV(.15,{-1000,-1000,2000,1000},{"1/1/2001","12/31/2001","4/15/
2002","12/31/2002"})
```

You could, however, rewrite this formula using equivalent serial date values (the serial date 36892 for 1/1/2001, the serial date value 37256 for 12/31/2001, and so on), and then Excel returns the correct net present value:

```
=XNPV(0.15,{-1000,-1000,2000,1000},{36892,37256,37361,37621})
```

Using the Coupon Dates Add-In Functions

Excel provides six functions that let you make coupon date calculations more easily: COUPDAYBS, COUPDAYS, COUPDAYSNC, COUPNCD, COUPNUM, and COUPPCD.

All six coupon date functions use four standard arguments: the settlement date, the maturity date, the frequency, and the basis.

The settlement date specifies thc date the bond is settled, or purchased. The maturity date specifies the date the bond matures, or expires. You may enter these date arguments either as text strings enclosed in quotation marks or as serial date values.

The frequency argument gives the number of coupon payments made each year: you specify 1 to indicate an annual coupon, 2 to indicate a semiannual coupon, and 4 to indicate a quarterly coupon.

The basis argument specifies the number of days in the month and year assumed for the date calculations. You specify the basis as 0 for the US (or NASD) version of 30 days in a month and 360 days in a year; as 1 for the actual number of days in the month and year; 2 for the actual number of days in the month but 360 days in a year; 3 for the actual number of days in the month and 365 days in a year; and 4 for the European version of 30 days in a month and 360 days in a year.

NOTE *Excel uses only the integer portion of the arguments you supply to the add-in coupon date functions. If you enter an argument with decimal values, Excel truncates the argument to just its integer component.*

The coupon date functions return an error value in several predictable cases:

- If you use an invalid date, Excel returns #VALUE.
- If you use a frequency argument other than 1, 2, or 4, Excel returns #NUM.
- If you use a day-count-basis switch other than 0, 1, 2, 3, or 4, Excel returns #NUM.
- If the settlement day follows the maturity date, Excel returns #NUM.

COUPDAYBS

The COUPDAYBS function calculates the number of days from the last coupon payment date to the settlement date given the settlement date, maturity date, coupon frequency, and basis. It uses the following syntax:

```
COUPDAYBS(settlement,maturity,frequency,basis)
```

For example, suppose you want to calculate the number of days from the last coupon payment date to the settlement date in the following situation: Someone purchases a 10-year bond on November 26, 2001, with a maturity date of April 30, 2009. The bond pays coupons twice a year based on the US, or NASD, assumption. To make this calculation, use the following formula:

```
COUPDAYBS("11/26/2000","4/30/2008",2,0)
```

The function returns the value 26.

COUPDAYS

The COUPDAYS function calculates the number of days in the coupon period that includes the settlement date given the settlement date, the maturity date, the coupon frequency, and the day-count basis. It uses the following syntax:

```
COUPDAYS(settlement,maturity,frequency,basis)
```

For example, suppose you want to calculate the number of days in the coupon payment in the following situation: Someone purchases a 10-year bond on November 26, 2001, with a maturity date of April 30, 2009. The bond pays its coupon twice a year based on the US, or NASD, assumption. To make this calculation, use the following formula:

```
=COUPDAYS("11/26/2001","4/30/2009",2,0)
```

The function returns the value 180.

COUPDAYSNC

The COUPDAYSNC function calculates the number of days from the settlement date to the next coupon date given the settlement date, the maturity date, the frequency, and the basis. It uses the following syntax:

```
COUPDAYSNC(settlement,maturity,frequency,basis)
```

For example, suppose you want to calculate the number of days from the settlement date to the next coupon payment in the following situation: Someone purchases a 10-year bond on November 26, 2001, with a maturity date of April 30, 2009. The bond pays its coupon twice a year based on the US, or NASD, assumption. To make this calculation, use the following formula:

```
=COUPDAYSNC("11/26/2001","4/30/2009",2,0)
```

The function returns the value 154.

COUPNCD

The COUPNCD function calculates the coupon date that follows the settlement date given the settlement date, the maturity date, the frequency, and the day-count-basis switch. It uses the following syntax:

```
COUPNCD(settlement,maturity,frequency,basis)
```

For example, suppose you want to calculate the next coupon payment after the settlement date in the following situation: Someone purchases a 10-year bond on November 26, 2001, with a maturity date of April 30, 2009. The bond pays its coupon twice a year based on the US, or NASD, assumption. To make this calculation, use the following formula:

```
=COUPNCD("11/26/2001","4/30/2009",2,0)
```

The function returns the value 37376, which is the serial date value for April 30, 2001.

NOTE *Excel uses serial values to represent dates: 1 for January 1, 1900, 2 for January 2, 1900, and so on. To format a serial date value to look like a date, select the cell, choose the Format menu's Cell command, click the Number tab, and choose a date format.*

COUPNUM

The COUPNUM function calculates the number of number of coupons, or interest payments, made between the settlement date and maturity date. The function, which rounds this result up to the nearest integer value, uses the following syntax:

```
COUPNUM(settlement,maturity,frequency,basis)
```

For example, suppose you want to calculate the number of coupons, or interest payments, in the following situation: Someone purchases a 10-year bond on November 26, 2001, with a maturity date of April 30, 2009. The bond pays its coupon twice a year based on the US, or NASD, assumption. To make this calculation, use the following formula:

```
=COUPNUM("11/26/2001","4/30/2009",2,0)
```

The function returns the value 15.

COUPPCD

The COUPPCD function calculates the coupon date before the settlement date given the settlement date, the maturity date, the frequency, and the basis. It uses the following syntax:

```
COUPPCD(settlement,maturity,frequency,basis)
```

For example, suppose you want to calculate the coupon payment date preceding the settlement date in the following situation: Someone purchases a 10-year bond on November 26, 2001, with a maturity date of April 30, 2009. The bond pays its coupon twice a year based on the US, or NASD, assumption. To make this calculation, use the following formula:

```
=COUPPCD("11/26/2001","4/30/2009",2,0)
```

The function returns the value 37195, which is the serial date value for October 31, 2001.

Using the Cumulative Interest and Principal Add-In Functions

Excel supplies two functions specifically for calculating cumulative interest and principal payments on a loan: CUMIPMT, which calculates the cumulative interest payments on a bond or note, and CUMPRINC, which calculates the cumulate principal payments on a bond or note.

Both functions use the same set of arguments, including the interest rate, the loan term (or number of periods), the loan balance (or present value), the starting date and the ending date of the period for which you want to calculate the cumulative interest or principal payments, and a type-of-annuity switch to indicate whether the stream of payments occurs as an ordinary annuity or an annuity due.

The interest rate, loan term, loan balance, and type-of-annuity-switch arguments work the same way for the CUMIPMT and CUMPRINC functions as they work for the standard financial functions.

NOTE *If you have questions about how the interest rate, loan term, loan balance, or type-of-annuity-switch arguments work, refer to the earlier section "Using the Payment Functions."*

The starting-date and ending-date arguments, as noted earlier, simply provide the starting and ending points for the period of time for which you want to calculate the cumulative interest or principal paid.

Both the CUMIPMT and CUMPRINC functions return an error value in several predictable situations as well as one surprising situation:

- If the interest rate or the loan term rate is less than or equal to zero.
- If the starting date or ending date is nonsensical or if the starting date follows the ending date.
- If the loan present value is less than or equal to zero. (Note that this means you *don't* use the convention of specifying the loan present value as a negative number to show that it's a cash outflow.)

CUMIPMT

The CUMIPMT function calculates the cumulative interest paid on a loan between two dates you specify given the interest rate, loan term, loan present value, the starting date and ending date, and the type-of-annuity switch. It uses the following syntax:

```
CUMIPMT(rate,nper,pv,start period,end period,type)
```

Suppose, for example, that you want to calculate the cumulative interest paid on a $1,000,000, 10-year equipment loan that charges 9% interest and requires monthly payments arranged as an annuity due. Further suppose that you want to calculate the cumulative interest payments made over the first 5 years, or 60 months. To make this calculation, use the following formula:

```
=CUMIPMT(.09/12,10*12,1000000,1,60,1)
```

The function returns the value −360094.

CUMPRINC

The CUMPRINC function calculates the cumulative principal paid on a loan between two dates you specify given the interest rate, loan term, loan present value, the starting date and ending date, and the type-of-annuity switch. It uses the following syntax:

```
CUMPRINC(rate,nper,pv,start period,end period,type)
```

Suppose, for example, that you want to calculate the cumulative principal paid on a $1,000,000, 10-year equipment loan that charges 9% interest and requires monthly payments arranged as an annuity due. Further suppose that you want to calculate the cumulative principal payments made over the first 5 years, or 60 months. To make this calculation, use the following formula:

```
=CUMPRINC(.09/12,10*12,1000000,1,60,1)
```

The function returns the value −394303.

Using the Dollar Pricing Add-In Functions

Excel's DOLLARDE and DOLLARFR functions let you easily convert security dollar prices from decimal prices to fractional prices or from fractional prices to decimal prices.

DOLLARDE

The DOLLARDE function, for example, converts a fractional dollar price to an equivalent decimal price based on the fractional price and the fraction's denominator. It uses the following syntax:

```
DOLLARDE(fractional price,fraction)
```

For example, to convert the fractional price 25 2/16ths to an equivalent decimal price, use the following formula:

```
=DOLLARDE(25.02,16)
```

The function returns the value 25.125.

And to convert the fractional price 25 1/8th to an equivalent decimal price, use the following formula:

```
=DOLLARDE(25.1,8)
```

This function returns the value 25.125.

DOLLARFR

The DOLLARFR functions converts a dollar decimal price into a dollar fractional price given the decimal price and the fraction's denominator. It uses the following syntax:

```
DOLLARFR(decimal price,fraction)
```

For example, to convert the price 10.125 to a fractional price in eighths, use the following formula:

```
=DOLLARFR(10.125,8)
```

The function returns the value 10.1.

Similarly, to convert the price 10.125 to a fractional price in sixteenths, use the following formula:

```
=DOLLARFR(10.125,16)
```

The function returns the value 10.02.

NOTE *When you work with the DOLLARDE and DOLLARFR functions, remember that Excel expects your fraction argument to be an integer. If it isn't, Excel uses just the integer portion. Also, Excel expects the fraction argument to be a positive value. If it isn't, Excel returns the #NUM! error value.*

Using the French Depreciation Add-In Functions

Excel supplies two special functions for making French depreciation calculations, AMORDEGRC and AMORLINC. Both functions use a similar sets of arguments, including the asset cost, purchase date, date at the end of the first period, salvage value, accounting period, depreciation rate, and basis. You specify the basis as 0 for the US (or NASD) version of 30 days in a month and 360 days in a year; as 1 for the actual number of days in the month and year; 2 for the actual number of days in the month but 360 days in a year; 3 for the actual number of days in the month and 365 days in a year; and 4 for the European version of 30 days in a month and 360 days in a year.

AMORDEGRC

The AMORDEGRC function uses the following syntax:

```
AMORDEGRC(cost,purchase date,first period,salvage,period,rate,basis)
```

For example, if you want to depreciate a piece of equipment purchased on July 15, 2001, for 3,000 French francs, using a salvage value of 600 French francs, a 15% depreciation rate, and the first accounting period ends on December 31, 2001, you use the following formula:

```
=AMORDEGRC(3000,"7/15/2001","12/31/2001",600,1,0.15,1)
```

The AMORDEGRC function returns the value 930.

You should know several points before using the AMORDEGRC function:

- The function uses different coefficients depending on the asset's estimated life. If the life of the asset falls between three and four years, the function uses a depreciation coefficient equal to 1.5. If the life of the asset falls between five and six years, the function uses a depreciation coefficient equal to 2. If the life of the asset is greater than six years, the function uses a depreciation coefficient equal to 2.5.
- To fully depreciate an asset, the depreciation rate grows to 50% for the next-to-last period and 100% for the last period.
- If you specify the estimated economic life of an asset as a non-integer value between 0 and 5—such as 4.5 for example—the AMORDEGRC function returns the #NUM! error value.

AMORLINC

The AMORLINC function uses the following syntax:

```
AMORLINC(cost,purchase date,first period,salvage,period,rate,basis)
```

For example, if you want to depreciate a piece of equipment purchased on July 15, 2001, for 3,000 French francs, using a salvage value of 600 French francs, a 15% depreciation rate, and the first accounting period ends on December 31, 2001, you use the following formula:

```
=AMORLINC(3000,"7/15/2001","12/31/2001",600,1,0.15,1)
```

The function returns the value 450.

Using the Future Value Add-In Functions

Two of the add-in functions don't really fit into one of the other categories, but because they both calculate the future value of some investment, we've grouped them together as future value functions: FVSCHEDULE and RECEIVED.

FVSCHEDULE

The FVSCHEDULE function calculates the future value of an investment given the present value of the investment and a schedule of interest rates. The function uses the following syntax:

```
FVSCHEDULE(principal,rate schedule)
```

As an example of how this function works, suppose you want to calculate the future value of an initial investment equal to $25,000 invested over the next five years at the following annual interest rates: .06, .07, .07, .08, .05. The following formula makes this calculation:

```
=FVSCHEDULE(25000,{.06,.07,.07,.08,.05})
```

If the annual interest rates are stored in the worksheet range B1:B5, as shown in Figure 5-7, you might also use the following formula:

```
=FVSCHEDULE(25000,B1:B5)
```

Both functions return the same value, 34405.39.

B7		f_x =FVSCHEDULE(25000,B1:B5)			
	A	B	C	D	E
1	Year 1 rate	0.06			
2	Year 2 rate	0.07			
3	Year 3 rate	0.07			
4	Year 4 rate	0.08			
5	Year 5 rate	0.05			
6					
7	Future Value	34405.39			
8					
9					

Figure 5-7 A worksheet set up to use the FVSCHEDULE function.

NOTE *The FVSCHEDULE function returns the #VALUE error value if you supply a nonnumeric interest rate argument. Note, however, that you can use zero or reference empty cells to show no interest.*

RECEIVED

The RECEIVED function calculates the future value amount of a fully invested, or zero-coupon, security given its settlement date, maturity date, the initial investment, the discount rate, and the basis. The function uses the following syntax:

```
RECEIVED(settlement,maturity,investment,discount,basis)
```

The settlement date specifies the date the bond is settled, or purchased. The maturity date specifies the date the bond matures, or expires. You may enter these date arguments either as text strings enclosed in quotation marks or as serial date values.

The investment is the initial amount invested, or the present value.

The discount rate specifies the annual discount rate used to price the bill.

Finally, the familiar basis argument specifies the number of days in the month and in the year assumed for the date calculations. You specify the basis as 0 for the US (or NASD) version of 30 days in a month and 360 days in a year; as 1 for the actual number of days in the month and year; 2 for the actual number of days in the month but 360 days in a year; 3 for the actual number of days in the month and 365 days in a year; and 4 for the European version of 30 days in a month and 360 days in a year.

NOTE *Excel uses only the integer portion of the arguments you supply to the add-in RECEIVED function. If you enter an argument with decimal values, Excel truncates the argument to just its integer component.*

For example, suppose you want to calculate the future value amount received for a bond you purchase on May 1, 2001, and that matures on October 31, 2003. Further suppose that you purchased the bond for $50,000 based on a 6% discount rate. If you want to use the US (or NASD) day-count-basis assumption, you use the following formula:

```
=RECEIVED("5/1/2001","10/31/2003",50000,.06,0)
```

The function returns the value 58823.53.

NOTE *The RECEIVED function returns an error value if a date argument or the set of date arguments is invalid or if the investment or discount rate is set to zero.*

Using the Interest Rate Add-In Functions

Excel provides four functions that let you make interest rate calculations: DISC, EFFECT, INTRATE, and NOMINAL.

The DISC and INTRATE functions, which are related, work from the same basic set of arguments: the settlement date, the maturity date, the redemption value, the price, the frequency, and the basis.

The settlement date specifies the date the bond is settled, or purchased. The maturity date specifies the date the bond matures, or expires. You may enter the date arguments either as text strings enclosed in quotation marks (for example, "7/4/00") or as serial date values (for example, 37365 for April 19, 2002.)

The redemption argument is the bond's redemption value per each $100 of face value.

The price argument shows the price of a bond expressed as a percentage of its face value. For example, a bond that cost $991.83 would be priced at 99.183.

The frequency argument gives the number of coupon payments made each year: you specify 1 to indicate an annual coupon, 2 to indicate a semiannual coupon, and 4 to indicate a quarterly coupon.

The basis argument specifies the number of days in the month and in the year assumed for the date calculations. You specify the basis as 0 for the US (or NASD) version of 30 days in a month and 360 days in a year; as 1 for the actual number of days in the month and year; 2 for the actual number of days in the month but 360 days in a year; 3 for the actual number of days in the month and 365 days in a year; and 4 for the European version of 30 days in a month and 360 days in a year.

The EFFECTIVE and NOMINAL functions, which are also related, work from a set of three arguments: the effective annual interest rate, the nominal interest rate, and the number of compounding periods in the year.

DISC

The DISC function calculates the discount rate for a security—the amount by which the redemption value is reduced expressed as an annual percentage—given its settlement date, maturity date, price, redemption, and basis. The function uses the following syntax:

```
DISC(settlement,maturity,price,redemption,basis)
```

For example, suppose you want to calculate the discount rate on a zero-coupon, $100 redemption-value bond that you purchased on July 10, 2001, for 99.875. If you choose to use the US (or NASD) day-count-basis assumption, you use the following formula to make this calculation:

```
=DISC("7/10/2001","11/30/2001",97.875,100,0)
```

The function returns the value .054643, which is equivalent to 5.4643%.

NOTE *The DISC function returns an error value if a date argument or the set of date arguments is invalid or if a bond price or redemption value is set to zero.*

EFFECT

The EFFECT function calculates the effective annual interest given the stated annual interest rate and the number of annual compounding periods. The function uses the following syntax:

```
EFFECT(nominal rate,compounding periods)
```

For example, if you want to calculate the effective interest rate when the nominal rate is 6%, but this rate is compounded daily (based on a 360-day year), you use the following formula:

```
=EFFECT(.06,360)
```

The function returns the value .061831, which is equivalent to 6.1831%.

NOTE *The EFFECT function returns an error value if you supply nonnumeric arguments, a nominal rate argument equal to 0, or a number of compounding periods argument equal to some value less than 1.*

INTRATE

The INTRATE function calculates the interest rate for a fully invested, or zero-coupon, security given its settlement date, maturity date, the initial investment amount, the redemption value, and the basis. The function uses the following syntax:

```
INTRATE(settlement,maturity,investment,redemption,basis)
```

For example, suppose you want to calculate the interest rate on a zero-coupon, $100 redemption-value bond that you purchased on July 10, 2001, for 99.875. If you choose to use the US (or NASD) day-count-basis assumption, you use the following formula to make this calculation:

```
=INTRATE("7/10/2001","11/30/2001",97.875,100,0)
```

The function returns the value .055829, which is equivalent to 5.5829%.

NOTE *The INTRATE function returns an error value if a date argument or the set of date arguments is invalid or if the investment or redemption value is set to zero.*

NOMINAL

The function calculates the nominal annual interest given the effective annual interest rate and the number of annual compounding periods. The function uses the following syntax:

```
NOMINAL(effective rate,compounding periods)
```

For example, if you want to calculate the nominal interest rate when the effective rate is 6.1831% and this rate is based on daily compounding (based on a 360-day year), you use the following formula:

```
=NOMINAL(.061831,360)
```

The function returns the value .06, which is equivalent to 6%.

NOTE *The EFFECT function returns an error value if you supply nonnumeric arguments, a nominal rate argument equal to 0, or a number of compounding periods argument equal to some value less than 1.*

Using the Price and Yield Add-In Functions

Excel provides 10 functions that let you make discount, yield, and price calculations for securities such as bonds more easily: ODDFPRICE, ODDFYIELD, ODDLPRICE, ODDLYIELD, PRICE, PRICEDISC, PRICEMAT, YIELD, YIELDDISC, and YIELDMAT.

NOTE *Excel's online help file supplies the actual formulas used for many of these yield and price functions.*

As a group, the 10 yield and price functions use a set of standard arguments: the settlement date, the maturity date, the frequency, and the basis.

The yield and price functions use several standard date arguments, for example. The settlement date specifies the date the bond is settled, or purchased. The maturity date specifies the date the bond matures, or expires. The issue date is the date on which a security is issued. You may enter the date arguments either as text strings enclosed in quotation marks (for example, "7/4/00") or as serial date values (for example, 37365 for April 19, 2002).

The functions for pricing odd-period securities—ODDFPRICE, ODDFYIELD, ODDLPRICE, and ODDLYIELD—also require the date of the first regular coupon payment or the date of the last regular coupon payment in order to calculate the first or last odd period.

The rate argument is the bond's interest rate. The yield argument is the bond's annual yield.

The redemption argument is the bond's redemption value per each $100 of face value.

The price argument shows the price of a bond expressed as a percentage of its face value. For example, a $1000 bond that cost $991.83 would be priced at 99.183.

The frequency argument gives the number of coupon payments made each year: you specify 1 to indicate an annual coupon, 2 to indicate a semiannual coupon, and 4 to indicate a quarterly coupon.

The basis argument specifies the number of days in the month and year assumed for the date calculations. You specify the basis as 0 for the US (or NASD) version of 30 days in a month and 360 days in a year; as 1 for the actual number of days in the month and year; 2 for the actual number of days in the month but 360 days in a year; 3 for the actual number of days in the month and 365 days in a year; and 4 for the European version of 30 days in a month and 360 days in a year.

NOTE *Excel uses only the integer portion of the arguments you supply to the add-in price and yield date functions. If you enter an argument with decimal values, Excel truncates the argument to just its integer component.*

The yield and price functions return the #NUM error value in several predictable cases:

- If you use an invalid date, Excel returns #VALUE. Note that this means your date arguments must make sense collectively, too. For example, your maturity date must follow the settlement date.

- If you use a frequency argument other than 1, 2, or 4, Excel returns #NUM.
- If you use a day-count-basis switch other than 0, 1, 2, 3, or 4, Excel returns #NUM.
- If the rate or yield or price is less than zero, Excel returns #NUM.

ODDFPRICE

The ODDFPRICE function calculates the price per $100 face value of a security when the first period is odd—shorter or longer than a typical coupon period—given the settlement date, maturity date, issue date, first coupon date, coupon rate, yield, redemption price, coupon frequency, and basis. It uses the following syntax:

```
ODDFPRICE(settlement,maturity,issue,first coupon,
rate,yield,redemption,frequency,basis)
```

Suppose, for example, that you want to calculate the price of an odd-period bond that you purchased on March 4, 2000, that will mature on May 31, 2011, was originally issued on December 7, 1999, pays a semiannual coupon of 3.5% starting on November 30, 2000, and is priced to yield 6.5% annually. Further assume that you want to use the European, 30-days-in-a-month, 360-days-in-a-year day-count basis. To make this calculation, use the following formula:

```
=ODDFPRICE("3/4/2000","5/31/2011","12/7/1999","11/30/2000",
.035*2,.065,100,2,4)
```

The function returns 100.5063.

ODDFYIELD

The ODDFYIELD function calculates the yield of a security when the first period is odd—shorter or longer than a typical coupon period—given the settlement date, maturity date, issue date, first coupon date, coupon rate, price, redemption price, coupon frequency, and basis. It uses the following syntax:

```
ODDFYIELD(settlement,maturity,issue,first coupon,rate,price,redemption,
frequency,basis)
```

Suppose, for example, that you want to calculate the price on an odd-period bond that you purchased on March 4, 2000, that will mature on May 31, 2011, was originally issued on December 7, 1999, pays a semiannual coupon of 3.5% starting on November 30, 2000, and is priced at 99.183 but will be redeemed at face value. Further assume that you want to use the European, 30-days-in-a-month, 360-days-in-a-year day-count basis. To make this calculation, use the following formula:

```
=ODDFYIELD("3/4/2000","5/31/2011","12/7/1999","11/30/2000",
.035*2,99.183,100,2,4)
```

The function returns 0.066599, which is equivalent to 6.6599%.

ODDLPRICE

The ODDLPRICE function calculates the price per $100 face value of a security when the last period is odd—shorter or longer than a typical coupon period—given the settlement date, maturity date, issue date, last coupon date, coupon rate, yield, redemption price, coupon frequency, and basis. It uses the following syntax:

```
ODDLPRICE(settlement,maturity,last coupon,
rate,yield,redemption,frequency,basis)
```

Suppose, for example, that you want to calculate the price on an odd-period bond that you purchased on March 4, 2000, that will mature on May 31, 2011, was originally issued on December 7, 1998, pays a semiannual coupon of 3.5%, last paid interest on November 30, 1999, and is priced to yield 6.5% annually. Further assume that you want to use the European, 30-days-in-a-month, 360-days-in-a-year day-count basis. To make this calculation, use the following formula:

```
=ODDLPRICE("3/4/2000","5/31/2011","11/30/1999",.035*2,.065,100,2,4)
```

The function returns 102.4757.

ODDLYIELD

The ODDLYIELD function calculates the yield of a security when the last period is odd—shorter or longer than a typical coupon period—given the settlement date, maturity date, issue date, last coupon date, coupon rate, price, redemption price, coupon frequency, and basis. It uses the following syntax:

```
ODDLYIELD(settlement,maturity,issue,last coupon,rate,price,redemption,
frequency,basis)
```

Suppose, for example, that you want to calculate the price on an odd-period bond that you purchased on March 4, 2000, that will mature on May 31, 2011, was originally issued on December 7, 1999, pays a semiannual coupon of 3.5%, last paid a coupon on November 30, 1999, and is priced at 99.183 but will be redeemed at face value. Further assume that you want to use the European, 30-days-in-a-month, 360-days-in-a-year day-count basis. To make this calculation, use the following formula:

```
=ODDLYIELD("3/4/2000","5/31/2011","11/30/1999",.035*2,99.183,100,2,4)
```

The function returns 0.070019, which is equivalent to 7.0019%.

PRICE

The PRICE function calculates the price per $100 face value of a security given the settlement date, maturity date, coupon rate, yield, redemption price, coupon frequency, and basis. It uses the following syntax:

```
PRICE(settlement,maturity,rate,yield,redemption,frequency,basis)
```

Suppose, for example, that you want to calculate the price on a bond that you purchased on March 4, 2001, that will mature on May 31, 2012, pays a semiannual coupon of 3.5%, is priced to yield 6.5% annually, and will be redeemed at face value, or 100. Further assume that you want to use the European, 30-days-in-a-month, 360-days-in-a-year day-count basis. To make this calculation, use the following formula:

```
=PRICE("3/4/2001","5/31/2012",.035*2,.065,100,2,4)
```

The function returns 103.9299.

PRICEDISC

The PRICEDISC function calculates the price per $100 face value of a discounted security given the settlement date, maturity date, discount rate, redemption price, and basis. It uses the following syntax:

```
PRICEDISC(settlement,maturity,discount,redemption,basis)
```

Suppose, for example, that you want to calculate the price on a discounted security that you purchased on March 4, 2001, that will mature on May 31, 2012, is discounted using a rate of 6.5% annually, and will be redeemed at face value, or 100. Further assume that you want to use the European, 30-days-in-a-month, 360-days-in-a-year day-count basis. To make this calculation, use the following formula:

```
=PRICEDISC("3/4/2001","5/31/2012",.065,100,4)
```

The function returns 26.9472.

PRICEMAT

The PRICEMAT function calculates the price per $100 face value of a security that will pay its interest upon maturity given the settlement date, maturity date, issue date, coupon rate, yield, and basis. It uses the following syntax:

```
PRICEMAT(settlement,maturity,issue,rate,yield,basis)
```

Suppose, for example, that you want to calculate the price on a security that you purchased on March 4, 2000, was first issued on March 4, 1999, that will mature on May 31, 2011, pays a coupon of 3.5% semiannually, and is discounted using a rate of 6.5% annually. Further assume that you want to use the European, 30-days-in-a-month, 360-days-in-a-year day-count basis. To make this calculation, use the following formula:

```
=PRICEMAT("3/4/2000","5/31/2011","3/4/1999",.035*2,.065,4)
```

The function returns 100.2923.

YIELD

The YIELD function calculates the yield of a security given the settlement date, maturity date, coupon rate, price, redemption price, coupon frequency, and basis. It uses the following syntax:

```
YIELD(settlement,maturity,rate,price,redemption,frequency,basis)
```

Suppose, for example, that you want to calculate the yield on a bond that you purchased on March 4, 2000, that will mature on May 31, 2011, pays a semiannual coupon of 3.5%, is priced at 101.1425, and will be redeemed at face value, or 100. Further assume that you want to use the European, 30-days-in-a-month, 360-days-in-a-year day-count basis. To make this calculation, use the following formula:

```
=YIELD("3/4/2000","5/31/2011",.035*2,101.1425,100,2,4)
```

The function returns 0.068507, which is equivalent to 6.8507%.

YIELDDISC

The YIELDDISC function calculates the yield of a discounted security given the settlement date, maturity date, price, redemption price, and basis. It uses the following syntax:

```
YIELDDISC(settlement,maturity,price,redemption,basis)
```

Suppose, for example, that you want to calculate the yield on a discounted security that you purchased on March 4, 2000, that will mature on May 31, 2011, is discounted at 56.1762, and will be redeemed at face value, or 100. Further assume that you want to use the European, 30-days-in-a-month, 360-days-in-a-year day-count basis. To make this calculation, use the following formula:

```
=YIELDDISC("3/4/2000","5/31/2011",56.1762,100,4)
```

The function returns 0.069412, which is equivalent to 6.9412%.

YIELDMAT

The YIELDMAT function calculates the yield of a security that will pay its interest upon maturity given the settlement date, maturity date, issue date, coupon rate, price, and basis. It uses the following syntax:

```
YIELDMAT(settlement,maturity,issue,rate,price,basis)
```

Suppose, for example, that you want to calculate the yield on a security that you purchased on March 4, 2000, was first issued on March 4, 1999, that will mature on May 31, 2011, pays a coupon of 3.5% semiannually, and is priced at 95.8194. Further assume that you want to use the European, 30-days-in-a-month, 360-days-in-a-year day-count basis. To make this calculation, use the following formula:

```
=YIELDMAT("3/4/2000","5/31/2011","3/4/1999",.035*2,95.8194,4)
```

The function returns 0.071698, which is equivalent to 7.1698%.

Using the Treasury Bill Add-In Functions

Excel provides three add-in financial functions for analyzing United States Treasury Bills: TBILLEQ, which calculates the bond-equivalent yields; TBILLPRICE, which calculates the price of a Treasury bill; and TBILLYIELD, which calculates the yield on a Treasury bill.

The Treasury bill functions use a set of standard arguments: the settlement date, the maturity date, the discount rate, and the price. The settlement date specifies the date the bill is settled, or purchased. The maturity date specifies the date the bill matures, or expires. (You may enter these date arguments either as text strings enclosed in quotation marks or as serial date values.) The discount rate specifies the annual discount rate used to price the bill. The price specifies the price per $100 of face value.

NOTE *Excel uses only the integer portion of the arguments you supply to the Treasury bill functions. If you enter an argument with decimal values, Excel truncates the argument to just its integer component.*

All three functions return an error value if the settlement or maturity date isn't a valid date, if the discount rate is less than zero, if the settlement date falls after the maturity date, or if the maturity date isn't within one year of the settlement date.

TBILLEQ

The TBILLEQ function calculates the bond-equivalent yield for a Treasury bill given its settlement date, maturity date, and a discount rate. It uses the following syntax:

```
TBILLEQ(settlement,maturity,discount)
```

For example, if you want to calculate the equivalent bond yield on a Treasury bill if the settlement date is April 8, 2002, the maturity date is July 15, 2002, and the discount rate is 3%, you use the following formula:

```
=TBILLEQ("4/8/2002","7/15/2002",.03)
```

The function returns the value .03067, or 3.067%.

TBILLPRICE

The TBILLPRICE function calculates the price per $100 of face value for a Treasury bill given the settlement date, the maturity date, and the discount rate. It uses the following syntax:

```
TBILLPRICE(settlement,maturity,discount rate)
```

For example, if you want to calculate the price on a Treasury bill if the settlement date is April 8, 2002, the maturity date is July 15, 2002, and the discount rate is 3%, you use the following formula:

```
=TBILLPRICE("4/8/2002","7/15/2002",.03)
```

The function returns the value 99.1833, which would mean that you would pay $99.1833 for each $100 of Treasury bill face value.

TBILLYIELD

The TBILLYIELD function calculates the yield delivered by a Treasury bill given the settlement date, maturity date, and price. It uses the following syntax:

```
TBILLYIELD(settlement,maturity,price)
```

For example, if you want to calculate the yield on a Treasury bill if the settlement date is April 8, 2002, the maturity date is July 15, 2002, and the price is 99.1833, you use the following formula:

```
=TBILLYIELD("4/8/2002","7/15/2002",99.1833)
```

The function returns the value 0.0302482, which is equivalent to 3.0248%.

Chapter 6

BUSINESS MODELING

Featuring:

- What-If Analysis with Data Tables
- What-If Analysis with Scenario Manager
- Simple Modeling with Goal Seek
- Optimization Modeling with Solver

This chapter describes how Excel's standard business modeling tools work. Although you can do plenty of powerful analysis without ever touching these tools, you probably should explore them at least a little. They give you new, powerful, relatively easy-to-use ways to analyze issues, problems, and opportunities.

NOTE *Excel also provides another powerful tool for modeling and analyzing your data: the PivotTable tool. Chapter 8 describes the PivotTable tool, including its PivotChart component.*

What-If Analysis with Data Tables

Excel lets you easily create simple data tables that show how changing a formula input affects the formula result. You can, for example, build simple one-variable data tables that show how changing a single input value affects one or more formulas. And you can also create more complicated two-variable data tables that show how changing two input values affect a single formula.

Working with One-Variable Data Tables

One-variable data tables let you experiment with how changing a single input variable can affect a formula's result or even several formulas' results. For example, suppose that you wanted to see how a changing interest rate would affect the loan payment on a $100,000 mortgage. Or suppose that you wanted to see how a changing interest rate would affect the loan payments on a $100,000 mortgage with two different repayment terms: repayment over 15 years and repayment over 30 years. Within Excel, the easiest way to make these calculations would be with a one-variable data table. Both what-if analyses look at the effect of a single changing input value—the interest rate—on a formula or formulas.

Setting Up a One-Variable Data Table

To set up a one-variable data table, you arrange the input values along either the left or top edge of a worksheet range and the formula or formulas you want to calculate along the other edge (top or left). Figure 6-1 shows how this looks with the input values—8.00%, 9.00%, 10.00%, 11.00%, and 12.00%—stored along the left edge of the worksheet range in A2:A6. Along the other edge of the worksheet range—in Figure 6-1, this means B1:C1—enter the formulas you want to test using the input values. In Figure 6-1, you'll see two formulas for calculating a monthly mortgage payment.

B1 fx =PMT(A1/12,15*12,-100000)

	A	B	C	D	E
1		$555.56	$277.78		
2	8.00%				
3	9.00%				
4	10.00%				
5	11.00%				
6	12.00%				
7					

Figure 6-1 An Excel worksheet range set up for creating a one-variable data table.

NOTE *Excel provides financial functions for calculating common formulas, including the formula for a loan payment. The PMT function, which is used in the workbook shown in Figure 6-1, uses the following syntax: PMT(rate,term,loan) in which* rate *is the periodic interest rate,* term *is the number of payments, and* loan *is the loan amount. If you have questions about the PMT function or any other Excel financial function, refer to Chapter 5.*

Cell B1 holds the formula shown below to calculate the monthly payment on a 15-year, $100,000 mortgage:

```
=PMT(A1/12,15*12,-100000)
```

Cell C1 holds the formula shown below to calculate the monthly payment on a 30-year, $100,000 mortgage:

```
=PMT(A1/12,30*12,-100000)
```

The key point to note about both of these formulas—*this is the secret to using a one-variable data table*—is that they refer to the empty corner cell of the worksheet that holds the data table.

Once you've arranged the input values and the formulas as shown in Figure 6-1, finish the data table by following these steps:

1. **Select the worksheet range that includes the input values and the formulas.**

   In Figure 6-1, this means you select the worksheet range A1:C6.

2. **Choose the Data menu's Table command.**

   Excel displays the Table dialog box shown in Figure 6-2.

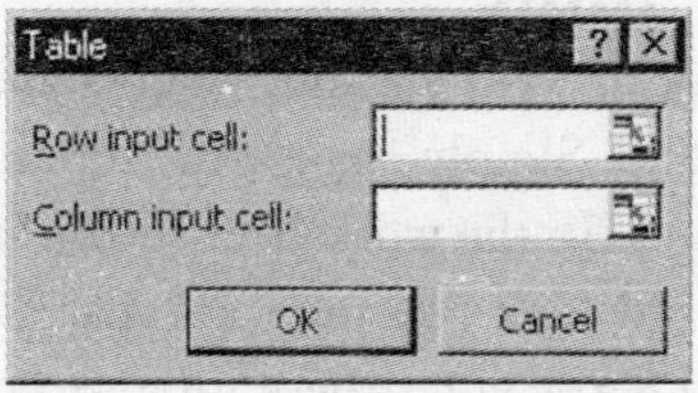

Figure 6-2 The Table dialog box.

3. **Provide the input cell location.**

   The input cell location tells Excel which cell address you've referenced in your what-if formulas. In the worksheet shown in Figure 6-1, the two what-if formulas use cell A1 as the changing, interest-rate input value. So this is the input cell. Because Figure 6-1 arranges the input values into a column, you enter this cell address in the Column Input Cell text box, as shown in Figure 6-2.

4. **Click OK.**

   Excel fills the data table with formula results for each input value, as shown in Figure 6-3. For example, Excel fills cell B2 by using the formula in cell B1 and the interest rate in cell A2 to calculate the monthly payment on a 15-year, $100,000 mortgage when the annual interest rate is 8.00%. Excel fills cell C3 by using the formula in cell C1 and the interest rate in cell A3 to calculate the monthly payment on a 30-year, $100,000 mortgage when the annual interest rate is 9.00%.

B1 =PMT(A1/12,15*12,-100000)

	A	B	C	D	E
1		$555.56	$277.78		
2	8.00%	$955.65	$733.76		
3	9.00%	$1,014.27	$804.62		
4	10.00%	$1,074.61	$877.57		
5	11.00%	$1,136.60	$952.32		
6	12.00%	$1,200.17	$1,028.61		
7					

Figure 6-3 The data table after calculating the what-if formula for each of the input values.

NOTE *Figure 6-1 and 6-3 show a one-variable data table that stores the input values along the left edge and the formulas along the top edge of the worksheet range. You can also store input values along the top edge and the formulas along the left edge. If you use this alternative organization, you enter the input cell address in the Table dialog box's Row Input Cell text box.*

Using the One-Variable Data Table

After you set up the one-variable data table, you can continue your what-if analysis without having to use the Data menu's Table command. Simply change the input values, and Excel updates the formula results for your changes. In the worksheet shown in Figure 6-3, for example, to see what loan payments would look like on a 15-year and 30-year, $100,000 mortgage at 6.5%, 7%, 7.5%, 8%, and 8.5%, enter these interest rate values in the worksheet range A2:A6.

While you might expect to have to reuse the Data menu's Table command to get Excel to recalculate the what-if formulas, you don't actually have to do this. When you initially choose the Data menu's Table command, Excel places the following formula in each of the cells inside the data table:

```
={TABLE(,A1)}
```

If you change an input value, Excel recalculates the TABLE function using the new input value.

Working with Two-Variable Data Tables

Two-variable data tables let you experiment with how changing two input variables can affect a single formula's result. For example, suppose that you wanted to see how a changing interest rate would affect the loan payment on 30-year mortgages of various sizes. For example, suppose that you wanted to calculate a loan payment using interest rates of 8%, 9%, 10%, 11%, and 12% and on mortgage amounts of $100,000, $200,000, and $300,000. Within Excel, the easiest way to make these calculations would be with a two-variable data table.

Setting Up a Two-Variable Data Table

To set up a two-variable data table, you arrange the two sets of input values along the left and top edge of a worksheet range. You then place the what-if formula in the top-left corner cell of the worksheet range. Figure 6-4 shows how this looks with the interest rate input values—8%, 9%, 10%, 11%, and 12%—stored along the left edge of the worksheet range in A2:A6 and the mortgage balance input values stored along the top edge of the worksheet range in B1:D1.

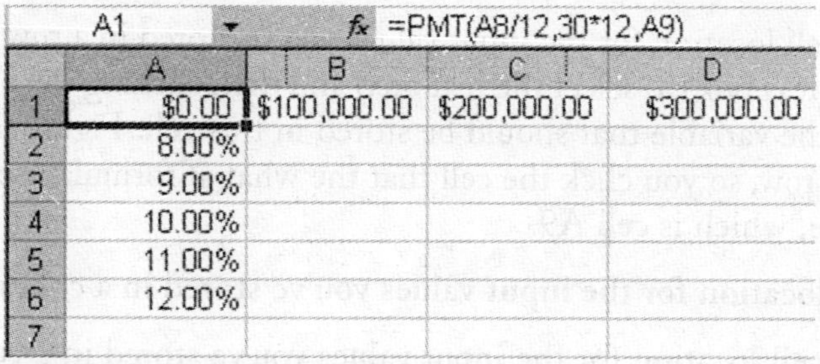

Figure 6-4 An Excel worksheet range set up for creating a two-variable data table.

Cell A1 holds the formula shown below to calculate the monthly payment on a 30-year mortgage:

```
=PMT(A8/12,30*12,A9)
```

NOTE *The PMT function uses the syntax PMT(rate,term,loan) in which* rate *is the periodic interest rate,* term *is the number of payments, and* loan *is the loan amount. If you have questions about the PMT function or any other Excel financial function, refer to Chapter 5.*

The key point to note about this formula—*and this is the secret to using a two-variable data table*—is that the formula refers to two empty cells below the worksheet range, A8 and A9, that will be used to store temporarily the what-if data as Excel makes its calculation.

Once you've arranged the input values and the formula as shown in Figure 6-4, finish the data table by following these steps:

1. **Select the worksheet range that includes the input values.**

   In Figure 6-4, this means you select the worksheet range A1:D6.

2. **Choose the Data menu's Table command.**

   Excel displays the Table dialog box shown in Figure 6-5.

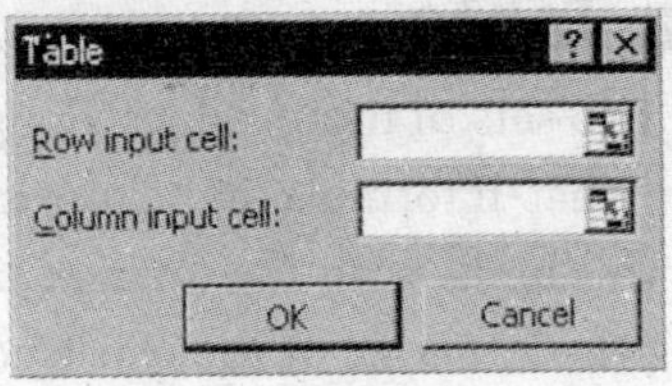

Figure 6-5 The Table dialog box.

3. **Provide the input cell location for the input values you've stored in a row.**

   You provide the input cell location for the input values you've stored in a row by clicking the Row Input Cell text box (to select the text box) and then clicking the empty cell you've used to refer to the variable that should be stored in this cell. Figure 6-4 stores mortgage amounts in a row, so you click the cell that the what-if formula uses to refer to the mortgage balance, which is cell A9.

4. **Provide the input cell location for the input values you've stored in a column.**

   You provide the input cell location for the input values you've stored in a column by clicking the Column Input Cell text box (to select the text box) and then clicking the empty cell you've used to refer to the variable that should be stored in this cell. Figure 6-4 stores interest rates in a row, so you click the cell that the what-if formula uses to refer to the interest rates, which is cell A8.

5. **Click OK.**

   Excel fills the data table with formula results for each input value, as shown in Figure 6-6. For example, Excel fills cell B2 by using the mortgage amount in cell B1 and the interest rate in cell A2 to calculate the monthly payment on a $100,000 mortgage when the annual interest rate is 8.00%. Excel fills cell C3 by using the mortgage amount in cell C1 and the interest rate in cell A3 to calculate the monthly payment on a $200,000 mortgage when the annual interest rate is 9.00%. Excel fills cell D4 by using the mortgage amount in cell D1 and the interest rate in cell A4 to calculate the monthly payment on a $300,000 mortgage when the annual interest rate is 10.00%.

A1 =PMT(A8/12,30*12,A9)

	A	B	C	D	E
1	$0.00	$100,000.00	$200,000.00	$300,000.00	
2	8.00%	($733.76)	($1,467.53)	($2,201.29)	
3	9.00%	($804.62)	($1,609.25)	($2,413.87)	
4	10.00%	($877.57)	($1,755.14)	($2,632.71)	
5	11.00%	($952.32)	($1,904.65)	($2,856.97)	
6	12.00%	($1,028.61)	($2,057.23)	($3,085.84)	
7					

Figure 6-6 The data table after you calculate the what-if formula for each of the input values.

Using the Two-Variable Data Table

As with a one-variable data table, you can continue your what-if analysis even after you've set up the two-variable data table—but without having to use the Data menu's Table command. Simply change the input values, and Excel updates the formula results for your changes. In the worksheet shown in Figure 6-6, for example, to see what loan payments would be using the same interest rates but with mortgage balances equal to $125,000, $150,000, and $175,000, simply enter these values in the worksheet range B1:D1.

What-If Analysis with Scenario Manager

Data tables, as discussed in the earlier sections of this chapter, let you perform what-if analysis when you change one variable and explore the effect on a small handful of formulas or when you change two variables and explore the effect on a single formula. But this approach doesn't work except in the simplest of situations. In most complex situations, you'll want to change several variables at a time and explore the effect on large numbers of formulas.

Suppose, for example, that you're using a workbook like the one shown in Figure 6-7 to perform break-even analysis. Each of the values in the worksheet range B4:B24 is an input to the formulas that show in the break-even analysis schedule contained in D2:G18. If you want to test several sets of input values, use Scenario Manager.

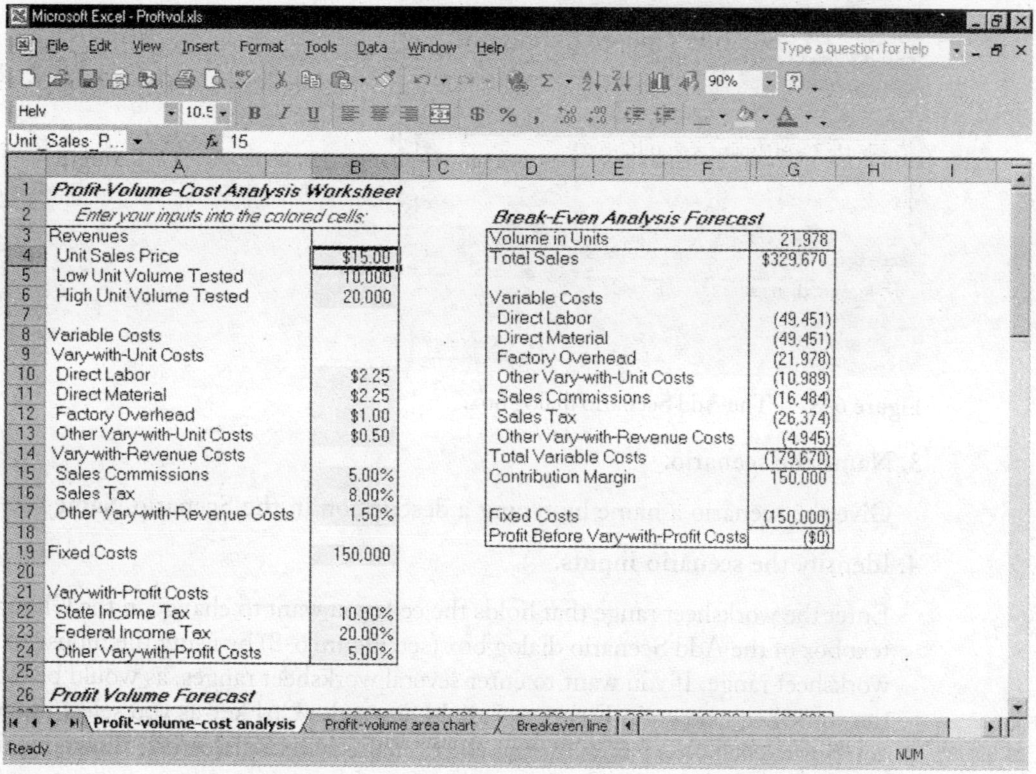

Figure 6-7 A simple profit-volume-cost analysis workbook.

NOTE *The workbook shown in Figure 6-7 is one of the starter workbooks supplied on the companion CD. Chapter 11 describes this workbook in detail.*

Creating a Scenario

To use Scenario Manager, you create sets of inputs called *scenarios*. To create a scenario, follow these steps:

1. Choose the Tools menu's Scenarios command.

Excel displays the Scenario Manager dialog box.

2. Click the Add button.

Excel displays the Add Scenario dialog box shown in Figure 6-8.

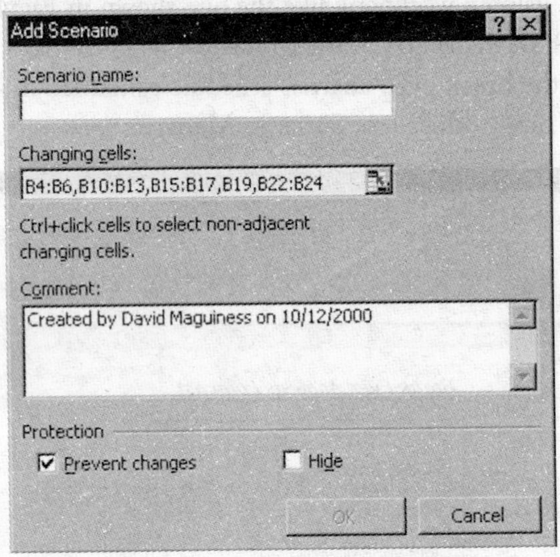

Figure 6-8 The Add Scenario dialog box.

3. Name the scenario.

Give the scenario a name by typing a description in the Scenario Name text box.

4. Identify the scenario inputs.

Enter the worksheet range that holds the cells you want to change in the Changing Cells text box of the Add Scenario dialog box (see Figure 6-8) by using the mouse to select the worksheet range. If you want to enter several worksheet ranges, as would be required for the worksheet shown in Figure 6-7, hold down the Ctrl key as you select ranges. When you finish, click OK. Excel displays the Scenario Values dialog box shown in Figure 6-9.

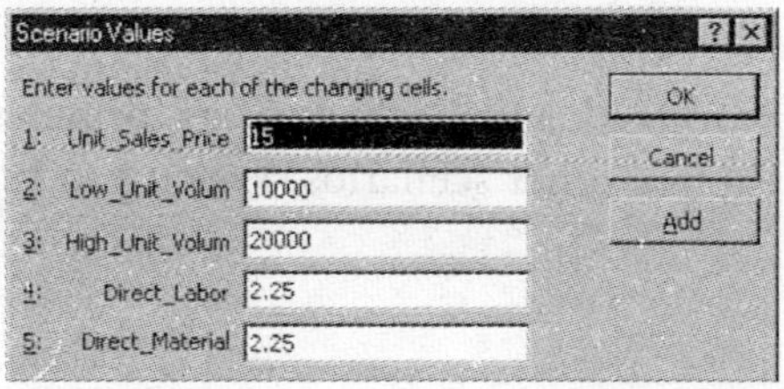

Figure 6-9 The Scenario Values dialog box.

5. Provide the input values.

Enter the input value you want to use for each scenario value. If you've selected more input cells than will fit within the Scenario Values dialog box, you'll need to scroll through the list. Click OK when you finish. Excel redisplays the Add Scenario dialog box.

Repeat steps 2 through 5 to create additional scenarios. After you complete step 5 for the last time, click Close.

Using a Scenario

Once you've created a scenario—again, this is just a set of input values—you can tell Excel to use the input values. To use a scenario, follow these steps:

1. Choose the Tools menu's Scenarios command.

Excel displays the Scenario Manager dialog box, which now displays the newly created scenario, as shown in Figure 6-10.

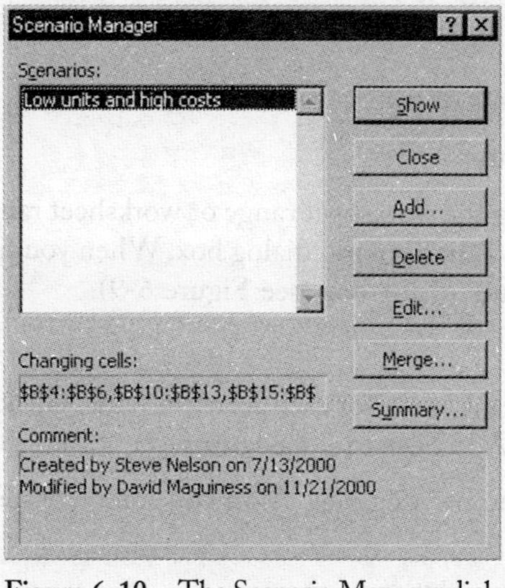

Figure 6-10 The Scenario Manager dialog box.

2. Select a scenario.

Select the scenario you want to explore by clicking its name in the Scenarios list box.

3. **Click the Show button.**

   Excel inputs the scenario values in your workbook and recalculates its formulas. You can repeat this step to experiment with or explore other scenarios. When you finish, click Close.

Editing a Scenario

As you would suspect, you can easily edit the scenarios you've created. You can also easily remove scenarios you no longer want to work with.

To remove an existing scenario, choose the Tools menu's Scenarios command so that Excel displays the Scenario Manager dialog box. Then select the scenario you want to delete, and click Delete.

To edit an existing scenario, follow these steps:

1. **Choose the Tools menu's Scenarios command.**

   Excel displays the Scenario Manager dialog box.

2. **Select a scenario.**

   Select the scenario you want to edit. You can do this most easily by clicking.

3. **Click the Edit button.**

   Excel displays the Edit Scenario dialog box, which closely resembles the Add Scenario dialog box shown in Figure 6-8.

4. **Optionally, edit the scenario name.**

   You can do this by editing the contents of the Scenario Name text box.

5. **Optionally, change the scenario inputs.**

   You can do this by editing or replacing the worksheet range or worksheet ranges shown in the Changing Cells text box of the Edit Scenario dialog box. When you finish, click OK. Excel displays the Scenario Values dialog box (see Figure 6-9).

6. **Provide the input values.**

   Edit or replace the input values you want to use for each scenario value. Click OK when you finish, and Excel redisplays the Add Scenario dialog box.

   Repeat steps 2 through 6 to edit additional scenarios. After you complete step 6 for the last time, click Close.

Summarizing Scenarios

Excel's Scenario Manager includes a Summary feature, which you can use to create either a separate worksheet or a PivotTable that lists selected input values and formula results. To create such a summary, follow these steps:

1. **Choose the Tools menu's Scenarios command.**

   Excel displays the Scenario Manager dialog box.

2. **Click the Summary button.**

   Excel displays the Scenario Summary dialog box, which asks whether you want to display a scenario summary or a PivotTable. Select the button that corresponds to the type of scenario summary you want. Then click OK.

3. **Click the Summary button.**

   Excel displays the Scenario Summary dialog box, shown in Figure 6-11, which asks whether you want to display a scenario summary or a PivotTable. Click the option button that corresponds to the type of scenario summary you want. Do not click OK until after step 4.

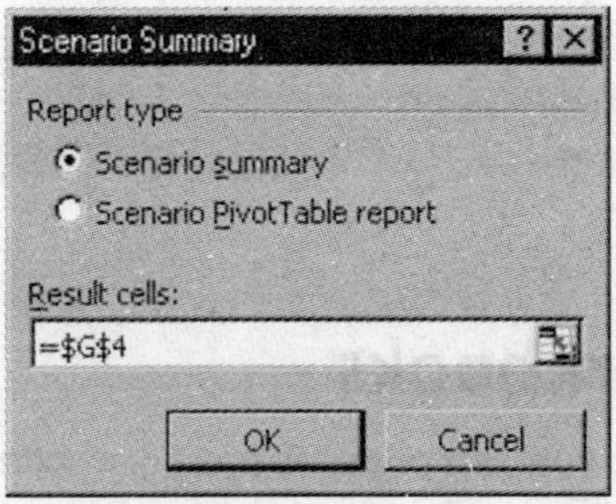

Figure 6-11 The Scenario Summary dialog box.

4. **Select the Result cells.**

   Specify which Result cells you want to see in the summary—these are the cells with the formulas that change as you explore different scenarios—by selecting them with the mouse. You can select nonadjacent cells by holding down the Ctrl key as you click. Click OK when you finish. Excel adds a scenario summary to your workbook that shows the scenario values and the selected Result cells, as shown in Figure 6-12.

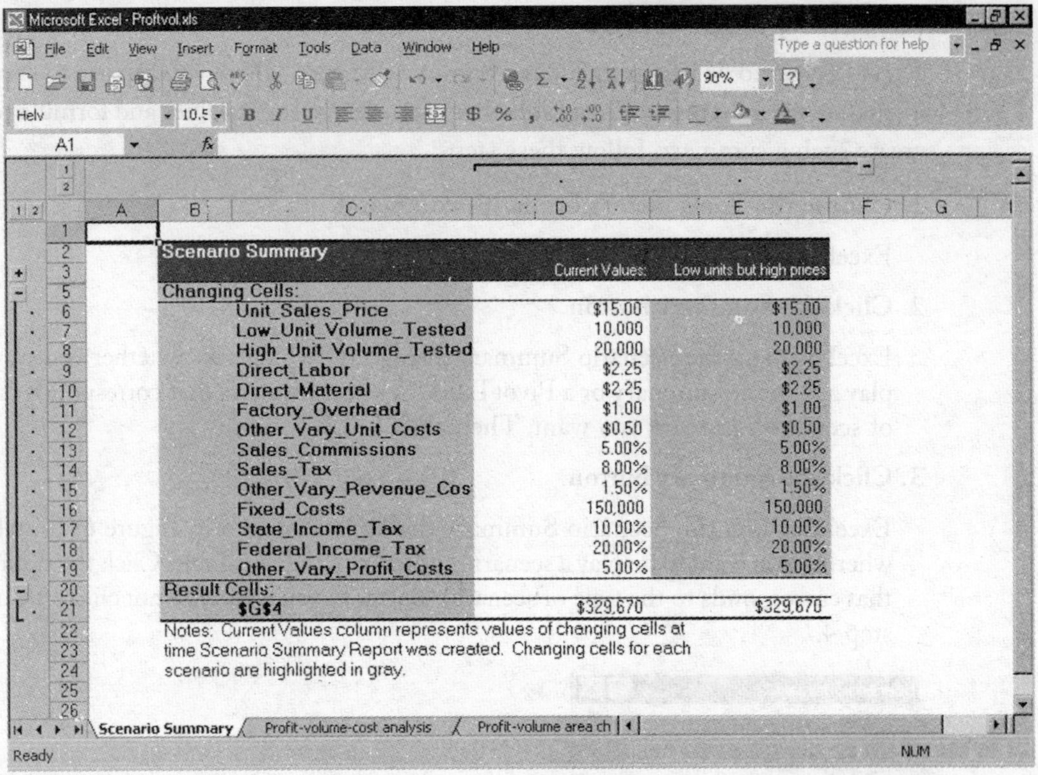

Figure 6-12 A Scenario Summary worksheet.

Merging Scenarios from Other Workbooks

If two workbooks use the same set of input cells, you can copy, or merge, a scenario from one open workbook to another open workbook. To merge scenarios, follow these steps:

1. **Activate the workbook to which you'll add a scenario.**

   When you merge scenarios, both workbooks need to be open, and you work from the workbook to which you'll add the scenarios.

2. **Choose the Tools menu's Scenarios command.**

   Excel displays the Scenario Manager dialog box.

3. **Click the Merge button.**

   Excel displays the Merge Scenarios dialog box shown in Figure 6-13.

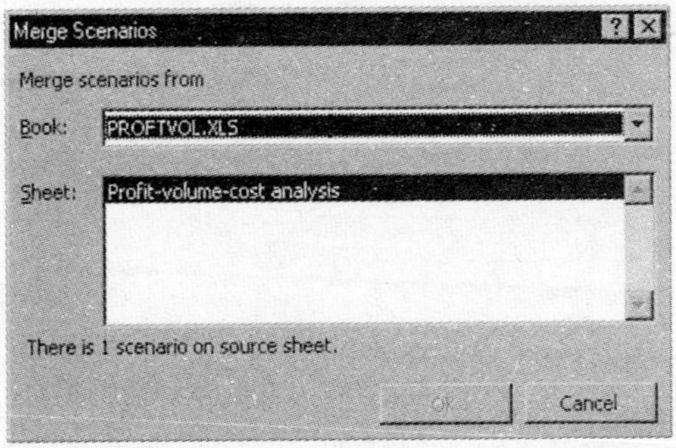

Figure 6-13 The Merge Scenarios dialog box.

4. Identify which workbook holds the scenarios you want.

Use the Book drop-down list box to select the workbook from which you want to retrieve a scenario.

5. Identify which scenario you want.

Use the Sheet list box to select the scenario you want to retrieve.

6. Click OK.

Excel merges the scenarios from the source workbook into the active workbook. You can now use these scenarios in the same way as those you create from scratch.

Simple Modeling with Goal Seek

You can use the Goal Seek command to determine which input value for a formula produces a specified formula result. Goal Seek, then, lets you quantify what needs to happen in order to achieve some specified result. Rather than supplying a set of formula inputs and letting Excel calculate the result, you supply a formula result, all of the input values except one, and then let Excel iteratively determine what the missing input value needs.

For example, suppose you want to determine the interest rate that would result in a $1,400-a-month payment on a $100,000 loan with a 10-year repayment term using the workbook shown in Figure 6-14. Cells B1, B2, and B3 hold values. Cell B5 holds the formula shown below to calculate the monthly interest payment:

```
=PMT(B1/12,B2,-B3)
```

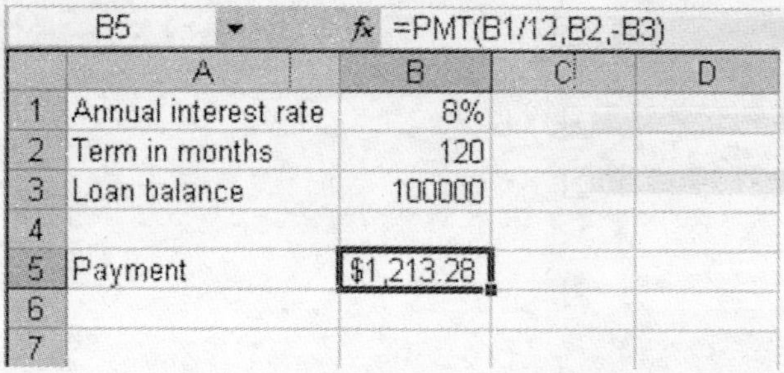

Figure 6-14 A simple loan payment workbook.

NOTE *If you have questions about the PMT function or any other Excel financial function, refer to Chapter 5.*

To determine the rate input value required for your specified formula result, follow these steps:

1. **Choose the Tools menu's Goal Seek command.**

   Excel displays the Goal Seek dialog box shown in Figure 6-15.

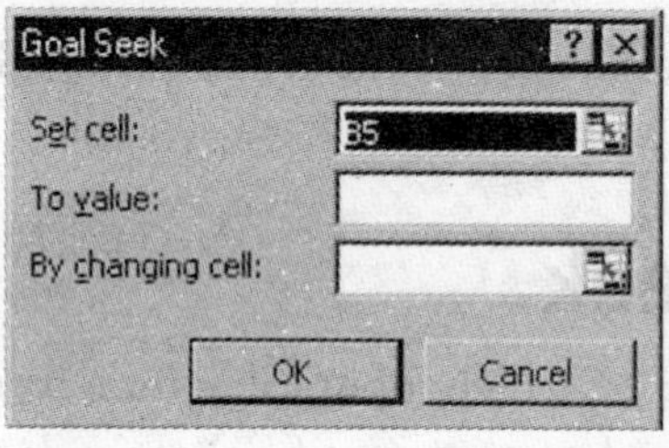

Figure 6-15 The Goal Seek dialog box.

2. **Specify which cell's formula you want to return a specified result.**

   Use the Set Cell text box to specify the cell that holds the formula Excel will attempt to set to the specified value. For the example workbook shown in Figure 6-14, you would specify the Set cell as B5.

3. **Specify this result.**

   Use the To Value text box to specify the formula result you want. For the example workbook shown in Figure 6-14, you would specify the To Value as 1400.

4. **Indicate which input cell should be adjusted.**

   Use the By Changing Cell text box to specify the input cell that Excel should adjust in an attempt to calculate the formula result you want. For the example workbook shown in Figure 6-14, you would specify the By Changing cell to B1. Then click OK. Excel adjusts the input cell to a value that produces the desired formula result and displays the results in the Goal Seek Status dialog box, as shown in Figure 6-16.

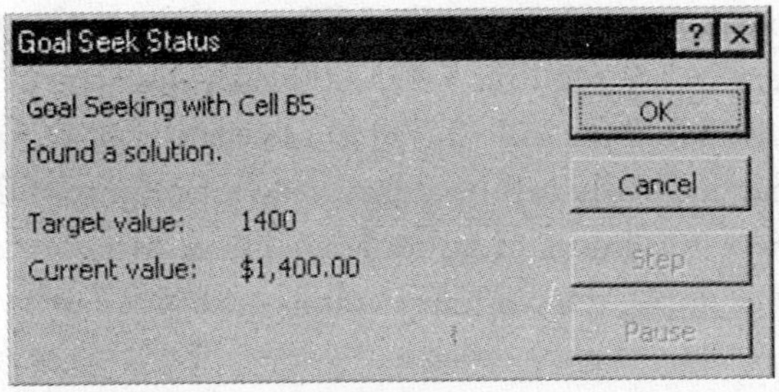

Figure 6-16 The Goal Seek Status dialog box.

Goal Seek typically finds the correct input cell value in a fraction of a second. If your calculations are very cumbersome, however, Goal Seek may take longer. When this happens, you can click the Goal Seek Status dialog box's Stop button to terminate the search. Or you can click the Pause button to temporarily suspend the search.

NOTE *Commonly, Goal Seek's calculations become more complicated or cumbersome when you have it calculate a string of formulas. For example, this might happen when you ask Goal Seek to calculate the input cell value to a first formula, which supplies a result to the second formula, which supplies a result to a third formula, which is the formula you want to produce a specified result.*

Optimization Modeling with Solver

Excel's Solver tool lets you solve optimization-modeling problems, also commonly known as linear programming problems. With an optimization-modeling problem, you want to optimize an objective function but at the same time recognize that there are constraints, or limits. While this abstract definition sounds complicated, at least at the conceptual level, optimization modeling makes common sense once you provide a concrete example.

EasyRefresher™: How Optimization Modeling Works

Suppose, for example, that you're a residential real-estate developer and contractor. You create and sell two products: building lots and houses. Suppose that you make $20,000 on each home you build and $15,000 on each building lot you develop and then sell. Your principal financial objective is to maximize your profits, and this objective can be expressed as an objective function, or equation, that you want to maximize:

```
$15,000*Lots+$20,000*Houses=Profits
```

Of course, any objective function is limited by certain constraints. To continue with the fictional case of residential development, suppose that you have two principal limiting factors: working capital and bulldozer capacity. Your working capital of $1,200,000 limits the number of lots and houses you can annually sell because every lot requires a $50,000 cash investment and every house requires a $25,000 cash investment. The fact that you have a single bulldozer available for only 3,000 hours each year also limits the number of lots and houses you can annually sell because every lot requires 80 hours of bulldozing and every house requires 200 hours of bulldozing. These two constraints can also be expressed as equations. For example, the working capital constraint can be expressed as follows:

```
$50,000*Lots+$25,000*Houses<=$1,200,000
```

This formula says the result of the formula $50,000 times the number of lots plus $25,000 times the number of houses must be less than or equal to the working capital limit of $1,200,000. The less than or equal to symbol is represented by the <= operator.

The bulldozer capacity constraint can be expressed as follows:

```
80*Lots+200*Houses<=3000
```

This formula says the result of the formula 80 times the number of lots plus 200 times the number of houses must be less than or equal to the bulldozer-hours limit of 3,000. Again, the less than or equal to symbol is represented by the <= operator.

Typically, you also have policy constraints when you work with an optimization-modeling problem. Suppose that as a matter of policy you want to maintain a certain level of activity both in developing lots and building houses. You might say, for example, that because you must maintain your team's expertise in both raw land development and residential contracting that you want to develop at least 10 lots every year and build at least 5 houses. These two constraints also need to be expressed as equations. The minimum-number-of-lots policy constraint can be expressed as follows:

```
Lots>=10
```

This formula says that you want to develop at least 10 building lots. Or, restated, this formula says that the *lots* variable must be greater than or equal to 10. The greater than or equal to symbol is represented by the >= operator.

The minimum-number-of-houses policy constraint can be expressed as follows:

```
Houses>=5
```

This formula says that you want to build at least 5 houses. Or, restated, this formula says that the *houses* variable must be greater than or equal to 10. Again, the greater than or equal to symbol is represented by the >= operator.

With the information provided in the preceding paragraphs of this EasyRefresher, we've described your fictional optimization-modeling problem. You want to maximize your profits, which can be described using the following objective function:

```
$15,000*Lots+$20,000*Houses=Profits
```

but you can't develop unlimited numbers of building lots or build unlimited numbers of houses. You are subject to the following constraints:

```
$50,000*Lots+$25,000*Houses<=$1,200,000

80*Lots+200*Houses<=3000

Lots>=10

Houses>=5
```

You can solve this equation in a variety of ways, including graphically, iteratively, or using a technique like simplex algebra. Or, you can provide the objective function and the constraint equations to Excel and have it solve the problem, which is the solution technique described in the paragraphs that follow.

Solving an Optimization Problem

To use Excel's Solver, you first build a workbook that describes your optimization-modeling problem, including its objective function and any constraints, and then you tell Solver to look for an optimal solution. As long as you understand the concepts of optimization modeling, as described in the preceding EasyRefresher, this process is simple.

Setting Up Your Workbook for Solver

You take three steps to set up a workbook for Solver: provide guesses of the variables that optimize your objective function, supply the objective function, and then supply the constraint functions. Figure 6-17 shows a workbook set up to solve the example problem discussed in the EasyRefresher.

B5 fx =15000*Lots+20000*Houses

	A	B	C
1	*Solver variables*		
2	Lots	15	
3	Houses	10	
4			
5	*Objective function*	=15000*Lots+20000*Houses	
6			
7	*Constraints*	*Formula*	*Constant*
8	Cash required limit	=Lots*50000+Houses*25000	1200000
9	Bulldozer hours limit	=Lots*80+Houses*200	3000
10	Minimum number of lots policy	=Lots	10
11	Minimum number of houses policy	=Houses	5
12			

Figure 6-17 A workbook set up for optimization modeling.

NOTE *If you want to experiment with Solver but don't want to construct the worksheet shown in Figure 6-17 from scratch, remember that all the workbook examples in this book are included on the companion CD.*

To build this or any optimization model workbook, follow these steps:

1. **Optionally, tell Excel to display the actual formulas rather than results.**

   You don't have to take this step, but because with optimization modeling you're really more interested in what the formulas look like as opposed to the results they produce, you probably want to tell Excel to display formulas rather than formula results. To do this, choose the Tools menu's Options command, click the View tab, and select the Formulas check box.

   NOTE *Figure 6-17 displays formulas instead of formula results.*

2. **Provide starting guesses for the variables.**

   You need to provide starting guesses for the variables you're trying to optimize. You can do this simply by entering values in cells, but we recommend you create a small schedule of variable names and variable guesses, as shown in Figure 6-17 in the worksheet range A1:B3.

   If you set up a worksheet range like that shown in Figure 6-17—and you really should—you'll also want to name the cells that hold your guesses. In this case, you can do this by selecting the worksheet range that holds the variable names (Lots, Houses) and guesses—A2:B3 in Figure 6-17—and then by choosing the Insert menu's Name command and then choosing Create. When Excel displays the Create Names dialog box, select the Left Column check box and click OK.

3. **Describe the objective function.**

   In Figure 6-17, the worksheet describes the equation with the following formula located in cell B5:

   ```
   =15000*Lots+20000*Houses
   ```

   Because the cells holding the variable guesses have been named Lots and Houses, the objective function uses these names in place of cell references. Note that the label in cell A5 identifies the equation, but you need to enter only the actual equation shown in cell B5.

4. **Describe each constraint.**

   In Figure 6-17, the constraints are described in the worksheet range B8:C11.

To describe a single constraint, you enter the constraint equation in one cell and the limiting constant value in another cell. For example, the working capital constraint mentioned in the earlier EasyRefresher says the formula $50,000 times the number of lots plus $25,000 times the number of houses must be less than or equal to $1,200,000 (the limiting constant).

To describe this first constraint, you enter the following formula in cell B8:

```
=Lots*50000+Houses*25000
```

and you enter the constant value which limits this formula in cell C8:

```
1200000
```

To describe the second constraint—the one that quantifies the limit on bulldozer capacity—you enter the following formula in cell B9:

```
=Lots*80+Houses*200
```

and you enter the constant value which limits this formula in cell C9:

```
3000
```

To describe the third constraint—which comes from your minimum-number-of-lots policy constraint—you enter the following formula in cell B10:

```
=Lots
```

and you enter the constant value which limits this formula in cell C10:

```
10
```

Finally, to describe the fourth constraint—which comes from your minimum-number-of-houses policy constraint—you enter the following formula in cell B11:

```
=Houses
```

and you enter the constant value which limits this formula in cell C11:

```
5
```

Once you've completed the preceding steps, you're ready to use Solver to look for an optimal solution to your objective function.

Using Solver

If you set up your workbooks similar to the one shown in Figure 6-17, you will find Solver easy to use. You simply follow these steps:

1. **Choose the Tools menu's Solver command.**

   Excel displays the Solver Parameters dialog box shown in Figure 6-18.

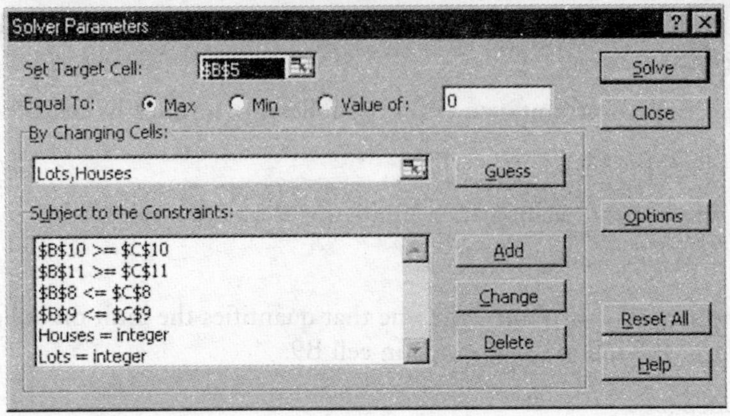

Figure 6-18 The Solver Parameters dialog box.

NOTE *If you don't see the Solver command on your Tools menu, it means the Solver add-in isn't yet installed. To install Solver, choose the Tools menu's Add-Ins command. When Excel displays the Add-Ins dialog box, scroll down the Add-Ins Available list box until you see the Solver Add-in entry. Select the Solver Add-in check box, click OK, and then if Excel requests it, provide the Excel or Office installation CD.*

2. **Identify the objective function.**

   Enter the address of the cell that holds your objective in the Set Target Cell box. For example, in Figure 6-17, cell B5 holds the objective function, so you would enter *B5* in the Set Target Cell box.

3. **Describe how Solver should optimize the objective function.**

   Use the Equal To option buttons to specify how Solver optimizes the objective function. In the case of a profit function, for example, you want to maximize the function, so you click the Max button. This is the case for the workbook shown in Figure 6-17. If your objective function described costs, you would instead want to minimize the function and so would click the Min button. You may also have situations in which you want to have the objective function return a specific value, and so you would click the Value Of button and then provide the specified value.

4. **Tell Solver which cells hold your variable guesses.**

   Use the By Changing Cells box to tell Excel where you've stored the variables used in the objective function and constraint equations. In Figure 6-17, for example, the workbook stores these variables in cells B2 and B3, so you could enter these two cell addresses in the By Changing Cells box. If you've named the variable cells, you can also type the cell names, as shown in Figure 6-18. Cell B2 is named Lots, and cell B3 is named Houses.

5. **Tell Solver you want to begin describing constraints.**

   Click the Add button. Excel displays the Add Constraint dialog box shown in Figure 6-19.

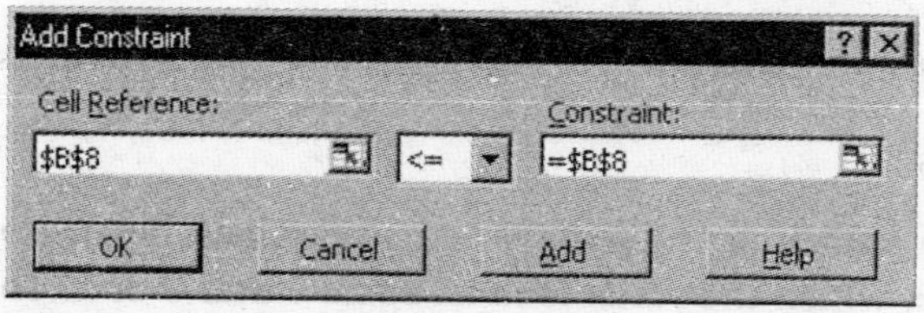

Figure 6-19 The Add Constraint dialog box.

6. **Describe the first constraint.**

   To add a constraint, use the Cell Reference box to identify the cell holding the first constraint's equation, use the unnamed operator box to select an appropriate constraint operator, and then use the Constraint box to identify the cell holding the first constraint's constant value. In the case of the workbook shown in Figure 6-17, for example, you might do this by clicking the Cell Reference box and then clicking cell B8, by selecting the <= operator, and then by clicking the Constraint box and then clicking cell C8. Figure 6-19 shows how the Add Constraint dialog box should look to specify this constraint. Click Add to add the constraint. Then repeat this task to add more constraints.

NOTE *The unnamed drop-down list box provides five constraint operators:* <= *for indicating less than or equal to,* = *for indicating equal to,* >= *for indicating greater than or equal to,* int *for indicating that a variable must be an integer, and* bin *for indicating that a variable must be binary (equal either to 1 or 0).*

7. **Add any implicit integer constraints.**

   In many optimization-modeling problems, you'll also have implicit integer constraints. What this means, for example, is that you can't use decimal values as part of the optimal solution. For example, you might say that you must develop an integer number of building lots or build an integer number of houses. Or restated slightly, you might say that you can't get to the end of the year and have one of your building lots only half-done or one of your houses only partially complete. To specify an integer constraint, use the Cell Reference box to identify the variable cell that must be an integer and then select the *int* operator from the unnamed drop-down list box. Figure 6-20 shows how the Add

Constraint dialog box looks when you specify an integer constraint. Note that you don't enter the word *integer* in the Constraint box. Excel does that.

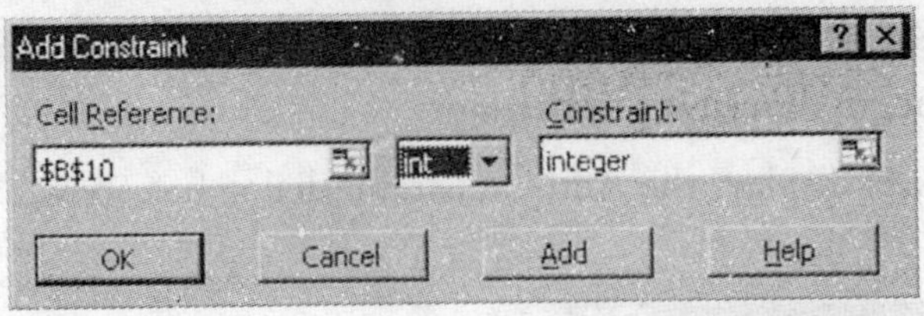

Figure 6-20 The Add Constraint dialog box, this time showing how an integer constraint looks.

8. Add any binary constraints.

In a handful of optimization modeling problems, you may also have binary constraints. A binary constraint is one in which the variable must equal either 0 or 1. To specify a binary constraint, use the Cell Reference box to identify the variable cell that must be binary and then select the *bin* operator from the unnamed drop-down list box.

9. Tell Excel you're done adding constraints.

To leave the Add Constraint dialog box after you finish describing your last constraint, click OK. Excel closes the Add Constraint dialog box and returns you to the Solver Parameters dialog box. Any constraints you've added show in the Subject To Constraints list box.

NOTE *If you add a constraint and later want to delete it, display the Solver Parameters dialog box, select the constraint, and then click the Delete button. If you add a constraint and later want to edit it, display the Solver Parameters dialog box, select the constraint, and then click the Change button. When Excel displays the Edit Constraint dialog box, use it to make your changes. The Edit Constraint dialog box works like the Add Constraint dialog box.*

10. Tell Excel to look for a solution.

Click the Solve button to direct Excel to look for a solution to your optimization-modeling problem. Excel looks for a solution and then displays the Solver Results dialog box shown in Figure 6-21.

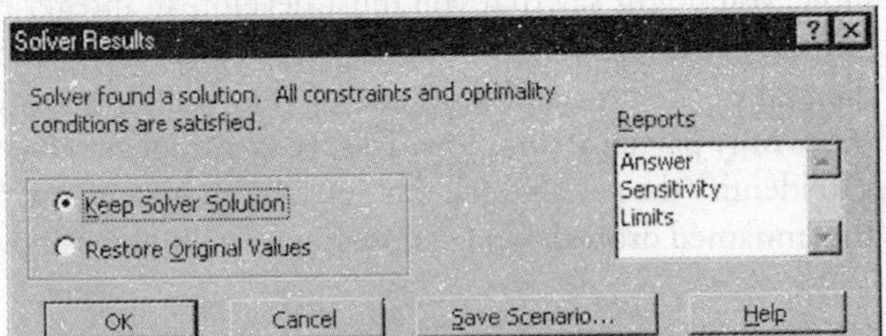

Figure 6-21 The Solver Results dialog box.

This dialog box identifies the variable values that optimize your objective function and asks what you want to do with these values.

- To save the solution, click the Keep Solver Solution option button and click OK.
- To discard the solution, click the Restore Original Values option button and click OK.
- To save the solution as a scenario, click the Save Scenario button and then provide a scenario name when prompted.

NOTE *The earlier section, "What-If Analysis with Scenario Manager," discusses how scenarios work.*

Reviewing Solver Reports

The Solver Results dialog box gives you the option of generating several reports on the optimization modeling that Solver performs. To generate these reports, select the report or reports you want from the list in the Solver Results dialog box, as shown in Figure 6-21.

NOTE *Excel does not allow integer constraints in Sensitivity and Limits Reports. You will need to return to the Solver Parameters dialog box (see Figure 6-18) and delete the integer parameters for Houses and Lots to get these reports. These reports involve graphing several parameters in several equations. When you graph a complex equation, not all of the results will have integer values.*

Understanding the Answer Report

The Answer Report, which Excel places on a separate worksheet, provides information about how close the optimal solution is to your original guesses and about which constraints bind, or limit, optimization. Figure 6-22 shows an example Answer Report. At the top of the report, Excel compares the original objection function formula result with the objection function result provided by original variable values. In Figure 6-22, for example, Excel shows the original objective function value as 425000 and the final objective function value as 440000. Solver, in this case, improves the objective function by 15000.

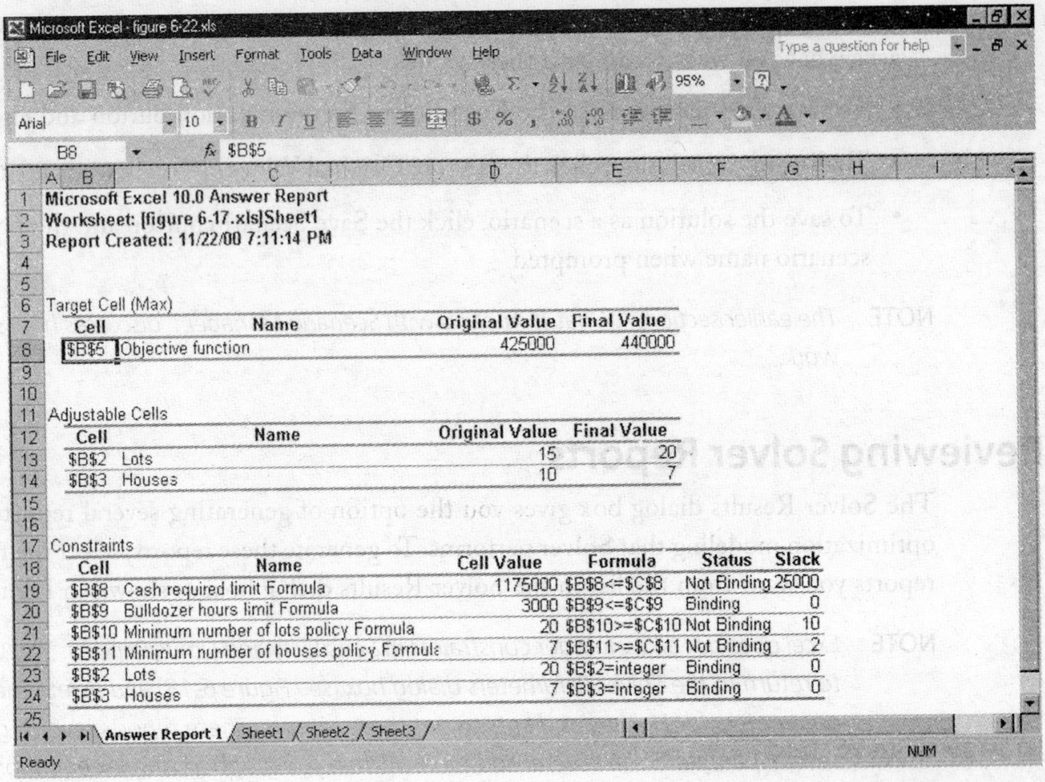

Figure 6-22 The Answer Report.

Beneath the comparison of the original and final values of the objective function's formula results, Excel compares the original values and final values of the variables (see Figure 6-22). This information lets you see exactly by how much Excel adjusts the variables in order to optimize your objective function.

At the bottom of the Answer Report, Excel analyzes the constraints by calculating the formula results for the constraints and then comparing these formula results to the constraint constants. This sounds like busywork at first blush, but this information is often very useful in two important ways: First, you can use the status information to see which constraints are binding, or limiting. In Figure 6-22, the binding constraint is the bulldozer hours. Second, you can use the slack information to see how close a given constraint comes to becoming binding. In Figure 6-22, the working capital constraint shows only 25000 for slack; in other words, you have only a 2% margin of error with your working capital ($25,000 / $1,200,000).

Understanding the Sensitivity Report

The Sensitivity Report, which Excel also places on a separate worksheet, shows reduced gradients for the variables and the Lagrange multipliers for the constraints, as shown in Figure 6-23. A reduced gradient value shows how the objective function would change if the variable value increased by 1. The Lagrange multiplier shows how the objective function would change if the constraint constant increased by 1.

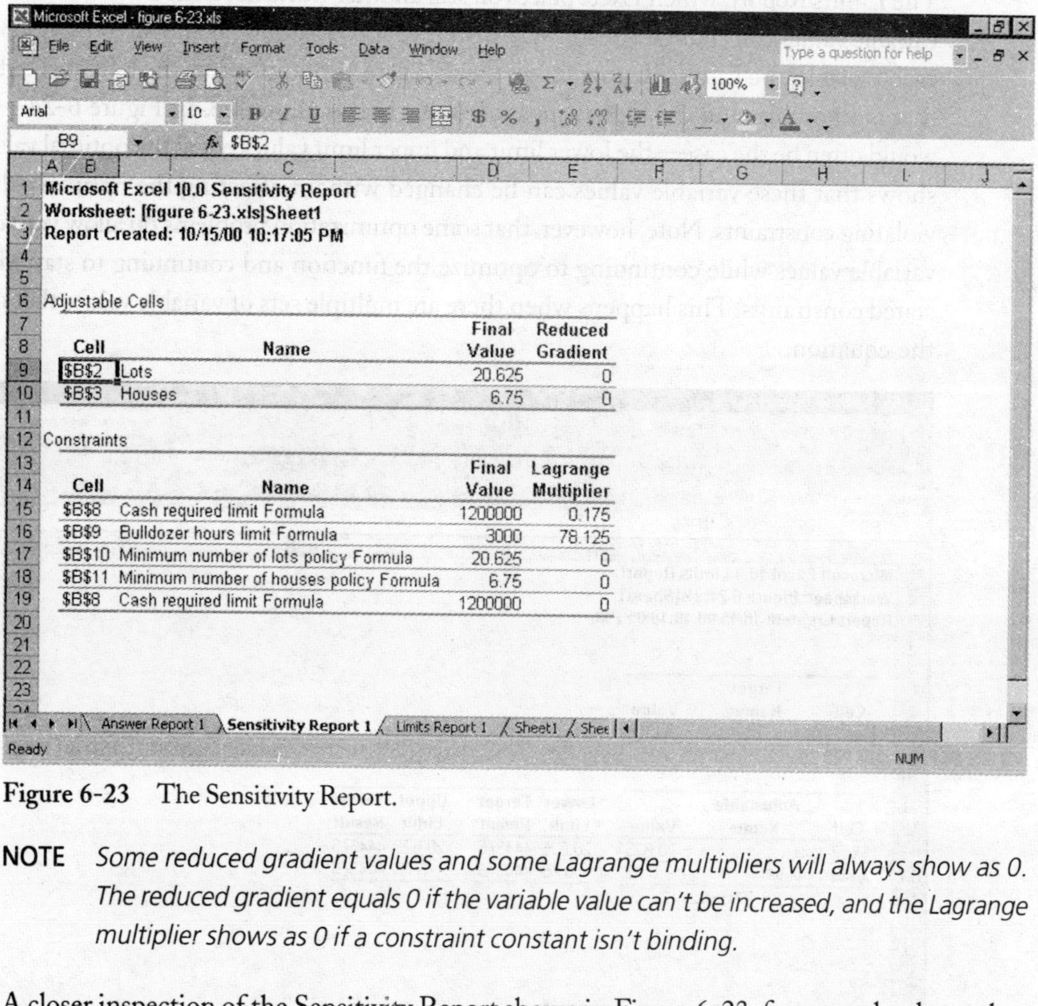

Microsoft Excel 10.0 Sensitivity Report
Worksheet: [figure 6-23.xls]Sheet1
Report Created: 10/15/00 10:17:05 PM

Adjustable Cells

Cell	Name	Final Value	Reduced Gradient
$B$2	Lots	20.625	0
$B$3	Houses	6.75	0

Constraints

Cell	Name	Final Value	Lagrange Multiplier
$B$8	Cash required limit Formula	1200000	0.175
$B$9	Bulldozer hours limit Formula	3000	78.125
$B$10	Minimum number of lots policy Formula	20.625	0
$B$11	Minimum number of houses policy Formula	6.75	0
$B$8	Cash required limit Formula	1200000	0

Figure 6-23 The Sensitivity Report.

NOTE *Some reduced gradient values and some Lagrange multipliers will always show as 0. The reduced gradient equals 0 if the variable value can't be increased, and the Lagrange multiplier shows as 0 if a constraint constant isn't binding.*

A closer inspection of the Sensitivity Report shown in Figure 6-23, for example, shows that the reduced gradient values for both the Lots and Houses variables equal 0. This indicates that neither value can be increased. The Sensitivity Report does show Lagrange multipliers for the working capital constraint and for the bulldozer-hours constraint. The Lagrange multiplier for the bulldozer-hours limit, 78.125, indicates that a 1 hour increase in the number of bulldozing hours available increases the objective function (your profits) by 78.125.

If you've created a linear optimization model—and we'll discuss linear models briefly in the next section, "Customizing Solver's Operation"—your Sensitivity Reports include several additional pieces of information, including reduced costs, shadow prices, objective coefficients, and constraint right-hand side ranges.

Understanding the Limits Report

The Limits Report, which Excel places on still another worksheet, shows you how much your variable values can change but still stay within your constraints, as shown in Figure 6-24. For each variable, the Limits Report shows the calculated optimal value, the lowest possible value that is allowable, and the highest possible value that is allowable. In Figure 6-24—and this would often be the case—the lower limit and upper limit values equal the optimal values. This shows that these variable values can be changed without affecting the optimal solution or violating constraints. Note, however, that some optimization problems do allow you to change variable values while continuing to optimize the function and continuing to stay within the stated constraints. This happens when there are multiple sets of variable values that optimize the equation.

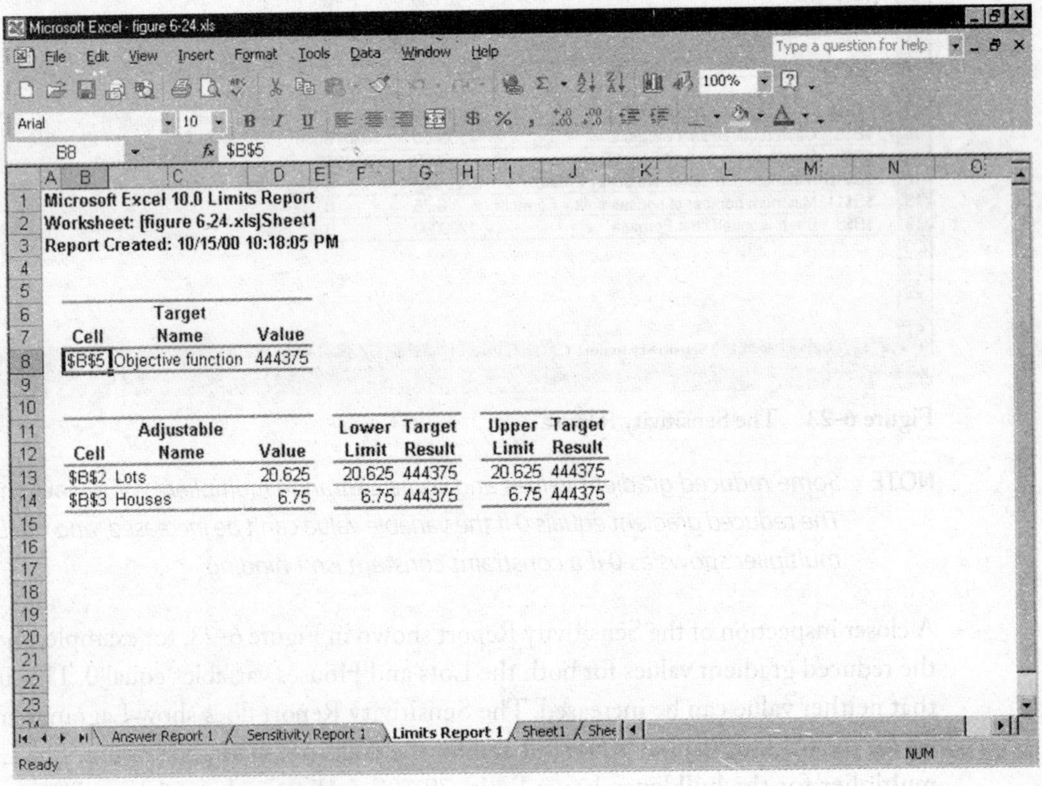

Figure 6-24 The Limits Report.

Customizing Solver's Operation

The Solver Parameters dialog box provides an Options button that you can click to display the Solver Options dialog box shown in Figure 6-25. The Solver Options dialog box lets you customize the way in which Solver works out your problem. The paragraphs that follow briefly describe each of the Solver options along with how and why you might change their settings.

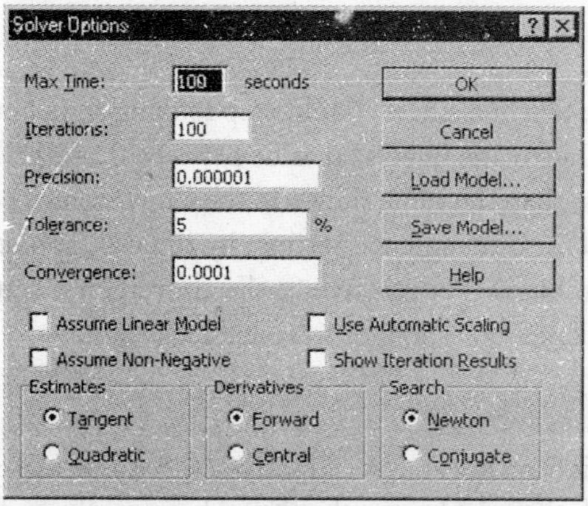

Figure 6-25 The Solver Options dialog box.

Max Time and Iterations

A handful of these options are essentially self-descriptive. The Max Time box, for example, lets you specify how long Solver should work on a problem, and it can be set as high as 32,767 seconds (which is over nine hours). The Iterations box lets you specify how many iterations Solver should work on a problem, and it can be set as high as 32,767.

Precision

The Precision box lets you specify how precise Solver should be in checking a possible optimal solution against your constraints. A precision setting of 0.000001, the default setting, tells Excel that if a constraint formula value is within 0.000001 of the constraint constant, it meets the constraint. You can set the Precision box to any value from 0 to 1. To loosen your precision, use a larger Precision value. To tighten your precision, use a smaller Precision value. As you boost your precision, predictably, Excel takes longer to reach a solution.

Tolerance

The Tolerance box lets you specify how precise Solver should be in making sure that any integer constraints are met. The default Tolerance setting of 5, or 5%, means that if an objective function variable is within 5% of an integer value—from 95% to 105%, in other words—Excel can consider it to be an integer. The Tolerance setting, by the way, applies only to optimization problems that use integer constraints. As you increase your precision, predictably, Excel takes longer to reach a solution.

Convergence

The Convergence box lets you indicate when Excel should stop looking for a better solution. You can set the Convergence value to any fractional value between 0 and 1. When the change in the objective function is less than the value shown in the Convergence box, Excel stops looking for a better solution. The Convergence setting, by the way, applies only to nonlinear optimization-modeling problems. As you reduce the convergence setting (i.e., increase the precision), predictably, Excel takes longer to reach a solution.

Assume Linear Model

If the relationships in your optimization are linear, you can select the Assume Linear Model check box. By doing this, you simplify the calculations that Excel has to make and, thereby, speed things up.

Assume Non-Negative

If you want to tell Excel that your variables must be equal to or greater than zero when you haven't set a lower limit constraint, you can select the Assume Non-Negative check box. In effect, when you check this box, you tell Excel to create another, implicit, set of constraints.

Use Automatic Scaling

You should select the Automatic Scaling check box when you're working with variables and formula results that differ in magnitude. An example of this situation is when you're solving for a rate of return (a percentage) using a set of large dollar variables.

Show Iteration Results

You can select the Show Iteration Results check box to direct Excel to pause after each calculation iteration. After each calculation iteration, Excel displays a Show Trial Solution dialog box. You can save the trial solution by clicking the Save Scenario button. Or you can continue to work toward the solution by clicking the Continue button. To terminate the iterations, click the Stop button.

Estimates

You use the Estimates option buttons—Tangent and Quadratic—to choose the approach that you want Excel to use to come up with the first trial solution. Select Tangent if you want Excel to extrapolate linearly from a tangent vector. Select Quadratic if you want Excel to extrapolate quadraticly—a technique which may yield better results for nonlinear optimization-modeling problems.

Derivatives

You use the Derivatives option buttons—Forward and Central—to specify the differencing used to estimate partial derivatives of the objective function and constraint function formulas. Typically, you can click the Forward button. However, if an optimization problem can't be solved with Forward derivatives, you can click the Central button. Using differentials near the center of a target often takes more calculations to solve, but can be better with highly constrained problems, such as airline ticket prices.

Search

The Search option buttons—Newton and Conjugate—let you choose the algorithm Excel uses to find an optimal solution. If your personal computer has lots of free memory, click the Newton button to reduce the number of calculation iterations (albeit at the expense of using more memory). If your personal computer doesn't have extra memory, click the Conjugate button to allow more time so that your computer doesn't use as much memory.

NOTE *Changing your Search setting to Conjugate should be necessary only on large, complicated optimization problems.*

Save Model and Load Model

The Save Model and Load Model buttons let you save an optimization model description. To save a model—such as the equations that you set up for the scenario with houses, lots, working capital, and bulldozers—click the Save Model button and then specify the empty worksheet range that Excel should use to save the model. To load a model, click the Load Model button and then specify the worksheet range holding the model.

Understanding Solver Error Messages

For most simple optimization problems, Excel rather quickly finds a solution to your problem and displays the Solver Results dialog box. In more complicated problems—unfortunately, those you're likely to encounter in real life—Excel may encounter difficulties. In these cases, it may display one of the error messages described in the following paragraphs.

Solver has converged to the current solution

This message means that while Excel has found what it appears to be a solution, there may be a better solution. To direct Excel to look for a better solution, reduce the Convergence setting using the Solver Options dialog box, as described in the preceding section, "Customizing Solver's Operations."

Solver cannot improve the current solution

This message indicates that Excel has calculated a rough, appropriate solution, but there may be a better solution. To direct Excel to look for a better solution, adjust the Precision setting to a larger value using the Solver Options dialog box. Again, the preceding section explains how to do this.

Stop chosen when the maximum time limit was reached

This message indicates that Excel ran out of time. You can attempt to retry solving the solution using a larger Max Time setting. To specify a larger Max Time value, use the Solver Options dialog box.

NOTE *To save the work that Excel has already performed when you encounter either this message or the next one, click the Keep Solver Results button.*

Stop chosen when the maximum iteration limit was reached

This message indicates that Excel ran out of iterations. You can attempt to retry solving the solution using a larger Iterations setting. To specify a larger Iterations value, use the Solver Options dialog box.

The Set Target Cell values do not converge

This message indicates that the objective function continues to increase or decrease even though all the constraints are already satisfied. In other words, with each iteration, Excel gets a better objective function value, but doesn't appear any closer to a final objective function value. If you encounter this error, review your objective function and constraints to make sure that you've correctly described the optimization-modeling problem.

Solver could not find a feasible solution

This message probably indicates that your optimization-modeling problem has no answer. Alternatively, this error message may suggest that you've incorrectly described the objective function or, perhaps more likely, one or more of the constraints. In the previous model, if your working capital was limited to $600,000, you would not have enough cash to work the minimum required number of lots and houses. There would be no feasible solution.

Conditions for Assume Linear Model are not satisfied

This message indicates you selected the Assume Linear Model check box, which appears on the Solver Options dialog box, but Excel, after reviewing the calculation results, concludes your model isn't linear. If you see this message, first display the Solver Options dialog box and select the Use Automatic Scaling check box. Then attempt to solve your optimization model again. If you get the message error a second time, display the Solver Options box again, but this time clear the Assume Linear Model check box. Then attempt to solve your problem again.

Solver encountered an error value in a target or constraint cell

This message indicates that one of your formulas results in an error value or that you've incorrectly specified an integer or binary constraint. To address this Solver problem, you need to fix the incorrect formula.

NOTE *The earlier section, "Using Solver," describes one way to correctly set up integer and binary constraints.*

There is not enough memory available to solve the problem

This message, as you would suspect, indicates that Excel doesn't have enough memory to successfully run Solver. To free up memory, try closing open documents and any other open programs. You may also want to add memory to your personal computer.

Chapter 7

SHARING WORKBOOKS

Featuring:

- Using OLE with Excel
- Sharing Workbook Files
- Sharing Excel Data over the Web
- Retrieving External Data with Excel

One of Excel distinguishing new features relates to sharing information—both between programs and within a workgroup. Excel now fully recognizes that many users—you may be one—use several programs in their work and use Excel in a workgroup environment. This chapter describes the tools and features that Excel provides for sharing data among users and between programs.

Using OLE with Excel

Microsoft Windows itself provides a powerful and easy-to-use tool for sharing data known as OLE, or Object Linking and Embedding. With OLE, you can transfer data between Excel and other Windows programs, as described in the paragraphs that follow.

How OLE Works

In order to make sense of OLE, it's helpful both to understand the basic operation of the Windows Clipboard and the terminology of OLE. The following paragraphs provide this background information.

The Clipboard is simply a temporary storage area in memory that's provided by Windows. Anytime you use the Copy or Cut command, Windows stores your copy of the copied or cut selection using the Clipboard. When you later choose the Paste command, the Windows program—this might be Excel, for example—retrieves whatever it stored on the Clipboard and pastes it into the worksheet at the location of the cell marker or insertion bar.

While you most often use the Clipboard to move and copy data within a program like Excel, you can also use the Clipboard to move and copy data between programs. In fact, the Clipboard is often the quickest and most convenient way to transfer data between programs.

NOTE *Microsoft Office programs store multiple selections on the Clipboard. When you choose the Paste command and the Clipboard holds multiple copied or cut selections, you can choose which selection gets pasted.*

Because the contents of the Clipboard are stored until you exit Windows, you can copy Excel data or formulas, leave Excel, start another program, and in that program choose the Edit menu's Paste command to paste the contents of the Clipboard into that program's document.

NOTE *Rather than exiting the Windows program before starting another one, you can run several applications at the same time.*

Once you understand the basic mechanics of the Clipboard, the terminology of OLE is easy to grasp. OLE is simply the name that Microsoft has given to this Clipboard-based method of sharing document data.

OLE works in roughly this way: The *source* (the document that contains the data you want to transfer elsewhere) in the *server application* (program used to create server document) provides data (such as a paragraph of text, a spreadsheet, or a chart) to the *container* (where you want to data to go) in the *client application* (the application used to create the container document).

For example, with OLE you can use a chart from an Excel workbook in a Microsoft Word document. In this case, Excel is the server application, the Excel workbook is the source, Word is the client application, and the Word document is the container.

OLE objects can be either static, or embedded, which means that what gets stored in the container document is simply a copy. And OLE objects can also be dynamic, or linked, which means that the client application actually retrieves a picture of the actual data from the server application. With a linked object, this "picture" changes as the data changes.

NOTE *You choose between embedded objects and linked objects on the basis of whether you want the object to change. If you don't want the object to change—perhaps because the container document shouldn't be revised—you embed. If you want the object to change—because you automate updating of the container document—you link.*

Although OLE provides you with powerful opportunities to share data between programs, you'll find it easy to use. You create an OLE connection by copying and pasting the data you want to share. Windows hides the complexity from you and takes care of the actual work of data sharing.

Creating an Embedded OLE Object

As an example of how to create an embedded OLE object, suppose that you do want to use an Excel chart in a Word document. To easily create such an embedded OLE object, follow these steps:

1. Open both the source and destination documents.

To most easily create embedded OLE objects, start both the server application and the client application. You should also open both the source document and the container document. If you're working with brand-new, as-yet unsaved documents, first save them.

NOTE *To easily create OLE connections, you need to run more than one program at the same time, which is called* multitasking. *The Windows Taskbar lets you easily run multiple programs at once. To start a second program, for example, use the Start button to start the program in the usual way. To switch between running programs, use the task buttons on the Taskbar.*

2. Select the chart object.

To select an object, simply click it. For example, to select the chart object shown in Figure 7-1, just click the chart.

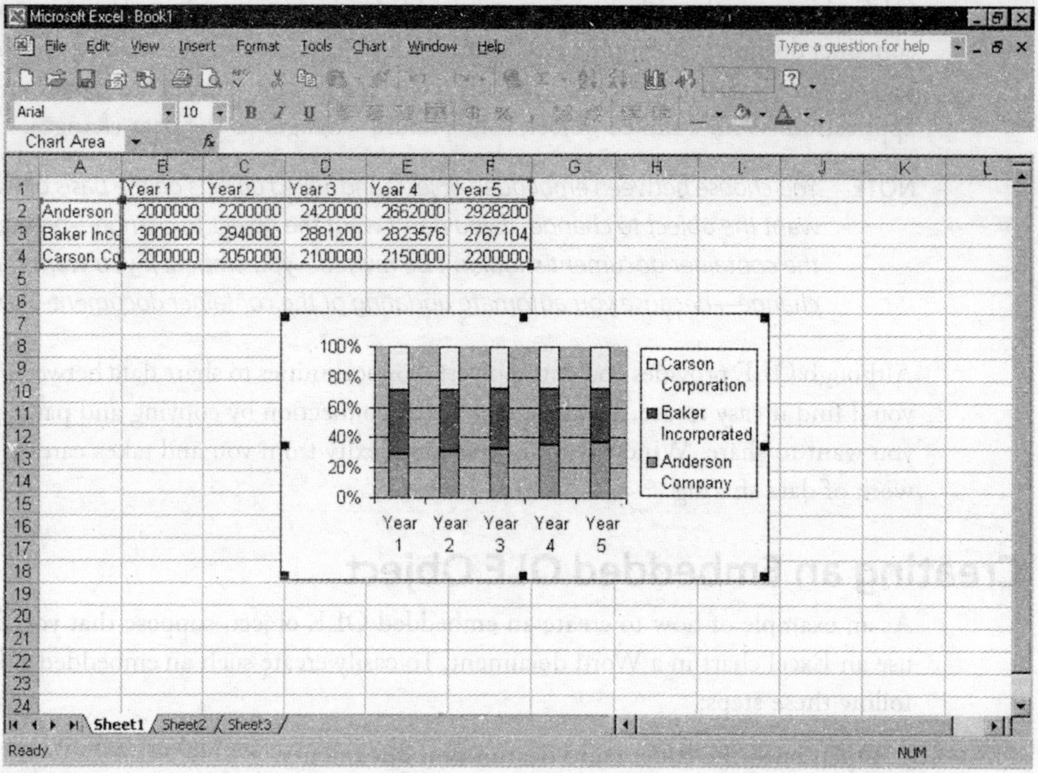

Figure 7-1 An Excel chart such as you might use for an OLE source document.

3. **Copy the object to the Clipboard.**

   You can copy an object to the Clipboard by clicking the Copy toolbar button. Or you can choose the Edit menu's Copy command.

4. **Display the source document.**

   You could do this by clicking the document's button on the Taskbar. If you wanted to copy the object to a Word document named Report, you would click the Report taskbar button.

5. **Position the insertion point at the location where you want to paste the object.**

   You can typically position the insertion point by clicking the point in the document where you want to place the object. For example, if you wanted to paste a chart object after the first paragraph, as shown in Figure 7-2, you would click on the line following the first paragraph.

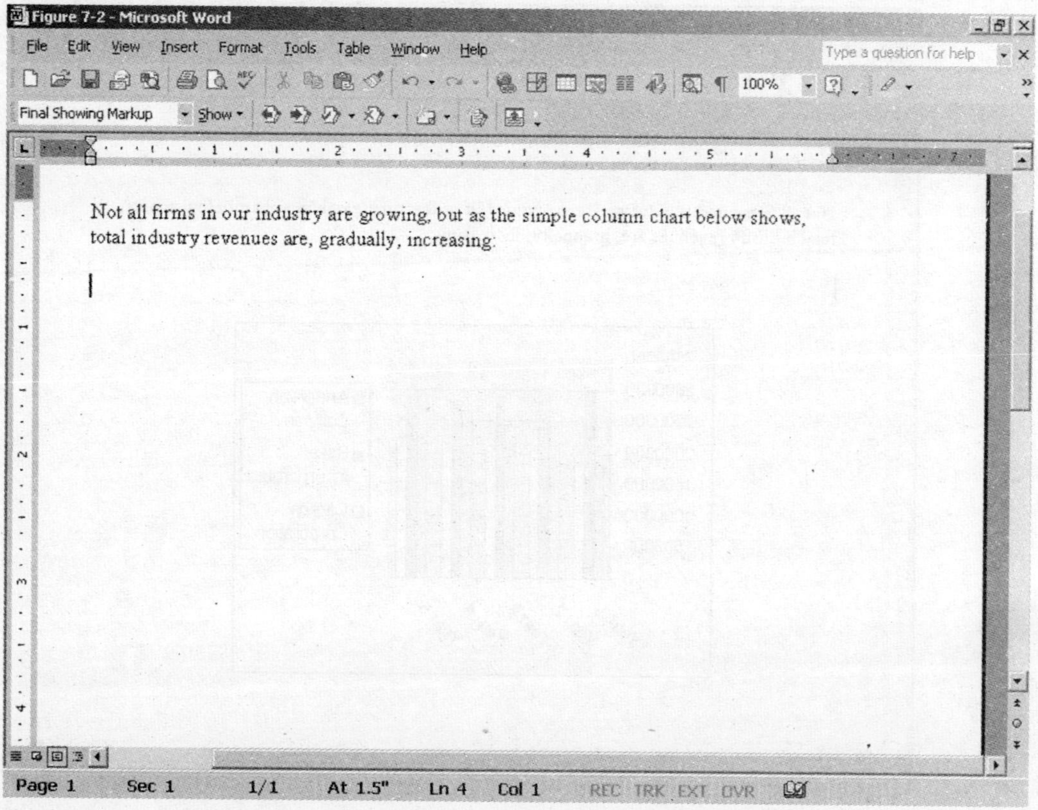

Figure 7-2 A Word document such as you might use for an OLE destination.

6. **Paste the chart object into the client application's container document.**

   You can paste an object to the Clipboard by clicking the Paste toolbar button. You can also choose the Edit menu's Paste command. When you do, the client application (with Windows' help) creates an embedded object that looks as much like the source document object as the server application, Windows, and the client application allow. In other words, Windows and Windows programs use the richest format available for the pasted object. Figure 7-3 shows the Excel chart from Figure 7-1 embedded in the Word document from Figure 7-2.

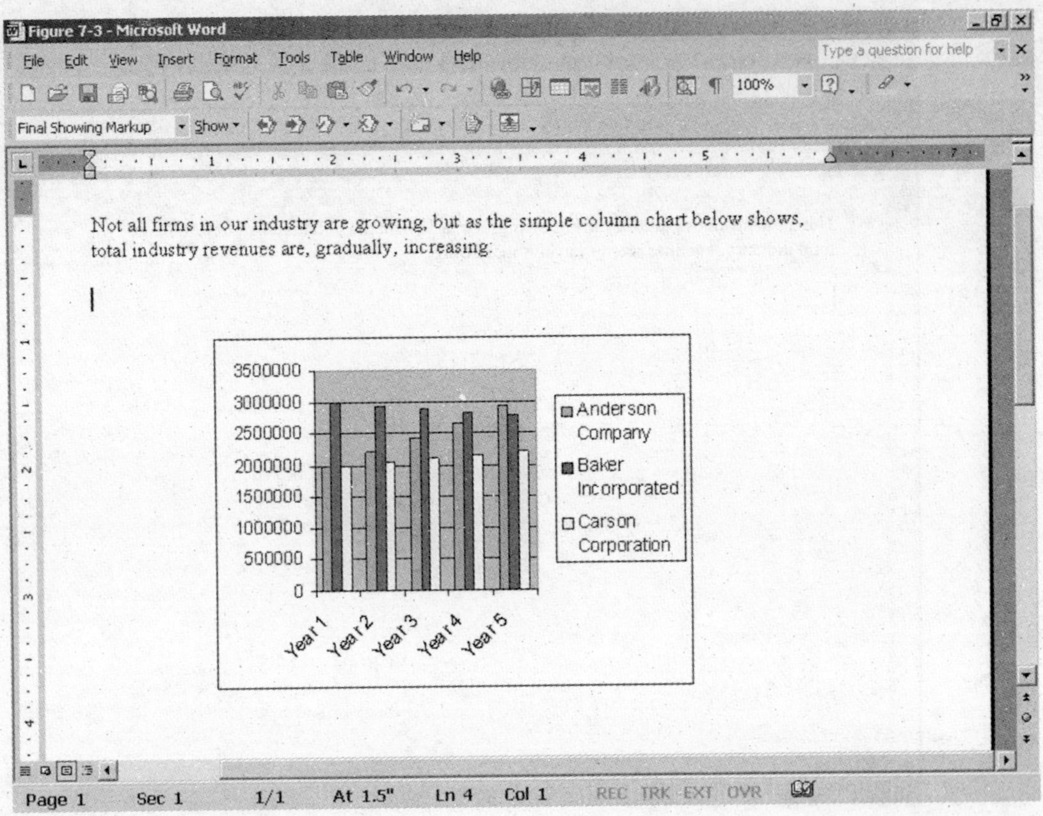

Figure 7-3 The Word document after adding the Excel chart object.

Creating a Linked OLE Object

You create a linked OLE object in almost the same way as you create an embedded OLE object. There's just one minor twist. You use the Edit menu's Paste Special command because it lets you indicate you want to create a linked object. For example, to create a linked OLE object using the same Excel chart shown in Figure 7-1 and the same Word document shown in Figure 7-2, follow these steps:

1. **Open both the source and container documents.**

   Again, to easily create embedded OLE objects, both the server application and the client application must be running and both the source document and container document should be open.

2. **Select the chart object.**

   As mentioned earlier, to select an object you simply click it.

3. **Copy the object to the Clipboard.**

   You can copy an object to the Clipboard by clicking the Copy toolbar button or by choosing the Edit menu's Copy command.

4. **Display the source document.**

   You could do this by clicking the document's button on the Taskbar.

5. **Position the insertion point at the location where you want to paste the object.**

   You can typically position the insertion point by clicking the point in the document where you want to place the object.

6. **Paste the chart object into the client application's container.**

   This is the only step that works differently from pasting an embedded object. When you paste a linked object, you need to use the Edit menu's Paste Special command. When you choose this command, the client program displays a Paste Special dialog box. (Figure 7-4 shows Microsoft Word's version of the Paste Special dialog box, but other programs' Paste Special dialog boxes look almost the same and work in the same basic way.) When the client program displays its Paste Special dialog box, click the Paste Link option button and click OK. Optionally, you can also select a format for the object from the As list box.

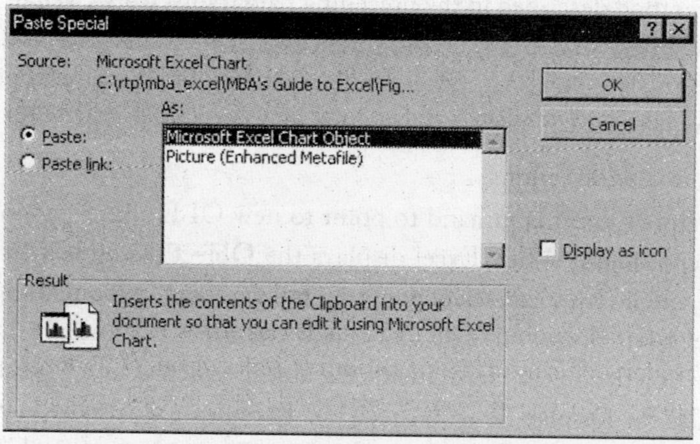

Figure 7-4 Microsoft Word's Paste Special dialog box.

When you open a document into which you've placed linked OLE objects, the program asks whether you want to update the links. If you do, click Yes, and the client application retrieves updated information from the source document.

NOTE *If you don't want the client application to automatically update links, you can tell it not to do so. To make this specification, in Excel, for example, choose the Tools menu's Options command, click the Calculation tab, and then clear the Update Remote References check box.*

By the way, it's possible to inadvertently break a link. For example, this may happen if the same source document is moved or renamed while the client application and container document are closed. In this case, you need to reestablish the link by repeating the steps you took to originally establish the link.

Editing OLE Objects

You can easily modify linked and embedded objects. To change an object, double-click it. The client application starts the server application and opens the appropriate source document. Once the server application is running and displaying the source, you can make your changes.

Inserting OLE Objects into Excel Workbooks

The object-sharing method described in the preceding paragraphs works well in situations in which you want to share data between programs and display that shared data in the container document. You should also know, however, that Excel's Insert menu provides an Object command, which you can use to place icons in a workbook that point to source documents.

To use the Insert menu's Object command to point to new OLE objects, choose the Insert menu's Object command. When Excel displays the Object dialog box, as shown in Figure 7-5, click the Create New tab, select the program necessary to create the object, and then click OK. Excel starts the server application, and you use it to create the new object. When you finish creating the object, click outside the object—such as on a worksheet cell—to return to Excel. Use the Display As Icon check box to indicate whether you want to see a picture of the object or simply a clickable icon you can use to access the object.

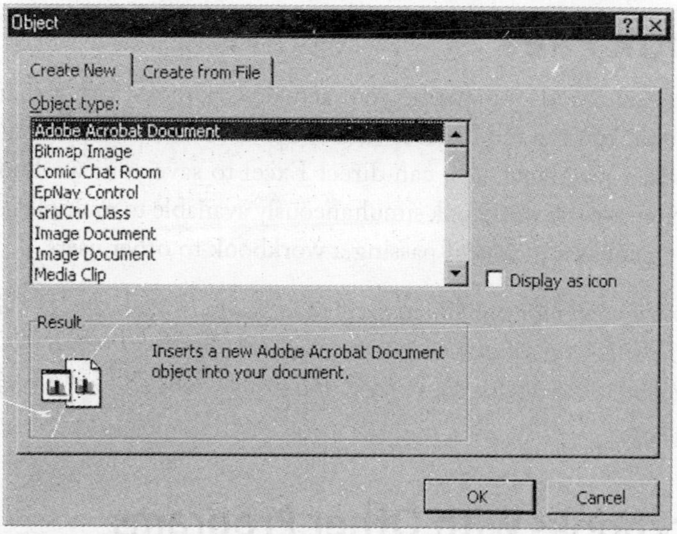

Figure 7-5 The Create New tab of the Object dialog box.

To use the Insert menu's Object command to point to an existing document, you also choose the Insert menu's Object command. When Excel displays the Object dialog box, however, you click the Create From File tab and then identify the file you want to use to create the object, as shown in Figure 7-6. To identify the file, enter the complete pathname in the File Name box or use the Browse button to display a dialog box you can use to search disks and folders for the file. Select the Link To File check box if you want to create a linked object. Select the Display As Icon check box to indicate whether you want to see a picture of the object or simply a clickable icon you can use to access the object.

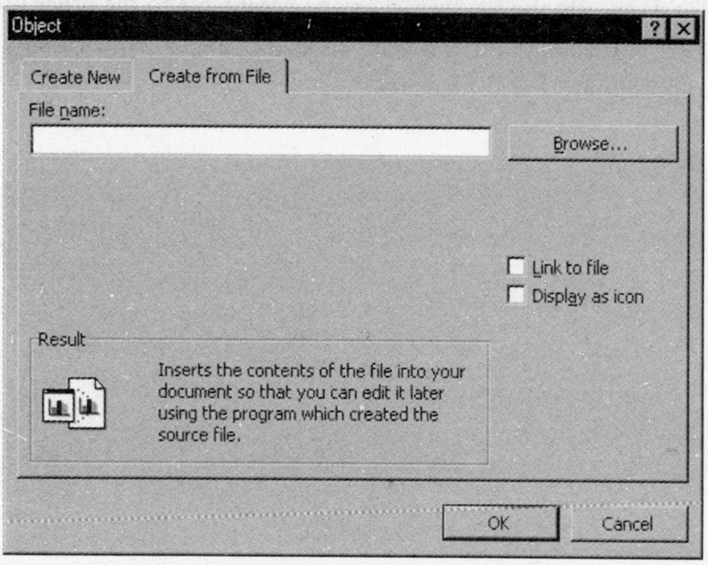

Figure 7-6 The Create From File tab of the Object dialog box.

Sharing Workbook Files

Excel provides several useful tools for sharing your actual workbooks, rather than just the information they contain. You can tell Excel to save or open workbooks in formats acceptable to other spreadsheet programs. You can direct Excel to save your workbooks on a network drive and then make the workbook simultaneously available to multiple users. And you can use electronic mail as a means of passing a workbook to other users.

NOTE *Excel also provides tools for publishing Excel workbooks to Web sites as Web pages, or HTML documents, and for placing interactive Excel objects into Web pages. At the end of this section, we'll discuss these tools and explain why you will probably never want to use them.*

Sharing Excel Workbooks with Other Programs

You can easily share an Excel workbook with other spreadsheet programs. You can, for example, export an Excel workbook so that someone using Lotus 1-2-3, another popular spreadsheet program, can open and work with the workbook. And you can also easily import spreadsheet documents created by other programs into Excel. For example, you can import a Quattro Pro workbook into Excel.

Exporting a Workbook

To export a workbook, you use the File menu's Save As command. When Excel displays the Save As dialog box, save the workbook file in the usual way—except use the Save As Type drop-down list to specify the file format as one acceptable to the other program, as shown in Figure 7-7. For example, if you want to export an Excel workbook to Lotus 1-2-3, choose the appropriate 1-2-3 file format.

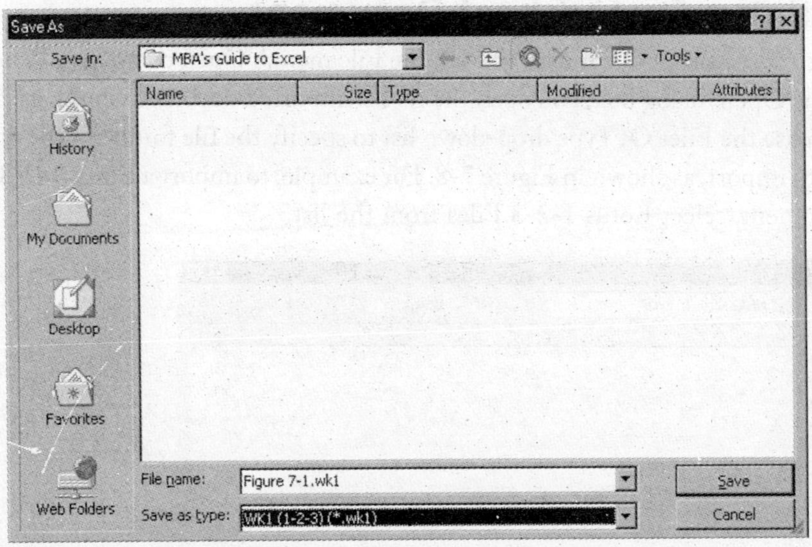

Figure 7-7 The Save As dialog box set to use the Lotus 1-2-3 format.

NOTE *You may need to determine the precise file format acceptable to the program that will later import the workbook you're exporting. Different versions of Lotus 1-2-3, for example, use different flavors of the standard 1-2-3 file format. Usually, if you know the file extension the spreadsheet program uses, you'll have enough information to select the appropriate format.*

If you can't determine the appropriate file format for the exported workbook file, you can try one of two tactics: You can use a simple standard spreadsheet format such as the tab-delimited format or the comma-separated value (CSV) format, which all spreadsheet programs understand. Or you can use a popular spreadsheet format, such as the Excel 95 file format or the Lotus 1-2-3 version 3 file format, which almost all spreadsheet programs understand.

NOTE *If you have questions about how to work with the other options on the Save As dialog box, refer to Chapter 1.*

Importing a Spreadsheet Document

To import a spreadsheet document, you use the File menu's Open command. When Excel displays the Open dialog box, you open the to-be-imported document in the usual way—except you use the Files Of Type drop-down list to specify the file format of the document you want to import, as shown in Figure 7-8. For example, to import a Lotus 1-2-3 spreadsheet document, select Lotus 1-2-3 Files from the list.

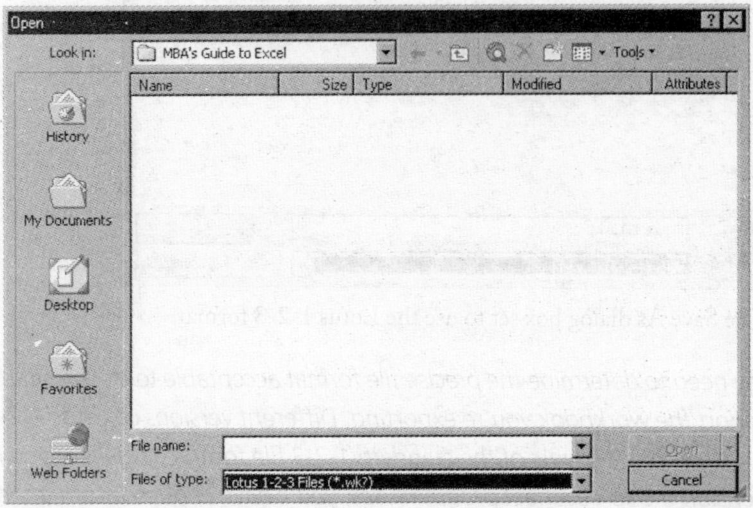

Figure 7-8 The Open dialog box with the Files Of Type list box indicating the Lotus 1-2-3 Files will be opened.

It's unlikely but not impossible that Excel won't recognize the other spreadsheet program's file format. In this case, before you save the spreadsheet document using this other spreadsheet program, you may need to choose a file format that Excel understands, such as any version of Excel, any version of Lotus 1-2-3, or a standard simple format such as CSV or tab-delimited.

NOTE *If you have questions about how to work with the other options in the Open dialog box, refer to Chapter 1.*

Sharing Excel Workbooks over a Network

You can share an Excel workbook with other Excel users over a network. In a nutshell, all you have to do is save the workbook in some accessible location, such as on a network drive or a shared local drive. With a workbook located on a network or shared local drive, network users with the appropriate level of authority and the requisite permissions can open, edit, and save the workbook.

NOTE *To view or open a network or shared local drive, you need to first map to the drive. You can map to a drive by clicking the Tools button in the Open or Save As dialog boxes, choosing the Map Network Drive command, and then entering the full pathname for the drive. If you have questions about the network pathname, ask your network administrator.*

If you do share a workbook over a network, you should be aware of a couple of points. First, and in general, if one user opens a workbook, other people can't open that same workbook except as a read-only document. What that means is that the person can't save the workbook using the same, original filename. The user can, however, save the workbook using a new filename or in a new location.

Excel tells you when you attempt to open a workbook that it's already being used, as shown in Figure 7-9. It then gives you the option of opening the workbook in read-only mode. You also have the option of asking Windows to notify you when the workbook document is fully available.

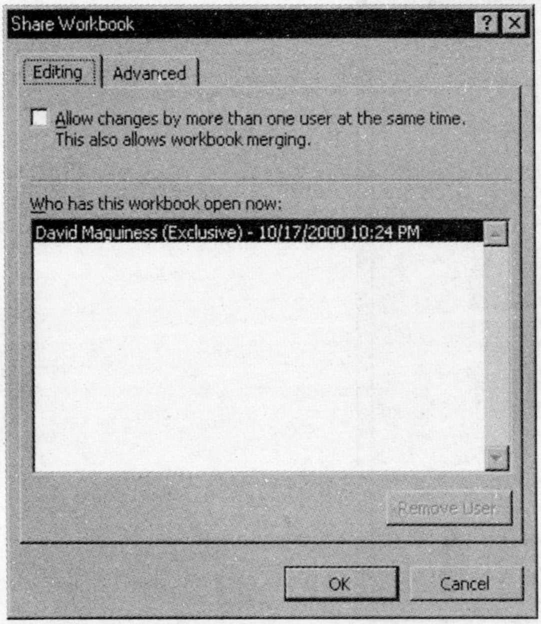

Figure 7-9 The Editing tab of the Share Workbook dialog box.

The second point you need to know about sharing a workbook over a network is that you have the option of telling Excel it's okay for multiple users to open and make changes to the same workbook. We can't emphasize enough that this option is extremely difficult to successfully use in a real-life work setting. You can just imagine all the trouble that can occur if people start making changes to the same parts of a workbook. If you want to do this, however, choose the Tools menu's Share Workbook command. When Excel displays the Share Workbook dialog box (see Figure 7-9), select the Allow Changes By More Than One User At The Same Time check box.

NOTE *The Share Workbook dialog box, as shown in Figure 7-9, also lists the names of the users who've opened a workbook.*

You can control many aspects of Excel's workbook sharing by using the Advanced tab of the Share Workbook dialog box, as shown in Figure 7-10. The Track Changes options, for example, let you tell Excel that it should keep a list of the changes made to a shared workbook and for how long this list should be kept. The Update Changes options let you specify when and how the shared workbook is updated for the changes that people make. Finally, the Conflicting Changes Between Users options let you specify what should happen when changes from different users are in conflict.

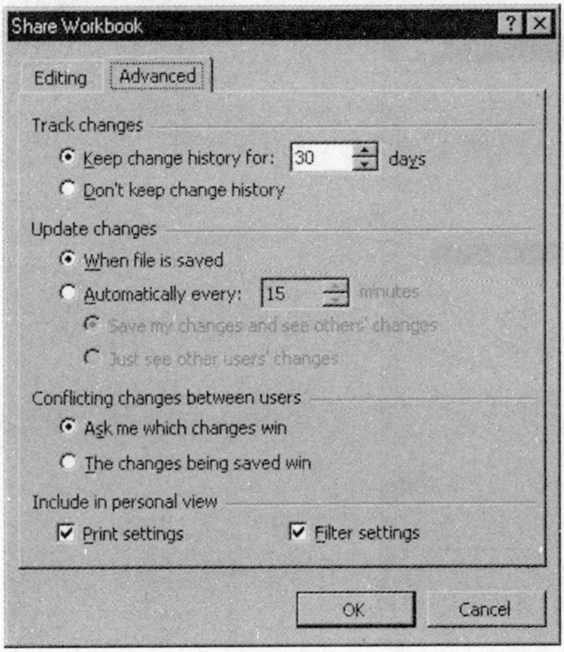

Figure 7-10 The Advanced tab of the Share Workbook dialog box.

Excel does attempt to resolve any conflicts that arise from workbook sharing. When a user saves a workbook, Excel looks for conflicts—such as the same cell being changed by different users. If Excel sees such a conflict, it displays the Resolve Conflicts dialog box, and asks how the conflict should be resolved. One important aspect of this conflict resolution, however, is that the person who saves the workbook and, therefore, sees the Resolve Conflicts dialog box, determines which changes should be saved and which should be discarded.

NOTE *If you choose to work with shared workbooks, you probably want to create a formal, perhaps written, policy to document how conflicts should be resolved. You may also want to plan for workbook sharing when you build the workbook. For example, you might build a workbook so different users would always be making changes to separate worksheets. This would prevent most conflicts.*

Sharing Excel Workbooks via E-Mail

Excel's File menu provides several commands, which you can use to share workbooks using electronic mail. When you share workbooks in this manner, you simply attach the workbook to an e-mail message and then send the message and its attachment, the workbook, to another person.

NOTE *If you can't e-mail someone a workbook, save the workbook to a floppy disk and deliver the disk.*

Sending a Workbook via E-Mail

If you regularly use e-mail, you'll find it very easy to share workbooks using mail. You simply send e-mail messages laden with Excel workbooks.

To e-mail the open Excel workbook, follow these steps:

1. **Choose the File menu's Send To command.**

   Excel displays the Send To submenu, which lists commands for sharing workbooks using electronic mail and, in some cases, other e-mail-like services, such as Microsoft's Exchange Server.

2. **Choose the Send To menu's Mail Recipient (As Attachment) command.**

   Excel opens your default e-mail client, opens a new message, and attaches the workbook. Figure 7-11 shows how the Microsoft Outlook Express e-mail client looks, but your e-mail client will probably look very similar even if you use one of the other popular e-mail programs.

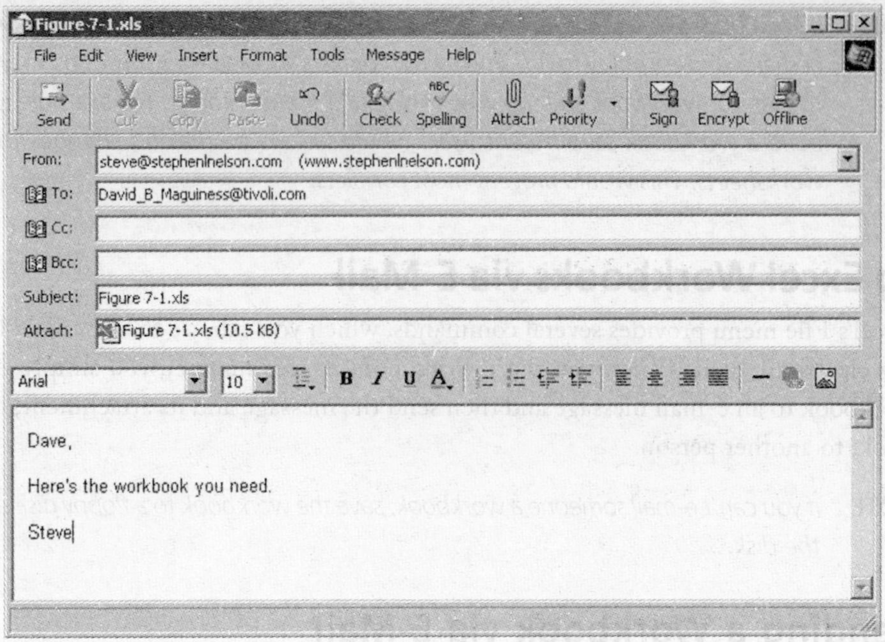

Figure 7-11 The Outlook Express message window with an Excel workbook attachment.

3. Complete and deliver the e-mail message in the usual way.

You complete your e-mail message in the usual way. For example, you need to provide the recipient's e-mail name or alias. And you probably want to provide a message subject and perhaps some message text to explain the message and your attachment. When you finish, send the message in the usual way.

NOTE *Some mail servers limit the size of the attachments they will accept. Some organizations discourage and even prohibit e-mail attachments because the attachments can contain viruses. Before you send an e-mail attachment, make sure that your recipient can accept an e-mail message with an attachment.*

Receiving a Workbook via E-Mail

You can also easily receive e-mail messages that contain Excel workbook attachments.

To receive and use an e-mailed Excel workbook, follow these steps:

1. **Start your e-mail program and retrieve your messages in the usual way.**

   Figure 7-12 shows the Outlook Express program window with the Inbox folder displayed. Other e-mail programs, however, typically show your incoming messages in a similar way. Notice that the first message includes a paperclip icon in front of it to indicate that a file is "attached."

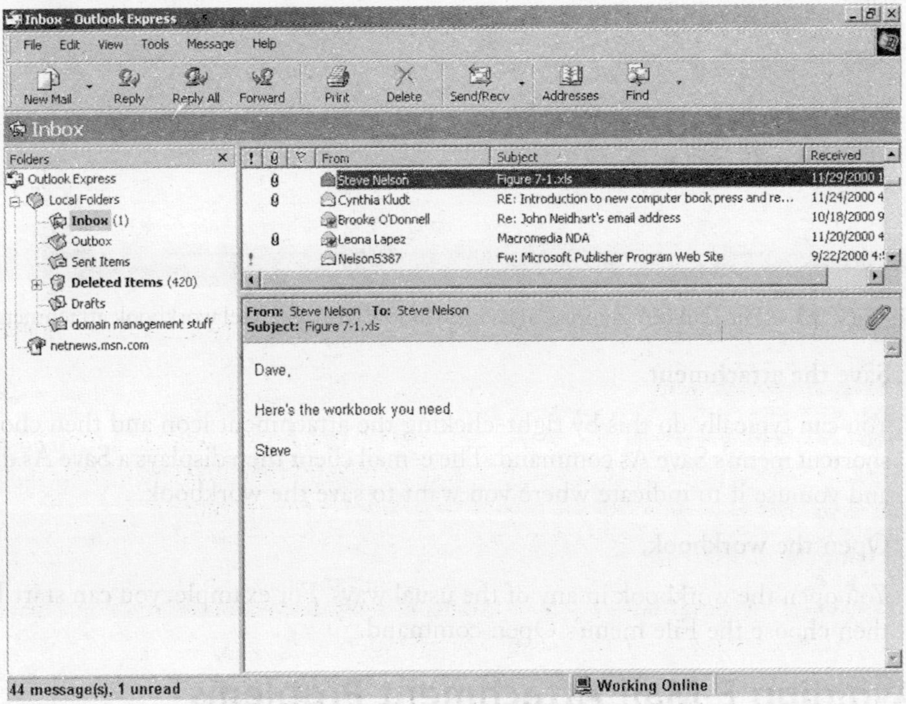

Figure 7-12 The Outlook Express Inbox folder showing incoming messages.

2. **Open the e-mail message with the attachment.**

   Figure 7-13 shows the Outlook Express message window displaying a sample message with an Excel workbook attachment. Again, your e-mail client will probably look very similar even if you use another program.

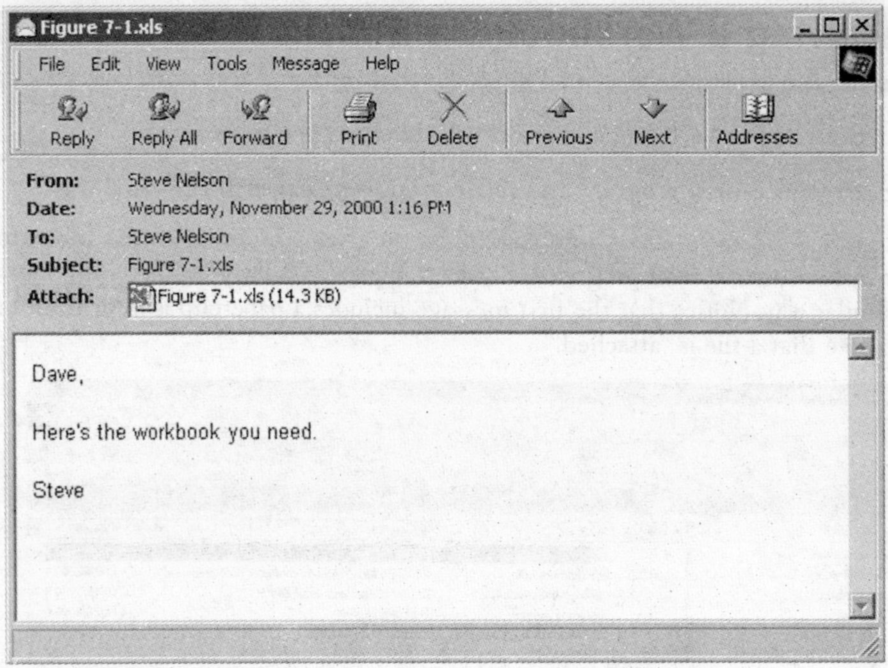

Figure 7-13 The Outlook Express message window with an Excel workbook attachment.

3. **Save the attachment.**

   You can typically do this by right-clicking the attachment icon and then choosing the shortcut menu's Save As command. The e-mail client then displays a Save As dialog box, and you use it to indicate where you want to save the workbook.

4. **Open the workbook.**

   You open the workbook in any of the usual ways. For example, you can start Excel and then choose the File menu's Open command.

Avoiding E-Mail Attachment Problems

E-mail attachment problems may be occurring more infrequently these days as the e-mail clients and the mail servers get smarter. Nevertheless, you should be aware that two problems are commonly encountered when sending attachments over the Internet: problems with attachment size and problems with attachment format.

Problems with attachment size stem from the fact that some mail servers limit attachment size. For example, a mail server may limit attachment size to less than one megabyte, and that may mean your largest Excel workbooks are too big to be attachments.

Problems with attachment format stem from the fact that an attachment can actually be included in a message in either of two formats: Uuencode or MIME. Some e-mail programs accept only one format or may by default assume that attachments use one of the formats. For example, an e-mail client may assume that attachments are Uuencode attachments and then become confused when trying to handle a MIME attachment.

While both problems are frustrating, fortunately neither problem is typically difficult to solve. If you encounter the first problem of attachment size, consult with the mail server administrators—and ask to have the attachment size limit changed. If you encounter the second problem of incompatible attachments, consult the e-mail client documentation to determine how to specify which format is used or assumed—and then make sure that both the sender's and recipient's e-mail clients use the same format.

Workbook Sharing with E-Mail

In the earlier chapter section "Sharing Excel Workbooks over a Network," we noted that if you enable workbook sharing, Excel will allow multiple users to simultaneously open a workbook. Then when these users attempt to save their changes, Excel looks for conflicts and attempts to help users resolve conflicting changes.

It turns out that you can have Excel also perform this same conflict resolution with workbooks you've shared, such as through e-mail or by physically delivering the workbook on a floppy disk. To use Excel's Workbook Sharing feature in these special cases, follow these steps:

1. **Turn on Workbook Sharing.**

   In order to merge workbooks, you need to first turn on Workbook Sharing in the workbook by using the Tools menu's Share Workbook command. This is described in the earlier chapter section "Sharing Excel Workbooks over a Network."

2. **Create identical copies of the same workbook.**

   You can create an identical copy by using the File menu's Save As command. Simply save the workbook using a new name.

3. **Distribute separate copies of the workbook you want to share.**

   You can do this by e-mailing the workbook, as described in the earlier chapter section "Sending a Workbook via E-Mail."

4. **Collect the workbooks after changes are made.**

   After people have made their changes, collect the workbooks. Save them in the same folder location.

5. **Open your master workbook.**

   The master workbook is the workbook in which you'll collect all the changes, and it's probably the same workbook you used to create the workbook copies you distributed.

6. **Choose the Tools menu's Compare And Merge Workbooks command.**

   Excel displays the Select Files To Merge Into Current Workbook dialog box shown in Figure 7-14.

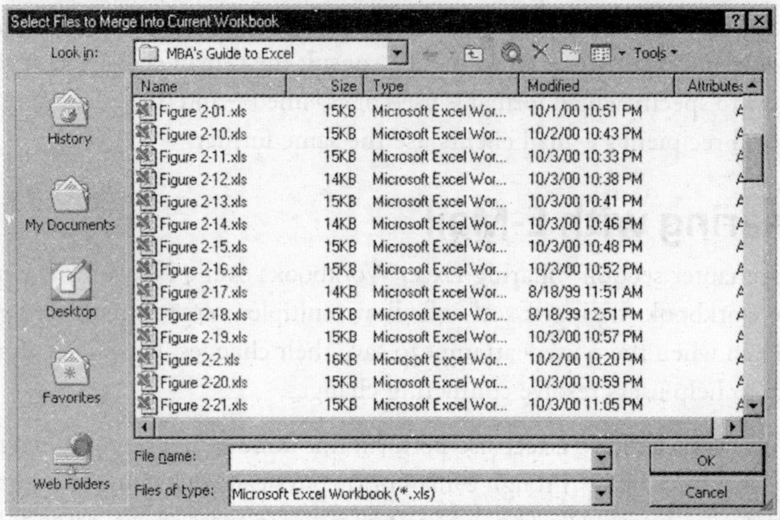

Figure 7-14 The Select Files To Merge Into Current Workbook dialog box.

7. **Select the workbooks you want to merge.**

   The Select Files To Merge Into Current Workbook dialog box works in the same basic way as the Save As and Open dialog boxes. You use the Look In drop-down list box to select the drive and folder you want to open. The main box of the dialog box lists the Excel workbooks in the open folder. To select a workbook, click it. To select multiple workbooks, hold down the Ctrl key and then click each workbook. Then click OK. Excel merges the changes from the selected workbooks into the master workbook.

Using E-Mail Routing Slips

If you choose the File menu's Send To command, you'll also notice a Routing Recipient command. The Routing Recipient command lets you build a list of e-mail addresses to which an Excel workbook can be sequentially routed, and then send the workbook to the first person on the list. When one recipient finishes with the workbook, Excel automatically routes, or sends, the workbook along to the next person on the list.

NOTE *The Routing Recipient command lets you have a group of people make workbook changes sequentially, which means that you avoid the sorts of conflicts described in the earlier discussions of workbook sharing and merging workbooks.*

Sending a Workbook Using Routing Slips

To use the Routing Recipient command, open the workbook you want to share and then follow these steps:

1. **Choose the Routing Recipient command.**

   Excel displays the Routing Slip dialog box shown in Figure 7-15.

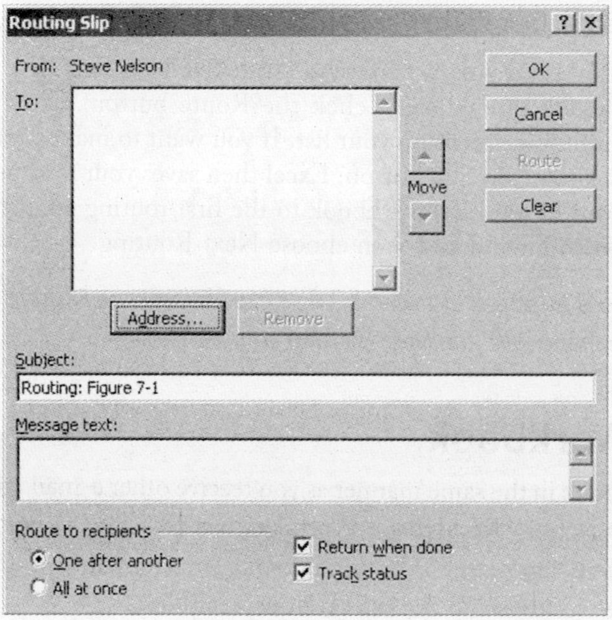

Figure 7-15 The Routing Slip dialog box you use to create a routing recipients list.

2. **Build your list of recipients.**

   Click the Address button to display the Address Book. To add a name, click it and then click the To button. If you want to send the workbook to someone not yet in your Address Book, first add his or her name to your Address Book. You should add names in the same order as you want to route the workbook, but if you don't, note that you can use the Move buttons to move a selected name up or down on the routing list.

3. **Optionally, provide a message subject and message text.**

   You can use the Subject and Message Text boxes to provide the e-mail message subject and message text. Each recipient sees this information.

4. **Indicate you want to use sequential routing.**

   Click the One After Another option button to indicate that you want to use sequential routing. You don't have to use sequential routing, but sequential routing is often desirable. Sequential routing eliminates the need to resolve conflicting edits to a workbook. (What happens, of course, is that recipients will effectively resolve conflicts as they review the previous recipient's work and make further changes.)

NOTE *If you want the workbook returned after the last person on the list finishes, select the Return When Done check box. If you want to receive notification each time the workbook is routed to the next recipient, select the Track Status check box.*

5. **Route the workbook to the first routing recipient.**

   You can begin routing the workbook in two ways: immediately or later. If you want to begin routing the workbook immediately, click the Route button; Excel sends the workbook to the first routing recipient on your list. If you want to make more changes or postpone routing, click the Add Slip button; Excel then saves your routing information. When you later want to send the workbook to the first routing recipient, choose the File menu's Send To command and then choose Next Routing.

NOTE *When a routing slip is attached to a workbook, Excel replaces the Send To submenu's Mail Recipient command with the Next Routing command.*

Receiving a Routed Workbook

You receive a routed workbook in the same manner as you receive other e-mail attachments, as described in the earlier section "Receiving a Workbook via E-Mail." When you finish with the workbook, however, choose the File menu's Send To command and then choose Next Routing to send the workbook to the next routing recipient.

NOTE *Excel provides these same instructions at the end of the e-mail message that goes along with your routed workbook.*

When you choose the Next Routing command, Excel displays the Routing Slip dialog box. Click the Route Document To option button, and then click OK to send the workbook to the next recipient.

NOTE *If you click the Send Copy Of Document Without Using The Routing Slip option button, Excel lets you send the workbook as an attachment to somebody besides the next person on the routing list and without a routing slip. This option is equivalent, then, to the Mail Recipient command, which appears on the Send To submenu when a workbook doesn't have a routing slip.*

Sharing Excel Data over the Web

Excel provides a special command—the File menu's Save As Web Page command—for creating a Web page version of an Excel workbook. You can also use the Save As Web Page command for creating interactive spreadsheet components for Web pages. The paragraphs that follow describe how you do both of these things—and also explain why you will rarely want to do either.

Creating a Web Page Version of an Excel Workbook

Excel lets you use hypertext markup language (HTML) as the format for your Excel workbooks. What this means is that you can create Excel workbooks that can both be opened and edited by Excel in almost the usual way and viewed using your Web browser. (If an Excel workbook is viewed with a Web browser, you can't edit the workbook data except in very limited circumstances, as described later in the section "Creating an Interactive Spreadsheet Component.")

Before we describe the steps for saving an Excel workbook using the Web page, HTML format, we need to emphasize that you don't want to use HTML as the default format for your workbooks. Much workbook information is lost and much workbook functionality is sacrificed when you use the HTML file format.

NOTE *You may be able to get a more complete list of the lost functionality that stems from using HTML as the Excel workbook file format from the Office Assistant. But know for starters that with HTML you lose the following items: the 1904 data system, arrays, cell comments, conditional formatting, custom views, data validation, external link references, formatting (including cell-level fonts, dashed and dotted borders, pattern fills, rotated and indented text), nested functions, password protection, precision-as-displayed options, range names, and scenarios.*

To create a Web page version of an Excel workbook, follow these steps:

1. Choose the File menu's Save As Web Page command.

Excel displays the Save As dialog box shown in Figure 7-16.

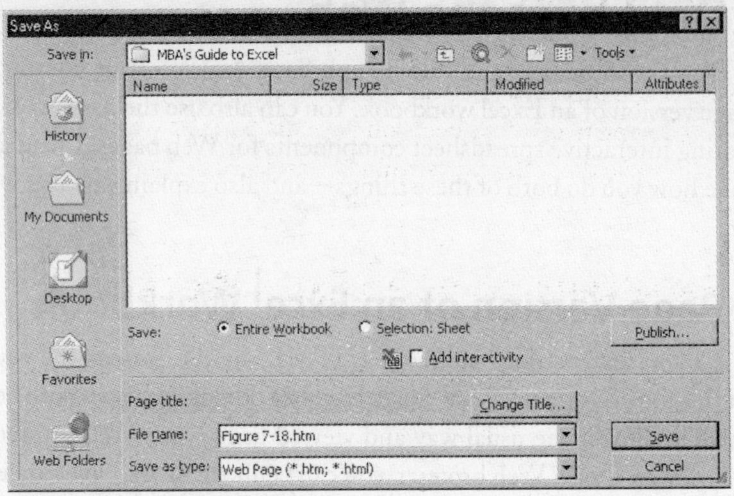

Figure 7-16 The Save As dialog box.

2. Name the Web page.

Click the File Name box, and enter the filename you want to use for the Web page.

3. Verify that the Save As Type box indicates the file format is Web Page, or HTML.

Excel lets you use either its standard binary file format, indicated by the .xls file extension, or its new Web page format, indicated by the .htm file extension. When you save a workbook as a Web page, predictably, you use the Web page format.

4. Specify where you want the Web page saved.

Use the navigation bar's clickable icons to open the folder location where you want to save the Web page. Most often, you click the My Documents icon so that Excel opens your My Documents folder. You can also click the Web Folders icon so that Excel displays a list of Web folders to which you can add files.

NOTE *If you don't see any Web folders listed when you click the Web Folder icon, click Create New Folder. When Excel displays the Add Web Folder dialog box, type the Web folder URL in the box provided. Or, click the Browse button, and then use your Web browser to open the Web folder location.*

5. **Click Publish to create the Web page.**

   When you click Publish, Excel creates an HTML, or Web page version, of the workbook in the specified location.

Once you create the Web page, you can view it using your Web browser. Or, you can open the Web page using Excel and then make the same general changes you make to any Excel workbook.

NOTE *If you do create Web page versions of Excel workbooks, you may want to develop proficiency in using the Insert menu's Hyperlink command. This command lets you add hyperlinks to a workbook—essentially by selecting the item you want to turn into a hyperlink, choosing the command, and then providing the Internet URL.*

Creating an Interactive Spreadsheet Component

Excel also lets you take Excel worksheets or worksheet ranges and convert them into miniature spreadsheet objects that can be placed in Web pages. These interactive spreadsheet components allow people to view the Web page with their Web browser. Figure 7-17, for example, shows a simple mortgage calculator workbook.

	A	B	C
1	Mortgage Payment Calculator		
2	Loan Balance	150000	
3	Repayment Term	360	
4	Annual Interest Rate	0.08	
5	Monthly Payment	($1,100.65)	
6			
7			

Figure 7-17 A simple workbook such as might be used to create an interactive spreadsheet component.

Figure 7-18 shows a Web page with a simple interactive spreadsheet component, which is actually the worksheet range A1:B5 from the workbook shown in Figure 7-17.

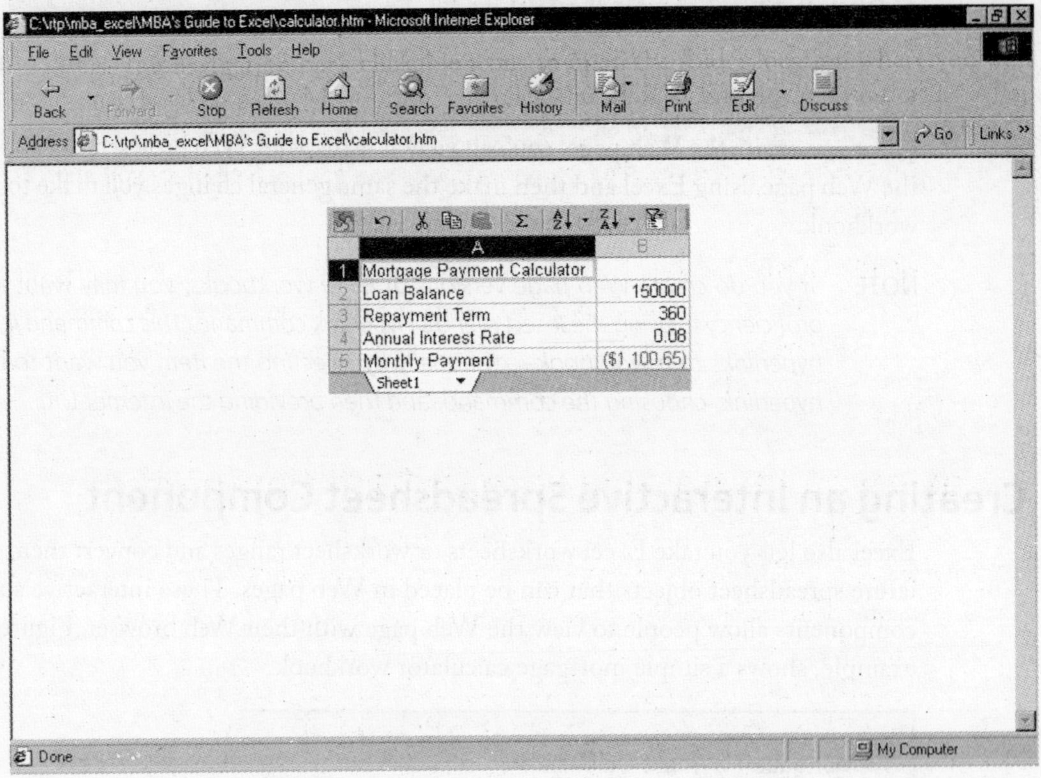

Figure 7-18 A Web page with a simple interactive spreadsheet component.

The unique feature of an interactive spreadsheet component is that when you view the component using Microsoft Internet Explorer version 4.1 (or a later version), you can make modest changes. In Figure 7-18, for example, if you enter a new interest rate, the interactive spreadsheet component calculates a new monthly mortgage payment.

In general, interactive spreadsheet components resemble Excel workbooks in their mechanics. Note, however, that even if you are familiar with Excel you will need to experiment a bit in order to become proficient with interactive spreadsheet components.

As with Excel Web pages, however, interactive spreadsheet components allow for only a subset of Excel's functionality. And, in fact, by using interactive spreadsheet components, you get only a very modest portion of Excel's functionality. What's more, to use interactive spreadsheet components, you must already have installed the Standard, Professional, or Premium version of Microsoft Office and the Office Web Components.

Accordingly, we wonder when interactive spreadsheet components would ever be the preferred method for sharing Excel data. Any time you can successfully share data using an interactive spreadsheet component, you've always got a superior solution that the recipient presumably already knows how to use: Excel.

Nevertheless, creating interactive spreadsheet components is easy. To create an interactive spreadsheet component, first select the worksheet range you want to use as an interactive spreadsheet component. Then follow these steps:

1. **Choose the File menu's Save As Web Page command.**

   Excel displays the Save As dialog box shown in Figure 7-19.

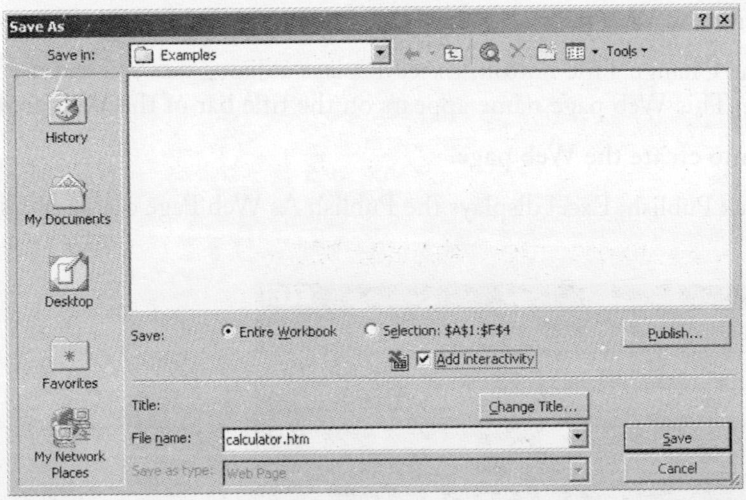

Figure 7-19 The Save As dialog box filled out to create an interactive spreadsheet component.

2. **Click the Selection: Sheet option button.**

   This tells Excel you want to create a Web component for the selected portion of the workbook.

3. **Select the Add Interactivity check box.**

   This tells Excel you want to create an interactive Web component for the selected portion of the workbook.

4. **Name the Web page.**

   Click the File Name box, and enter the filename you want to use for the Web page.

5. **Specify where you want the Web page saved.**

   Use the navigation bar's clickable icons to open the folder location where you want to save the Web page. Most often, you click the My Documents icon so that Excel opens your My Documents folder. You can also click the Web Folders icon so that Excel displays a list of Web folders to which you can add files.

NOTE *If you don't see any Web folders listed when you click the Web Folder icon, click Create New Folder. When Excel displays the Add Web Folder dialog box, type the Web folder URL in the box provided. Or, click the Browse button, and then use your Web browser to open the Web folder location.*

6. **Optionally, give the Web page a name.**

   If you click the Change Title button, Excel displays a dialog box you can use to name the Web page. This Web page name appears on the title bar of the Web browser.

7. **Click Publish to create the Web page.**

   When you click Publish, Excel displays the Publish As Web Page dialog box shown in Figure 7-20.

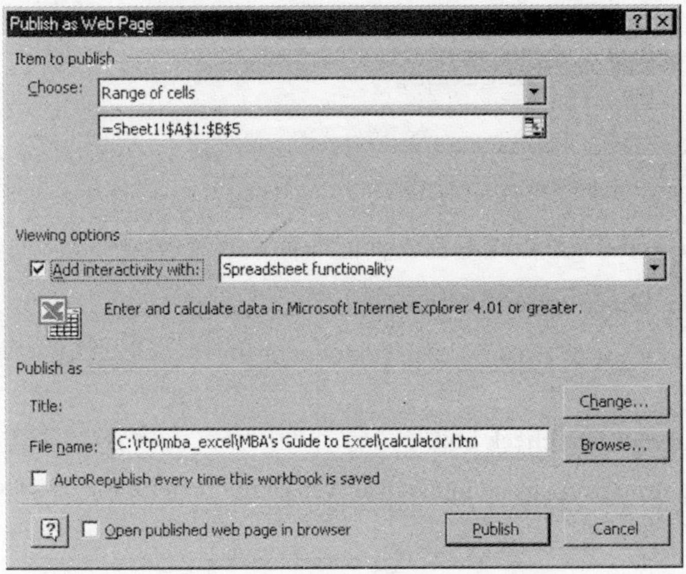

Figure 7-20 The Publish As Web Page dialog box.

8. **Verify the worksheet selection.**

   Review the Choose boxes to confirm that these correctly identify the worksheet selection you want to publish as an interactive spreadsheet component. Edit the contents if needed.

9. **Verify the form of interactivity.**

   Confirm that the Add Interactivity With check box shows the correct form of interactivity. For example, if you're creating an interactive spreadsheet component, the list box should show Spreadsheet Functionality.

10. **Verify the filename.**

    Confirm that the file pathname shows in the File Name box. If the correct file pathname doesn't show in the File Name box, edit the contents as needed.

11. **Publish the interactive spreadsheet component.**

    Click the Publish button.

Retrieving External Data with Excel

Most of the earlier sections of this chapter presuppose you use Excel to create data you then pass along to other programs and people. While many people are very likely to use Excel in this way, you may use Excel to retrieve data created or stored by some other program.

In the final pages of this chapter, then, we'll briefly explain how to use Excel to collect external data so you can exploit Excel's analytical power to examine the data. Specifically, the chapter discusses two tools: Excel's Import Wizard and its Get External Data commands.

Importing Textual Data into Excel

Excel lets you easily import textual data into an Excel workbook. This capacity may not sound interesting, but it means that anything you can get as a text file—such as a financial report generated by the mainframe accounting system—can be imported into Excel and then examined.

To import a text file into Excel, follow these steps:

1. **Open the text file.**

   Using the File menu's Open command, tell Excel that you want to open the text file. When Excel displays the Open dialog box, select the All Files item or the Text File items in the List Files Of Type box so that your text file is listed. Once you find the file, click it and then click the Open button. Excel displays the first Text Import Wizard dialog box, shown in Figure 7-21.

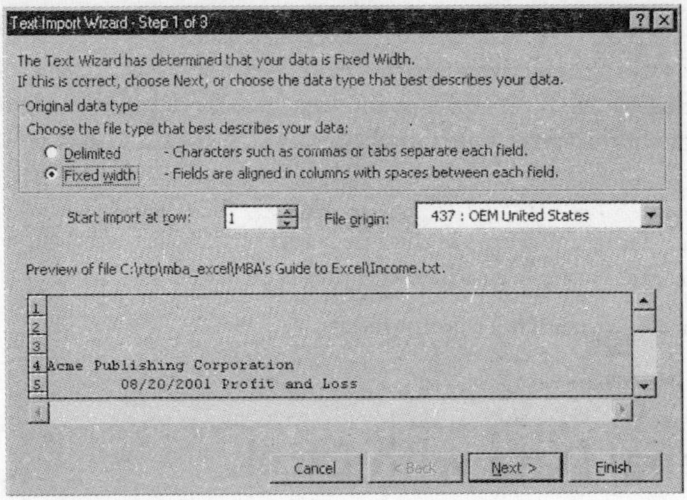

Figure 7-21 The first Text Import Wizard dialog box.

2. **Indicate whether the file uses the fixed-width format or delimiting characters.**

   Use the Original Data Type option buttons—Fixed Width or Delimited—to indicate whether the file uses a fixed-width format, which is the same thing as a straight text file, or uses delimiting characters. Excel can usually guess correctly about which format your text file uses, by the way, so if you're not sure which option to select, accept Excel's default suggestion.

3. **Indicate the first row that should be imported.**

   Use the Start Import At Row box to indicate which row of the text file is the first row you want to have imported. For example, you might not want to import reader header and title information, and might instead want only to begin importing the first row with the data.

4. **Identify the file origin.**

   Use the File Origin box to identify the source of the file. If you're importing data created by another Windows program, select the Windows (ANSI) entry from the File Origin box. If you're importing data from a mainframe, select the MS-DOS (PC-8) entry from the File Origin box.

NOTE *You can use the Preview box to see how Excel interprets your to-be-imported data.*

5. **Verify the fixed-width assumptions or delimited character assumptions made by Excel.**

   Once you finish with the first Text Import Wizard dialog box, you click Next. Excel then displays the second Text Import Wizard dialog box. If you're importing a fixed-width file, Excel displays the dialog box shown in Figure 7-22. You use this dialog box to verify how Excel breaks the text file into columns. You can create new break lines by clicking. You can remove an existing break line by double-clicking. You can also move an existing break line by dragging.

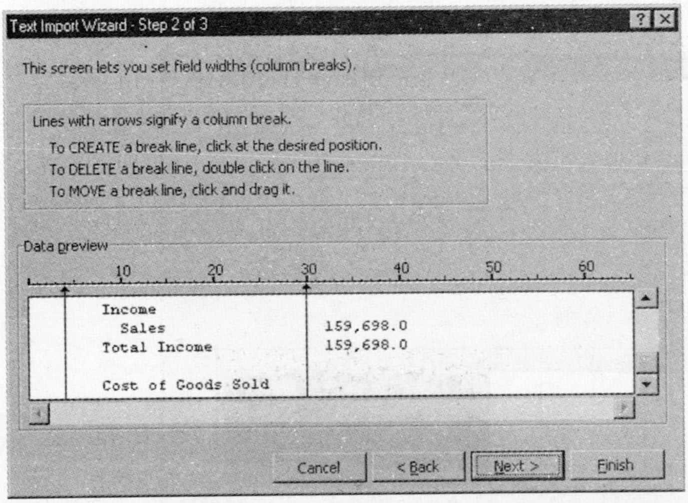

Figure 7-22 The second Text Import Wizard dialog box if you're importing a fixed-width file.

If you're importing a delimited character file, Excel displays the dialog box shown in Figure 7-23. You use this dialog box principally to verify that Excel has correctly identified the delimiter: The checked Delimiters box should identify the delimiter. You can also indicate if the text file uses a character (such as a quotation mark) to identify text. Note that you can tell whether Excel's delimiter assumptions correctly describe the text file because the preview box shows how your data look given the delimiter specifications.

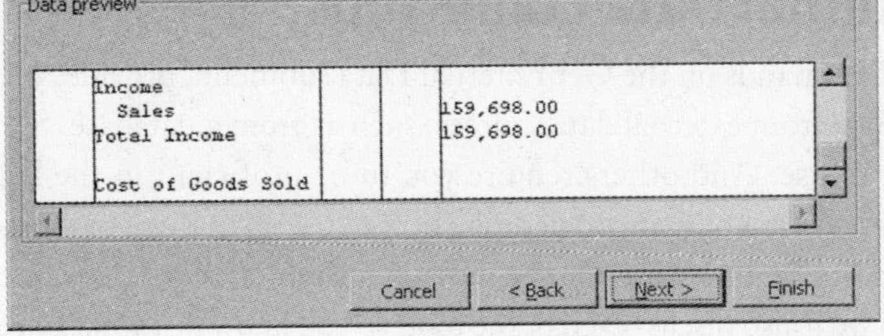

Figure 7-23 The second Text Import Wizard dialog box if you're importing a delimited character file.

6. **Select formatting for each column.**

   After you've verified the fixed-width or delimited character assumptions of Excel—and fixed any incorrect assumptions—click Next. Excel displays the third Text Import Wizard shown in Figure 7-24. You use this dialog box to specify the formatting assumptions Excel should make about the to-be-imported text file.

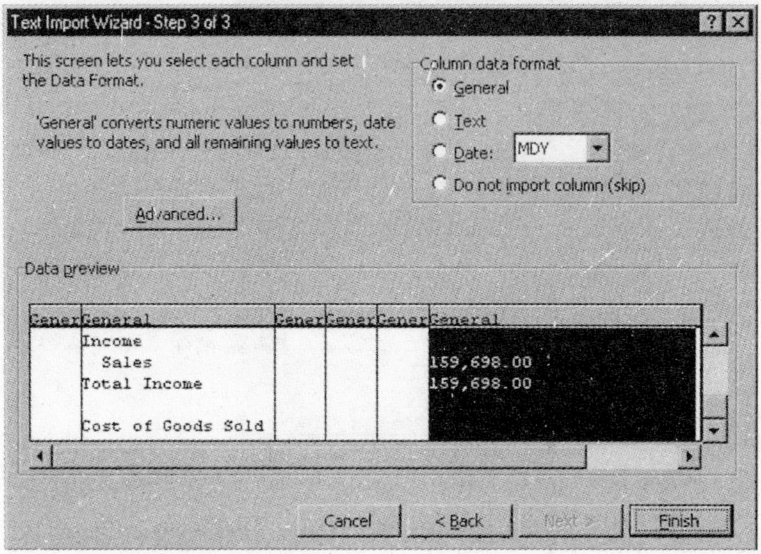

Figure 7-24 The third Text Import Wizard dialog box.

   Excel also guesses about the default formatting that it should use for each column of the text file you import. You should verify that each column uses the best default formatting. To change a column's format, click the column header and then the appropriate Column Data Format button. If you don't want to import a column, click it and then click the Do Not Import Column option button.

7. **Click Finish when you're finished.**

   Excel imports the text file into a new, blank, open workbook. At this point, you're ready to begin cleaning up the data so you can start working with it.

Using the Get External Data Commands

Excel, through the commands on the Get External Data submenu, provides tools that you can use to retrieve data from external data sources, such as from a database. Some of these tools are quite easy to use. And others require you to be proficient in the language and structure of databases. We're not going to describe how to use all of these tools in detail here. We will, however, describe how you use the most common of these tools, including the Query Wizard. And we'll also discuss each of the tools so you know just what Excel is capable of and about features you may want to explore in more detail.

Importing Text Files

If you choose the Data menu's Get External Data command and then choose the Get External Data submenu's Import Text File command, Excel lets you identify a text file you want to import. Once you've identified this text file, Excel starts the same Text Import Wizard described in the previous section, "Importing Textual Data into Excel."

When you use the Import Text File command, however, Excel does one thing differently from starting the Text Import Wizard from the File menu's Open command. When you use the Import Text File command, Excel maintains a link to the original text file by using external references. This means that if you want to re-import the text file—perhaps because the data has changed—you can easily do so. To re-import the data, click the Refresh All toolbar button on the External Data toolbar.

NOTE *If you don't see the External Data toolbar, right-click another toolbar and choose the shortcut menu's External Data command.*

Using the Query Wizard

Excel's Import External Data submenu provides access to the Query Wizard, which is the tool you'll most often use to retrieve external data. The Query Wizard, in effect, provides an interface you use from inside Excel to query an external database.

The Query Wizard works with most common databases. Excel provides database drivers for connecting to most (perhaps all) of the popular database engines, including the Microsoft Access, Excel, FoxPro, and SQL Server products and the third-party database products dBASE, Oracle and Paradox.

If you want to retrieve information from an external database that isn't on the list contained in the preceding paragraph, you can still retrieve data from the database. For example, almost surely, you can use the database program to create a text file that holds the information you want to query. And you may also be able to create database files, or tables, that use a format that mimics one of the databases listed.

NOTE *To import a text file, you use the Text Import Wizard. As noted in the preceding paragraphs, you can start the Text Import Wizard indirectly by choosing the File menu's Open command and then attempting to open the text file. Or you can start the Text Import Wizard directly by choosing the Data menu's Get External Data command and then choosing Import Text File.*

To use the Query Wizard, follow these steps:

1. **Open a blank workbook.**

   Excel places the external data you retrieve in the open workbook. This means you'll probably want to start with a blank, open workbook. If you want to place the data in an existing workbook, make sure you've got an empty worksheet on which to store the data.

2. **Start the Query Wizard.**

   To start the Query Wizard, choose the Data menu's Import External Data command and then choose New Database Query. Excel displays the Choose Data Source dialog box shown in Figure 7-25.

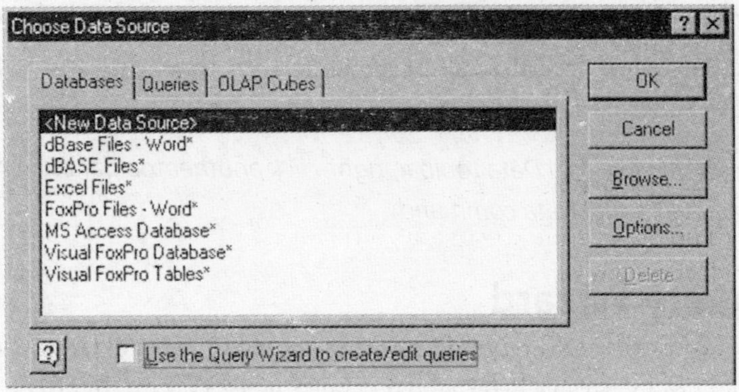

Figure 7-25 The Choose Data Source dialog box.

3. **Indicate you want to use the Query Wizard.**

   Check the Use The Query Wizard To Create/Edit Queries box to indicate you'll use the Query Wizard.

4. **Indicate the data source from which you'll retrieve the data.**

   To select the data source from which you want to retrieve data, first click the Databases tab. Then select the type of database from which you'll retrieve data. For example, if you're retrieving data from a dBASE database, click the dBASE Files entry in the list box. Click OK after you've selected your data source. The Query Wizard displays the Choose Columns dialog box shown in Figure 7-26.

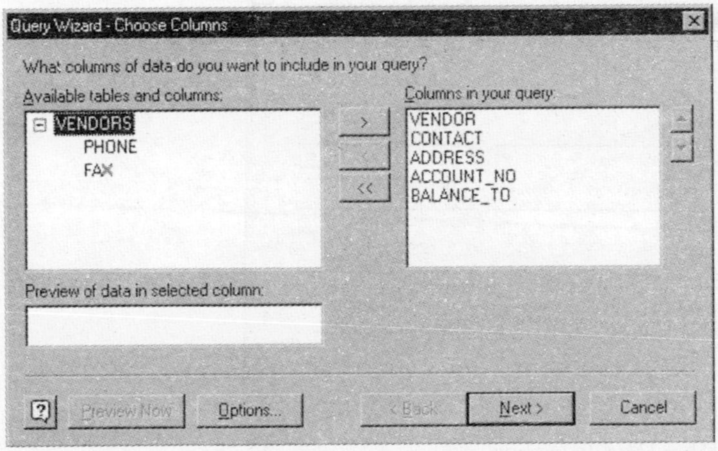

Figure 7-26 The Choose Columns dialog box.

NOTE *If you want to rerun an existing query, click the Queries tab to see a list of defined queries you can use to get external data. You can also click the OLAP Cubes tab to see a list of OLAP data sources that may be available.*

5. Select the table or tables that you want to query.

When Excel displays the Choose Columns dialog box, use the Available Tables And Columns list box to select the tables and columns, or fields, that you want to import. To see the columns that a table uses, click the plus symbol next to the table name.

6. Select the columns that you want to retrieve.

Select the columns you want to retrieve by clicking the column and then clicking the Add button. The Add button shows a single arrow pointing to the Columns In Your Query list box. To remove a column from the Columns In Your Query list box, click the column and then click the Remove button, which shows a single arrow pointing to the Available Tables And Columns List box. To start over, click the Remove All button, which shows a double arrow pointing to the Available Tables And Columns List box. When you finish selecting the columns you want to retrieve, click Next. The Query Wizard displays the Filter Data dialog box shown in Figure 7-27.

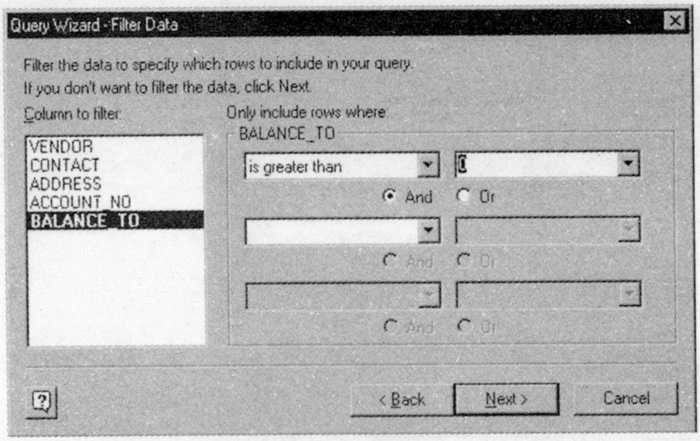

Figure 7-27 The Filter Data dialog box.

7. **Describe the data the Query Wizard should retrieve.**

   To describe the data you want to retrieve, use filters based on the columns, or fields, that you're querying. To create a filter, select the column you want the query to examine. Then use the Only Include Rows Where boxes and buttons to indicate how this column is examined. Figure 7-27, for example, shows a filter that looks at the BALANCE_TO column to see whether this value is greater than or equal to zero. The first drop-down list box in the Only Include Rows Where area provides other logical operators you can also use. If you want to create a filter based on more than one comparison of the same column, use the And and Or option buttons and the next row of boxes. If you want to create a filter based on another column, select the column from the Columns To Filter list box and then repeat the preceding steps. When you finish specifying the filters you want to use, click Next. The Query Wizard displays the Sort Order dialog box shown in Figure 7-28.

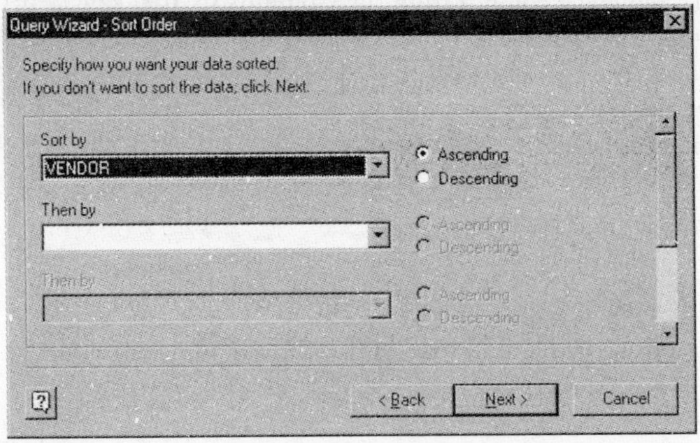

Figure 7-28 The Sort Order dialog box.

8. **Select a sort order for the retrieved data.**

   When Excel displays the Sort Order dialog box, use the Sort By box and the Ascending and Descending option buttons to indicate how the retrieved data should be arranged in your worksheet. If some of the records, or rows, will use the same first sort key—this is what you specified using the Sort By box—you can provide a second sort key using the first Then By box and buttons. You can also provide additional sort keys using the other Then By box and buttons. When you finish specifying the sort order, click Next. The Query Wizard displays the Finish dialog box shown in Figure 7-29.

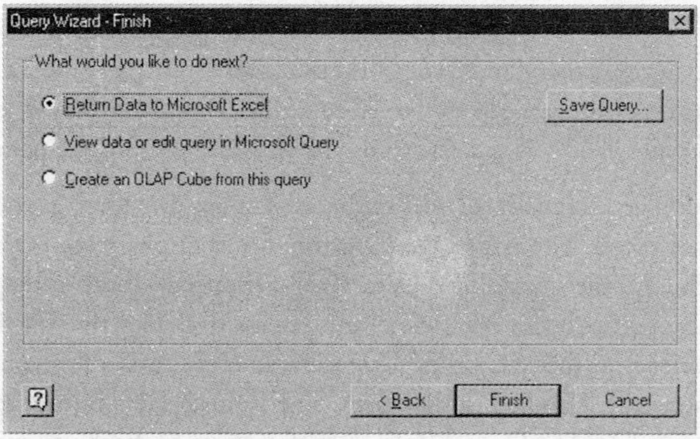

Figure 7-29 The Finish dialog box.

9. **Tell the Query Wizard where you want to place the data that the query returns.**

   When the Query Wizard displays the Finish dialog box, use the What Would You Like To Do Next option buttons to select a location for the data. Presumably, you want to place the retrieved data in an Excel worksheet so you can use Excel's analytical tools to examine the data in ways that the database program doesn't allow. To do this, click the Return Data To Microsoft Excel button. Then click Finish. Excel runs the query and asks where the retrieved data should be stored using the Import Data dialog box shown in Figure 7-30.

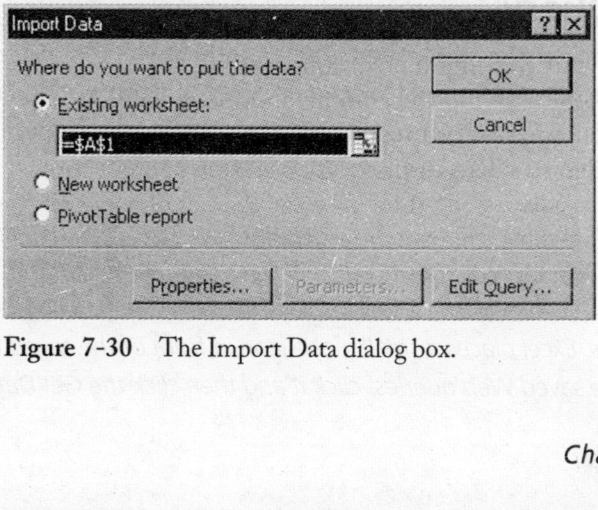

Figure 7-30 The Import Data dialog box.

NOTE *If you want to save the query so you can use it again, click the Finish dialog box's Save button. Then when Excel displays the Save As dialog box, use the File Name box to give the query a name. Once you've done this, click Save to save the query for future use.*

10. Select a location for the retrieved data.

When Excel asks where the retrieved data should be placed, use the Where Do You Want To Put The Data option buttons to select a location for the data: in the open workbook at the location of the cell selector, in a new workbook, or in a PivotTable report. Then click OK. Excel places the data in the indicated location.

After you place the retrieved data in an Excel workbook, you can begin to work with the data using Excel's features. You can use statistical functions to look closely at the data's characteristics, for example. And you can use charts to view and present the data visually.

The External Data toolbar, which Excel will probably display, provides several toolbar buttons you'll find useful, too. The Edit Query button, for example, restarts the Query Wizard so you can change the query. The Data Range Properties button displays the External Data Range Properties dialog box, which you can use to change the way that Excel handles the data it retrieves in the query. The Query Parameters button lets you describe how any query parameters are handled in the query. The Refresh Data button reruns the query to retrieve any new data. The Cancel Refresh button stops a refresh you might have started. The Refresh All button reruns all the queries in a workbook. Finally, the Refresh Status button displays a dialog box that reports information such as how long a refresh operation took.

NOTE *A query parameter is a value that you've said you will supply to the query before or as it runs. The Query Wizard doesn't let you create query parameters. If you create from-scratch queries using Microsoft Query, which is discussed briefly in the later section "Running Microsoft Query," you can use query parameters.*

Running a Web Query

The Get External Data submenu provides a Web Query tool that you can use to retrieve tabular data from a Web page. To run a simple Web query, open a blank workbook, choose the Data menu's Import External Data command, and then choose the Import External Data submenu's New Web Query command.

NOTE *Excel also comes with several Web queries already set up and saved, which you can run by choosing the Data menu's Import External Data command and then choosing Run Saved Query. When you do this, Excel displays the Run Query dialog box, which lists the saved queries. Excel places a small globe icon in front of the saved Web queries. To run one of the saved Web queries, click it and then click the Get Data button.*

If you choose the New Web Query command, Excel displays the New Web Query dialog box, as shown in Figure 7-31. To use the New Web Query dialog box, type or select the address in the Address box to open the Web page with the table from which you want to retrieve information. If you want to import more than one table, select the arrow next to the table. At this point, you can click Import and Excel will retrieve the table data. When Excel asks where the data should be placed using the Import Data dialog box (see Figure 7-30), indicate the appropriate location.

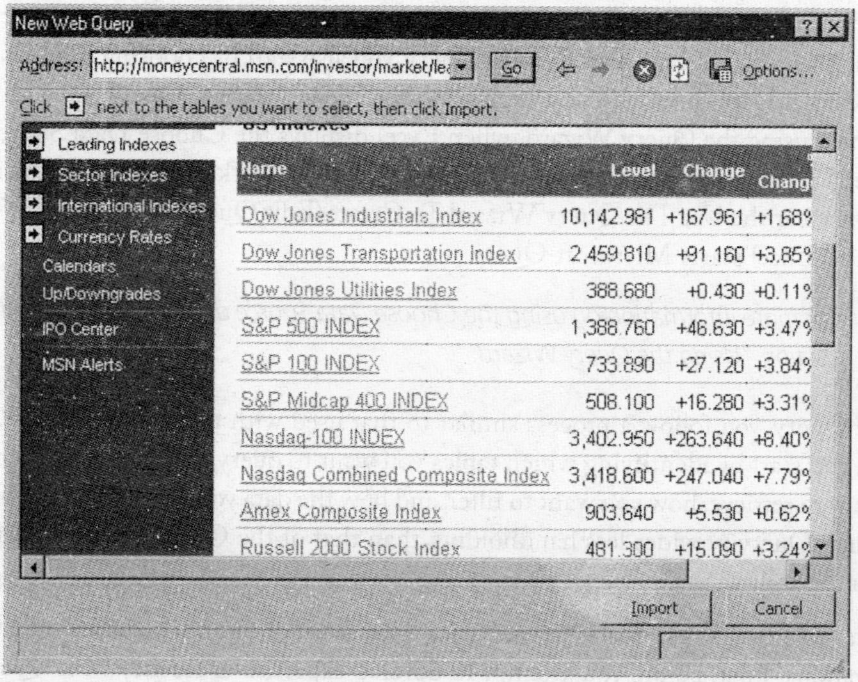

Figure 7-31 The New Web Query dialog box.

You can use the other option buttons in the New Web Query dialog box to control the Web query. In addition, the Options button enables you to choose how this data is formatted as it is imported into your workbook. Your best bet in working with these options is probably just to experiment and see which option settings produce the best results.

NOTE *The more you know about HTML, the more you can do with the Web Query tool. If you know HTML well, for example, you can use the New Web Query dialog box to specify that only specific tables should be retrieved from a Web page.*

Running Microsoft Query

The Query Wizard, described in the earlier chapter section "Using the Query Wizard," provides you with a simple way to access external data. You should know, however, that the Query Wizard is a tool you use to tell another program, Microsoft Query, how you want to query an external database. While the Query Wizard works well in most simple situations, you don't get access to all of Microsoft Query's power when you work through the wizard.

When you want more control over how a query operates, you can work directly with Microsoft Query. To work directly with Query, you also start by choosing the Data menu's Get External Data command and then choosing New Database Query. As with a query performed using the Query Wizard, when Excel displays the Choose Data Source dialog box (see Figure 7-25), you select the database source. To work directly with Query, however, you clear the Use The Query Wizard To Create/Edit Queries check box. When you click OK, Excel starts Microsoft Query.

NOTE *For more information on using the Choose Data Source dialog box, refer to the earlier section "Using the Query Wizard."*

To use Query, you follow a process similar to that used with the Query Wizard. For example, you start by identifying which tables you want to query, which columns, (or fields) you want to retrieve, how you want to filter, and how the data you retrieve should be sorted. Although Query provides less handholding than that of the Query Wizard, it offers you greater flexibility.

A more detailed discussion of Query is beyond the scope of this book, but here are two final observations: First, before you attempt to develop expertise or fluency with Query, make sure that you won't get farther, faster, simply by learning how to use the external data source's query capabilities. For example, Access is easier to learn (in part because it's better documented) and more useful than Query. It may not be a good use of your time to learn Query so that you can then query an Access database. Instead, you might be better off learning Access.

Second, the Excel help file provides detailed information about how to use Microsoft Query. To access this information, ask the Office Assistant a question such as, "How do I work with Microsoft Query?" Then explore the help topics that the Office Assistant provides.

Chapter 8

PIVOTTABLES AND PIVOTCHARTS

Featuring:

- Using the PivotTable Wizard
- Editing PivotTables
- Creating PivotCharts

This chapter describes how you can use Excel's PivotTable features to work with data bases in Excel. If you use Excel to list records, you can use the PivotTables feature to sort, filter, and pivot fields so you can better focus on the information you want.

NOTE *Excel databases are simply worksheets that list information, as shown in Figure 8-1. The first row names the fields of the data. Subsequent rows hold the database. To sort a database, select the worksheet range holding the database and then choose the Data menu's Sort command. To filter a database, select the worksheet range holding the database and then choose the Data menu's AutoFilter command or its Filter command.*

Using the PivotTable Wizard

Figure 8-1 shows three years' worth of sales data for a microbrewery that sells six types of beer on the West Coast. The company recorded sales for each type of beer by state and by season. You can see that with the large amounts of information in the database, it's difficult to spot trends. Creating a PivotTable allows you to see which type of beer sells best in which region or during which season.

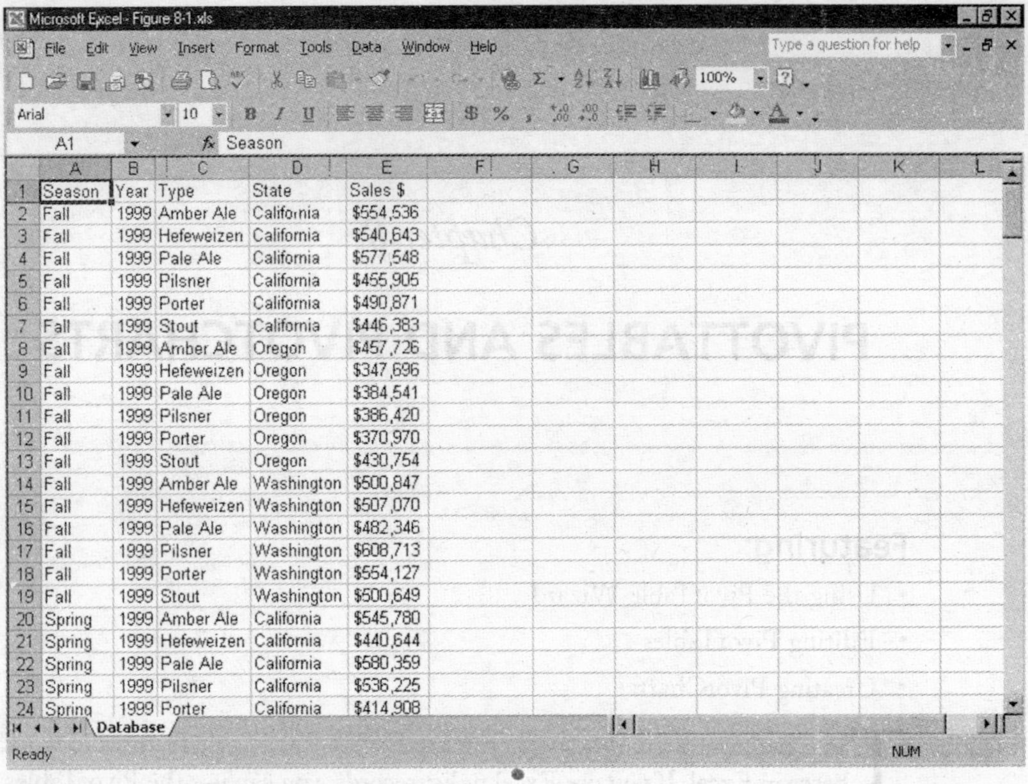

	A	B	C	D	E
1	Season	Year	Type	State	Sales $
2	Fall	1999	Amber Ale	California	$554,536
3	Fall	1999	Hefeweizen	California	$540,643
4	Fall	1999	Pale Ale	California	$577,548
5	Fall	1999	Pilsner	California	$455,905
6	Fall	1999	Porter	California	$490,871
7	Fall	1999	Stout	California	$446,383
8	Fall	1999	Amber Ale	Oregon	$457,726
9	Fall	1999	Hefeweizen	Oregon	$347,696
10	Fall	1999	Pale Ale	Oregon	$384,541
11	Fall	1999	Pilsner	Oregon	$386,420
12	Fall	1999	Porter	Oregon	$370,970
13	Fall	1999	Stout	Oregon	$430,754
14	Fall	1999	Amber Ale	Washington	$500,847
15	Fall	1999	Hefeweizen	Washington	$507,070
16	Fall	1999	Pale Ale	Washington	$482,346
17	Fall	1999	Pilsner	Washington	$608,713
18	Fall	1999	Porter	Washington	$554,127
19	Fall	1999	Stout	Washington	$500,649
20	Spring	1999	Amber Ale	California	$545,780
21	Spring	1999	Hefeweizen	California	$440,644
22	Spring	1999	Pale Ale	California	$580,359
23	Spring	1999	Pilsner	California	$536,225
24	Spring	1999	Porter	California	$414,908

Figure 8-1 Database of beer sales.

To start the PivotTable Wizard, select any cell in the database and choose the Data menu's PivotTable And PivotChart Report command. Excel displays the dialog box shown in Figure 8-2.

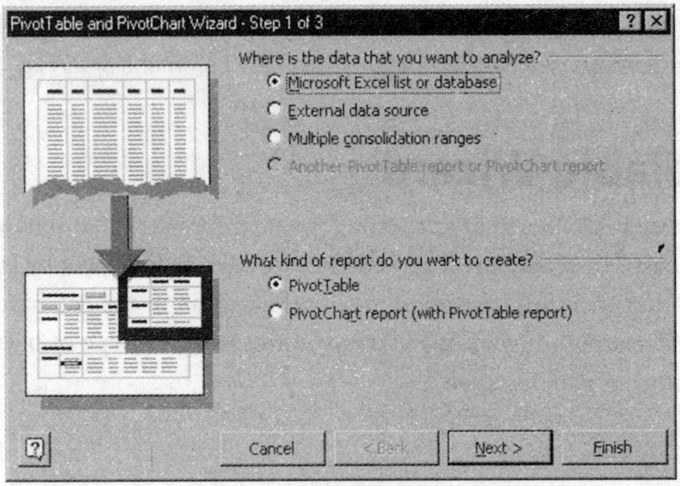

Figure 8-2 The first step of the PivotTable And PivotChart Wizard.

If your data is in a single range on a single worksheet in the current workbook, click the Microsoft Excel List Or Database option button. Then click the PivotTable option button, and click Next.

The second step of the PivotTable And PivotChart Wizard asks you to select the data you want to include in the PivotTable. Do so, and then click Next.

In the third and last step of the PivotTable And PivotChart Wizard, specify where you want Excel to put the PivotTable you're creating and click Finish. As shown in Figure 8-3, Excel displays the new, empty PivotTable in the location you specified. It also displays the PivotTable toolbar and PivotTable Field List dialog box, which you use to lay out and edit the PivotTable.

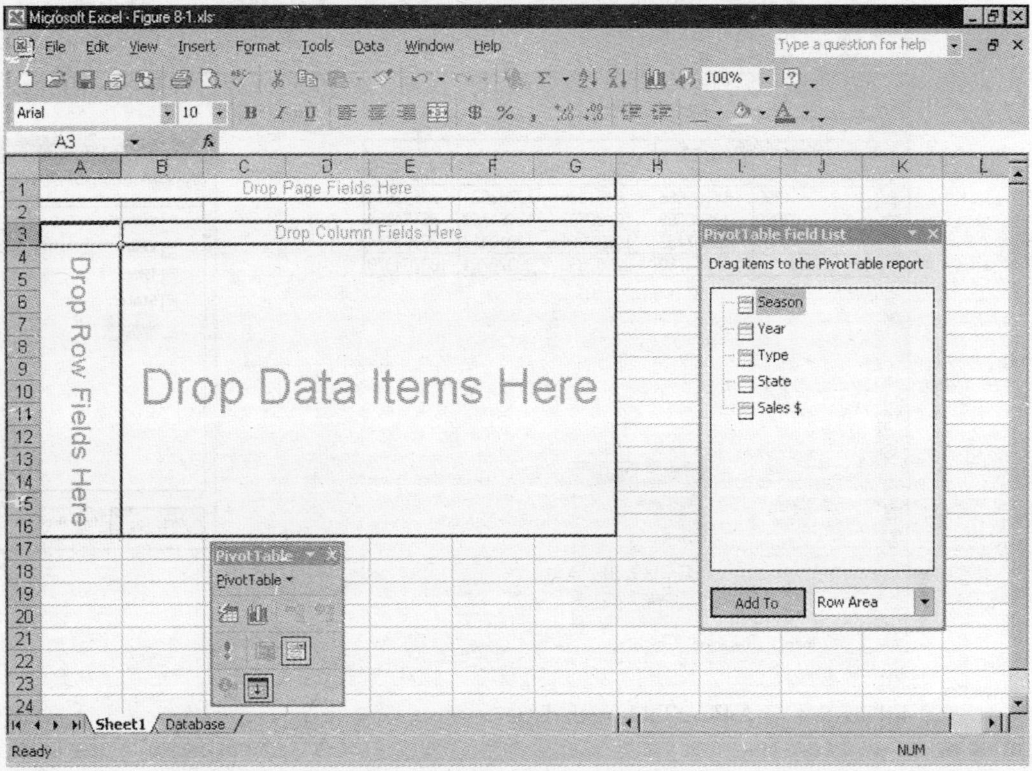

Figure 8-3 The new, empty PivotTable, the PivotTable toolbar, and the PivotTable Field List dialog box.

Specifying PivotTable Layout

To begin laying out your PivotTable, use the buttons on the PivotTable toolbar to drag fields to set up row and column headings. In the example shown in Figure 8-3, you could drag the Year field to the box labeled Drop Row Fields Here and the State field to the box labeled Drop Column Fields Here. You could then drag the Sales field to the Drop Data Items Here box. After you drag the Sales field to the Data area, Excel adds the data to the PivotTable. Figure 8-4 shows fields on a PivotTable filled with data.

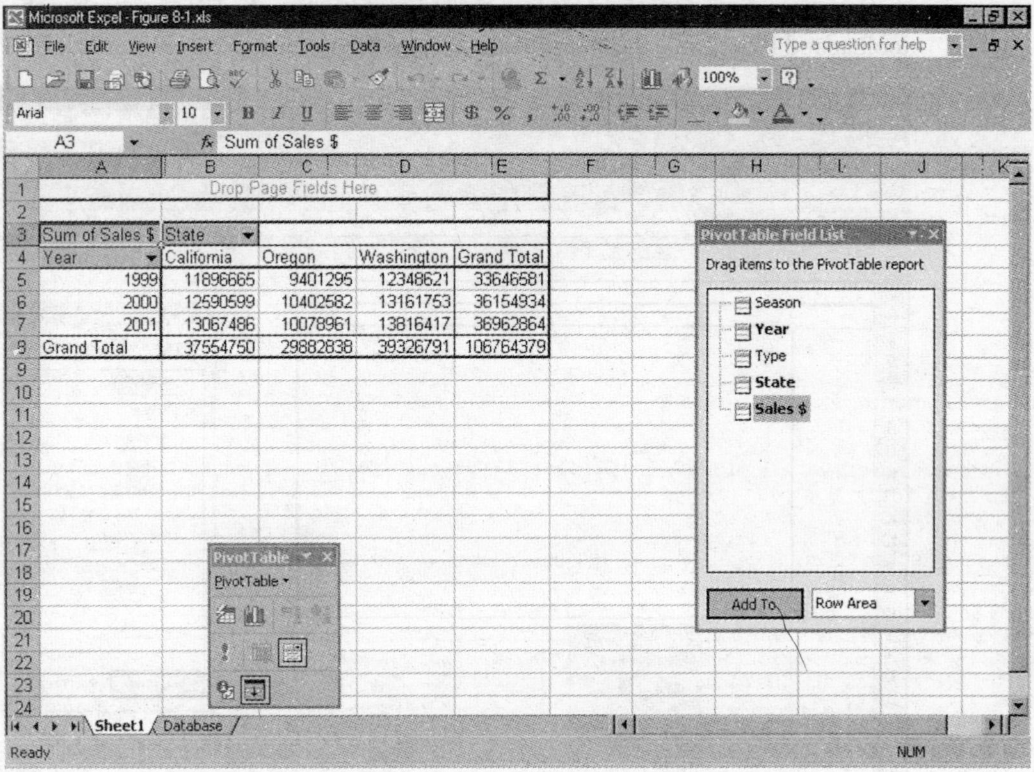

Figure 8-4 A PivotTable with data.

The box in the upper left corner reads Sum Of Sales $. This is because Excel assumes you want to subtotal and total sales figures. If you were to drag a label field instead of a value field into the Data area, Excel would by default count the occurrences of that label. You can change the operation performed on the data included in a PivotTable by selecting a cell in the part you want to change and clicking the PivotTable toolbar's Field Settings button. Excel displays the PivotTable Field dialog box shown in Figure 8-5. This dialog box's options differ slightly depending on the type of data presented in the part of the PivotTable you selected.

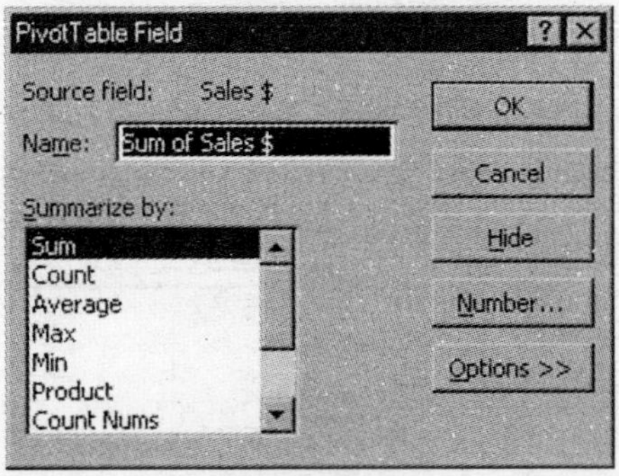

Figure 8-5 The PivotTable Field dialog box.

TIP *To rename a field, enter a new name in the Name text box in the PivotTable Field dialog box.*

To change the operation performed on items in the field, select an item from the Summarize By drop-down list box and click OK. For comparative operations, click the Options button. You can then list item data as a percentage of another item or as a difference from another item, for example.

You can drag multiple fields to a heading. To add another field to a PivotTable, just drag the field's button from the PivotTable Field List dialog box. For example, you could drag the Season field to the right of the Year column to sort by year and then by season. Figure 8-6 shows how the PivotTable looks when you do this. To remove a field from a table, just drag the field outside the table area.

NOTE *If you don't see the field buttons on the PivotTable toolbar, click the Display Fields button.*

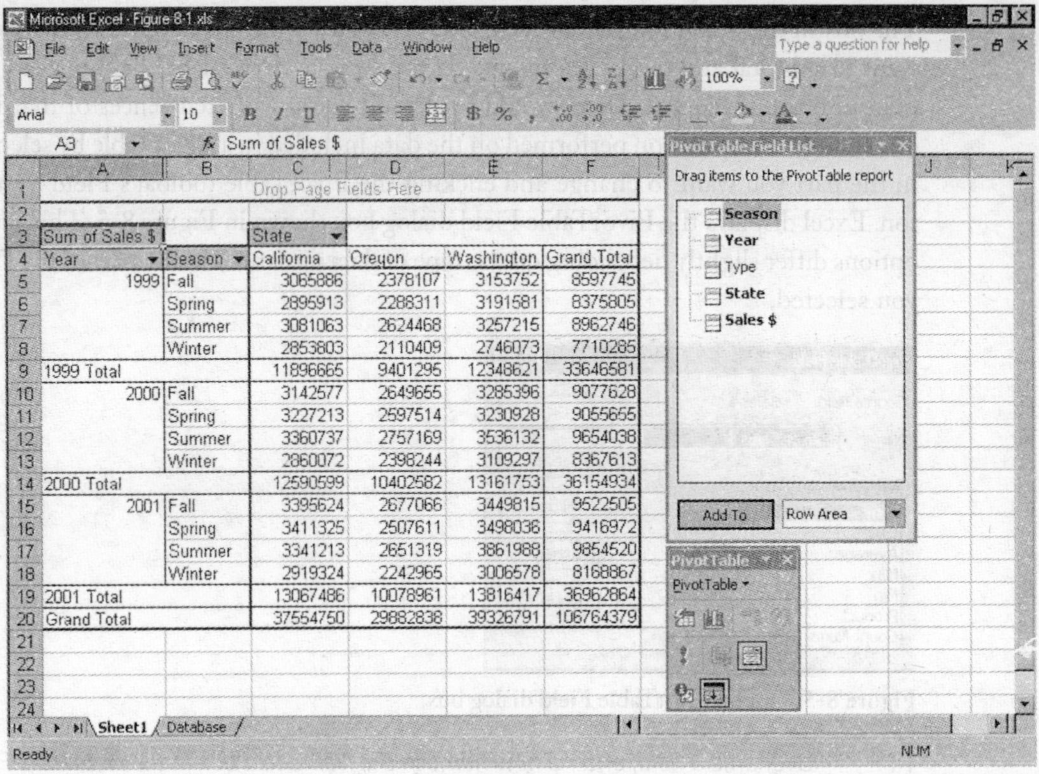

Sum of Sales $		State			
Year	Season	California	Oregon	Washington	Grand Total
1999	Fall	3065886	2378107	3153752	8597745
	Spring	2895913	2288311	3191581	8375805
	Summer	3081063	2624468	3257215	8962746
	Winter	2853803	2110409	2746073	7710285
1999 Total		11896665	9401295	12348621	33646581
2000	Fall	3142577	2649655	3285396	9077628
	Spring	3227213	2597514	3230928	9055655
	Summer	3360737	2757169	3536132	9654038
	Winter	2860072	2398244	3109297	8367613
2000 Total		12590599	10402582	13161753	36154934
2001	Fall	3395624	2677066	3449815	9522505
	Spring	3411325	2507611	3498036	9416972
	Summer	3341213	2651319	3861988	9854520
	Winter	2919324	2242965	3006578	8168867
2001 Total		13067486	10078961	13816417	36962864
Grand Total		37554750	29882838	39326791	106764379

Figure 8-6 A PivotTable with multiple row fields.

NOTE *If you attempt to change the data summarized in a PivotTable (for example, the value in cell D7), Excel prevents you from doing so. This safeguard, of course, is because this cell sums the data for the various types of beer in the database, and you cannot change the sum without changing the values that make up the sum. If you want to change the values in the PivotTable, you must make the changes to the database upon which the PivotTable is based. Then return to the PivotTable and click the Refresh Data button on the PivotTable toolbar to update the PivotTable.*

Editing PivotTables

PivotTables got their name because you can easily rearrange, or "pivot," them. For example, you can move row headings to become column headings, or vice versa, or you can change the hierarchy of fields within a row or column heading. You can also separate PivotTable data among pages.

TIP *You can improve the visual appeal of a table by applying a style to it. To do so, click the Format Report button on the PivotTable toolbar, select a style from the AutoFormat dialog box, and click OK.*

Pivoting

To pivot a PivotTable, just drag a heading to a different axis. For example, you can drag the Season field to the column heading to create a long, narrow table, as shown in Figure 8-7. By doing this, each state has its own subtable within the table.

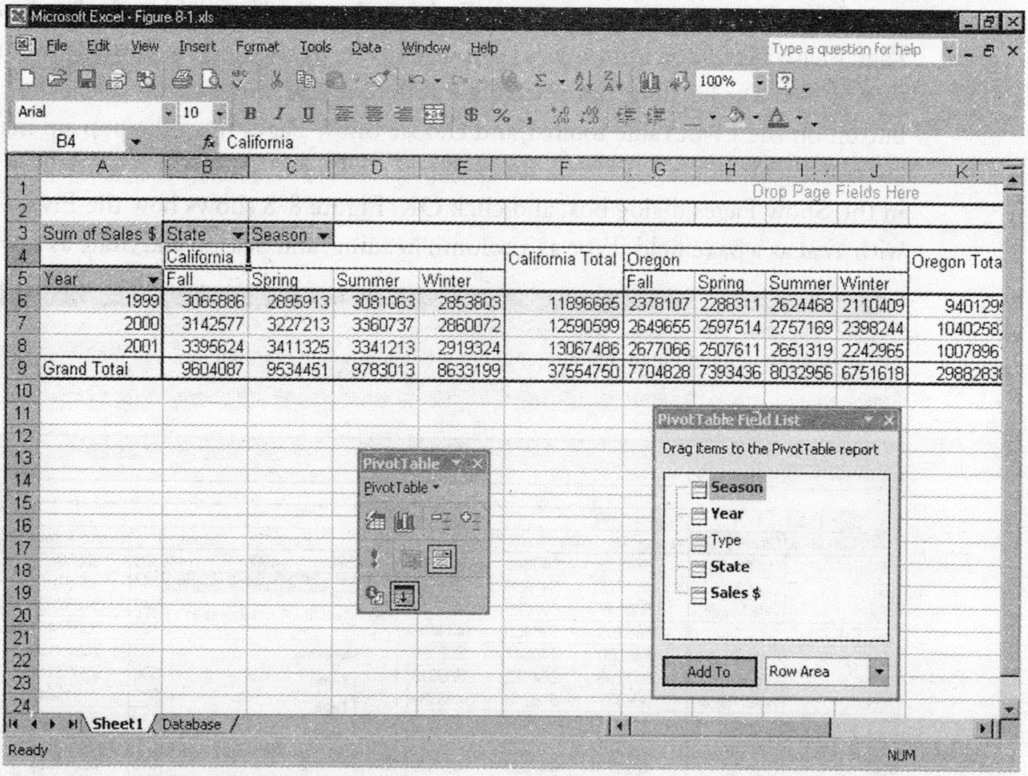

Figure 8-7 Pivoting a PivotTable.

You can also reorganize a PivotTable by changing the hierarchy of fields in a heading. For example, if you look back at the PivotTable in Figure 8-6, sales are grouped first by year and then by season within each year. However, if you drag the Season field to the left of the Year field, you can group first by season, and then within each season, by year.

Filtering Items in a Field

You can tell Excel which items you want to include in a PivotTable for each field. For example, if you don't want to worry about sales in California for the moment, you can exclude California from the table. To do so, click the down arrow on the right side of the State heading and clear the California check box. Then click OK.

Separating Data Between Pages

If your database is so large that your PivotTable is too long or wide to easily read without scrolling back and forth, you might want to view only certain parts of the data on a single worksheet page. For example, in the microbrewery database, you might want to put sales data for each year on a separate page. To do so, drag the Year field to the box labeled Drop Page Fields Here. You can view data for other years by clicking the down arrow on the right side of the Year heading and selecting a different year. You can also click the PivotTable button on the PivotTable toolbar and choose Show Pages from the pop-up menu to create new sheets in the workbook for each page field. Just select the page field from the list in the Show Pages dialog box, and click OK. Figure 8-8 shows how the PivotTable looks with Year as a page field, Type as a column heading, and Season and State as row headings.

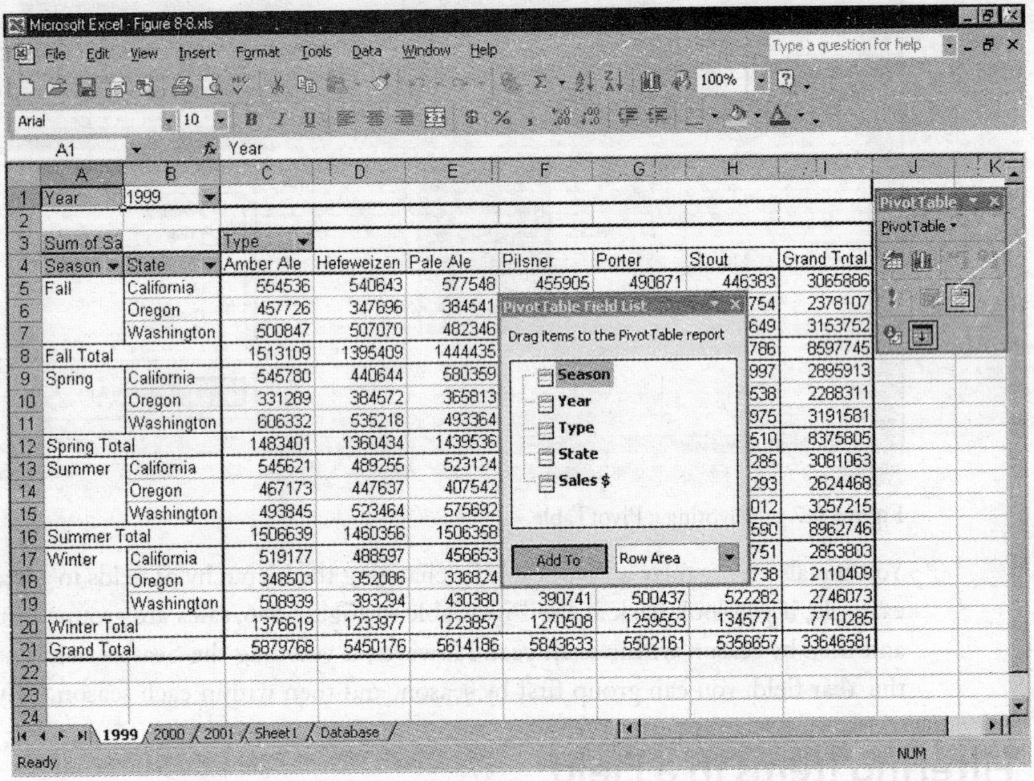

Figure 8-8 Pivoting a PivotTable once again.

Grouping PivotTable Data

With some fields, you can create subgroups. For example, you may want to group the Types shown in Figure 8-8 into ales and lagers or dark beers and light beers. To create a group for the ales and another for the lagers, select all the types you want to include in the group. (You can select nonadjacent items by holding down the Ctrl key as you click.) Choose the Data menu's Group And Outline command and then choose Group. Excel names the groups Group1, Group2, and so forth. You can rename the groups to something more descriptive by selecting the heading and typing a new name. Excel names the new field according to the field from which you're creating the Groups. In this example, Excel names the new groups of fields Type2 because the Type field was grouped. You can change the name of the group field by selecting a group name and clicking the Field Settings button on the PivotTable toolbar. Figure 8-9 shows how the PivotTable looks after grouping the types into Ales and Pilsners and naming the group field Fermentation.

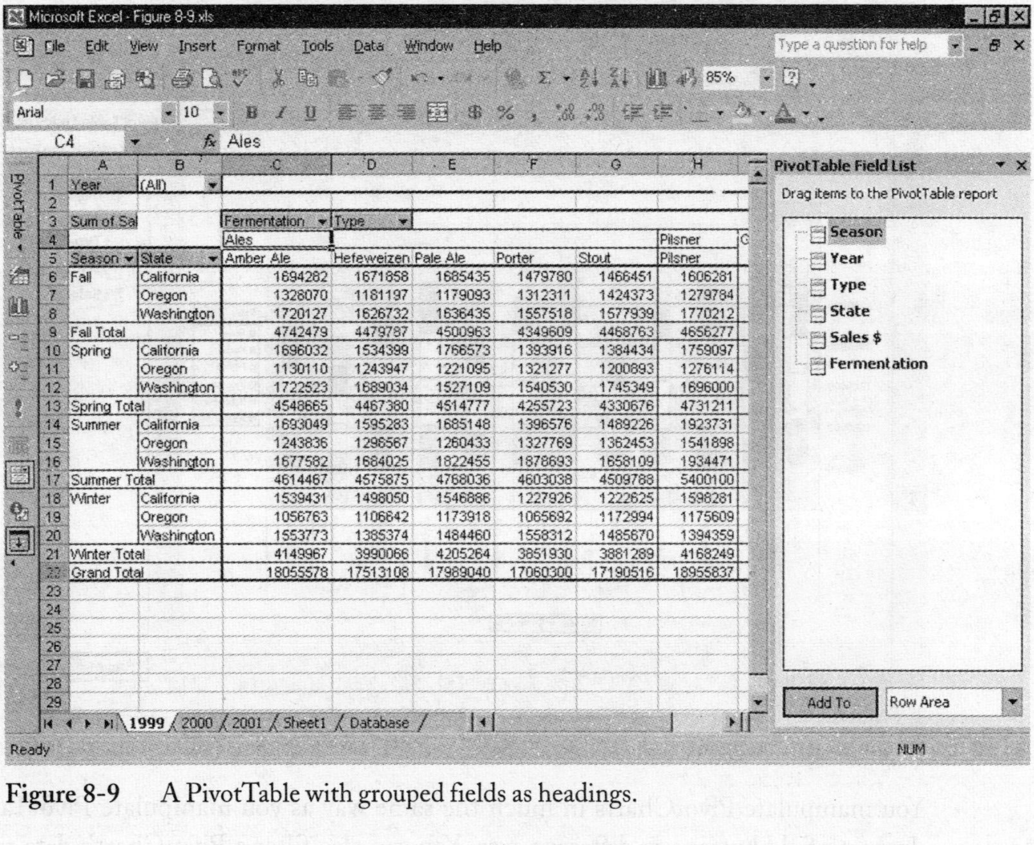

	A	B	C	D	E	F	G	H
1	Year	(All)						
2								
3	Sum of Sal		Fermentation	Type				
4			Ales					Pilsner
5	Season	State	Amber Ale	Hefeweizen	Pale Ale	Porter	Stout	Pilsner
6	Fall	California	1694282	1671858	1685435	1479780	1466451	1606281
7		Oregon	1328070	1181197	1179093	1312311	1424373	1279784
8		Washington	1720127	1626732	1636435	1557518	1577939	1770212
9	Fall Total		4742479	4479787	4500963	4349609	4468763	4656277
10	Spring	California	1696032	1534399	1766573	1393916	1384434	1759097
11		Oregon	1130110	1243947	1221095	1321277	1200893	1276114
12		Washington	1722523	1689034	1527109	1540530	1745349	1696000
13	Spring Total		4548665	4467380	4514777	4255723	4330676	4731211
14	Summer	California	1693049	1595283	1685148	1396576	1489226	1923731
15		Oregon	1243836	1296567	1260433	1327769	1362453	1541898
16		Washington	1677582	1684025	1822455	1878693	1658109	1934471
17	Summer Total		4614467	4575875	4768036	4603038	4509788	5400100
18	Winter	California	1539431	1498050	1546886	1227926	1222625	1598281
19		Oregon	1056763	1106642	1173918	1065692	1172994	1175609
20		Washington	1553773	1385374	1484460	1558312	1485670	1394359
21	Winter Total		4149967	3990066	4205264	3851930	3881289	4168249
22	Grand Total		18055578	17513108	17989040	17060300	17190516	18955837

Figure 8-9 A PivotTable with grouped fields as headings.

Creating PivotCharts

Excel provides two ways of creating PivotCharts. If you've already created a PivotTable and want to chart the information on which it focuses, you can save time and space by creating a PivotChart directly from the PivotTable. If you haven't created a PivotTable and are instead more interested in creating a PivotChart, you can create the PivotChart using the PivotTable and PivotChart Wizard without specifying the layout of a PivotTable.

Creating a PivotChart from an Existing PivotTable

To create a PivotChart from an existing PivotTable, select a cell in the PivotTable and click the Chart Wizard button on the PivotTable toolbar. Figure 8-10 shows a PivotChart based on the PivotTable in Figure 8-8.

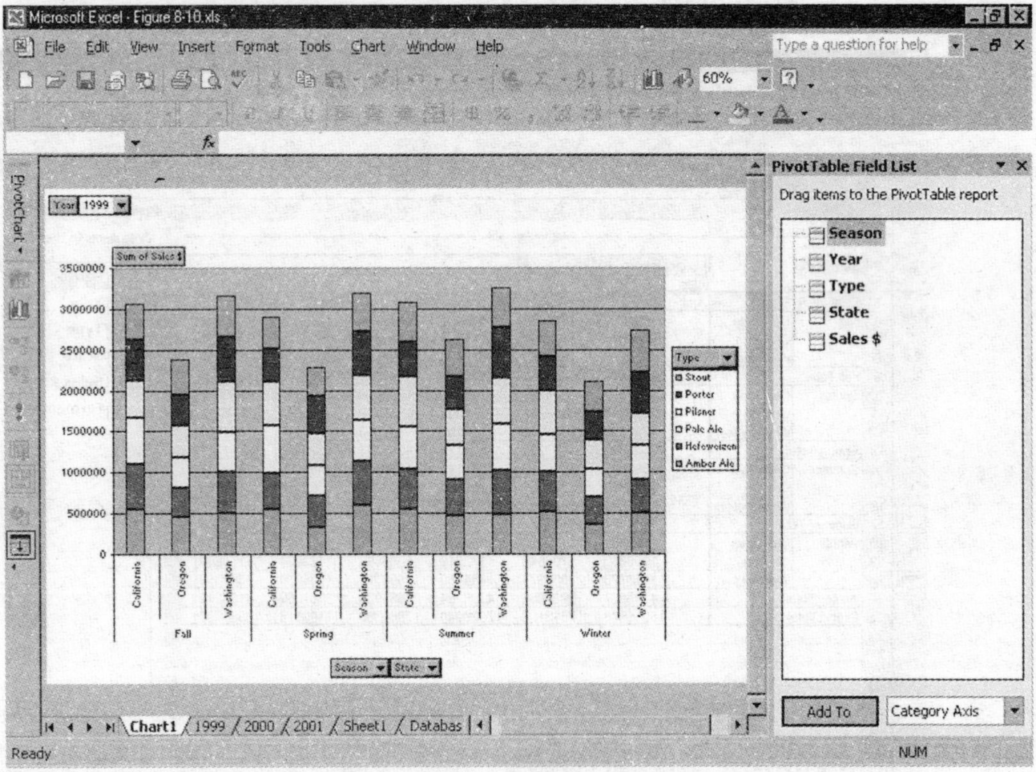

Figure 8-10 A PivotChart.

You manipulate PivotCharts in much the same way as you manipulate PivotTables—by dragging field buttons to different axes. You can also filter a PivotChart's data to include only certain items in a field. To do this, click the down arrow on the right side of the field button and select or clear the check boxes to include or omit items from the PivotChart. Click OK to redraw the chart.

After you've created the PivotChart, you can click the Chart Wizard button on the PivotTable toolbar again to start the Chart Wizard and customize the PivotChart. Using the Chart Wizard, you can specify such items as chart type, axis titles, and legend placement.

NOTE *For more information about chart types and customizing charts in Excel, see Chapter 2.*

Creating a PivotChart Directly from a Database

To create a PivotChart directly from a database, open the database and choose the Data menu's PivotTable And PivotChart Report command. In step one of the wizard, click the PivotChart (With PivotTable Report) option button. In the second step, select the data you want to include in the PivotChart. In the last step, specify where you want Excel to put the new PivotChart. When you click Finish, Excel displays a new, blank PivotChart, as shown in Figure 8-11.

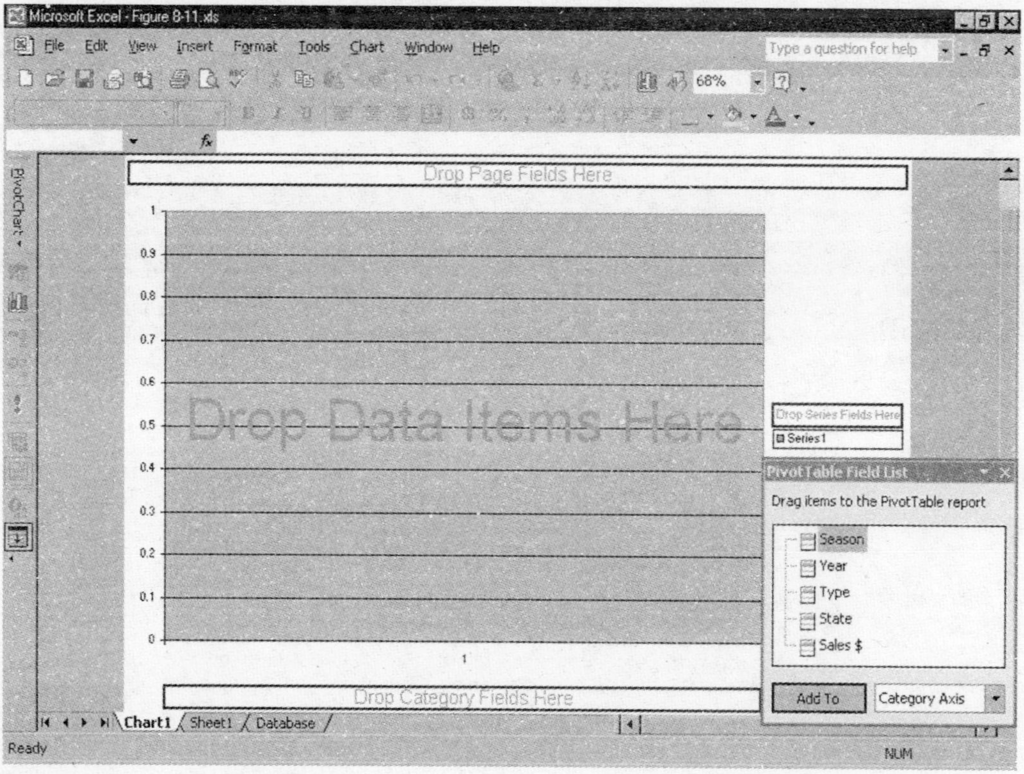

Figure 8-11 A new PivotChart.

To add data to the PivotChart, drag the field buttons from the PivotTable toolbar to the various parts of the PivotChart until it displays the information you want. You can move fields to other axes by dragging them as well. To remove a field from a chart, drag its button off the chart area.

After you've created the PivotChart, you can click the Chart Wizard button on the PivotTable toolbar again to start the Chart Wizard and customize the PivotChart. Using the Chart Wizard, you can specify such items as chart type, axis titles, and legend placement.

Chapter 9

SMALL BUSINESS FINANCIAL MANAGER

Featuring:

- Installing and Starting the Small Business Financial Manager
- Importing Financial Data
- Working with the Report Wizard
- Working with the Financial Analysis Tools
- Refreshing Imported Data
- Rearranging and Modifying Imported Data

This chapter describes how you can use the Small Business Financial Manager that comes with the Small Business, Professional, and Premium versions of Microsoft Office. The Small Business Financial Manager lets you retrieve financial data from popular small business accounting programs, including QuickBooks and Peachtree Accounting, and then analyze this data using Excel.

Unfortunately, the Small Business Financial Manager was not available at the time of publication. The information presented in this chapter was based on an earlier version of the Small Business Financial Manager but should apply very closely to the version in the future update.

NOTE *As soon as a new version of the Small Business Finance Manager is available, we will post an updated version of this chapter at the Redmond Technology Press web site,* www.redtechpress.com.

Installing and Starting the Small Business Financial Manager

The Small Business Tools, which include Small Business Financial Manager, aren't automatically installed when you install Office applications. These extra programs come on Disk 2 of the Office CD set. You may therefore need to install these tools.

To install the Small Business Tools, insert Disk 2 in your CD-ROM drive and then follow the onscreen instructions.

NOTE *The Small Business Tools include four distinct tools: Business Planner, Direct Mail Manager, Small Business Customer Manager (which works with Microsoft Outlook), and Small Business Financial Manager.*

After you install the Small Business Tools, you can start the Small Business Financial Manager directly by clicking the Start button, choosing Programs, choosing Small Business Tools, and then choosing the Small Business Financial Manager. Or, you can start the Small Business Financial Manager by starting Excel and then choosing one of the Financial Manager menu commands.

NOTE *When you install Small Business Financial Manager, you add the Financial Manager menu of commands to the Excel menu bar.*

Importing Financial Data

Before you can begin using the Small Business Financial Manager, you import the financial data stored in your accounting system and store it in a database. You may also need to reorganize the data slightly once it's in this database. And, of course, as your accounting records change, you'll want to update the database used by Excel and the Small Business Financial Manager.

NOTE *Excel doesn't change your accounting; it only creates a copy of the data that can be used by the Small Business Financial Manager.*

Importing Data for the First Time

To import your data for the first time, follow these steps:

1. **Choose the Financial Manager menu's Import Wizard command, or click the Import button on the Startup Screen.**

   Excel displays the New Database Wizard dialog box, as shown in Figure 9-1. Click Next to begin the process of importing your accounting data.

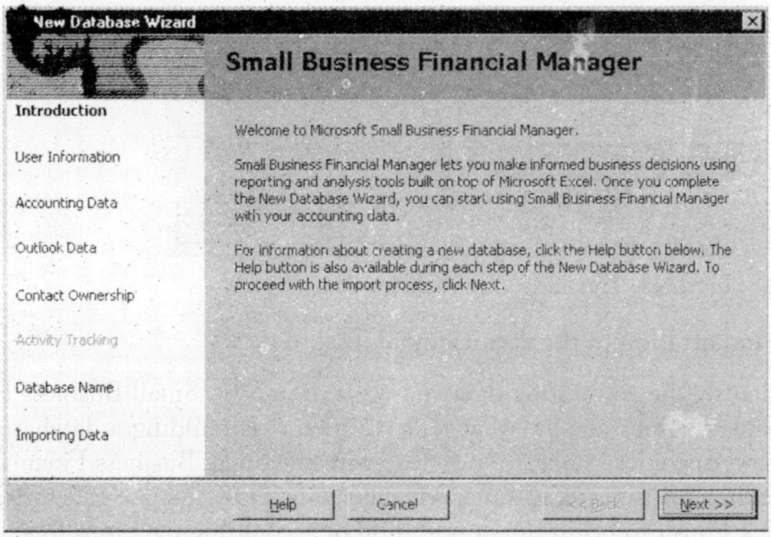

Figure 9-1 The first New Database Wizard dialog box.

2. **Provide a user name and password.**

   Excel asks for a password and then asks you to type the password again to confirm what you typed the first time. Excel uses this password to limit access to the financial data you're creating using the Financial Manager. Click Next to continue.

3. **Select the correct accounting data.**

   After you provide a password, the Small Business Financial Manager reviews your local hard disk drive for any accounting data files and then displays a list of the accounting data files it finds, as shown in Figure 9-2. Typically, the Small Business Financial Manager finds at least two files: your actual accounting data files and the sample data files that come with the accounting software. To select the accounting data files that you want to import, click the data files and then click Next.

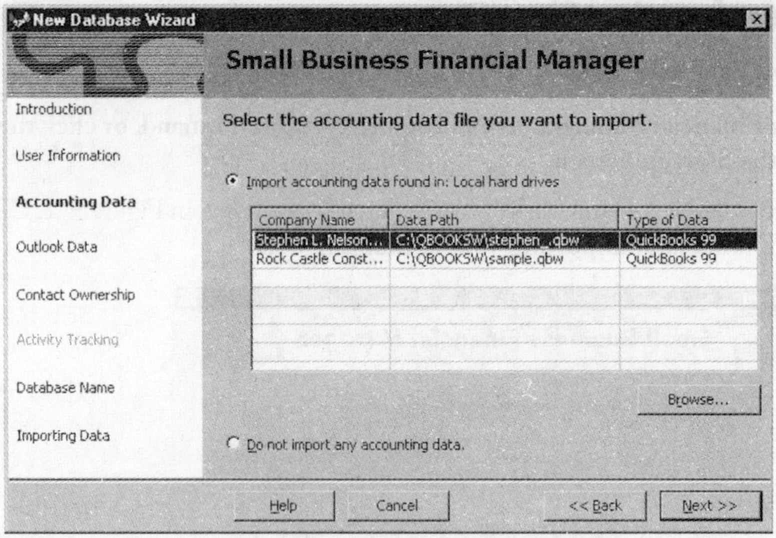

Figure 9-2 The third New Database Wizard dialog box.

4. **Initiate the importation of the accounting data.**

   After you identify the accounting data you want to import, Small Business Financial Manager displays a message box that tells you that it is building a database of your accounting and customer information for use with the Small Business Financial Manager and the Small Business Customer Manager. Click OK to close this message box, and then click Finish to begin the importation of accounting data into this database.

NOTE *If you restrict access to your accounting data using a password, the Small Business Financial Manager asks for this password before it begins importing data.*

Depending on the size of your accounting database, the importation will probably take several minutes—and perhaps longer. When the New Database Wizard finishes importing your data, it displays another message box. Click OK to close the message box and begin working with the data.

Working with the Report Wizard

After you've imported your accounting data, you use the Report Wizard to produce a financial report based on the imported accounting data.

Reviewing the Report Wizard Reports

The Report Wizard produces reports that fall into one of seven categories: balance sheets, cash flow statements, change in stockholders' equity, income statements, ratio reports, sales analysis reports, and trial balance reports. Table 9-1 briefly summarizes the types of reports that the Report Wizard produces in each of these categories.

CATEGORY	REPORT OPTIONS AVAILABLE
Balance Sheet	Simple balance sheets, balance sheets with prior-year comparisons, and balance sheets with scenarios you've created using the what-if analysis tools.
Cash Flow	Simple one-period cash flow statements with year-to-date and prior-period comparisons, rolling 12-period cash flow reports, and one-period cash flow reports and year-to-date cash flow reports with scenarios created using the what-if analysis tools.
Change in Stockholders' Equity	One-period reports and year-to-date reports of the changes in stockholders' equity.
Income Statement	Simple income statements with one-period and year-to-date comparisons, income statements with 12-period and four-quarter trends, income statements for a fiscal year and periods, income statements for a fiscal year and quarters, and income statements with scenarios created using the what-if analysis tools.
Ratios	A rolling 12-period report showing trends in financial ratios.
Sales Analysis	Sales reports from a variety of perspectives, including by customers and by types of services.
Trial Balance	Simple trial balance reports with one-period and year-to-date comparisons and trial balance with scenarios created using what-if analysis tools.

Table 9-1 The Report Wizard report categories and report options.

Using the Report Wizard

To use the Report Wizard to create one of its reports, follow these steps:

1. Start the Report Wizard.

You can do this either by choosing the Financial Manager menu's Report Wizard command or by clicking the Report button on the Startup Screen, as shown in Figure 9-3.

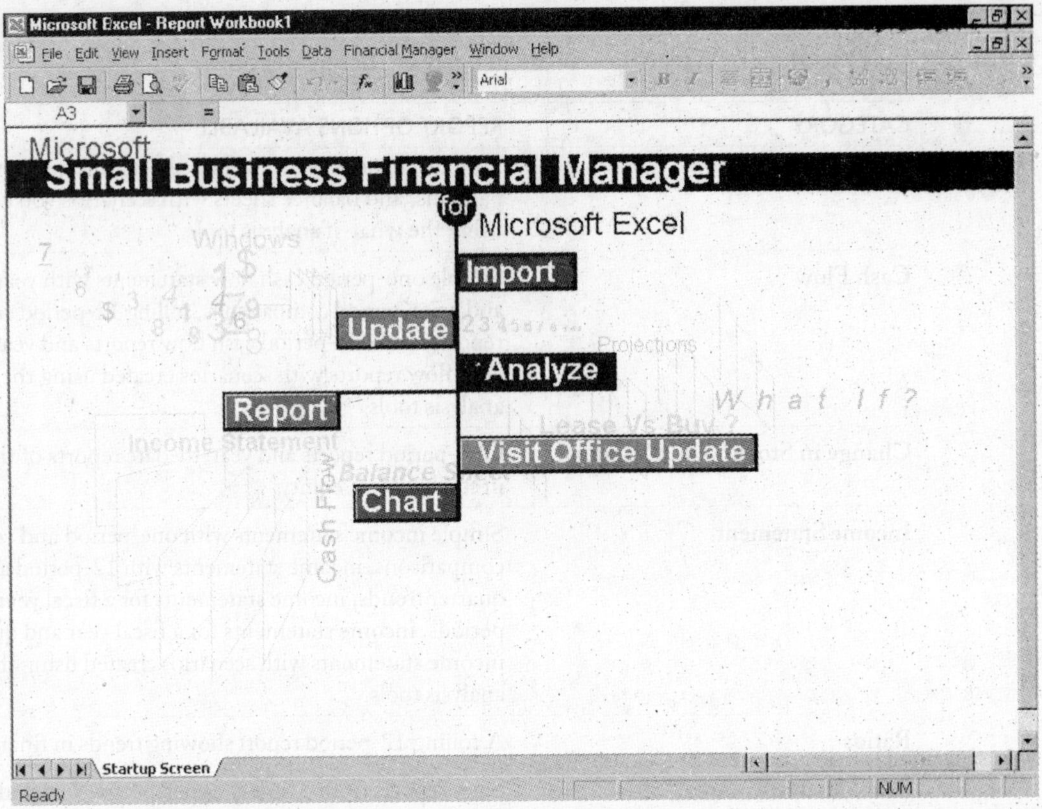

Figure 9-3 The Small Business Financial Manager Startup Screen.

2. Select the category of financial reports you want to create.

To select a financial report category, click an entry in the Financial Reports list box, as shown in Figure 9-4. After you select a financial report category, click Next.

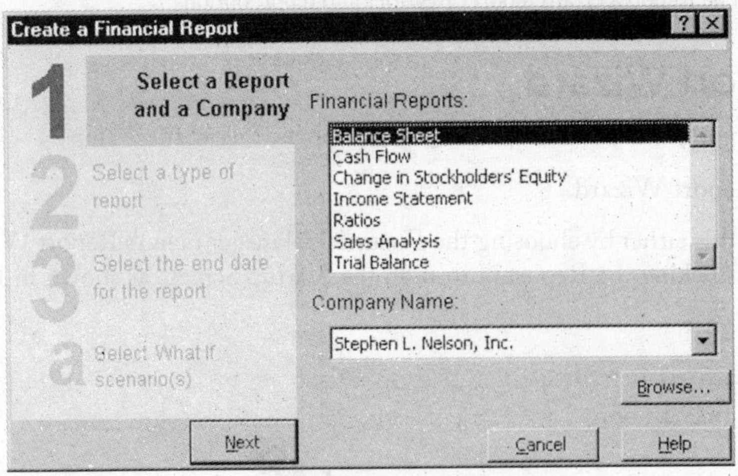

Figure 9-4 The first Report Wizard dialog box.

3. **Provide the user name and database password.**

   If Small Business Financial Manager requests it, provide the user name and database password you created during the importation of your accounting data.

4. **Select the type of report you want.**

   When Excel asks what type of report you want, select an entry from the Report Types list box. Then click Next.

NOTE *You can't select a report type that relies on a scenario unless you've already created the scenario using the what-if analysis tools.*

5. **Select an end date for the report.**

   When Excel asks for the report end date, select an entry from the End Date For This Report list box. Then click Finish.

The Report Wizard creates a financial report based on your parameters and places the report on a new worksheet in the open workbook. Figure 9-5 shows an example of one such financial report, an income statement for December 1998 with year-to-date and prior-period comparisons.

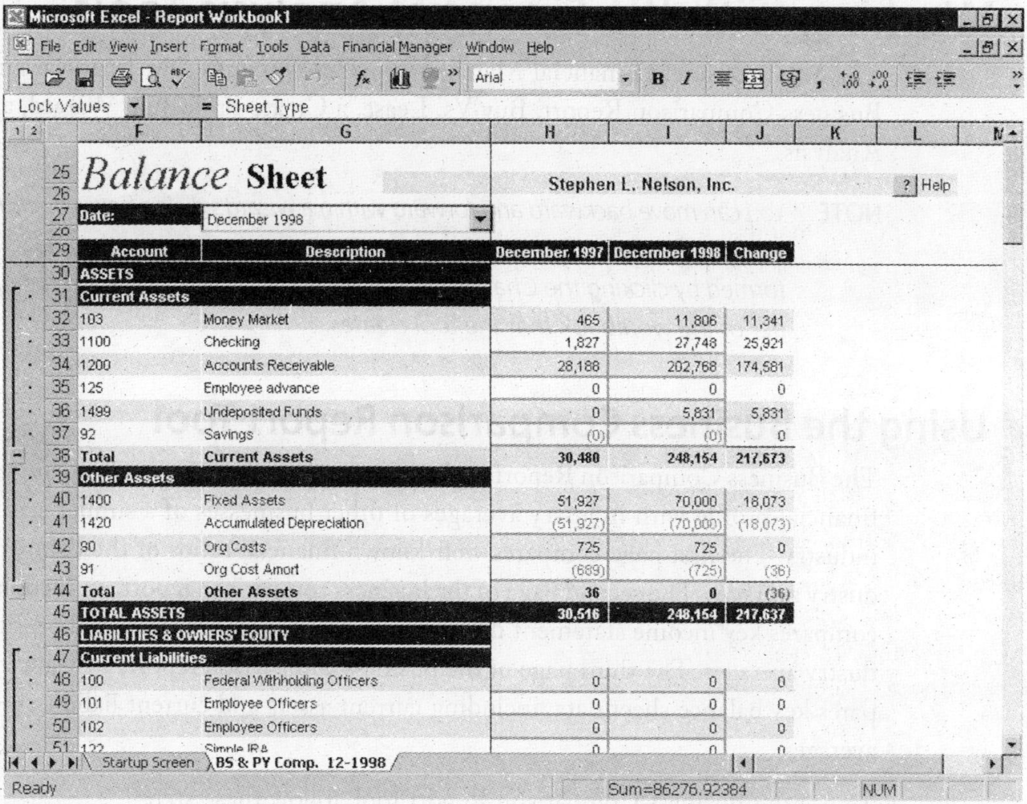

Figure 9-5 An example financial report created by the first Report Wizard.

Using the Report Wizard's Reports

The principal reason for using the Report Wizard is to generate a report so that you can analyze the report using Excel. This may mean simply viewing the report, perhaps onscreen or in a printed copy. If you're using Small Business Financial Manager in this way, however, you may be doing so only because the reporting capabilities of your accounting software are very limited or restricting.

The other way you can use the Report Wizard reports, of course, is to use the now-in-a-workbook financial data for making your own calculations. This work is something you can't do with your accounting program's reports. Once you've got a report stored in an Excel workbook, it's relatively easy to create formulas that manipulate the data, extract information so it can be analyzed, and chart information so it can be visually analyzed or shared. This type of work requires the basic Excel skills discussed in Chapters 1 and 2.

NOTE *If the information on which a report is based changes, choose the Financial Manager menu's Recalculate Reports command.*

Working with the Financial Analysis Tools

The Small Business Financial Manager provides you with four financial analysis tools: Business Comparison Report, Buy Vs. Lease, a Create Projection Wizard, and What-If Analysis.

NOTE *You can move backward and forward within a wizard's dialog boxes by clicking the Back and Next buttons. You can also return to a wizard to change the analysis you've performed by clicking the Change Wizard hyperlink, which appears in the upper left corner of the workbook that the tool creates.*

Using the Business Comparison Report Tool

The Business Comparison Report tool creates a report that lets you compare one business's financial profile with industry averages of other businesses of a similar size in the same industry. The first page compares well-known financial ratios of the company to the industry averages. The second page of the business comparison report, an Income Statement, compares key income statement data—such as sales, gross margin, and profit—to the industry averages. The third page of the business comparison report, a Balance Sheet, compares key balance sheet data, including current assets and current liabilities—to industry averages.

To use the Business Comparison Report tool, follow these steps:

1. **Start the Business Comparison Wizard.**

   Click the Analyze button on the Startup Screen, and then select a Business Comparison item from the list box in the Select A Financial Manager Analysis Tool dialog box and click Next. Excel displays the first Business Comparison Wizard dialog box, as shown in Figure 9-6.

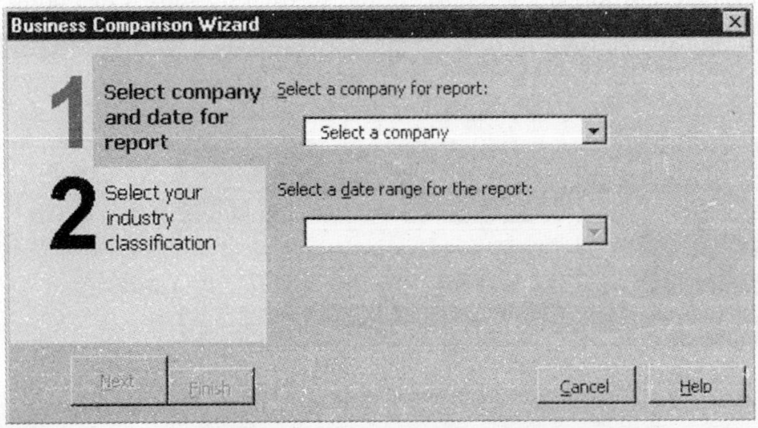

Figure 9-6 The first Business Comparison Wizard dialog box.

2. **Select the company and the period you want to compare.**

   Select the company you want to compare, if necessary, from the Select A Company For Report box. Select an accounting period you want to compare from the Select A Date Range For The Report box, and then click Next. Excel displays the second Business Comparison Wizard dialog box, as shown in Figure 9-7.

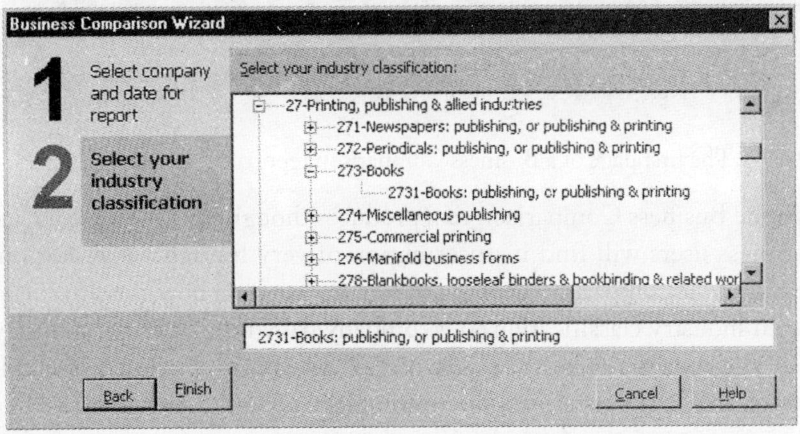

Figure 9-7 The second Business Comparison Wizard dialog box.

3. **Select the industry in which the company operates.**

The Business Comparison Wizard organizes industries into a tree diagram. To expand a tree branch, click its plus sign. To collapse a tree branch, click its minus sign. When you find the industry that most closely matches your company, click it and then click the Finish button. The Business Comparison Wizard compares your company to the industry averages, producing a report similar to the one shown in Figure 9-8.

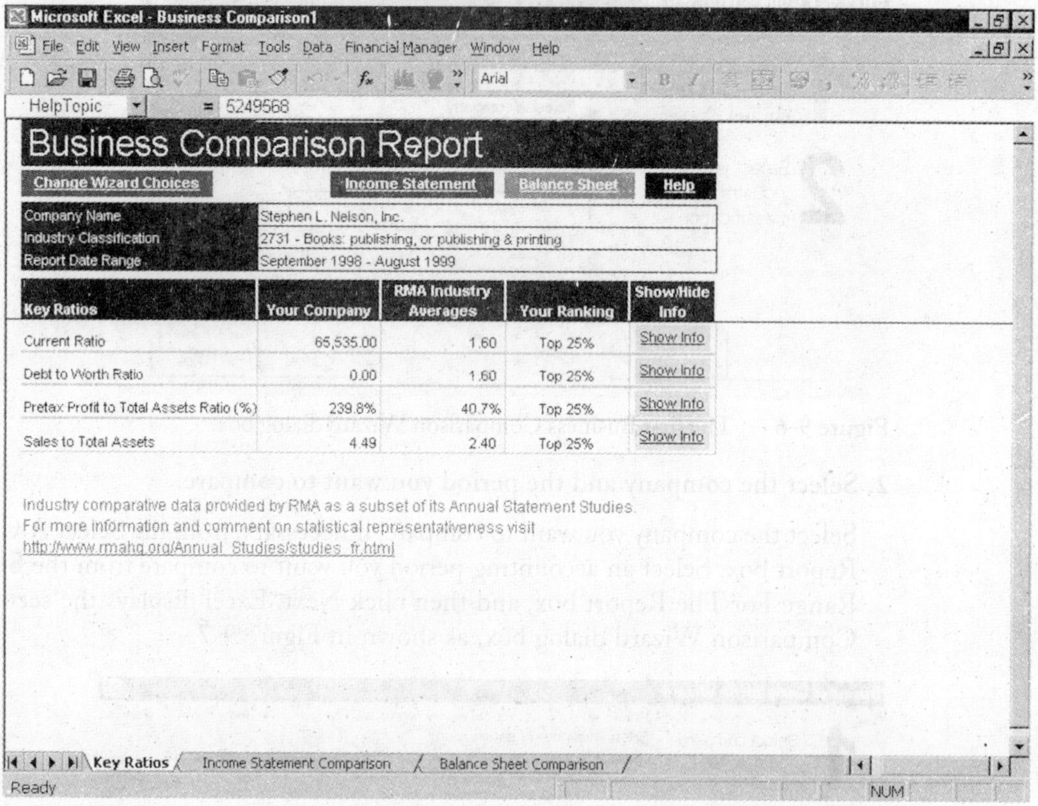

Figure 9-8 The first page of a Business Comparison report.

Although the Business Comparison tool produces thought-provoking data, unfortunately, many business users will find its information of very limited value. For one thing, the effectiveness of the comparison depends to a great extent on how closely a business matches the selected industry classification. If a company truly resembles the industry into which it's placed, the comparison may be very useful. If a company doesn't resemble the industry, however, the comparison may be meaningless.

Another issue concerns the accounting policies and conventions used both by the company and the industry. Even large companies show considerable variety and creativity in the accounting policies they adopt and the conventions they follow. And we can only assume that small companies show even more variety and creativity. Differences in accounting treatment, of course, also make comparisons more difficult.

Using the Buy Vs. Lease Tool

The Buy Vs. Lease tool helps you choose between buying or leasing some asset. The Buy Vs. Lease Wizard is perhaps most useful for forecasting the cash flows that stem from an asset purchase. Predictably, the wizard suggests that you borrow to buy an asset when the cost of borrowing is less than the cost of capital. For this reason, you don't really need to use the wizard to determine which financing option works best: the cheapest financing option is the cheapest financing option.

The Buy Vs. Lease Wizard is more useful, however, when you want to explore the effects of a purchase on your cash flows. In small companies, perhaps especially those that are growing, the cash flow effect of an asset purchase becomes a major issue—sometimes one that's more important than net present value measures.

To use the Buy Vs. Lease tool, follow these steps:

1. **Start the Buy Vs. Lease Wizard.**

   Click the Analyze button on the Startup Screen, and then select a Buy Vs. Lease item from the list box in the Select A Financial Manager Analysis Tool dialog box. Excel displays the first Buy Vs. Lease Wizard dialog box, as shown in Figure 9-9.

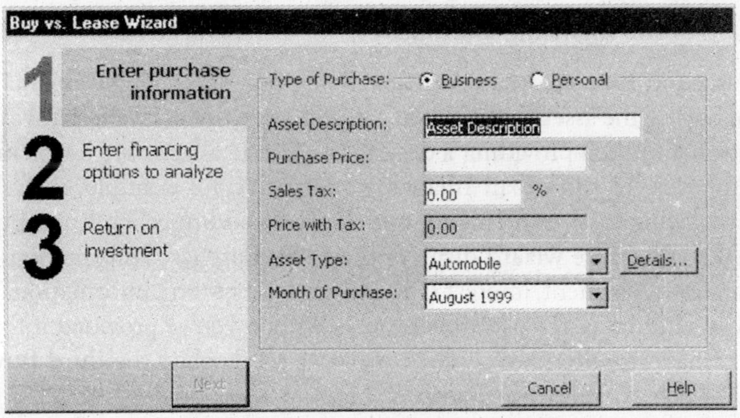

Figure 9-9 The first Buy Vs. Lease Wizard dialog box.

2. **Describe the asset.**

   Use the first Buy Vs. Lease Wizard dialog box to describe the asset you may buy or lease. Use the Type Of Purchase buttons to indicate whether the asset is a business or personal asset. Use the Asset Description box to name the asset. Use the Purchase Price box to provide the asset's purchase price. Use the Sales Tax box to provide the sales tax percentage that will be charged in addition to the purchase price. Use the Asset Type drop-down list box to identify the asset category. Finally, use the Month Of Purchase box to indicate when you'll purchase the asset. When you've provided this information, click Next. Excel displays the second Buy Vs. Lease Wizard dialog box, as shown in Figure 9-10.

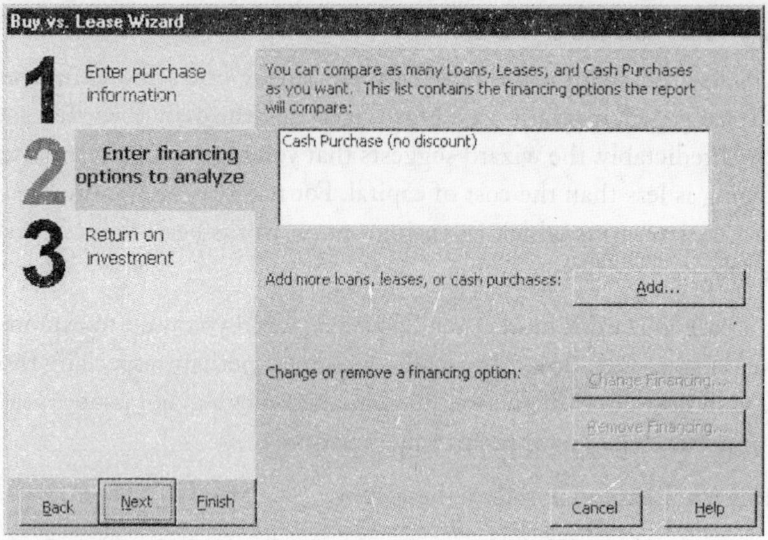

Figure 9-10 The second Buy Vs. Lease Wizard dialog box.

NOTE *The Asset Type and Month Of Purchase information lets the wizard correctly calculate the tax effects of your purchase.*

3. Describe each of the financing alternatives.

Initially the second Buy Vs. Lease Wizard dialog box lists a single financing alternative—that of buying the asset for cash. You can add more financial alternatives by clicking the Add button and then providing a description of the alternative by clicking buttons and filling in boxes. To add a loan-financing alternative, for example, click Add. When the wizard asks what kind of financing option you're adding, click Loan Purchase and then click OK. When the wizard displays the Loan Purchase Information dialog box, enter the loan down payment, interest rate, and repayment term information. To describe other financial alternatives, repeat this process. When you've provided information on each of your financing alternatives, click Next. Excel displays the third Buy Vs. Lease Wizard dialog box, as shown in Figure 9-11.

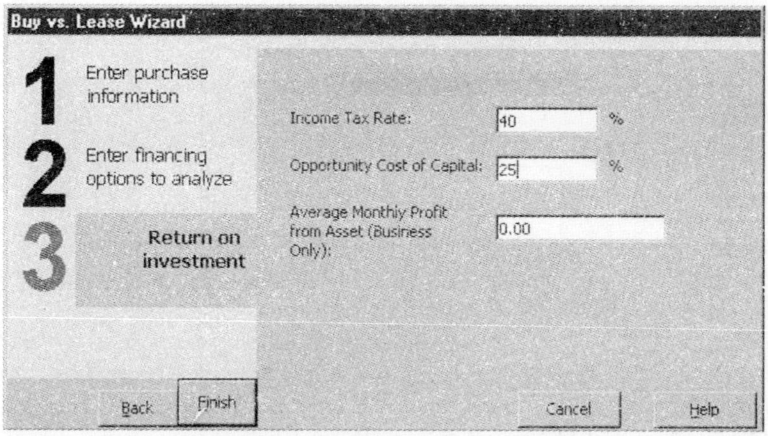

Figure 9-11 The third Buy Vs. Lease Wizard dialog box.

The Buy Vs. Lease Wizard provides a multipage report that summarizes the financial effects of the asset purchase under each of your financing alternatives. In addition, the wizard creates a depreciation schedule for a purchased asset and an amortization schedule for any loans.

4. Describe each of the financing alternatives.

Use the third Buy Vs. Lease Wizard dialog box to describe your income tax rate, the cost of capital that the wizard should use in its discounted cash flow calculations, and the average monthly profit of an asset if the asset is one you'll use for business. Then click Finish.

Using the Create Projection Wizard Tool

The Create Projection Wizard tool helps you create a financial projection by inflating or deflating historical accounting data.

NOTE *After you create a financial projection, you view it by using the Projection Reports tool, which is described in the next section, "Using the Projection Reports Tool."*

To use the Create Projection Wizard tool, follow these steps:

1. Start the Create Projection Wizard tool.

Click the Analyze button on the Startup Screen, select the Create Projection Wizard item from the list box in the Select A Financial Manager Analysis Tool dialog box, and then click Next. Excel displays the first Financial Manager Projection Wizard dialog box, as shown in Figure 9-12.

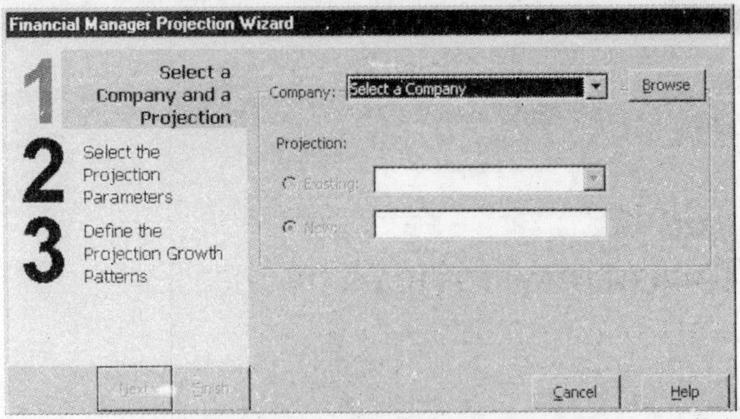

Figure 9-12 The first Financial Manager Projection Wizard dialog box.

2. **Select the company, and indicate that you want to create a new projection.**

   Select the company you want to compare, if necessary, from the Company box, and then click the New button. Name your projection using the Name box, and then click Next. Excel displays the second Financial Manager Projection Wizard dialog box, as shown in Figure 9-13.

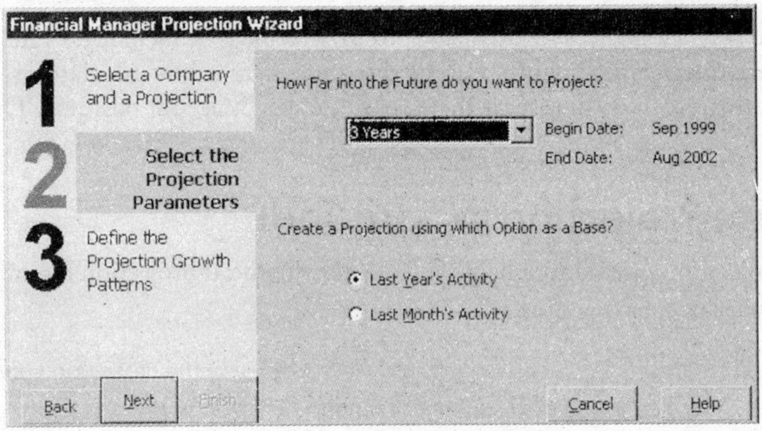

Figure 9-13 The second Financial Manager Projection Wizard dialog box.

3. **Describe the forecasting horizon.**

   Use the How Far Into The Future Do You Want To Project box to indicate how many months or years into the future you want to project.

4. **Tell the wizard what the projection should be based on.**

   Use the Last Year's Activity and Last Month's Activity option buttons to indicate what data you want to base your projection on. Then click Next. Excel displays the third Financial Manager Projection Wizard dialog box, as shown in Figure 9-14.

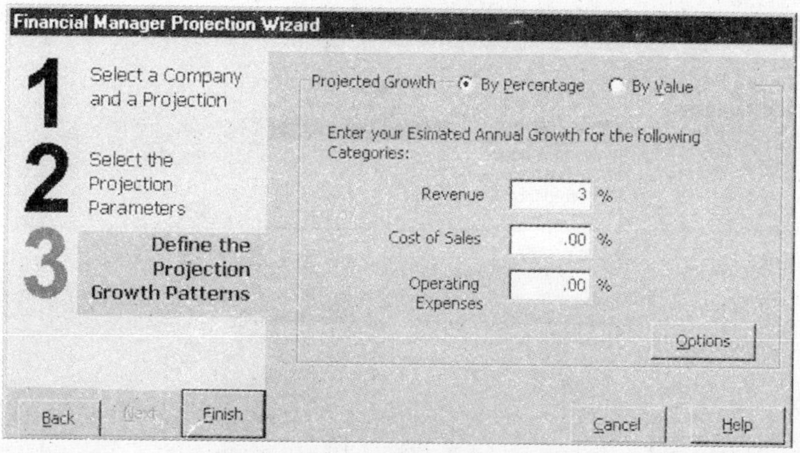

Figure 9-14 The third Financial Manager Projection Wizard dialog box.

5. **Tell the wizard how to change the base values.**

   Click the By Percentage option button if you want the wizard to inflate or deflate base values by a set percentage. Alternatively, click the By Value option button if you want the wizard to inflate or deflate base values by some stated value. Once you indicate whether you want to change the base values based by a percentage or value, use the Revenue, Cost Of Sales, and Operating Expenses boxes to provide the percentage or value. Click the Finish button to direct the wizard to create the projection based on your directions.

NOTE *You can click the Options button, which appears on the third Financial Manager Projection Wizard dialog box, to display still another dialog box which gives you far finer control over the way that base values are adjusted.*

When the wizard finishes creating your projection, click OK. You can use the Projection Reports tool, which is described in the next section, to view the projection.

Using the Projection Reports Tool

After you create a projection—which is actually just a set of numbers created by the Create Projection Wizard—you can produce a report based on the projection. To produce such a report, follow these steps:

1. **Start the Projection Reports tool.**

   Click the Analyze button on the Startup Screen, and then select the Projection Reports item from the list box in the Select A Financial Manager Analysis Tool dialog box. Excel displays the first Create A Projection Report dialog box, as shown in Figure 9-15.

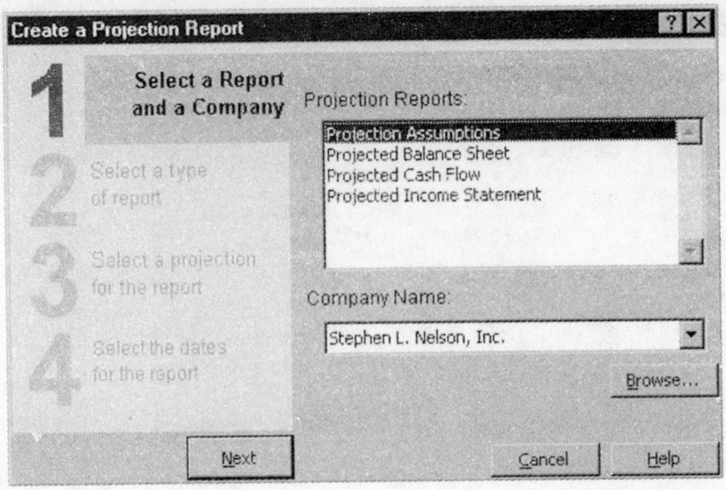

Figure 9-15 The first Create A Projection Report dialog box.

2. **Select a report category.**

   Select a report category by clicking one of the entries in the Projection Reports list box.

3. **Select the company.**

   If necessary, select the company you want to compare from the Company box. Then click Next. Excel displays the second Create A Projection Report dialog box, as shown in Figure 9-16.

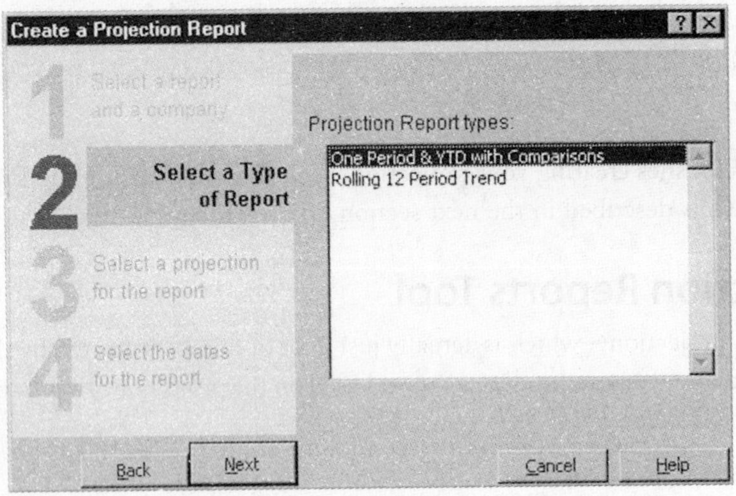

Figure 9-16 The second Create A Projection Report dialog box.

4. **Select the specific report.**

   Select the specific type of report you want to prepare by clicking one of the reports listed in the Projection Report Types list box. Then click Next. Excel displays the third Create A Financial Report dialog box, as shown in Figure 9-17.

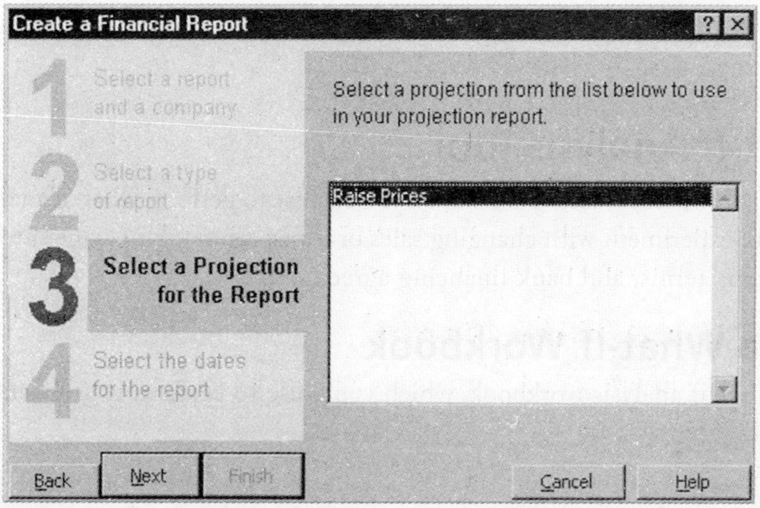

Figure 9-17 The third Create A Financial Report dialog box.

5. **Select the projection to use.**

   Select the projection you want to use to create the report by clicking it in the only list box provided by the third Create A Financial Report dialog box. Then click Next. Excel displays the fourth Create A Financial Report dialog box, as shown in Figure 9-18.

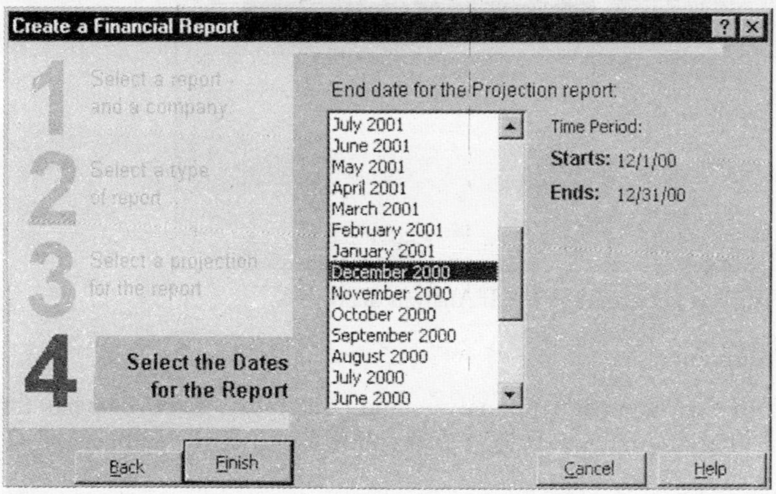

Figure 9-18 The fourth Create A Financial Report dialog box.

6. **Select an end date for the projection report.**

   Select an end date for the projection report by clicking one of the end dates listed in the fourth Create A Financial Report dialog box. Click the Finish button to direct the wizard to create the projection report using the specified projection.

Excel adds new worksheets to the workbook showing pro forma financial statements based on your projections.

Using the What-If Analysis Tool

The What-If Analysis tool creates a workbook you can use to perform what-if analysis. For example, you can experiment with changing sales or expenses, vendor payment terms and customer financing terms, and bank financing agreements.

Creating a What-If Workbook

To create the what-if analysis workbook, which you'll use to perform your what-if modeling, follow these steps:

1. **Start the What-If Analysis tool.**

   Click the Analyze button on the Startup Screen, and then select the What-If Analysis item from the list box in the Select A Financial Manager Analysis Tool dialog box. Excel displays the first Perform A What-If Analysis dialog box, as shown in Figure 9-19.

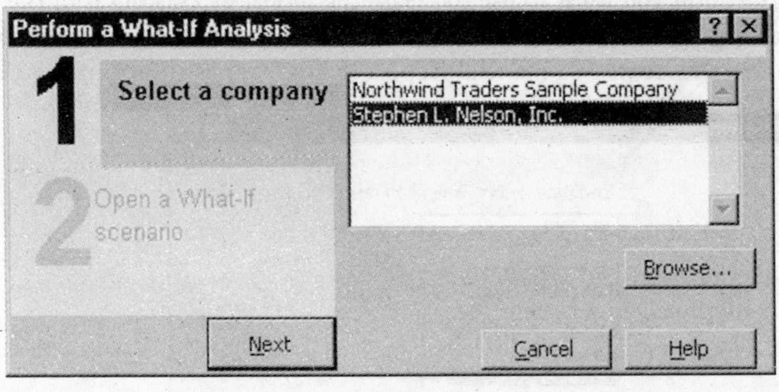

Figure 9-19 The first Perform A What-If Analysis dialog box.

2. **Select the company.**

   Select the company you want to analyze, and click Next. Excel displays the second Perform A What-If Analysis dialog box, as shown in Figure 9-20.

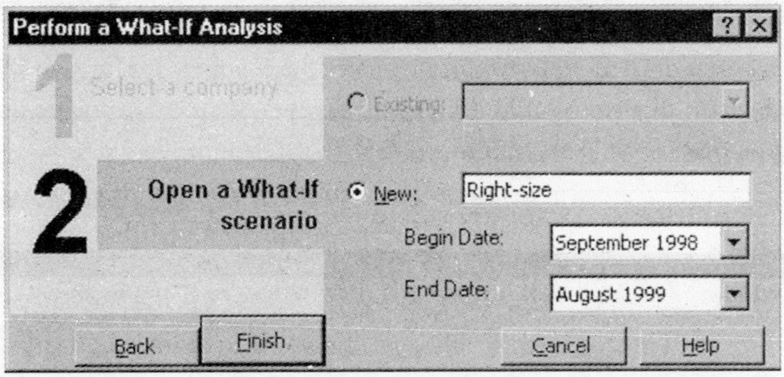

Figure 9-20 The second Perform A What-If Analysis dialog box.

3. Indicate that you want to create a new what-if analysis.

Click the New option button, and then give a name to your what-if analysis. Provide begin and end dates for the analysis using the Begin Date and End Date boxes, and then click Next. Excel displays the Save As dialog box.

NOTE *After you create a what-if projection, you can also use the second Perform A What-If Analysis dialog box to select a what-if analysis from the Existing box.*

4. Save the what-if analysis.

Use the Save As dialog box to save your what-if analysis. Use the File Name box to name the new what-if analysis workbook. And use the Save In box to choose a folder location. After you specify the name and location of the what-if analysis, click the Save button. Excel creates and saves the what-if analysis workbook and displays its overview worksheet, as shown in Figure 9-21.

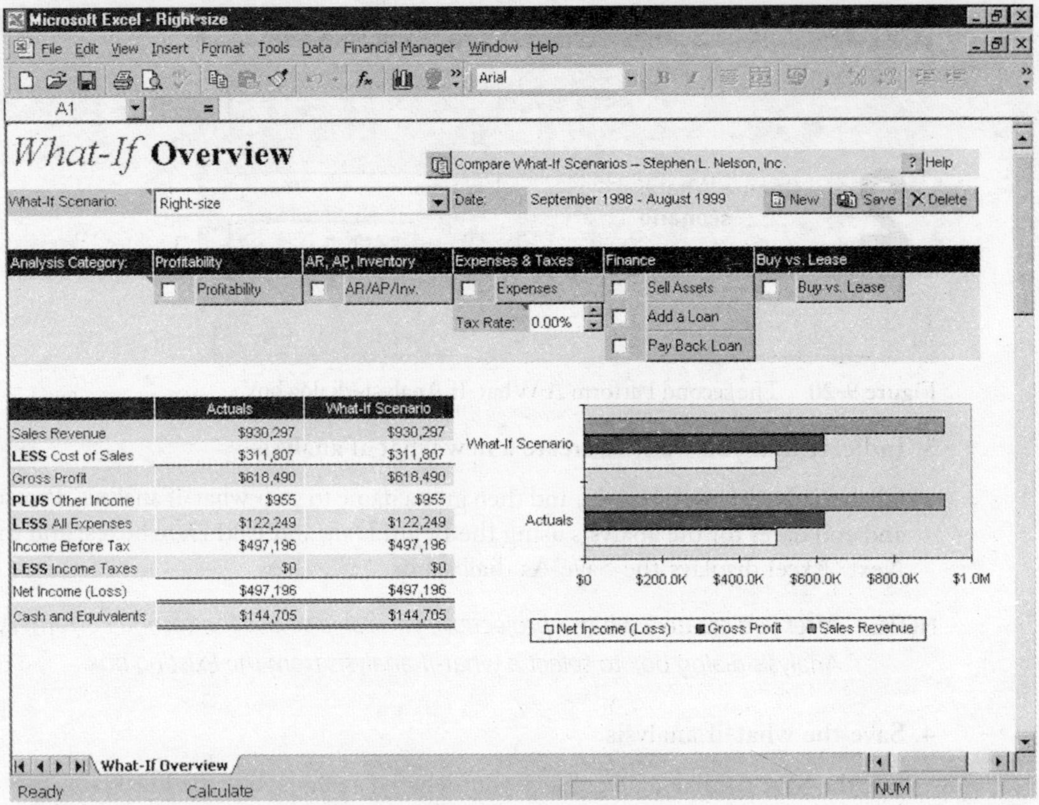

Figure 9-21 The what-if analysis overview worksheet.

Using a What-If Workbook

Once you create the what-if analysis workbook, you use the analysis boxes and buttons to ask your what-if questions.

To ask what-if questions about how sales affect your profitability, for example, click the Profitability button. When Excel displays a dialog box listing the ways that your accounting data reports sales, select a sales category and click OK. Excel next displays a new worksheet, as shown in Figure 9-22, that lets you see sales by the selected category. To change some number, click the cell and then type your new number. To return to the overview worksheet, click the What-If Overview button.

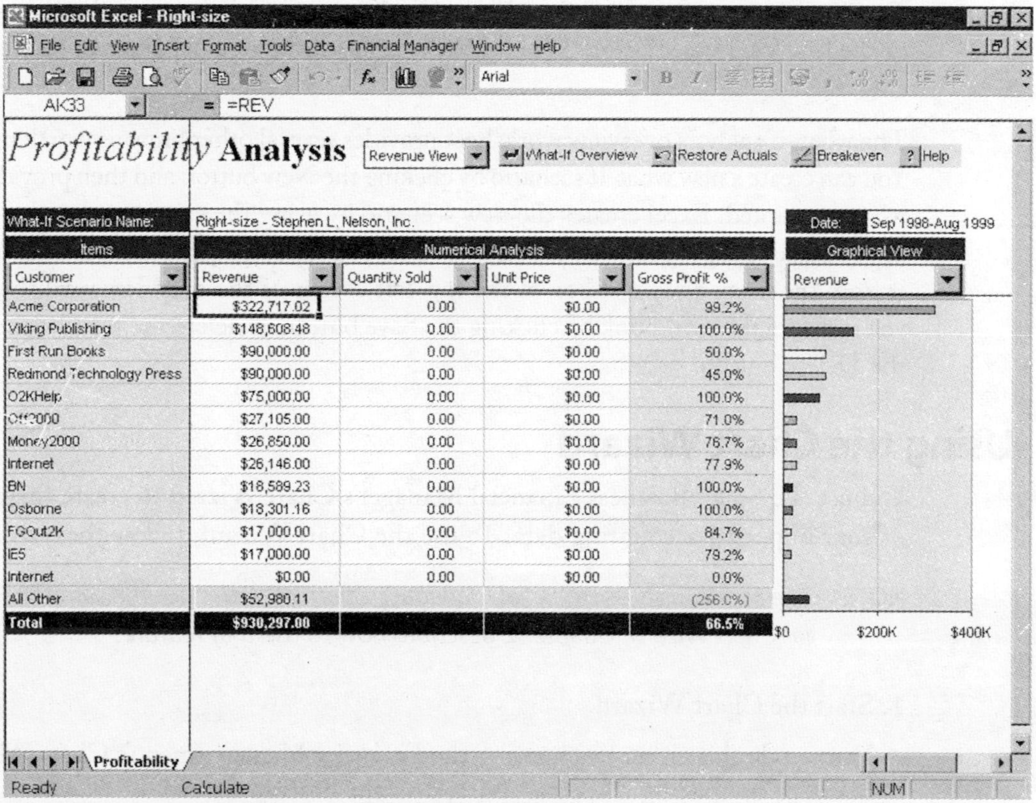

Figure 9-22 The what-if analysis profitability worksheet.

NOTE *You can change the information displayed in the what-if profitability worksheet by clicking the column heading drop-down list boxes and selecting an entry.*

To ask what-if questions about how accounts payable and accounts receivable payment terms and inventory balances affect your cash flow, click the AR/AP/Inv. button. When Excel displays a new worksheet that lets you see accounts receivable, accounts payable, and inventory detail, change these asset or liability values by clicking cells and then typing your new numbers. Or, adjust the slider button that corresponds to the item you want to experiment with.

To ask what-if questions about how expenses affect your profitability, click the Expenses button. When Excel displays a new worksheet that lets you see expenses by account, change expense values by clicking cells and then typing your new numbers. Or, adjust the slider button that corresponds to an expense.

To create asset purchase and financing what-if scenarios, click one of the Finance buttons or the Buy Vs. Lease button. When Excel displays a dialog box, describe the scenario and click OK.

The what-if analysis overview worksheet provides several other buttons worth mentioning. You can create a new what-if scenario by clicking the New button and then providing a name when prompted. Excel creates the new scenario by using the existing scenarios values, but as you make changes your new scenario evolves. You can display another scenario by choosing it from the drop-down list box in the top-left corner of the overview worksheet. Finally, you can save the workbook by clicking the Save button or delete the workbook by clicking the Delete button.

Using the Chart Wizard

You use the Small Business Financial Manager's Chart Wizard to create financial charts of your imported accounting data. To use the Chart Wizard, follow these steps:

NOTE *The Small Business Financial Manager's Chart Wizard is not the same as Excel's regular Chart Wizard. Chapter 2 describes how to use that feature.*

1. **Start the Chart Wizard.**

   You can do this either by choosing the Financial Manager menu's Chart Wizard command or by clicking the Chart button on the Startup Screen.

2. **Select the category of financial chart you want to create.**

   To select a financial chart category, click an entry in the Financial Charts list box, as shown in Figure 9-23. After you select a financial chart category and select the company name, if necessary, click Next.

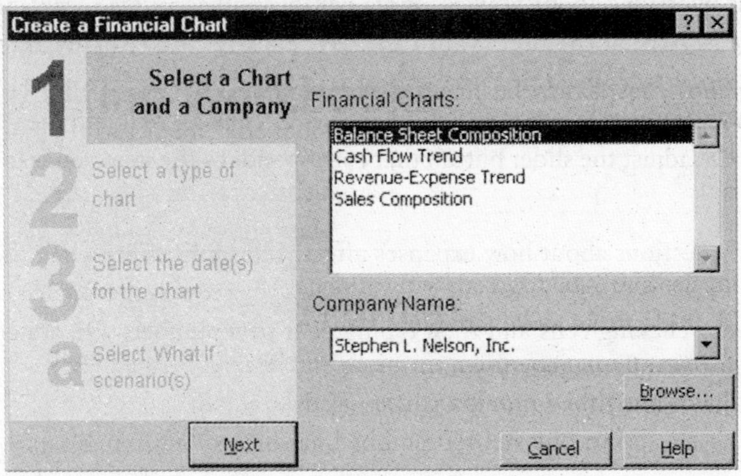

Figure 9-23 The first Create A Financial Chart dialog box.

NOTE *If Small Business Financial Manager requests it, provide the user name and database password you created during the importation of your accounting data.*

3. Select the type of report you want.

When Excel asks what type of chart you want, use the boxes and buttons provided to describe it. Then click Next.

NOTE *Different financial chart categories provide you with different reporting options.*

4. Select an end date for the report.

When Excel asks for the chart end or as-of date, select an entry from the list box. Then click the Finish button.

The Chart Wizard creates a financial chart according to your instructions and places the chart on a new sheet in the open workbook. Figure 9-24 shows an example of a financial chart, a cash flow trend chart for January 1998 through August 1999.

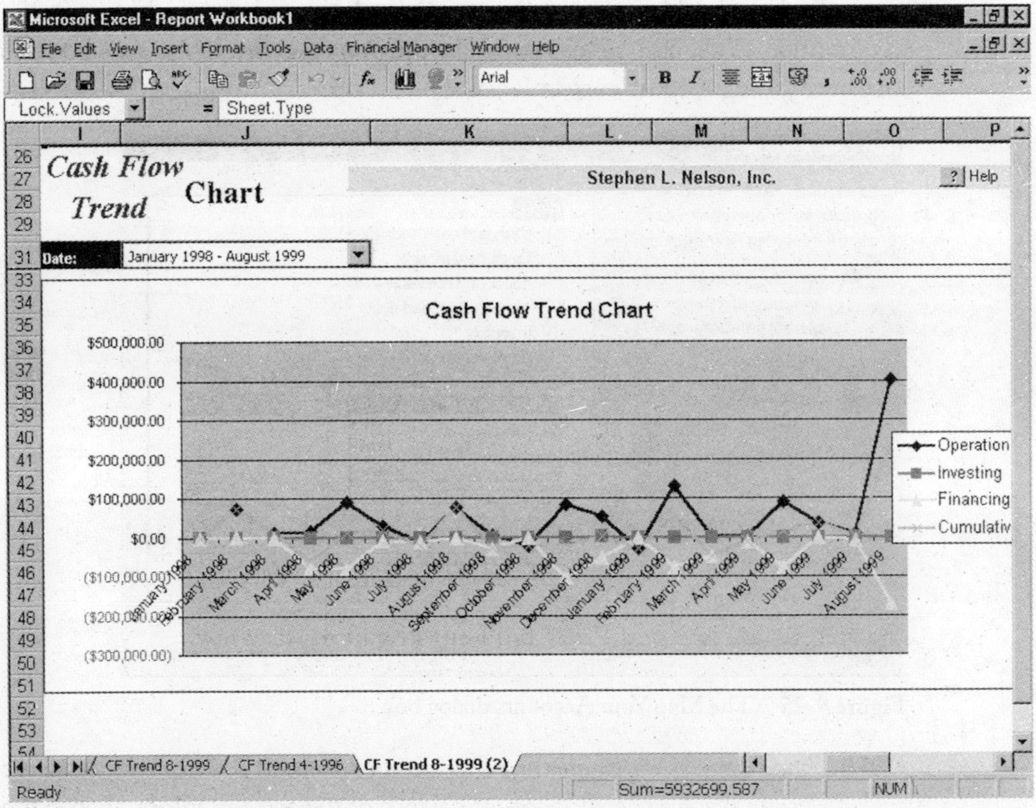

Figure 9-24 An example financial chart created by the Chart Wizard.

Refreshing the Imported Data

Over time, of course, your accounting database changes as it's updated to reflect new activity. To refresh the imported data for these changes, simply click the Update button, which appears on the Startup Screen of the Small Business Financial Manager workbook. The Small Business Financial Manager prompts you for your password, and then it imports any new data needed to refresh the database used by the Small Business Financial Manager.

Rearranging and Modifying Imported Data

One problem of working with the Small Business Financial Manager is that it expects your chart of accounts—the list of accounts you use—to be organized in a very conventional way. If you haven't organized your chart of accounts this way, you may need to rearrange, or remap, the data.

To remap the data, choose the Financial Manager menu's Remap Data command. When Excel displays the Map Your Accounts dialog box, as shown in Figure 9-25, review the oıganization of the accounts as shown in the tree diagram. If you see an account grouped incorrectly, drag it to its correct location.

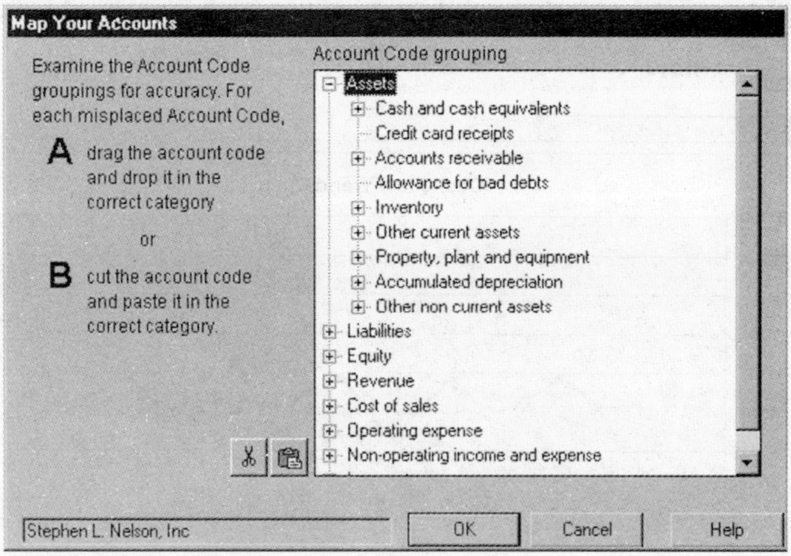

Figure 9-25 The Map Your Accounts dialog box.

NOTE *The Financial Manager menu also provides an Insert Balance command, which you can use to place a specific account balance or full account information in the active cell.*

Part 3

USING THE STARTER WORKBOOKS

In This Part

Chapter 10

BUILDING A BUSINESS PLANNING WORKBOOK

Featuring:

- EasyRefresher™: Financial Statements and Ratios
- Using the Business Planning Starter Workbook
- Understanding the Starter Workbook's Calculations
- Customizing the Starter Workbook

Pro forma financial statements—income statements, balance sheets, and cash flow statements—usually constitute an integral part of business planning and the overall budgeting process. Financial ratios are usually applied to these statements to assist both the builder and the user of the pro forma financial statements in assessing the strengths, weaknesses, and performance of the business and the reasonableness of the model.

The business planning starter workbook (BIZPLAN.XLS), described in this chapter, provides a framework to use in constructing pro forma financial statements and in applying ratio analysis to the pro forma statements. This starter workbook, with minor modifications, lets you apply ratio analysis to a set of existing financial statements. This chapter shows how to use the business planning starter workbook, modify it, and combine it with subsidiary spreadsheets.

EasyRefresher™: Financial Statements and Ratios

Financial statements describe either the past or the future financial condition and performance of a business. The term *financial statement* can refer to one of several types of schedules and summaries of economic information. Typically, however, the term describes a set of documents that include an income statement (also called a statement of operations), a balance sheet (also called a statement of financial condition), and a cash flow statement.

An income statement details the profits and losses of a business for a specific period. For example, you might want to know the profits or losses of your business over the past month. Therefore, you would prepare an income statement that lists your revenues and expenses and calculates the profits or losses for the month.

A balance sheet identifies and lists the assets and liabilities of a business as of a specific time. It paints a clear picture of what the business owns, what the business owes, and the difference between the two (often called the net worth or owner equity). Typically, you prepare a balance sheet as of the end of the period for which an income statement is prepared. For example, if you prepare an income statement for a month, you might also want to prepare a balance sheet as of the last day of the month.

A cash flow statement outlines the cash inflows and outflows of a business for a specific period. Generally, you prepare a cash flow statement for the same period for which you prepare an income statement.

Financial ratios express relationships among the amounts reported in the financial statements. The ratios can offer insights into the economic health of a business. The ratios can also indicate the reasonableness of the assumptions implicit in a forecast. For example, by comparing the ratios of your business with the ratios of similar businesses, you can compare the financial characteristics of your business with those of other businesses. By comparing the ratios in your pro forma model with industry averages and standards, you also test your modeling assumptions for reasonableness.

Two general categories of financial ratios exist: common size ratios and intrastatement or interstatement ratios. Common size ratios convert a financial statement—usually a balance sheet or an income statement—from dollars to percentages. Common size ratios allow for comparisons of the assets, liabilities, revenues, owner equity, and expenses of businesses of various sizes. The comparison can be either at a point in time or as a trend over time. Intrastatement or interstatement ratios quantify relationships among amounts from different financial statements or from different parts of the same financial statement. Intrastatement and interstatement ratios are an attempt to account for the fact that amounts usually cannot be interpreted alone, but must be viewed in the context of other key financial factors and events. In general, both categories of ratios are most valuable when compared with industry averages and trends.

Using the Business Planning Starter Workbook

You can use the business planning starter workbook, shown in Figures 10-1 through 10-5, to construct pro forma financial statements that let you forecast profits and losses, financial condition, and cash flows for a business or organization. To use the workbook, you develop and then enter information on the assets; the creditor and owner equities at the start of the forecasting horizon; the expected changes in the assets and equities over the forecasting horizon; and the revenues and expenses for each period on the forecasting horizon.

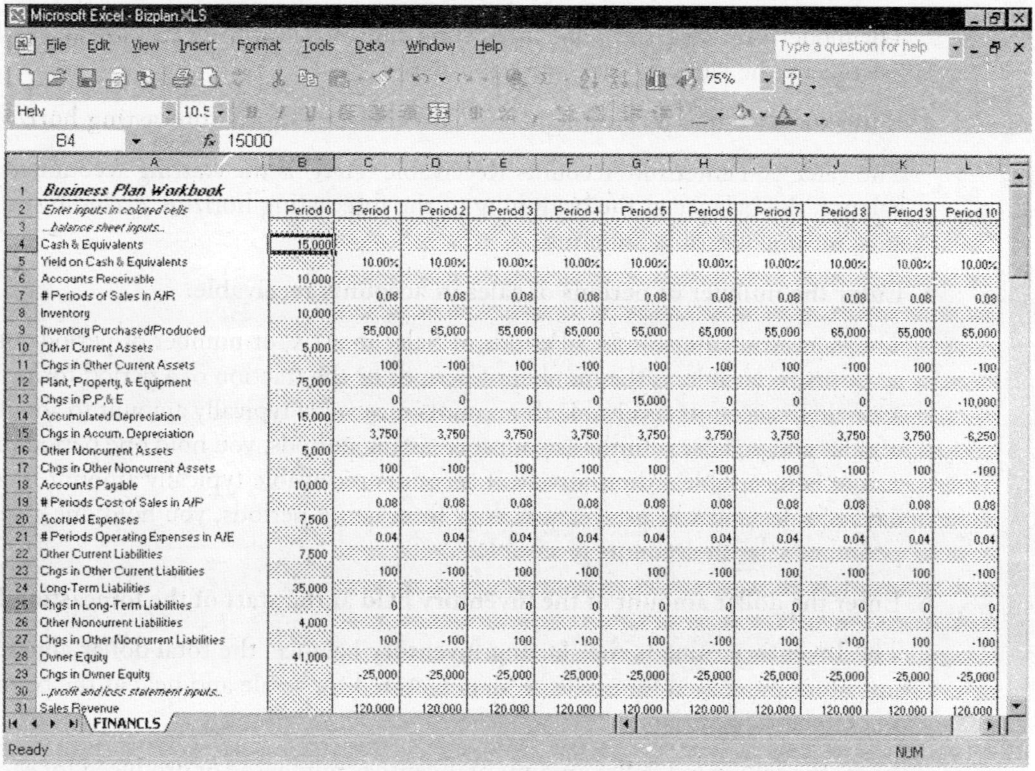

Figure 10-1 The inputs area of the business planning starter workbook.

Given data that includes your starting assets, liabilities, owner equity balances, and expected changes in these amounts for the forecasting horizon, this workbook constructs a balance sheet. Given data that includes sales and costs of sales, operating expenses, interest income and expenses, and marginal income tax rates, this workbook constructs an income statement. From the balance sheet and income statement, this workbook constructs a cash flow statement.

To enter your own data in the business planning starter workbook, use the following steps. Enter positive balances or increases as positive amounts, and enter negative balances or decreases as negative amounts.

1. **Open the business planning starter workbook, BIZPLAN.XLS, from the companion CD.**

   The starter workbook initially contains the default inputs shown in Figure 10-1.

2. **Enter the Cash & Equivalents balance for the start of the forecasting horizon.**

   The value you enter for Cash & Equivalents is the starting cash and cash equivalents (marketable securities), the dollar total of all the cash held at the beginning of the forecasting period.

3. **Enter the forecasted period yield that you expect the cash and equivalents to deliver.**

   The model estimates the period interest income by multiplying the cash and equivalents balance by the yield on cash and equivalents.

4. **Enter the accounts receivable balance for the start of the forecasting horizon.**

   The value you enter for Accounts Receivable (A/R) is the starting accounts receivable balance, the balance at the beginning of the forecasting horizon, excluding any allowance for uncollectible amounts.

5. **Enter the number of periods of sales in accounts receivable.**

   The value you enter for # of Periods of Sales in A/R, or number of periods of sales in accounts receivable, is the number of periods or the fraction of a period for which sales are held in accounts receivable. If accounts receivable typically amount to about 30 days of sales and you use months as your forecasting periods, you hold one period of sales in accounts receivable. Alternatively, if accounts receivable typically amount to about 30 days of sales and you use years as your forecasting periods, you hold one-twelfth of a period of sales in accounts receivable.

6. **Enter the dollar amount of the inventory held at the start of the forecasting horizon.**

   The Inventory value is the starting inventory balance, the total dollar amount of the inventory purchased for resale or manufactured for resale and held at the beginning of the forecasting horizon.

7. **Enter the forecasted dollar amount of inventory purchased or produced for each period of the forecasting horizon.**

   The Inventory Purchased/Produced value is the dollar total of items purchased or produced over the period.

8. **Enter the amount of the other current assets held at the start of the forecasting horizon.**

   The Other Current Assets starting balance is the dollar total of any other current assets with which you begin the forecasting horizon. These other current assets might include prepaid expenses, short-term investments, and deposits made with vendors.

9. Enter the amount of the change in the other current assets for each period in the forecasting horizon.

The value for Chgs in Other Current Assets, or changes in other current assets for the period, is the dollar total of increases or decreases in the accounts included in the starting other Current Assets balance.

10. Enter the amount of the plant, property, and equipment at the start of the forecasting horizon.

The starting Plant, Property, & Equipment balance is the dollar total of the fixed assets. This amount includes such items as realty, manufacturing equipment, and furniture.

11. Enter the amount of the change in the plant, property, and equipment (P, P, & E) for each period of the forecasting horizon.

The Chgs in P, P, & E value is the dollar total of decreases or increases in the plant, property, and equipment accounts for the period. Increases in these accounts probably stem from purchases of additional fixed assets. Decreases in these accounts probably stem from disposal of assets.

12. Enter the amount of the accumulated depreciation on the plant, property, and equipment at the start of the forecasting horizon.

The starting Accumulated Depreciation balance represents the depreciation expenses charged to date on the assets identified in the starting Plant, Property, & Equipment balance.

13. Enter the amount of the change in the accumulated depreciation for each period of the forecasting horizon.

The Chgs in Accum. Depreciation value is the dollar total of increases and decreases in the accumulated depreciation account for the period. Increases in the accumulated depreciation balance probably stem from the current period depreciation expense. Decreases in the accumulated depreciation balance probably stem from removing the accumulated depreciation attributed to a fixed asset that you disposed of.

14. Enter the amount of the other noncurrent assets at the start of the period.

The starting other Noncurrent Assets balance is the dollar total of all other noncurrent assets held at the start of the forecasting period. Other noncurrent assets might include copyrights, patents, and goodwill.

15. **Enter the amount of the change in the other noncurrent assets for each period of the forecasting horizon.**

    The Chgs in Other Noncurrent Assets value is the dollar total increase or decrease for the period in the accounts included in the starting Other Noncurrent Assets balance.

16. **Enter the amount of the accounts payable balance at the start of the forecasting horizon.**

    The starting Accounts Payable (A/P) balance is the dollar total of amounts owed vendors for inventory at the start of the forecasting horizon. This starter workbook calculates future Accounts Payable balances, based on the cost of sales volumes. To add precision to the forecasts of accounts payable, the model assumes that accounts payable represent debt incurred for the cost of sales.

17. **Enter the number of periods of the cost of sales in accounts payable.**

    The # Periods Cost of Sales in A/P is the number of periods or the fraction of a period for which the cost of sales is held in accounts payable. If accounts payable typically amount to about 30 days of cost of sales and you use months as your forecasting periods, you hold one period of cost of sales in accounts payable. Alternatively, if accounts payable typically amount to about 30 days of cost of sales and you use years as your forecasting periods, you hold one-twelfth of a period of cost of sales in accounts payable.

18. **Enter the amount of the accrued expenses balance at the start of the forecasting horizon.**

    The starting Accrued Expenses (A/E) balance is the dollar total of amounts owed vendors for operating expenses at the start of the forecast horizon. This starter workbook calculates future Accrued Expenses balances, based on the operating expenses levels. To add precision to the forecasts of accrued expenses, the model assumes that accrued expenses represent debt incurred for operating expenses.

19. **Enter the number of periods of operating expenses in accrued expenses.**

    The # Periods Operating Expenses in A/E value is the number of periods or the fraction of a period for which operating expenses are held in accrued expenses. If accrued expenses typically amount to 30 days of operating expenses and you use months as your forecasting periods, you hold one period of operating expenses in accrued expenses. Alternatively, if accrued expenses typically amount to about 30 days of operating expenses and you use years as your forecasting periods, you hold one-twelfth of a period of operating expense in accrued expenses.

20. **Enter the amount of the other current liabilities at the start of the forecasting period.**

    The Other Current Liabilities starting balance is the dollar total of all other current liabilities held at the start of the forecasting period. Other current liabilities might include income tax payable, product warranty liability, and the current portion of a long-term liability.

21. **Enter the amount of the change in the other current liabilities for each period of the forecasting horizon.**

    The Chgs in Other Current Liabilities value is the dollar total of increases or decreases for the period in the accounts included in the starting Other Current Liabilities balance.

22. **Enter the amount of the long-term liabilities balance at the start of the forecasting horizon.**

    The starting Long-Term Liabilities balance is the dollar total of debt that will be paid back sometime after the next year.

23. **Enter the amount of the change in the long-term liabilities for each period of the forecasting horizon.**

    The Chgs in Long-Term Liabilities value is the increase or decrease for the period in the outstanding long-term debt. These changes might include decreases stemming from the amortization of principal through debt service payments and increases stemming from additional funds provided by creditors. You need to include the principal component of debt service payments as negative amounts because they decrease the amount of long-term liability.

24. **Enter the amount of the other noncurrent liabilities at the start of the forecasting horizon.**

    The Other Noncurrent Liabilities starting balance is the dollar total of all other noncurrent liabilities held at the start of the forecasting period. These might include deferred income tax, employee pension plan liabilities, and capitalized lease obligations.

25. **Enter the amount of the change in the other noncurrent liabilities for each period of the forecasting horizon.**

    The Chgs in Other Noncurrent Liabilities value is the dollar total of increases or decreases for the period in the accounts included in the starting Other Noncurrent Liabilities balance. These changes might include decreases stemming from the amortization of principal through debt service payments and increases stemming from additional funds provided by creditors.

26. **Enter the amount of the owner equity balance at the start of the forecasting horizon.**

    The Owner Equity starting balance is the dollar total of the capital originally contributed by owners and the earnings retained by the business at the start of the forecasting horizon.

27. **Enter the amount of the change in the owner equity balance for each period of the forecasting horizon stemming from additional capital contributions, dividends, and other special distributions to owners.**

    The Chgs in Owner Equity value is the dollar total of increases for the period in owner equity, other than those stemming from the profits of a business and all decreases in owner equity. For example, increases in the Owner Equity balance might result from additional offerings of common or preferred stock and treasury stock transactions; decreases in the Owner Equity balance might result from dividends and other distributions to stockholders.

NOTE *Changes to owner equity balance resulting from the profit or loss for the period are calculated in the income statement; they are not entered.*

28. **Enter the sales revenue forecasted for each period of the forecasting horizon.**

    The Sales Revenue values represent the forecasted sales revenues generated by the business over each period of the forecasting horizon.

29. **Enter the cost of sales forecasted for each period of the forecasting horizon.**

    The Cost of Sales values represent the forecasted costs of the inventory sold for the forecasting horizon.

30. **Enter those costs that fall into the first, second, and third operating expense classification or category for each period of the forecasting horizon.**

    The operating expenses for Cost Centers 1, 2, and 3 represent the operating expenses for the forecasting horizon. These figures might be three expense classifications related to operating the business, or they might be the total expenses for three groups of expenses.

31. **Enter the interest expense of carrying any debt used to fund operations or asset purchases.**

    The Interest Expense values represent the period interest expenses of carrying any debt related to the business.

32. **Enter the marginal income tax rate that, when multiplied against the profit or loss for the period, calculates the income tax expense (or savings).**

    The Marginal Income Tax Rate value is the percentage that, when multiplied by the operating profit (or loss), calculates the income tax expense (or savings). If you are interested only in calculating pretax profits and losses, enter this amount as 0.

After you enter the required inputs, the starter workbook makes the calculations necessary to construct pro forma financial statements and calculate a set of rather standard financial ratios.

Understanding the Starter Workbook's Calculations

The business planning starter workbook has seven parts: the inputs forecast, Balance Sheet, Common Size Balance Sheet, Income Statement, Common Size Income Statement, Cash Flow Statement, and Financial Ratios Table. I want to briefly describe the calculations that occur within each of these parts in case you have questions or in case you want to modify the starter workbook so it works for your situation.

Forecasting Inputs

The inputs area of the business planning starter workbook has one set of formulas. The second row identifies the period for which the results are calculated. The period identifier numbers the periods for which values are entered. The start of the first period is stored in cell B2 as the integer 0. Periods that follow are stored as the previous period plus 1.

The period identifiers in the Balance Sheet, Common Size Balance Sheet, Income Statement, Cash Flow Statement, and Financial Ratios Table schedules use similar formulas.

NOTE *The cells that hold the period identifiers use a custom number format that precedes each period with identification with the word* Period. *To remove this, reformat the cells using another number format.*

Balance Sheet

The Balance Sheet schedule has 20 rows with calculated data, but the first row contains only the text label Period (see Figure 10-2). (As in the inputs area of the business planning starter workbook, the period identifier numbers the periods for which values are forecasted.) The rest of the Balance Sheet's values are described in the paragraphs that follow.

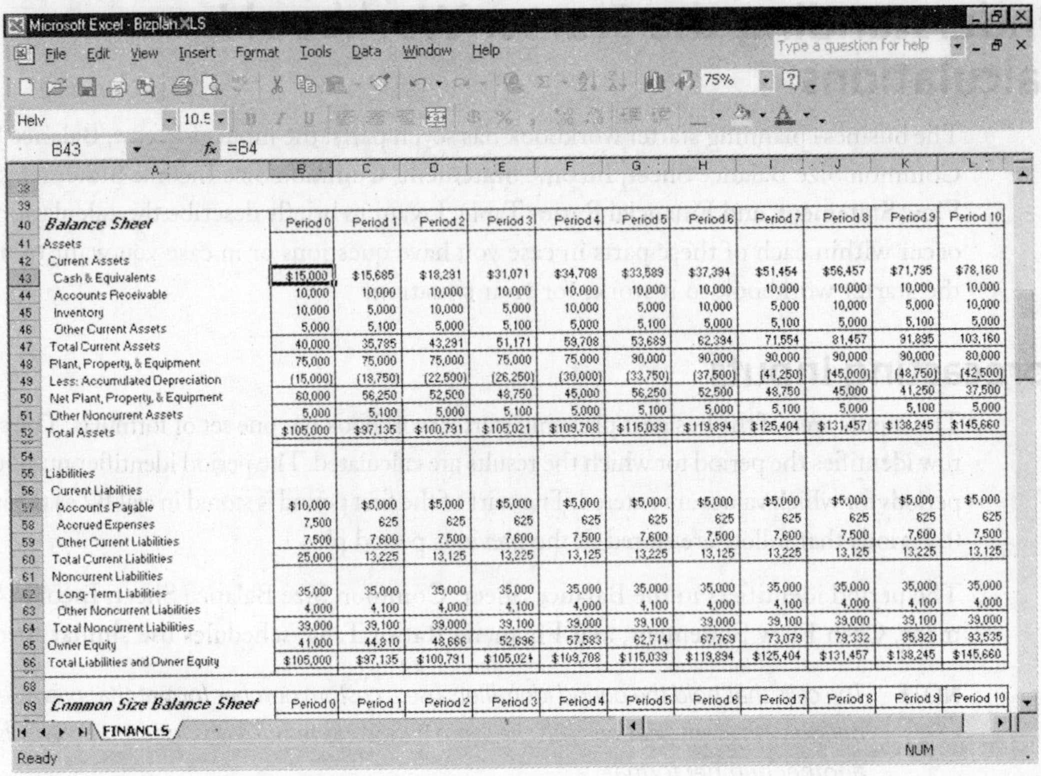

		Period 0	Period 1	Period 2	Period 3	Period 4	Period 5	Period 6	Period 7	Period 8	Period 9	Period 10
40	***Balance Sheet***											
41	Assets											
42	Current Assets											
43	Cash & Equivalents	$15,000	$15,685	$18,291	$31,071	$34,708	$33,589	$37,394	$51,454	$56,457	$71,795	$78,160
44	Accounts Receivable	10,000	10,000	10,000	10,000	10,000	10,000	10,000	10,000	10,000	10,000	10,000
45	Inventory	10,000	5,000	10,000	5,000	10,000	5,000	10,000	5,000	10,000	5,000	10,000
46	Other Current Assets	5,000	5,100	5,000	5,100	5,000	5,100	5,000	5,100	5,000	5,100	5,000
47	Total Current Assets	40,000	35,785	43,291	51,171	59,708	53,689	62,394	71,554	81,457	91,895	103,160
48	Plant, Property, & Equipment	75,000	75,000	75,000	75,000	75,000	90,000	90,000	90,000	90,000	90,000	80,000
49	Less: Accumulated Depreciation	(15,000)	(18,750)	(22,500)	(26,250)	(30,000)	(33,750)	(37,500)	(41,250)	(45,000)	(48,750)	(42,500)
50	Net Plant, Property, & Equipment	60,000	56,250	52,500	48,750	45,000	56,250	52,500	48,750	45,000	41,250	37,500
51	Other Noncurrent Assets	5,000	5,100	5,000	5,100	5,000	5,100	5,000	5,100	5,000	5,100	5,000
52	Total Assets	$105,000	$97,135	$100,791	$105,021	$109,708	$115,039	$119,894	$125,404	$131,457	$138,245	$145,660
54												
55	Liabilities											
56	Current Liabilities											
57	Accounts Payable	$10,000	$5,000	$5,000	$5,000	$5,000	$5,000	$5,000	$5,000	$5,000	$5,000	$5,000
58	Accrued Expenses	7,500	625	625	625	625	625	625	625	625	625	625
59	Other Current Liabilities	7,500	7,600	7,500	7,600	7,500	7,600	7,500	7,600	7,500	7,600	7,500
60	Total Current Liabilities	25,000	13,225	13,125	13,225	13,125	13,225	13,125	13,225	13,125	13,225	13,125
61	Noncurrent Liabilities											
62	Long-Term Liabilities	35,000	35,000	35,000	35,000	35,000	35,000	35,000	35,000	35,000	35,000	35,000
63	Other Noncurrent Liabilities	4,000	4,100	4,000	4,100	4,000	4,100	4,000	4,100	4,000	4,100	4,000
64	Total Noncurrent Liabilities	39,000	39,100	39,000	39,100	39,000	39,100	39,000	39,100	39,000	39,100	39,000
65	Owner Equity	41,000	44,810	48,666	52,696	57,583	62,714	67,769	73,079	79,332	85,920	93,535
66	Total Liabilities and Owner Equity	$105,000	$97,135	$100,791	$105,024	$109,708	$115,039	$119,894	$125,404	$131,457	$138,245	$145,660
68												
69	***Common Size Balance Sheet***	Period 0	Period 1	Period 2	Period 3	Period 4	Period 5	Period 6	Period 7	Period 8	Period 9	Period 10

Figure 10-2 The Balance Sheet portion of the business planning starter workbook.

Cash & Equivalents

The Cash & Equivalents figures show the projected cash on hand at the end of each of the forecasting periods. The starting balance is the value you enter in the inputs area of the business planning starter workbook. The balance for the first and subsequent periods is pulled from the Cash Flow Statement schedule, where it is calculated.

Accounts Receivable

The Accounts Receivable (A/R) figures show the net receivables held as of the end of each forecasting period. The starting balance is the value you enter in the inputs planning area of the business starter worksheet. The balance for the first and subsequent periods is based on the Sales Revenue and the # Periods of Sales in A/R values you enter in the inputs area of the business planning starter workbook. For example, the formula for the first period is:

```
=C7*C31
```

The formula for the second period is:

```
=D7*D31
```

and so on.

Inventory

The Inventory values show the dollar total of the inventory held at the end of each forecasting period. The starting balance is the value you enter in the inputs area of the business planning starter workbook. The balance for the first and subsequent periods is the previous period balance plus any inventory purchases or production costs minus any cost of sales. For example, the formula for the first period is:

```
=B45+C9-C32
```

The formula for the second period is:

```
=C45+D9-D32
```

and so on.

Other Current Assets

The Other Current Assets figures show the dollar total of the other current assets held at the end of each forecasting period. The starting balance for Other Current Assets is the value you enter in the inputs area of the business planning starter workbook. The balance for the first and subsequent periods is the previous balance plus the change in the balance. For example, the formula for the first period is:

```
=B46+C11
```

The formula for the second period is:

```
=C46+D11
```

and so on.

Total Current Assets

The Total Current Assets figures show the dollar total of the current assets at the end of each of the forecasting horizons. The balance at any time is the sum of Cash & Equivalents, Accounts Receivable, Inventory, and Other Current Assets. For example, the formula for the starting Total Current Assets balance is:

```
=SUM(B43:B46)
```

The formula for the first period is:

```
=SUM(C43:C46)
```

and so on.

Plant, Property, & Equipment

The Plant, Property, & Equipment figures show the original dollar cost of the plant, property, and equipment at the end of each forecasting horizon. The starting Plant, Property, & Equipment balance is the value you enter in the inputs area of the business planning starter workbook. The balance for the first and subsequent periods is the previous balance plus any additions to the plant, property, and equipment accounts. For example, the formula for the first period is:

```
=B48+C13
```

The formula for the second period is:

```
=C48+D13
```

and so on.

Less: Accumulated Depreciation

The Accumulated Depreciation figures show the cumulative depreciation expenses charged through the current period for the plant, property, and equipment. The starting balance is the value you enter in the inputs area of the business planning starter workbook. The balance for the first and subsequent periods is the previous balance minus the current period's changes in accumulated depreciation. For example, the formula for the first period is:

```
=B49-C15
```

The formula for the second period is:

```
=C49-D15
```

and so on. Because the accumulated depreciation is shown as a negative amount, you need to subtract the positive number pulled from the forecasting inputs.

Net Plant, Property, & Equipment

The Net Plant, Property, & Equipment figures show the difference between Plant, Property, & Equipment and Accumulated Depreciation at the end of each of the forecasting horizons. For example, the formula for the starting balance is:

```
=B48+B49
```

The formula for the first period is:

```
=C48+C49
```

and so on. Because the Accumulated Depreciation balance is shown as a negative amount, you simply add these two amounts in the formula for the Net Plant, Property, & Equipment amount.

Other Noncurrent Assets

The Other Noncurrent Assets figures show the dollar total of any other noncurrent assets held at the end of each of the forecasting periods. The starting balance is the value you enter in the inputs area of the business planning starter workbook. The balance for the first and subsequent periods is the previous period balance plus the change in the account in the current period. For example, the formula for the first period is:

```
=B51+C17
```

The formula for the second period is:

```
=C51+D17
```

and so on.

Total Assets

The Total Assets figures show the dollar total of all the assets held at the end of the forecasting periods. The balance at any time is the sum of Current Assets; Net Plant, Property, & Equipment; and Other Noncurrent Assets. For example, the formula for the starting balance is:

```
=B47+B50+B51
```

The formula for the first period is:

```
=C47+C50+C51
```

and so on.

Accounts Payable

The Accounts Payable figures show the debt that is related to the cost of sales outstanding at the end of each forecasting period. The starting balance is the value you enter in the inputs area of the business planning starter workbook. The balance for the first and subsequent periods is Cost of Sales for the period times # of Periods of Cost of Sales in A/P. For example, the formula for the first period is:

```
=C19*C32
```

The formula for the second period is:

```
=D19*D32
```

and so on.

Accrued Expenses

The Accrued Expenses figures show the debt that is related to the operating expenses outstanding at the end of each forecasting period. The starting balance is the value you enter in the inputs area of the business planning starter workbook. The balance for the first and subsequent periods is the operating expenses times # of Periods Operating Expenses in A/E. For example, the formula for the first period is:

```
=C21*SUM(C33:C35)
```

The formula for the second period is:

```
=D21*SUM(D33:D35)
```

and so on.

Other Current Liabilities

The Other Current Liabilities figures show the dollar total of other debts outstanding at the end of the forecasting periods that will be paid within the current year or business cycle. The starting balance is the value you enter in the inputs area of the business planning starter workbook The balance for the first and subsequent periods is the previous balance plus the change in the current period. For example, the formula for the first period is:

```
=B59+C23
```

The formula for the second period is:

```
=C59+D23
```

and so on.

Total Current Liabilities

The Total Current Liabilities figures show the dollar total of all the current liabilities at the end of each of the forecasting periods. The balance at any time is the sum of Accounts Payable, Accrued Expenses, and Other Current Liabilities. For example, the formula for the starting balance is:

```
=SUM(B57:B59)
```

The formula for the first period is:

```
=SUM(C57:C59)
```

and so on.

Long-Term Liabilities

The Long-Term Liabilities figures show the dollar total of the long-term outstanding debt at the end of each forecasting period. The starting balance is the value you enter in the inputs area of the business planning starter workbook. The balance for the first and subsequent periods is the previous balance plus any changes in the Long-Term Liabilities balance in the current period. For example, the formula for the first period is:

```
=B62+C25
```

The formula for the second period is:

```
=C62+D25
```

and so on.

Other Noncurrent Liabilities

The Other Noncurrent Liabilities figures show the dollar total of any other noncurrent outstanding debt at the end of each forecasting period. The starting balance is the value you enter in the inputs area of the business planning starter workbook. The balance for the first and subsequent periods is the previous period balance plus the change in the current period. For example, the formula for the first period is:

```
=B63+C27
```

The formula for the second period is:

```
=C63+D27
```

and so on.

Total Noncurrent Liabilities

The Total Noncurrent Liabilities figures show the dollar totals of the long-term debt and the other noncurrent outstanding debt at the end of each of the forecasting periods. The balance at any time is the sum of Long-Term Liabilities and Other Noncurrent Liabilities. For example, the formula for the starting balance is:

```
=B62+B63
```

The formula for the first period is:

```
=C62+C63
```

and so on.

Owner Equity

The Owner Equity figures show the dollar totals of the owner equity accounts at the end of each forecasting period. The starting balance is the value you enter in the inputs area of the business planning starter workbook. The balance for the first and subsequent periods is the previous period balance plus Net Income After Taxes for the period plus other adjustments, such as additional capital contributions and dividends. For example, the formula for the first period is:

```
=B65+C29+C116
```

The formula for the second period is:

```
=C65+D29+D116
```

and so on.

Total Liabilities and Owner Equity

The Total Liabilities and Owner Equity figures show the dollar totals of Current Liabilities, Noncurrent Liabilities, and Owner Equity at the end of each forecasting period. For example, the formula for the starting balance is:

```
=B60+B64+B65
```

The formula for the first period is:

```
=C60+C64+C65
```

and so on.

TIP *The Total Assets value should equal the Total Liabilities and Owner Equity value. If they differ, your model contains an error.*

Common Size Balance Sheet

The Common Size Balance Sheet schedule lists, in the balance sheet format, what percentage of the total assets each individual asset represents and what percentage of the total liabilities and owner equity each individual liability and the owner equity represents (see Figure 10-3). When you compare these percentages with those of business peers, you can see the relative financial strength or weakness of your business. Trends in the percentages over time can indicate improvement or deterioration in the overall financial condition of your business.

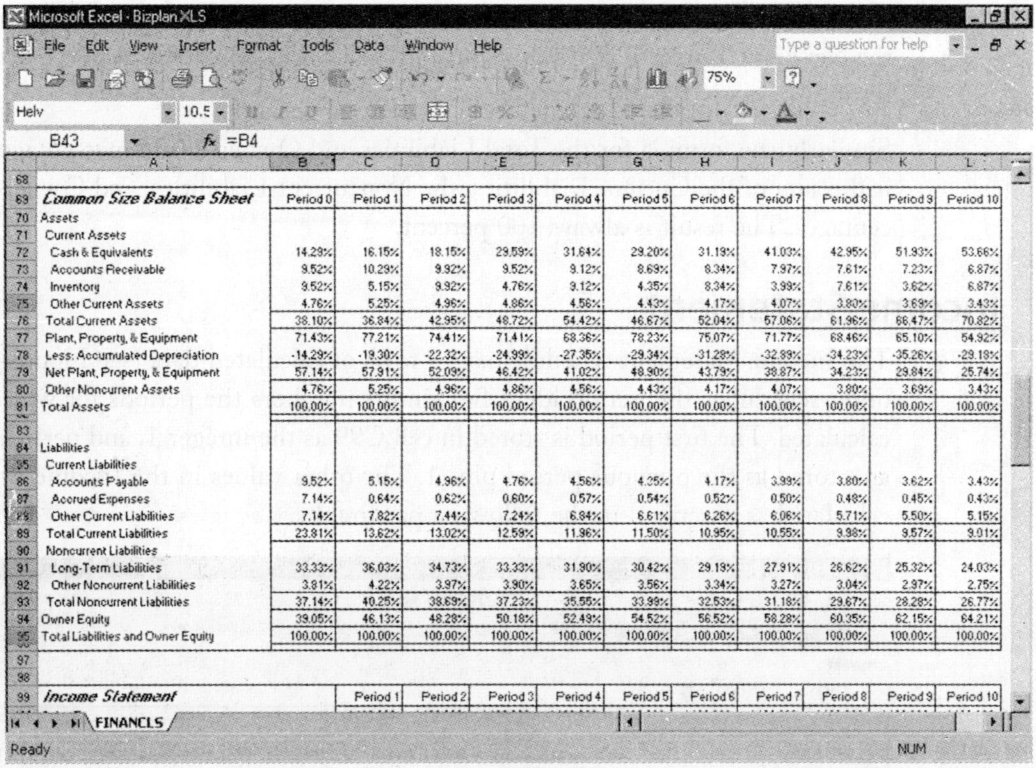

Common Size Balance Sheet	Period 0	Period 1	Period 2	Period 3	Period 4	Period 5	Period 6	Period 7	Period 8	Period 9	Period 10
Assets											
Current Assets											
Cash & Equivalents	14.29%	16.15%	18.15%	29.59%	31.64%	29.20%	31.19%	41.03%	42.95%	51.93%	53.66%
Accounts Receivable	9.52%	10.29%	9.92%	9.52%	9.12%	8.69%	8.34%	7.97%	7.61%	7.23%	6.87%
Inventory	9.52%	5.15%	9.92%	4.76%	9.12%	4.35%	8.34%	3.98%	7.61%	3.62%	6.87%
Other Current Assets	4.76%	5.25%	4.96%	4.86%	4.56%	4.43%	4.17%	4.07%	3.80%	3.69%	3.43%
Total Current Assets	38.10%	36.84%	42.95%	48.72%	54.42%	46.67%	52.04%	57.06%	61.96%	66.47%	70.82%
Plant, Property, & Equipment	71.43%	77.21%	74.41%	71.41%	68.36%	78.23%	75.07%	71.77%	68.46%	65.10%	54.92%
Less: Accumulated Depreciation	-14.29%	-19.30%	-22.32%	-24.99%	-27.35%	-29.34%	-31.28%	-32.89%	-34.23%	-35.26%	-29.18%
Net Plant, Property, & Equipment	57.14%	57.91%	52.09%	46.42%	41.02%	48.90%	43.79%	38.87%	34.23%	29.84%	25.74%
Other Noncurrent Assets	4.76%	5.25%	4.96%	4.86%	4.56%	4.43%	4.17%	4.07%	3.80%	3.69%	3.43%
Total Assets	100.00%	100.00%	100.00%	100.00%	100.00%	100.00%	100.00%	100.00%	100.00%	100.00%	100.00%
Liabilities											
Current Liabilities											
Accounts Payable	9.52%	5.15%	4.96%	4.76%	4.56%	4.35%	4.17%	3.98%	3.80%	3.62%	3.43%
Accrued Expenses	7.14%	0.64%	0.62%	0.60%	0.57%	0.54%	0.52%	0.50%	0.48%	0.45%	0.43%
Other Current Liabilities	7.14%	7.82%	7.44%	7.24%	6.84%	6.61%	6.26%	6.06%	5.71%	5.50%	5.15%
Total Current Liabilities	23.81%	13.62%	13.02%	12.59%	11.96%	11.50%	10.95%	10.55%	9.98%	9.57%	9.01%
Noncurrent Liabilities											
Long-Term Liabilities	33.33%	36.03%	34.73%	33.33%	31.90%	30.42%	29.19%	27.91%	26.62%	25.32%	24.03%
Other Noncurrent Liabilities	3.81%	4.22%	3.97%	3.90%	3.65%	3.56%	3.34%	3.27%	3.04%	2.97%	2.75%
Total Noncurrent Liabilities	37.14%	40.25%	38.69%	37.23%	35.55%	33.99%	32.53%	31.18%	29.67%	28.28%	26.77%
Owner Equity	39.05%	46.13%	48.28%	50.18%	52.49%	54.52%	56.52%	58.28%	60.35%	62.15%	64.21%
Total Liabilities and Owner Equity	100.00%	100.00%	100.00%	100.00%	100.00%	100.00%	100.00%	100.00%	100.00%	100.00%	100.00%

Income Statement		Period 1	Period 2	Period 3	Period 4	Period 5	Period 6	Period 7	Period 8	Period 9	Period 10

Figure 10-3 The Common Size Balance Sheet portion of the business planning starter workbook.

The Common Size Balance Sheet schedule has 19 rows with calculated data that express line-item amounts as percentages of the total. For the asset side of the Balance Sheet, assets are expressed as a percentage of the total assets. For the creditor and owner equity side of the Balance Sheet, equities are expressed as a percentage of the total liabilities and owner equity. The formulas for all rows except Total Assets and Total Liabilities and Owner Equity simply convert the Balance Sheet values to percentages. For example, the Cash & Equivalents formula for the first period is:

```
=B43/B$52
```

The formula for the second period is:

```
=C43/C$52
```

and so on. All asset percentages are derived from dividing by total assets, which explains why the absolute reference to row $52 is used in all asset formulas. Similarly, the absolute reference to row $66 appears in all formulas in the liabilities and equity formulas.

The formula for the Total Assets percentage at any time is the sum of the Current Assets; the Net Plant, Property, & Equipment; and the Other Noncurrent Assets percentages. The result always equals 100 percent.

Similarly, the formula for the Total Liabilities and Owner Equity percentage at any time is the sum of the Current Liabilities, the Noncurrent Liabilities, and Owner Equity percentages. The result is always 100 percent.

Income Statement

The Income Statement schedule has 14 rows of calculated data (see Figure 10-4). As in other schedules, the period identifier simply numbers the periods for which values are calculated. The first period is stored in cell C99 as the integer 1, and periods that follow are stored as the previous period plus 1. The other values in the Income Statement are calculated as described in the following paragraphs.

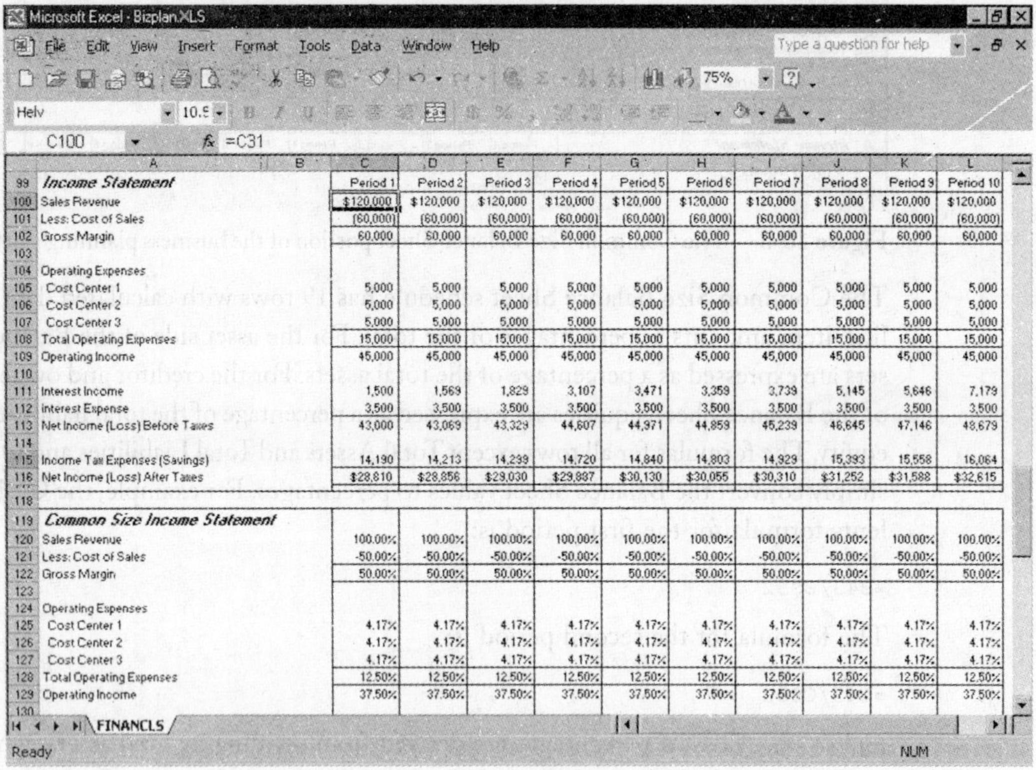

	A	C	D	E	F	G	H	I	J	K	L
99	*Income Statement*	Period 1	Period 2	Period 3	Period 4	Period 5	Period 6	Period 7	Period 8	Period 9	Period 10
100	Sales Revenue	$120,000	$120,000	$120,000	$120,000	$120,000	$120,000	$120,000	$120,000	$120,000	$120,000
101	Less: Cost of Sales	(60,000)	(60,000)	(60,000)	(60,000)	(60,000)	(60,000)	(60,000)	(60,000)	(60,000)	(60,000)
102	Gross Margin	60,000	60,000	60,000	60,000	60,000	60,000	60,000	60,000	60,000	60,000
103											
104	Operating Expenses										
105	Cost Center 1	5,000	5,000	5,000	5,000	5,000	5,000	5,000	5,000	5,000	5,000
106	Cost Center 2	5,000	5,000	5,000	5,000	5,000	5,000	5,000	5,000	5,000	5,000
107	Cost Center 3	5,000	5,000	5,000	5,000	5,000	5,000	5,000	5,000	5,000	5,000
108	Total Operating Expenses	15,000	15,000	15,000	15,000	15,000	15,000	15,000	15,000	15,000	15,000
109	Operating Income	45,000	45,000	45,000	45,000	45,000	45,000	45,000	45,000	45,000	45,000
110											
111	Interest Income	1,500	1,569	1,829	3,107	3,471	3,359	3,739	5,145	5,646	7,179
112	Interest Expense	3,500	3,500	3,500	3,500	3,500	3,500	3,500	3,500	3,500	3,500
113	Net Income (Loss) Before Taxes	43,000	43,069	43,329	44,607	44,971	44,859	45,239	46,645	47,146	48,679
114											
115	Income Tax Expenses (Savings)	14,190	14,213	14,299	14,720	14,840	14,803	14,929	15,393	15,558	16,064
116	Net Income (Loss) After Taxes	$28,810	$28,856	$29,030	$29,887	$30,130	$30,055	$30,310	$31,252	$31,588	$32,615
118											
119	*Common Size Income Statement*										
120	Sales Revenue	100.00%	100.00%	100.00%	100.00%	100.00%	100.00%	100.00%	100.00%	100.00%	100.00%
121	Less: Cost of Sales	-50.00%	-50.00%	-50.00%	-50.00%	-50.00%	-50.00%	-50.00%	-50.00%	-50.00%	-50.00%
122	Gross Margin	50.00%	50.00%	50.00%	50.00%	50.00%	50.00%	50.00%	50.00%	50.00%	50.00%
123											
124	Operating Expenses										
125	Cost Center 1	4.17%	4.17%	4.17%	4.17%	4.17%	4.17%	4.17%	4.17%	4.17%	4.17%
126	Cost Center 2	4.17%	4.17%	4.17%	4.17%	4.17%	4.17%	4.17%	4.17%	4.17%	4.17%
127	Cost Center 3	4.17%	4.17%	4.17%	4.17%	4.17%	4.17%	4.17%	4.17%	4.17%	4.17%
128	Total Operating Expenses	12.50%	12.50%	12.50%	12.50%	12.50%	12.50%	12.50%	12.50%	12.50%	12.50%
129	Operating Income	37.50%	37.50%	37.50%	37.50%	37.50%	37.50%	37.50%	37.50%	37.50%	37.50%

Figure 10-4 The Income Statement and Common Size Income Statement areas of the business planning starter workbook.

Sales Revenue

The Sales Revenue figures are the estimates you enter in the inputs area of the business planning starter workbook. The amount for the period is the value you enter in the inputs area of the business planning starter workbook.

Less: Cost of Sales

The Cost Of Sales figures are the Cost of Sales estimates you enter in the inputs area of the business planning starter workbook.

Gross Margin

The Gross Margin figures show the amounts left over from the sales proceeds after subtracting Cost of Sales. Subtracting your other expenses from the Gross Margin amount gives you your profit figure. The Gross Margin formula is Sales Revenue for the period minus Cost of Sales. For example, the formula for the first period is:

```
=C100+C101
```

The formula for the second period is:

```
=D100+D101
```

and so on. Notice that because the Cost of Sales figures are pulled into the Income Statement schedule as negative amounts, the Gross Margin formula simply adds the Sales Revenue figure to the negative Cost of Sales figure.

Operating Expenses – Cost Centers 1, 2, and 3

The Operating Expenses figures for Cost Centers 1, 2, and 3 show the amount for each operating expense classification or category that you enter in the inputs area of the business planning starter workbook.

Total Operating Expenses

The Total Operating Expenses figures show the sums of the operating expenses you enter in the inputs area of the business planning starter workbook for these three operating expense categories or classifications. The total for each period is the sum of the operating expenses for Cost Centers 1, 2, and 3. For example, the formula for the first period is:

```
=SUM(C105:C107)
```

The formula for the second period is:

```
=SUM(D105:D107)
```

and so on.

Operating Income

The Operating Income figures show the sales dollar amounts left after paying the Cost of Sales and the Operating Expenses. The Operating Income figures represent the amounts that go toward paying your financing expenses and income tax, and the amount that constitutes your profits. The amount for each period is the Gross Margin figure for the period minus the Total Operating Expenses figure. For example, the formula for the first period is:

```
=C102-C108
```

The formula for the second period is:

```
=D102-D108
```

and so on.

Interest Income

The Interest Income figures show the earnings from investing the cash of the business. The amount for each period is the beginning Cash & Equivalents balance from the inputs area of the business planning starter workbook times the period yield on Cash & Equivalents. For example, the formula for the first period is:

```
=B43*C5
```

The formula for the second period is:

```
=C43*D5
```

and so on.

Interest Expense

The Interest Expense figures show the costs of using borrowed funds for operations and asset purchases. The amount for each period is the value you enter in the inputs area of the business planning starter workbook.

Net Income (Loss) Before Taxes

The Net Income (Loss) Before Taxes figures show the amount of operating income left after receiving any interest income and paying any interest expense. The amount for each period is the Operating Income figure for the period plus the Interest Income figure for the period minus the Interest Expense figure for the period. For example, the formula for the first period is:

```
=C109+C111-C112
```

The formula for the second period is:

```
=D109+D111-D112
```

and so on.

Income Tax Expenses (Savings)

The Income Tax Expenses (Savings) figures show the income tax expenses (or savings) that use the calculated Net Income (Loss) Before Taxes figures and the Marginal Income Tax Rate figures you forecasted in the inputs area of the business planning starter workbook. Notice that the model calculates a current period savings in income taxes when there is a net loss before taxes. This might be the case when a current period loss is carried back to a prior period or when the current period loss is consolidated with the current period income of related businesses. Basically, then, the model assumes that a net loss before income taxes results in a current period tax refund—that is, an overall tax savings—because you can deduct a loss in one business from the profits of another business. However, if a current period loss does not result in a current period income tax savings, you need to modify the formula, as described in the section "Customizing the Starter Workbook."

The amount for each period is the Net Income (Loss) Before Taxes times the Marginal Income Tax Rate figure. For example, the formula for the first period is:

```
=C37*C113
```

The formula for the second period is:

```
=D37*D113
```

and so on.

Net Income (Loss) After Taxes

The Net Income (Loss) After Taxes figures calculate the after-tax profits of operating the business. The amount for each period is the Net Income (Loss) Before Taxes figure minus the Income Tax Expenses (Savings) figure. For example, the formula for the first period is:

```
=C113-C115
```

The formula for the second period is:

```
=D113-D115
```

and so on.

Common Size Income Statement

The Common Size Income Statement schedule lists, in income statement format, what percentage of the total sales revenue each income statement line item represents (see Figure 10-4). When you compare these percentages against those of business peers, you can see the relative financial performance of your business. Trends in the percentages over the forecasting horizon can indicate improvement or deterioration in the financial performance of your business.

The Common Size Income Statement schedule has 13 rows of calculated data that express the component line-item amount for each period as a percentage of the sales revenue figure for the period. The formulas for all rows except Sales Revenue simply convert the Income Statement values to percentages.

The Sales Revenue figures add the Cost of Sales, Total Operating Expenses, Interest Income, Interest Expense, Income Tax Expenses (Savings), and Net Income (Loss) After Taxes percentages. The results always equal 100 percent.

NOTE *The Sales Revenue percentage calculations adds the expense and profit percentages. Those expenses shown as negative amounts, therefore, are subtracted.*

Cash Flow Statement

The Cash Flow Statement schedule has 18 rows of calculated data (see Figure 10-5). As in other schedules, a period identifier numbers the periods for which values are calculated. The first period is stored in cell C141 as integer 1. Periods that follow are stored as the previous period plus 1. Other Cash Flow Statement values are calculated as described in the paragraphs that follow.

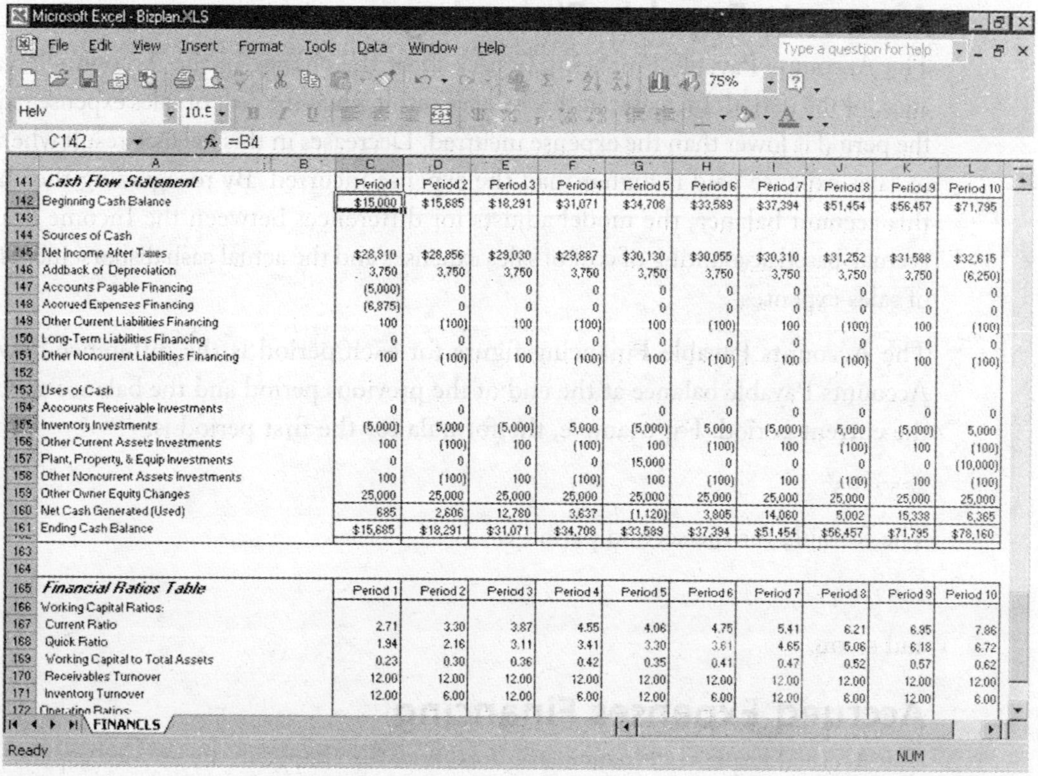

	Cash Flow Statement	Period 1	Period 2	Period 3	Period 4	Period 5	Period 6	Period 7	Period 8	Period 9	Period 10
142	Beginning Cash Balance	$15,000	$15,685	$18,291	$31,071	$34,708	$33,589	$37,394	$51,454	$56,457	$71,795
143											
144	Sources of Cash										
145	Net Income After Taxes	$28,810	$28,856	$29,030	$29,887	$30,130	$30,055	$30,310	$31,252	$31,588	$32,615
146	Addback of Depreciation	3,750	3,750	3,750	3,750	3,750	3,750	3,750	3,750	3,750	(6,250)
147	Accounts Payable Financing	(5,000)	0	0	0	0	0	0	0	0	0
148	Accrued Expenses Financing	(6,875)	0	0	0	0	0	0	0	0	0
149	Other Current Liabilities Financing	100	(100)	100	(100)	100	(100)	100	(100)	100	(100)
150	Long-Term Liabilities Financing	0	0	0	0	0	0	0	0	0	0
151	Other Noncurrent Liabilities Financing	100	(100)	100	(100)	100	(100)	100	(100)	100	(100)
152											
153	Uses of Cash										
154	Accounts Receivable Investments	0	0	0	0	0	0	0	0	0	0
155	Inventory Investments	(5,000)	5,000	(5,000)	5,000	(5,000)	5,000	(5,000)	5,000	(5,000)	5,000
156	Other Current Assets Investments	100	(100)	100	(100)	100	(100)	100	(100)	100	(100)
157	Plant, Property, & Equip Investments	0	0	0	0	15,000	0	0	0	0	(10,000)
158	Other Noncurrent Assets Investments	100	(100)	100	(100)	100	(100)	100	(100)	100	(100)
159	Other Owner Equity Changes	25,000	25,000	25,000	25,000	25,000	25,000	25,000	25,000	25,000	25,000
160	Net Cash Generated (Used)	685	2,606	12,780	3,637	(1,120)	3,805	14,060	5,002	15,338	6,365
161	Ending Cash Balance	$15,685	$18,291	$31,071	$34,708	$33,589	$37,394	$51,454	$56,457	$71,795	$78,160

	Financial Ratios Table	Period 1	Period 2	Period 3	Period 4	Period 5	Period 6	Period 7	Period 8	Period 9	Period 10
166	Working Capital Ratios:										
167	Current Ratio	2.71	3.30	3.87	4.55	4.06	4.75	5.41	6.21	6.95	7.86
168	Quick Ratio	1.94	2.16	3.11	3.41	3.30	3.61	4.65	5.06	6.18	6.72
169	Working Capital to Total Assets	0.23	0.30	0.36	0.42	0.35	0.41	0.47	0.52	0.57	0.62
170	Receivables Turnover	12.00	12.00	12.00	12.00	12.00	12.00	12.00	12.00	12.00	12.00
171	Inventory Turnover	12.00	6.00	12.00	6.00	12.00	6.00	12.00	6.00	12.00	6.00

Figure 10-5 The Cash Flow Statement and Financial Ratios Table areas of the business planning starter workbook.

Beginning Cash Balance

The Beginning Cash Balance figures show the forecasted cash and equivalents balance at the start of each forecasting period. The starting balance is the value you enter in the inputs area of the business planning starter workbook. For subsequent periods, the Beginning Cash Balance is the previous period's Ending Cash Balance.

Net Income After Taxes

The Net Income After Taxes figures show the amounts calculated in the Income Statement schedule as the business profits for each forecasting period.

Addback of Depreciation

The Addback of Depreciation figures show the change in the accumulated depreciation balance for each forecasting period. Normally, this change stems from the period depreciation expense; it must be added back into the Net Income After Taxes figure because the depreciation expense uses no cash. The depreciation added back for each period is the value you enter in the inputs area of the business planning starter workbook as the change in accumulated depreciation.

Accounts Payable Financing

The Accounts Payable Financing figures show the change in the Accounts Payable balance for the period. Increases in this balance result when the cost of sales expense paid during the period is lower than the expense incurred. Decreases in this balance result when the cost of sales expense paid is higher than the expense incurred. By recognizing the changes in this account balance, the model adjusts for differences between the Income Statement's accrual-based accounting of cost of sales expenses and the actual cash disbursements for costs of sales expenses.

The Accounts Payable Financing figure for each period is the difference between the Accounts Payable balance at the end of the previous period and the balance at the end of the current period. For example, the formula for the first period is:

```
=C57-B57
```

The formula for the second period is:

```
=D57-C57
```

and so on.

Accrued Expenses Financing

The Accrued Expenses Financing figures show the change in the accrued expenses balance for the period. Increases in this balance result when the operating expense paid during the period is lower than the expense incurred. Decreases in this balance result when the operating expense paid during the period is higher than the expense incurred. By recognizing the changes in this account balance, the model adjusts for differences between the Income Statement's accrual-based accounting expenses and the actual cash disbursements for operating expenses.

The Accrued Expenses Financing figure for each period is the difference between the Accrued Expenses balance at the end of the previous period and the balance at the end of the current period. For example, the formula for the first period is:

```
=C58-B58
```

The formula for the second period is:

```
=D58-C58
```

and so on.

Other Current Liabilities Financing

The Other Current Liabilities Financing figures show the change in the Other Current Liabilities balance for the period. This amount increases when, either directly or indirectly, cash is generated by borrowing. This amount decreases when, either directly or indirectly, cash is used to pay off short-term borrowing.

The Other Current Liabilities Financing figure for each period is the difference between the Other Current Liabilities balance at the end of the previous period and the balance at the end of the current period. For example, the formula for the first period is:

```
=C59-B59
```

The formula for the second period is:

```
=D59-C59
```

and so on.

Long-Term Liabilities Financing

The Long-Term Liabilities Financing figures show the changes in the long-term liabilities amount for the period. This balance increases when, either directly or indirectly, cash is generated by long-term borrowing. This amount decreases when, either directly or indirectly, cash is used to pay off long-term borrowing.

The Long-Term Liabilities Financing figure for each period is the difference between the Long-Term Liabilities balance at the end of the previous period and the balance at the end of the current period. For example, the formula for the first period is:

```
=C62-B62
```

The formula for the second period is:

```
=D62-C62
```

and so on.

Other Noncurrent Liabilities Financing

The Other Noncurrent Liabilities Financing figures show the changes in the Other Noncurrent Liabilities balance for the period. This amount increases when, either directly or indirectly, cash is generated by other long-term borrowing. This amount decreases when, either directly or indirectly, cash is used to pay off other long-term borrowing.

The Other Noncurrent Liabilities Financing figure for each period is the difference between the Other Noncurrent Liabilities balance at the end of the previous period and the balance at the end of the current period. For example, the formula for the first period is:

```
=C63-B63
```

The formula for the second period is:

```
=D63-C63
```

and so on.

Accounts Receivable Investments

The Accounts Receivable Investments figures show the change in the Accounts Receivable balance for each forecasting period. This amount increases when the sales revenue collected during the period is less than the revenue recorded. This amount decreases when the sales revenue collected during the period is more than recorded. By recognizing the changes in the account balance, the model adjusts for differences between the income statement's accrual-based accounting of sales revenues and the actual cash collections for sales.

The Accounts Receivable Investments figure for each period is the difference between the Accounts Receivable balance at the end of the previous period and the balance at the end of the current period. For example, the formula for the first period is:

```
=C44-B44
```

The formula for the second period is:

```
=D44-C44
```

and so on.

Inventory Investments

The Inventory Investments figures show the change in the inventory balance for each forecasting period. This amount increases when the inventory sold is less than the inventory acquired. This amount decreases when the inventory sold is more than the inventory acquired. By recognizing the changes in this account balance, the model recognizes the cash effects of changing inventory balances.

The Inventory Investments figure for each period is the difference between the Inventory balance at the end of the previous period and the balance at the end of the current period. For example, the formula for the first period is:

```
=C45-B45
```

The formula for the second period is:

```
=D45-C45
```

and so on.

Other Current Assets Investments

The Other Current Assets Investments figures show the changes in the Other Current Assets balance for the period. This amount increases when, either directly or indirectly, cash is used to acquire current assets. This amount decreases when indirectly or directly cash is generated by converting current assets to cash.

The Other Current Assets Investments figure for each period is the difference between the Other Current Assets balance at the end of the previous period and the balance at the end of the current period. For example, the formula for the first period is:

```
=C46-B46
```

The formula for the second period is:

```
=D46-C46
```

and so on.

Plant, Property & Equip Investments

The Plant, Property, & Equip Investments figures show the change in the Plant, Property, & Equipment balance for the period. This amount increases when, either directly or indirectly, cash is used to acquire plants, property and equipment. This amount decreases when, either directly or indirectly, cash is generated by converting plants, property, and equipment to cash.

The Plant, Property, & Equip Investments figure for each period is the difference between the Plant, Property, & Equipment balance at the end of the previous period and the balance at the end of the current period. For example, the formula for the first period is:

```
=C48-B48
```

The formula for the second period is:

```
=D48-C48
```

and so on.

Other Noncurrent Assets Investments

The Other Noncurrent Assets Investments figures show the changes in the Other Noncurrent Assets balance for the period. This amount increases when, either directly or indirectly, cash is used to acquire other noncurrent assets. This amount decreases when, either directly or indirectly, cash is generated by converting other noncurrent assets to cash.

The Other Noncurrent Assets Investments figure for each period is the difference between the Other Noncurrent Assets balance at the end of the previous period and the balance at the end of the current period. For example, the formula for the first period is:

```
=C51-B51
```

The formula for the second period is:

```
=D51-C51
```

and so on.

Other Owner Equity Changes

The Other Owner Equity Changes figures show the cash flows stemming from any additional capital contributions made by the owners to the business or from dividends and other distributions made by the business to the owners. The Other Owner Equity Changes figure is the value you enter in the inputs area of the business planning starter workbook. The Other Owner Equity Changes figures are pulled into the Uses of Cash section as negative values because a positive change in the owner equity, such as an additional capital contribution, such as from a stock offering, doesn't use cash but provides cash; and a negative change in the owner equity, such as a dividend, does use cash.

Net Cash Generated (Used)

The Net Cash Generated (Used) figures show the total cash flow for each period of the forecasting horizon, based on the listed sources and uses of cash. The amount for each period is the sources of cash for the period less the uses of cash for the period. For example, the formula for the first period is:

```
=SUM(C145:C151)-SUM(C154:C159)
```

The formula for the second period is:

```
=SUM(D145:D151)-SUM(D154:D159)
```

and so on.

Ending Cash Balance

The Ending Cash Balance figures show the forecasted cash and equivalents balance at the end of each period. The balance is the Beginning Cash Balance figure for the period plus the Net Cash Generated (Used) figure for the period. For example, the formula for the first period is:

```
=C142+C160
```

The formula for the second period is:

```
=D142+D160
```

and so on.

Financial Ratios Table

The Financial Ratios Table has 12 rows of calculated data (see Figure 10-5). As in other schedules, the period identifier numbers the periods for which values are calculated. The first period is stored in cell C165 as the integer 1, and periods that follow are stored as the previous period plus 1. The other values in the Financial Ratios Table are calculated as described in the following paragraphs.

Current Ratio

The Current Ratio figures show the ratio of current assets to current liabilities. The current ratio provides one measure of a business's ability to meet its short-term obligations. The Current Ratio figure for each period is the Total Current Assets figure from the Balance Sheet schedule divided by the Total Current Liabilities figure. For example, the formula for the first period is:

```
=C47/C60
```

The formula for the second period is:

```
=D47/D60
```

and so on.

Quick Ratio

The Quick Ratio figures show the ratio of the sum of the cash and equivalents plus the accounts receivable to the current liabilities. The quick ratio provides a more stringent measure of a business's ability to meet its short-term financial obligations than other ratios. The Quick Ratio figure for each period is the sum of the Cash & Equivalents figure and the Accounts Receivable figure divided by the Total Current Liabilities figure. For example, the formula for the first period is:

```
=(C43+C44)/C60
```

The formula for the second period is:

```
=(D43+D44)/D60
```

and so on.

Working Capital to Total Assets

The Working Capital to Total Assets figures show the ratio of working capital (the current assets minus the current liabilities) to the total assets. The Working Capital to Total Assets ratio is another measure of a firm's ability to meet its financial obligations and gives an indication as to the distribution of a business's assets into liquid and nonliquid resources.

The Working Capital to Total Assets ratio for each period is calculated by dividing the difference between the Current Assets and Current Liabilities figures by the Total Assets figure. For example, the formula for the first period is:

```
=(C47-C60)/C52
```

The formula for the second period is:

```
=(D47-D60)/D52
```

and so on.

Receivables Turnover

The Receivables Turnover figures show the ratio of sales to the accounts receivable balance. The Receivables Turnover ratio indicates the efficiency of sales collections. One problem with the measure as it's usually applied is that both credit and cash sales might be included in the ratio denominator. Two potential shortcomings exist with this approach. First, the presence of the cash sales might make the receivables collections appear more efficient than is the case. Also, mere changes in the mix of credit and cash sales might affect the ratio, even though the efficiency of the receivables collections process has not changed.

The Receivables Turnover figure for each period is calculated by dividing the Sales Revenue figure for the period by the Accounts Receivable balance outstanding at the end of the period. For example, the formula for the first period is:

```
=C100/C44
```

The formula for the second period is:

```
=D100/D44
```

and so on.

Inventory Turnover

The Inventory Turnover row shows the ratio of the cost of sales to the inventory balance. The Inventory Turnover ratio calculates how long inventory is held. It can indicate depleted or excessive inventory balances. The Inventory Turnover ratio for each period is calculated by dividing the Cost of Sales figure for the period by the inventory held at the end of the period. For example, the formula for the first period is:

```
=-C101/C45
```

The formula for the second period is:

```
=-D101/D45
```

and so on.

Times Interest Earned

The Times Interest Earned row shows the ratio of the sum of the net income after taxes plus the interest income to the interest expense. The ratio indicates the relative ease with which the business is paying its financing costs. The Times Interest Earned ratio for each period is calculated by dividing the sum of the Operating Income and Interest Income figures from the Income Statement schedule by the Interest Expense figure. For example, the formula for the first period is:

```
=(C109+C111)/C112
```

The formula for the second period is:

```
=(D109+D111)/D112
```

and so on.

Sales to Operational Assets

The Sales to Operational Assets row shows the ratio of sales of sales revenue to net plant, property, and equipment. The ratio indicates the efficiency with which a business uses its operational assets to generate sales revenue. The Sales to Operational Assets ratio for each period is the Sales Revenue figure you enter in the inputs area of the business planning starter workbook divided by the Net Plant, Property, & Equipment figure from the Balance Sheet schedule. For example, the formula for the first period is:

```
=C100/C50
```

The formula for the second period is:

```
=D100/D50
```

and so on.

Return on Total Assets

The Return on Total Assets row shows the ratio of the sum of the net income after taxes plus the interest expense to the total assets for each period. The ratio indicates the overall operating profitability of the business, expressed as a rate of return on the business assets. The formula for the first period is:

```
=(C16+C112)/C52
```

The formula for the second period is:

```
=(D116+D112)/D52
```

and so on.

Return on Equity

The Return on Equity row shows the ratio of the net income after taxes to the owner equity for each period. The ratio indicates the profitability of the business as an investment of the owners. The Return on Equity ratio for each period is the Net Income (Loss) After Taxes figure from the Income Statement schedule divided by the Owner Equity figure from the Balance Sheet schedule. For example, the formula for the first period is:

```
=C116/C65
```

The formula for the second period is:

```
=D116/D65
```

and so on.

Investment Turnover

The Investment Turnover row shows the ratio of the sales revenue to the total assets. The ratio, like the Sales to Operational Assets ratio, indicates the efficiency with which a business uses its assets (in this case, its total assets) to generate sales. The Investment Turnover ratio for each period is the Sales Revenue figure you enter in the inputs area of the business planning starter workbook divided by the Total Assets figure from the Balance Sheet schedule. For example, the formula for the first period is:

```
=C100/C52
```

The formula for the second period is:

```
=D100/D52
```

and so on.

Financial Leverage

The Financial Leverage row shows the difference between the return on the owner equity and the return on the total assets. The ratio indicates the increase or decrease in an equity return as a result of borrowing. A positive value indicates an improvement in the return on owner equity by using financial leverage; a negative value indicates deterioration in the return on owner equity. The Financial Leverage figure for each period is the Return on Total Assets figure minus the Return on Equity figure. For example, the formula for the first period is:

```
=C176-C175
```

The formula for the second period is:

```
=D176-D175
```

and so on.

Customizing the Starter Workbook

You can use the business planning starter workbook for many business projections. However, you might want to change the starter workbook so that it more closely matches your requirements. For example, you can add text that describes the business and the forecasting horizon. You can increase or decrease the number of periods. For example, you can increase the number of periods to 12 if your periods are months and you want to forecast an entire year. Before you change anything on the starter workbook other than the forecasting inputs, unprotect the document.

NOTE *Unless you turn off cell protection, input cells in the inputs area of the business planning starter workbook are the only cells into which you can enter data.*

Changing the Number of Periods

You can rather easily increase or decrease the number of forecasting periods. To increase the number of periods, remove the borders from the last column; then copy the current last column to the right as needed. To decrease the number of periods, simply delete any unneeded column from the right side of the schedule. When you finish these steps, you can replace the borders on the right and reinstate cell protection as needed.

Ratio Analysis on Existing Financial Statements

If you want to perform financial ratio analysis on a set of existing financial statements, copy the contents of column C, from the row in the inputs area of the business planning starter workbook that contains the sales revenue forecast (row 31) through the last row of the ratios table, into column B. Then remove the columns for periods 1 through 10 (columns C through L), following the steps described in the preceding section, "Changing the Number of Periods." Optionally, you can delete the Cash Flow Statement and add appropriate column headings as needed.

To use the modified starter workbook, enter the necessary Balance Sheet and Income Statement data in each of the unshaded cells in column B of the inputs area of the business planning starter workbook. (Typically, the "as of" date of the Balance Sheet and the ending date of the Income Statement period are the same.)

Calculating Taxes for a Current Net Loss Before Taxes

To calculate the income tax expense as 0 when there is a current period net loss before income taxes, you need to edit the formula in the cell that calculates the income tax expense (or savings) for the first period (cell C115) so that it takes the maximum of the calculated expense amount or 0 by using the MAX function:

```
=MAX(C37*C113,0)
```

Once you've done this, you can copy the formula into the rest of the cells in the forecasting horizon that calculate the income tax expense (or savings).

Combining This Workbook with Other Workbooks

Other starter workbooks on the *MBA's Guide to Excel's* companion CD are specifically designed to provide data to the financial statements with ratios workbook. For example, you might construct an asset depreciation schedule that uses the straight-line depreciation convention for a $25,000 asset representing your entire plant, property, and equipment investment and then use this data in the business planning starter workbook.

If you want to use workbooks together in this manner, you should combine the workbooks into a single workbook. The easiest way to copy one of the workbooks is to copy the workbook's worksheet to a blank worksheet in the other workbook. (Each of the starter workbooks uses only a single worksheet to make this process both easy and possible.)

If you wanted to combine an asset depreciation workbook with the business planning workbook, for example, you might open both workbooks, copy the asset depreciation worksheet to the Clipboard, add a new sheet to the business planning starter workbook (such as by choosing the Insert menu's Worksheet command), and then paste the asset depreciation worksheet into the newly added, blank worksheet in the business planning workbook.

Chapter 11

BUILDING A PROFIT VOLUME AND BREAK-EVEN ANALYSIS WORKBOOK

Featuring:

- EasyRefresher™: Profit Volume and Break-Even Analysis
- Using the Profit Volume and Break-Even Analysis Starter Workbook
- Understanding the Starter Workbook's Calculations
- Customizing the Starter Workbook
- Charting Profit Volume Analysis Data

Profit volume analysis lets you look at the revenues, costs, and profits of a business for a range of business volumes, or revenues. By using profit volume analysis, you can see how sensitive profits are to changes in business volume and where break-even points occur. The profit volume and break-even analysis starter workbook described in this chapter provides a framework to use in performing profit volume analysis and in calculating break-even points. This chapter shows how to use the workbook and modify it. In addition, this chapter includes two charts useful in portraying profit volume and break-even analysis data.

EasyRefresher™: Profit Volume and Break-Even Analysis

Profit volume analysis, sometimes called cost-profit-volume analysis, is the process of calculating the profits of a business at different volumes, or revenue levels. Break-even analysis is estimating the revenue level that provides exactly enough contribution margin to cover fixed costs. In this calculation, because no profits exist, none of the costs that vary with profits exist. At the break-even point, revenues leave exactly enough contribution margin to cover fixed costs. The general formula used to calculate the break-even point is as follows:

```
Break-even point in units=Fixed costs/Contribution margin per unit
```

If you use more than one of the vary-with-profit cost categories presented in the profit volume and break-even analysis starter workbook, you need to recognize the correct relationships between variables as you input them. Basically, three types of relationships exist: independent-independent, independent-dependent, and dependent-dependent. Independent-independent is easiest to calculate because all of the costs that vary with profits are calculated independent of the other. The other two types of relationships can be more difficult. With the independent-dependent relationship, you need to calculate one cost so that you can calculate the next. As an example of this relationship and how you might recognize it in your inputs, suppose that the state income tax rate is 10% and is deducted from the Profit Before Vary-with-Profits Costs (PBVPC) and that after deducting the state income tax from the PBVPC, the federal income tax rate of 20% is applied to the PBVPC. The correct input percentage for the state income tax rate is 10%, because 10% of the PBVPC calculates the correct state income tax cost, as follows:

```
State Income Tax=10%*PBVPC
```

However, the federal income tax percentage must recognize the state income tax costs:

```
Federal Income Tax=20%*(PBVPC-(10%*PBVPC))
```

This formula can be further modified as follows to express the federal income tax rate as a percentage of the PBVPC and, therefore, your input to the profit volume and break-even analysis starter workbook:

```
Federal Income Tax=18%*PBVPC
```

A third type of relationship that might exist between the costs that vary with profits is a dependent-dependent, or circular, relationship. For example, suppose that you have an employee bonus cost equal to 10% of the after-tax profits. You need to know the amount of the bonus before you can calculate the federal income taxes because it's a tax-deductible expense, and you need to know the federal income tax because it determines the after-tax profits, upon which the bonus is calculated, before you can calculate the bonus. Assuming that your only tax is a federal income tax rate of 20%, you calculate your federal income tax as follows:

```
Federal Income Tax=20%*(PBVPC-bonus)
```

Assuming that the employee bonus is 10% of the after-tax profits, your employee bonus cost equals:

```
Bonus=10%*(PBVPC-Federal Income Tax)
```

Given these definitions, you can define the federal income tax percentage by substituting the formula for the bonus in the federal income tax formula, as follows:

```
Federal Income Tax=20%*(PBVPC-(10%*(PBVPC-Federal Income Tax)))
```

You could state this formula algebraically as:

```
Federal Income Tax=20%*(PBVPC-(10%*PBVPC)+(10%*Federal Income Tax))
```

or:

```
Federal Income Tax=20%*((90%*PBVPC)+(10%*Federal Income Tax))
```

or:

```
Federal Income Tax=(18%*PBVPC)+(2%*Federal Income Tax)
```

or:

```
98%*Federal Income Tax=18%*PBVPC
```

or to show the federal income tax as a percentage of the PBVPC:

```
Federal Income Tax=18.3673%*PBVPC
```

Given this number, it's easy to define the bonus as a percentage of the PBVPC by substituting the following formula for federal income tax in the bonus formula:

```
Bonus=10%*(PBVPC-(18.3673%*PBVPC))
```

or, to show the bonus as a percentage of the PBVPC:

```
Bonus=10%*(81.6327%*PBVPC)
```

or, to show the bonus as a percentage of the PBVPC in another way:

```
Bonus=8.16372%*PBVPC
```

Using the Profit Volume and Break-Even Analysis Starter Workbook

You can use the profit volume and break-even analysis starter workbook (PROFITVOL), shown in Figures 11-1 through 11-4, to test the effect of changing revenues on business profits. To complete the schedule, you define the following:

- Revenue variables, including the unit sales price, the low revenue in unit volume tested, and the high revenue in unit volume tested.

- Variable costs best expressed as an amount per unit, including the direct labor, the direct materials, and the factory overhead.
- Variable costs best expressed as a percentage of revenue, including sales commissions and sales tax.
- Any costs commonly calculated as a percentage of profits, including state income tax and federal income tax.

The starter workbook shown in Figure 11-1 calculates the break-even point in units; shows the revenues, costs, and profits for the break-even point; and calculates the revenues, costs, and profits for the low units volume, the high units volume, and four intervals between the low and high volumes.

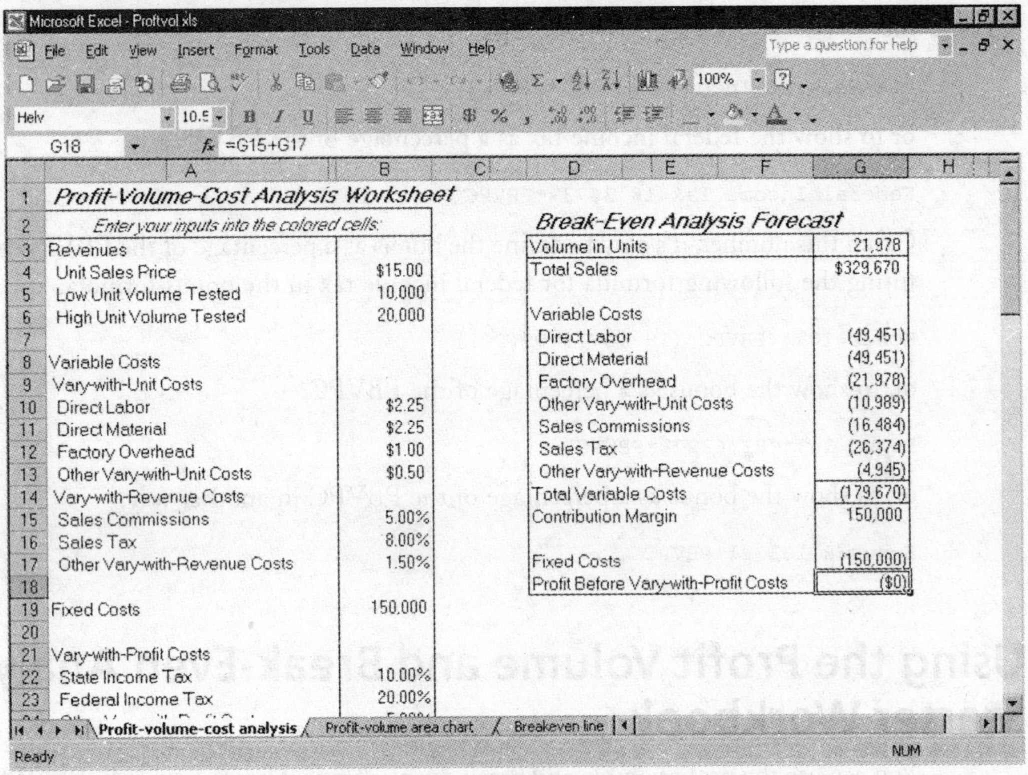

Figure 11-1 The inputs area and Break-Even Analysis Forecast of the profit volume and break-even analysis starter workbook.

Two charts included with the starter workbook let you look at the results of your profit volume analysis graphically. The first chart shows the revenues, costs, and profits at various revenue levels. The second shows the revenues plotted against the total fixed and variable costs; the point at which the revenue line intersects the total fixed and variable costs identifies the break-even point.

To enter your own data in the profit volume and break-even analysis starter workbook, follow these steps:

1. **Open the profit volume and break-even analysis starter workbook, PROFTVOL, from the companion CD.**

   The workbook initially contains the default inputs shown in Figure 11-1.

2. **Estimate the unit sales price of the product or service you sell.**

   In cell B4, enter the Unit Sales Price value as the amount per unit you will receive from the sales of the product or service for which you are performing profit volume and break-even analysis.

3. **Estimate the lowest business volume in units for which you want to calculate total sales, costs, and profits.**

   You enter this value in cell B5. Low Unit Volume Tested is the minimum revenue level (in units) for which you will calculate revenues, costs, and profits.

4. **Estimate the highest business volume in units for which you want to calculate total sales, costs, and profits.**

   You enter this value in cell B6. High Unit Volume Tested is the maximum revenue level (in units) for which you will calculate revenues, costs, and profits.

5. **Estimate any direct labor costs that vary with the units sold and that are calculated as an amount per unit.**

   Enter this value in cell B10. Direct Labor is the dollar amount of labor per unit.

6. **Estimate any direct material costs that vary with the units sold and that are calculated as an amount per unit.**

   Enter this value in cell B11. Direct Material is the dollar amount of materials per unit.

7. **Estimate any factory overhead costs that vary with the units sold and that are calculated as an amount per unit.**

   Enter this value in cell B12. Factory Overhead is the dollar amount of factory overhead per unit.

8. **Estimate any other costs that vary with the units sold and that are calculated as an amount per unit.**

   If you have other costs that you want to express as a dollar amount per unit, enter the dollar amount of these other costs as the Other Vary-with-Unit Costs amount in cell B13.

9. **Estimate any sales commissions as a percentage of the price or the total sales.**

   Enter this value as a percentage in cell B15.

10. **Estimate any sales tax as a percentage of the unit sales price or the total sales.**

    Enter this value as a percentage in cell B16.

11. **Estimate any other costs that vary with revenues as a percentage of the unit sales price or the total sales.**

    If you have other costs that you want to express as a percentage of revenues, enter that percentage as the Other Vary-with-Revenue Costs amount in cell B17.

12. **Estimate the total fixed costs.**

    Enter the Fixed Costs value in cell B19. Fixed costs are those costs that will not change, given the range of revenue levels for which you are testing.

13. **Estimate the state income tax as a percentage of profits before federal income tax and other costs that vary with profits.**

    Enter this value in cell B22. The workbook assumes that state income taxes are a percentage of your profits before federal income taxes and any other costs that vary with profits (such as profit-sharing plans).

14. **Estimate the federal income tax as a percentage of profits before state income tax and other costs that vary with profits.**

    Enter this value in cell B23. The workbook assumes that federal income taxes are a percentage of your profits before state income taxes and other costs that vary with profits (such as profit-sharing plans).

15. **Estimate as a percentage any other costs that vary with the profits before taxes.**

    If you have other costs that you want to express as a percentage of profits, enter that percentage as the Other Vary-with-Profit Costs amount in cell B24.

Understanding the Starter Workbook's Calculations

The profit volume and break-even analysis starter workbook has six parts: the Profit-Volume Inputs box and the Break-Even Analysis Forecast (shown in Figure 11-1), the Profit Volume Forecast (shown in Figure 11-2), the Common Size Profit Volume Forecast (shown in Figure 11-3), and the Profit Volume Area and the Break-Even Analysis Line Chart Data (shown in Figure 11-4).

For convenience and good documentation within the model, cell B4 contains the Unit Sales Price amount and is named Unit_Sales_Price, cell B5 contains the Low Unit Volume Tested amount and is named Low_Unit_Volume_Tested, cell B6 contains the High Unit Volume Tested amount and is named High_Unit_Volume_Tested, cell B10 contains the Direct Labor amount and is named Direct_Labor, cell B11 contains the Direct Material amount and is named Direct_Material, cell B12 contains the Factory Overhead amount and is named Factory_Overhead, cell B13 contains the Other Vary-with-Unit Costs amount and is named Other_Vary_Unit_Costs, cell B15 contains the Sales Commissions percentage and is named Sales_Commissions, cell B16 contains the Sales Tax percentage and is named Sales_Tax, cell B17 contains the Other Vary-with-Revenue Costs percentage and is named Other_Vary_Revenue_Costs, cell B19 contains the Fixed Costs amount and is named Fixed_Costs, cell B22 contains the State Income Tax percentage and is named State_Income_Tax, cell B23 contains the Federal Income Tax percentage and is named Federal_Income_Tax, and cell B24 contains the Other Vary-with-Profit Costs percentage and is named Other_Vary_Profit_Costs. The formulas within the starter workbook use these cell names rather than the cell addresses.

NOTE *To confirm these variables in the PROFITVOL.XLS workbook, click on one of these cells. In a toolbar near the upper left corner of the spreadsheet, you will see a drop-down box with all of the variable names listed here.*

Break-Even Analysis Forecast

The Break-Even Analysis Forecast calculates the volume level in units at which you break even and displays the revenues, variable costs, and fixed costs forecasted at this volume level (see Figure 11-1). The schedule has only one column containing calculated data. Within it, revenues appear as positive amounts, and expenses appear as negative amounts.

Volume in Units

The Volume in Units amount is the number of units at which the break-even point occurs. The amount is rounded to the nearest whole unit, because selling partial units usually is impossible. This Volume in Units amount is calculated by dividing the Fixed Costs amount by the contribution margin per unit. The contribution margin per unit is calculated by subtracting each of the variable costs (expressed as an amount per unit) from the Unit Sales Price value. Those variable costs, which you enter as a percentage of the Unit Sales Price amount, are converted to an amount per unit. Because the calculated revenue level is the level at which no profits are generated, no costs based on profits are included in the formula or are shown in the forecast of revenues and costs and the break-even point. The formula for the break-even point in units (in cell G3) is:

```
=ROUND(Fixed_Costs/(Unit_Sales_Price-
(Direct_Labor+Direct_Material+Factory_Overhead+Other_Vary_Unit_Costs)-
(Unit_Sales_Price*(Sales_Commissions_+Sales_Taxes+Other_Vary_Revenue_Costs))),0)
```

which is essentially the break-even point equation from the EasyRefresher section, where:

```
Break-even point in units=Fixed costs/Contribution margin per unit
```

Total Sales

The Total Sales amount shows the revenue in dollars for the break-even point. The Total Sales amount is the break-even Volume in Units times the Unit Sales Price value. The Total Sales formula (in cell G4) is:

```
=G3*Unit_Sales_Price
```

Direct Labor

The Direct Labor figure shows the direct labor costs for the break-even volume. The amount is the break-even Volume in Units amount times the Direct Labor cost per unit. The Direct Labor formula (in cell G7) is:

```
=-G3*Direct_Labor
```

Direct Material

The Direct Material figure shows the direct material costs for the break-even volume. The amount is the break-even Volume in Units amount times the Direct Material cost per unit. The Direct Material formula (in cell G8) is:

```
=-G3*Direct_Material
```

Factory Overhead

The Factory Overhead figure shows the factory overhead costs for the break-even volume. The amount is the break-even Volume in Units amount times the Factory Overhead cost per unit. The Factory Overhead formula (in cell G9) is:

```
=-G3*Factory_Overhead
```

Other Vary-with-Unit Costs

The Other Vary-with-Unit Costs figure shows any other costs you have expressed as an amount per unit for the break-even volume. The amount is the break-even Volume in Units amount times the Other Vary-with-Unit Costs per unit. The Other Vary-with-Unit Costs formula (in cell G10) is:

```
=-G3*Other_Vary_Unit_Costs
```

Sales Commissions

The Sales Commissions figure shows the sales commissions costs for the break-even volume. The amount is the break-even revenue level times the Sales Commissions percentage. The Sales Commissions formula (in cell G11) is:

```
=-G4*Sales_Commissions
```

Sales Tax

The Sales Tax figure shows the sales tax costs for the break-even volume. The amount is the break-even revenue level times the Sales Tax percentage. The Sales Tax formula (in cell G12) is:

```
=-G4*Sales_Tax
```

Other Vary-with-Revenue Costs

The Other Vary-with-Revenue Costs figure shows any other costs you have expressed as a percentage of revenues for the break-even volume. The amount is the break-even revenue level times the Other Vary-with-Revenue Costs percentage. The Other Vary-with-Revenue Costs formula (in cell G13) is:

```
=-G4*Other_Vary_Revenue_Costs
```

Total Variable Costs

The Total Variable Costs figure shows the total variable costs for the break-even volume. The Total Variable Costs formula (in cell G14) is:

```
=SUM(G7:G13)
```

Contribution Margin

The Contribution Margin figure shows the difference between the total sales and the total variable costs. For break-even analysis, this amount must equal the fixed costs. However, because the break-even point in unit volume is rounded to an integer, this amount might differ. The formula (in cell G15) is:

```
=G4+G14
```

Fixed Costs

The Fixed Costs figure shows the fixed costs at the break-even volume. The formula (in cell G17) is:

```
=-Fixed_Costs
```

Profit Before Vary-with-Profit Costs

The Profit Before Vary-with-Profit Costs figure shows the amount of profit for the break-even volume and is the Contribution Margin amount minus the Fixed Costs figure. None of the costs that vary with profits are included, because profits must equal 0. In some situations, the profit will equal some amount other than 0, even though, by definition, the true break-even point is the revenue volume at which profits equal 0. Typically, however, firms cannot sell fractional units of products or services. Accordingly, the break-even Volume in Units is rounded to an integer, and the starter workbook assumes that this is the closest to a break-even volume that you can actually operate. The Profit Before Vary-with-Profit Costs formula (in cell G18) is:

```
=G15+G17
```

Profit Volume Forecast

The Profit Volume Forecast shown in Figure 11-2 calculates the revenue, costs, and profits at the low unit volume you specify, the high unit volume you specify, and four intermediate volumes between these two boundaries. In the forecast, revenues appear as positive amounts and expenses appear as negative amounts.

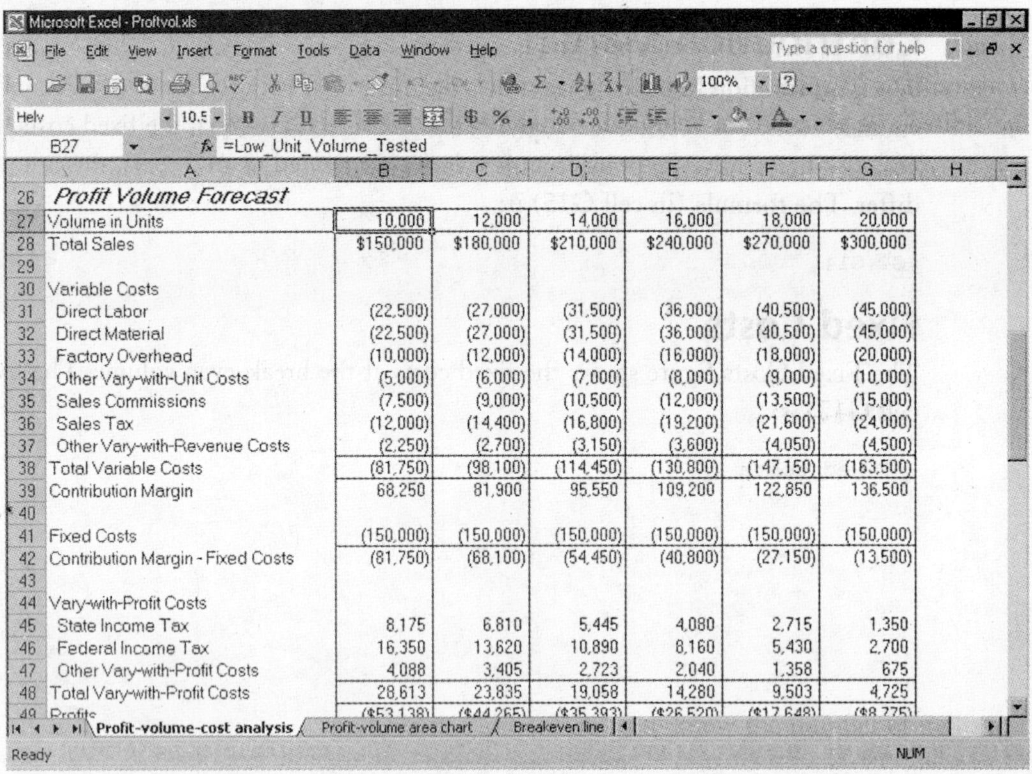

	A	B	C	D	E	F	G
26	*Profit Volume Forecast*						
27	Volume in Units	10,000	12,000	14,000	16,000	18,000	20,000
28	Total Sales	$150,000	$180,000	$210,000	$240,000	$270,000	$300,000
29							
30	Variable Costs						
31	Direct Labor	(22,500)	(27,000)	(31,500)	(36,000)	(40,500)	(45,000)
32	Direct Material	(22,500)	(27,000)	(31,500)	(36,000)	(40,500)	(45,000)
33	Factory Overhead	(10,000)	(12,000)	(14,000)	(16,000)	(18,000)	(20,000)
34	Other Vary-with-Unit Costs	(5,000)	(6,000)	(7,000)	(8,000)	(9,000)	(10,000)
35	Sales Commissions	(7,500)	(9,000)	(10,500)	(12,000)	(13,500)	(15,000)
36	Sales Tax	(12,000)	(14,400)	(16,800)	(19,200)	(21,600)	(24,000)
37	Other Vary-with-Revenue Costs	(2,250)	(2,700)	(3,150)	(3,600)	(4,050)	(4,500)
38	Total Variable Costs	(81,750)	(98,100)	(114,450)	(130,800)	(147,150)	(163,500)
39	Contribution Margin	68,250	81,900	95,550	109,200	122,850	136,500
40							
41	Fixed Costs	(150,000)	(150,000)	(150,000)	(150,000)	(150,000)	(150,000)
42	Contribution Margin - Fixed Costs	(81,750)	(68,100)	(54,450)	(40,800)	(27,150)	(13,500)
43							
44	Vary-with-Profit Costs						
45	State Income Tax	8,175	6,810	5,445	4,080	2,715	1,350
46	Federal Income Tax	16,350	13,620	10,890	8,160	5,430	2,700
47	Other Vary-with-Profit Costs	4,088	3,405	2,723	2,040	1,358	675
48	Total Vary-with-Profit Costs	28,613	23,835	19,058	14,280	9,503	4,725
49	Profits	($53,138)	($44,265)	($35,393)	($26,520)	($17,648)	($8,775)

Figure 11-2 The Profit Volume Forecast of the profit volume and break-even analysis starter workbook.

Volume in Units

The Volume in Units figure shows the business volume in units for each of the six volume levels for which revenues, costs, and profits are calculated. The first Volume in Units amount is pulled into the Profit Volume Forecast as the Low Unit Volume Tested amount you enter in the Profit Volume inputs box. The second through the sixth Volume in Units amounts, however, are calculated as the previous Volume in Units amounts plus an increase equal to the range of volumes tested, divided by the number of volumes tested. The range of volumes tested is the High Unit Volume Tested figure minus the Low Unit Volume Tested figure. The number of volumes tested is set at 5 and is defined with the reference name Increments within the starter workbook. The formula for the second Volume in Units figure (in cell C27) is:

```
=B27+((High_Unit_Volume_Tested-Low_Unit_Volume_Tested)/Increments)
```

The formula for the third volume is:

```
=C27+((High_Unit_Volume_Tested-Low_Unit_Volume_Tested)/Increments)
```

and so on.

Total Sales

The Total Sales amount shows the revenue in dollars for each volume tested. The Total Sales figure is the Volume in Units figure times the Unit Sales Price figure. For example, the Total Sales formula for the first volume tested (in cell B28) is:

```
=B27*Unit_Sales_Price
```

The formula for the second volume tested is:

```
=C27*Unit_Sales_Price
```

and so on.

Direct Labor

The Direct Labor figure shows the direct labor costs for each of the volumes tested. The amount is the Volume in Units figure times the Direct Labor cost per unit. The Direct Labor formula for the first volume (in cell B31) is:

```
=-B27*Direct_Labor
```

The formula for the second volume is:

```
=-C27*Direct_Labor
```

and so on.

Direct Material

The Direct Material figure shows the direct material costs for each of the volumes. The amount is the Volume in Units figure times the Direct Material cost per unit. The Direct Material formula for the first volume (in cell B32) is:

```
=-B27*Direct_Material
```

The formula for the second volume is:

```
=-C27*Direct_Material
```

and so on.

Factory Overhead

The Factory Overhead figure shows the factory overhead costs for each of the volumes. The amount is the Volume in Units figure times the Factory Overhead cost per unit. The Factory Overhead formula for the first volume (in cell B33) is:

```
=-B27*Factory_Overhead
```

The formula for the second volume is:

```
=-C27*Factory_Overhead
```

and so on.

Other Vary-with-Unit Costs

The Other Vary-with-Unit Costs figure shows any other costs you have expressed as an amount per unit for each volume tested. The amount is the Volume in Units figure times the Other Vary-with-Unit Costs per unit. The other Vary-with-Unit Costs formula (in cell B34) is:

```
=-B27*Other_Vary_Unit_Costs
```

The formula for the second volume is:

```
=-C27*Other_Vary_Unit_Costs
```

and so on.

Sales Commissions

The Sales Commissions figure shows the sales commissions costs for each of the volumes tested. The amount is the Total Sales figure times the Sales Commissions percentage. The Sales Commissions formula for the first volume (in cell B35) is:

```
=-B28*Sales_Commissions
```

The formula for the second volume is:

```
=-C28*Sales_Commissions
```

and so on.

Sales Tax

The Sales Tax figure shows the sales tax costs for each of the volumes tested. The amount is the Total Sales figure times the Sales Tax percentage. The Sales Tax formula for the first volume (in cell B36) is:

```
=-B28*Sales_Tax
```

The formula for the second volume is:

```
=-C28*Sales_Tax
```

and so on.

Other Vary-with-Revenue Costs

The Other Vary-with-Revenue Costs figure shows any other costs you have expressed as a percentage of revenues for each of the volumes tested. The amount is the Total Sales figure times the Other Vary-with-Revenue Costs percentage. The Other Vary-with-Revenue Costs formula for the first volume (in cell B37) is:

```
=-B28*Other_Vary_Revenue_Costs
```

The formula for the second volume is:

```
=-C28*Other_Vary_Revenue_Costs
```

and so on.

Total Variable Costs

The Total Variable Costs figure shows the total variable costs for each of the volumes tested. The Total Variable Costs formula for the first volume (in cell B38) is:

```
=SUM(B31:B37)
```

The formula for the second volume is:

```
=SUM(C31:C37)
```

and so on.

Contribution Margin

The Contribution Margin figure shows the difference between the Total Sales figure and the Total Variable Costs figure. The Contribution Margin formula for the first volume (in cell B39) is:

```
=B28+B38
```

The formula for the second volume is:

```
=C28+C38
```

and so on.

Fixed Costs

The Fixed Costs figure shows the fixed costs you enter for the range of volumes tested. The formula is simply a named cell reference and is the same for each of the volumes tested. The formula for the first volume (in cell B41) is:

```
=-Fixed_Costs
```

Contribution Margin – Fixed Costs

This figure is the Contribution Margin figure minus the Fixed Costs figure. It is the amount used to calculate any costs that vary with profits. The Contribution Margin – Fixed Costs formula for the first volume (in cell B42) is:

```
=B39+B41
```

The formula for the second volume is:

```
=C39+C41
```

and so on.

State Income Tax

The State Income Tax figure shows the state income tax costs for each of the volumes tested. The amount is the Contribution Margin – Fixed Costs figure times the State Income Tax percentage. The State Income Tax formula for the first volume (in cell B45) is:

```
=-B42*State_Income_Tax
```

The formula for the second volume is:

```
=-C42*State_Income_Tax
```

and so on.

Federal Income Tax

The Federal Income Tax figure shows the federal income tax costs for each of the volumes tested. The amount is the Contribution Margin – Fixed Costs figure times the Federal Income Tax percentage. The Federal Income Tax formula for the first volume (in cell B46) is:

```
=-B42*Federal_Income_Tax
```

The formula for the second volume is:

```
=-C42*Federal_Income_Tax
```

and so on.

Other Vary-with-Profit Costs

The Other Vary-with-Profit Costs figure shows any other costs that are calculated as a percentage of profits for each of the volumes tested. The amount is the Contribution Margin – Fixed Costs figure times the Other Vary-with-Profit Costs percentage. The Other Vary-with-Profit Costs formula for the first volume (in cell B47) is:

```
=-B42*Other_Vary_Profit_Costs
```

The formula for the second volume is:

```
=-C42*Other_Vary_Profit_Costs
```

and so on.

Total Vary-with-Profit Costs

The Total Vary-with-Profit Costs figure shows the total of the costs that vary with profits for each of the volumes tested. The formula for the first volume (in cell B48) is:

```
=SUM(B45:B47)
```

The formula for the second volume is:

```
=SUM(C45:C47)
```

and so on.

Profits

The Profits figure shows the profits for each of the volumes tested and is the Contribution Margin – Fixed Costs amount minus the Total Vary-with-Profit Costs amount. The Profits formula for the first volume (in cell B49) is:

```
=B42+B48
```

The formula for profits for the second volume is:

```
=C42+C48
```

and so on.

Common Size Profit Volume Forecast

The Common Size Profit Volume Forecast shown in Figure 11-3 simply converts the costs and profits in the Profit Volume Forecast to percentages of the total sales for each of the volumes for which revenue, costs, and profits are calculated.

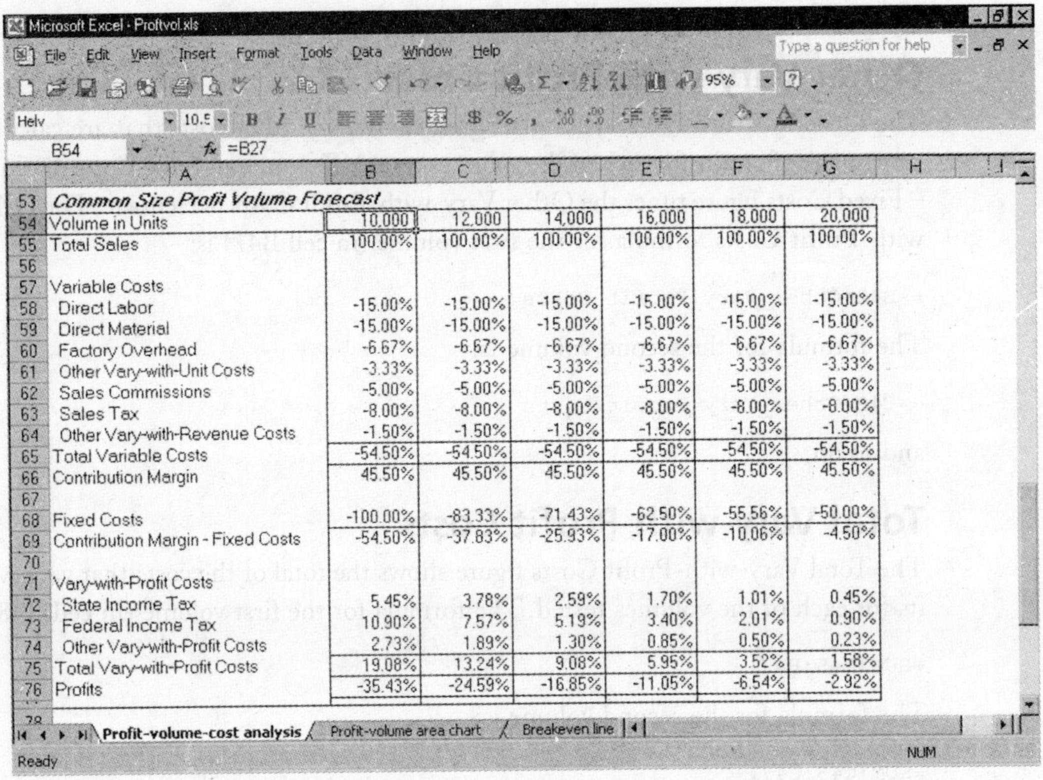

	A	B	C	D	E	F	G
53	*Common Size Profit Volume Forecast*						
54	Volume in Units	10,000	12,000	14,000	16,000	18,000	20,000
55	Total Sales	100.00%	100.00%	100.00%	100.00%	100.00%	100.00%
56							
57	Variable Costs						
58	Direct Labor	-15.00%	-15.00%	-15.00%	-15.00%	-15.00%	-15.00%
59	Direct Material	-15.00%	-15.00%	-15.00%	-15.00%	-15.00%	-15.00%
60	Factory Overhead	-6.67%	-6.67%	-6.67%	-6.67%	-6.67%	-6.67%
61	Other Vary-with-Unit Costs	-3.33%	-3.33%	-3.33%	-3.33%	-3.33%	-3.33%
62	Sales Commissions	-5.00%	-5.00%	-5.00%	-5.00%	-5.00%	-5.00%
63	Sales Tax	-8.00%	-8.00%	-8.00%	-8.00%	-8.00%	-8.00%
64	Other Vary-with-Revenue Costs	-1.50%	-1.50%	-1.50%	-1.50%	-1.50%	-1.50%
65	Total Variable Costs	-54.50%	-54.50%	-54.50%	-54.50%	-54.50%	-54.50%
66	Contribution Margin	45.50%	45.50%	45.50%	45.50%	45.50%	45.50%
67							
68	Fixed Costs	-100.00%	-83.33%	-71.43%	-62.50%	-55.56%	-50.00%
69	Contribution Margin - Fixed Costs	-54.50%	-37.83%	-25.93%	-17.00%	-10.06%	-4.50%
70							
71	Vary-with-Profit Costs						
72	State Income Tax	5.45%	3.78%	2.59%	1.70%	1.01%	0.45%
73	Federal Income Tax	10.90%	7.57%	5.19%	3.40%	2.01%	0.90%
74	Other Vary-with-Profit Costs	2.73%	1.89%	1.30%	0.85%	0.50%	0.23%
75	Total Vary-with-Profit Costs	19.08%	13.24%	9.08%	5.95%	3.52%	1.58%
76	Profits	-35.43%	-24.59%	-16.85%	-11.05%	-6.54%	-2.92%

Figure 11-3 The Common Size Profit Volume Forecast of the profit volume and break-even analysis starter workbook.

Predictably, the formulas used in this forecast are all very simple. For example, the formula for the Total Sales percentage for the first volume shown (in cell B55) is:

```
=B28/B$28
```

The volume in Units formulas are simply cell references to the Volume in Units figures calculated in the Break-Even Analysis Forecast. For example, the Volume in Units formula for the first volume shown (in cell B54) is:

```
=B27
```

Interpreting the Profit Volume Charts and Chart Data

The Profit Volume Area Chart Data shown in Figure 11-4 provides the data graphed in the profit volume area chart discussed later in the chapter.

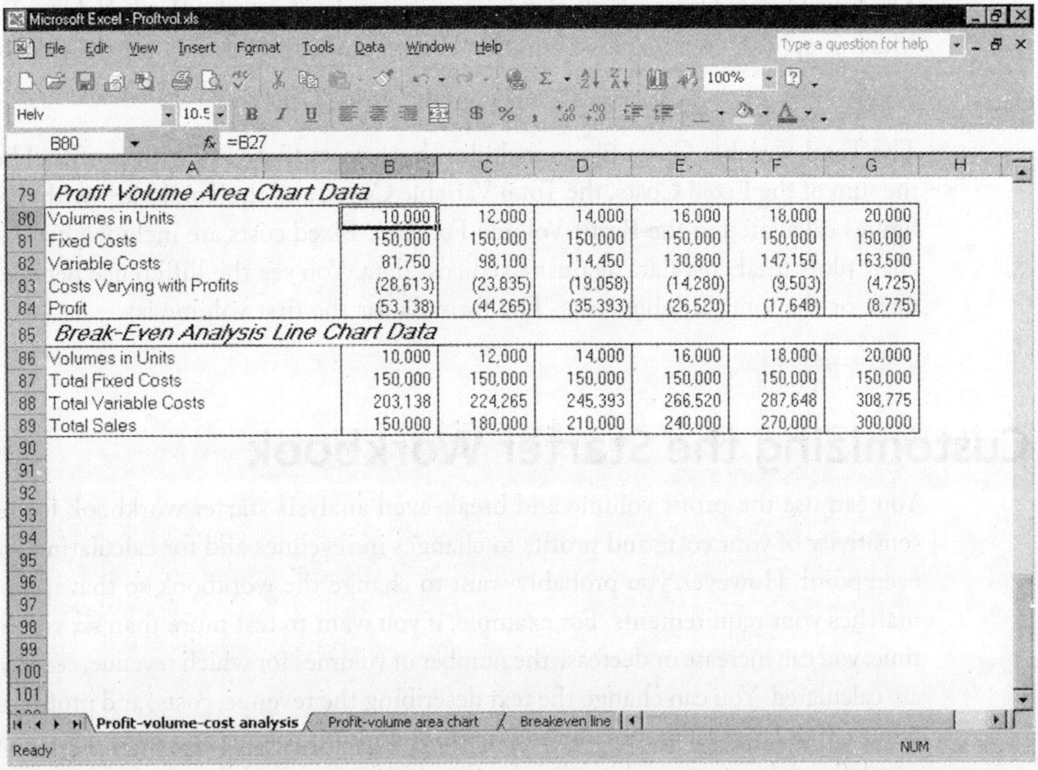

	A	B	C	D	E	F	G
79	*Profit Volume Area Chart Data*						
80	Volumes in Units	10,000	12,000	14,000	16,000	18,000	20,000
81	Fixed Costs	150,000	150,000	150,000	150,000	150,000	150,000
82	Variable Costs	81,750	98,100	114,450	130,800	147,150	163,500
83	Costs Varying with Profits	(28,613)	(23,835)	(19,058)	(14,280)	(9,503)	(4,725)
84	Profit	(53,138)	(44,265)	(35,393)	(26,520)	(17,648)	(8,775)
85	*Break-Even Analysis Line Chart Data*						
86	Volumes in Units	10,000	12,000	14,000	16,000	18,000	20,000
87	Total Fixed Costs	150,000	150,000	150,000	150,000	150,000	150,000
88	Total Variable Costs	203,138	224,265	245,393	266,520	287,648	308,775
89	Total Sales	150,000	180,000	210,000	240,000	270,000	300,000

Figure 11-4 The Profit Volume Area Chart Data portion of the profit volume and break-even analysis starter workbook.

All the figures are simply pulled from the Profit Volume Forecast by cell references. For example, the Volume in Units figure for the first volume is pulled from the Profit Volume Forecast by the following formula:

```
=B27
```

The Fixed Costs, Variable Costs, and Costs Varying with Profits figures are pulled as positive numbers from the Profit Volume Forecast, in which they appear as negative numbers. For example, the formula for the first volume of the Fixed Costs row is:

```
=-B41
```

The Break-Even Analysis Line Chart Data (also shown in Figure 11-4) provides the data to the line chart discussed later in the chapter, which identifies the break-even point by showing the intersection of the total sales line with total costs line. The Volume in Units, Total Fixed

Costs, and Total Sales figures are pulled from the Profit Volume Forecast by cell references. For example, the formula for the first volume of the Volume in Units row is:

```
=B27
```

The Fixed Costs figure is pulled as a positive number from the Profit Volume Forecast, in which it appears as a negative number. For example, the formula for the first volume is:

```
=-B41
```

The Total Variable Costs figure includes those costs that vary with profits. The figure is the sum of the Fixed Costs, the Total Variable Costs, and the Total Vary-with-Profit Costs figures calculated in the Profit Volume Forecast. Fixed costs are included because the line chart plots total cost data against fixed cost data. You see the difference between the two lines, or the total variable costs. The formula for the first volume is:

```
=-B38-B41-B48
```

Customizing the Starter Workbook

You can use the profit volume and break-even analysis starter workbook for testing the sensitivity of your costs and profits to changes in revenues and for calculating your break-even point. However, you probably want to change the workbook so that it more closely matches your requirements. For example, if you want to test more than six volumes at one time, you can increase or decrease the number of volumes for which revenue, costs, and profits are calculated. You can change the text describing the revenue, costs, and profits, or you can remove those cost categories unnecessary to your profit volume and break-even analysis. You can define minimums and maximums for specific costs and then include these minimums and maximums in your profit volume analysis. Before you change anything on the schedule other than the inputs, unprotect the document.

Changing the Number of Volumes Tested

You can rather easily increase or decrease the number of volumes tested in the profit volume analysis workbook. For example, to increase the number of volumes for which you test revenue, costs, and profits, follow these steps:

1. Remove the right border from the last column of the Profit Volume Forecast.
2. Copy the current last column to the right into as many additional columns as there are additional volumes for which you want to test revenue, costs, and profits.

3. Redefine the reference name Increments so that it equals one number less than the number of different unit volumes you show in your new Profit Volume Forecast. (For example, with six unit volumes in the Profit Volume Forecast, Increments is set to 5.)

To decrease the number of volumes in the Profit Volume Forecast, follow these steps:

1. Clear any unneeded columns from the right side of the forecast.
2. Redefine the reference name Increments so that it equals the one number less than the number of different unit volumes you now show in your new Profit Volume Forecast. (For example, with six unit volumes in the schedule, Increments is set to 5.)

NOTE *After you add or subtract volumes from the starter workbook, you may want to add back the right border and reinstate cell protection as needed.*

Removing Forecasts from the Starter Workbook

You can remove the Break-Even Analysis Forecast, the Common Size Profit Volume Forecast, or both the Profit Volume Forecast and the Common Size Profit Volume Forecast. (The Common Size Profit Volume Forecast uses information in the Profit Volume Forecast, so if you remove the Profit Volume Forecast, also remove the Common Size Profit Volume Forecast.) To remove any of these forecasts from the starter workbook, simply clear the forecast you want to remove.

Adding Minimums and Maximums to the Profit Volume Forecast

In your business, you might need to keep certain expenses below or above certain amounts. If so, you can, for example, specify that those costs the starter workbook calculates as a percentage of profits not become positive if the expenses should be expressed as negatives. To set a minimum expense as 0, edit the formula in the first volume column in the Profit Volume Forecast so that it checks for a minimum, as follows:

```
=MIN("old formula", "minimum amount")
```

in which the old formula is the formula currently in the cell and the minimum amount is the dollar amount shown as 0, or a negative value, which you don't want the calculated result to fall below. For example, you could set the State Income Tax formula to never fall below 0 by editing the formula currently in cell B45 to read:

```
=MIN(-B42*State_Income_Tax,0)
```

Notice that to keep an expense amount from falling below a certain floor value you use a MIN function because the starter workbook calculated expenses as negative amounts. To set a maximum amount, use a MAX function, with the maximum amount specified as 0, or a negative value in the formula:

```
=MAX("old formula","maximum amount")
```

NOTE *Because expenses are expressed as negative amounts, setting an amount above which an expense should not rise uses a MAX function with one of the arguments set as 0 or a negative "ceiling" value. Setting an amount below which an expense should never fall uses a MIN function, with one of the arguments set as 0 or a negative "floor" value.*

Charting Profit Volume Analysis Data

Two charts are included with the starter workbook let you look at the results of your profit-volume analysis graphically. The first chart shows the revenues, costs, and profits at various revenue levels. The second shows the revenues plotted against the total fixed and variable costs; the point at which the revenue line intersects the total fixed and variable costs identifies the break-even point.

Using the Profit Volume Area Chart

Figure 11-5 shows an area chart of the variable costs, fixed costs, costs varying with profits, and profits forecasted for volumes modeled in a profit volume analysis. To use the area chart for your own profit volume analysis, simply follow the instructions in the earlier section "Using the Profit Volume and Break-Even Analysis Starter Workbook" to enter inputs for the profit volume and break-even analysis starter workbook.

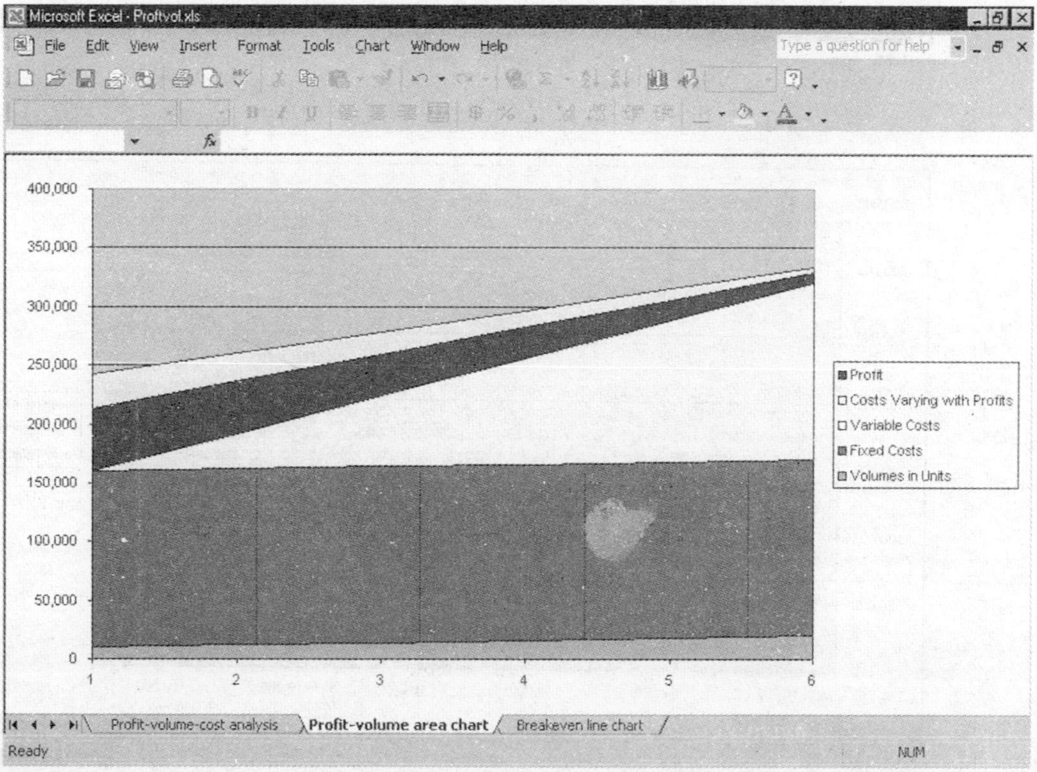

Figure 11-5 The profit volume area chart.

The profit volume area chart resides on the Profit-Volume Area Chart tab of the workbook. Click the Profit-Volume Area Chart sheet tab to view the chart once you've collected and entered the starter workbook's input data.

Notice that although the total sales are not explicitly included in the chart, they are implicitly included because the sum of the variable costs, fixed costs, costs varying with profits, and profits add up to the total sales.

Using the Break-Even Line Chart

Figure 11-6 shows a line chart of total sales plotted against total costs, including variable costs, fixed costs, and costs varying with profits. To use the line chart for your own break-even analysis, first follow the instructions in the section "Using the Profit Volume and Break-Even Analysis Starter Workbook" to enter inputs for the profit volume and break-even analysis starter workbook.

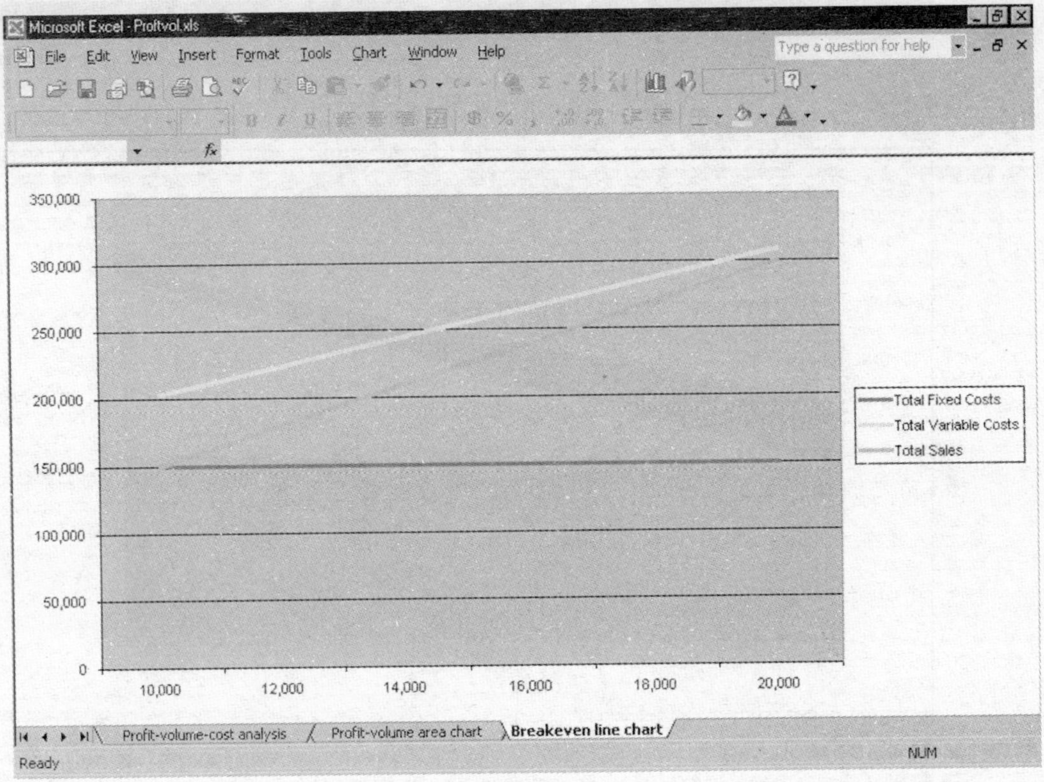

Figure 11-6 The break-even line chart.

The break-even line chart resides on the Breakeven Line Chart tab of the workbook. Click the Breakeven Line Chart sheet tab to view the chart once you've collected and entered the starter workbook's input data.

NOTE *Because area and line charts emphasize the differences in a variable or variables over time, the scaling for the values axis greatly affects the perceived differences. By using small scaling units, you increase the perceived change in the variable or variables. By using large scaling units, you decrease the perceived change. In general, common sense suggests that the scaling units for charts of financial information be determined by the materiality of the changes. This means that you might need to override the automatic scaling provided by Excel because it scales the data based on the minimum and maximum values, not on your subjective definition of materiality.*

Chapter 12

FORECASTING SALES AND COST OF SALES

Featuring:

- EasyRefresher™: Sales and Cost of Sales Forecasting
- Using the Sales Forecasting Starter Workbook
- Understanding the Starter Workbook's Calculations
- Customizing the Starter Workbook

Business planning usually requires detailed forecasts of sales and related variables, such as cost of sales, gross margins, and the inventory levels required to support the forecasted sales. The sales forecasting starter workbook (SALESRPT.XLS) described in this chapter provides a framework for you to use in forecasting sales, cost of sales, gross margins, and inventory levels in a variety of businesses, including manufacturing, wholesaling and retailing, and service firms. This chapter shows how to use the sales forecasting starter workbook, print it, modify it, and link it with subsidiary spreadsheets.

EasyRefresher™: Sales and Cost of Sales Forecasting

Sales forecasting is basic to any business plan or budget and to some investment analysis. Essentially, you need to collect information for or make forecasts concerning as many as five related variables.

For example, you typically need to collect the units and dollars of inventory that you already hold or that you estimate you will hold at the beginning of the sales forecast. In a manufacturing firm, these amounts are the sum of the work in process, or partially manufactured, inventory and the finished goods, or ready to sell, inventory. In a wholesaling or retailing firm, these amounts are the sum of those items purchased for resale. You need to collect both the units of inventory and the dollars of inventory. (In a service business, no inventory is manufactured or purchased, so these amounts are 0.)

Second, for each period in the forecasting horizon, you need to forecast the number of units produced if you're a manufacturer or the number of units purchased if you're a wholesaler or retailer. Typically, the amounts cannot be forecasted independent of sales, but sales isn't the only variable that affects production or purchases. Other important variables such as manufacturing capacities and availability of inventory items to be purchased also impact planned production and purchases.

Third, you need to forecast the costs of producing or purchasing the inventory for each period over the forecasting horizon. For a manufacturing firm, costs are often forecasted by classifications such as direct labor (the wages and employee benefits incurred in making the item), direct material (the raw materials and components that go into the finished product), and factory overhead (the miscellaneous and incidental costs associated with making the item, such as electricity to run the manufacturing equipment). For wholesalers and retailers, forecasted costs are the amounts paid to suppliers for those items purchased for resale. In a service business, no inventory is manufactured or purchased, so no production or purchase costs exist.

Fourth, you need to forecast the number of units sold and the price per unit sold for each period over the forecasting horizon. For manufacturers, wholesalers, and retailers, the unit forecast simply is the number of cars, shirts, or basketballs sold; the unit price forecast is simply the price at which these items are sold to the customer. For service firms, the unit forecast simply is the number of times a service is provided or the hours of work performed; the unit price forecast is simply the price at which the service or work is billed to the customer.

Fifth, you need to forecast any other variable costs associated with sales. For any type of business, these other costs might include sales commissions incurred as a result of the sale, taxes on the sale, and any other costs incurred and directly tied to the sale.

With this information, you should be able to forecast total sales, cost of sales, and margins. Usually when you forecast sales and cost of sales, you use either the financial accounting or managerial accounting format. Using the financial accounting format, you calculate sales revenue, cost of goods sold, and gross sales margin.

Using the managerial accounting format, you calculate the marginal sales revenue, the variable costs, and the marginal contribution. The marginal sales revenue is the number of units sold times the unit price at which the sales are made. The variable costs include both the cost of goods sold, which is the sum of the production or purchasing costs of the items sold, and also any other variable costs incurred as a result of the sale. The marginal contribution is the marginal sales revenue minus the variable costs. The marginal contribution is that amount generated by your sales to pay your fixed costs, those costs that do not vary with sales volumes. You might want to use a combination of both formats in your forecasting, so the sales and cost of sales starter workbook amounts to a hybrid of the two formats. You can use sales revenue for either the financial accounting sales revenue or the managerial accounting marginal sales revenue. You can use the cost of sales for either the financial accounting cost of goods sold or the managerial accounting variable costs. Depending on how you use the workbook's sales revenue and cost of sales, you can use the gross margin for either the financial accounting gross sales margin or the managerial accounting marginal contribution. Total sales simply are the number of units sold times the unit price at which the sales are made. The cost of the goods sold is the sum of the production or purchasing costs of the items sold. The gross sales margin is the total sales less the cost of sales. The gross sales margin is that amount actually generated by your sales to pay for your operating and financing costs. Any amounts left over after paying these costs represent your profit.

Using the Sales Forecasting Starter Workbook

You can use the sales forecasting starter workbook (SALESRTP.XLS), as shown in Figures 12-1 and 12-2, to construct sales forecast schedules for each product or service for which you want to estimate sales and production activity separately. This starter workbook provides a framework for the development of your own sales forecasts. To complete it for a product or service line, you develop and then enter your sales forecasts, your manufacturing or purchasing forecasts, and your beginning inventory levels for work in process and finished goods.

Given the beginning inventory (expressed both in units and in dollars), the number of units produced or purchased and their costs by period, and the sales volumes and unit sales prices by period, this workbook details and calculates the total sales, production activity, and inventory balances by period on the forecasting horizon. You need this information to calculate product sales and gross margins, business profits and losses, and business cash flows, and you need it to report the inventory balance on the balance sheet.

To enter your own data in sales forecasting starter workbook, follow these steps:

1. **Open the sales forecasting starter workbook, SALESRPT.XLS, from the companion CD.**

   The workbook initially contains the default inputs shown in Figure 12-1.

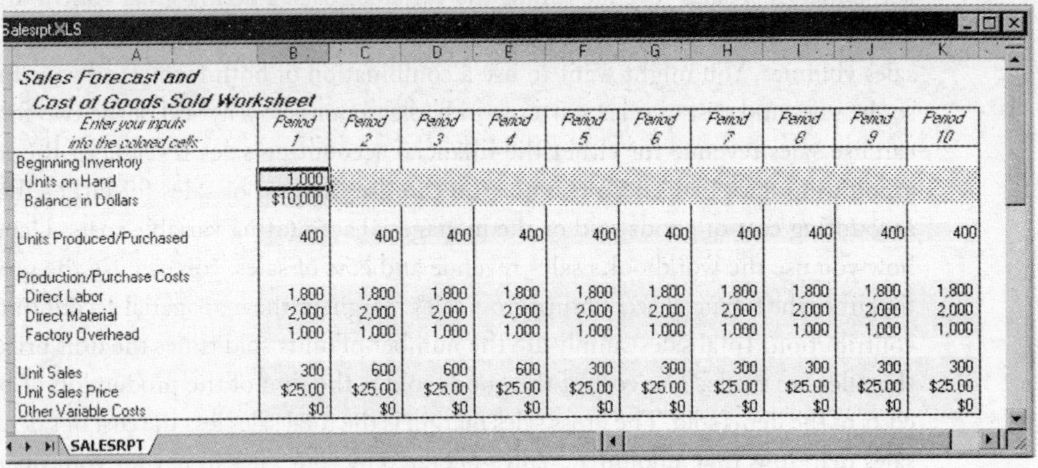

Salesrpt.XLS

A	B	C	D	E	F	G	H	I	J	K
Sales Forecast and Cost of Goods Sold Worksheet										
Enter your inputs into the colored cells:	*Period 1*	*Period 2*	*Period 3*	*Period 4*	*Period 5*	*Period 6*	*Period 7*	*Period 8*	*Period 9*	*Period 10*
Beginning Inventory										
Units on Hand	1,000									
Balance in Dollars	$10,000									
Units Produced/Purchased	400	400	400	400	400	400	400	400	400	400
Production/Purchase Costs										
Direct Labor	1,800	1,800	1,800	1,800	1,800	1,800	1,800	1,800	1,800	1,800
Direct Material	2,000	2,000	2,000	2,000	2,000	2,000	2,000	2,000	2,000	2,000
Factory Overhead	1,000	1,000	1,000	1,000	1,000	1,000	1,000	1,000	1,000	1,000
Unit Sales	300	600	600	600	300	300	300	300	300	300
Unit Sales Price	$25.00	$25.00	$25.00	$25.00	$25.00	$25.00	$25.00	$25.00	$25.00	$25.00
Other Variable Costs	$0	$0	$0	$0	$0	$0	$0	$0	$0	$0

SALESRPT

Figure 12-1 The inputs area of the sales forecasting starter workbook.

2. **Enter the beginning inventory balance in dollars and in units on hand for the first period.**

   The values you enter for Units on Hand and Balance in Dollars under Beginning Inventory come from your accounting records; they document your starting inventory balances.

   Notice that subsequent periods' beginning inventory figures are calculated, not entered, using the forecasts of sales and manufacturing or purchasing activity.

3. **Enter the units produced or purchased for each period over the forecasting horizon.**

   The period production figures stem from your forecasts of the anticipated manufacturing or the anticipated purchasing volumes necessary to support the sales plan.

TIP *For manufacturing firms, the number of units in the starting inventory balance and the number of units produced should be expressed in equivalent units. For example, 100 units that are 50% complete are included in the schedule instead as 50 units that are 100% complete. This approach is necessary because if you don't use equivalent units, only a percentage of the costs are included and the calculated unit cost will be too low.*

4. **Enter the production costs (direct labor, direct material, and factory overhead) associated with manufacturing or purchasing volumes forecasted for each period over the forecasting horizon.**

   The production costs—Direct Labor, Direct Material, and Factory Overhead—are those costs associated with manufacturing or purchasing the product. If you are in a wholesale or retail business that has no manufacturing activity, enter only the Direct Material value (which should be called purchases).

5. **Enter the units sold and the unit sales price forecasted for each period over the forecasting horizon.**

   Forecast the Unit Sales and Unit Sales Price amounts based on your sales and marketing research. In general, you estimate future sales based on your past sales history and expectations about future orders.

6. **Enter any other variable costs associated with consummating a sale for each period over the forecasting horizon.**

   Other Variable Costs amounts associated with a sale might include commissions or bonuses owed to the salespeople who close the sale, bad debt expense that might be expressed as a function of the sale, and marketing costs related to packaging and distributing the product. You'll often enter this item as a formula that is calculated from Unit Sales, Unit Sales Price, or the Production/Purchase Costs.

Understanding the Starter Workbook's Calculations

The sales forecasting starter workbook has five parts: the Sales Forecast heading box, the Sales Forecast Inputs (discussed above), Cost Totals and Statistics, Sales and Gross Margin Forecast, and Inventory Forecast.

Sales Forecast

The Sales Forecast schedule heading box provides column headings for the schedules in the starter workbook. It uses a single formula to calculate the period number. The period identifier simply numbers the time periods for which sales, manufacturing or purchasing, and inventory levels are forecasted. You'll probably want the number of periods in your Sales Forecast Inputs schedule to correspond to the number of periods in the other schedules that make up your financial forecasting model. The first period is stored in cell B4 as the integer 1. Subsequent period numbers are calculated as 1 plus the previous period.

Cost Totals and Statistics

The Cost Totals and Statistics schedule calculates the total production and purchase costs, as well as the beginning, produced or purchased, and weighted average unit costs shown in Figure 12-2. It has four rows that contain calculated data.

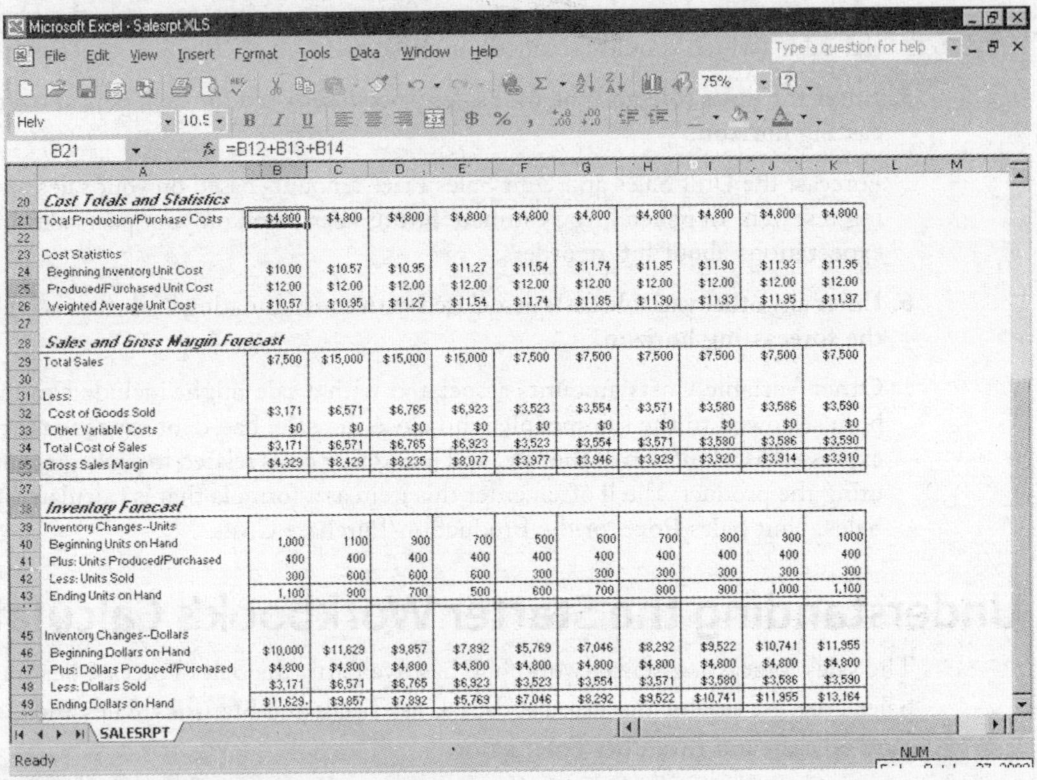

B21 =B12+B13+B14

	A	B	C	D	E	F	G	H	I	J	K
20	*Cost Totals and Statistics*										
21	Total Production/Purchase Costs	$4,800	$4,800	$4,800	$4,800	$4,800	$4,800	$4,800	$4,800	$4,800	$4,800
22											
23	Cost Statistics										
24	Beginning Inventory Unit Cost	$10.00	$10.57	$10.95	$11.27	$11.54	$11.74	$11.85	$11.90	$11.93	$11.95
25	Produced/Furchased Unit Cost	$12.00	$12.00	$12.00	$12.00	$12.00	$12.00	$12.00	$12.00	$12.00	$12.00
26	Weighted Average Unit Cost	$10.57	$10.95	$11.27	$11.54	$11.74	$11.85	$11.90	$11.93	$11.95	$11.97
27											
28	*Sales and Gross Margin Forecast*										
29	Total Sales	$7,500	$15,000	$15,000	$15,000	$7,500	$7,500	$7,500	$7,500	$7,500	$7,500
30											
31	Less:										
32	Cost of Goods Sold	$3,171	$6,571	$6,765	$6,923	$3,523	$3,554	$3,571	$3,580	$3,586	$3,590
33	Other Variable Costs	$0	$0	$0	$0	$0	$0	$0	$0	$0	$0
34	Total Cost of Sales	$3,171	$6,571	$6,765	$6,923	$3,523	$3,554	$3,571	$3,580	$3,586	$3,590
35	Gross Sales Margin	$4,329	$8,429	$8,235	$8,077	$3,977	$3,946	$3,929	$3,920	$3,914	$3,910
37											
38	*Inventory Forecast*										
39	Inventory Changes--Units										
40	Beginning Units on Hand	1,000	1100	900	700	500	600	700	800	900	1000
41	Plus: Units Produced/Purchased	400	400	400	400	400	400	400	400	400	400
42	Less: Units Sold	300	600	600	600	300	300	300	300	300	300
43	Ending Units on Hand	1,100	900	700	500	600	700	800	900	1,000	1,100
45	Inventory Changes--Dollars										
46	Beginning Dollars on Hand	$10,000	$11,629	$9,857	$7,892	$5,769	$7,046	$8,292	$9,522	$10,741	$11,955
47	Plus: Dollars Produced/Purchased	$4,800	$4,800	$4,800	$4,800	$4,800	$4,800	$4,800	$4,800	$4,800	$4,800
48	Less: Dollars Sold	$3,171	$6,571	$6,765	$6,923	$3,523	$3,554	$3,571	$3,580	$3,586	$3,590
49	Ending Dollars on Hand	$11,629	$9,857	$7,892	$5,769	$7,046	$8,292	$9,522	$10,741	$11,955	$13,164

Figure 12-2 The schedule calculated by the sales forecasting starter workbook.

Total Production/Purchase Costs

The Total Production/Purchase Costs value is simply the sum of the Direct Labor, Direct Material, and Factory Overhead values. For a wholesaler or retailer, because the Direct Labor and Factory Overhead figures, by definition, are 0, the total cost is the same as the Direct Material cost. For a service firm, no inventory might be manufactured or purchased for resale. Therefore, this amount might be 0.

The formula for the first period is:

```
=B12+B13+B14
```

The formula for the second period is:

```
=C12+C13+C14
```

and so on.

Beginning Inventory Unit Cost

The Beginning Inventory Unit Cost value represents the cost of producing one of the units held in the beginning inventory. It is calculated by dividing the Beginning Dollars on Hand value by the Beginning Units on Hand value calculated in the Inventory Forecast schedule. For example, the formula for the first period is:

```
=B46/B40
```

The formula for the second period is:

```
=C46/C40
```

and so on.

Produced/Purchased Unit Cost

The Produced/Purchased Unit Cost value represents the cost of producing or purchasing one of the units manufactured or bought during the period. Although the inventory balances reported on this schedule use an average cost inventory assumption, you can use this value to construct alternative inventory costing methods, such as First-In-First-Out (FIFO) and Last-In-First-Out (LIFO). (FIFO assumes that the first items purchased or produced are the first items sold; LIFO assumes that the last items purchased or produced are the first items sold. In a period of rising prices, FIFO calculates lower cost of goods sold and higher ending inventory.)

The formula for the first period is:

```
=B21/B9
```

The formula for the second period is:

```
=C21/C9
```

and so on.

Weighted Average Unit Cost

The Weighted Average Unit Cost value represents the average cost of the product units, considering both the beginning inventory balance and the period production or purchase inventory. This is the per unit cost used to calculate both the cost of sales and next period's beginning inventory levels.

The formula divides the total of the inventory Beginning Dollars on Hand and the Total Production/Purchase Costs values by the total of the inventory Beginning Units on Hand and the Units Produced/Purchased values. For example, the formula for the first period is:

```
=(B46+B21)/(B40+B9)
```

The formula for the second period is:

```
=(C46+C21)/(C40+C9)
```

and so on.

Sales and Gross Margin Forecast

The Sales and Gross Margin Forecast schedule calculates the total sales, cost of goods sold, other variable costs, total cost of sales, and gross sales margin. It has five rows of data.

Total Sales

The Total Sales figure represents the total sales made over the period. The Total Sales formula multiplies the Unit Sales value by the Unit Sales price value. For example, the first period total sales formula is:

```
=B16*B17
```

The second period total sales formula is:

```
=C16*C17
```

and so on.

Cost of Goods Sold

The Cost of Goods Sold figure shows the total cost of manufacturing or purchasing the items sold during the period. The formula multiplies the Unit Sales value for the period by the Weighted Average Unit Cost value for the period. For example, the formula for the first period is:

```
=B16*B26
```

The formula for the second period is:

```
=C16*C26
```

and so on.

Other Variable Costs

The Other Variable Costs figure shows the other direct costs associated with consummating a sale. The value is simply pulled from the cell in which you entered this figure in the Sales Forecast Inputs schedule.

Total Cost of Sales

The Total Cost of Sales figure shows the total cost of goods sold and other costs related to the sales. The value is the sum of the Cost of Goods Sold and Other Variable Costs values. For example, the formula for the first period is:

```
=B32+B33
```

The formula for the second period is:

```
=C32+C33
```

and so on.

Gross Sales Margin

The Gross Sales Margin figure shows the amount remaining from sale proceeds after deducting the cost of sales. The Gross Sales Margin figure represents the funds that go toward paying your fixed costs and profits. The formula is the Total Sales value less the Total Cost of Sales value. For example, the formula for the first period is:

```
=B29-B34
```

The formula for the second period is:

```
=C29-C34
```

and so on.

Inventory Forecast

The Inventory Forecast schedule calculates the beginning inventory balance, the change in inventory balance, and the ending inventory balance, each in dollars and in units. The schedule has eight rows that contain calculated data.

Beginning Units on Hand

The Beginning Units on Hand figure shows the number of complete products you have available for resale at the beginning of the period. For the first forecasting period, the Beginning Units on Hand figure is simply pulled from the Sales Forecast Inputs schedule. In subsequent periods, it is taken from the cell containing the previous period's Ending Units on Hand.

Plus: Units Produced/Purchased

The Units Produced/Purchased figure shows the number of equivalent units manufactured or the number of units bought during the period. The number is pulled from the Sales Forecast Inputs schedule.

Less: Units Sold

The Units Sold figure shows the number of units in inventory sold during the period. The number is pulled from the Unit Sales forecast in the Sales Forecast Inputs schedule.

Ending Units on Hand

The Ending Units on Hand figure shows the number of units of inventory held at the end of the period. This number is always the same as the number of units held at the beginning of the next period.

The number is the Beginning Units on Hand value plus the Units Produced/Purchased value for the period minus the Units Sold value for the period. For example, the formula for the first period is:

```
=B40+B41-B42
```

The formula for the second period is:

```
=C40+C41-C42
```

and so on.

Beginning Dollars on Hand

The Beginning Dollars on Hand figure shows the dollar cost of the completed and partially completed products that you have available in inventory for resale. The number for the first period is pulled from the Sales Forecast Inputs schedule. In subsequent periods, the number is taken from the previous period's Ending Dollars on Hand.

Plus: Dollars Produced/Purchased

The Dollars Produced/Purchased figure shows the dollar cost of the units manufactured or bought during the period, using the weighted average unit cost as the cost per unit. The number is pulled from Total Production/Purchase Costs in the Cost Totals and Statistics schedule.

Less: Dollars Sold

The Dollars Sold figure shows the dollar cost of the units sold during the period, using the weighted average unit cost as the cost per unit. This amount is pulled from Cost of Goods Sold in the Sales and Gross Margin Forecast.

Ending Dollars on Hand

The Ending Dollars on Hand figure shows the dollar cost of the inventory held at the end of the period. This number is always the same as the dollar cost of the inventory held at the beginning of the next period.

If you are in a manufacturing business, you can use this amount as the dollar cost of the work in process and finished inventory that is included in the Balance Sheet. If you are in a wholesale or retail business, you use this amount as the dollar cost of all the inventory that is included in the balance sheet.

The Ending Dollars on Hand formula adds the Beginning Dollars on Hand and Dollars Produced/Purchased values and then subtracts the Dollars Sold value. For example, the formula for the first period is:

```
=B46+B47-B48
```

The formula for the second period is:

```
=C46+C47-C48
```

and so on.

Customizing the Starter Workbook

You can use the sales forecasting starter workbook without modification for many sales forecasts. However, you might want to change the workbook so that it more closely matches your requirements. For example, you can add text that describes the product being manufactured or purchased and for which sales are forecasted. You can also increase or decrease the number of periods. For example, you can increase the number of periods to 12 if your periods are months and you want to forecast an entire year.

NOTE *Before you change anything in the starter workbook other than the Sales Forecast Inputs schedule, unprotect the document.*

To increase the number of periods, remove the borders from the last column; then copy the current last column to the right as needed. To decrease the number of periods, simply delete any unneeded column from the right side of the schedule. When you finish these steps, you can replace the borders on the right and reinstate cell protection as needed.

Chapter 13

BUILDING A CAPITAL BUDGETING WORKBOOK

Featuring:

- EasyRefresher™: Cash Flow Forecasting and Analysis
- Using the Cash Flow Forecast and Analysis Starter Workbook
- Understanding the Starter Workbook's Calculations
- Customizing the Starter Workbook

Capital budgeting and investment analysis require that you forecast pretax and after-tax cash flows based on both holding and disposing of each asset or investment. Financial measures of profitability and liquidity are applied to these cash flows. The cash flow forecast and analysis starter workbook (CASHFLOW.XLS) described in this chapter provides a framework for forecasting pretax and after-tax cash flows, internal rates of return, internal rates of return adjusted for reinvestment of interim cash flows, net present values, and payback periods. You should find this starter workbook useful for cash flow forecasts for both capital assets and financial investments. This chapter shows how to use the cash flow forecast and analysis starter workbook, print it, modify it, and combine it with subsidiary spreadsheets.

EasyRefresher™: Cash Flow Forecasting and Analysis

Cash flow forecasting and analysis, a basic component of capital budgeting and investment analysis, requires that you forecast each of the variables that might affect cash flows on the forecasting horizon. These variables include the initial outlay to acquire an asset or investment, the cash inflows and the cash outflows from holding an asset or investment, and any cash flows from disposing of an asset or investment. Using these variables, you can forecast the initial cash investment, the operating cash flows, and any liquidation cash flows.

To these cash flows, you apply profitability and liquidity measures. Because all the profitability measures use discounting, it's important to understand what discounting means. Discounting is the technique of reducing future cash to its equivalent in current cash, thereby providing a basis for an "apples-to-apples" comparison. To convert future cash amounts to current cash amounts, you first need to determine the time value of money, commonly called the interest rate, or the discount rate. The discount rate applied one period at a time is the period discount rate. To discount future cash into equivalent current cash, you divide the cash flow by the sum of one plus the period discount rate as many times as there are periods. For example, if the period discount rate equals 10% and you want to convert a $2,300 cash flow two years from now into equivalent current cash, you make the following calculation:

```
2300/(1+10%)/(1+10%)
```

or:

$$2300/\ (1+10\%)^2$$

Similarly, if you have a cash flow of $5,000 occurring five years from now, you make the following calculation:

```
5000/(1+10%)/(1+10%)/(1+10%)/(1+10%)/(1+10%)
```

or:

$$5000/(1+10\%)^5$$

In any of the discounted cash flow profitability measures, this is the basic calculation: discounting future cash into its equivalent in current cash by using the time value of money expressed as an interest rate. With this background, you will be better able to understand the definitions of the profitability measures employed in the cash flow forecast and analysis starter workbook.

The internal rate of return, another term used in the starter workbook, is the discount rate that equates all the future cash flows to the initial cash investment. In other words, given a stated initial cash investment and a set of stated cash flows, the internal rate of return calculates the assumed interest rate delivered by the investment.

The internal rate of return adjusted for reinvestment of the interim cash flows, sometimes called the adjusted rate of return, is like the internal rate of return measure except that it assumes cash flows occurring between the beginning and the end of the forecasting horizon are reinvested until the end of the forecasting horizon at some stated reinvestment rate and then are paid at the end of the forecasting horizon with the final cash flow.

Although the internal rate of return and adjusted rate of return measures calculate the assumed interest rate based on the stated initial investment and the stated future cash flows, the net present value measure calculates an assumed initial investment based on the stated future cash flows and a stated interest rate. By comparing the actual investment with the assumed investment, you discover whether the investment is falling short of, meeting, or exceeding your stated interest rate. When the assumed initial investment falls short of the actual initial investment, the internal rate of return that the asset delivers falls short of the discount rate. When the assumed initial investment equals the actual initial investment, the internal rate of return that the asset delivers equals the discount rate. When the assumed initial investment exceeds the actual investment, the internal rate of return delivered by the asset exceeds the discount rate.

The starter workbook also incorporates a common liquidity, or closeness to cash, measure: the payback period. The payback period measure indicates how many periods are required to pay back or return the initial cash investment. Although liquidity is generally less important than profitability, in some situations businesses prefer more-liquid investments to less-liquid investments.

Using the Cash Flow Forecast and Analysis Starter Workbook

You can use the cash flow forecast and analysis starter workbook, as shown in Figures 13-1 through 13-5, to construct cash flow forecasts and analysis summaries for assets or investments for which you want to measure profitability and liquidity. To complete it for an asset or investment, develop and then enter information on the initial cash outlay needed to acquire the asset or investment, information on the cash inflows and outflows resulting from holding the asset or investment, and information on any residual cash flows from disposing of the asset or investment.

Given a set of data that includes your initial cash investment, sales and cost of sales, operating expenses, interest expenses, marginal income tax rates, depreciation and other noncash expenses, and debt principal payments and other cash nonexpenses, this starter workbook calculates the operating profit (or loss) and cash flows stemming from holding an investment. (Noncash expenses are those expenses, such as depreciation, that do not require any cash outflow. Other noncash expenses include the depletion expense of using up an intangible asset. Cash nonexpenses are those cash payments, such as debt principal payments, that represent a cash outflow but that are not considered an expense when calculating profit.) Given a set of data that includes gross residuals, transaction/disposal costs, outstanding debt, nontaxable portions of the residual, and marginal capital gains tax rates, this starter workbook calculates the capital gain (or loss) and cash flows stemming from disposing of an asset or investment. (The gross residual is the amount you can sell the asset or investment for. The marginal capital gains tax rate is the percentage that, when multiplied by the capital gains, correctly calculates the capital gains tax.) Given all of this data and your reinvestment and discount rates, the workbook calculates pretax and after-tax internal rates of return, pretax and after-tax adjusted rates of return, pretax and after-tax net present values, and the asset or investment payback period. You need some or all of this information to evaluate the economics of alternative investments and assets and to calculate overall profits (or losses), overall capital gains (or losses), and overall cash flows.

To enter your own data in the cash flow forecast and analysis starter workbook, follow these steps:

1. **Open the cash flow forecast and analysis starter workbook, CASHFLOW.XLS, from the companion CD.**

   The starter workbook initially contains the default inputs shown in Figure 13-1.

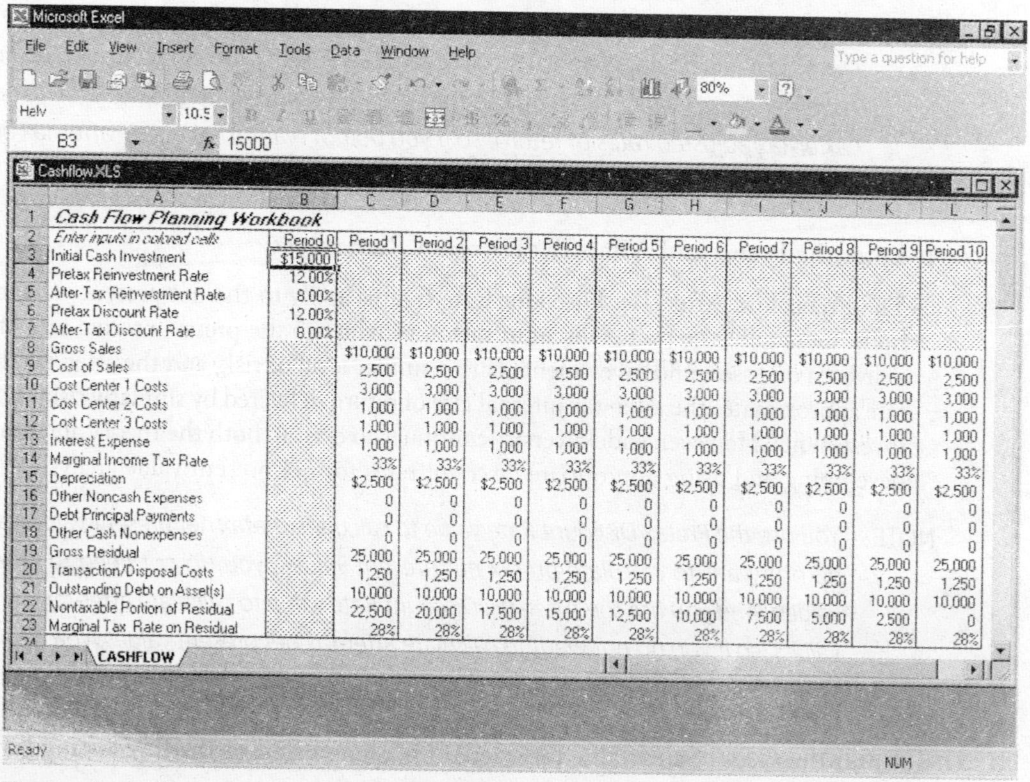

	A	B	C	D	E	F	G	H	I	J	K	L
1	*Cash Flow Planning Workbook*											
2	*Enter inputs in colored cells*	Period 0	Period 1	Period 2	Period 3	Period 4	Period 5	Period 6	Period 7	Period 8	Period 9	Period 10
3	Initial Cash Investment	$15,000										
4	Pretax Reinvestment Rate	12.00%										
5	After-Tax Reinvestment Rate	8.00%										
6	Pretax Discount Rate	12.00%										
7	After-Tax Discount Rate	8.00%										
8	Gross Sales		$10,000	$10,000	$10,000	$10,000	$10,000	$10,000	$10,000	$10,000	$10,000	$10,000
9	Cost of Sales		2,500	2,500	2,500	2,500	2,500	2,500	2,500	2,500	2,500	2,500
10	Cost Center 1 Costs		3,000	3,000	3,000	3,000	3,000	3,000	3,000	3,000	3,000	3,000
11	Cost Center 2 Costs		1,000	1,000	1,000	1,000	1,000	1,000	1,000	1,000	1,000	1,000
12	Cost Center 3 Costs		1,000	1,000	1,000	1,000	1,000	1,000	1,000	1,000	1,000	1,000
13	Interest Expense		1,000	1,000	1,000	1,000	1,000	1,000	1,000	1,000	1,000	1,000
14	Marginal Income Tax Rate		33%	33%	33%	33%	33%	33%	33%	33%	33%	33%
15	Depreciation		$2,500	$2,500	$2,500	$2,500	$2,500	$2,500	$2,500	$2,500	$2,500	$2,500
16	Other Noncash Expenses		0	0	0	0	0	0	0	0	0	0
17	Debt Principal Payments		0	0	0	0	0	0	0	0	0	0
18	Other Cash Nonexpenses		0	0	0	0	0	0	0	0	0	0
19	Gross Residual		25,000	25,000	25,000	25,000	25,000	25,000	25,000	25,000	25,000	25,000
20	Transaction/Disposal Costs		1,250	1,250	1,250	1,250	1,250	1,250	1,250	1,250	1,250	1,250
21	Outstanding Debt on Asset(s)		10,000	10,000	10,000	10,000	10,000	10,000	10,000	10,000	10,000	10,000
22	Nontaxable Portion of Residual		22,500	20,000	17,500	15,000	12,500	10,000	7,500	5,000	2,500	0
23	Marginal Tax Rate on Residual		28%	28%	28%	28%	28%	28%	28%	28%	28%	28%

Figure 13-1 The inputs area of the cash flow forecast and analysis starter workbook.

2. **Enter the Initial Cash Investment value.**

   The initial cash investment is the amount required to acquire the investment. Enter a cash outflow as a positive amount and a cash inflow as a negative amount. If you use debt to fund a portion of the purchase, the initial cash investment is probably the gross sales price of the asset less the amount of the debt.

3. **Enter the Pretax and After-Tax Reinvestment Rates.**

   The Pretax and After-Tax Reinvestment Rate figures apply to the adjusted rate of return calculations. The rates represent the forecasted returns at which interim cash flows will be reinvested over the holding period. Generally, pretax rates approximate the yields delivered by intermediate-term taxable bonds, and the after-tax rates approximate the yields delivered by intermediate-term tax-exempt bonds. You don't want to commingle returns with different tax treatment. Both the pretax return and the interest income from a taxable bond are taxable. Both the after-tax return and the interest income from a tax-exempt bond are nontaxable. You pick bonds with intermediate maturities because the maturity of the asset or investment is typically intermediate.

NOTE *You use the Pretax Reinvestment Rate value to calculate pretax adjusted rates of return, so if you do not want to calculate pretax adjusted rates of return, you do not need to enter these values. And you use the After-Tax Reinvestment Rate value to calculate after-tax adjusted rates of return, so if you do not want to calculate after-tax adjusted rates of return, you do not need to enter these values.*

4. Enter the Pretax and After-Tax Discount Rate values.

The Pretax and After-Tax Discount Rate figures apply to the net present value calculations. Generally, the pretax discount rate approximates the pretax internal rate of return delivered on assets and investments with a similar level of risk, and the after-tax discount rate approximates the after-tax internal rate of return delivered by similarly risky assets and investments. However, wide diversity continues to exist in both the theory and practice of developing and using appropriate discount rates for net present value analysis.

NOTE *You use the Pretax Discount Rate value to calculate pretax net present values, so if you do not want to calculate pretax net present values, you do not need to enter these values. And you use the After-Tax Discount Rate value to calculate after-tax net present values, so if you do not want to calculate after-tax net present values, you do not need to enter these values.*

5. Enter the Gross Sales value forecasted for each period of the forecasting horizon.

The Gross Sales values represent the forecasted sales generated by the asset or investment over each of the periods of the forecasting horizon. You use these forecasts to estimate the income tax expense and the cash flows. Accordingly, implicit in the construction of the starter workbook is the assumption that you use cash-basis accounting for income tax purposes and for development of the sales forecasts.

Enter cash inflows as positive amounts and cash outflows as negative amounts. (If you are analyzing the cash flows from financial assets, this amount might be the investment revenue forecasted for each period. If you are analyzing the cash flows from assets that deliver productivity or efficiency gains, this amount might be the cost savings forecasted for each period.)

6. Enter the Cost of Sales values forecasted for each period of the forecasting horizon.

The Cost of Sales values represent the forecasted costs that are tied to sales generated over the forecasting horizon. These values might include cost of goods sold, selling costs, and perhaps other variable sales costs, such as commissions owed salespeople. You use these forecasts to estimate the taxable income and the cash flows.

Enter cash outflows as positive amounts and cash inflows as negative amounts. (If you are analyzing the cash flows from a financial asset or an asset that delivers productivity gains, this amount might be 0 for each period.)

7. **Enter the Cost Center costs for Cost Centers 1, 2, and 3.**

   The operating expenses for Cost Centers 1, 2, and 3 represent the cash basis operating expenses for the forecasting horizon. These values might be three expense classifications related to holding the asset or investment, or they might be the total expenses for three groups of expenses. You use these forecasts to estimate the taxable income and the cash flows.

   In the Cost Center 1 Costs row, enter those costs that fall into the first classification or category. In the Cost Center 2 Costs row, enter those costs that fall into the second classification or category. In the Cost Center 3 Costs row, enter those costs that fall into the third classification or category. Be sure to enter cash outflows as positive amounts and cash inflows as negative amounts.

8. **Enter the Interest Expense value, the cost of carrying any debt used to fund a portion of the asset or investment purchase.**

   The Interest Expense values represent the period interest expense of carrying any debt related to the asset purchase. The interest expense equals 0 when you use no debt in the asset or investment purchase. You use these forecasts to estimate the taxable income and the cash flows.

9. **Enter the Marginal Income Tax Rate values.**

   The Marginal Income Tax Rate value is the percentage that, when multiplied by the operating profit (or loss) for the period, calculates the income tax expense (or savings). If you are interested only in calculating pretax profit measures, enter 0 as this amount.

10. **Enter the Depreciation expenses included in the expense categories 1, 2, or 3 of the forecasting horizon.**

    The Depreciation expenses represent the amounts of depreciation included in operating expenses for Cost Centers 1, 2, and 3 for the forecasting horizon. When no depreciation is included in the operating expenses for Cost Centers 1, 2, and 3, this amount equals 0.

11. **Enter the Other Noncash Expenses values for the forecasting horizon.**

    The Other Noncash Expenses values represent the amounts of noncash expenses other than depreciation, included in operating expenses for Cost Centers 1, 2, and 3 for the forecasting horizon. Examples of such noncash expenses include the depletion of natural resource assets and the amortization of intangible assets. When no other noncash expenses exist in the operating expenses for Cost Centers 1, 2, and 3, these amounts equal 0.

12. **Enter the Debt Principal Payments values.**

    The Debt Principal Payments values represent the cash paid out to reduce any debt used to fund any portions of the asset or investment purchase. If you use no debt in the asset or investment purchase or you use debt for which the payments you made include only interest, these amounts equal 0.

13. **Enter the Other Cash Nonexpenses values.**

    The Other Cash Nonexpenses values represent the amounts of cash nonexpenses, other than debt principal payments, that affect cash flows but not profits. Examples of such noncash expenses include the expenses that are not deductible for calculation of taxable profits, such as life insurance on key employees, and expenditures that are not expenses, such as deposits paid to vendors and suppliers.

14. **Enter the Gross Residual value forecasted for each period of the forecasting horizon.**

    The Gross Residual values represent the figures at which you can dispose of the asset or investment on the forecasting horizon. You use these amounts to calculate the capital gains (or losses) and the liquidation cash flows. If the asset or investment cannot be liquidated except at the end of the holding period, you need to enter only the final residual forecast.

15. **Enter the Transaction/Disposal Costs values.**

    The Transaction/Disposal costs values represent any incidental expenses or costs of disposing of the asset or investment. Examples include removal costs and brokerage fees. You use these amounts to calculate the capital gains (or losses) and the liquidation cash flows. You need only enter Transaction/Disposal Costs figures for those periods for which you forecast a gross residual.

16. **Enter the Outstanding Debt on Asset(s) values.**

    The Outstanding Debt on Asset(s) values represent the debt that you will pay off as a result of disposing of the asset. You need to enter outstanding debt figures only for those periods for which you forecast a gross residual.

17. **Enter the Nontaxable Portion of Residual values.**

    The Nontaxable Portion of Residual values represent those amounts of the cash received upon disposal that are not subject to capital gains taxes. You use these amounts to calculate the capital gains (or losses) and the liquidation cash flows. Typically, the nontaxable portion of the residual is the net book value of the asset or investment. If no depreciation has been charged, this means the nontaxable portion equals the original cost. You need to enter the Nontaxable Portion of Residual figures only for those periods for which you forecast a gross residual.

18. **Enter the Marginal Tax Rate on Residual value.**

    The Marginal Tax Rate on Residual, or capital gains rate, represents the percentage that, when multiplied by the net gain or loss stemming from the disposal of the asset, calculates the capital gains tax expense (or savings). You need to enter Marginal Tax Rate on Residual figures only for those periods for which you forecast a gross residual.

After you enter the required inputs, the starter workbook makes the calculations necessary to construct pro forma cash flow forecasts and calculate a standard set of investment measures.

Understanding the Starter Workbook's Calculations

The cash flow forecast and analysis starter workbook has eight parts: the inputs area, the Profit and Loss Statement, the Gain and Loss Statement, the Operating Cash Flows Statement, the Liquidation Cash Flows Statement, the Cash Flow Analysis, the Pretax Cash Flow Scenarios, and the After-Tax Cash Flow Scenarios.

Cash Flow Forecasting Inputs

Only one set of formulas exists in the inputs area of the cash flow forecast and analysis starter workbook: the one in the second row that identifies the period for which the results are calculated. The rest of the rows contain input cells where you can enter your own data. Unless you turn off cell protection, these are the only cells in which you can enter data.

The period identifier simply numbers the periods forecasted. The start of the first period is stored as the integer 0. (Using 0 as the starting balance is the traditional way to identify those cash flows that are not discounted because they occur at the beginning of the forecasting horizon.) Periods that follow are stored as the previous period plus 1.

NOTE *The period identifiers are formatted with a custom format that places the word* period *in front of the period identifier. If you want to change this, simply use another number format.*

Profit and Loss Statement

The Profit and Loss Statement schedule has 12 rows that contain calculated data, as shown in Figure 13-2.

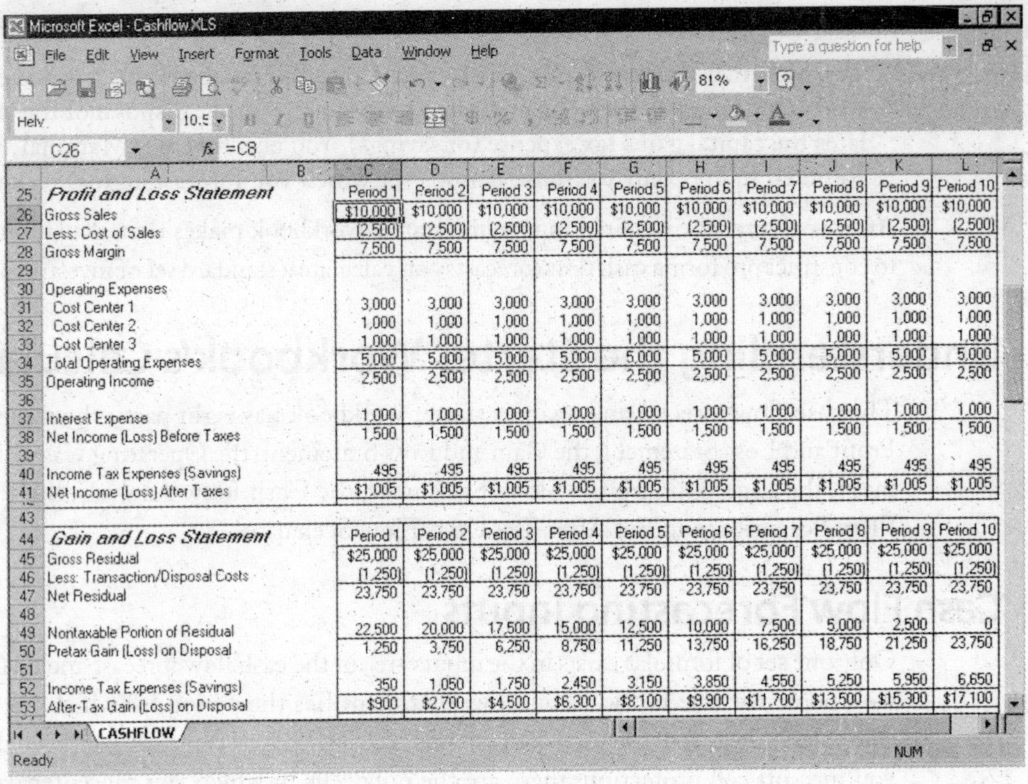

Microsoft Excel - Cashflow.XLS

C26 =C8

	A	C	D	E	F	G	H	I	J	K	L
25	***Profit and Loss Statement***	Period 1	Period 2	Period 3	Period 4	Period 5	Period 6	Period 7	Period 8	Period 9	Period 10
26	Gross Sales	$10,000	$10,000	$10,000	$10,000	$10,000	$10,000	$10,000	$10,000	$10,000	$10,000
27	Less: Cost of Sales	(2,500)	(2,500)	(2,500)	(2,500)	(2,500)	(2,500)	(2,500)	(2,500)	(2,500)	(2,500)
28	Gross Margin	7,500	7,500	7,500	7,500	7,500	7,500	7,500	7,500	7,500	7,500
29											
30	Operating Expenses										
31	Cost Center 1	3,000	3,000	3,000	3,000	3,000	3,000	3,000	3,000	3,000	3,000
32	Cost Center 2	1,000	1,000	1,000	1,000	1,000	1,000	1,000	1,000	1,000	1,000
33	Cost Center 3	1,000	1,000	1,000	1,000	1,000	1,000	1,000	1,000	1,000	1,000
34	Total Operating Expenses	5,000	5,000	5,000	5,000	5,000	5,000	5,000	5,000	5,000	5,000
35	Operating Income	2,500	2,500	2,500	2,500	2,500	2,500	2,500	2,500	2,500	2,500
36											
37	Interest Expense	1,000	1,000	1,000	1,000	1,000	1,000	1,000	1,000	1,000	1,000
38	Net Income (Loss) Before Taxes	1,500	1,500	1,500	1,500	1,500	1,500	1,500	1,500	1,500	1,500
39											
40	Income Tax Expenses (Savings)	495	495	495	495	495	495	495	495	495	495
41	Net Income (Loss) After Taxes	$1,005	$1,005	$1,005	$1,005	$1,005	$1,005	$1,005	$1,005	$1,005	$1,005
43											
44	***Gain and Loss Statement***	Period 1	Period 2	Period 3	Period 4	Period 5	Period 6	Period 7	Period 8	Period 9	Period 10
45	Gross Residual	$25,000	$25,000	$25,000	$25,000	$25,000	$25,000	$25,000	$25,000	$25,000	$25,000
46	Less: Transaction/Disposal Costs	(1,250)	(1,250)	(1,250)	(1,250)	(1,250)	(1,250)	(1,250)	(1,250)	(1,250)	(1,250)
47	Net Residual	23,750	23,750	23,750	23,750	23,750	23,750	23,750	23,750	23,750	23,750
48											
49	Nontaxable Portion of Residual	22,500	20,000	17,500	15,000	12,500	10,000	7,500	5,000	2,500	0
50	Pretax Gain (Loss) on Disposal	1,250	3,750	6,250	8,750	11,250	13,750	16,250	18,750	21,250	23,750
51											
52	Income Tax Expenses (Savings)	350	1,050	1,750	2,450	3,150	3,850	4,550	5,250	5,950	6,650
53	After-Tax Gain (Loss) on Disposal	$900	$2,700	$4,500	$6,300	$8,100	$9,900	$11,700	$13,500	$15,300	$17,100

CASHFLOW

Ready NUM

Figure 13-2 The Profit and Loss Statement area of the cash flow forecast and analysis starter workbook.

Gross Sales

The Gross Sales figures show the sales estimates. You enter this amount in the inputs area of the starter workbook. The Profit and Loss Statement simply references the input value you supply.

Less: Cost of Sales

The Cost of Sales figures show the cost of sales estimates. You enter this amount in the inputs area of the starter workbook. Again, the Profit and Loss Statement simply references the input value you supply.

Gross Margin

The Gross Margin figures show the amounts left over from the sales proceeds after paying for the cost of sales. The Gross Margin figures represent the amount of cash that goes toward paying your other expenses and your profits.

The Gross Margin value for each period is the Gross Sales figure for the period less the Cost of Sales figure. But because the Cost of Sales figures are pulled into the Profit and Loss

Statement as negative amounts, the Gross Margin formula simply adds the positive Gross Sales figure to the negative Cost of Sales figure. For example, the formula for the first period is:

```
=C26+C27
```

The formula for the second period is:

```
=D26+D27
```

and so on.

Operating Expenses – Cost Centers 1, 2, and 3

The figures in these three rows show the amounts of the operating expenses for the three categories entered in the inputs area of the starter workbook.

Total Operating Expenses

The Total Operating Expenses figures show the sums of the operating expenses entered in the inputs area of the starter workbook for the three expense categories. For example, the formula for the first period is:

```
=SUM(C31:C33)
```

The formula for the second period is:

```
=SUM(D31:D33)
```

and so on.

Operating Income

The Operating Income figures show the amounts of sales dollars left after paying the cost of sales and the operating expenses. The Operating Income figures represent the amounts that go toward paying you financing expenses, income taxes, and profits.

The Operating Income value for each period is the Gross Margin figure for the period minus the Total Operating Expenses figure. For example, the formula for the first period is:

```
=C28-C34
```

The formula for the second period is:

```
=D28-D34
```

and so on.

Interest Expense

The Interest Expense figures show the amounts required to carry any debt used to fund portions of your asset or investment purchase. If you used no debt to fund the purchase, these amounts are 0.

The Interest Expense value for each period is the value you enter in the inputs area of the starter workbook.

Net Income (Loss) Before Taxes

The Net Income (Loss) Before Taxes figures represent the amounts of operating income left after paying any interest expense. These amounts represent your taxable operating profits.

The Net Income (Loss) Before Taxes figure for each period is the Operating Income figure minus the Interest Expense figure. For example, the formula for the first period is:

```
=C35-C37
```

The formula for the second period is:

```
=D35-D37
```

and so on.

Income Tax Expenses (Savings)

The Income Tax Expenses (Savings) figures show the forecasted income tax expenses (or savings) using the pretax operating profits calculated and the marginal income tax rates entered in the inputs area of the starter workbook.

The Income Tax Expenses (Savings) figure for each period is the Net Income (Loss) Before Taxes figure multiplied by the Marginal Income Tax Rate figure. For example, the formula for the first period is:

```
=C14*C38
```

The formula for the second period is:

```
=D14*D38
```

and so on.

Net Income (Loss) After Taxes

The Net Income (Loss) After Taxes figures show the after-tax profits of holding the asset or investment.

The Net Income (Loss) After Taxes value for each period is the Net Income (Loss) Before Taxes figure minus the Income Tax Expenses (Savings) figure. For example, the formula for the first period is:

```
=C38-40
```

The formula for the second period is:

```
=D38-D40
```

and so on.

Gain and Loss Statement

The Gain and Loss Statement schedule has seven rows of calculated data (see Figure 13-2).

Gross Residual

The Gross Residual figures show the total amounts for which the asset or investment can be liquidated for each period of the forecasting horizon. You enter these figures in the inputs area of the starter workbook.

Less: Transaction/Disposal Costs

The Transaction/Disposal Costs figures show the costs associated with liquidating the asset or investment for each period of the forecasting horizon. You enter these figures in the inputs area of the starter workbook.

Net Residual

The Net Residual figures are the amounts left over from liquidating an asset or investment after paying any transaction or disposal costs, using the Gross Residual figures and the Transaction/Disposal Costs figures.

The Net Residual figure for each period is the Gross Residual figure minus the Transaction/Disposal Costs figure. But because the Transaction/Disposal Costs figure is pulled into the Gain and Loss Statement schedule as a negative amount, the Net Residual formula simply adds the positive Gross Residual figure to the negative Transaction/Disposal Costs figure. For example, the formula for the first period is:

```
=C45+C46
```

The formula for the second period is:

```
=D45+D46
```

and so on.

Nontaxable Portion of Residual

The Nontaxable Portion of Residual figures show the amounts of the residuals that are not included in capital gains or losses calculations. You enter these figures in the inputs area of the starter workbook.

Pretax Gain (Loss) on Disposal

The Pretax Gain (Loss) on Disposal figures are the capital gains or losses that must be included in capital gains tax calculations.

The Pretax Gain (Loss) on Disposal figure for each period is the Net Residual figure minus the Nontaxable Portion of Residual figure. For example, the formula for the first period is:

```
=C47-C49
```

The formula for the second period is:

```
=D47-D49
```

and so on.

Income Tax Expenses (Savings)

The Income Tax Expenses (Savings) figures represent the tax effect of the liquidation of the asset or investment, calculated by using the Pretax Gain (Loss) on Disposal figures and the Marginal Income Tax Rate figures entered in the inputs area of the starter workbook.

The Income Tax Expenses (Savings) value for each period is calculated by multiplying the Marginal Tax Rate on Residual figure by the Pretax Gain (Loss) on Disposal figure. For example, the formula for the first period is:

```
=C50*C23
```

The formula for the second period is:

```
=D50*D23
```

and so on.

After-Tax Gain (Loss) on Disposal

The After-Tax Gain (Loss) on Disposal figures show the after-tax profit (or loss) from liquidating the asset or investment.

The After-Tax Gain (Loss) on Disposal value for each period is the Pretax Gain (Loss) on Disposal figure minus the Income Tax Expenses (Savings) figure stemming from the disposal. For example, the formula for the first period is:

```
=C50-C52
```

The formula for the second period is:

```
=D50-D52
```

and so on.

Operating Cash Flows Statement

The Operating Cash Flows Statement schedule has eight rows with calculated data, as shown in Figure 13-3.

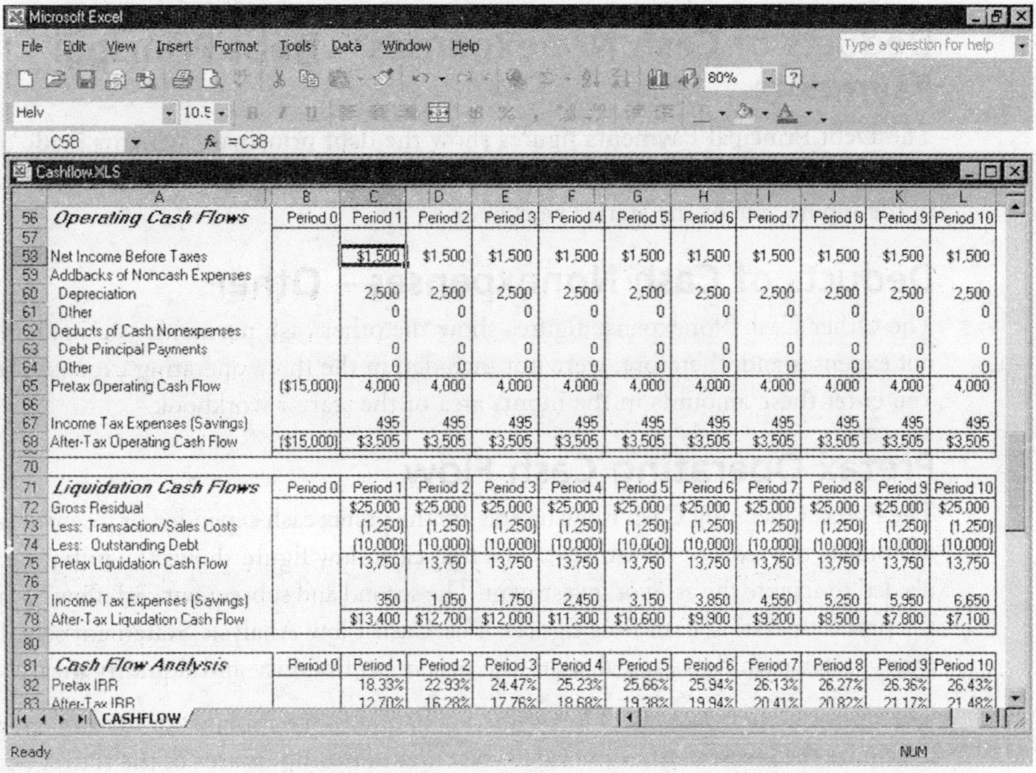

	A	B	C	D	E	F	G	H	I	J	K	L
56	*Operating Cash Flows*	Period 0	Period 1	Period 2	Period 3	Period 4	Period 5	Period 6	Period 7	Period 8	Period 9	Period 10
57												
58	Net Income Before Taxes		$1,500	$1,500	$1,500	$1,500	$1,500	$1,500	$1,500	$1,500	$1,500	$1,500
59	Addbacks of Noncash Expenses											
60	Depreciation		2,500	2,500	2,500	2,500	2,500	2,500	2,500	2,500	2,500	2,500
61	Other		0	0	0	0	0	0	0	0	0	0
62	Deducts of Cash Nonexpenses											
63	Debt Principal Payments		0	0	0	0	0	0	0	0	0	0
64	Other		0	0	0	0	0	0	0	0	0	0
65	Pretax Operating Cash Flow	($15,000)	4,000	4,000	4,000	4,000	4,000	4,000	4,000	4,000	4,000	4,000
66												
67	Income Tax Expenses (Savings)		495	495	495	495	495	495	495	495	495	495
68	After-Tax Operating Cash Flow	($15,000)	$3,505	$3,505	$3,505	$3,505	$3,505	$3,505	$3,505	$3,505	$3,505	$3,505
70												
71	*Liquidation Cash Flows*	Period 0	Period 1	Period 2	Period 3	Period 4	Period 5	Period 6	Period 7	Period 8	Period 9	Period 10
72	Gross Residual		$25,000	$25,000	$25,000	$25,000	$25,000	$25,000	$25,000	$25,000	$25,000	$25,000
73	Less: Transaction/Sales Costs		(1,250)	(1,250)	(1,250)	(1,250)	(1,250)	(1,250)	(1,250)	(1,250)	(1,250)	(1,250)
74	Less: Outstanding Debt		(10,000)	(10,000)	(10,000)	(10,000)	(10,000)	(10,000)	(10,000)	(10,000)	(10,000)	(10,000)
75	Pretax Liquidation Cash Flow		13,750	13,750	13,750	13,750	13,750	13,750	13,750	13,750	13,750	13,750
76												
77	Income Tax Expenses (Savings)		350	1,050	1,750	2,450	3,150	3,850	4,550	5,250	5,950	6,650
78	After-Tax Liquidation Cash Flow		$13,400	$12,700	$12,000	$11,300	$10,600	$9,900	$9,200	$8,500	$7,800	$7,100
80												
81	*Cash Flow Analysis*	Period 0	Period 1	Period 2	Period 3	Period 4	Period 5	Period 6	Period 7	Period 8	Period 9	Period 10
82	Pretax IRR		18.33%	22.93%	24.47%	25.23%	25.66%	25.94%	26.13%	26.27%	26.36%	26.43%
83	After-Tax IRR		12.70%	16.28%	17.76%	18.68%	19.38%	19.94%	20.41%	20.82%	21.17%	21.48%

Figure 13-3 The Operating Cash Flows and Liquidation Cash Flows schedules of the cash flow forecast and analysis starter workbook.

Net Income Before Taxes

The Net Income Before Taxes figure shows the pretax profits calculated on the Profit and Loss Statement.

Addbacks of Noncash Expenses – Depreciation

The Depreciation figures show the depreciation expenses included in the three operating expense classifications or categories. You enter these amounts in the inputs area of the starter workbook.

Addbacks of Noncash Expenses – Other

The Other Noncash Expenses figures show the other noncash expenses included in the three operating expense categories. You enter these amounts in the inputs area of the starter workbook.

Deducts of Cash Nonexpenses – Debt Principal Payments

The Debt Principal Payments figures show the debt principal payments made to reduce the debt used to fund a portion of the asset or investment purchase. You enter these amounts in the inputs area of the starter workbook.

Deducts of Cash Nonexpenses – Other

The Other Cash Nonexpense figures show the other cash payments you made that were not expenses and, therefore, were not included in the three operating expense categories. You enter these amounts in the inputs area of the starter workbook.

Pretax Operating Cash Flow

The Pretax Operating Cash Flow figures are the pretax cash expended or received as a result of holding the asset or investment. The first cash flow figure shows the initial cash outlay needed to acquire the asset or investment. The second and subsequent cash flow figures show the pretax operating cash flow figures. The Cash Flow Analysis Statement schedule uses these pretax cash flows to calculate the pretax profitability and liquidity measures.

The Pretax Operating Cash Flow value for Period 0, the initial cash investment required to acquire the investment, is the value you enter in the inputs area of the starter workbook. Notice that this amount is pulled into the Operating Cash Flows Statement schedule as a negative amount because it is an outflow. The Pretax Operating Cash Flow values for subsequent periods are calculated by adding noncash expenses to the net income (Loss) Before Taxes figure and subtracting the Other Cash Nonexpenses figure from the Net Income (Loss) Before Taxes figure. For example, the formula for the first period is:

```
=C58+C60+C61-C63-C64
```

The formula for the second is:

```
=D58+D60+D61-D63-D64
```

and so on.

Income Tax Expenses (Savings)

The Income Tax Expenses (Savings) figures show the income tax expenses (or savings) calculated in the Profit and Loss Statement schedule.

After-Tax Operating Cash Flow

The After-Tax Operating Cash Flow figures are calculated by using the Pretax Operating Cash Flow figures and the Income Tax Expenses (Savings) figures. The Cash Flow Analysis schedule uses these after-tax cash flows to calculate the after-tax profitability and liquidity measures.

The After-Tax Operating Cash Flow value for Period 0, the initial cash investment, is pulled from the cell containing the pretax operating cash flow (B65). The figures for subsequent periods are calculated as the Pretax Operating Cash Flow figure minus the Income Tax Expenses (Savings) figure. For example, the first-period formula is:

```
=C65-C67
```

The formula for the second period is:

```
=D65-D67
```

and so on.

Liquidation Cash Flow Statement

The Liquidation Cash Flow Statement schedule has six rows with calculated data (see Figure 13-3).

Gross Residual

The Gross Residual figures show the amounts for which the asset or investment can be sold. You enter these amounts in the inputs area of the starter workbook.

Less: Transaction/Sales Costs

The Transaction/Sales Costs figures show the expenses of liquidating the asset or investment. You enter these amounts in the inputs area of the starter workbook.

Less: Outstanding Debt

The Outstanding Debt figures show the principal balances of any debt used to fund portions of the asset or investment purchase. You enter these amounts in the inputs area of the starter workbook.

Pretax Liquidation Cash Flow

The Pretax Liquidation Cash Flow figure is calculated as the Gross Residual figure minus the Transaction/Sales Costs figure and minus the Outstanding Debt figure. But because the Transaction/Sales Costs figure and the Outstanding Debt figure are pulled into the Liquidation Cash Flow Statement schedule as negative amounts, the Pretax Liquidation Cash Flow formula simply adds the Gross Residual figure to the negative Transaction/Sales Costs figure and the negative Outstanding Debt figure. For example, the formula for the first period is:

```
=C72+C73+C74
```

The formula for the second period is:

```
=D72+D73+D74
```

and so on.

Income Tax Expenses (Savings)

Income Tax Expenses (Savings) figures show any capital gains taxes associated with liquidating the asset or investment.

The figure for each period is the value calculated in the Gain and Loss Statement schedule.

After-Tax Liquidation Cash Flow

The After-Tax Liquidation Cash Flow figures are the after-tax cash received as a result of liquidating an asset or investment at the end of the period.

The After-Tax Liquidation Cash Flow value for each period is the Pretax Liquidation Cash Flow figure minus the Income Tax expenses (Savings) figure. For example, the formula for the first period is:

```
=C75-C77
```

The formula for the second period is:

```
=D75-D77
```

and so on.

Cash Flow Analysis

The Cash Flow Analysis schedule calculates the profitability and liquidity measures for each of the alternative holding periods, as shown in Figure 13-4. The schedule has 10 rows with calculated data. The values for Pretax IRR, After-Tax IRR, Pretax Adjusted IRR, After-Tax Adjusted IRR, Pretax Net Present Value, and After-Tax Net Present Value are similar in that the value shown in the Period 1 column assumes that the asset or investment is purchased at the beginning of the first period (Period 0), is held for one period, and then is sold at the end of the first period. Similarly, the values shown in the subsequent period columns assume that the asset or investment is purchased at the beginning of the first period and then is sold at the end of the indicated period. These values often fluctuate, depending on the holding period. By developing and examining the values delivered by the asset or investment under alternative holding periods, you can choose holding periods that enhance profits. For example, a 10% pretax internal rate of return of an asset or investment held for three years means you get back not only all your initial investment but a dime a year for every dollar invested. An 8% pretax internal rate of return for the same asset or investment held for four years means you get back all your initial investment but only eight cents for every dollar invested a year.

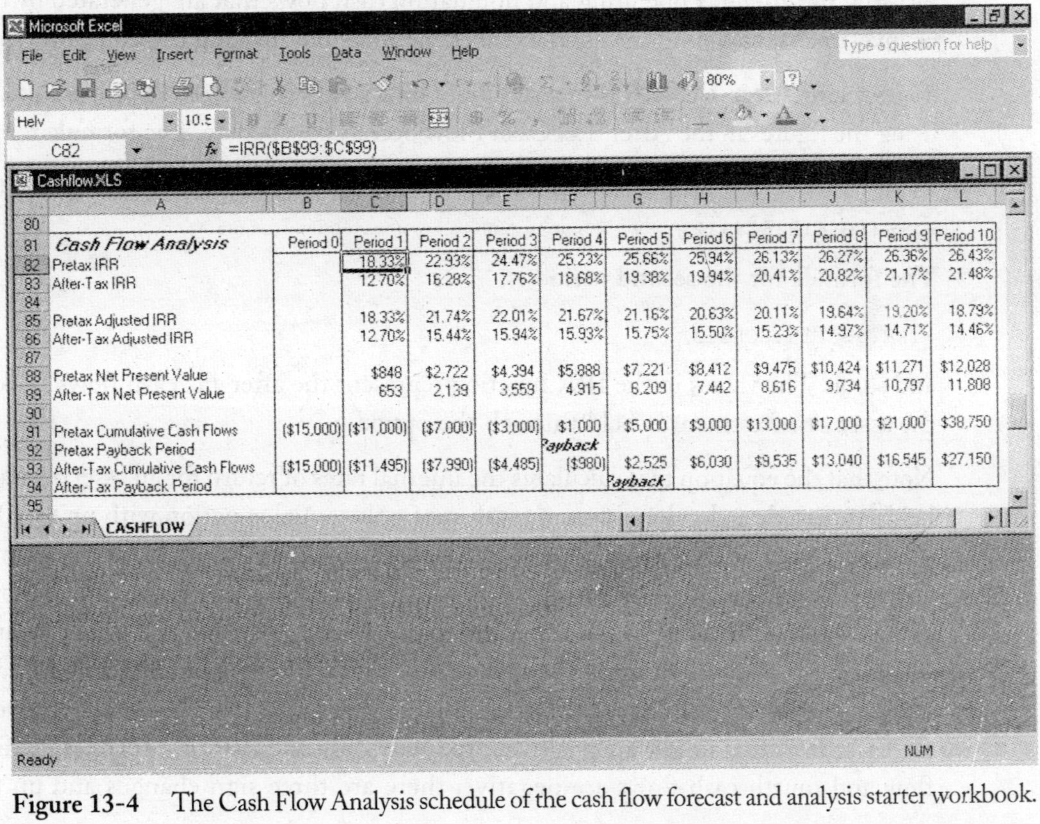

Figure 13-4 The Cash Flow Analysis schedule of the cash flow forecast and analysis starter workbook.

Pretax IRR

The Pretax IRR figures are the pretax internal rates of return, which are calculated by using the pretax operating and liquidation cash flows that are generated by the asset or investment, assuming the asset or investment is held through the end of the period.

The specific Pretax IRR (internal rate of return) figure for each period is calculated by using the figures in the Pretax Cash Flow Scenarios schedule. The formula for the first period is:

```
=IRR($B$99:$C$99)
```

The formula for the second period is:

```
=IRR($B$100:$C$100)
```

and so on. The values in the IRR function represent the pretax cash flows forecasted if the asset or investment is held through the period.

After-Tax IRR

The After-Tax IRR figures are the after-tax internal rates of return, which are calculated by using the after-tax operating and liquidation cash flows that are generated by the asset or investment, assuming the asset or investment is held through the end of the period.

The specific After-Tax IRR (internal rate of return) figure for each period is calculated by using the figures in the After-Tax Cash Flow Scenarios schedule. The formula for the first period is:

```
=IRR($B$112:$C$112)
```

The formula for the second period is:

```
=IRR($B$113:$C$113)
```

and so on. The values in the IRR function represent the after-tax cash flows forecasted if the asset or investment is held through the period.

Note that the equation that calculates the internal rates of return for an asset or investment held 10 periods is, by definition, a tenth root polynomial equation with up to 10 correct solutions. Accordingly, several internal rates of return can be correct for any investment you analyze. Be particularly careful in applying the internal rate of return measure to those assets or investments for which cash flows fluctuate between positive and negative amounts. Generally, an asset or investment has as many correct IRRs as sign changes in the cash flow. If there is only one sign change—for example, if the initial investment is negative and all the cash flows that follow are positive—you have only one IRR. However, if the first cash flow and fourth cash flows are negative, there are three sign changes and up to three correct IRRs. (The first sign change is the initial negative cash flow changing to positive, the second is the third-period changing to the fourth-period negative, and the third is the fourth-period negative changing to the fifth-period positive cash flow.) For this reason, you might want to use the adjusted rate of return or the net present value profit measure instead of the internal rate of return measure.

Pretax Adjusted IRR

The Pretax Adjusted IRR figures are the pretax internal rates of return, which are calculated by using the pretax operating and liquidation cash flows that are generated by the asset or investment, assuming that the asset or investment is held through the end of the period and assuming that any interim cash flows are reinvested at the pretax reinvestment rate specified in the inputs area of the starter workbook. (Notice that in Period 1, because there would be no interim cash flows—both the operating and liquidation cash flows occur at the end of the first period—the pretax adjusted IRR equals the pretax IRR.) This schedule assumes that when you buy an asset or make an investment at the beginning of the first period and sell at the end of the second period, you reinvest the operating cash flow generated by the investment in the first period at the pretax reinvestment rate specified in the inputs area of the starter workbook until the end of the second period.

The figure for each period's Pretax Adjusted IRR (internal rate of return adjusted for reinvestment of the interim cash flows) is calculated by using the figures in the Pretax Cash Flow Scenarios schedule and the Pretax Reinvestment Rate figure specified in the inputs area of the starter workbook. The formula for the first period is:

```
=MIRR($B$99:$C$99,,$B$4)
```

The formula for the second period is:

```
=MIRR($B$100:$C$100,,$B$4)
```

and so on. The values used in the MIRR function represent the pretax cash flows forecasted if the asset or investment is held through the period. The contents of the cell referenced by $B$4 is the pretax reinvestment rate.

After-Tax Adjusted IRR

The After-Tax Adjusted IRR figures are the after-tax internal rates of return, which are calculated by using the after-tax operating and liquidation cash flows that are generated by the asset or investment, assuming the asset or investment is held through the end of the period and assuming that any interim cash flows are reinvested at the after-tax reinvestment rate specified in the inputs area of the starter workbook. (Notice that in Period 1, because there would be no interim cash flows—both the operating and liquidation cash flows occur at the end of the first period—the after-tax adjusted IRR equals the after-tax IRR.) This schedule assumes that when you buy an asset or make an investment at the beginning of the first period and sell at the end of the second period, you reinvest the operating cash flow generated by the investment in the first period at the after-tax reinvestment rate specified in the inputs area of the starter workbook until the end of the second period.

The figure for each period's After-Tax Adjusted IRR (internal rate of return adjusted for reinvestment of the interim cash flows) is calculated by using the figures in the After-Tax Cash Flow Scenarios schedule and the After-Tax Reinvestment Rate figure specified in the inputs area of the starter workbook. The formula for the first period is:

```
=MIRR($B$112:$C$112,,$B$5)
```

The formula for the second period is:

```
=MIRR($B$113:$C$113,,$B$5)
```

and so on. The values in the MIRR function represent the after-tax cash flows forecasted if the asset or investment is held through the period. The contents of the cell referenced by $B$5 is the after-tax reinvestment rate.

Pretax Net Present Value

The Pretax Net Present Value figures are calculated by using the pretax operating and liquidation cash flows generated by the asset or investment, assuming the asset or investment is held through the end of the period, and by using the pretax discount rate specified in the inputs area of the starter workbook. Pretax net present values are significant in that they express in current cash the amount by which the investment falls short of or exceeds the time value of money specified by the pretax discount rate. For example, a $1,000 net present value of an asset or investment held for three years means that holding the investment for three years returns $1,000 more (in the current dollar value) than the pretax discount rate specifies. A negative $500 net present value for the same asset or investment held four years means that holding the asset or investment for four years returns $500 less (in current dollar value) than the pretax discount rate specifies. The pretax net present values often fluctuate, depending on the holding period. By developing and examining the pretax net present values delivered by the asset or investment under alternative holding periods, you can choose holding periods to enhance pretax profits.

For instance, in the example introduced in the preceding sentences, you actually lose $1,500 by holding the investment an additional (fourth) year. (The $1,500 of loss is the difference between making $1,000, which is what happens if you hold the investment for three years, and losing $500, which is what happens if you hold the investment for four years.)

The Pretax Net Present Value figure for each period is calculated by using the figures in the Pretax Cash Flow Scenarios schedule and the Pretax Discount Rate figure specified in the inputs area of the starter workbook. The formula for the first period is:

```
=NPV($B$6,$C$99:$C$99)+$B$99
```

The formula for the second period is:

```
=NPV($B$6,$C$100:$C$100)+$B$100
```

and so on. The values in the NPV function represent the pretax cash flows forecasted if the asset or investment is held through the period. The contents of the cell referenced by $B$6 is the pretax discount rate. The amount added to the NPV function is the initial investment.

After-Tax Net Present Value

The After-Tax Net Present Value figures are calculated by using the after-tax operating and liquidation cash flows generated by the asset or investment, assuming the asset or investments held through the end of the period, and by using the after-tax discount rate specified in the inputs area of the starter workbook. After-tax net present values are significant in that they express in current cash the amount by which the investment falls short of or exceeds the time value of money specified by the after-tax discount rate. For example, a $1,000 net present value of an asset or investment held for three years means that holding the investment for three years returns $1,000 more (in current dollar value) than the after-tax discount rate specifies. A negative $500 net present value for the same asset or investment held four years means that holding the asset or investment for four years returns $500 less (in current dollar value) than the after-tax discount rate specifies. The after-tax net present value often fluctuates, depending on the holding period. By developing and examining the after-tax net present values delivered by the asset or investment under alternative holding periods, you can choose holding periods to enhance after-tax profits. For example, in the example introduced in the preceding sentences, you lose $1,500 by holding the investment an additional (fourth) year.

The After-Tax Net Present Value figure for each period is calculated by using the figures in the After-Tax Cash Flow Scenarios schedule and the After-Tax Discount Rate figure specified in the inputs area of the starter workbook. The formula for the first period is:

```
=NPV($B$7,$C$112:$C$112)+$B$112
```

The formula for the second period is:

```
=NPV($B$7,$C$113:$C$113)+$B$113
```

and so on. The values in the NPV function represent the after-tax cash flows forecasted if the asset or investment is held through the period. The contents of the cell referenced by $B$7 is the after-tax reinvestment rate. The amount added to the NPV function is the initial investment.

Pretax Cumulative Cash Flows

The Pretax Cumulative Cash Flows figures represent the cumulative cash flows that result from holding the asset or investment, which are calculated by using the pretax cash flows from the Pretax Cash Flows Scenarios schedule, assuming the investment is held for 10 periods. The period during which the cumulative cash flow figure turns from a negative amount to a positive amount indicates the period in which the investment pays back the original cash invested—a common measure of liquidity.

The Pretax Cumulative Cash Flows figure for each period is calculated by using the 10-period holding scenario in the Pretax Cash Flow Scenarios schedule. The formula in the Period 0 column for the initial investment is:

```
=SUM($B$108:B108)
```

The formula for the first period is:

```
=SUM($B$108:C108)
```

The formula for the second period is:

```
=SUM($B$108:D108)
```

and so on. The results represent the cumulative pretax cash flows through the period.

Pretax Payback Period

The Pretax Payback Period is a text flag (the word *Payback*) that identifies the period during which the initial investment and any negative operating cash flows are finally paid back. The text flag appears in the column for the period in which the cumulative cash flow changes from negative to positive.

The Pretax Payback Period formulas determine whether the cumulative pretax cash flow has turned from a negative amount, indicating that the initial investment has not been fully paid back, to a positive amount, indicating that the initial investment has been paid back. The formula for the first period is:

```
=IF((AND(B91<0,C91>=0))=TRUE(),"Payback","")
```

The formula for the second period is:

```
=IF((AND(C91<0,D91>=0))=TRUE(),"Payback","")
```

and so on. For the period during which the initial investment is finally paid back, the text flag *Payback* appears in the column.

After-Tax Cumulative Cash Flows

The After-Tax Cumulative Cash Flows figures represent the cumulative cash flows that result from holding the asset or investment calculated by using the after-tax cash flows as calculated in the After-Tax Cash Flow Scenarios schedule, assuming the investment is held for 10 periods. The period during which the cumulative cash flow figure turns from a negative amount to a positive amount indicates the period in which the investment pays back the original cash invested—a common measure of liquidity.

The After-Tax Cumulative Cash Flows figure for each period is calculated by using the 10-year holding period scenario in the After-Tax Cash Flow Scenarios schedule. The formula for the initial investment is:

```
=SUM($B$121:B121)
```

The formula for the first period is:

```
=SUM($B$121:C121)
```

The formula for the second period is:

```
=SUM($B$121:D121)
```

and so on. The results represent the cumulative after-tax cash flows through the period.

After-Tax Payback Period

The After-Tax Payback Period is a text flag (the word *Payback*) that identifies the period during which the initial investment and any negative operating cash flows are finally paid back. The text flag appears in the column for the period in which the cumulative cash flow moves from a negative amount to a positive amount.

The After-Tax Payback Period formulas determine whether the cumulative after-tax cash flow has turned from a negative amount, indicating that the initial investment has not been fully paid back, to a positive amount, indicating that the initial investment has been paid back. The formula for the first period is:

```
=IF((AND(B93<0,C93>=0))=TRUE(),"Payback","")
```

The formula for the second period is:

```
=IF((AND(C93<0,D93>=0))=TRUE(),"Payback","")
```

and so on. For the period during which the initial investment is finally paid back, the text flag *Payback* appears in the column.

Pretax Cash Flow Scenarios

The Pretax Cash Flow Scenarios schedule has 12 rows (see Figure 13-5). These are the forecasted cash flows for the alternative holding periods and are used to calculate the profitability and liquidity measures in the Cash Flow Analysis schedule. You will probably use this schedule only indirectly because it provides the raw data used to calculate the profitability measures. However, to read the schedule, you simply look down column A, which describes the various lengths of time you can hold the asset or investment, until you come to the number of periods held that you want to examine—that row then shows the cash flows occurring each period for the number-of-periods-held scenario. For example, suppose you want to view the pretax cash flows if the investment is held for 5 periods. You first look down the first column of the Pretax Cash Flow Scenarios column. When you come to 5, you're at the row that shows the cash flows that assume you hold the asset or investment for 5 periods. The negative amount in column B shows the period 0 cash flow ($15,000 in Figure 13-5). The positive amounts in columns C through F in Figure 13-5 show the operating cash flow $4,000. The positive cash flow in column G shows the combined operating and liquidation cash flows as $17,750. Notice that in columns H and beyond, representing periods and beyond, the amounts appear as 0 because the asset or investment has been disposed of and, therefore, no longer results in cash flows.

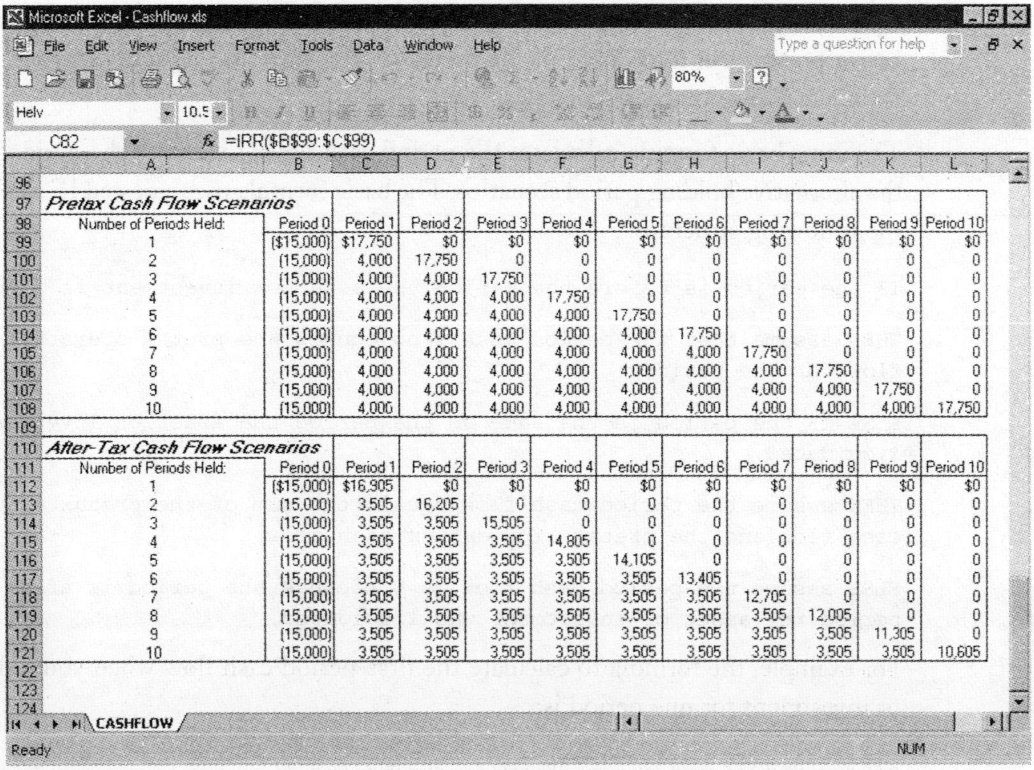

Pretax Cash Flow Scenarios											
Number of Periods Held:	Period 0	Period 1	Period 2	Period 3	Period 4	Period 5	Period 6	Period 7	Period 8	Period 9	Period 10
1	($15,000)	$17,750	$0	$0	$0	$0	$0	$0	$0	$0	$0
2	(15,000)	4,000	17,750	0	0	0	0	0	0	0	0
3	(15,000)	4,000	4,000	17,750	0	0	0	0	0	0	0
4	(15,000)	4,000	4,000	4,000	17,750	0	0	0	0	0	0
5	(15,000)	4,000	4,000	4,000	4,000	17,750	0	0	0	0	0
6	(15,000)	4,000	4,000	4,000	4,000	4,000	17,750	0	0	0	0
7	(15,000)	4,000	4,000	4,000	4,000	4,000	4,000	17,750	0	0	0
8	(15,000)	4,000	4,000	4,000	4,000	4,000	4,000	4,000	17,750	0	0
9	(15,000)	4,000	4,000	4,000	4,000	4,000	4,000	4,000	4,000	17,750	0
10	(15,000)	4,000	4,000	4,000	4,000	4,000	4,000	4,000	4,000	4,000	17,750

After-Tax Cash Flow Scenarios											
Number of Periods Held:	Period 0	Period 1	Period 2	Period 3	Period 4	Period 5	Period 6	Period 7	Period 8	Period 9	Period 10
1	($15,000)	$16,905	$0	$0	$0	$0	$0	$0	$0	$0	$0
2	(15,000)	3,505	16,205	0	0	0	0	0	0	0	0
3	(15,000)	3,505	3,505	15,505	0	0	0	0	0	0	0
4	(15,000)	3,505	3,505	3,505	14,805	0	0	0	0	0	0
5	(15,000)	3,505	3,505	3,505	3,505	14,105	0	0	0	0	0
6	(15,000)	3,505	3,505	3,505	3,505	3,505	13,405	0	0	0	0
7	(15,000)	3,505	3,505	3,505	3,505	3,505	3,505	12,705	0	0	0
8	(15,000)	3,505	3,505	3,505	3,505	3,505	3,505	3,505	12,005	0	0
9	(15,000)	3,505	3,505	3,505	3,505	3,505	3,505	3,505	3,505	11,305	0
10	(15,000)	3,505	3,505	3,505	3,505	3,505	3,505	3,505	3,505	3,505	10,605

Figure 13-5 The Pretax and After-Tax Cash Flow Scenarios schedules of the cash flow forecast and analysis starter workbook.

Period 0

The values in the Period 0 cash flows column show the initial cash outlay to acquire the asset or investment and are the same for each of the alternative holding periods.

The Period 0 cash flow, which is the initial cash outlay to acquire the asset or investment, is the same for each of the holding periods in the Pretax Cash Flow Scenarios schedule.

Period 1 Through 10

The period cash flows show the forecasted pretax cash flow stemming from holding and perhaps disposing of an asset or investment for each of 10 periods. For example, the Period 1 pretax cash flow for holding period 1 equals the sum of both the pretax operating cash flow and the pretax liquidation cash flow for the first period; cash flows beyond the first period equal 0, signifying that asset or investment has been liquidated. Similarly, the Period 2 pretax cash flow for holding period 2 equals the sum of the pretax operating cash flow and the pretax liquidation cash flow for the second period; cash flows for Period 3 and beyond for holding Period 2 equal 0. The Period 1 pretax cash flow for holding period 2 equals the pretax operating cash flow for the first period. This schedule provides the alternative pretax cash flows used in the pretax profitability and liquidity measures shown in the Cash Flow Analysis schedule.

The same basic formula calculates the period cash flows for any of the periods in each of the alternative holding period scenarios. The basic formula uses a nested IF statement with the following structure:

```
IF the period is before the period the asset or investment is liquidated,

THEN assume that the period cash flow equals the pretax operating cash
flow for the period,

ELSE IF the period is the same as the period the asset or investment is
liquidated,

THEN assume the period cash flow equals the sum of the pretax operating
cash flow and the pretax liquidation cash flow,

ELSE assume the period cash flow is 0 because the period is after the
period the asset or investment was liquidated.
```

For example, the formula to calculate the first-period cash flow when you hold the asset or investment for one period is:

```
=IF(C$98<$A99,C$65,IF(C$98=$A99,C$65+C$75,0))
```

The formula to calculate the second-period cash flow when you hold the asset or investment for one period is:

```
=IF(D$98<$A99,D$65,IF(D$98=$A99,D$65+D$75,0))
```

The formula to calculate the first-period cash flow when you hold the asset or investment for two periods is:

```
=IF(C$98<$A100,C$65,IF(C$98=$A100,C$65+C$75,0))
```

The formula to calculate the second-period cash flow when you hold the asset or investment for two periods is:

```
=IF(D$98<$A100,D$65,IF(D$98=$A100,D$65+D$75,0))
```

and so on.

After-Tax Cash Flow Scenarios

The After-Tax Cash Flow Scenarios schedule has 12 rows (see Figure 13-5). These are the forecasted cash flows for the alternative holding periods and are used to calculate the profitability and liquidity measures in the Cash Flow Analysis schedule.

Period 0

The values in the Period 0 cash flow column show the initial cash outlay to acquire the asset or investment and are the same for each of the alternative holding periods.

The Period 0 cash flow, which is the initial cash outlay to acquire the asset or investment, is the same for each of the holding periods in the After-Tax Cash Flow Scenarios schedule.

Period 1 Through 10

The period cash flows show the forecasted after-tax cash flow stemming from holding and perhaps disposing of an asset or investment for each of 10 periods. For example, the Period 1 after-tax cash flow for holding period 1 equals the sum of both the after-tax operating cash flow and the after-tax liquidation cash flow for the first period; cash flows beyond the first period equal 0, signifying that the asset or investment has been liquidated. Similarly, the Period 2 after-tax cash flow for holding period 2 equals the sum of the after-tax liquidation cash flow for the second period; cash flows for Period 3 and beyond for holding period 2 equal 0. The Period 1 after-tax cash flow for holding period 2 equals the after-tax operating cash flow for the first period. This schedule provides the alternative after-tax cash flows used in the after-tax profitability and liquidity measures shown in the Cash Flow Analysis schedule.

The same basic formula calculates the period cash flows for any of the periods in each of the alternative holding period scenarios. The basic formula uses a compound IF function statement with the following structure:

```
IF the period is before the period the asset or investment is liquidated,

THEN assume that the period cash flow equals the after-tax operating cash
flow for the period,

ELSE IF the period is the same as the period the asset or investment is
liquidated,

THEN assume the period cash flow equals the sum of the after-tax operating
cash flow and the after-tax liquidation cash flow,

ELSE assume the period cash flow is 0 because the period is after the
period the asset or investment was liquidated.
```

For example, the formula to calculate the first-period cash flow when you hold the asset or investment for one period is:

```
=IF(C$111<$A112,C$68,IF(C$111=$A112,C$68+C$78,0))
```

The formula to calculate the second-period cash flow when you hold the asset or investment for one period is:

```
=IF(D$111<$A112,D$68,IF(D$111=$A112,D$68+D$78,0))
```

The formula to calculate the first-period cash flow when you hold the asset or investment for one period is:

```
=IF(C$111<$A113,C$68,IF(C$111=$A113,C$68+C$78,0))
```

The formula to calculate the second-period cash flow when you hold the asset or investment for two periods is:

```
=IF(D$111<$A113,D$68,IF(D$111=$A113,D$68+D$78,0))
```

and so on.

Customizing the Starter Workbook

You can use the cash flow forecast and analysis starter workbook without modification for many cash flow forecasts and analyses. However, you might want to change the workbook so that it more closely matches your requirements. For example, you can add text that describes the asset or investment for which cash flows are forecasted and analyzed. You can increase or decrease the number of periods. For example, you can increase the number of periods to 12 if your periods are months and you want to forecast an entire year. You might also want to remove either the pretax or the after-tax profitability and liquidity measures if you don't consider one or the other in your decision making. Before you change anything in the workbook other than the forecasting inputs, unprotect the document.

Changing the Number of Forecasting Periods

You can rather easily increase and decrease the number of forecasting periods shown in the cash flow forecast and analysis starter workbook.

To increase the number of periods, follow these steps:

1. Remove the border from the last column of the cash flow forecast and analysis schedules.
2. Copy the current last column of the cash flow forecast and analysis schedules to the right as needed.
3. Replace the border on the right of the cash flow forecast and analysis schedules.
4. Insert the same number of rows below the Pretax Cash Flow Scenarios matrix in the same way that you added columns to the cash flow forecast and analysis summary.
5. Remove the bottom borders of the Pretax Cash Flow Scenarios and After-Tax Cash Flow Scenarios schedules.
6. Copy the last row of both the Pretax Cash Flow Scenarios and After-Tax Cash Flow Scenarios into the same number of rows in the same way that you added columns to the cash flow forecast and analysis summary.
7. Replace the bottom borders on both the Pretax Cash Flow Scenarios and the After-Tax Cash Flow Scenarios schedules.
8. Adjust the pretax and after-tax internal rate of return, adjusted rate of return, and net present value formulas for the new columns so that the cash flow value arguments in the IRR, MIRR, and NPV functions use the correct row of the Pretax Cash Flow Scenarios or After-Tax Cash Flow Scenarios.

To decrease the number of periods, follow these steps:

1. Delete any unneeded columns from the right side of the schedule.
2. In the Pretax Cash Flow Scenarios and After-Tax Cash Flow Scenarios schedules, delete the rows that correspond to the columns you deleted.

Removing the Pretax Profitability and Liquidity Measures

To remove the pretax profitability and liquidity measures from the spreadsheet, follow these steps:

1. Delete the Pretax Cash Flow Scenarios schedule.
2. From the Cash Flow Analysis schedule, delete the Pretax IRR, the Pretax Adjusted IRR, the Pretax Net Present Value, the Pretax Cumulative Cash Flows, and the Pretax Payback Period rows.

Removing the After-Tax Profitability and Liquidity Measures

To remove the after-tax profitability and liquidity measures from the spreadsheet, follow these steps:

1. Delete the After-Tax Cash Flow Scenarios schedule.
2. From the Cash Flow Analysis schedule, delete the After-Tax IRR, the After-Tax Adjusted IRR, the After-Tax Net Present Value, the After-Tax Cumulative Cash Flows, and the After-Tax Payback Period rows.

Combining This Workbook with Other Workbooks

Other workbooks on the companion CD are specifically designed to provide data for the cash flow forecast and analysis starter workbook. In fact, each of the starter workbooks described in the next two chapters provides data that can be used as input for this starter workbook: one of the asset depreciation workbooks can provide the depreciation expenses and the net book value (representing the nontaxable portion of the residual), one of the debt amortization workbooks can provide the interest expense and debt principal payments for each period and the outstanding debt amount, the cost center workbook can be used to construct detailed forecasts of various categories of expenses, and the sales forecasting workbook can be used to develop the sales and cost of sales figures.

NOTE *For detailed instructions on combining one worksheet with another, refer to Chapter 10.*

Chapter 14

BUILDING AMORTIZATION SCHEDULES

Featuring:

- EasyRefresher™: Amortizing Debt
- Using the Debt Amortization Starter Workbooks
- Understanding the Fixed Rate, Ordinary Annuity Amortization Starter Workbook
- Understanding the Fixed Rate, Annuity Due Amortization Starter Workbook
- Understanding the Variable Rate, Ordinary Annuity Amortization Starter Workbook
- Understanding the Variable Rate, Annuity Due Amortization Starter Workbook
- Customizing the Debt Amortization Starter Workbooks

Debt amortization schedules ensure that your financial models and accounting records of amortized debt instruments are precise and accurate. Using an amortization schedule lets you track the principal balance, debt service payments, and principal and interest components of the payments on a debt instrument.

The debt amortization starter workbooks in this chapter automate the preparation of debt amortization schedules and provide foundations for customizing schedules. These starter workbooks (and the amortization conventions they use) are as follows:

- FIXRATE.XLS (fixed interest rate, ordinary annuity)
- FIXDUE.XLS (fixed interest rate, annuity due)
- VARIRATE.XLS (variable interest rate, ordinary annuity)
- VARIDUE.XLS (variable interest rate, annuity due)

EasyRefresher™: Amortizing Debt

Debt amortization is the systematic reduction in debt principal made over the term, or life, of the debt through periodic debt service payments. In general, five variables can determine the amortization of a debt: principal, interest rate, amortization term, debt term, and debt service payment. The principal is the amount to be amortized, or paid back. The interest rate is the percentage that, when multiplied by the principal at the beginning of the period, calculates the amount of interest. The amortization term is the number of payment periods over which the principal can be completely paid back, given a constant debt service payment. The debt term is the number of time periods over which the debt is outstanding. Although the debt term is generally the same as the amortization term, it can be shorter. In those cases, a balloon payment equal to the unamortized principal is made at the end of the debt term. The debt service payment is the combined principal and interest payment made every period over the debt term.

The timing of a payment—whether it's at the beginning or at the end of the period—also affects the amortization of a debt. Payments made at the end of the period are called payments in arrears, or ordinary annuities. Payments made at the beginning of the period are called payments in advance, or annuities due.

Excel's PMT function calculates the payment that, given the interest rate and the principal, completely pays off the debt principal over the amortization term.

The payment is calculated by using the PMT function, which uses the following formulas:

```
Payment for an ordinary annuity=Principal/Present Value factor of the ordinary annuity for i and n
Payment for an annuity due=Principal/Present Value factor of the annuity due for i and n
```

where i is the period interest rate and n is the number of periods.

All of the variables are defined by the terms of the contract that describes the debt instrument. Accordingly, your best source for determining these variables is the debt contract.

TIP *Be consistent in the financial measurement time periods you use. If you're building a debt amortization schedule with monthly payments, express your debt and amortization terms in months and use a monthly interest rate. If you're building a debt amortization schedule with quarterly or yearly payments, express your debt and amortization terms in quarters or years and use a quarterly or yearly interest rate.*

Using the Debt Amortization Starter Workbooks

You can use the debt amortization starter workbooks, as shown in Figures 14-1 through 14-4, to construct debt amortization schedules for a variety of debt instruments.

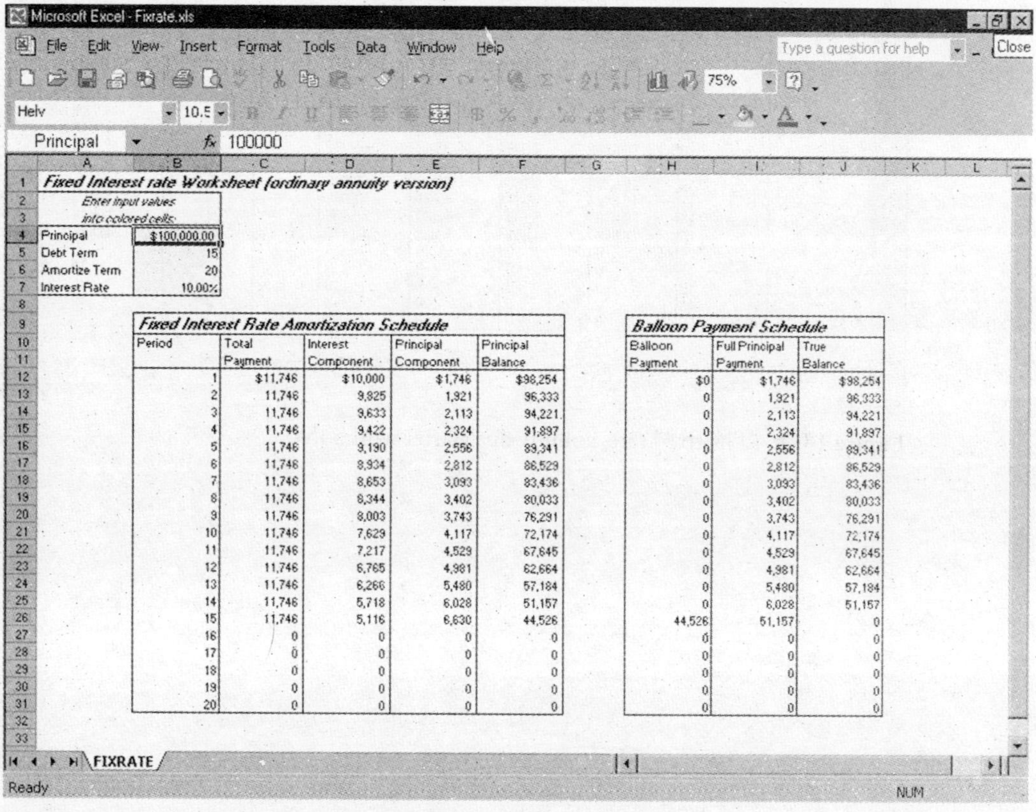

Fixed Interest rate Worksheet (ordinary annuity version)

Enter input values into colored cells:

Principal	$100,000.00
Debt Term	15
Amortize Term	20
Interest Rate	10.00%

Fixed Interest Rate Amortization Schedule					Balloon Payment Schedule		
Period	Total Payment	Interest Component	Principal Component	Principal Balance	Balloon Payment	Full Principal Payment	True Balance
1	$11,746	$10,000	$1,746	$98,254	$0	$1,746	$98,254
2	11,746	9,825	1,921	96,333	0	1,921	96,333
3	11,746	9,633	2,113	94,221	0	2,113	94,221
4	11,746	9,422	2,324	91,897	0	2,324	91,897
5	11,746	9,190	2,556	89,341	0	2,556	89,341
6	11,746	8,934	2,812	86,529	0	2,812	86,529
7	11,746	8,653	3,093	83,436	0	3,093	83,436
8	11,746	8,344	3,402	80,033	0	3,402	80,033
9	11,746	8,003	3,743	76,291	0	3,743	76,291
10	11,746	7,629	4,117	72,174	0	4,117	72,174
11	11,746	7,217	4,529	67,645	0	4,529	67,645
12	11,746	6,765	4,981	62,664	0	4,981	62,664
13	11,746	6,266	5,480	57,184	0	5,480	57,184
14	11,746	5,718	6,028	51,157	0	6,028	51,157
15	11,746	5,116	6,630	44,526	44,526	51,157	0
16	0	0	0	0	0	0	0
17	0	0	0	0	0	0	0
18	0	0	0	0	0	0	0
19	0	0	0	0	0	0	0
20	0	0	0	0	0	0	0

Figure 14-1 The fixed rate, ordinary annuity starter workbook.

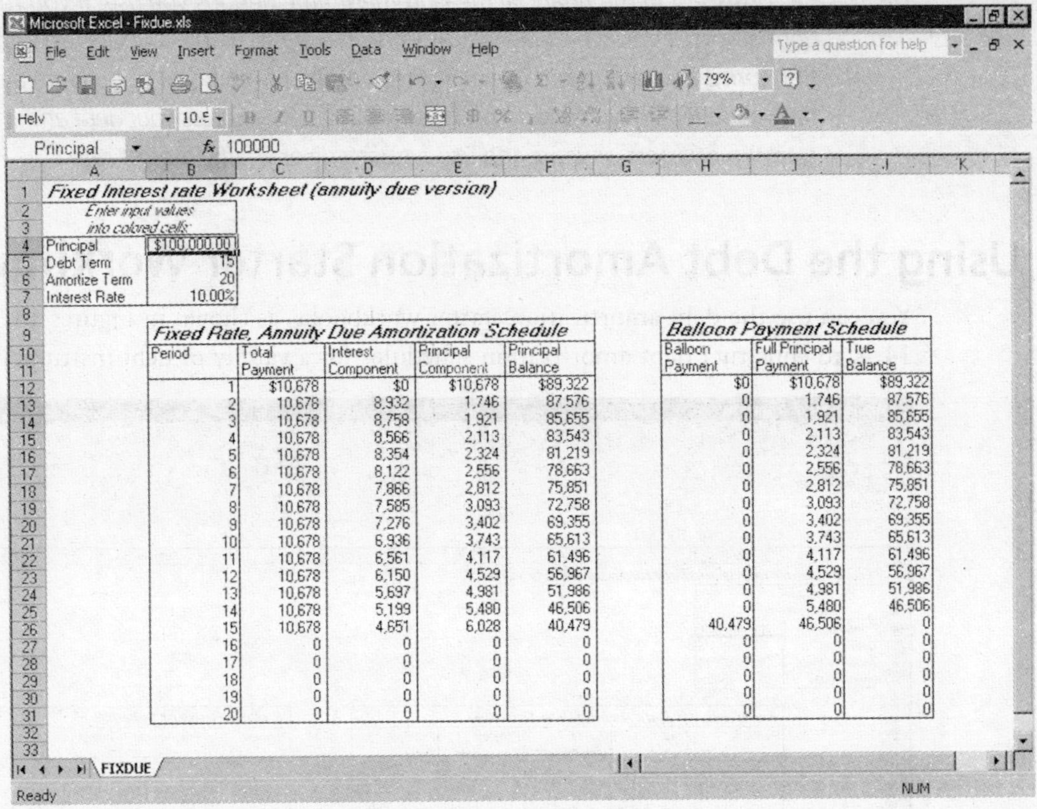

Fixed Interest rate Worksheet (annuity due version)

Enter input values into colored cells

Principal	$100,000.00
Debt Term	15
Amortize Term	20
Interest Rate	10.00%

Fixed Rate, Annuity Due Amortization Schedule

Period	Total Payment	Interest Component	Principal Component	Principal Balance
1	$10,678	$0	$10,678	$89,322
2	10,678	8,932	1,746	87,576
3	10,678	8,758	1,921	85,655
4	10,678	8,566	2,113	83,543
5	10,678	8,354	2,324	81,219
6	10,678	8,122	2,556	78,663
7	10,678	7,866	2,812	75,851
8	10,678	7,585	3,093	72,758
9	10,678	7,276	3,402	69,355
10	10,678	6,936	3,743	65,613
11	10,678	6,561	4,117	61,496
12	10,678	6,150	4,529	56,967
13	10,678	5,697	4,981	51,986
14	10,678	5,199	5,480	46,506
15	10,678	4,651	6,028	40,479
16	0	0	0	0
17	0	0	0	0
18	0	0	0	0
19	0	0	0	0
20	0	0	0	0

Balloon Payment Schedule

Balloon Payment	Full Principal Payment	True Balance
$0	$10,678	$89,322
0	1,746	87,576
0	1,921	85,655
0	2,113	83,543
0	2,324	81,219
0	2,556	78,663
0	2,812	75,851
0	3,093	72,758
0	3,402	69,355
0	3,743	65,613
0	4,117	61,496
0	4,529	56,967
0	4,981	51,986
0	5,480	46,506
40,479	46,506	0
0	0	0
0	0	0
0	0	0
0	0	0
0	0	0

Figure 14-2 The fixed rate, annuity due starter workbook.

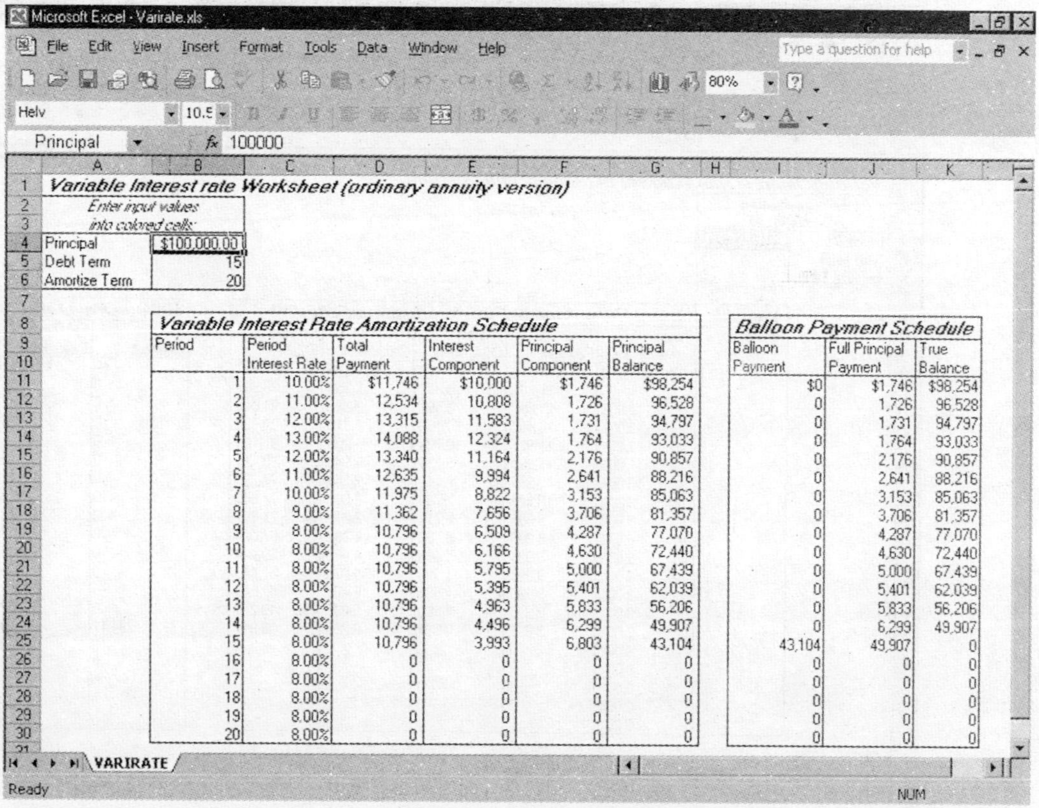

Variable Interest rate Worksheet (ordinary annuity version)

Enter input values into colored cells:

Principal	$100,000.00
Debt Term	15
Amortize Term	20

Period	Period Interest Rate	Total Payment	Interest Component	Principal Component	Principal Balance	Balloon Payment	Full Principal Payment	True Balance
1	10.00%	$11,746	$10,000	$1,746	$98,254	$0	$1,746	$98,254
2	11.00%	12,534	10,808	1,726	96,528	0	1,726	96,528
3	12.00%	13,315	11,583	1,731	94,797	0	1,731	94,797
4	13.00%	14,088	12,324	1,764	93,033	0	1,764	93,033
5	12.00%	13,340	11,164	2,176	90,857	0	2,176	90,857
6	11.00%	12,635	9,994	2,641	88,216	0	2,641	88,216
7	10.00%	11,975	8,822	3,153	85,063	0	3,153	85,063
8	9.00%	11,362	7,656	3,706	81,357	0	3,706	81,357
9	8.00%	10,796	6,509	4,287	77,070	0	4,287	77,070
10	8.00%	10,796	6,166	4,630	72,440	0	4,630	72,440
11	8.00%	10,796	5,795	5,000	67,439	0	5,000	67,439
12	8.00%	10,796	5,395	5,401	62,039	0	5,401	62,039
13	8.00%	10,796	4,963	5,833	56,206	0	5,833	56,206
14	8.00%	10,796	4,496	6,299	49,907	0	6,299	49,907
15	8.00%	10,796	3,993	6,803	43,104	43,104	49,907	0
16	8.00%	0	0	0	0	0	0	0
17	8.00%	0	0	0	0	0	0	0
18	8.00%	0	0	0	0	0	0	0
19	8.00%	0	0	0	0	0	0	0
20	8.00%	0	0	0	0	0	0	0

Figure 14-3 The variable rate, ordinary annuity starter workbook.

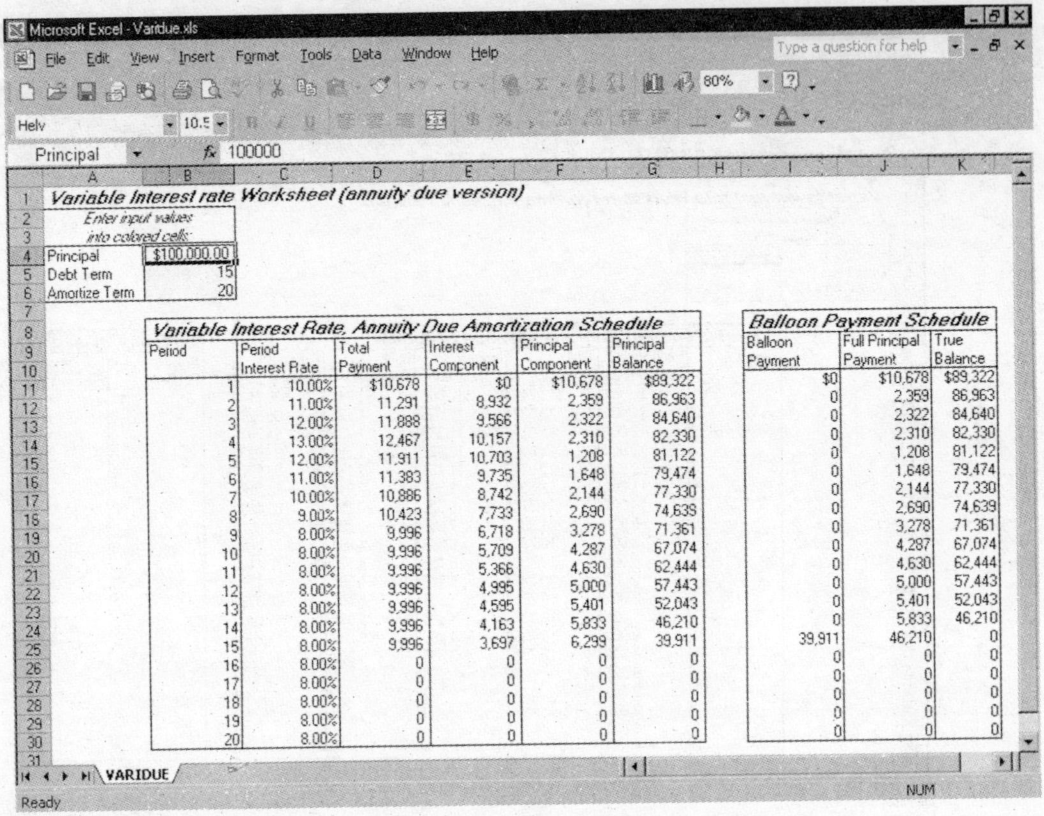

Figure 14-4 The variable rate, annuity due starter workbook.

Given four parameters—principal, debt term, amortization term, and interest rate—these starter workbooks calculate payment amounts, the interest and principal components of each payment, the outstanding principal balance for each period, and any balloon payments necessary to pay off the unamortized principal at the end of the debt term. You need this information to calculate profits and losses, to calculate cash flows, to report asset or liability balances on the balance sheet, and to calculate any gains or losses on the disposal of the asset or the refunding of the liability.

To enter your own data in a debt amortization starter workbook, follow these steps:

1. Open the appropriate debt amortization starter workbook from the companion CD.

Use the fixed rate, ordinary annuity starter workbook if your debt instrument uses a fixed, or constant, interest rate and payments occur at the end of the payment period. Use the fixed rate, annuity due starter workbook if your debt instrument used a fixed interest rate but payments occur at the beginning of the payment period. Use the variable interest rate, ordinary annuity starter workbook if your debt instrument uses a variable, or floating, interest rate and payments occur at the end of the payment period. Finally, use the variable interest rate, annuity due starter workbook if your debt instrument uses a variable interest rate but payments occur at the beginning of the payment period.

NOTE *The fixed rate, ordinary annuity starter workbook initially contains the default inputs shown in Figure 14-1. The fixed rate, annuity due starter workbook initially contains the default inputs shown in Figure 14-2. The variable rate, ordinary annuity starter workbook initially contains the default inputs shown in Figure 14-3. Finally, the variable rate, annuity due starter workbook initially contains the default inputs shown in Figure 14-4.*

2. **Specify the starting principal balance of the debt.**

   In cell B4, enter the starting principal balance of the debt.

3. **Specify the debt term.**

   In cell B5, enter the debt term, in payment periods.

4. **Specify the amortization term.**

   In cell B6, enter the amortization term, in payment periods.

5. **Specify the interest rate or interest rates that should be used to calculate the interest.**

   For the fixed interest rate, ordinary annuity and the fixed interest rate, annuity due starter workbooks, enter the per-period interest rate in cell B7.

   For the variable interest rate, ordinary annuity and the variable interest rate, annuity due starter workbooks, enter the period interest rates in the Period Interest Rate column of the amortization schedule starting in cell C11.

After you enter the required inputs, the starter workbook makes the calculations necessary to create the debt amortization schedule.

Understanding the Fixed Rate, Ordinary Annuity Amortization Starter Workbook

The fixed rate, ordinary annuity amortization starter workbook has three parts: the Fixed Interest Rate Amortization Inputs box, the Fixed Interest Rate Amortization Schedule, and the Balloon Payment Schedule.

Fixed Interest Rate Amortization Inputs

The amortization inputs are the only four variables you enter, and, unless you turn off cell protection, the four cells containing these values are the only cells in which you can enter data.

NOTE *These variables are defined by the debt contract.*

For convenience and good documentation within the starter workbook, cell B4 contains the starting debt amount and is named Principal, cell B5 contains the debt term in payment periods and is named Debt_Term, cell B6 contains the amortization term in payment periods and is named Amortize_Term, and cell B7 contains the per-period interest rate and is named Interest_Rate. The formulas within the actual schedules use these cell names rather than the cell addresses.

Fixed Interest Rate Amortization Schedule

The amortization schedule has five columns: Period, Total Payment, Interest Component, Principal Component, and Principal Balance.

Period

The period identifier simply numbers the time periods over which the debt is outstanding and paid down. The first period identifier is stored in cell B12 as the integer 1. Periods that follow are stored as the previous period plus 1.

Total Payment

The total payment is the payment for the current period. If you're using the starter workbook for liability bookkeeping, this is the amount you enter as a credit to the cash account. If you're using this starter workbook for receivables or investment bookkeeping, this is the amount you enter as a debit to your cash account. If you're using the starter workbook as part of a financial forecast and, from your perspective, the debt being amortized represents an asset, you can add the payment amount to other debt service payments in the section of a cash flow forecast that details sources of funds.

The Total Payment formula for the first period uses the PMT function as follows:

```
=-PMT(Interest_Rate,Amortize_Term,Principal)
```

The minus sign to the left of the PMT function is needed because, when the principal amount included is a positive number, the payment calculated is negative. The formula for subsequent periods is modified to display 0 after the debt is paid off. Starting in the second period, the basic formula is enclosed in an IF statement that first verifies that the debt term hasn't already expired. Therefore, in the second period of the forecasting horizon, the Total Payment formula is:

```
=IF(B13<=Debt_Term,-PMT(Interest_Rate,Amortize_Term,Principal),0)
```

B13 contains the period identifier. In subsequent periods, this part of the formula is changed so that the formula always uses the current period identifier.

Interest Component

The interest component is the amount of income or expense accrued over the payment period. If you're using the starter workbook for liability bookkeeping, this is the amount you enter as a debit to the interest expense account. If you're using the starter workbook for receivables or investment bookkeeping, this is the amount you enter as a credit to the interest income account. If you're using the starter workbook for a financial forecast, you can include this amount in either the financing income or financing expense portion of your profit and loss statement.

Each period's Interest Component amount is the previous period's Principal Balance amount times the Interest Rate value. The formula for the first period is:

```
=Principal*Interest_Rate
```

The formula for subsequent periods is modified to display 0 after the debt is paid off. Starting in the second period, the basic formula is enclosed in an IF statement that first verifies that the debt term hasn't already expired. Therefore, in the second period of the forecasting horizon, the total payment formula is:

```
=IF(B13<=Debt_Term,F12*Interest_Rate,0)
```

As in the total payment formula, B13 contains the period identifier. F12 contains the ending balance in the previous period. In subsequent periods, these parts of the formula are changed so that the formula always uses the current period identifier and the Principal Balance amount for the previous period.

Principal Component

The principal component is the amount subtracted from the outstanding principal balance when the total payment exceeds the accrued interest. If you're using the starter workbook for receivables or investment bookkeeping, this is the amount you enter as a credit to the asset account, reflecting a reduction in the amount owed you. If you're using the starter workbook for liability bookkeeping, this is the amount you enter as a debit to the liability account, reflecting a reflecting in the amount you owe.

For each period, the Principal Component amount is the Total Payment amount less the Interest Component amount. The formula for the first period is:

```
=C12-D12
```

The formula for the second period is:

```
=C13-D13
```

and so on.

Principal Balance

The principal balance is the outstanding balance of the debt at the end of the period. If you're using the starter workbook for financial forecasts, this is the amount you include in the balance sheet as either an asset or a liability.

The Principal Balance amount is the previous period's Principal Balance amount minus the Principal Component amount for the current period. The formula for the first period is:

```
=Principal-E12
```

The formula for subsequent periods is modified to display 0 for the Principal Balance amount after the debt is paid off. This modification is necessary for those situations in which a balloon payment is paid. Starting in the second period, the basic formula is enclosed in an IF statement that first verifies that the debt term hasn't already expired. Therefore, in the second period of the forecasting horizon, the Principal Balance formula is:

```
=IF(B13<=Debt_Term,F12-E13,0)
```

Again, B13 contains the period identifier. F12 contains the ending balance for the previous period. E13 contains the Principal Component amount for the current period. In subsequent periods, these parts of the formula are changed so that the formula always uses the current period identifier, the Principal Balance amount for the previous period, and the Principal Component amount for the current period.

Balloon Payment Schedule

Use the Balloon Payment Schedule when you're working with a debt that contains a balloon payment. The bookkeeping and forecasting method for balloon payments and principal reductions are the same as the methods for the total payment and principal component described on the amortization schedule.

The Balloon Payment Schedule has three columns: Balloon Payment, Full Principal Payment, and True Balance.

Balloon Payment

The balloon payment is the principal balance outstanding when the debt term ends. The formula for the first period is:

```
=IF (B12=Debt_Term,F12,0)
```

The formula for the second period is:

```
=IF(B13=Debt_Term,F13,0)
```

and so on.

Full Principal Payment

The full principal payment for each period is the principal component of the regular payment plus any balloon payment. The schedule uses the Full Principal Payment value as the full principal reduction stemming from regular payments and any balloon payment due. The formula for the first period is:

```
=H12+E12
```

The formula for the second period is:

```
=H13+E13
```

and so on.

True Balance

The true principal balance is the principal balance in the amortization schedule less any balloon payment made. The schedule uses the True Balance value as the principal balance outstanding because it includes both the principal components of the regular debit service payments and the balloon payment. The formula for the first period is:

```
=F12-H12
```

The formula for the second period is:

```
=F13-H13
```

and so on.

Understanding the Fixed Rate, Annuity Due Amortization Starter Workbook

The fixed rate annuity due amortization starter workbook has three parts: the Fixed Interest Rate, Annuity Due Amortization Inputs box; the Fixed Interest Rate, Annuity Due Amortization Schedule; and the Balloon Payment Schedule.

Fixed Interest Rate, Annuity Due Amortization Inputs

The amortization inputs are the only four variables you enter, and, unless you turn off cell protection, the four cells containing these values are the only cells in which you can enter data.

As with the other debt amortization schedules, cell B4 contains the starting debt amount and is named Principal, cell B5 contains the debt term in payment periods and is named Debt_Term, cell B6 contains the amortization term in payment periods and is named

Amortize_Term, and cell B7 contains the per-period interest rate and is named Interest_Rate. The formulas within the actual schedule use these cell names rather than the cell addresses.

Fixed Interest Rate, Annuity Due Amortization Schedule

The amortization schedule has five columns: Period, Total Payment, Interest Component, Principal Component, and Principal Balance.

Period

The period identifier simply numbers the time periods over which the debt is outstanding and paid down. The first period identifier is stored in cell B12 as the integer 1. Periods that follow are stored as the previous period plus 1.

Total Payment

The total payment is the current period payment. If you're using the starter workbook for liability bookkeeping, this is the amount you enter as a credit to the cash account. If you're using this starter workbook for receivables or investment bookkeeping, this is the amount you enter as a debit to your cash account. If you're using the starter workbook as part of a financial forecast and, from your perspective, the debt being amortized represents a liability, you can add the payment amount to other debt service payments in the section of a cash flow forecast that details uses of funds. If you're using the starter workbook as part of a financial forecast and, from your perspective, the debt being amortized represents an asset, the payment amount would probably be added to other debt service payments in the section of a cash flow forecast that details sources of funds.

The Total Payment formula for the first period uses the PMT function as follows:

```
=-PMT(Interest_Rate,Amortize_Term,Principal,0,1)
```

The minus sign to the left of the PMT function is needed because, when the Principal Component amount is a positive number, the Total Payment amount that is calculated is negative.

The formula for subsequent periods is also modified to display 0 after the debt is paid off. Starting in the second period, the basic formula is enclosed in an IF statement that first verifies that the debt term hasn't already expired. If it has, the payment amount is zero; the debt has already expired. Therefore, in the second period of the forecasting horizon, the Total Payment formula is:

```
=IF(B13<=Debt_Term,-PMT(Interest_Rate,Amortize_Term,Principal,0,1),0)
```

B13 contains the period identifier. In subsequent periods, this part of the formula is changed so that it always uses the current period identifier.

Interest Component

The interest component is the amount of income or expense accrued over the previous payment period and paid at the beginning of the current payment period. If you're using the starter workbook for liability bookkeeping, this is the amount you enter as the debit to the interest expense account. If you're using the starter workbook for receivables or investment bookkeeping, this is the amount you enter as a credit to the interest income account. If you're using the starter workbook for a financial forecast, you can include this amount in either the financing income or financing expense portion of your profit and loss statement.

Each period's interest is the previous Principal Balance amount times the Interest Rate value. But because no time has passed between the start of the debt term and the first payment, letting interest accrue, the first-period formula is 0. Starting in the second period, the Interest Component amount is the previous period's Principal Balance times the Interest Rate value. Also, the basic formula is enclosed in an IF statement that verifies that the debt term hasn't already expired. Therefore, in the second period of the forecasting horizon, the Total Payment formula is:

```
=IF(B13<=Debt_Term,F12*Interest_Rate,0)
```

B13 contains the period identifier. F12 contains the previous period's Principal Balance amount. In subsequent periods, these parts of the formula change so that the formula always uses the current period identifier and the previous period Principal Balance amount.

NOTE *Remember that the balances reported on the amortization schedule are as of the beginning of the payment period. If you need to know the balance at the end of the payment period—as might be the case if you use the amortization schedule for accounting or financial forecasting—you need to add the interest accrued during the previous period to show the correct balance at the end of the period. For example, the ending balance for the first period is calculated:*

=F12+D13

The formula for the second period is:

=F13+D14

and so on. Notice also that any balloon payment is assumed to be made at the beginning of the payment period.

Principal Component

The principal component is the amount subtracted from the outstanding principal balance when the total payment exceeds the accrued interest. If you're using the starter workbook for receivables or investment bookkeeping, this is the amount you enter as the credit to the asset account, reflecting a reduction in the amount owed to you. If you're using the starter workbook for liability bookkeeping, this is the amount you enter as the debit to the liability account, reflecting a reduction in the amount you owe.

For each period, the Principal Component amount is the Total Payment amount less the Interest Component amount. The formula for the first period is:

```
=C12-D12
```

The formula for the second period is:

```
=C13-D13
```

and so on.

Principal Balance

The principal balance is the outstanding balance of the debt at the beginning of the period immediately after the payment is made. If you're using the starter workbook for financial forecasts, this is the amount you enter, along with any interest accrued as of the balance sheet date, on the balance sheet as either an asset or a liability. (For example, if you're reporting the balance for the end of the first period, you add the beginning Principal Balance amount for the first period and the interest accrued during the first period but paid in the second period.)

The Principal Balance amount is the previous period's Principal Balance amount minus the Principal Component amount for the current period. The formula for the first period is:

```
=Principal-E12
```

The formula for subsequent periods is modified to display 0 after the debt is paid off. This modification is necessary for those situations in which a balloon payment is paid. Starting in the second period, the basic formula is enclosed in an IF statement that verifies that the debt term hasn't already expired. Therefore, in the second period of the forecasting horizon, the Principal Balance formula is:

```
=IF(B13<=Debt_Term,F12-E13,0)
```

Again, B13 contains the period identifier. F12 contains the Principal Balance amount for the previous period. E13 contains the Principal Component amount for the current period. In subsequent periods, these parts of the formula change so that the formula always uses the current period identifier, the Principal Balance amount for the previous period, and the Principal Component amount for the current period.

Balloon Payment Schedule

Use the Balloon Payment Schedule when you're working with debt that contains a balloon payment. The bookkeeping and forecasting methods for balloon payments and principal reduction are the same as the methods for the total payment and principal component described on the amortization schedule. The Balloon Payment Schedule has three columns: Balloon Payment, Full Principal Payment, and True Balance.

Balloon Payment

The balloon payment is the principal balance outstanding when the debt term ends. The formula for the first period is:

```
=IF(B12=Debt_Term, F12,0)
```

The formula for the second period is:

```
=IF(B13=Debt_Term, F13,0)
```

and so on.

Full Principal Payment

The full principal payment is the principal component of the regular payment and any balloon payment. The schedule uses the Full Principal Payment value as the total principal reduction stemming from regular payments and any balloon payment made. The formula for the first period is:

```
=H12+E12
```

The formula for the second period is:

```
=H13+E13
```

and so on.

True Balance

The true principal balance is the principal balance in the amortization schedule less any balloon payment made. The schedule uses the True Balance value as the principal balance outstanding because it includes both the principal components of the regular debt service payments and the balloon payment. The formula for the first period is:

```
=F12-H12
```

The formula for the second period is:

```
=F13-H13
```

and so on.

Understanding the Variable Rate, Ordinary Annuity Amortization Starter Workbook

The variable rate ordinary annuity amortization starter workbook has three parts: the Variable Interest Rate Amortization Inputs box, the Variable Interest Rate Amortization Schedule, and the Balloon Payment Schedule.

Variable Interest Rate Amortization Inputs

The amortization inputs, along with the Period Interest Rate values in the amortization schedule, are the variables you enter, and, unless you turn off cell protection, these are the only cells in which you can enter data.

As with the other debt amortization schedules, cell B4 contains the starting debt amount and is named Principal, cell B5 contains the debt term in payment periods and is named Debt_Term, and cell B6 contains the amortization in payment periods and is named Amortize_Term. The formulas within the actual schedules use these cell names rather than the cell addresses.

Variable Interest Rate Amortization Schedule

The amortization schedule has six columns: Period, Period Interest Rate, Total Payment, Interest Component, Principal Component, and Principal Balance.

Period

The period identifier simply numbers the time periods over which the debt is outstanding and paid down. The first period identifier is stored in cell B11 as the integer 1. Periods that follow are stored as the previous period plus 1.

Period Interest Rate

The period interest rates are the interest rates that, when multiplied by the outstanding balance at the beginning of the payment period, produce the amount of interest expense or interest income for the period. Period interest rates typically are tied to a market-sensitive interest rate index that is based on a widely traded or widely used interest rate, such as the one-year U.S. Treasury bill or the one-year London interbank offer rate. You enter either the actual or the forecasted interest rates for each payment period over the debt term in this column.

Total Payment

The total payment is the current period payment. If you're using the starter workbook for liability bookkeeping, this is the amount you enter as a credit to the cash account. If you're using this starter workbook for receivables or investment bookkeeping, this is the amount you enter as a debit to your cash account. If you're using the starter workbook as part of a financial forecast and, from your perspective, the debt being amortized represents a liability, you can add the payment amount to other debt service payments in the section of a cash flow forecast that details uses of funds. If you're using the starter workbook as part of a financial forecast and, from your perspective, the debt being amortized represents an asset, you can add the payment amount to other debt service payments in the sources of funds section of a cash flow forecast.

The Total Payment formula for the first period uses the PMT function, as follows:

```
=-PMT(C11,Amortize_Term,Principal)
```

The minus sign to the left of the PMT function is needed because, when the Principal amount is positive, the Total Payment amount is negative. C11 contains the first-period interest rate. In subsequent periods, this part of the formula changes so that the formula always uses the appropriate period's interest rate. However, the formula is modified to display 0 after the debt is paid off. The formula also is modified so that the payment amount that is calculated not only includes the new Period Interest Rate value but also reflects the remaining amortization term and the current Principal Balance amount. Starting in the second period, then, this formula is enclosed in an IF statement that verifies that the debt term hasn't already expired. In the second period of the forecasting horizon, the Total Payment formula is:

```
=IF(B12<=Debt_Term,-PMT(C12,Amortize_Term-B11,G11),0)
```

B12 contains the period identifier. The Amortize_Term-B11 portion of the formula calculates the remaining amortization term over which the amount in cell G11, the previous period's Principal Balance amount, must be amortized. C12 contains the Period Interest Rate value for the current period. In subsequent periods, these parts of the formula are changed so that the formula always uses the current period identifier, the remaining amortization term, and the previous period's Principal Balance amount.

Interest Component

The interest component is the amount of income or expense accrued over the payment period. If you're using the starter workbook for liability bookkeeping, this is the amount you enter as a debit to the interest expense account. If you're using the starter workbook for receivables or investment bookkeeping, this is the amount you enter as a credit to the interest income account. If you're using the starter workbook for a financial forecast, you can add this amount in either the financing income or financing expense portion of your profit and loss statement.

Each period's Interest Component value is the Principal Balance amount times the Period Interest Rate value. The formula for the first period is:

```
=Principal*C11
```

However, the formula for subsequent periods is modified to display 0 after the debt is paid off. Starting in the second period, then, the basic formula is enclosed in an IF statement that first verifies that the debt term hasn't already expired. In the second period of the forecasting horizon, the Interest Component formula is:

```
=IF(B12<=Debt_Term,G11*C12,0)
```

Again, B12 contains the period identifier. G11 contains the Principal Balance amount for the previous period. C12 contains the Period Interest Rate value for the current period. In subsequent periods, these parts of the formula are changed so that the formula always uses the current period identifier, the previous period Principal Balance amount, and the current Period Interest Rate value.

Principal Component

The principal component is the amount subtracted from the outstanding principal balance when the total payment exceeds the accrued interest. If you're using the starter workbook for receivables or investment bookkeeping, this is the amount you enter as a credit to the asset account, reflecting a reduction in the amount owed you. If you're using the starter workbook for liability bookkeeping, this is the amount you enter as a debit to the liability account, reflecting a reduction in the amount you owe.

For each period, the Principal Component value is the Total Payment amount less the Interest Component amount. The formula for the first period is:

```
=D11-E11
```

The formula for the second period is:

```
=D12-E12
```

and so on.

Principal Balance

The principal balance is the outstanding balance of the debt at the end of the period. If you're using the starter workbook for financial forecasts, this is the amount you include in the balance sheet either as an asset or as a liability.

The Principal Balance amount for each period is the previous period's Principal Balance amount minus the Principal Component amount for the current period. The formula for the first period is:

```
=Principal-F11
```

The formula for subsequent periods is modified to display 0 after the debt is paid off. Starting in the second period, then, the basic formula is enclosed in an IF statement that first verifies that the debt term hasn't already expired. In the second period of the forecasting horizon, the Principal Balance formula is:

```
=IF(B12<=Debt_Term,G11-F12,0)
```

Once again, B12 contains the period identifier. G11 contains the Principal Balance amount for the previous period. F12 contains the Principal Component amount for the current period. In subsequent periods, theses parts of the formula are changed so that the formula always uses the current period identifier, the Principal Balance amount for the previous period, and the current Interest Component amount.

Balloon Payment Schedule

Use the Balloon Payment Schedule when you're working with debt that contains a balloon payment. The bookkeeping and forecasting methods for balloon payments and principal reduction are the same as the methods for the total payment and principal component described on the amortization schedule.

The Balloon Payment Schedule has three columns: Balloon Payment, Full Principal Payment, and True Balance.

Balloon Payment

The balloon payment is the principal balance outstanding when the debt term ends. The formula for the first period is:

```
=IF(B11=Debt_Term,G11,0)
```

The formula for the second period is:

```
=IF(B12=Debt_Term,G12,0)
```

and so on.

Full Principal Payment

The full principal payment is the principal component of the regular payment plus any balloon payment. The schedule uses the Full Principal value as the full principal reduction stemming from both regular payments due over the debt term and any balloon payment due during the last payment period of the debt term. The formula for the first period is:

```
=I11+F11
```

The formula for the second period is:

```
=I12+F12
```

and so on.

True Balance

The true principal balance is the principal balance per the amortization schedule less any balloon payment made. The schedule uses the True Balance value as the principal balance outstanding, including the principal components of both the regular debt service payment and the balloon payment. The formula for the first period is:

```
=G11-I11
```

The formula for the second period is:

```
=G12-I12
```

and so on.

Understanding the Variable Rate, Annuity Due Amortization Starter Workbook

The variable rate, annuity due amortization starter workbook has three parts: the Variable Interest Rate, Annuity Due Amortization Inputs box; the Variable Interest Rate, Annuity Due Amortization Schedule; and the Balloon Payment Schedule.

Variable Interest Rate, Annuity Due Amortization Inputs

The amortization inputs, along with the Period Interest Rate values in the amortization schedule, are the variables you enter, and, unless you turn off cell protection, these are the only cells in which you can enter data.

As with the other debt amortization schedules, cell B4 contains the starting debt amount and is named Principal, cell B5 contains the debt term in payment periods and is named Debt_Term, and cell B6 contains the amortization in payment periods and is named

Amortize_Term. The formulas within the actual schedule use these cell names rather than the cell addresses.

Variable Interest Rate, Annuity Due Amortization Schedule

The amortization schedule has six columns: Period, Period Interest Rate, Total Payment, Interest Component, Principal Component, and Principal Balance.

Period

The period identifier simply numbers the time periods over which the debt is outstanding and paid down. The first period is stored in cell B11 as the integer 1. Periods that follow are stored as the previous period plus 1.

Period Interest Rate

The period interest rates are the interest rates that, when multiplied by the outstanding balance at the beginning of the payment period, result in the amount of interest expense or interest income for the period. The period interest rates typically are tied to a market-sensitive interest rate index that is based on a widely traded or used interest rate, such as the one-year U.S. Treasury bill or one-year London interbank offered rate. You enter actual or forecasted interest rates for each payment period over the debt term in this column. (Although no time has elapsed and no interest has accrued before the first payment is made, you still need the Period Interest Rate value for the first period to calculate the Total Payment amount for the first period.)

Total Payment

The total payment is the current period payment. If you're using the starter workbook for liability bookkeeping, this is the amount you enter as a credit to the cash account. If you're using this starter workbook for receivables or investment bookkeeping, this is the amount you enter as a debit to your cash account. If you're using the starter workbook as part of a financial forecast and, from your perspective, the debt being amortized represents a liability, you can add the payment amount to other debt service payments in the section of a cash flow forecast that details uses of funds. If you're using the starter workbook as part of a financial forecast and, from your perspective, the debt being amortized represents an asset, you can add the payment amount to other debt service payments in the section of a cash flow forecast that details sources of funds.

The Total Payment formula for the first period uses the PMT function, as follows:

```
=-PMT(C11,Amortize_Term,Principal,0,1)
```

C11 contains the first-period interest rate. The minus sign to the left of the PMT function is needed because, when the Principal Component amount is a positive number, the Total Payment amount that is calculated is negative. In subsequent periods, this part of the formula changes so that the formula always uses the appropriate period's interest rate. However, the formula is modified in subsequent periods to display 0 after the debt is paid off. The formula also is modified so that the calculated payment amount not only includes the new period Interest Rate value but also reflects the remaining amortization term and the current Principal Balance amount. Starting in the second period, then, this formula is enclosed in an IF statement that verifies that the debt term hasn't already expired. In the second period of the forecasting horizon, the Total Payment formula is:

```
=IF(B12<=Debt_Term,-PMT(C12,Amortize_Term-B11,G11+E12,0,1),0)
```

B12 contains the period identifier. C12 contains the Period Interest Rate value for the current period. The Amortize_Term-B11 portion of the formula calculates the remaining amortization term over which the amount in cells G11 and E12, the previous period's Principal Balance and the current period's Interest Component, must be amortized. In subsequent periods, these parts of the formula are changed so that the formula always uses the current period identifier, the remaining amortization term, and the appropriate principal and accrued interest balances.

Interest Component

The interest component is the amount of income or expense that is accrued over the previous payment period and that is paid at the beginning of the current payment period. If you're using the starter workbook for liability bookkeeping, this is the amount you enter as a debit to the interest expense account. If you're using the starter workbook for receivables or investment bookkeeping, this is the amount you enter as a credit to the interest income account. If you're using the starter workbook for a financial forecast, you can add this amount in either the financing income or financing expense portion of your profit and loss statement.

Except for the Interest Component amount for the first period, which is entered as 0, each period's Interest Component amount is the previous period's Principal Balance amount times the previous Period Interest Rate value. However, the formula is modified to display 0 after the debt is paid off. Accordingly, the basic formula is enclosed in an IF statement that verifies that the debt term hasn't already expired. In the second period of the forecasting horizon, the Interest Component formula is:

```
=IF(B12<=Debt_Term,G11*C11,0)
```

Again, B12 contains the period identifier. G11 contains the Principal Balance amount for the previous period. C11 contains the Period Interest Rate value for the previous period. In subsequent periods, these parts of the formula change so that the formula always uses the current period identifier, the previous period's Principal Balance amount, and the previous Period Interest Rate value.

Principal Component

The principal component is the amount subtracted from the outstanding principal balance when the total payment exceeds the accrued interest. If you're using the starter workbook for receivables or investment bookkeeping, this is the amount you enter as a credit to the asset account, reflecting a reduction in the amount owed to you. If you're using the starter workbook for liability bookkeeping, this is the amount you enter as a debit to the liability account, reflecting a reduction in the amount you owe.

For each period, the Principal Component amount is the Total Payment amount less the Interest Component amount. The formula for the first period is:

```
=D11-E11
```

The formula for the second period is:

```
=D12-E12
```

and so on.

Principal Balance

The principal balance is the outstanding balance of the debt at the beginning of the period, immediately after the payment is made. If you're using the starter workbook for financial forecasts, this amount, plus any accrued interest, is what you include on the balance sheet either as an asset or as a liability.

The Principal Balance amount is the previous period's Principal Balance minus the Principal Component of the current period's payment. The formula for the first period is:

```
=Principal-F11
```

The formula for subsequent periods is modified to display 0 after the debt term is paid off. Starting in the second period, then, the basic formula is enclosed in an IF statement that verifies that the debt term hasn't already expired. In the second period of the forecasting horizon, the Principal Balance formula is:

```
=IF(B12<=Debt_Term,G11-F12,0)
```

Once again, B12 contains the period identifier. G11 contains the Principal Balance amount for the previous period. F12 contains the Principal Component amount for the current period. In subsequent periods, these parts of the formula change so that the formula always uses the current period identifier, the Principal Balance amount for the previous period, and the current Principal Component amount.

NOTE *Remember that the balances reported on the amortization schedule are as of the beginning of the period. If you need to know the balances for the end of the period—as might be the case if you use the amortization schedule for accounting—you need to add the interest accrued from the previous period to show the principal balance for the end of the period. For example, the ending balance formula for the first period is:*

=G11+E12

The ending balance formula for the second period is:

=G12+E13

and so on. Notice that any balloon payment is assumed to be made at the beginning of the payment period.

Balloon Payment Schedule

You use the Balloon Payment Schedule when you're working with debt that contains a balloon payment. The bookkeeping and forecasting methods for balloon payments and principal reductions are the same as the methods for the total payment and principal component described on the amortization schedule. The Balloon Payment Schedule has three columns: Balloon Payment, Full Principal Payment, and True Balance.

Balloon Payment

The balloon payment is the principal balance outstanding when the debt term ends. The formula for the first period is:

```
=IF(B11=Debt_Term,G11,0)
```

The formula for the second period is:

```
=IF(B12=Debt_Term,G12,0)
```

and so on.

Full Principal Payment

The full principal payment is the principal component of the regular payment plus any balloon payment. The schedule uses this value as the total principal reduction stemming from both regular payments made over the debt term and any balloon payment made during the last payment period of the debt term. The formula for the first period is:

```
=I11+F11
```

The formula for the second period is:

```
=I12+F12
```

and so on.

True Balance

The true principal balance is the principal balance in the amortization schedule, less any balloon payment made. The schedule uses this value as the principal balance outstanding, including both principal components of the regular debt service payments and the balloon payment. The formula for the first period is:

```
=G11-I11
```

The formula for the second period is:

```
=G12-I12
```

and so on.

Customizing the Debt Amortization Starter Workbooks

You can use the debt amortization starter workbooks without modification for many debt instruments. However, you will still want to regularly make several changes to the workbooks.

NOTE *Before you change anything in the starter workbook other than the input parameters, unprotect the document. As needed, reinstate cell protection when you finish making your changes.*

Changing the Number of Periods

You can easily increase or decrease the number of periods in any of the debt amortization schedules. To increase the number of periods, remove the border from the last row of the amortization schedule. Then copy the current last row of the amortization schedule down as needed. Finally, replace the border at the bottom of the amortization schedule.

TIP *You'll probably want either as many rows in the schedules as there are forecasting periods in your overall model or as many rows as there are payment periods in the debt term.*

To decrease the number of periods, delete any unneeded rows from the bottom of the schedule. Then add a border at the new bottom of the amortization schedule.

Removing the Balloon Payment Schedule

If the debt you want to track doesn't have a balloon payment, you might want to remove the Balloon Payment Schedule. To do so, simply clear all the cells in the Balloon Payment Schedule.

Adding Data Values

Column A is empty along the left edge of the amortization schedules. You can use this empty range to store payment due dates or actual payment transaction dates. To enter a date value, click the cell and type the date.

Chapter 15

BUILDING ASSET DEPRECIATION SCHEDULES

Featuring:

- EasyRefresher™: Asset Depreciation
- Using the Asset Depreciation Starter Workbooks
- Understanding the Straight-Line Depreciation Starter Workbook
- Understanding the Declining Balance Depreciation Starter Workbook
- Understanding the Sum-of-the-Years'-Digits Depreciation Starter Workbook
- Understanding the Annuity Depreciation Starter Workbook
- Understanding the Activity Depreciation Starter Workbook
- Customizing the Asset Depreciation Starter Workbooks

Financial accounting standards and tax accounting laws require that you depreciate an asset in the process of calculating profits. Methods and conventions for doing this vary depending on the asset, the industry, and the party to whom profits are reported. The purpose, however, remains the same: to allocate the cost of the asset over the years it will be used. The five asset depreciation starter workbooks, described in this chapter, automate the preparation of asset depreciation schedules and provide foundations for customizing depreciation schedules. These starter workbooks (and the depreciation convention each uses) are as follows:

- STRAIGHT.XLS (straight-line)
- DECLIN'G.XLS (declining balance)
- SUMYEARS.XLS (sum-of-the-years'-digits)
- ANNUITY.XLS (annuity or sinking fund)
- ACTIVITY.XLS (activity)

EasyRefresher™: Asset Depreciation

Asset depreciation answers the question, "How much does the asset cost per period?" To answer that question, you need to: know the cost of the asset, estimate the number of periods in the asset's useful life, project any salvage value the asset will have at the end of its useful life, and choose a depreciation method. For example, suppose your business purchases a delivery truck for $10,000, uses it for five years, and then sells it for $2,000. Using the simplest depreciation method, straight-line depreciation, you calculate the cost of the truck over the five years as the $10,000 original cost less the $2,000 salvage value for a result of $8,000. Now divide the $8,000 by the five years of useful life. The result—$1,600—is the depreciation expense.

Straight-line depreciation is the most popular method because it's easy to apply and intuitive. The other methods—declining balance, sum-of-the-years'-digits, annuity/sinking fund, and activity—simply allocate the asset cost over the asset's useful life in different ways.

The declining balance depreciation method expenses more of the cost of the asset in the early periods of an asset's estimated life than in the later periods. It does so using the following formula:

```
(Declining Balance Percentage)*(Net Book Value)/(Estimated Life)
```

For example, suppose you want to recalculate the first year's depreciation expense for the delivery truck using 200% declining balance depreciation. The declining balance percentage is 200%. The net book value, because no depreciation has occurred, is $10,000. The estimated life is five years. Accordingly, you calculate the first year's depreciation expense as:

```
200%*($10,000/5 years)
```

or

```
$4,000.
```

The declining balance percentage is always greater than 100%. Accordingly, the formula accelerates the depreciation of an asset. Often, federal and state income tax laws determine usage of the declining balance depreciation method. Tax laws allow declining balance depreciation for many types of assets and specify a variety of declining balance percentages to be used, including 125, 150, 175, and 200%, depending on which year you acquire and begin using an asset. Generally, the tax law in effect when you buy and begin using an asset determines the types of assets for which you can use the declining balance method, as well as the declining balance percentage.

The sum-of-the-years'-digits depreciation method, like the declining balance method, also expenses more of the cost of an asset in the early periods of an asset's estimated life than in the later periods. It does so using the following formula:

```
(Periods Left in Estimated Life)/(Sum of the Periods' Digits)*(Original
Cost-Salvage Value)
```

For example, suppose you want to recalculate the first year's depreciation expense for the delivery truck using the sum-of-the-years'-digits method. The periods left in the estimated life, because the asset is still new, is five years. The sum of the periods' (or years') digits is 1+2+3+4+5, or 15. The original cost less the salvage value is $10,000–$2,000, or $8,000. Accordingly, you calculate the first year's depreciation expense as:

```
(5/15)*$8,000
```

or

```
$2,667.
```

Because the fraction becomes smaller in each succeeding period, the amount of depreciation expensed each year becomes smaller.

The annuity and sinking fund depreciation methods are mechanically identical, so this book supplies the same starter workbook for both. Both of these methods expense less of the cost of an asset in the early periods of an asset's life than in the later periods, so they are roughly the opposite of the declining balance and sum-of-the-years'-digits methods in this regard. The annuity and sinking fund methods also include in their depreciation expenses a specified return on the investment. Generally, the annuity and sinking fund methods violate the Generally Accepted Accounting Principles (GAAP). (Generally Accepted Accounting Principles are the rules and methods that certified public accountants, with help from business and the government, develop and use for financial accounting. Usually, when people refer to Generally Accepted Accounting Principles, they mean the pronouncements of the Financial Accounting Standards Board, an independent professional group.) Because they are contrary to GAAP and because they are complex, these methods are rarely used in practice except in heavily regulated industries such as public utilities in which Governmental rate-setting agencies often specify returns on investment. The annuity and sinking fund depreciation methods use the following formula to calculate depreciation expenses:

```
(Original Cost-(Present Value of the Salvage Value))/(Present Value Factor
of an Ordinary Annuity for n Periods at i%)
```

where n equals the estimated life, and i equals the specified return on investment.

For example, suppose you want to recalculate the first year's depreciation expense for the delivery truck using the annuity or sinking fund method. Also suppose that you are assured a 10% return on assets by a state regulatory agency. The 10% is the specified return on investment. The original cost is $10,000. The estimated life is five years. The present value of the salvage value is calculated as follows: For each year in the asset's estimated life, the $2,000 salvage value is divided by the sum of 1 plus the specified return on investment, or (1+10%)^5, or $1,241.84.

You can then calculate the present value of an ordinary ($1) annuity for 5 periods using a 10% discount rate using the PV function as follows:

```
=PV(.10,5,1)
```

for a result of 3.7908. Accordingly, you calculate the depreciation expense as:

```
($10,000-$1,241.84)/3.7908
```

or

```
$2,310.37.
```

This depreciation amount also includes assumed investment revenue of 10% on the asset cost of $10,000, or $1,000, meaning the actual amount of the asset being expensed in this period is $2,310.37 minus $1,000 or $1,310.37. In other words, the depreciated value of the truck after one year under this method is $8,689.63.

As the net book value of the asset becomes smaller over its useful life, the assumed investment revenue becomes smaller. Consequently, the $2,310.37 of depreciation represents less assumed investment revenue and more actual asset being expensed. The assumed investment revenue amounts to the assumed return on assets allowed by the regulatory agency.

The activity method depreciates an asset as it's used, instead of as time passes, by calibrating the estimated life of an asset in units of use. It does so by using the following formula:

```
(Period Units of Use/Estimated Life in Units of Use)* (Original Cost-
Salvage Value)
```

For example, suppose you want to recalculate the first year's depreciation expense for the delivery truck using the activity depreciation method. If a delivery truck lasts for 100,000 miles and you anticipate driving the truck 30,000 miles the first year, you calculate the first year's depreciation expense as:

```
30,000/100,000*($10,000-$2,000)
```

or

```
$2,400.
```

In general, financial accounting standards and the tax laws guide you in determining asset cost, useful life, and salvage value and in selecting a depreciation method. Accordingly, if you're building a depreciation schedule to use for tax accounting, your best resources are the publications of the Internal Revenue Service and your tax adviser. Alternatively, if you're building a depreciation schedule to use for financial accounting, your best resources are the publications of the Financial Accounting Standards Board and your certified public accountant.

TIP *Be consistent in the financial measurement periods you use in depreciating assets. If you're building a monthly forecast, calculate depreciation expenses on a monthly basis and enter the useful life in months. Alternatively, if you're building a quarterly or yearly forecast, calculate your depreciation expenses on a quarterly or yearly basis and enter the estimated life of an asset in quarters or years.*

Using the Asset Depreciation Starter Workbooks

You can use the asset depreciation starter workbooks shown in Figures 15-1 through 15-5 to construct depreciation schedules using a variety of asset depreciation conventions. Given three parameters—original cost, salvage value, and estimated life—these starter workbooks calculate the period depreciation, the accumulated depreciation, and the net book value for each period of the forecasting horizon. You need this information to calculate business profits and losses, to report asset balances on the balance sheet, and to calculate any gains or losses on the disposal of assets.

To enter your own data in an asset depreciation starter workbook, follow these steps:

1. Open the appropriate asset depreciation starter workbook from the companion CD.

Use the straight-line depreciation starter workbook if you want to use straight-line depreciation. Use the declining balance depreciation starter workbook if you want to use declining balance, such as double-declining balance, depreciation. Use the sum-of-the-years'-digits depreciation starter workbook if you want to use sum-of-the-years' digits depreciation. Use the annuity depreciation starter workbook if you want to use annuity or sinking fund depreciation. Finally, use the activity-based depreciation starter workbook if you want to use activity-based depreciation.

NOTE *The straight-line depreciation starter workbook initially contains the default inputs shown in Figure 15-1. The declining balance depreciation starter workbook initially contains the default inputs shown in Figure 15-2. The sum-of-the-years'-digits depreciation starter workbook initially contains the default inputs shown in Figure 15-3. The annuity or sinking fund depreciation starter workbook initially contains the default inputs shown in Figure 15-4. Finally, the activity depreciation starter workbook initially contains the default inputs shown in Figure 15-5.*

2. Enter the original cost of the asset.

In cell B4, enter the original cost of acquiring an asset and placing it into service. In general, the Original Cost value should be the cost of acquiring and placing into service the asset that you are depreciating. This amount might include the asset purchase price, sales tax, shipping insurance costs, freight charges, and installation costs.

3. **Enter the salvage, or residual value, of the asset.**

   In cell B5, enter the salvage value of the asset or group of assets. If you're using group or composite depreciation, enter the total cost of all the assets in the group. The Salvage Value figure is the residual value of the asset at the end of its estimated useful life.

4. **Enter the estimated useful life, or economic life, of the asset.**

   In cell B6, enter the estimated life of the asset. For tax accounting purposes, the useful life and salvage value sometimes are defined by tax law. For financial accounting purposes, previous experience with an asset might provide historical data for estimating the useful life.

   When you're using sum-of-the-years'-digits or annuity depreciation, express the estimated life in integer format. Accordingly, if you're depreciating an asset over 2 ½ years, instead of entering the estimated life as 2.5 (years), enter the estimated life as 30 (months).

NOTE *If you are using the Annuity Depreciation Worksheet, remember to adjust the specified return on investment in accordance with the guidelines from your regulatory agency.*

   If you're using activity-based depreciation, note that you need to specify the useful life in units of useful life.

5. **Provide any other data required for the depreciation calculations.**

   If you're calculating declining balance depreciation, for example, enter the declining balance percentage you've selected or have been directed to use by your tax adviser in cell B7.

   If you're calculating annuity-based depreciation, enter the specified return on investment in cell B7.

   If you're calculating activity-based depreciation, enter the period units of use, starting in cell B11.

TIP *If you want to fully depreciate the asset using activity-based depreciation, be sure the sum of the period units of use equals the estimated life, calibrated in units of use.*

After you enter the required inputs, the starter workbook makes the calculations necessary to produce a depreciation schedule.

Understanding the Straight-Line Depreciation Starter Workbook

The straight-line depreciation starter workbook has two parts: the Straight-Line Depreciation Calculation Inputs box in the range A2:B6 and the Straight-Line Depreciation Schedule, starting with the title in row 8.

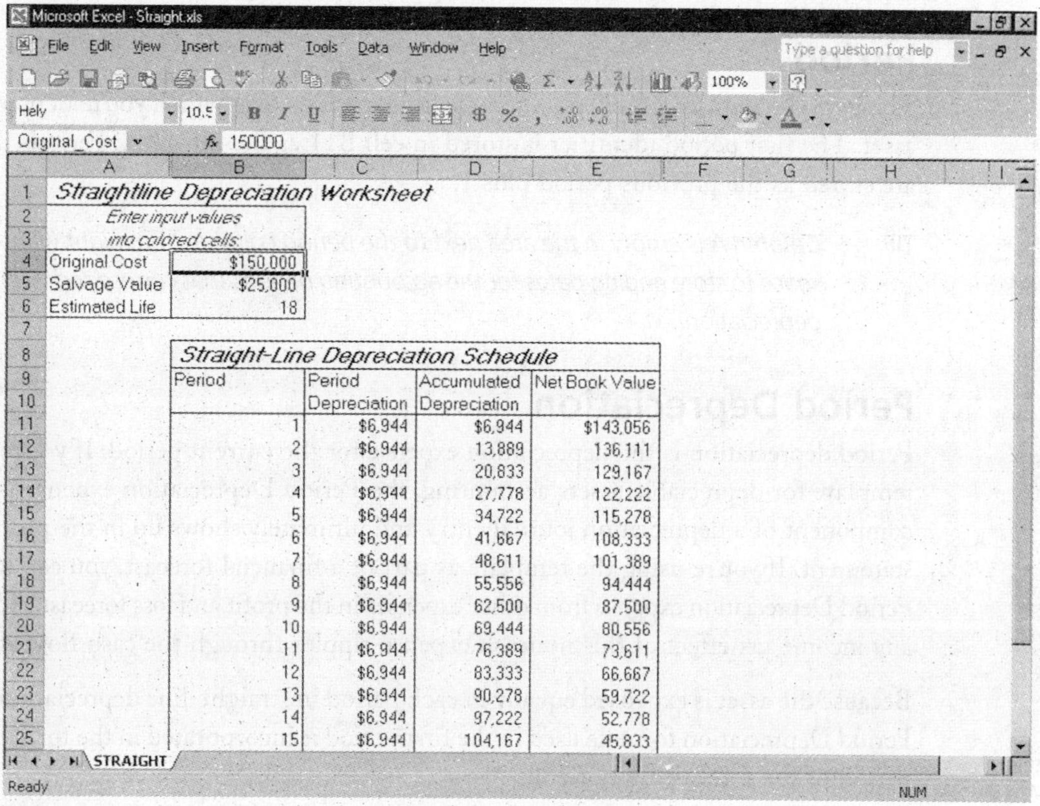

Figure 15-1 The straight-line depreciation starter workbook.

Straight-Line Depreciation Calculation Inputs

The calculation inputs are Original Cost, Salvage Value, and Estimated Life. These are the only three variables you enter, and, unless you turn off cell protection, the three cells containing these values are the only cells within the spreadsheet in which you can enter data.

For convenience and good documentation within the starter workbook, cell B4 contains the original cost and is named Original_Cost, cell B5 contains the salvage value and is named Salvage_Value, and cell B6 contains the estimated life and is named Estimated_Life. The formulas within the Straight-Line Depreciation Schedule use these cell names rather than the cell addresses.

Straight-Line Depreciation Schedule

The Straight-Line Depreciation Schedule has four columns: Period, Period Depreciation, Accumulated Depreciation, and Net Book Value.

Period

The period identifier simply numbers the time periods over which you're depreciating the asset. The first period identifier is stored in cell B11 as the integer 1. Periods that follow are stored as the previous period plus 1.

TIP *Column A is empty in the area next to the period column. You might want to use this space to store ending dates for the accounting periods that correspond with the period depreciation.*

Period Depreciation

Period depreciation is the depreciation expense for the current period. If you're using the template for depreciable assets accounting, the Period Depreciation expense is the debit component of a depreciation journal entry and ultimately shows up in the profit and loss statement. If you're using the template as part of a financial forecast, you can include the Period Depreciation expense from other expenses in the profit and loss forecast. Additionally, any income tax effect of this noncash expense ripples through the cash flow statement.

Because the asset is expensed equally in each period in straight-line depreciation, the basic Period Depreciation formula used in the first period is incorporated in the formula for each period of the forecasting horizon:

```
=SLN(Original_Cost,Salvage_Value,Estimated_Life)
```

This formula for subsequent periods is modified to prevent an asset from being depreciated below its salvage value and to deal with an estimated life expressed as a noninteger. Starting in the second period, the basic formula is enclosed in a MIN statement, which selects the smaller of two amounts: the straight-line depreciation expense or the amount yet to be depreciated. For example, the Period Depreciation formula for the second period is:

```
=MIN(SLN(Original_Cost,Salvage_Value,Estimated_Life), E11-Salvage_Value)
```

The E11–Salvage_Value portion of the formula calculates the amount yet to be depreciated. In subsequent periods, this part of the formula uses the Net Book Value amount from previous periods.

Accumulated Depreciation

If you're using the starter workbook for depreciable assets accounting, the incremental increase in accumulated depreciation is the credit component of a depreciation journal entry and ultimately shows up on the balance sheet as an adjustment to the asset's carrying cost. If you're using the starter workbook as part of a financial forecast, you can include the accumulated depreciation from the original cost of the asset in the balance sheet forecast to show the asset's net book value. Alternatively, you might simply use the Net Book Value amount calculated by this schedule.

The formula for the accumulated depreciation balance in the first period is:

```
=SUM(C$11:C11)
```

The formula for the second period is:

```
=SUM(C$11:C12)
```

and so on.

Net Book Value

The net book value is an asset's carrying cost and is the amount that you report either individually or with other assets' net book values on any historical or pro forma balance sheets.

For each period, the Net Book Value amount is the Original Cost amount less any accumulated depreciation. The formula for the first period is:

```
=Original_Cost-D11
```

The formula for the second period is:

```
=Original_Cost-D12
```

and so on.

Understanding the Declining Balance Depreciation Starter Workbook

In general, you use the declining balance depreciation starter workbook if you've selected or been counseled by your tax adviser to use a declining balance convention, such as Accelerated Cost Recovery System (ACRS) or modified Accelerated Cost Recovery System (MACRS), for tax accounting. You can also use this starter workbook if you're calculating depreciation for financial accounting and you feel that the declining balance method of depreciation allocates costs in a way that matches economic reality.

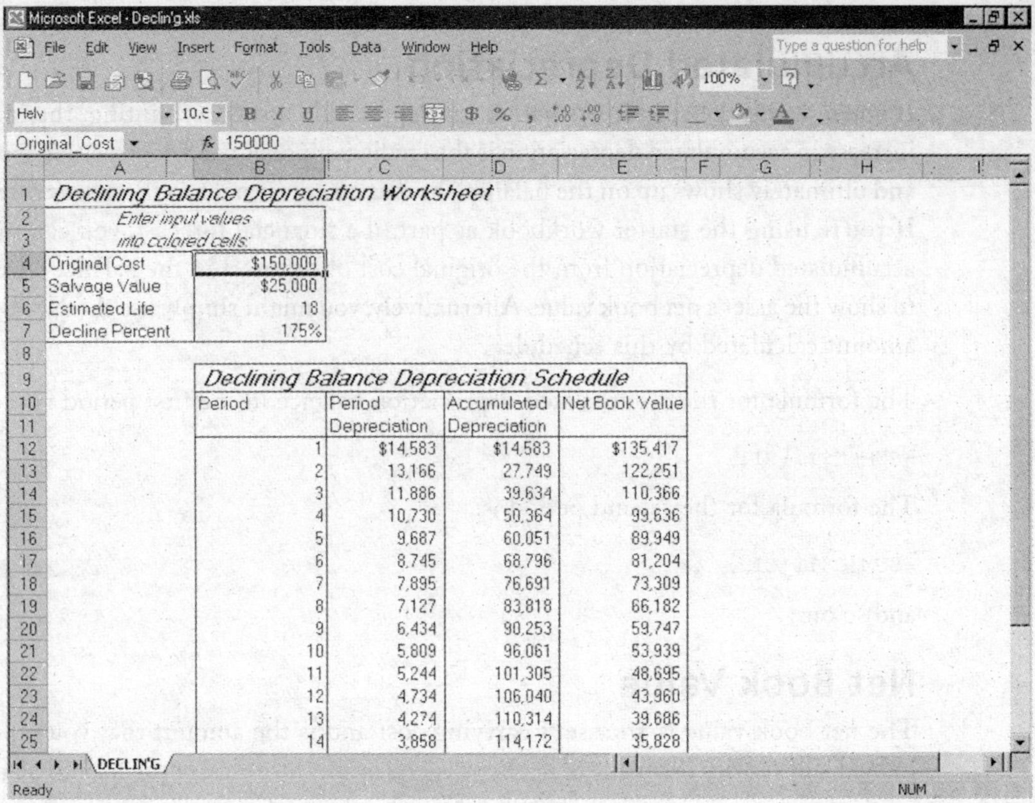

	A	B	C	D	E
1	*Declining Balance Depreciation Worksheet*				
2	*Enter input values*				
3	*into colored cells:*				
4	Original Cost	$150,000			
5	Salvage Value	$25,000			
6	Estimated Life	18			
7	Decline Percent	175%			
8					
9		*Declining Balance Depreciation Schedule*			
10		Period	Period	Accumulated	Net Book Value
11			Depreciation	Depreciation	
12		1	$14,583	$14,583	$135,417
13		2	13,166	27,749	122,251
14		3	11,886	39,634	110,366
15		4	10,730	50,364	99,636
16		5	9,687	60,051	89,949
17		6	8,745	68,796	81,204
18		7	7,895	76,691	73,309
19		8	7,127	83,818	66,182
20		9	6,434	90,253	59,747
21		10	5,809	96,061	53,939
22		11	5,244	101,305	48,695
23		12	4,734	106,040	43,960
24		13	4,274	110,314	39,686
25		14	3,858	114,172	35,828

Figure 15-2 The declining balance depreciation starter workbook.

Given four parameters—original cost, salvage value, estimated life, and the decline percentage—this starter workbook calculates the depreciation expense, the accumulated depreciation, and the net book value for each period of the forecasting horizon.

NOTE *This starter workbook uses the VDB functions default setting, which switches to the straight-line depreciation convention when that method maximizes the expense charged. This convention is employed because the declining balance depreciation formula does not completely depreciate assets with very low salvage values. Without this feature, an asset might not be completely depreciated over its estimated life.*

WARNING *Declining balance depreciation calculated with the declining balance depreciation starter workbook will not perfectly match the declining balance depreciation calculated using the Internal Revenue Service's rules. The Internal Revenue Service modifies the standard declining balance calculations for a variety of reasons related to technical tax laws and tax regulations.*

The declining balance starter workbook has two parts: the Declining Balance Depreciation Calculation Inputs box and the Declining Balance Depreciation Schedule.

Declining Balance Depreciation Calculation Inputs

The calculation inputs are Original Cost, Salvage Value, Estimated Life, and Decline Percent. These are the only four variables you enter, and, unless you turn off cell protection, the four cells containing these values are the only cells within the spreadsheet in which you can enter data.

For convenience and good documentation within the starter workbook, cell B4 contains the original cost and is named Original_Cost, cell B5 contains the salvage value and is named Salvage_Value, cell B6 contains the estimated life and is named Estimated_Life, and cell B7 contains the declining balance percentage and is named Decline_Percent. The formulas within the schedules use these cell names rather than the cell addresses.

Declining Balance Depreciation Schedule

The Declining Balance Depreciation Schedule has four columns: Period, Period Depreciation, Accumulated Depreciation, and Net Book Value.

Period

The period identifier simply numbers the time periods over which you're depreciating the asset. The first period identifier is stored in cell B12 as the integer 1. Periods that follow are stored as the previous period plus 1.

TIP *Column A is empty in the area next to the period column. You might want to use this space to store ending dates for the accounting periods that correspond with the period depreciation.*

Period Depreciation

If you're using declining balance depreciation over the asset's entire estimated life, period depreciation is the depreciation expense for the current period. If you're using the template for depreciable assets bookkeeping, the Period Depreciation expense is the debit component of a depreciation journal entry and ultimately shows up in the profit and loss statement. If you're using the template as part of a financial forecast, you can add the Period Depreciation expense to other expenses in the profit and loss forecast. Additionally, any income tax effect of this noncash expense ripples through the cash flow statement.

The Period Depreciation formula for the first period in the forecasting horizon is:

```
=VDB(Original_Cost,Salvage_Value,Estimated_Life,B12-2,B12,Decline_Percent)
```

The formula simply supplies the needed input values for calculating declining balance depreciation to the VDB function. (If you have questions about how the VDB works, refer to Chapter 5.)

Accumulated Depreciation

If you're using the starter workbook for depreciable assets accounting, the incremental increase in accumulated depreciation is the credit component of a depreciation journal entry and ultimately shows up on the balance sheet as an adjustment of the asset's carrying cost. If you're using the starter workbook as part of a financial forecast, you can deduct the accumulated depreciation from the original cost of the asset in the balance sheet forecast to show the asset's net book value. Alternatively, you might simply use the Net Book Value amount calculated by this schedule.

The formula for the Accumulated Depreciation balance in the first period is:

```
=SUM(C$12:C12)
```

The formula for the second period is:

```
=SUM(C$12:C13)
```

The formula for the third period is:

```
=SUM(C$12:C14)
```

and so on.

Net Book Value

The net book value is an asset's carrying cost and is the amount that you report either individually or with other assets' net book values on any historical or pro forma balance sheets.

For each period, the Net Book Value amount is the Original Cost amount less any accumulated depreciation. The net book value formula for the first period is:

```
=Original_Cost-D12
```

The formula for the second period is:

```
=Original_Cost-D13
```

The formula for the third period is:

```
=Original_Cost-D14
```

and so on.

Understanding the Sum-of-the-Years'-Digits Depreciation Starter Workbook

You can use the sum-of-the-years'-digits depreciation starter workbook shown in Figure 15-3 to construct depreciation schedules with the sum-of-the-years'-digits method. In general, you use this starter workbook if you've selected or been counseled by your tax adviser to use the sum-of-the-years'-digits convention for tax accounting. You can also use this starter workbook if you're calculating depreciation for financial accounting and you feel that this depreciation method allocates costs in a way that matches economic reality.

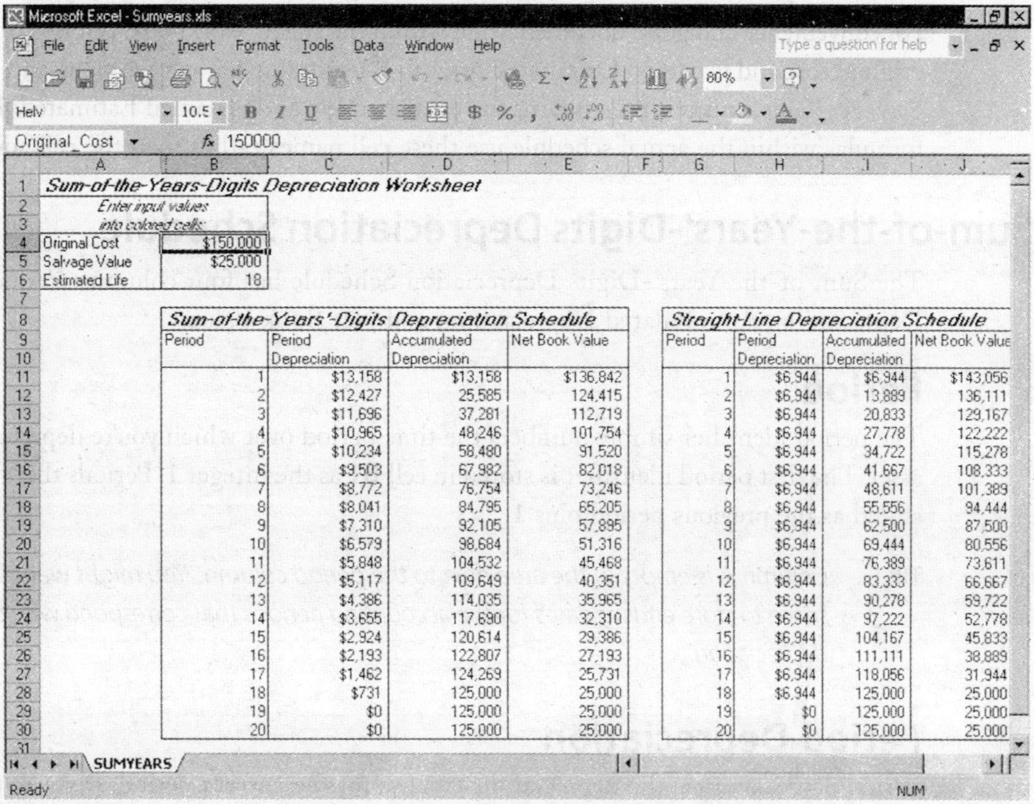
Microsoft Excel - Sumyears.xls

Original_Cost | 150000

Sum-of-the-Years-Digits Depreciation Worksheet

Enter input values into colored cells:	
Original Cost	$150,000
Salvage Value	$25,000
Estimated Life	18

Sum-of-the-Years'-Digits Depreciation Schedule				Straight-Line Depreciation Schedule			
Period	Period Depreciation	Accumulated Depreciation	Net Book Value	Period	Period Depreciation	Accumulated Depreciation	Net Book Value
1	$13,158	$13,158	$136,842	1	$6,944	$6,944	$143,056
2	$12,427	25,585	124,415	2	$6,944	13,889	136,111
3	$11,696	37,281	112,719	3	$6,944	20,833	129,167
4	$10,965	48,246	101,754	4	$6,944	27,778	122,222
5	$10,234	58,480	91,520	5	$6,944	34,722	115,278
6	$9,503	67,982	82,018	6	$6,944	41,667	108,333
7	$8,772	76,754	73,246	7	$6,944	48,611	101,389
8	$8,041	84,795	65,205	8	$6,944	55,556	94,444
9	$7,310	92,105	57,895	9	$6,944	62,500	87,500
10	$6,579	98,684	51,316	10	$6,944	69,444	80,556
11	$5,848	104,532	45,468	11	$6,944	76,389	73,611
12	$5,117	109,649	40,351	12	$6,944	83,333	66,667
13	$4,386	114,035	35,965	13	$6,944	90,278	59,722
14	$3,655	117,690	32,310	14	$6,944	97,222	52,778
15	$2,924	120,614	29,386	15	$6,944	104,167	45,833
16	$2,193	122,807	27,193	16	$6,944	111,111	38,889
17	$1,462	124,269	25,731	17	$6,944	118,056	31,944
18	$731	125,000	25,000	18	$6,944	125,000	25,000
19	$0	125,000	25,000	19	$0	125,000	25,000
20	$0	125,000	25,000	20	$0	125,000	25,000

SUMYEARS

Figure 15-3 The sum-of-the-years'-digits depreciation starter workbook.

Given three parameters—original cost, salvage value, and estimated life—this starter workbook calculates the period depreciation, the accumulated depreciation, and the net book value for each period of the forecasting horizon.

The schedule also calculates the excess accelerated depreciation taken as a result of using the sum-of-years'-digits method, because this amount might be subject to special tax treatment either on a current basis or at disposal. To calculate the excess, this starter workbook incorporates a straight-line depreciation schedule.

The sum-of-the-years'-digits depreciation starter workbook has four parts: the Sum-of-the-Years'-Digits Calculation Inputs box, the Sum-of-the-Years'-Digits Depreciation Schedule, the Straight-Line Depreciation Schedule, and the Excess Accelerated Depreciation Schedule.

Sum-of-the-Years'-Digits Calculation Inputs

The calculation inputs are Original Cost, Salvage Value, and Estimated Life. These are the only three variables you enter, and, unless you turn off cell protection, the three cells containing these values are the only cells within the spreadsheet in which you can enter data.

For convenience and good documentation within the starter workbook, cell B4 contains the original cost and is named Original_Cost, cell B5 contains the salvage value and is named Salvage_Value, and cell B6 contains the estimated life and is named Estimated_Life. The formulas within the actual schedule use these cell names rather than the cell addresses.

Sum-of-the-Years'-Digits Depreciation Schedule

The Sum-of-the-Years'-Digits Depreciation Schedule has four columns: Period, Period Depreciation, Accumulated Depreciation, and Net Book Value.

Period

The period identifier simply numbers the time period over which you're depreciating the asset. The first period identifier is stored in cell B1 as the integer 1. Periods that follow are stored as the previous period plus 1.

TIP *Column A is empty in the area next to the period column. You might want to use this space to store ending dates for the accounting periods that correspond with the period depreciation.*

Period Depreciation

Period depreciation is the depreciation expense for the current period. If you're using the starter workbook for depreciable assets accounting, the Period Depreciation expense is the debit component of a depreciation journal entry and ultimately shows up in the profit and loss statement. If you're using the starter workbook as part of a financial forecast, you can add the Period Depreciation expense to other expenses in the profit and loss forecast. Additionally, any income tax effect of this noncash expense ripples through the cash flow statement.

The Period Depreciation formula for the first period in the forecasting horizon is:

```
=SYD(Original_Cost,Salvage_Value,Estimated_Life,B11)
```

The formula for the second period, however, is modified so that the asset is not depreciated below its salvage value. Starting with the second period, the formula to calculate the Period Depreciation expense is enclosed in an IF statement that first verifies that the asset hasn't already been fully depreciated. For the comparison, rounded amounts are used so that trailing digits of insignificance don't affect the test. The formula for the second period is:

```
=IF(ROUND(Original_Cost-D11,0)=ROUND(Salvage_Value,0),),SYD(Original_Cost,
Salvage_Value,Estimated_Life,B12)
```

The Original_Cost–D11 portion is the Net Book Value amount at the end of the previous period. B12 contains the period identifier for the expense that is calculated. In subsequent periods, these parts of the formula change so that the formula always uses the Net Book Value amount from the previous period and the period identifier from the current period.

In other words, this equation states that if the net book value after depreciation equaled the salvage value after the last period, set the depreciation for this period to 0.

Accumulated Depreciation

If you're using the starter workbook for depreciable assets accounting, the incremental increase in the Accumulated Depreciation amount is the credit component of a depreciation journal entry and ultimately shows up on the balance sheet as an adjustment to the asset's carrying cost. If you're using the starter workbook as part of a financial forecast, you can deduct the Accumulated Depreciation amount from the original cost of the asset in the balance sheet forecast to show the asset's net book value. Alternatively, you might simply use the Net Book Value amount calculated by this schedule.

The formula for the Accumulated Depreciation balance in the first period is:

```
=SUM(C$11:C11)
```

The formula for the second period is:

```
=SUM(C$11:C12)
```

The formula for the third period is:

```
=SUM(C$11:C13)
```

and so on.

Net Book Value

The net book value is an asset's carrying cost and is the amount that you report either individually or with other assets' net book values on any historical or pro forma balance sheets.

For each period, the Net Book Value amount is the Original Cost amount less any accumulated depreciation. The formula for the first period is:

```
=Original_Cost-D11
```

The formula for the second period is:

```
=Original_Cost-D12
```

The formula for the third period is:

```
=Original_Cost-D13
```

and so on.

Straight-Line Depreciation Schedule

The Straight-Line Depreciation Schedule has four columns: Period, Period Depreciation, Accumulated Depreciation, and Net Book Value.

Period

The period identifier simply numbers the time periods over which you're depreciating the asset. The first period is stored as the integer 1. Periods that follow are stored as the previous period plus 1.

Period Depreciation

Period depreciation is the depreciation expense for the current period. If you're using the template for depreciable assets accounting, the Period Depreciation expense is the debit component of a depreciation journal entry and ultimately shows up in the profit and loss statement. If you're using the starter workbook as part of a financial forecast, you can add the Period Depreciation expense to other expenses in the profit and loss forecast. Additionally, any income tax effect of this noncash expense ripples through the cash flow statement.

Because the asset is expensed equally in each period in straight-line depreciation, the basic Period Depreciation formula used in the first period is incorporated in the formula for each period of the forecasting horizon:

```
=SLN(Original_Cost,Salvage_Value,Estimated_Life)
```

The formula for subsequent periods is modified to prevent an asset from being depreciated below its salvage value. Starting in the second period, the basic formula is enclosed in a MIN statement, which selects the smaller of two amounts: the straight-line depreciation expense or the amount yet to be depreciated. For example, the period expense formula for the second period is:

```
=MIN(SLN(Original_Cost,Salvage_Value,Estimated_Life),J11-Salvage_Value)
```

The J11–Salvage_Value portion calculates the amount yet to be depreciated. In subsequent periods, this part of the formula uses the Net Book Value amount from the previous period.

Accumulated Depreciation

If you're using the starter workbook for depreciable assets accounting, the incremental increase in the Accumulated Depreciation amount is the credit component of a depreciation journal entry and ultimately shows up on the balance sheet as an adjustment to the asset's carrying cost. If you're using the starter workbook as part of a financial forecast, you can deduct the accumulated depreciation from the original cost of the asset in the balance sheet forecast to show the asset's net book value. Alternatively, you might simply use the Net Book Value amount calculated by this schedule.

The formula for the Accumulated Depreciation balance in the first period is:

```
=SUM(H$11:H11)
```

The formula for the second period is:

```
=SUM(H$11:H12)
```

and so on.

Net Book Value

The net book value is an asset's carrying cost and is the amount that you report either individually or with other assets' net book values on any historical or pro forma balance sheets.

For each period, the Net Book Value amount is the Original Cost amount less any accumulated depreciation. The formula for the first period is:

```
=Original_Cost-I11
```

The formula for the second period is:

```
=Original_Cost-I12
```

and so on.

Excess Accelerated Depreciation Schedule

In certain situations, excess accelerated depreciation is accorded special income tax treatment. The calculated results in the one-column Excess Accelerated Depreciation Schedule are simply the difference between the Net Book Value amount for each period calculated in the Sum-of-the-Years'-Digits Depreciation Schedule and the Net Book Value amount calculated in the Straight-Line Depreciation Schedule. The formula for the first period is:

```
=J11-E11
```

The formula for the second period is:

```
=J12-E12
```

and so on.

Understanding the Annuity Depreciation Starter Workbook

You can use the annuity or sinking fund depreciation starter workbook, shown in Figure 15-4, to construct depreciation schedules with the annuity or sinking fund depreciation methods. The annuity and sinking fund depreciation methods include, as part of the depreciation expense, a return on the asset being depreciated. In general, this method violates the Generally Accepted Accounting Principles, and, for this reason, you are unlikely to need this starter workbook. However, public utilities sometimes use these methods for calculating depreciation expenses—a practice that's defensible because the rate-setting process often assumes a guaranteed return on investment. In general, you can use this template if management feels that the rate setting virtually assures a specific return on assets and the annuity or sinking fund method has been selected and approved by management, appropriate regulatory agencies, and your external auditors.

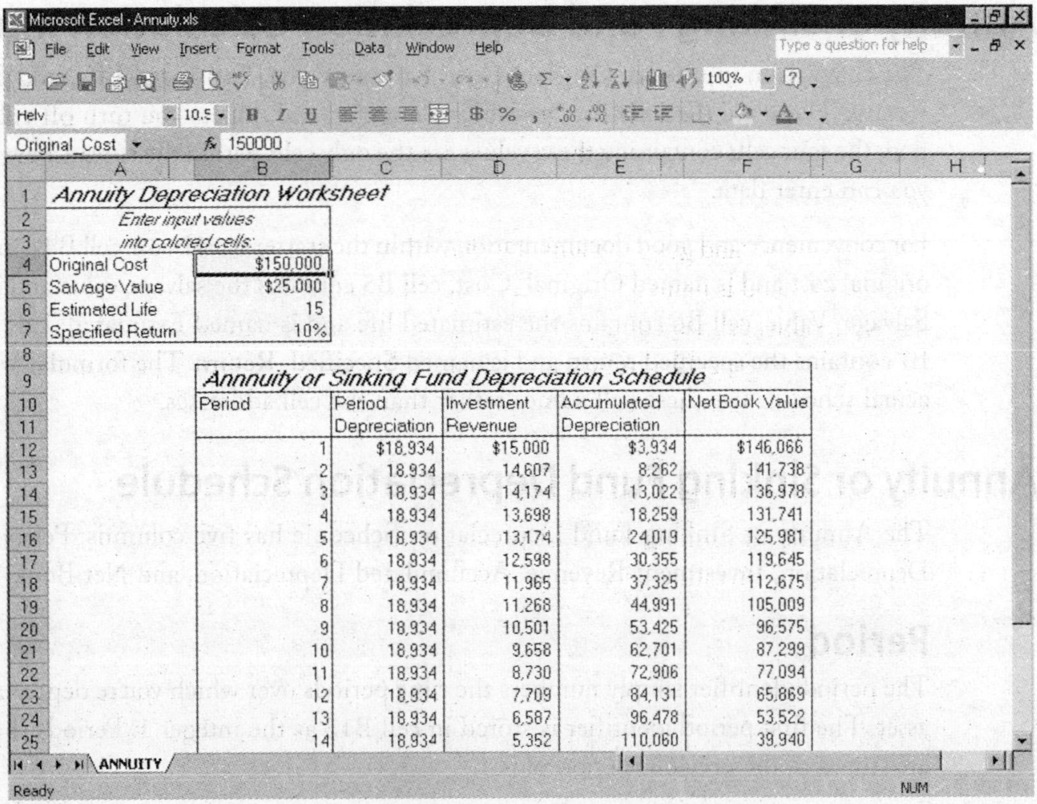

Original Cost	$150,000
Salvage Value	$25,000
Estimated Life	15
Specified Return	10%

Annnuity or Sinking Fund Depreciation Schedule

Period	Period Depreciation	Investment Revenue	Accumulated Depreciation	Net Book Value
1	$18,934	$15,000	$3,934	$146,066
2	18,934	14,607	8,262	141,738
3	18,934	14,174	13,022	136,978
4	18,934	13,698	18,259	131,741
5	18,934	13,174	24,019	125,981
6	18,934	12,598	30,355	119,645
7	18,934	11,965	37,325	112,675
8	18,934	11,268	44,991	105,009
9	18,934	10,501	53,425	96,575
10	18,934	9,658	62,701	87,299
11	18,934	8,730	72,906	77,094
12	18,934	7,709	84,131	65,869
13	18,934	6,587	96,478	53,522
14	18,934	5,352	110,060	39,940

Figure 15-4 The annuity or sinking fund depreciation starter workbook.

Given four parameters—original cost, salvage value, the estimated useful life, and the specified return on investment—this schedule calculates the period depreciation, the accumulated depreciation, the imputed (or assumed) investment revenue, and the net book value for each period of the forecasting horizon. You need this information to calculate business profits and losses, to report asset balances on the balance sheet, and to calculate any gains or losses on the disposal of assets.

The annuity or sinking fund depreciation starter workbook has two parts: the Annuity or Sinking Fund Depreciation Calculation Inputs box and the Annuity or Sinking Fund Depreciation Schedule.

Annuity or Sinking Fund Depreciation Calculation Inputs

The calculation inputs are Original Cost, Salvage Value, Estimated Life, and Specified Return. These are the only four variables you enter, and, unless you turn off cell protection, the four cells containing these values are the only cells within the spreadsheet in which you can enter data.

For convenience and good documentation within the starter workbook, cell B4 contains the original cost and is named Original_Cost, cell B5 contains the salvage value and is named Salvage_Value, cell B6 contains the estimated life and is named Estimated_Life, and cell B7 contains the specified return and is named Specified_Return. The formulas within the actual schedule use these cell names rather than the cell addresses.

Annuity or Sinking Fund Depreciation Schedule

The Annuity or Sinking Fund Depreciation Schedule has five columns: Period, Period Depreciation, Investment Revenue, Accumulated Depreciation, and Net Book Value.

Period

The period identifier simply numbers the time periods over which you're depreciating the asset. The first period identifier is stored in cell B12 as the integer 1. Periods that follow are stored as the previous period plus 1.

TIP *Column A is empty in the area next to the period column. You might want to use this space to store ending dates for the accounting periods that correspond with the period depreciation.*

Period Depreciation

Period depreciation is the depreciation expense for the current period. If you're using the template for depreciable assets accounting, the Period Depreciation expense is the debit component of a depreciation journal entry and ultimately shows up in the profit and loss statement. If you're using the template as part of a financial forecast, you can include the Period Depreciation expense with other expenses in the profit and loss forecast. Additionally, any income tax effect of this noncash expense ripples through the cash flow statement.

The basic Period Depreciation formula is:

```
=-(Original_Cost -(Salvage_Value/(1+Specified_Return)^Estimated_Life))/
PV(Specified_Return,Estimated_Life,1)
```

The minus sign at the beginning of this formula is necessary because the PV function returns a negative value when all of its arguments are positive. You may note how this corresponds to the original equation for Period Depreciation as explained earlier in this chapter:

```
(Original Cost-(Present Value of the Salvage Value))/(Present Value Factor
of an Ordinary Annuity for n Periods at i%)
```

The Present Value of the Salvage Value variable takes the final Salvage Value and factors it based on the specified return for the estimated life of the asset.

The formula for the second period, however, is modified so that the asset is not depreciated below its salvage value. Starting with the second period, the formula to calculate the Period Depreciation expense is enclosed in an IF statement that first verifies that the asset hasn't already been fully depreciated. For the comparison, rounded amounts are used so that trailing digits of insignificance don't affect the test. The formula for the second period is:

```
IF(ROUND(Original_Cost-E12,0)=ROUND(Salvage_Value,0)0,
-(Original_Cost-(Salvage_Value/
(1+Specified_Return)^Estimated_Life))/
PV(Specified_Return,Estimated_Life,1))
```

In other words, this equation states that if the net book value after depreciation equaled the salvage value after the last period, set the depreciation for this period to 0.

Investment Revenue

Investment revenue is the assumed investment return on the asset. If you're using the template for depreciable assets accounting and have selected the annuity depreciation method, the investment revenue for a period is credited to an investment revenue account and ultimately shows up in the profit and loss statement. If you're using the template for depreciable assets accounting and have selected the sinking fund depreciation method, the investment revenue for a period is credited to the depreciation expense account. This results in a net debit to the depreciation expense account equal to the return of the asset principal and the increase in the accumulated depreciation expense for the period. The net depreciation expense ultimately shows up in the profit and loss statement. If you're using the template as part of a financial forecast, you can add the investment revenue to other miscellaneous revenues in the profit and loss forecast.

The first-period Investment Revenue value is the Original Cost value times the Specified Return value. The formula for the first period is:

```
=Specified_Return*Original_Cost
```

The formula for the second period, however, is modified so that the previous Net Book Value amount is used and so that investment revenue isn't calculated when the asset is fully depreciated. Starting in the second period, the formula to calculate the Investment Revenue amount is enclosed in an IF statement that first verifies that the asset hasn't already been fully depreciated. For the comparison, rounded amounts are used so that trailing digits of insignificance don't affect the test. The formula for the second period is:

```
=IF(ROUND(Original_Cost-E12,0)=ROUND(Salvage_Value,0)0,
Specified_Return*(Original-Cost-E12))
```

The Original_Cost–E12 portion is the Net Book Value amount at the end of the previous period. In subsequent periods, this part of the formula changes so that it always uses the Accumulated Depreciation amount from the previous period.

Accumulated Depreciation

If you're using the template for depreciable assets accounting, the incremental increase in the Accumulated Depreciation amount is the credit component of a depreciation journal entry and ultimately shows up on the balance sheet as an adjustment to the asset's carrying cost. If you're using the template as part of a financial forecast, you can include the Accumulated Depreciation amount with the original cost of the asset in the balance sheet forecast to show the asset's net book value. Alternatively, you might simply use the Net Book Value amount calculated in this schedule.

The first period's Accumulated Depreciation balance is the cumulative return of principal calculated as the cumulative depreciation expense net of the cumulative assumed investment revenue. The formula for the first period is:

```
=SUM(C$12:C12)-SUM(D$12:D12)
```

The formula for the second period is:

```
=SUM(C$12:C13)-SUM(D$12:D13)
```

and so on.

Net Book Value

The net book value is an asset's carrying cost and is the amount that you report either individually or with other assets' net book values on any historical or pro forma balance sheets.

For each period, the Net Book Value amount is the Original Cost amount less any accumulated depreciation. The formula for the first period is:

```
=Original_Cost-E12
```

The formula for the second period is:

```
=Original_Cost-E13
```

and so on.

Understanding the Activity Depreciation Starter Workbook

You can use the activity depreciation starter workbook shown in Figure 15-5 to construct depreciation schedules with the activity method. The activity method is unique among depreciation methods because it expenses the original cost of an asset based on use rather than on time. In general, you use this starter workbook if you're calculating depreciation for financial or managerial accounting and you feel that its allocation of costs matches economic reality.

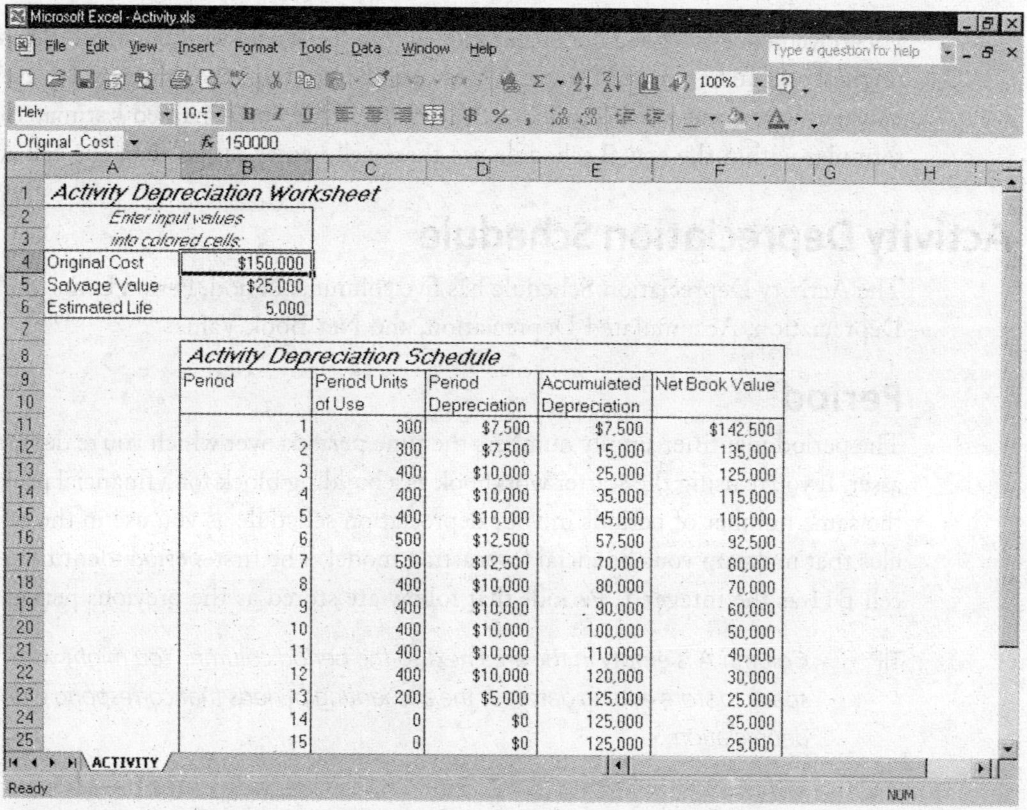

Activity Depreciation Worksheet

Enter input values into colored cells.

Original Cost	$150,000
Salvage Value	$25,000
Estimated Life	5,000

Activity Depreciation Schedule

Period	Period Units of Use	Period Depreciation	Accumulated Depreciation	Net Book Value
1	300	$7,500	$7,500	$142,500
2	300	$7,500	15,000	135,000
3	400	$10,000	25,000	125,000
4	400	$10,000	35,000	115,000
5	400	$10,000	45,000	105,000
6	500	$12,500	57,500	92,500
7	500	$12,500	70,000	80,000
8	400	$10,000	80,000	70,000
9	400	$10,000	90,000	60,000
10	400	$10,000	100,000	50,000
11	400	$10,000	110,000	40,000
12	400	$10,000	120,000	30,000
13	200	$5,000	125,000	25,000
14	0	$0	125,000	25,000
15	0	$0	125,000	25,000

Figure 15-5 The activity depreciation starter workbook.

Given the four parameters—original cost, salvage value, estimated useful life (expressed in units of use rather than time), and period units of use—this schedule calculates the depreciation expense, the accumulated depreciation, and the net book value for each period of the forecasting horizon.

The activity depreciation starter workbook has two parts: the Activity Depreciation Calculation Inputs box and the Activity Depreciation Schedule.

Activity Depreciation Calculation Inputs

The calculation inputs and the period units of use are the only variables you enter, and, unless you turn off cell protection, these are the only cells in which you can enter data.

Most often, the financial accounting standards or internal managerial accounting conventions that apply to your modeling assumptions determine the method you use to calculate these variables.

For convenience and good documentation within the starter workbook, cell B4 contains the original cost and is named Original_Cost, cell B5 contains the salvage value and is named Salvage_Value, and cell B6 contains the estimated life and is named Estimated_Life. The formulas within the actual schedule use these cell names rather than the cell addresses.

Activity Depreciation Schedule

The Activity Depreciation Schedule has five columns: Period, Period Units of Use, Period Depreciation, Accumulated Depreciation, and Net Book Value.

Period

The period identifier simply numbers the time periods over which you're depreciating the asset. If you're using the starter workbook as a building block for a financial projection, use the same number of periods in your depreciation schedule as you use in the other schedules that make up your financial forecasting model. The first-period identifier is stored in cell B11 as the integer 1. Periods that follow are stored as the previous period plus 1.

TIP *Column A is empty in the area next to the period column. You might want to use this space to store ending dates for the accounting periods that correspond with the period depreciation.*

Period Units of Use

The Period Units of Use isn't calculated by a formula. You enter either the actual or the forecasted units of use for each period of the forecast as input values. You should check that the total of this column equals the value that you entered for estimated life; it is not absolutely required, as you will see in the following discussion on Period Depreciation.

Period Depreciation

Period depreciation is the depreciation expense for the current period. If you use the template for depreciable assets accounting, the Period Depreciation expense is the debit component of a depreciation journal entry and ultimately shows up in the profit and loss statement. If you use the template as part of a financial forecast, you'll probably add the Period Depreciation expense with other expenses in the profit and loss forecast.

The activity depreciation method expenses a portion of an asset's depreciable cost based on the ratio of that period's units of use to the estimated life, calibrated in units of use. For example, the formula for the first period is:

```
=(C11/Estimated_Life)*(Original_Cost-Salvage_Value)
```

The formula for subsequent periods is modified to prevent an asset from being depreciated below its salvage value (as might be the case if you accidentally entered more period units of use than the estimated life in units of use). Starting in the second period, the basic formula is enclosed in the MIN statement, which selects the smaller of two amounts: the activity depreciation expense or the amount yet to be depreciated. For example, the period expense formula for the second period is:

```
=MIN(C12/Estimated_Life*(Original-Cost-Salvage_Value),F11-Salvage_Value)
```

The F11–Salvage_Value portion calculates the amount yet to be depreciated. In subsequent periods, this part of the formula uses the Net Book Value amount from the previous period.

Accumulated Depreciation

If you use the template for depreciable assets accounting, use the incremental increase in accumulated depreciation as the credit component of a depreciation journal entry, and it will ultimately show up on the balance sheet as an adjustment to the asset's original cost. If you use the template as part of a financial forecast, you might deduct the accumulated depreciation from the original cost of the asset on the balance sheet forecast to show the asset's net book value. Alternatively, you can use the Net Book Value amount calculated in this schedule.

The first period's Accumulated Depreciation balance is the first Period Depreciation expense. The formula is:

```
=SUM(D$11:D11)
```

The formula for the second period is:

```
=SUM(D$11:D12)
```

and so on.

Net Book Value

Net book value is an asset's original cost minus its accumulated depreciation and is the amount that you would report, either individually or with other assets' net book values, on any historical or pro forma balance sheets.

For each period, the Net Book Value figure is the Original Cost amount less any accumulated depreciation. The formula for the first period is:

```
=Original_Cost-E11
```

The formula for the second period is:

```
=Original_Cost-E12
```

and so on.

Customizing the Asset Depreciation Starter Workbooks

You can use the asset depreciation starter workbooks for a wide variety of depreciation calculations. However, you might want to change the starter workbooks so that they more precisely meet your requirements. For example, you can add text that describes the asset, describes the units of use that calibrate its estimated life, or identifies the supporting documentation for the schedule. You can also increase or decrease the number of periods.

NOTE *Before you change anything in the activity depreciation starter workbook other than the input parameters, unprotect the document.*

Changing the Number of Periods

You can easily increase or decrease the number of periods shown in any of the asset depreciation schedules. To increase the number of periods, remove the border from the last row of the depreciation schedule and then copy the current last row of the schedule (the row for Period 20) down as needed. To decrease the number of periods, simply delete any unneeded rows from the bottom of the schedule.

TIP *If you're using the starter workbook for accounting and bookkeeping, use a number of periods that is equal to or greater than the estimated life of the asset. However, if you're using the starter workbook as a building block for a financial projection, you'll probably want the number of periods in your depreciation schedule to correspond to the number of periods in the other schedules that make up your financial forecasting model.*

Index

A

B

C

D

E

F

G

H

I

K

L

M

N

O

P

Q

R

S

T

U

V

X

Y

Z

The manuscript for this book was prepared and submitted to Redmond Technology Press in electronic form. Text files were prepared using Microsoft Word 2000. Pages were composed using PageMaker 6.5 for Windows, with text in Frutiger and Caslon. Composed files were delivered to the printer as electronic prepress files.

Project Editor
Paula Thurman

Technical Editor / Layout

Minh-Tam S. Le

Indexer

Julie Kawabata